TRIPLE CROSS

Also by Peter Lance

Cover Up

1000 Years for Revenge

The Stingray

First Degree Burn

"TRIPLE CROSS"

HOW BIN LADEN'S MASTER SPY PENETRATED
THE CIA, THE GREEN BERETS, AND THE FBI—AND
WHY PATRICK FITZGERALD FAILED TO STOP HIM

PETER LANCE

REGAN

An Imprint of HarperCollins*Publishers*

Timeline photograph credits: Sadat Assassination: Al Akhbar/Gamma Press; al-Zawahiri: CNN; Chapel of the Bells: courtesy of Chapel of the Bells; Ronnie Bucca: courtesy of Eve Bucca; bin Laden and al-Zawahiri: AP Images; Spetsnaz Commando: Musa/AP images; Kahane: Corbis; Sphinx mailboxes, Sphinx business card: Peter Lance; Shalabi's house: Nancy Siesel/ *New York Times/Redux;* Nancy Floyd: courtesy of Nancy Floyd; Dana Ewell: Kurt Hegre/*Fresno Bee*; Monica Zent, Ewell family: courtesy of detectives John Souza and Chris Curtice; Salem and Rahman: Corbis; World Trade Center: Peter Lance; John Anticev: Christine Cornell; Lou Napoli: ABC News; Carson Dunbar: Brian Price/AP World Wide; Ronnie Bucca close up: courtesy of Eve Bucca; bomb damage at WTC: Richard Drew/AP World Wide; Kevin Shea: courtesy of Kevin Shea; TWA #847 hijacking: Herve Merliac/AP Images; Khobar Bombing: U.S. Navy/AP World Wide; Siddig Siddig Ali: Chester Higgins/*New York Times*/Redux; Hampton-El: © Jolie Stahl; Ahmed Abdel Sattar: AP Images; War Victim: Peter Lance; Brad Smith: courtesy of Rob Born; Aida Fariscal and Rodolfo Mendoza: Peter Lance; Mohammed Abouhalima: Corbis; Egyptian Embassy: CNN; Edwin Angeles: Peter Lance; Valerie Caproni: Lucy Nicholson/AFP/Getty Images; Ellen Corcella: courtesy of WNDU; Jack Cloonan: PBS; Dan Coleman: CNN; Mike Scheuer; J. Scott Applewhite/AP World Wide; Kallstrom: Department of Homeland Security; Jamal Ahmad al-Fadl: Christine Cornell; Alkhifah Center: Larry Schwartz; Yousef at trial: Jane Rosenberg; the defendants: Christine Cornell; DIAC Link Chart: courtesy of Jacob L. Bosen; Reena Raggi: Jim Estrin/*New York Daily News;* Refai and Rahman; ABC News; Anthony Shaffer: Dennis Cook/AP Images; Barbara Bodine: M. O'Sullivan/VOA; Harry Ellen, '96 meeting place: Peter Lance; Mohammed El-Atriss: Mike Durer/AP Images; Sphinx sign: Peter Lance; George W. Bush: AP Images; Bucca on 9/11: Magnum Photos; Dietrich Snell; Morris Mac Matzen/AP Images; KSM captured: AP Images; Angela Clemente and Mary Bari: Peter Lance.

HarperCollins books may be purchased for educational, business, or sales promotional use. For information please write: Special Markets Department, HarperCollins Publishers, 10 East 53rd Street, New York, NY 10022.

For editorial inquiries, please contact Regan, 10100 Santa Monica Blvd., 10th floor, Los Angeles, CA 90067.

FIRST EDITION

Designed by Publications Development Company of Texas

Library of Congress Cataloging-in-Publication Data has been applied for.

ISBN 10: 0-06-088688-9

ISBN 13: 978-0-06-088688-2

06 07 08 09 10 11 PDC/RRD 10 9 8 7 6 5 4 3 2 1

To Christopher, Mallory, and Alison, my children,
in the fervent hope that by the time they are old enough
to write their own books, U.S. intelligence agencies
like the FBI will have learned from their mistakes and
restructured sufficiently to protect our country from the next attack.

"I think you or I would have a better chance of winning the Powerball lottery than an Egyptian major in the unit that assassinated Sadat would have getting a visa, getting to California, getting into the army, and getting assigned to a Special Forces unit. That just doesn't happen."[1]

> —Lt. Col. Robert Anderson, former commanding
> officer of Ali Mohamed, John F. Kennedy Special
> Warfare Center, Fort Bragg, North Carolina

"Ali Mohamed is one of the most frightening examples of the infiltration of terrorists into the infrastructure of the United States.[2] Like [the villain in] a John Le Carré thriller, he played the role of a triple agent and nearly got away with it."[3]

> —Steven Emerson, author of *American Jihad*

"You have a man that's working for us and being paid by us at the same time as he's working for Osama bin Laden, who is the greatest enemy that this country has had since 1941. We had him, and he played us."[4]

> —Roger L. Stavis, attorney for Ali Mohamed's
> al Qaeda trainee El Sayyid Nosair

"Ali Mohamed is the most dangerous man I have ever met. We cannot let this man out on the street."[5]

> —Patrick Fitzgerald, U.S. Attorney for the Northern
> District of Illinois and Special Prosecutor in the
> Valerie Plame CIA leak case

CONTENTS

THIS IS A TRUE STORY ...

PREFACE

9/11 has become a cold case.

The biggest mass murder in U.S. history remains unsolved, and five years after the attacks that killed 2,973 Americans in New York, Washington, and Pennsylvania, few in official Washington or New York seem determined to "clear" it. The only federal case associated directly with the attacks—that of Zacarias Moussaoui—ended in a plea bargain, and in the penalty phase, one of the FBI's own agents accused the Bureau of "criminal negligence."[1]

Just a week before the fifth anniversary of 9/11, President Bush pledged that he would seek authority to try terror suspects in "military tribunals." But many of those same "high value" detainees—including Khalid Shaikh Mohammed, the alleged 9/11 "mastermind"—have been held in secret CIA prisons and subjected to torture for years without giving up any substantive intelligence on the whereabouts of Osama bin Laden. Now any effort to try them in U.S. courts would take a significant change in constitutional due process guarantees—an outcome that this strict constructionist Supreme Court is unlikely to approve.[2] So the case stays cold as the war on terror heats up.

As recently as August 2006, al Qaeda resurrected a fiendish plan to smuggle liquid-based explosive bombs aboard a series of transatlantic flights—mimicking the notorious Bojinka plot designed in 1994 by Ramzi Yousef, the true 9/11 mastermind. Probative evidence derived from Yousef in 1996 was covered up on President Clinton's watch when multiple opportunities to eliminate Osama bin Laden were squandered. Meanwhile, al Qaeda's post-9/11 bombings in Bali, Madrid, Istanbul, London, Casablanca, and Riyadh, along with its deadly involvement in the ongoing Iraqi insurgency, are stark testimony to the terror network's lethal resilience.

With each new audio recording or video fatwa, bin Laden and his second in command, Dr. Ayman al-Zawahiri, seem to get bolder. Yet the Bush administration recently closed the CIA's bin Laden unit,[3] and, astonishingly, to this day the Saudi billionaire has never even been *charged* for the 9/11 attacks.[4]

The final report of the 9/11 Commission, the last official body to investigate the attacks, has proven vastly incomplete. Although the idea of a plot using planes as missiles had its genesis with Yousef in Manila during the fall of 1994, the commission elected to focus its investigation from 1998 forward,[5] leaving out major elements of the story. Their report reduced to a footnote details of the three major war games being conducted on 9/11, including an exercise by the Northeast Air Defense Sector of NORAD that initially confused officials responsible for protecting New York.[6] Worse, it ignored a remarkable account cited earlier by the commission's own chairman, Thomas Kean, that F-16s from his home state of New Jersey were moments away from Lower Manhattan but never called by NORAD to interdict the Twin Towers attack.[7]

Now, more than five years after "Black Tuesday," a number of crucial questions remain unanswered. Could the attacks have been prevented? If so, who in our government should be blamed for the failure? Most important, have our intelligence agencies undergone sufficient reform to prevent future assaults on America by al Qaeda? Since 9/11 I have devoted virtually every working moment to an investigation designed to answer those questions.

For me, like most Americans, that day started out uneventfully. On the morning of September 11, 2001, I was on the West Coast. I got up early to write and turned on CNN.

Then, as I watched the South Tower go down, a cold dull pain formed at the base of my spine. My son Christopher's high school was located just a few blocks away from Ground Zero. After several agonizing hours fighting my way through jammed phone circuits, word came from a relative out-of-state that Chris was safe. After he was released with his classmates, he walked more than ninety blocks uptown to join his mother and sisters in safety.

But the next morning, I learned that Ronnie Bucca, a fire marshal I'd met years before, wasn't so lucky. I had called the FDNY headquarters at Brooklyn's Metrotech complex, hoping for word about another friend of mine, Chief Fire Marshal Lou Garcia. As it turned out, Garcia had escaped, if narrowly: He had rushed to Ground Zero as soon as he saw smoke licking from the North Tower, and almost died when the South Tower collapsed. I have known Louie for years. In fact, he'd introduced me to Ronnie Bucca back in 1997.

One of the house marshals answered the phone when I called.

"Lou's okay," he said. "But we lost Ronnie."

"Ronnie *Bucca?*" I said in disbelief. Ronnie wasn't just an arson investigator. He was a member of an army reserve intelligence unit with TOP SECRET clearance. And he'd been predicting, for *years,* that terrorists would return to hit the Towers again.

"He's still missing," said the house marshal. "Our guys are down at the pile right now searching."

The loss of Ronnie Bucca turned out to be one of the cruelest ironies of all the bitter stories from September 11. I'd met Ronnie in September 1997, when I'd attended a fund-raiser for the FDNY's burn fund at the Fire Museum in Soho. I'd just written *First Degree Burn,* a novel about a fictional New York City fire marshal,[8] and was signing some copies when Ronnie walked up to the table and handed me one. He cocked his head, smiled, and said, "I'm expecting something really clever, now. After all, you're a writer."

I hesitated for a moment, then inside on the cover page I wrote: "This is fiction. You're the real thing."

I had no idea at the time what an understatement that was.

The Paul Revere of the War on Terror

In the months that followed 9/11, I was astonished by the contours of Bucca's story. He was a former Green Beret paratrooper who worked Rescue One, the oldest heavy rescue company in the world. In 1986, he had survived a four-story fall from a burning tenement on the Upper West Side, while trying to rescue a lieutenant trapped above the fire floor. Bucca emerged from the fall with a broken back, wrists, and legs. Back then he could have retired on a three-quarter, tax-free pension, the Holy Grail for members of service in New York City. But Ronnie vowed to go back, not just to the fire department but to Rescue One, the "special forces" of the FDNY. And within a year he did just that—earning legendary status in a company of legendary men.

Henceforth, Ronnie was known to his "brothers" in ladder and engine companies throughout the city as "The Flying Firefighter."[9]

By 1992, tired of pulling bodies out of buildings where the fires were intentionally set, Ronnie Bucca had become a marshal with the FDNY's Bureau of Fire Investigation. On the night of the 1993 World Trade Center (WTC) bombing, he promised one of his buddies from Rescue One who'd been injured in the blast that he'd find out who did it.

The Feds would later learn that the device had been planted beneath the Twin Towers by Ramzi Yousef, an engineer trained in Wales who grew up in Kuwait with an abiding hatred of Israel. In the early days after the bombing, however, Yousef remained a phantom, known only by the code name "Rashed." He fled New York for Pakistan the night of the blast and was the object of a worldwide manhunt, but the FBI seemed stymied. Bucca wanted in on the investigation, but the Bureau excluded FDNY arson investigators from the official probe.

So Ronnie Bucca, who was in an army reserve intelligence detachment, got himself assigned to the Defense Intelligence Analysis Center (DIAC) at Bolling Air Force Base in Washington. There, as he began to examine the intel, he learned that the FBI actually had an informant inside the bombing cell months before the blast, but after a falling-out with a Bureau supervisor, he'd withdrawn. At that point Yousef was sent to New York by al Qaeda. His 1,500-pound, urea-nitrate-fuel oil bomb, driven to the Towers in a yellow Ryder truck, killed six and injured one thousand.

Working back-to-back tours so that he could go to the New York Public Library and educate himself on the history of Islamic terror, Bucca made a shocking discovery: An accountant who appeared to be an al Qaeda mole had been working inside the FDNY. The man, an Egyptian American and an intimate of the radical cleric Sheikh Omar Abdel Rahman, had obtained the blueprints of the WTC from the FDNY back in 1992—a year before the Trade Center bombing. Ronnie even found videotape of the man on the arm of the Sheikh, who was the spiritual mufti[10] behind Yousef's cell. But the FBI's New York Office ignored his evidence.

Now, days after the greatest mass murder in American history, I learned from Chief Garcia that one of the New York dead was this heroic fire marshal who had warned everybody it was coming.

One night in the late 1990s while standing outside a bar on First Avenue, Ronnie had actually pointed to the Towers and referenced King Richard the Lionheart. This was payback, he said. Osama bin Laden had been referring to the West collectively as the "Crusaders." The way Ronnie saw it, this modern terror war was just the latest round in a thousand-year grudge match.

He reminded his fellow firefighters—who wear the Maltese Cross on their uniforms—that the worldwide symbol of firefighting had derived from the Knights of Malta. They had organized the first fire brigades in the eleventh century as they stormed the battlements of Saladin and the other Islamic princes.

Outside the bar, looking down First Avenue at the Towers that night, Ronnie said, "We took *their* castles and now they're gonna come back and take *ours*."

When word came that they'd found Ronnie's remains, I thought back to what he'd said and began asking the same questions millions of Americans were then asking: How could this happen? How could the best and brightest in U.S. intelligence ignore year after year of warnings? How did they get caught so off guard?

Or did they?

Back to Investigative Journalism

Now, after more than a decade writing fiction, I was back developing sources inside and outside of the Bureau, poring over the 40,000-plus pages of trial transcripts from the al Qaeda cases in the Southern District of New York and cashing in markers from my days as a trial preparation assistant in the Manhattan D.A.'s office when I was at Fordham Law School. The hunt took me from Ground Zero to the teeming slums of Manila in search of al Qaeda turncoats who might talk. I was the first print reporter to do an extensive interview with Col. Rodolfo Mendoza, the chief interrogator of Ramzi Yousef's partner Abdul Hakim Murad, a pilot trained in four U.S. flight schools. It was Murad who first revealed that Yousef and his uncle Khalid Shaikh Mohammed had sent up to ten jihadis to aviation schools back in the winter of 1995.

Out of that work came *1000 Years for Revenge*.[11] That book presented documentary evidence that Yousef, the original WTC bomber, was also the architect of 9/11. After Yousef's conviction in 1997, responsibility for the plot had merely been shifted to his uncle Khalid Shaikh Mohammed, whom the Feds called KSM. I also proved, by a preponderance of the evidence, that the FBI could have stopped Yousef in 1992 before his first date with the Trade Center.

But there were major unanswered questions:

1. Why did the FBI and the U.S. Justice Department ignore probative evidence from Col. Mendoza and the Philippines National Police in 1995 that the Yousef-KSM cell had set in motion this planes-as-missiles plot?

2. Yousef had been brought to ground in Islamabad in 1995 via a tip to the Rewards for Justice program, He'd been arrested after a worldwide search in which his wanted poster was plastered on tens of thousands of matchbook covers airdropped throughout the Middle East. Yet the Justice Department and the Bureau had kept secret the identity of KSM—not even mentioning him in the press—until 1998, when the planes-as-missiles plot was well underway. Again, why?

"Testifying" Before the 9/11 Commission

After reading *1000 Years for Revenge,* the chairman of the 9/11 Commission, former New Jersey Governor Thomas Kean, suggested that I share my findings with his staff.[12] As it turned out, however, the commission elected to take my "testimony" in secret, in a windowless conference room at 26 Federal Plaza on March 15, 2004. In fact, the man who interviewed me, Dietrich Snell, was the former prosecutor of Ramzi Yousef, whose very office had failed to act on the evidence from the Philippines National Police that Yousef was tied to the planes operation.

As I saw it, Dietrich Snell should have been a *witness* before the 9/11 Commission, subpoenaed to testify under oath in open session. Instead he was hired as its senior counsel, and given the job of determining "the origin of the plot"—the most important question facing the 9/11 Commission. After all, if they couldn't tell when the plot commenced, they couldn't rightfully hold U.S. intelligence agencies responsible for not stopping it. But it soon became clear that the commissioners, and investigators like Snell, had little interest in assessing blame. Almost half of the commission's staff was made up of alumni from the very agencies that failed to stop the attacks. In short, the foxes had been hired to guard the chicken coop.

In the end, Snell relegated the evidence I submitted from the Philippines National Police to a footnote in the 9/11 Commission's final report. Worse, he flushed remarkable documentary evidence that al Qaeda may have been involved in the crash of TWA Flight 800 in 1996. A cache of memos from the Bureau's own files strongly suggested that a bomb had been planted aboard the Paris-bound flight in order to secure a mistrial for Yousef in the first of two federal prosecutions. The forensic investigator who had shared the documents with me had also presented them to the commission, but there wasn't a word about that 1996 al Qaeda-related evidence from Ramzi Yousef in their final report.

Operation Able Danger

What I didn't know at the time was that, in late 1999 and early 2000, the chairman of the Joint Chiefs of Staff and the head of the U.S. Army's Special Operations Command (SOCOM) had authorized a data-mining operation called Able Danger, in which vast amounts of classified and open-source intelligence on al Qaeda was being processed using powerful "search bots" that surfed the Web around the clock. Within months, the Able Danger analysts had amassed 2.5 terabytes of data, equal to 12 percent of all the printed pages in the Library of Congress.

By mid-2000, working out of Fort Belvoir, Virginia, the Able Danger investigators had found key links to four of the 9/11 hijackers. They also found direct ties between bin Laden and the New York cell of Ramzi Yousef and Sheikh Omar Abdel Rahman. This dovetailed with my findings that the two attacks on the World Trade Center were perpetrated by the same core group of al Qaeda operatives. The Able Danger data miners later found a major al Qaeda presence in the port city of Aden, Yemen.

The active pursuit of that intelligence in the early fall of 2000 could have prevented the attack on the U.S.S. *Cole* in October, and tipped Bureau agents to the 9/11 plot more than a year before the attacks. But for reasons as yet undetermined, this vast cache of data-mined intelligence was ordered destroyed. Worse, when two decorated Able Danger operatives, an army lieutenant colonel and a navy captain, sought to share this scandal with the 9/11 Commission, they were effectively spurned.

The senior counsel on the 9/11 Commission staff who rejected the Able Danger intel, and kept it out of the final report, was Dietrich Snell—the same ex-prosecutor who had buried my evidence that the two attacks on the Twin Towers were directly funded and controlled by bin Laden and al Qaeda.

A Different Finding

The 9/11 Commission Report, published in July 2004 and later nominated for a National Book Award, concluded that the original World Trade Center bombing cell was made up of a "loosely based group of Sunni Islamists";[13] further, that the 9/11 plot had originated not with Ramzi Yousef in Manila in 1994, as I had demonstrated, but with Yousef's uncle Khalid Shaikh Mohammed, who—according to Snell's account—pitched the planes-as-missiles operation to Osama bin Laden in 1996.[14] The evidence I'd obtained from the Philippines National Police demonstrated that the Yousef-KSM Manila cell was funded directly by bin Laden via his brother-in-law, but the commission, with the backing of Snell and other ex-Feds, concluded that KSM wasn't even a member of al Qaeda in 1996. By mid-2004, I was getting closer to the truth. The 1996 FBI 302 memos I'd tried to share with the commission showed that the Bureau, and prosecutors from the Justice Department, had affirmatively covered up evidence of an active al Qaeda cell in New York City. The same intelligence revealed the existence of a bin Laden-sponsored plot to hijack U.S. airliners, designed to pressure the United States to free the blind Sheikh and Ramzi Yousef, who was locked up in the Metropolitan Correctional Center (MCC) in Lower Manhattan. Similar threat reporting would show up in Presidential Daily Briefings in 1998 and 2001—a fact that later made headlines—but my findings revealed that the FBI had buried identical intelligence years before.

Why would America's most elite law enforcement and investigative agencies suppress such critical intelligence?

Their motive could be traced to a most surprising quarter: organized crime. As a phone-book-sized file of documentary evidence from prosecutors in the Eastern District of New York reveals, FBI investigators and federal prosecutors were desperate to avoid a scandal over an alleged corrupt relationship between R. Lindley DeVecchio, a senior supervisory special agent in the Bureau's New York Office (NYO) and a notorious hit man named Gregory Scarpa Sr., whose two-year war of succession in the Colombo crime family had left twelve people dead, including two innocent bystanders.

Through a bizarre turn of events, the Yousef evidence came from the killer's own son, Greg Scarpa Jr., a junior wiseguy who happened to inhabit a jail cell adjacent to Yousef's at the MCC. But rather than risk losing a series of sixty Mafia cases in the Eastern District built on tainted evidence from Scarpa Sr., the Feds decided to bury the intel.

One of the lead prosecutors who disconnected those dots, I learned, was Patrick Fitzgerald, then the head of Organized Crime and Terrorism in New York's Southern District. Considered the Justice Department's leading authority on bin Laden, Fitzgerald would go on to become U.S. Attorney in Chicago, and special prosecutor in the ongoing investigation of media leaks regarding former CIA operative Valerie Plame, which ultimately cleared White House aide Karl Rove, while indicting Lewis "Scooter" Libby, a top aide to Vice President Cheney.

Al Qaeda Meets the Mob

Much of this tangled tale was laid out in great detail in my second investigative book *Cover Up*, published in September 2004. It documented an ends/means decision by senior FBI and Justice Department officials to suppress the DeVecchio scandal, preserve those mob cases, and brand the Yousef-Scarpa Jr. intelligence a "hoax" and a "scam." Until the cover up, that intelligence—chronicled in dozens of FBI 302s and notes from Yousef—was considered so important to the Feds that they gave Scarpa Jr. a camera to photograph it and even set up a phony Mafia front company, "Roma Corporation," allowing them to monitor Yousef's outside calls.

By the fall of 1996, the Bureau's internal affairs probe on DeVecchio was closed and Yousef was convicted along with Murad and a third conspirator. Dietrich Snell and Mike Garcia, the current U.S. Attorney for the SDNY, had won a decisive victory and the Feds soon began to believe that they were winning the war against al Qaeda. But the burial of that evidence, which prevented other U.S. intelligence agencies from appreciating al Qaeda's true breadth and depth, would have shocking repercussions.

As I looked back on the Justice Department's counterterrorism track record, I concluded that many of the dots left unconnected by the FBI and Department of Justice (DOJ) on the road to 9/11 appeared to have been the result of an *intentional* obscuring of the evidence.

Continuing to work sources and examine the reams of documentary evidence generated in the SDNY al Qaeda cases, I came to the conclusion that the FBI's failure to prevent the African embassy bombings in 1998, the deadly assault on U.S.S. *Cole* in 2000, and the 9/11 attacks themselves, went beyond gross negligence. It seemed as if a number of FBI officials and federal prosecutors at the heart of the bin Laden hunt realized that they had been outgunned for years. So they had acted affirmatively to partition the intelligence.

I believe that their motive was to sanitize the record and thus prevent the public from understanding the full depth of the FBI/DOJ missteps in the years leading up to September 11. So "walls" were intentionally built, and key intelligence was withheld from other agencies, including the CIA and DIA. In any other government enterprise, the consequences might have been more benign, but in the realm of national security that compartmentalization of intelligence proved fatal.

By the third anniversary of 9/11, the Scarpa-Yousef evidence had been published in *Cover Up*.[15] Sixteen months later, DeVecchio would finally be arraigned on murder charges stemming, in part, from that investigation. But many unanswered questions remained. I wanted to know the names of the men and women in the shadows at DOJ who had suppressed the evidence and hidden the truth behind al Qaeda all those years. I also wanted to learn why the Bush administration would act to obstruct an investigation into the destruction of the Able Danger intel, a scandal that took place during the Clinton years.

It took me months of further digging before the depth of the government's deception started to become clear.

Ali Mohamed Was the Key

In the years leading to the 9/11 attacks, no single agent of al Qaeda was more successful in compromising the U.S. intelligence community than a former Egyptian army captain turned CIA operative, Special Forces advisor, and FBI informant named Ali Mohamed. Spying first for the Central Intelligence Agency (CIA) and later the FBI, Mohamed even succeeded in penetrating the John F. Kennedy Special Warfare Center at Fort Bragg— while simultaneously training the cell that blew up the World Trade Center in 1993. He went on to train Osama bin Laden's personal bodyguard, and photographed the U.S. embassy in Kenya taking the surveillance pictures bin Laden himself used to target the suicide truck bomb that killed 224 and injured thousands there in 1998.[16]

Mohamed accomplished all that fully *nine years* after the FBI first photographed the cell he trained using automatic weapons at a firing range on Long Island. He lived the quiet life of a Silicon Valley computer executive while slipping off to Afghanistan and the Sudan to train some of al Qaeda's most lethal terrorists in bomb-making and assassination tradecraft. He was so trusted by bin Laden that Ali was given the job of moving the Saudi "Emir" from Afghanistan to Khartoum in 1991 and then back to Jalalabad in 1996—much of that time maintaining his status as an FBI informant who worked his Bureau control agent like a mole.

Mohamed twice played host to al Qaeda's second-in-command, Dr. Ayman al-Zawahiri, who traveled to the United States in the 1990s to raise money for the Jihad. He used his army vacation to hunt down elite Soviet Spetsnaz commandos in Afghanistan, and later toyed with gullible special agents in New York and San Francisco while he learned the inner workings of the FBI's al Qaeda playbook. In the annals of espionage, few men have moved in an out of the deep black world between the hunters and the hunted with as much audacity as Ali Mohamed—known to his al Qaeda brothers as *Ali Amiriki,* or "Ali the American." A deep-penetration al Qaeda sleeper, he succeeded as a triple agent, gaining access to the most sensitive intelligence in the U.S. counterterrorism arsenal.

Next to Ramzi Yousef, the bomb maker who plotted both attacks on the Twin Towers, Mohamed remains the greatest enigma in the war on terror. Brazenly slipping past watch lists, he moved in and out of the United States with impunity for years, marrying an American woman, becoming a naturalized citizen, seeking TOP SECRET security clearance from a Silicon Valley defense contractor, and working for the FBI while servicing the top echelons of al Qaeda.

The story of Ali Mohamed holds the key to the full truth about how bin Laden planned, financed, and executed the 9/11 attacks. He's also a living witness to how the best and the brightest in the U.S. intelligence community were repeatedly outflanked for two decades, from the death of Egyptian president Anwar Sadat in 1981 through the attacks of September 11, 2001.

My conclusion in *Cover Up* was that the FBI had buried key al Qaeda intelligence to avoid a scandal over tainted Mafia evidence. But as unbelievable as that story seemed, the investigation took on even stranger twists and turns when Ali Mohamed came into focus. For example, almost from the moment the Bureau "opened" him as an informant back in 1992, Ali's main control agent on the West Coast became embroiled in a grisly triple murder case that distracted him from fully appreciating Mohamed's lethal dedication to stealing America's secrets for the jihad. Patrick Fitzgerald himself called Ali "the most dangerous man I ever met," and soon, as I began to fill in the blanks on him, I encountered evidence more astonishing than any fiction I had ever written.

Working the "Murder Book"

For this phase of the investigation I decided to work the research the way cold case detectives work a homicide file, known in many squad rooms as "the murder book." To begin with, I reread more than twenty-five four-inch-thick three-ring binders of research from my first two books. I then went back through the summaries I'd made of the forty thousand pages of trial testimony in the SDNY's al Qaeda-related cases, including the first WTC bombing trial in 1994; the Day of Terror trial of Sheikh Omar Abdel Rahman and eleven others in 1995; the Bojinka trial of Ramzi Yousef and his Manila coconspirators in 1996; the second WTC trial—this one with Yousef as a defendant—in 1997; and the African embassy bombing trial, known formally as *United States v. bin Laden*, which began in February 2001, seven months before 9/11.

Then, as cold case detectives do, I read the "book" out of order, examining whole files randomly in the hope that the exercise would provoke a new lead. I soon realized that there was still a major case missing: the 1991 murder trial of El Sayyid Nosair, who had gunned down Rabbi Meier Kahane the night of November 5, 1990. Incredibly, despite a wealth of evidence pointing to an international terrorist conspiracy with al Qaeda at its core, that case had been tried as a "lone gunman" shooting by the office of the New York County District Attorney. Examining that transcript, and the later coverage of the trial by the *New York Times,* led me to the discovery of a New Jersey check-cashing store where Nosair had rented a mailbox in 1990. As unbelievable as it may seem, that precise location, doors away from the blind Sheikh's New Jersey mosque, was where two of the 9/11 hijackers, associated with Hani Hanjour, picked up their fake IDs in July 2001.

All the Bureau had to do was sit on that check-cashing business and they would have been able to penetrate the 9/11 plot.

The Nosair mailbox discovery was proof positive that in order to fully understand the 9/11 plot, any thorough investigation had to go back years before the time period covered by the 9/11 Commission. When I did that, and reread the "murder book" on Yousef's suicide-hijack plot, the eureka moment came when I realized that the key to the FBI failures—and to the subsequent cover-up of evidence that disconnected the dots—was Ali Mohamed. With further probing, I discovered that this man, known by fifteen aliases, was the enigma behind the destruction of the Able Danger intelligence as well.

Ali Mohamed could have been a one-man 9/11 Commission. He held the key to how the best and the brightest in the FBI and Department of Justice failed to stop bin Laden's juggernaut. And yet the Feds had him buried, confined in witness protection somewhere near New York—the perfect al Qaeda spy who knew all the secrets. When I had finished reworking the "murder book" on 9/11, I knew that if I could tell his story, I would get closer to the truth.

The Investigators Who Paved the Way

All investigative reporters stand on the shoulders of those who came before them, and the Ali Mohamed story is no exception. As I began to piece together the fragments of intelligence on his triple life, a series of seminal news pieces helped me form a grid. Among the first investigators to fully appreciate Mohamed's deception was Steven Emerson, who examined him in *American Jihad* back in 2002.[17] In the *San Francisco Chronicle*, Lance Williams and Erin McCormick did an outstanding series on Ali and his Silicon Valley cohort Khalid Dahab.[18] Joseph Neff and John Sullivan did a pair of excellent investigative stories for the *Raleigh News & Observer* on Ali's years at Fort Bragg.[19] Additional pieces that helped form my initial blueprint came from Associated Press writers Tom Hays and Sharon Theimer;[20] Peter Waldman, Gerald F. Seib, and Jerry Markon in the *Wall Street Journal*;[21] and *Chicago Tribune* reporters Andrew Martin and Michael J. Berens.[22]

But by far the most comprehensive reporting on Mohamed was done by Benjamin Weiser, who covers the SDNY for the *New York Times*. His cowriter on several key pieces was Pulitzer Prize winner James Risen.[23] To the degree I've been able to add to the body of knowledge on al Qaeda's master spy, I remain indebted to all of them.

The Spy of Many Names

What follows is the most thorough examination to date of one of the most secret espionage failures in American history: the story of Ali Abdel Saoud Mohamed, aka Ali Abul Saoud Mustafa, aka Ali Aboualacoud,[24] aka Abu Omar,[25] aka Haydara,[26] aka Ahmed Bahaa Adam,[27] aka Abu Mohammed ali Amriki,[28] aka Ali Nasser Mohamed Taymour,[29] aka Abu Osama,[30] aka Bakhbola, aka Bili Bili.[31] Diamond merchant, army sergeant, leather dealer, suburban husband, special ops assassin, security guard, computer specialist, CIA asset, FBI informant—and the man who literally wrote al Qaeda's book on terror—Ali Mohamed wore many faces, perhaps none as secretive as the one he presented to his American wife, Linda, who talked to me for the first time during this investigation.

Because Ali Mohamed supplies the puzzle pieces that complete the story of FBI negligence on the road to 9/11, I will briefly cover some of the ground examined in *1000 Years for Revenge* and *Cover Up*. It's now clear that Ramzi Yousef was Osama bin Laden's chief operational point man, followed after his capture by Khalid Shaikh Mohammed. But over the years Ali Mohamed emerged as al Qaeda's chief intelligence officer, and the man bin Laden trusted with his life. In bin Laden's ingenious but diabolical plan to attack America, the roles of these two men meshed perfectly. The bomb maker and the spy, two lethal components in al Qaeda's thirteen-year war against the "Crusaders." Which terrorist was more important? That is for the reader to decide. But as Sun Tzu wrote in the sixth century BC, "all war is deception," and Ali Mohamed was one of the most capable deceivers this nation has ever embraced.

PETER LANCE
New York City
October 1, 2006

CAST OF CHARACTERS

The Feds

Patrick Fitzgerald	Assistant U.S. Attorney, Southern District New York (SDNY).
	Chief of Organized Crime & Terrorism Unit, SDNY.
	Later became U.S. Attorney in Chicago and special prosecutor in the CIA leak probe.
Jamie Gorelick	Deputy Attorney General under President Bill Clinton.
	Author of the "wall memo."
	Supported 1995 extradition from the United States of bin Laden's brother-in-law.
	Later became one of the ten 9/11 Commissioners.
Jack Cloonan	Special Agent, Squad I-49 (the bin Laden squad), Federal Bureau of Investigation (FBI).
	Assigned in 1996 to build a file on Ali Mohamed, but failed to recognize him as an al Qaeda spy prior to his 1998 arrest.
	Debriefed Mohamed after his arrest in 1998.
Dan Coleman	Special Agent, Squad I-49, FBI.
	Assigned to Alec Station, the CIA's dedicated bin Laden unit.

Frank Pellegrino — Special Agent, FBI.
Debriefed Abdul Hakim Murad.
Later worked in Squad I-49.

Andrew McCarthy — Assistant U.S. Attorney.
With Patrick Fitzgerald, coprosecuted Sheikh Omar Abdel Rahman and eleven others in the "Day of Terror" trial.

Dietrich Snell — Assistant U.S. Attorney, SDNY.
Coprosecuted Ramzi Yousef, Abdul Hakim Murad, and Wali Khan in the Bojinka trial.
Later became senior counsel to the 9/11 Commission.

Mary Jo White — U.S. Attorney, SDNY, 1993–2002.

Louis Freeh — Director, Federal Bureau of Investigation, 1993–2001.
Former Special Agent, New York Office (NYO), FBI.
Former Assistant U.S. Attorney, SDNY.

Nancy Floyd — Special Agent, FBI Foreign Counterintelligence Division, FBI's NYO.
Recruited Egyptian asset Emad Salem.

John Anticev — Special Agent, FBI's New York Office.
Member, FBI-NYPD Joint Terrorism Task Force (JTTF).
Control agent for Salem, 1991–1992.
Partner of Detective Lou Napoli.

Lou Napoli — NYPD detective, Member, JTTF.
Failed to follow Salem's advice and track Abouhalima and Salameh in the months before 1993 WTC bombing.

Emad Salem	Former Egyptian intelligence officer recruited by SA Nancy Floyd as an FBI asset.
	Infiltrated Sheikh Omar Abdel Rahman's cell in 1991–1992.
Jamal al-Fadl	Former assistant to Osama bin Laden in Sudan.
	Became a U.S. witness in 1996 and gave Feds the roadmap to al Qaeda.
Neal Herman	Head of the JTTF in the FBI's NYO in the fall 1992, before the WTC bombing.
	Led hunt for Ramzi Yousef after the bombing.
Carson Dunbar	Assistant Special Agent in Charge (ASAC), FBI's NYO.
	Mistrusted Salem and Floyd; blamed for Salem's withdrawal from the cell in 1992.
Brian Parr	Agent, U.S. Secret Service.
	Debriefed Yousef during rendition to the United States from Pakistan in 1995.
Thomas Donlon	Special Agent, FBI. Conducted airborne interrogation in which Yousef admitted his role in the 1993 WTC bombing.
Bradley Garrett	Special Agent, FBI.
	In Islamabad the day of Yousef's capture.
	Arrived late at guesthouse from which Khalid Shaikh Mohammed escaped, but later took credit for the Yousef takedown.
Harry Samit	Special Agent, FBI, Minneapolis. Begged FBI to approve FISA warrant on Zacarias Moussaoui, 2001.
	Later accused FBI of "criminal negligence" at Moussaoui trial.

David Frasca	Head of FBI's Radical Fundamentalist Unit. Failed to act on the Phoenix memo in July 2001 and rejected Samit's FISA request before 9/11.
Michael Rolince	Chief of counterintelligence, FBI Headquarters, Washington, D.C. Told NSC officials that Ali Mohamed's tour with Ayman al-Zawahiri in 1995 was "covered." Failed to read Samit's FISA request.
Ken Williams	Special Agent, FBI, Phoenix. Issued July 2001 memo urging monitoring of flight schools. Accused by FBI asset Harry Ellen of sending memo more than four years too late.

Al Qaeda

Osama bin Laden	Saudi billionaire, leader of al Qaeda. Morphed the Egyptian Islamic Jihad (EIJ) and the Mujahadeen funding network (MAK) into al Qaeda in 1988. Used Ali Mohamed to train his personal body-guard and to move him with his entourage from Afghanistan to Sudan in 1991. Personally selected ground zero point for 1998 African embassy bomb using Ali Mohamed's 1993 surveillance photos.
Ali Mohamed	Former major, Egyptian army. Infiltrated CIA and the Green Berets. Became FBI informant while serving as al Qaeda's top U.S. spy and bin Laden's security chief. Undetected by the Bureau for nine years before his arrest.

Ayman al-Zawahiri	Egyptian surgeon and deputy chief of al Qaeda. Leader of EIJ, jailed for Sadat assassination. Sent Mohamed to U.S. in 1985 as an EIJ spy.
Omar Abdel Rahman	Muslim cleric, the so-called "blind Sheikh." Led the radical Islamic Group (IG). Religious leader who inspired both attacks on World Trade Center.
Mohamed Atef	Former Egyptian police officer. Military commander, al Qaeda. His daughter married bin Laden's son.
Khalid Dahab	Protégé of Ali Mohamed in California. Helped to recruit ten U.S. sleepers. Sentenced to death in 1999 during Egyptian terror trial in which Ali Mohamed was also condemned.
Wadih El-Hage	Chief secretary to Osama bin Laden in Khartoum. Became a key operative in the Kenyan embassy bombing cell.
Mohammed Jamal Khalifa	Brother-in-law of Osama bin Laden. Captured by INS in 1994 but extradited to Jordan with full support of Dep. A.G. Jamie Gorelick.
Ramzi Yousef	Chief al Qaeda bomb maker. Planted first WTC bomb. Designed planes-as-missiles plot that led to 9/11. Passed intelligence to Mafia informant Greg Scarpa Jr., in 1996 while in federal jail in lower Manhattan.

Khalid Shakhi Mohammed	Uncle of Ramzi Yousef. Often referred to as "KSM." Executed Yousef's "planes operation" on 9/11.
Abdul Hakim Murad	Cohort of Ramzi Yousef. Trained as pilot in four U.S. flight schools. Confessed planes-as-missiles plot to Philippines police in 1995. Predicted to FBI that Yousef would strike WTC again.
Wali Khan Amin Shah	Fourth member of Yousef/KSM Manila cell behind plot to kill Pope, Bojinka plot, and Ramzi Yousef's planes-as-missiles operation in 1995. Beloved by bin Laden, aka "the lion."
El Sayyid Nosair	Egyptian EIJ member, follower of Omar Abdel Rahman. Trained by Ali Mohamed. Murdered Rabbi Meier Kahane in 1990 in New York City. First al Qaeda blood spilled on U.S. soil.
Mahmud Abouhalima	New York cell member, known as "the Red." Trained by Ali Mohamed. Convicted in WTC bombing plot. Intended getaway driver for Nosair.
Mohammed Salameh	Partner of Abouhalima. Trained by Ali Mohamed. Monitored by FBI at shooting range in 1989. Eluded FBI in months before 1993 bombing. Drove getaway car for Yousef after WTC bombing.

Nidal Ayyad	Kuwaiti national, graduated from Rutgers University, New Jersey.
	Trained by Ali Mohamed.
	Convicted of abetting Yousef in 1993 WTC bombing.
Ibrahim El-Gabrowny	Egyptian cousin of El Sayyid Nosair.
	Raised $20,000 from bin Laden for Nosair's legal bills in Kahane murder case.
Mohammed Atta	Egyptian terrorist.
	Succeeded Abdul Hakim Murad, Yousef's original lead pilot, in 9/11 plot.
Khalid al-Midhar Nawaf al-Hazmi	"Muscle hijackers" present at 2000 9/11 summit in Kuala Lumpur, Malaysia.
	Lived openly in San Diego in home rented to them by FBI informant Abdussattar Shaykh.
Ihab Ali aka Nawawi	U.S. citizen, Florida resident and sleeper recruited by Ali Mohamed.
	Trained at Oklahoma flight school associated with 9/11 hijackers.
	Copiloted bin Laden's plane in 1994.
Khallad bin Atash	Leader of al Qaeda plot to bomb U.S.S. *Cole* in October 2000.
	Monitored ten months earlier by CIA at 9/11 planning meeting in January 2000.
Riduan Isamuddin	Also known as "Hambali." Fund-raiser for al Qaeda.
	On board of Malaysian front company funding Yousef/KSM Manila cell.
	Present at 9/11 planning session.
	Key figure in 2002 Bali bombings.

PART I

PART

ONE

1

THE DEEP
BLACK HOLE

On October 20, 2000, after tricking the U.S. intelligence establishment for years, Ali Mohamed stood in handcuffs, leg irons, and a blue prison jumpsuit before Judge Leonard B. Sand in a Federal District courtroom in Lower Manhattan. Over the next thirty minutes he pleaded guilty five times, admitting to his involvement in plots to kill U.S. soldiers in Somalia and Saudi Arabia, U.S. ambassadors in Africa, and American civilians "anywhere in the world."[1] The goal of the al Qaeda terrorists he trained, he said, was to "kidnap, murder and maim." His career in espionage had earned him a death sentence in an Egyptian trial the year before. But now, before the federal judge, Ali was seeking mercy.

In short but deliberate sentences, Mohamed peeled back the top layer of the secret life he'd led since 1981, when radical members of his Egyptian army unit gunned down Nobel Prize winner Anwar Sadat. A highly educated master spy, fluent in four languages, Mohamed told of how he had risen from a young recruit in the virulently anti-American Egyptian Islamic Jihad to become Osama bin Laden's most trusted security adviser. He described how al Qaeda cell members from Kenya had infiltrated Mogadishu, Somalia, in the 1993 campaign that ultimately downed two U.S.

Black Hawk helicopters; how he had brokered a terror summit between al Qaeda and the hyper-violent Iranian Party of God known as Hezbollah; and how he had trained al Qaeda jihadis in Afghanistan and Sudan, teaching them improvised bomb building while schooling them in the creation of secret cells so that they could operate in the shadows. On this last bit of tradecraft, he'd literally written the book.[2] If there was ever a shadow man in the dark reaches of al Qaeda, it was the triple spy born Ali Abdel Saoud Mohamed.[3]

Because there is so little on the public record about him and because his career resulted in so much terror and death, we will reproduce his words from that plea session throughout this book, verbatim.

Perhaps Ali's most telling admission came when Judge Sand asked his objectives. Mohamed answered by restating al Qaeda's longstanding goal of driving the U.S. out of the Middle East—particularly Saudi Arabia, where troops had been stationed since August 7, 1990.[4] What would make Mohamed's leader, Osama bin Laden, think he could *achieve* that goal? At that point, without naming him, Mohamed cited the example of how President Ronald Reagan had withdrawn U.S. troops from Lebanon following the deadly Marine barracks bombing in 1983—an act of terror that some suspect Ali himself may have had a hand in:[5]

THE COURT: The overall objective of all of these activities you described was, what?

MOHAMED: . . . just to attack any Western target in the Middle East; to force the government of the Western countries just to pull out . . . not interfere in the—

THE COURT: And to achieve that objective, did the conspiracy include killing nationals of the United States?

MOHAMED: Yes, sir. Based on the Marine explosion in Beirut in 1983 and the American pull-out from Beirut, they will be the same method, to force the United States to pull out from Saudi Arabia.

THE COURT: And it included conspiracy to murder persons who were involved in government agencies and embassies overseas?

MOHAMED: Yes, your honor.

THE COURT: And to destroy buildings and properties of the United States?

MOHAMED: Yes, your honor.

THE COURT: And to attack national-defense utilities?

MOHAMED: Yes, your honor.

But the most important aspect of that plea session was what was left *unsaid.* In that Southern District Courtroom nearly two years before the attacks of September 11, Ali Mohamed uttered *nothing* on the record about his most stunning achievements: how he had slipped past a State Department Watch List and into America, seduced a Silicon Valley medical technician into marriage, joined the U.S. Army, and gotten himself posted to the highly secure base where the Green Berets and Delta Force train. He didn't say a word about how he'd moved in and out of contract spy work for the CIA and fooled FBI agents for six years as he smuggled terrorists across U.S. borders, and guarded the tall Saudi billionaire who had personally declared war on America: Osama bin Laden.

"Those who know Ali Mohamed say he is regarded with fear and awe for his incredible self-confidence, his inability to be intimidated, [his] absolute ruthless determination to destroy the enemies of Islam and his zealous belief in the tenets of militant Islamic Fundamentalism."[6]

That's how terrorism expert Steven Emerson described Mohamed after the FBI finally arrested him in 1998. Though the Bureau had been onto his terrorist connections since 1989, it took the simultaneous attacks on the embassies in Dar es Salaam and Nairobi to jolt them into the admission that the Justice Department had been conned; that whatever intelligence crumbs he'd thrown to the FBI, Mohamed had gotten back ten times more. Worse, he'd led a campaign of disinformation that lulled the Bureau into a vast underestimation of the al Qaeda threat.

Mohamed's commanding officer at Fort Bragg, Lt. Col. Robert Anderson, was more specific: "Ali Mohamed is probably the most dangerous person that I ever met in my life."

He wasn't the devil himself, Anderson said, in an interview for this book.[7] He was more like "The aide to the devil. He was a fanatic. He had an air about him; a stare, a very coldness that was pathological." But Anderson noted that Ali "would shift into a very nice polite individual when it was to his advantage."

Now, in the courtroom, as he stood cuffed and stooped over, feigning humility, Ali Mohamed played yet another role—that of the contrite and broken jihadi, a man willing to cooperate with the Feds. Finally, once and for all, the hope was that he would give up his secrets. But in the poker game between "asset" and FBI control agent, Mohamed held most of the face cards. He had stung the Bureau repeatedly over the years and he knew that in the end, they would want to hide the truth.

"Ali knew where the bodies were buried," said one former FBI agent. "In fact, he dug most of the graves himself. There was just no way that [FBI] management wanted that story to come out."[8]

"With his connections to U.S. law enforcement and intelligence," says Emerson, "I've never seen a terrorist with such a storied background."[9] As the man who had sat in a room with the "terror prince," while bin Laden personally targeted the Nairobi embassy back in 1994, Mohamed should have been the star witness in the embassy bombing trial, which was just months away. Yet Patrick Fitzgerald, the lead prosecutor, never called him.

Why did the Feds let Ali Mohamed sit out that trial? Why did they make a secret plea agreement with him; yet not force him to testify? Because Mohamed wasn't just the government's best witness to al Qaeda's *successes,* he was also the best witness to the *failures* of the FBI and the CIA to stop bin Laden's terror campaign.

It was a string of attacks that stretched from the murder of Rabbi Meier Kahane in 1990 through the bombing of the World Trade Center in 1993, up through the assault on the U.S.S. *Cole* in 2000, and on to the second attack on the Twin Towers in 2001. Mohamed had been an FBI snitch for much of that decade and he'd been on the Bureau's radar since 1989. What he knew about the FBI's missteps could fill a metaphorical book, and the U.S. Justice Department was determined that it would never be published.

And yet even today, years after pleading guilty to crimes that would have ended any other terrorist's life via lethal injection, Ali Mohamed remains a legal black hole. Minutes after that hearing he was locked away, hidden from public scrutiny. It's been nearly six years and one of the discoveries made in this investigation is that Judge Sand has yet to pronounce sentence.[10]

Today Mohamed exists in a kind of legal no-man's-land, a prisoner of the Feds whose name appears nowhere on the Bureau of Prisons inmates roster. His case file in the Southern District is heavily redacted or otherwise sealed. Only a handful of people in the Justice Department know the full details of his plea agreement.

His wife, Linda Sanchez, remains loyal to him and hopeful that some day the Feds will set him free. "He's done a lot for the government," she said in an exclusive interview for this book. "Someday you'll know it all, but I can't discuss it."[11]

Mohamed's lawyers, James Roth and Lloyd Epstein, have steadfastly resisted any attempts by journalists to get the full story. But from interviews with those who knew him in North Carolina and Silicon Valley, the depth of Mohamed's deception is becoming clearer. "It boggles the mind that anyone who lived this close here could possibly have anything to do with something this horrible," said an old acquaintance from California. "It makes you wonder about anyone else we were so taken in by."[12] Another U.S. official who crossed Mohamed's path had a different opinion. "You could sit and have lunch with him and he'd be as nice as pie. But if the call came to blow you up, there is no question in my mind that Ali would blow you up."[13]

Death of a Pharaoh

On October 6, 1981, Anwar Sadat, the Egyptian president who had won a Nobel Prize for making peace with Israel, sat in a reviewing stand near Cairo's unknown soldier tomb. Surrounded by four layers of bodyguards during an annual troop review commemorating the Yom Kippur War, Sadat looked upward as an elite Egyptian Air Force squadron performed flybys overhead. Suddenly, one of the troop carriers passing the reviewing stand came to an abrupt stop. Five men jumped off, led by a radical army lieutenant named Khalid al-Islambouli.[14] They rushed the reviewing stand, throwing grenades and firing bursts from automatic weapons. Thirty-five seconds later, a bullet ripped through an artery in Sadat's chest. "Impossible," he exclaimed, "impossible." Then he fell dead.[15]

On the day of the assassination, one of the shooters was gunned down immediately. A second escaped, but was captured shortly thereafter; three of the others were wounded. Still, the ringleader, al-Islambouli, was ecstatic. "I have slain Pharaoh," he cried, "and I do not fear death."

The murder of Sadat was a seminal event in what would become a decades-long *jihad,* or holy war, against the West. The assassination came a year after Sheikh Omar Abdel Rahman, the assassins' spiritual leader, issued a *fatwa*—a religious order, condemning Sadat.[16] Rahman was arrested, but later acquitted in the assassination plot. He would go on to make an indelible mark on the future of radical Islam.

The Blind Sheikh

Blinded shortly after birth, Omar Abdel Rahman had memorized the Koran by the age of eleven. He earned a degree in Koranic studies in 1972 from the Al Azhar University in Cairo, where he was influenced by the writings of Sayyid Qutb, an intellectual who was an early adherent of the Muslim Brotherhood.[17]

The Brotherhood, or Ikhwan, was founded in 1928. It spawned two of Egypt's most virulent terror sects: The al Gamma'a Islamayah (Islamic Group), run by Rahman, and the Egyptian Islamic Jihad (EIJ), led by Dr. Ayman al-Zawahiri, the scion of a prominent Cairo family. Begun as a student movement within the Brotherhood, the EIJ splintered off in the early 1970s to become a covert military arm, while the Ikhwan sought more mainstream political legitimacy. Because al-Islambouli, the lead Sadat shooter, was an outspoken EIJ member, al-Zawahiri was jailed as a coconspirator. One of three hundred arrested, the bespectacled surgeon stood trial as "Defendant No. 113."[18] He was convicted on weapons charges and sentenced to three years in an Egyptian prison, where he later claimed that he was severely tortured.

But incarceration only served to radicalize the young doctor. He emerged in 1984 as a leading spokesman for jailed Islamic militants.[19] One of his fellow inmates was Mustafa Shalabi, a thirty-year-old red-headed electrical contractor who, years later, would establish an early beachhead for the jihad at a mosque in Brooklyn.[20]

In the decade to come, Rahman, al-Zawahiri, and Shalabi would collaborate with Osama bin Laden, weaving the threads of the IG and the EIJ into the radical new terror network called al Qaeda. Each of the three Egyptian leaders would have a significant impact on the life of Ali Mohamed, offering him direct access to bin Laden, the terror prince, himself.

Lighting Ali's Fuse

Born in Kafr El Sheikh, Lower Egypt in 1952, Mohamed seems to have been launched on his trajectory after an incident that occurred in 1966, when he was fourteen. According to Jack Cloonan, the FBI agent who debriefed him after 9/11, "That's when his fuse was lit."

"He was up there in the Sinai," says Cloonan, "with a very trusted uncle of his [who] was a goat herder, and the goats wandered over the border and somehow got into Israel. The Israeli army troops who were up there guarding that part of Sinai thought that these guys were driving the goats and crossing the border to cover up the tracks of infiltrators. So they came to Ali's uncle and roughed him up. They killed some of his livestock, and then they took his uncle's sandals off and took hot water that they were boiling for tea, and poured it over his feet."

From that moment as a teenager, says Cloonan, Ali Mohamed decided "he was going to get revenge." Years later, after he'd infiltrated Silicon Valley, Ali would recruit a young Egyptian medical student with a similar revenge story involving an accidental border crossing. Khalid Dahab was the son of an airline pilot and a female medical doctor from a wealthy family in Alexandria. As a schoolboy in 1973, Dahab became radicalized after his father's Cairo-bound flight was reportedly shot down by Israeli fighter jets.[21] As Cloonan observes, such revenge motivations are "a para-mount driving force" for much of modern radical Islam.[22] As another source with the State Department's Diplomatic Security Service puts it: "A man on the West Bank is killed by Israeli tanks. His daughter grows up and just lives to avenge that death. One night she straps on a suicide vest and blows up a café full of innocent people celebrating a wedding in Tel Aviv. The next day a village gets leveled in Gaza in retaliation. It's a circle of hate."[23]

For Ali Mohamed, the circle was more like a straight line. After attending Cairo Military Academy, he earned two bachelors degrees and a master's degree in psychology from the University of Alexandria; then, in 1971, he joined the Egyptian army. Over the next thirteen years he became an intelligence officer, rising to the rank of major in an Egyptian special forces unit.[24] Fluent in Egyptian and Arabic from an early age, Ali soon mastered English and Hebrew as well.[25] He was frequently assigned to protect Egyptian diplomats overseas, where his experience broadened.[26] But he longed to play a more active role in special operations. "This guy loves action. Loves the intrigue," says Cloonan. So Mohamed volunteered for a series of dangerous clandestine missions, participating in operations in Libya and elsewhere. "He landed with helicopters to take over a jail and shoot it out with the Libyans," Cloonan says. It was only one of many special ops he would conduct in the years that followed.

The Perfect Alibi

By 1981, Ali Mohamed had joined al-Zawahiri's Egyptian Islamic Jihad. In fact, the man who later became his commanding officer in the U.S. Army says that Ali once confessed to being in the very same unit that shot Sadat. But if he was ever a suspect in that slaying, he had the perfect alibi: at the time of the assassination, Mohamed was assigned to a U.S.-Egyptian officer exchange program at Fort Bragg, North Carolina.[27]

Training alongside the Fifth Special Forces, Mohamed was tutored by Green Beret officers in reconnaissance, unconventional warfare, and counterinsurgency tactics.[28] As Joseph Neff and John Sullivan reported in the Raleigh *News & Observer*, he graduated from the program after four months, collecting a diploma with a Green Beret on it. He also participated in Operation Bright Star, a semiannual U.S./Egyptian joint military exercise.

Yet, as a devoted Muslim who prayed five times a day—and wasn't afraid to express his political views—Mohamed was under increasing pressure in the Egyptian army.

"Being Special Forces made him of real interest to certain cells within the Brotherhood," says Cloonan. "But his religious fervor also made Ali a target in the Egyptian army." Mohamed's association with the Egyptian Islamic Jihad raised suspicions. According to Nabil Sharef, a former intelligence officer, now a university professor, Mohamed was considered too religious, and potentially radical.[29]

By 1984, as Egypt's new president, Hosni Mubarak, sought to thin the Egyptian army's ranks of Islamic zealots, Ali's brand of religious fervor forced his discharge.

"He got mustered out," says Cloonan, "and he was bitter." But soon, after leaving uniform, Ali attracted the attention of Dr. Ayman al-Zawahiri, who assigned him a series of missions to test his capabilities and prove his bona fides.

"One of the first things they asked him to do," Cloonan says, "is surveillance on airplanes, because they want to hijack a plane. So Ali goes out—because he's got some of the best training going—and does surveillances on aircraft in Cairo. How you bridge the fence, how you get on board, how you're going to do it from A to Zed. That's pretty scary, because guess what happens down the road when you talk about airplanes and hijacking?"

Ali soon swore a *bayat*, an Islamic oath of allegiance, to al-Zawahiri and the EIJ. "You're my sheikh. You're my Emir," says Cloonan, quoting Mohamed's pledge to the doctor. "I pledge my *bayat* to you." Working for the doctor as a *de facto* spy, Mohamed proved himself further by getting hired by Egyptair, the Egyptian state airline His job description was security adviser.[30]

"It gives him access" says Cloonan.[31]

During his eighteen-month tenure at Egyptair, Mohamed was able to study the latest air piracy countermeasures. As the disciple of a radical Islamic leader like al-Zawahiri, Mohamed was undergoing his first real test as a double agent, and he passed with flying colors. His next assignment from the doctor was more of a challenge. "Zawahiri says, *infiltrate the United States government,*" says Cloonan, "*an intelligence service.*"[32]

So Ali Mohamed set his sights on the Cairo station of the Central Intelligence Agency.

2

A COMPANY JOB

As a radical Sunni Muslim, Ali Mohamed was spiritually at war with the Shiites who made up the Iranian based "Party of God," known as Hezbollah. But he was adaptive and responsive to outside forces. Penetrating the Central Intelligence Agency would prove more daunting than Egyptair, but deception was fast becoming Ali's stock in trade, and he took advantage of a series of terrorist events in Beirut to snooker the CIA as well.

On April 18, 1983, in what would become a model for similar suicide attacks, a delivery van pulled up outside the U.S. embassy in Beirut. The van had been stolen from the embassy the year before, so it was admitted to the protected compound and parked under the portico at the front of the seven-story building. Inside was a suicide bomber bearing four hundred pounds of explosives. When the device detonated, the sides of the embassy pancaked down. Sixty-three people died, including seventeen Americans—eight of them CIA staff.[1] Though a group calling itself "Islamic Jihad" took responsibility, the attack was the work of Hezbollah. Six months and five days later, they struck again. On Sunday morning, October 28, simultaneous suicide truck bombs exploded outside the Marine Barracks at the Beirut airport and a nearby French garrison. Two hundred and forty-one leathernecks and other U.S. personnel were killed and eighty seriously wounded. The French lost fifty-eight troops.

These Hezbollah attacks were the chilling precursors of the simultaneous truck bombings that targeted the American embassies in East Africa fifteen years later—an al Qaeda operation that Ali Mohamed himself would play a key role in executing.[2] Indeed, according to the FBI's Cloonan, "some people have thought that Ali might have been involved in the '83 [Marine] bombing."[3]

Morale at the CIA's headquarters in Langley, Virginia, slipped even lower on March 16, 1984, when Beirut station chief William Buckley was kidnapped at gunpoint by a Hezbollah cadre led by Imad Mugniyah. Buckley was held captive in the Sheikh Abdullah camp in the Bekaa valley. He knew virtually all of the Agency's Middle East secrets, and for months his disappearance haunted CIA director William Casey. The Agency was determined to find him, and the hunt grew even more intense after reports that Buckley had been severely tortured.

For Mugniyah, too, the motivation was revenge. "Imad had a good reason to retaliate," a source told the London *Sunday Times*. "A car bomb killed his brother Jihad, who had taken Imad's old job as a bodyguard to Hezbollah's spiritual leader." Rightly or wrongly, Mugniyah blamed the CIA for his brother's death—and Buckley paid the price. His disfigured body was later found dumped unceremoniously after his murder.[4]

Hezbollah would ultimately arrange the kidnapping of eighteen hostages in Lebanon during the 1980s. Buckley was one of three killed[5] along with Lt. Col William R. Higgens, another of Mugniyah's victims.[6] Described as "the ultimate faceless terrorist,"[7] Mugniyah would go on to command Hezbollah's overseas operations and execute some of the most infamous acts in the history of terrorism—including the July 14, 1985, hijacking of TWA Flight 847, an incident remembered for the murder of U.S. Navy diver Robert Stethem, and the riveting image of the airliner's pilot being held in the cockpit with a gun to his head.

Munigyah's tactics and core Islamic Shiite-based beliefs were anathema to the Sunni Islamists of the EIJ and al Qaeda, but as a measure of Ali Mohamed's capabilities, he would later broker an historic "terror summit" between the Hezbollah leader and Osama bin Laden in the early 1990s. The Sunnis and Shiites were then throat-cutting adversaries, but many analysts believe that that meeting—which we'll explore in Chapter 14—laid the groundwork for the cooperation between the two sects in the early months of the Iraqi insurgency.

Into the Fold

After the devastating assault on its staff and leadership in Beirut, the CIA found itself playing catch-up in 1984. The Cold War was winding down; the new enemy spoke Arabic and used the Koran as a weapon to inspire U.S. hatred in *madrassas*; militant schools from Islamabad and Kabul to Doha and Riyadh. The Agency was hungry for insights into this new violent Islamic mindset—and so, when Ali Mohamed walked into the CIA station in Cairo, he had a distinct advantage.

"He ends up connecting," says Cloonan. "Having been around the Egyptian military, having participated in Operation Bright Star, he has extensive contacts." Mohamed came to the Station Chief's attention, quickly but his acceptance by CIA was hardly a foregone conclusion.

"The Agency [people], to their credit, are a little bit suspect of him," says Cloonan. "They're wondering, 'Is this a provocation? Is this something that the Egyptians are running against us?' The Cairo chief of station is very concerned now about Ali's Islamic and fundamentalist leanings, because they obviously go to their Egyptian counterparts [to vet him]. Nevertheless, and this is an important point, [the station chief] sends out an Agency-wide cable that says, 'This is the guy [and] this is what his background is. I'm a little bit suspect of him, but is anybody interested in him?'"

Cloonan says that the CIA station in Bonn, center for all Iranian-based operations, responded. "They express interest and Ali ends up being brought into the fold."

But perhaps as evidence of the CIA's desperation for Islamic human intelligence (HUMINT), they apparently accepted Mohamed without subjecting him to a polygraph.

"It gets worse," says Cloonan. "He meets his CIA handler. They go through what they want him to do. He's supposed to infiltrate the Hamburg mosque that's being run by an Imam named Mohtashemi, with strong ties to Hezbollah.

"To the Agency's credit, they've got a second source in the mosque. Ali goes in and out for a week. He has a couple of meetings with his CIA handlers who come down from Bonn."

But within the week, says Cloonan, Mohamed betrayed the CIA. "He essentially gives up the operation. Based on what the second source says, Ali tells Mohtashemi and others that he is a plant."

Given the CIA's standing policy neither to confirm nor deny any details regarding case officers or assets, the full story behind Mohamed's CIA tenure may never be known. But Cloonan's rendering dovetails with several published accounts. In the *New York Times,* Weiser and Risen reported that Ali was found to be "untrustworthy."[8] Neff and Sullivan quoted a U.S. official in the Raleigh *News & Observer:* "Some time later, we found out [that Mohamed] had been talking to known terrorists and had identified himself as a CIA agent. We felt him to be untrustworthy and we put him on a Watch List." The source went on to say that "The CIA also warned other U.S. government agencies about Mohamed and urged them to detain him if possible."[9]

Cloonan corroborates that account. "The Agency musters him out and ends their relationship with him. They *do* send a cable out saying 'You've got to be very concerned about this guy.' So that is out there. But they don't do anything else at this point." And that apparent failure to act would have fatal implications down the line.

Why? Because at that point in 1984 the FBI had no knowledge of Ali Mohamed—and yet al-Zawahiri, the head of the radical Egyptian Islamic Jihad, was now vectoring him toward the United States.

After his abortive infiltration of the Hamburg mosque, Cloonan says, Mohamed's association with terrorists was "out there in the domain"; word of his suspect behavior was spreading to other intelligence services. "But what we *don't* know at this point in time is that Ali has been told by al-Zawahiri to infiltrate the United States government."

Still, with his name on the State Department's Watch List, one would think that Mohamed, now a bona fide EIJ spy, would have had a difficult time obtaining a U.S. entry visa.

He didn't.

Why not? The answer isn't so simple. In the shadowy world of Mideast espionage, where assets go in and out of favor with agencies like the CIA, the story gets murky—and troubling. One account, reported by Paul-Quinn Judge and Charles M. Sennot in a 1995 *Boston Globe* article, quoted unnamed "government sources" as saying that Ali's 1985 entry into the United States "was the result of an action initiated by Langley"— that is, the CIA.[10]

"Senior officials say Mohamed, who is of Egyptian origin, benefited from a little-known visa-waiver program that allows the CIA and other security agencies to bring valuable agents into the country, bypassing the usual immigration formalities. Intelligence sources say that waivers are controlled by the CIA's Department of Operations, the clandestine side of the agency, and have been used 'sparingly' in recent years."[11]

Three years later, in 1998, James Risen of the *New York Times* challenged the *Globe's* account, but suggested an alternative explanation: "American officials said today that there was no evidence that the agency arranged for Mr. Mohamed's visa. Officials could, not however, rule out the possibility that some other Federal agency helped Mr. Mohamed."[12]

Jack Cloonan calls it "a hiccup in the system."

"He slipped off the Watch List," he says. In any case, "Ali decides, 'What's my next move. I'm going to come to the United States.'"

Officially spurned by the CIA, did Ali Mohamed nonetheless maintain his ties to the Agency? Did he get a leg up with his visa and help slipping past that Watch List? Others, including his commanding officer at Fort Bragg, believe that he did. Given Mohamed's tenure with the CIA, that question may be impossible to answer at this point. But we can get a hint if we consider the Agency circa 1984 in the context of the shifting global geopolitics of that time.

Helping the "Muj"

By the mid-1980s, the CIA was secretly providing a fortune in arms and equipment to a guerrilla army that Ali Mohamed would later fight alongside in the nine-year war against the Soviet Union. After Russian tanks rolled into the Afghan capital of Kabul on Christmas Day 1979, the incoming Reagan administration strategized that a surrogate battle against the Soviets might hasten an end to the Cold War. The same president who turned tail in the face of Islamic terrorists in Beirut, now began arming their spiritual "brothers," the mujahadeen rebels. The Saudis matched the U.S. contribution dollar for dollar.[13]

"You've got to understand those days," says one retired State Department agent who served in Pakistan.[14] "We were battling the Evil Empire. This was their Vietnam. It was going to be the last surrogate battle of the Cold War. Against the invading Russian forces, the Muj *did* look like freedom fighters. This was an easy war to get behind. But at the time none of us—and I mean *nobody*—had the forward radar to see these guys as our once and future enemy."

In April 1985, President Reagan signed NSD 166, a secret national security directive calling for the CIA to expel the Russians from Afghanistan "by all means available."[15] Later dubbed the "Spanish Civil War of Islam" by journalist Mary Anne Weaver,[16] the Afghan struggle attracted Islamic fundamentalists from throughout the Middle East, including Osama bin Laden, the seventeenth son of a Saudi construction billionaire. Bin Laden arrived in Peshawar in 1987[17] at the age of thirty, with a C-123 transport plane full of arms and equipment to help his "brothers" battle the Russian "infidels."[18]

Not long after that, Dr. Ayman al-Zawahiri showed up and began serving as a medical officer for the mujahadeen. His subsequent meeting with bin Laden would prove historic. The modern terror network al Qaeda would be the progeny of their alliance. But making it work took the support of other key Egyptians who had traveled to Peshawar— among them former police officer Mohammed Atef, aka Abu Hafs al Masri, and Sheikh Omar Abdel Rahman, who eventually escaped house arrest in Egypt. They all made their way to Peshawar, the key staging area for covert CIA aid.

"It was like the early days in 'Nam," says one retired army officer who served with the Special Forces. "If you wanted to move up the food chain you did multiple tours. I have to think that, loyal to Allah or not, some of these people who poured into Peshawar back then were thinking career move."[19]

Another key player who found his way to the teeming city near the Afghan border was Mustafa Shalabi, who had done time with al-Zawahiri in prison after the Sadat murder. Shalabi's spiritual *mufti* was the radical Palestinian scholar Abdullah Azzam, who had taught at Al-Azhar University in Cairo, where blind Sheikh Rahman had been a fellow professor.[20]

By the late 1980s, Azzam had set up a worldwide funding network called the Services Office for the mujahadeen, or Makhtab al-Khidimat (MAK).[21] With storefront locations at mosques in a dozen countries and more than thirty U.S. cities, the MAK raised millions of dollars in cash for the anti-Soviet struggle or "alkifah." The flagship U.S. office, located at the Al Farooq Mosque on Atlantic Avenue in Brooklyn, even adopted that very name. London's *Independent* later described the Brooklyn center as "a place of pivotal importance to Operation Cyclone, the clandestine American training effort to support the mujahadeen."[22] There was another Alkifah branch at 2824 Kennedy Boulevard in Jersey City, New Jersey.

"All throughout the 1980s, Abdullah Azzam would come to the United States," says defense lawyer Roger Stavis, who later participated in the Day of Terror case.[23] "He would go to mosques like the Al Farooq and various other mosques in Chicago and Los Angeles, and speak at Friday prayers. He would raise consciousness about the mission in Afghanistan and he would raise funds."

Back then, Azzam and blind Sheikh Rahman were united in their devotion to Ibn Taymiyah, a fourteenth-century Muslim philosopher who believed that Islam was the successor religion to Judaism and Christianity.[24] It's believed that they both worked directly with the CIA in the Muj funding operation.[25] In a compelling *New Yorker* piece on the Alkifah Center by Robert Friedman, Barnett Rubin of Columbia University asserted that "Sheikh Azzam was 'enlisted' by the CIA to unite fractious rebel groups operating in Peshawar."

In 1989, Rubin contends, the CIA sent Sheikh Rahman to Peshawar to "preach to the Afghans about the need for unity in dislodging the Kabul regime."[26]

The combination of the blind Sheikh as radical interpreter of the Koran, al-Zawahiri as political tactician, and Atef as military commander would make for an extremely lethal Egyptian triad, and bin Laden would use it to full advantage in the birth and growth of al Qaeda.

During the 1980s, the Sheikh emerged as spiritual mufti to both the EIJ and the al Gamma'a Islamiyah, his own bloody Islamic Group.[27] He was also tightly aligned with Afghani warlord Gulbuddin Hekmatyar, the conduit for many of the billions in U.S. covert military aid to the mujahadeen.

"That put Sheikh Omar in the Company's good books," said one source who worked with the CIA supply operation in that era. "And believe me, later on when the Sheikh wanted to come to the States, he cashed in those chips."[28]

The Sheikh's close relationship with Hekmatyar would be underscored in an April 2002 FBI affidavit that offers probative evidence linking bin Laden and al Qaeda directly to both attacks on the World Trade Center.[29] Later, Ali Mohamed would be so closely aligned with the blind Sheikh that he would train Abdel Rahman's New York cell. That relationship, coupled with the CIA's secret funding for the mujahadeen through Hekmatyar, helps to explain why the Agency may have run interference for Ali as he sought entry to the United States and a position of influence at Fort Bragg, the heart of the U.S. military's black operations.

The "Muj" Were Our Buddies

The Reagan administration's deal with the devil to thwart the Soviets drew broad support from both Democrats and Republicans. In contrast to the CIA's illegal Contra supply operation, ongoing at the same time in Nicaragua, the mujahadeen were fighting "the good war."[30]

"The Muj were our buddies," recalled one former member of the House Armed Services Committee. "Once we'd sent them those Stingers back in '86, they kicked Russian butt."

The hundreds of shoulder-fired Stinger missiles supplied by the CIA were particularly effective against the deadly Soviet Hind-D helicopter gunships, reportedly responsible for three hundred confirmed Stinger "kills" in the Afghan theater of ops.[31]

As an experienced Special Forces commando, Ali Mohamed would have been a tremendous asset to the anti-Soviet jihad, especially since his training had been refined at Fort Bragg. Yet al-Zawahiri, ever the long-range planner, was already casting around for a radical Islamic "sleeper" to send to America—a mole who might burrow into one of our clandestine intelligence services. There was no better candidate than Ali Mohamed, a multilingual student of psychology and a hardened Special Forces commando with years of operational experience.

On September 6, 1985, with his visa approved by unknown U.S. officials, Ali bought a ticket on TWA and boarded a flight for New York City.

3

"SO . . . CHARISMATIC"

In the early fall of 1985, Linda Lee Sanchez, a medical technician from Santa Clara, California, boarded a TWA flight in Athens bound for New York. The forty-three-year-old divorcée was returning from a vacation in Greece. As the rest of the passengers filed onto the plane, a tall, dark-haired, well-built man in cargo pants dropped into the seat next to her. He looked to be in his early thirties—about ten years younger than she—and very attractive. Linda hesitated, unsure whether to say anything to him at the start of what would be the long flight to the United States.

The man eyed her and got up, turning so that she could see him in full figure. He put his hand into his pocket and pulled out a small booklet.

"I made some comment that I can't remember," Linda recalls. "He just smiled at me and sat down."

The man took out a pen and began making marks in the booklet. Sneaking another glance, Linda realized he was doing a crossword puzzle in some foreign language. What is it, she wondered? Finally she asked him.

"It's Arabic," he said. The man seemed strong, but somehow vulnerable. Gentle, she thought. She nodded and smiled tentatively.

He extended his hand. "Hello. I'm Ali." The man stressed the second syllable: Al*ee*.

As Linda took his hand, she could feel the power in his grip.

"I'm from Egypt," he said.

"That's how it started," Linda remembers. "He was just so . . . charismatic. We got to talking, and I said, 'Oh, that's too bad about Sadat.' He just laughed at me and said, 'You only hear the good things. People think he was such a good guy but he was really very oppressive.'"[1]

It was a conversation that would change Linda Sanchez's life. They talked for the next ten and a half hours, as the 747 headed west. Ali left the flight at JFK. He had his own agenda—making sure he could clear customs with his new visa. But if he was worried about getting past the Watch List, he didn't show it when they parted company. Just before she headed off for the final leg of her flight home to Santa Clara via San Francisco, Ali asked for her number. Linda wondered if she would ever see him again.

He didn't wait long to call. Six weeks later, they were married in Reno, Nevada.

"He was very good to me and he was very kind," Linda says. "He was always a gentleman." Linda Sanchez will say nothing now about that whirlwind courtship; in fact, despite her husband's confession to committing multiple acts of terrorism for al Qaeda, she remains loyal to him, making cross-country trips to visit him in federal custody and speaking to him regularly by phone.

For years reporters have been after her to tell his story, and for years she has turned them away. That's how our first conversation began in late March 2006.

"What are you going to write about Ali that hasn't been written?" she asked me.[2]

"The whole story," I said. "You were with this man for a number of years. He obviously had an impact on your life, and he's clearly had an impact on the Justice Department and the FBI. I want to try and get to the truth."

"Nobody Can Get to Ali"

There was a pause on the line. "Yeah . . . he's an interesting fellow," she finally said. "But you know, he's still not sentenced yet, and without him being sentenced I really can't say much. He can't talk to anybody. Nobody can get to him. A guy from *60 Minutes* tried to get to him and he thought, 'Well, I have connections,' but he had none. They [the Feds] have got Ali pretty secretive."

I told Linda that I'd digested all of the news pieces on her husband, including profiles in the *New York Times,* the *Chicago Tribune,* and the *San Francisco Chronicle,* but I still felt I didn't really know him.

Sanchez said she'd read the articles, too. "It's like he just kind of vanished [into] thin air."

All the more reason to help me tell his story in full, I suggested—as gently as possible. After all, Sanchez's life had been upended in the fall of 1998, when she learned that her husband was an al Qaeda spy.

"I guess it was kind of surreal," she says now thinking back on the discovery. "I knew that he had been speaking to the FBI off and on over the years. So I guess it wasn't a *shock,* but it was a big disappointment." Linda says she never saw it coming—particularly the storm of attention that followed. "From the time he got arrested . . . all hell broke loose," she says. "There were reporters coming in and out." At Ali's request, though, Sanchez never talked to them. "He doesn't want me to say anything," she reminded me.

I kept pushing.

When it hit the papers that he had worked for al Qaeda, I asked, what was the reaction?

"I lost a lot of friends," she said. "I guess you find out who your friends really are. One called the day [Ali] pleaded guilty and it was all over the television. She said, 'Sanchez, I can't believe what I just heard on TV. And if you don't *leave* him, if you don't *divorce* him, I will *never* talk to you again.'"

Linda laughed. "She's never talked to me again."

Another close friend from Reno read about Ali's guilty plea in a newspaper.

"She was kind of cool to me and I didn't understand why," Sanchez says. "I said, 'Have I done something to you? Are you *upset* with me?' She wrote me back and said, 'I'm a *true* American and I can't be your friend anymore.'"

The more I spoke to Linda Sanchez, the more I began to appreciate her mixed sense of loyalty and betrayal. But her devotion to Ali years after 9/11 was surprising. Was it possible that she never suspected him? In the thirteen years he served as al Qaeda's "California connection," Ali Mohamed spent long periods out of the country—sometimes as much as six months at a time. He associated with a tightly knit group of Islamic fundamentalists and met regularly with the FBI. Was his wife really that much in the dark?

Sanchez did admit to me that Ali told her he "knew bin Laden." Yet until the African embassy bombings in 1998, when Ali got arrested, most Americans had never heard of the Saudi billionaire or his terror network. At that, point, as Steven Emerson has said, "bin Laden was still on the periphery of the radar screen, not considered a key player."[3]

The more I pressed her, the more Linda insisted that she had little knowledge of her husband's secret life, other than the fact that he had interacted on a regular basis with the FBI.

"I knew some details," she said. "I mean, I knew that he had been talking to the government, but Ali never discussed what really went on over there. He always tried to keep me out of it. It's still hard for me to picture what he was involved in. He never told me what he talked to the government about. I guess he just never wanted me to be involved."

At that point, Linda referred me to Jack Cloonan, the retired special agent who debriefed Ali after 9/11. Cloonan worked in Squad I-49, the so-called bin Laden squad in the FBI's New York Office.

"He and Ali became pretty good friends," she said. "He knows the most."

Later, I asked Cloonan whether he thought Sanchez had any true sense of who she was married to.

"I don't think she was involved in anything," he said during a wide-ranging interview on May 4, 2006. "Clearly Ali didn't tell her much and we have no reason to believe otherwise," says Cloonan. "Was it a marriage of convenience? I think it probably was. And then I think it evolved and morphed into something different. You and I may not understand the relationship, but I think she cares for the guy."

Today Linda remains steadfastly loyal to the man who pleaded guilty to planning the Nairobi bombing, where 213 people died. But the source of her devotion seems to be simple gratitude to a man who treated her with kindness. "He has *nobody* else in this country," she says. "I'm the *only* person and he was very good to me. He was very kind. He was always a gentleman."

But did he use her? What we know about Ali Mohamed, and the infiltration protocol he recommended to other jihadis, suggests that he did. Meeting and quickly marrying an American citizen like Linda Sanchez gave Mohamed an immediate place to live—her condo in Santa Clara—and an advantage in securing U.S. citizenship, something he accomplished by 1989. The Santa Clara address also gave him a base in Silicon Valley with the potential of yielding important defense secrets for al-Zawahiri and the Egyptian Islamic Jihad. Later we'll see how Ali applied for a security clearance that allowed him to work as a guard for a key defense contractor. He also worked the Islamic community in the San Jose–Santa Clara area to help raise thousands of dollars for the jihad, established a key sleeper cell to plan future acts of terror in the United States, and even spirited al-Zawahiri into the area twice under false cover. Further, as we'll see, Mohamed interfaced with the FBI via one of the most gullible control agents any spy could hope to have watching over him.[4] Whether that relationship happened as a result of luck or intent is unclear. But Ali Mohamed's profile is that of a cold-blooded deep cover operative who left little to chance.

Was Linda Sanchez hopelessly naïve? Did she have blinders on in their marriage from the start? Consider the facts surrounding their marriage:

Mohamed was thirty-three when they met, Sanchez a decade older. He was a fervently religious Islamic fundamentalist who performed the daily Islamic prayer cycle,[5] and never smoked, drank, or ate pork.[6] Linda was raised a Protestant, a passionate Latina with Navajo blood on her grandmother's side. The Chapel of the Bells in Reno, where they exchanged vows, bills itself as "Reno's first drive-thru chapel."[7] A wedding there costs $75, plus $55 for a Nevada marriage license, $12.50 for a "Nevada Legal Witness fee," and $20 for paperwork and filing. Pictures and flowers are extra.

Ali was careful not to force his wife toward the Koran, allowing her, for the most part, to live a relatively full California lifestyle. Linda attributed that to Ali's kindness. What she didn't realize was that he was adhering to the rules of deep cover Islamic operatives—rules that he himself had helped to translate and write.[8]

Writing the Book on Terror

In the spring of 2000, a 180-page manual entitled "Military Studies in the Jihad against the Tyrants" was found in Manchester, England. Similar copies turned up in the London office of Khalid Fawwaz,[9] the same al Qaeda spokesman and financier who paid for the surveillance equipment that Ali Mohamed used to photograph the Nairobi embassy in 1993.[10] A how-to book on espionage for aspiring terrorists, it offers an indispensable window into al Qaeda's motives and strategies.

Ali later admitted to writing and translating much of the manual.

"Spying on the enemy is permitted and it may even be a duty in the case of war between Moslems and others," the manual instructs. "Winning the battle is dependent on knowing the enemies' secrets, movements and plans."[11] The manual notes that, "The Prophet Allah—bless and keep him—used that method. He would send spies and informants."

According to the manual, anyone willing to "undergo martyrdom" should be "able to act, pretend and mask himself" behind enemy lines. It instructs jihadis on how to become what Ali would later call "sleepers" or "submarines,"[12] offering tips on how to "act, change positions and conceal oneself."

Ironically, the terror manual cites among its sources *By Way of Deception*, former Israeli Mossad operative Victor Ostrovsky's memoir on double-agent tradecraft.[13] The rules in the chapters on espionage advise future al Qaeda spies to keep low profiles. As such they should:

• Not talk with their wives about Jihad work.

• Not address others with traditional Islamic greetings in which Allah's name is invoked.

- Not cause trouble in one's neighborhood.

- Not appear to be overly inquisitive.

- Not speak loudly.

The manual also advises would-be sleepers to:

- Have a general appearance that does not indicate Islamic orientation (beard, Koran).

- Burn letters immediately after reading them and get rid of the ashes, too.

- Use codes when talking on the telephone.

- Married brothers should not add their wives to their passports.

The book even cites Islamic scripture to justify deceiving one's wife:

It was said in the Proverbs, "The hearts of freemen are the tombs of secrets" and [that to] "Moslems secrecy is faithfulness, and talking about it is faithlessness." [Mohammed]—God bless and keep him—used to keep work secrets from the closest people, even from his wife A'isha—may Allah's grace be on her.

Silicon Valley Spy

Deception was Ali's stock in trade, and it's clear that his first successful mission in the United States was his conquest of Linda Sanchez, the trusting, older woman from Silicon Valley. By mid-October 1985, with no other visible means of support, he was living in Linda's new duplex apartment at 720 Harvard Avenue in Santa Clara, right in the middle of the exploding high-tech heartland. He quickly made contacts in the Islamic community and followed the first rule of all deep-cover agents: keep the story simple, and as close to the truth as possible. Among his fellow Muslims, Ali was openly vocal in his support for mujahadeen; to some he even hinted that he had official connections to the group. "Everyone in the community knew he was working as a liaison between the CIA and the

Afghan cause," said Dr. Ali Zaki, a San Jose obstetrician.[14] To other neighbors, Ali was a bit more circumspect, saying that he was a former Egyptian army officer who "hoped" to do intelligence work for the United States.

With the bravado of a true spy, he even dropped audacious hints to his new wife about his true purpose,[15] telling fragments of the truth to accompany his lies. Early in their marriage, Ali revealed to her his true purpose for coming to the United States—though she didn't understand the significance of his revelation at the time. "Everything he knew was military," she said. "He wanted to join the army so that maybe he could get into the Secret Service or the FBI. That was his goal. To work in some kind of intelligence."

In the early months of their marriage, Mohamed was careful to give Linda a lot of space, despite the cultural void that divided them. "Ali never pushed me to try become a Muslim," she says, "'Cause it used to just upset me to go to somebody's home and the men would be in one room and women would be separate."[16] Linda described visiting the small home of one of Ali's Islamic friends: "It was just a one-bedroom apartment. But all the men were in the living room and the women were sitting in the bedroom eating on the bed. And that just irritated me to no end." Ultimately she left the party, alone: "We had our own cars."

Linda drove a VW Cabriolet. Ali drove a Hyundai.

Later that night, she says, "He came home and he said, 'How come you left?'"

"I said, 'I can't do this. You know? This is America. We eat together.'"

Ali was careful not to provoke a confrontation. Later that week, she remembers, they were invited to a friend's going-away party together. "I said, 'No, you go, 'cause I don't want to do this. And, so then, after that, I was never invited."

Still, Sanchez acknowledges that she deferred to Ali on *some* issues—including her diet. Ali wouldn't allow her to keep any pork in the house.

"I'd have to get my bacon fix somewhere else." She laughed. "I didn't want to cause a fight."

At the same time, Ali didn't seem interested in expanding their circle of friends beyond the Zakis and other Muslims from the local An-Noor mosque[17] and Linda thought it wise not to push him to become more "western." To hear her speak now, it's clear that he lectured her on why he wanted to keep his circle of friends Islamic and tight.

"You have to live there," she says. "You have to be Middle Eastern, to understand the language and to understand their culture. Ali said, 'Nobody will ever understand it unless you are born there, raised there, and live amongst the government and amongst the people.'"

Santa Clara's Sleeper Cell

But Mohamed's isolation from Americans in Silicon Valley was self-imposed. Not long after his arrival he began to establish a radical Islamic cell, beginning with Khalid Dahab, the twenty-one-year-old former medical student he'd met in Alexandria in 1984 during his stint with the Egyptian Special Forces.[18]

Entering the United States on a student visa in 1986, ostensibly to study medicine, Dahab also sought marriage to an American wife as a quick path to a green card.[19] In fact, it was Linda Sanchez who introduced the handsome Dahab to his first wife, but the marriage failed within the month after Dahab pushed her to convert to Islam. A second marriage, which court records labeled primarily one of "convenience" ended in divorce in less than a year, after Dahab reportedly assaulted his new bride with a stick.

According to *San Francisco Chronicle* reporter Lance Williams' detailed account, Dahab later dropped his last name and often referred to himself by the identity of his Silicon Valley cell leader, "Mohamed."[20]

In a confession after his October 1988 arrest in Egypt, Dahab admitted that he'd helped his namesake recruit up to ten al Qaeda sleeper operatives to be stationed in the United States to execute future acts of terror.[21] The jihadis were expected to "fade into the woodwork," says terror expert Khaled Duran, whom Williams interviewed.

It's no wonder, given their mission, that Mohamed and Dahab, who sold cars and drove a used Volvo,[22] wanted to avoid alliances with non-believers.[23] In his confession, Dahab said that Ali gave him training in military fundamentals and letter-bomb construction. Dahab and Ali would get together regularly with other "brothers" to clean their rifles and handguns.[24]

But Linda Sanchez insists that she wasn't exposed to all that, and retired FBI agent Jack Cloonan seems to agree. As an American woman who was literally sleeping with the enemy, Linda seems to have been another victim of Ali Mohamed's Janus-faced talent for deception. Terrorism analyst Steven Emerson describes how Ali used that skill to full advantage when penetrating the nation's top intelligence services.

"Intelligence agencies, by their nature, are compartmentalized and, therefore, have an institutional interest in erecting barriers between different divisions, units, and the functions that they carry out," says Emerson.[25] "When you couple that with the proliferation of different agencies that are involved in intelligence gathering, you end up with this incredible ocean of different vessels that are all involved in basically the same function, but don't talk to one another and have a vested interest in not talking to one another. Ali Mohamed was able to exploit that system with murderous efficiency."

Having established his beachhead in California, Mohamed now set his sights on renewing his connection to the American military. His officer exchange experience at Fort Bragg in 1981 ` spared him legal scrutiny after the Sadat assassination, and soon getting inside the TOP SECRET confines of one of America's most clandestine bases would become his next goal.

4

PLACATING LINDA WITH GOLD

By 1986, Linda Sanchez remembers, Ali Mohamed had begun to grow restless in his new suburban home. "When he first came over here he couldn't find a job," she says. "Everything he knew was military. And so then he thought, well, maybe he would join the army."

In his early months in Santa Clara, the only success he had with employment was some temporary work as a security guard for a nondescript computer company. Then, over the next few months, Ali began to disappear. He made frequent trips to the Middle East, often returning with expensive gold bracelets to placate his wife.[1] He soon applied to become a naturalized citizen;[2] and in between classes where he studied the Constitution and the Declaration of Independence, he would slip off to Africa and the Afghan theater of ops.

"For five years he was moving back and forth between the U.S. and Afghanistan," says Nabil Sharef, a former Egyptian intelligence officer who now works as a university professor. "It's impossible the CIA thought he was going there as a tourist." In fact, he adds, "If the CIA hadn't caught onto him, it should be dissolved and its budget used for something worthwhile."[3]

At some point, early on, Mohamed even started a home computer business, hoping to gain intelligence from the ever-expanding computer industry based in his new backyard.[4] But whatever success he may have had seemed too limiting. "Mohamed was a doer," says Steven Emerson. "He couldn't sit still." He needed to get back into an environment where he'd have access to pure military intelligence.

On August 15, 1986, less than a year after arriving in California, Ali Mohamed drove to an army recruiting station in Oakland.[5] As a resident alien he was entitled to enter the U.S. military, so he enlisted under the name Ali Aboualacoud Mohamed (a variation on Ali Abdel Saoud).

Mohamed entered the U.S. Army as an enlisted man, despite the fact that he was a decorated ex-major in the Egyptian Special Forces.[6] Was it to avoid the sort of vetting he would get in officer candidate school? His wife Linda has a more benign explanation:

"He was over the age," she says.[7]

A foreign national joining the army at the age of thirty-four was a sight to turn heads, but after thirteen years in uniform back in Egypt, Mohamed knew the chain of command. He completed basic training in A Company of the 4th Battalion at Fort Jackson, South Carolina. Rock-hard, and with the mindset of an enemy in an occupied zone, he blew past most of the young recruits. The FBI's Jack Cloonan recalls that he may have set a record for the two-mile run.[8] With lightning speed, Mohamed rose to the rank of E-4, one pay grade under sergeant. He qualified as an expert marksman with the M-16,[9] went through jump school and won the Army Service Ribbon, the Army Achievement Medal, and a Commendation Medal for his spit-and-polish performance.[10]

But Mohamed's next feat in the military defies conventional practice. With no apparent outside contacts and what his wife called "the luck of the draw," Ali Mohamed, the chief spy for the Egyptian Islamic Jihad, ended up posted again at Fort Bragg, North Carolina, the home of the Fifth Special Forces. More shocking, he fulfilled his goal of penetrating U.S. intelligence by somehow getting himself assigned to the John F. Kennedy Special Warfare Center, the advanced officer training school for the ultra-secret Delta Force and the Green Berets.

"Imagine what you could do if you're working for Zawahari in arguably one of the more sensitive military operations that the U.S. Army staffs," asks retired FBI agent Cloonan.

He attributes Mohamed's posting at Bragg to the spy's skills at "self promotion." But the ease at which Ali got past the Watch List and navigated the treacherous waters of U.S. counterintelligence, suggests something more. Clearly Mohamed had some kind of official help (CIA or not) bypassing the State Department's Watch List on entry to the United States. His commanding officer at Fort Bragg believes that strings were also pulled to get him into the JFK Special Warfare Center.

"You or I would have a better chance of winning the Powerball lottery than Ali Mohamed getting assigned to a Special Forces unit at Fort Bragg," says Lt. Col. Robert Anderson, now retired.[11]

"Consider what happened," Anderson marvels. "This individual was a major in the Egyptian army. He left the Egyptian army, got a visa to the United States. That is difficult. At some point, he joins the United States Army. He does not have a security clearance. He's assigned to a Special Forces unit at Fort Bragg. If you proposed this to any army non-commissioned officer [or] commissioned officer, they'[d] tell you, it didn't happen without support from an outside agency. Now, what outside agency? I would say that it would have to be the CIA getting him into the United States. And then once in the United States, the Federal Bureau of Investigation."

Steven Emerson believes that Mohamed exploited the culture of secrecy among the intelligence agencies.

"He figured out early on [that] once he got in the front door at Fort Bragg and was able to play a dual role there, he [could] exploit the system perfectly. He could play one bureaucracy versus the other. He knew how compartmentalized they were. They [agencies] didn't talk to one another. And he knew the different thresholds at which his background would be checked."[12]

By April 1987, Ali Mohamed, now a supply sergeant, was crossing the red clay parade grounds of the base, assigned to the same elite center that had shielded him from the Sadat murder indictment back in 1981.

"Not a Bomb Thrower"

Ali Mohamed was regular army, not a member of the Special Forces. He began as an E4 working in a supply unit assigned to the Green Berets;

then, when he made sergeant, he got assigned to the JFK Special Warfare Center (SWC). At that point, Mohamed was not yet a U.S. citizen, so he couldn't get a security clearance. But he didn't let that stop him. Without having to undergo rigorous Special Forces training, he got close to them anyway, by wrangling an appointment as an assistant lecturer in Islamic studies. It was his job to train officers who were destined for the Middle East theater of ops.

"Think Jack the Ripper teaching at the London College of Surgeons," said one ex-Green Beret, who now works near the base. "Knowing what we know now about [him], it's unreal that he made it so deep, given the level of security there."[13]

Mohamed didn't always hide his radical light under a bushel. He confided to friends at the base that he was deeply upset by the Mubarak regime's hard line against the Egyptian Islamic jihad. Lt. Col. Anderson remembers a disagreement he had with Ali over Anwar Sadat's legacy.

"I told him that I thought that Anwar Sadat was a great patriot for Egypt, and [with] a very cold stare he said to me, 'No. He was a traitor and he had to die.' At that point I realized that he was a religious fanatic. His beliefs were so strong that if you disagreed with [him], he would feel very free to go ahead and kill you."[14]

Anderson contends that Ali "was a little afraid of me," because "I had the power to remove him at any time that I so desired." Anderson, in return, was wary of Mohamed's "extreme views." But he also felt that exposure to Ali could be "beneficial to the department," serving as a kind of "training aid" for the officers at SWC who might soon confront Islamic fanaticism in the Middle East.

Another source at Bragg, who remembers Ali from his earlier tour in 1981, described something Mohamed said about Sadat that was almost *identical* to one of the opening lines he would use on Linda Sanchez four years later on that TWA incoming flight.

"I know when Anwar Sadat died people would say, 'Too bad about Sadat,' and Ali would just go, 'You guys only heard the good things. You don't know the bad things over there—all the political prisoners.'"[15]

Just as he had won over Linda, Ali made a number of conquests at Bragg. His immediate supervisor Norvell "Tex" De Atkine remembers him as "a good soldier, quite intelligent. If we had a lecture on Islam, rather than *me* give it, I would have him teach that particular class. The man was a fundamentalist, all right, but not a bomb thrower."[16]

It was De Atkine who decided to feature Mohamed in a series of training videos. Set in a kind of talk-show format, they showed the Egyptian wearing a business suit, a measure De Atkine took to ensure that he wouldn't be diminished by his sergeant's uniform.

In a transcript of one of these videos I obtained, Ali demonstrates an astonishing knowledge of Middle Eastern history and geopolitics. But he also reveals a theory of Islamic expansionism that should have set off alarms among officers at the highly secure base. In one speech, Mohamed, a would-be U.S. citizen and active duty army sergeant, declares his allegiance to Islam, over all other creeds, and makes it clear that any country where Islam does *not* rule should be considered in a state of "war." Though he mentions Egypt, the subtext of his threat would include the United States:

> Islam cannot survive in an area without political domination. Islam itself, as a religion, cannot survive. If I live in one area, we *have* to establish an Islamic state, because Islam without political domination cannot survive. We have what we call a *dar ul harp,* which is the world of war, and *dar ul Islam,* which is the world of Islam. *Dar ul harp,* the world of war, comprises all the territory that doesn't have Islamic law. So if I live in an area of Egypt, for example, or in the Middle East, I will consider it *dar ul harp.* I will consider it the world of war, because actually it doesn't apply the Islamic law one hundred percent. As a Muslim I have *an obligation* to change *darl ul harp* to *dar ul Islam* and establish Islamic law. It's an obligation. It's not a choice.

Officers like De Atkine seemed oblivious to Mohamed's true intentions, even when stated explicitly. Yet there were enlisted men on the base who saw through him.

"To be in the [enlisted ranks] and have so much training was weird," said Jason T. Fogg, a fellow G.I. at Bragg who remembers Mohamed for his arrogance.[17] Now a supervisor with a freight company in Spring Hill, Tennessee, Fogg remembers Mohamed routinely comparing the U.S. Army to the Egyptian army and finding it wanting. "To have so much hate toward the U.S. was odd," says Fogg. "He never referred to America as his country."

Outspoken as he was, though, Mohamed never seemed worried about blowing his cover. It was as if he felt protected at the base, which has a strong CIA presence—a fact that might seem less surprising in light of the CIA's investment in the mujahadeen during those years.[18]

Mohamed also seemed especially talented at presenting himself as a skilled and valuable player in whatever context he found himself, says Emerson. "He was a chameleon. He could appear to be part of a loyal network and be trusted. It's the same way he had insinuated himself in the U.S. law enforcement and intelligence community. He was being protected as an asset, not being suspected as being a terrorist."

So Mohamed's occasional lapses could be understood. He rightfully felt he was among anti-Soviet, pro-mujahadeen sympathizers, and whenever he sensed the danger of exposure he had the ability to transform himself into a kind of Islamic Eddie Haskell who could kiss ass with the best of them. He seemed particularly adept at snowing senior officers like De Atkine, who even to this day refers to Mohamed as "an adventurer" rather than a spy.[19] Other senior staff members at the JFK Special Warfare Center seemed to agree.

"He told me on several occasions that he would never betray the United States, as far as breaking U.S. law or trying to undermine the government," says Lt. Col. Steven Neely, who ran the Middle East studies section at the JFK Center. "He was, in many, many ways, as loyal a soldier as you'd find coming off the farm in the Carolinas or out of New York City."[20]

As for Mohamed's *personal* devotion—to his wife—it's some measure of how he viewed their relationship that Mohamed chose to live as a bachelor at Bragg. During the entire thirty-one months he was stationed in North Carolina, Linda Sanchez remained across the country in Santa Clara. By her own admission, she visited him only two to three times a year.[21] The only way De Atkine knew Ali was married was that he saw his marital status on his pay slip.

"He never once mentioned his wife," he says.[22]

Sanchez wasn't the only one Ali Mohamed was able to fool. Other senior officers seemed equally taken with him. In a December 1987 commendation letter citing Mohamed's performance on a physical readiness test, Capt. Brian Layer wrote, "You have separated yourself from your peers and I have taken notice."[23]

Downplaying Ali's Security Breaches at Bragg

For years, senior U.S. counterterrorism officials have been in denial about Ali Mohamed's penetration of Fort Bragg. In early January 2006, I had dinner with Michael Sheehan, who recently retired as the New York City Police Department's Deputy Commissioner for Counterterrorism. A decorated former Special Forces colonel who served two tours in the White House on the National Security Council, Sheehan is now a distinguished fellow at NYU's Center on Law and Security and teaches at West Point where he graduated in 1977.[24]

During our dinner, I mentioned to Sheehan that I was writing a book about Ali Mohamed. He immediately shot back at me across the table, "Oh, come on, That guy was just a Spec. 4. He didn't even have a security clearance. Reporters are always hyping his importance. It's so overblown. He was a *supply sergeant* at Bragg, for God's sake."[25] Sheehan's underestimation of Mohamed was typical of senior U.S. counterterrorism officials, who downplayed his threat to U.S. security for years. As we'll see, a veteran FBI agent in the San Francisco office trusted Ali as an informant beginning in 1992, while at the same time the FBI's New York Office had evidence that Mohamed trained the original World Trade Center bombing cell. Yet for unexplained reasons, he was allowed to live freely for six more years.

It was this mindset that allowed Mohamed to compromise security at Fort Bragg—and, as we'll see, the army's efforts at covering up Ali's penetration at Bragg may well have compromised intelligence sharing between the Defense Intelligence Agency (DIA) and the FBI at a crucial time, when bin Laden's operatives were planning both the attack on the *Cole* and the 9/11 plot.

Ali Mohamed's infiltration of the John F. Kennedy Special Warfare Center would have consequences for years to come. Retired agent Cloonan describes how Ali used his proximity to top secret intelligence at Bragg to steal the army's most important secrets. "He was basically a supply sergeant," says Cloonan. "But they realized at Bragg, because of his language ability, that he [was] much more than that. Not just your normal recruit. This is a guy who was a standing flag officer [in the army of] one of our allies. He's multifaceted." They figured, "we ought to utilize him to our advantage. So, what he did, even though he didn't have security clearance, was go out to the map shack and take the maps [of] Afghanistan— pretty good resolution—and take them to the local Kinko's store, downsize them, and send them off to the 'brothers.'"

In similar fashion, Mohamed also gained access to top secret training manuals and other communiqués on U.S. troop strength from the highest levels of the Pentagon. He then passed them on to his cell members in New York and abroad.

There's little doubt that Ali's presence at Bragg gave Dr. al-Zawahiri and the Egyptian Islamic Jihad inside access to an array of military tactics, not to mention a keen sense of U.S. military readiness. In fact, via consolidation, the Pentagon made Ali's job easier. At the time he was stationed at Bragg, the Pentagon was in the process of combining all special operations units from each of the service branches under one central command.

As retired general David J. Baratto recalls, "The JFK School was the architect for [that] structure—how it would operate; the missions it would undertake and how it would train."[26]

At one point, according to reporters Joseph Neff and John Sullivan, Mohamed got hold of plans for a Special Operations Staff Officer Course Command Post Exercise (SOSOC CPX) focused on Baluchistan, an area the size of France that encompasses parts of Pakistan, Afghanistan, and Iran.[27] A hotbed of Islamic radicalism, Baluchistan was the home of Ramzi Yousef and his uncle Khalid Shaikh Mohammed, and was later reported to be a post-9/11 hiding place for Osama bin Laden.[28]

The object of the SOSOC CPX war game was to teach Green Beret officers how to fight rebel insurgents in the Baluchi mountains. According to Lonnie Poole, a retired lieutenant colonel, the exercise involved Special Forces, psychological operations, and civil affairs. In a Raleigh *News & Observer* article, retired air force reserve colonel Chester Richards confirmed that bin Laden and other al Qaeda strategists would have coveted such a document.

Even if it were out of date, says Richards, "it would be quite valuable . . . allow[ing] him to get inside our minds and how we do battle."[29]

With access to that level of classified intelligence, Ali Mohamed had become Ayman al-Zawahiri's most lethal mole inside the base. It happened at just the moment when al-Zawahiri was allying himself closely with Osama bin Laden. In the years that followed, Mohamed would stay under the radar, but at times his loyalty to the jihad would surface and he'd risk blowing his cover. In 1988, as the war against the Soviets ground on, he pressed the edge of the tolerance envelope once again—when he informed his superiors at Bragg that he was going to go off to Afghanistan and kill Russians.

5

LIT UP LIKE A
CHRISTMAS TREE

Operation Bright Star began as a joint ground troop exercise between the United States and Egypt after the signing of the Camp David Peace Accord in 1979.[1] That historic treaty, in which Egypt recognized Israel's right to exist, earned Anwar Sadat his Nobel Prize and led to the issuance of his death warrant by the Egyptian Islamic jihad. By 1983, Bright Star had grown to a biennial event involving both air and ground forces, run by the U.S. Central Command (CENTCOM), based in Tampa, Florida.[2] Today the exercise comprises up to 78,000 troops from eleven countries, but in the summer of 1988, when Bright Star was still a bilateral exercise between Egypt and the United States, Ali Mohamed was sent back to his former country in the uniform of a U.S. Army sergeant. Naturally, his supporters at Bragg, like Tex De Atkine, hoped that he would be an asset in the war games.

But it was not to be. Just three days into the Bright Star exercises of 1988, Ali Mohamed was abruptly sent home; indeed, the entire exercise was almost cancelled. "There was some trouble there," remembers Lamar A. Wood, who worked in the motor pool attached to the Fifth Special Forces Group.[3]

What happened? "When he shows up at Operation Bright Star," says Cloonan, "the Egyptians are offended. They know of his reputation. They know of his Islamic leanings."[4] As Cloonan notes, the warning signals about Mohamed were unmistakable. "I mean, this guy is lit up like a Christmas tree. The whole thing is almost shut down. The army had to get Ali out of Dodge very quickly and they did within twenty-four hours."[5]

That wasn't Mohamed's last disruption. Later that year, the ever-audacious Ali, who seemed to operate at Fort Bragg under some kind of protection, informed De Atkine that he had decided to use a month's leave to travel to the Middle East and fight in the "Holy War" alongside his "brothers."

Mohamed's commanding officer, Robert Anderson, reacted to the news with shock.

"The Middle Eastern seminar director came in and told me, 'Ali is going to go to Afghanistan and kill Russians.' And I said, 'I know the answer to this question but I have to ask it. Did you tell him that E-5s in the United States Army [don't] go on their own anywhere to kill Russians?' He said, 'Of course I did.'"

Anderson examined Ali's application for leave, which gave a temporary address in France. So Anderson called Mohamed in for a meeting.

"He said, 'Oh, no, I just want to go to Paris and have a vacation.'" Anderson recalls.

"I might like to go to Paris on vacation, only I don't have the money. But this Spec 4 does. Where was he getting [it]?"

So Anderson contacted a lawyer at the army's Judge Advocate General's (JAG) office. "He said, 'You really can't stop him.'" At that point, Anderson prepared an eight-page report on Mohamed. "We put in his leave forms," he says. "We got copies of his airline tickets. And I sent the intelligence report through our normal chain of command. I also sent it through another intelligence agency at Fort Bragg so that I was sure that everybody in the world would have an opportunity to read it."

Anderson says that he never got a response from the army, or the "other intelligence agency at Fort Bragg," which he chooses not to name.[6]

The prospect an active-duty U.S. soldier in a theater of ops where the United States wasn't officially involved raised the threat of another Francis Gary Powers incident. The pilot of an ultra-secret U-2 reconnaissance aircraft, Powers was shot down over Russia on May 1, 1960, provoking a major showdown between the United States and the Soviet Union at the height of the Cold War. Now, the United States was shipping billions in covert arms to the mujahadeen in an off-the-books conflict against the U.S.S.R. that would leave no room for deniability if Mohamed should be killed or wounded in action.

And yet Ali Mohamed defied his commanding officer and prepared to go anyway.

At that point, it seems clear that he was serving two sets of masters at Bragg. According to Jack Cloonan, Mohamed prepared a military plan of attack for Afghanistan before he left. He actually "submitted [the] plan to his colleagues," says Cloonan. "I've no way of verifying this, but according to Ali it was a good plan." In addition to whatever he might have stolen from the "map shack" at Bragg, Ali asked Captain Michael Asimos for some unclassified maps of Afghanistan before he left.[7] "This was vintage Ali," says Cloonan. "He is so ops-minded."

Before departing, Mohamed also contacted Mustafa Shalabi, the trusted Egyptian associate of Abdullah Azzam who ran the Alkifah Center at the Al Farooq Mosque in Brooklyn.[8] At the time, Shalabi was pulling in tens of thousands of dollars in cash each month that he was funneling to the mujahadeen. According to the 1999 confession of Ali's Santa Clara protégé Khalid Dahab, Mohamed's relationship with Shalabi dated back to 1987.[9]

As the days until his leave counted down, Lt. Col. Anderson directly ordered Ali not to go. But Mohamed defied him and flew to Paris anyway, presumably traveling on his resident alien U.S. visa. He then used "other" documents to get from Europe to the Mideast and into the mountains near Kandahar. Once in country, he passed his intelligence directly to Ahmad Shah Massoud, the legendary mujahadeen warlord who later became the leader of the Northern Alliance. Massoud was another CIA favorite. Over the years, the legendary "Lion of Panjshir" would receive briefcases from Agency operatives filled with hundreds of thousands of U.S. dollars. Ironically, Massoud, a fierce Afghani nationalist, ended up as a bitter foe of the al Qaeda-backed Taliban regime. He was assassinated by suicide bombers just days before 9/11.

According to Cloonan, during his time in Afghanistan, Mohamed "planned an operation against the Spetznaz," the elite Soviet special forces, and "killed a bunch of them." When he returned to Fort Bragg, it was with an air of triumph. Mohamed flashed two belts he claimed he'd taken off Spetsnaz commandos whom he'd personally ambushed.[10] Though such belts were readily available in the bazaars of Kabul, Mohamed's Green Beret buddies seemed convinced that he'd made the kills. "He had lost twenty, twenty-five pounds," said one source, "which indicated to me that he had done something rather strenuous."[11]

Mohamed even gave one of the belts to Lt. Col. Anderson, who had forbidden him to make the trip. "He said that he'd killed this Russian special forces soldier," says Anderson. "And that he'd killed numerous Russian special forces." With an air of smugness, he gave his C.O. a debriefing, complete with maps. "And after he told us all this, we sat down and wrote another eight-page intelligence report," says Anderson. "To this day, I've never heard a response about either [report,] except that a Federal Bureau of Investigation agent [later] said to me that he had seen the reports and had them."

Anderson was astonished by Mohamed's brazen defiance of army protocol.

"It's pretty much unthinkable that an American soldier would go unpunished after fighting in a foreign war," says Anderson, who says that he consulted a JAG officer about court martialing Mohamed. "I mentioned to the JAG that [Mohamed had given him] a Russian special forces belt." The JAG responded that one belt wouldn't be sufficient "to convict anyone of anything."

Anderson believes that the FBI was secretly supervising Mohamed throughout this period. "I believe that there was an agent that controlled Ali and knew Ali Mohamed's actions. I can't prove that, but I believe it." The FBI's own Jack Cloonan, who investigated Ali's service at Bragg years later, underscores that Mohamed was a spy who "hid in plain sight."

"There's an interesting dynamic that happens at this point," says Cloonan, "because as Ali befriends the people of the JFK Special Warfare School, they're promoting him. I mean, they don't hesitate to bring him in when they have visiting military officers there from liaison services, some of whom know Ali. In fact, one gentleman from Jordan was flabbergasted when he saw Ali there. He couldn't figure it out. *What are you doing here?* Again, no bells and whistles go off, but Ali being who he is, uses all of this to his advantage. When you think about it, he was amazingly transparent when he was there."

The evidence suggests that the love-hate relationship Mohamed experienced at Fort Bragg was a function of his support for our covert allies. But soon the geopolitical wind shifted radically—and with it, the dynamic in Afghanistan.

The Disposal Problem

By February 1989, with the help of the United States, Saudi Arabia, and more than ten thousand "Afghan Arabs"—the term used to describe all non-Afghanis who battled the Soviets—the last Russian troops pulled out of Afghanistan. It was a stunning victory for the forces of radical Islam.

"The Soviet Union, armed to the teeth, was falling apart," recalls Milt Bearden, the CIA's former station chief in Islamabad, Pakistan. "A shooting war then erupted in the Persian Gulf. Afghanistan was off the front burner."[12] That left a lot of battle-hardened Islamic radicals, trained and equipped with CIA munitions, to bring the fight to a new enemy—their former benefactor, the United States.

French scholar Giles Kepel says that the Muslim victory over the Soviets "intoxicated" the Afghan veterans. "They believed that it could be replicated elsewhere," he says. "That the whole world was ripe for jihad."[13] Richard Murphy, the assistant secretary of state for Near East and South Asian relations at the State Department during the Reagan years, concurs.[14] "We did spawn a monster in Afghanistan," he acknowledged.

But the bloodthirsty zeal of Islamic radicals might not have taken hold across the Middle East if U.S. intelligence agencies hadn't ignored this emerging new threat.

"We steered and encouraged these people. Then we dropped them," says Jack Blum, a former investigative counsel for the Senate Foreign Relations Committee. "Now we've got a disposal problem. When you motivate people to fight for a cause—jihad—the problem is, how do you shut them off?"[15]

The Afghan war had set off a firestorm in the world of radical Islam and the new leader stoking the flames was Osama bin Laden. To finance the emerging global jihad, the Saudi billionaire envisioned taking over the Services Office network (MAK), which by 1989 was still providing a multimillion dollar annual war chest to the mujahadeen. The problem was that MAK founder Abdullah Azzam had other plans. He wanted the continuing cash flow to be used to set up a "pure" Islamic regime in Kabul.

But the Egyptians around bin Laden—including al-Zawahiri, Mohammed Atef, and Sheikh Omar Abdel Rahman—coveted a portion of the funds for use against Egyptian President Hosni Mubarak, whom they bitterly called the "Wicked Pharaoh."[16]

Mysterious forces saw to it that the obstacle was soon eliminated.

On November 24, 1989, Azzam and his two sons were murdered in a car bombing on their way to Friday prayers. The triple homicide has never been solved, and[17] bin Laden officially professed grief over the incident. But the EIJ knew that Azzam was the one man standing between bin Laden and the capital he needed, So, in what amounted to little more than a mob takeover, the Egyptians cemented their position with bin Laden at the top of the jihad power structure. They have dominated the war on terror ever since.

Within months, al Qaeda, which bin Laden and al-Zawahiri had founded in 1988, effectively absorbed the MAK and its worldwide network of storefront fund-raising centers like the Alkifah in Brooklyn and another center with the same name in Jersey City.

The phrase *al Qaeda* is literally translated as "the base" or "the foundation," but Robin Cook, the late British M.P. and former foreign secretary, contended that the real meaning of the name was more like "the database," in reference to the computer file of thousands of mujahadeen who'd been recruited and trained—with CIA help—to fight the Soviets.[18] The loyal alumni of the EIJ, al-Zawahiri's group, were rewarded with positions of prominence in the new hierarchy. And one of the names near the top of the list was Ali Mohamed's.

The importance of Egyptians surrounding bin Laden—not just to al Qaeda's leadership but to its long-term goals—cannot be underestimated.

The blind Sheikh, as we'll see, became a spiritual icon for al Qaeda and a prime motivator for both attacks on the World Trade Center. Mohammed Atef's daughter would later marry bin Laden's son. The territorial Atef would later run afoul of Ali Mohamed,[19] but "Ali the American," the California spy born in Egypt, soon became a rising star.

Apparently protected by a kind of "get out of jail free" card of unknown origin, Ali continued his tour at the JFK Special Warfare Center untouched. By the summer of 1989, he was taking audacity to new heights.

Fully five months after the Soviets pulled out of Afghanistan—while he was still on active duty with the Green Berets—Mohamed began commuting up to New York City on weekends. His mission: to train members of a hand-picked cell that Osama bin Laden and al-Zawahiri were funding to "devise a scheme and plan of unimaginable horror," as the Feds would later put it.[20] Al Qaeda was setting out to create a "jihad army" in New York City, and Ali Mohamed's job was to train its first foot soldiers.

AK-47s Above the Hamptons

On those weekend trips to New York, Ali would stop in at the Alkifah Center in Brooklyn to visit his fellow Egyptian Mustafa Shalabi, the man Abdullah Azzam had sent to Brooklyn to oversee the MAK fund-raising network for the mujahadeen.[21]

Ali's trainees were a mixed group of Egyptians and Afghan war veterans. Mahmud Abouhalima was a six-foot-two redheaded Egyptian who worked as a cab and limo driver. Known as "the Red," Abouhalima was always seen in the company of the tiny Mohammed Salameh, a slow-witted Palestinian who grew up in Jordan and studied *Sharia* (Islamic law) under the "martyred" Abdullah Azzam. Abouhalima and Salameh would weave in and out of the FBI's sights for the next four years.

Several members of the group were U.S. citizens: Clement Rodney Hampton-El, a medical technician also known as "Dr. Rashid," was an American-born black Muslim who claimed to have been wounded in Afghanistan. Nidal Ayyad, born in Kuwait, had taken classes to become a citizen (like Ali Mohamed). He worked for Allied Signal, a chemical company in New Jersey. But perhaps the most tightly wired member of the group was El Sayyid Nosair, a thirty-four-year-old janitor from Port Said, Egypt, who popped Prozac[22] and worked in the basement of the Civil Courthouse on Centre Street in Manhattan. His cousin, an electrical contractor named Ibrahim El-Gabrowny, later reportedly met bin Laden himself in Afghanistan.[23]

"Ali Mohamed would come up from North Carolina to train these Muslim brothers here in the New York area," says Roger Stavis, who later represented Nosair. "He would bring with him a satchel full of military manuals and documents. It was Ali Mohamed who taught the men how to engage in a guerrilla war. He would give courses in how to make bombs, how to use guns, how to make Molotov cocktails."[24]

Khalid Ibrahim, another of the trainees, later told a federal jury that Mohamed used the name "Abu Omar" during the guerrilla warfare sessions.[25] The earliest of these were held in the apartment of a would-be jihadi named Abdel Aziz Hassan, on Harrison Avenue in Jersey City.[26] On another trip up from Fort Bragg, Ali took Nosair and Ibrahim to the Alkifah Center at the Kennedy Boulevard mosque. Affectionately referred to as "The Jersey Jihad Office,"[27] it was there, on June 4, 1989, that he screened his training videos from Fort Bragg for the "brothers."

"Understand what this means," says a former FBI agent in the New York Office who asked not to be identified. "You have an al Qaeda spy who's now a U.S. citizen, on active duty in the U.S. Army, and he brings along a video paid for by the U.S. government to train Green Beret officers and he's using it to help train Islamic terrorists so they can turn their guns on us. Keep in mind that this is when Bush 41 is in the White House. By now the Afghan war is over."[28]

Mohamed's gun training exercises took place at five separate ranges in upstate New York, Connecticut, New Jersey, and Pennsylvania.[29] But the best-documented sessions occurred over four successive Sundays in July 1989.

After meeting up at the storefront office of the Brooklyn Alkifah Center at 552 Atlantic Avenue, a group of "brothers" loaded cases of ammo and duffel bags filled with semiautomatic weapons into a series of vehicles. Heading off to the Long Island Expressway, they would drive for more than an hour out to Exit 71 near the township of Brookhaven on the North Shore.[30] There, at a ninety-one-acre undeveloped sand pit known as the Calverton Shooting Range, the men disembarked and began destroying paper targets with pistols and machine guns.[31]

At these sessions, El Sayyid Nosair brandished a chrome-plated .357 Magnum. Mahmud Abouhalima wore an NRA cap and wielded an AK-47; his Islamic brothers joked that the big curly redhead was born with "Crusader's blood." Down the firing line at the range, Clement Rodney Hampton-El wore a T-shirt with a map of Afghanistan and the slogan "A Muslim to a Muslim Is a Brick Wall."[32] Ayyad, the Rutgers graduate, alternated between handguns and rifles. The diminutive Mohammed Salameh had trouble loading the magazines.[33]

But each of them had received small arms training from Ali Mohamed, the veteran intelligence officer who had qualified as an expert marksman back when he was a teenager at the Cairo Military Academy.

"Ali Mohamed would come up to New York from Fort Bragg," says Roger Stavis. "He came quite often and became a real presence in that [Alkifah] office, which later metastasized into al Qaeda."[34]

A Warning of the Violence to Come

As these Islamic radicals blasted away a half-hour north of East Hampton, they presented the first early warning signs of the incipient jihad that would soon erupt in America. In November of the following year, Nosair would storm into a hotel in midtown Manhattan and murder controversial Jewish rabbi Meier Kahane.[35]

Two years later, Ramzi Yousef would come to New York and enlist the help of Abouhalima, Salameh, and Ayyad to build the urea nitrate-fuel oil bomb to be set off beneath the World Trade Center.[36] Hampton-El would conspire with blind Sheikh Rahman in a plot to blow up the bridges and tunnels into Manhattan, the United Nations headquarters, and the very building in Foley Square that houses the New York Office of the FBI.[37]

Ali Mohamed, their leader, would generate a record of terrorism even more astounding. In 1991, he would personally escort bin Laden out of Afghanistan and train his personal bodyguards. In 1993, he would scout the Nairobi embassy, where a suicide truck bomb would explode four and a half years later.[38]

The question that haunts terrorism analysts to this day is *What if:* What if Mohamed's shooters had been pulled over; questioned about their gun permits, even their U.S. residence status? Mohammed Salameh was an illegal alien, and thus subject to immediate arrest by the INS; that could have given the authorities probable cause to search him and the vehicle he rode out in, and question his cohorts as material witnesses. What if such routine police work had been done to determine why a group of foreign nationals was firing automatic weapons at the height of the Long Island summer season?

How, you may ask, would they have attracted official attention? That's the extraordinary part of this story: They already *had.* On each of those Sundays in July, those terrorists-in-training were being followed by the FBI's Special Operations Group (SOG), the same elite unit from the New York Office that "got Gotti." From July 2 to July 23, 1989, FBI agents banged off dozens of color shots of Nosair, Abouhalima, Salameh, Ayyad and Hampton-El, suspects later dubbed "ME's" for "Middle Eastern men" in FBI files.[39] As one criminal defense lawyer familiar with the surveillance put it: "One can only imagine the furor if a social club full of Gambino family members headed out to Calverton every Sunday and fired off Kalashnikovs and Ruger nines."[40]

The SOG clearly knew that these men were terrorists in training. Tommy Corrigan, a former senior member of the NYPD-FBI Joint Terrorism Task Force, says that the surveillance stemmed from a tip that PLO terrorists were threatening to blow up casinos in Atlantic City[41]—a lead that almost seems comical now, in light of the crimes that these men would later commit. Years later, James Fogle, one of the FBI agents on the detail, admitted in federal court that the Special Operations Group had been assigned to follow the convoys as a result of a "terrorism" assignment.[42]

Whatever the details, however, the chance to interdict their activities soon evaporated when the surveillance was ended. By the end of that summer, the "ME's" and their Green Beret-linked leader simply faded back into the shadows, and the FBI's NYO reportedly closed its file on Ali Mohamed's trainees.

The FBI's Jack Cloonan, who began building a profile of Ali in 1996, claims that even *he* didn't become aware of the 1989 Calverton training until his bin Laden squad went back "and did the data mining" seven years later.[43]

That's when Ali's association with Nosair, Abouhalima, Salameh, and the others got "included in the file."

But Ali Mohamed's trainees would soon come to the attention of other investigators in the FBI's NYO. It would happen in a hail of gunfire in a Manhattan hotel function room fourteen months later. Before it was over, an international political figure would lay dead—and the shooter, trained by Ali Mohamed, would give the FBI its next best chance to stop bin Laden's incipient war.

6

THE LONE
GUNMAN

Four months after the Calverton shooting sessions, Ali received his honorable discharge from the U.S. Army. One of the commendations in his file was for "patriotism, valor, fidelity and professional excellence."[1] In light of what he now knows about Mohamed, Lt. Col. Robert Anderson, his commanding officer, says that he intends to ask the secretary of the army to reverse Mohamed's discharge status to "dishonorable."

"It's terrible," he says. "In retrospect, it's just beyond the pale."

But in November 1989, Ali moved back to Santa Clara, California, still receiving full benefits as a member of the army reserve.

Before long he resumed his trips to Afghanistan and the Middle East.[2] Though he'd been away from his wife, Linda, for more than two and a half years, Mohamed began taking extended stays out of the country—trips that would last up to six months.[3]

His return to California amped up Khalid Dahab, who had done his best to maintain Mohamed's cell of "sleepers" while he was away.[4] In this period, Mohamed often used the alias "Omar" or "Abu [father of] Omar."

The earliest known record that he had shown up on the FBI's radar was when a Bureau confidential source known as "CS-3" met "Omar" at a Santa Clara mosque, describing him later as "someone who received American military experience in bomb-making, who served as bin Laden's bodyguard and who then lived in California."[5]

Enter the Blind Sheikh

In July 1990, following a similar path to Ali Mohamed, Sheikh Omar Abdel Rahman got a CIA-approved visa, slipped past the same State Department Watch List, and landed at John F. Kennedy International Airport in New York.[8] He was met at the airport by Mustafa Shalabi, the trusted Egyptian associate of the murdered Abdullah Azzam who ran the Brooklyn Alkifah Center.[9] Mahmud Abouhalima, "the Red," one of Ali's star pupils, used his limo license to chauffeur the Sheikh around the tristate area.

"Prior to that time—1988, '89—terrorism for all intents and purposes didn't exist in the United States," says Corrigan, the retired JTTF investigator. "But Abdel Rahman's arrival in 1990 really stoked the flames of terrorism in this country. This was a major-league ballplayer in what at the time was a minor-league ballpark. He was . . . looked up to worldwide. A mentor to bin Laden, he was involved with the MAK over in Pakistan."

In Corrigan's view, the arrival of the blind Sheikh was "a real coup for the local crew members like Shalabi, Nosair, Abouhalima, and Ayyad."[10]

Before long, Rahman was preaching at three separate mosques: the Al Farooq at Atlantic Avenue; the Abu Bakr on Foster Avenue in Brooklyn— a mosque his radical followers soon took over—and the dingy Al-Salaam (Mosque of Peace), located on the third floor of a Jersey City building above a cell-phone store.

Shalabi, whose help Ali Mohamed sought before his Afghan war leave, welcomed the Sheikh with open arms, even installing him in a Brooklyn apartment. But the cleric coveted the thousands in cash still rolling into

Shalabi's Alkifah Center,[11] and as the months went by, he began quarreling with him openly in the mosques.[12]

Curiously, during this period, Ali Mohamed entered into another, previously unreported, dispute with the U.S. government. He was having trouble with an agency that had nothing to do with terrorism: the IRS. From 1988, Mohamed owed taxes of $2,632.94. The following year his unpaid balance with the IRS had escalated by an additional $7,825.61 to a combined debt of just under $10,500.00.[13] Based on the standard salary for an army sergeant in those years, that tally seems well beyond what his tax burden should have been—raising questions as to what other income sources Mohamed may have enjoyed during those years.[14] Whatever the source, it would take another five years before the debt was paid and the IRS wiped Mohamed's slate clean.

Meanwhile, Ali Mohamed had other things to worry about. By the fall of 1990, one of his Egyptian students was growing more and more restless. El Sayyid Nosair, the janitor who worked in the courthouse basement, had joined the IG, the blind Sheikh's ultra-violent anti-Western terrorist group, and he was itching to make his bones for the jihad.

A Lead to the 9/11 Plot—Ten Years Early

Nosair kept a mailbox at a check-cashing store in Jersey City called Sphinx Trading. It was located at 2828 Kennedy Boulevard in Jersey City, four doors down from Sheikh Rahman's al-Salaam Mosque. One of the most extraordinary discoveries of this investigation is that Sphinx Trading held a key that could have put the FBI right into the middle of the 9/11 plot, months before September 11.

That mailbox of Nosair's is a symbol of how so many roads in the 9/11 story lead back to the blind Sheikh and his cell members. It underscores why the 9/11 Commission was bound to get only part of the truth when it focused on the years 1998 forward in trying to untangle the "planes as missiles" plot. As we'll see, El Sayyid Nosair and Sphinx

Trading were each enormous "dots" on the road to 9/11 that the FBI left disconnected.

During the penalty phase of the Moussaoui trial in March 2006, Minneapolis agent Harry Samit accused FBI officials of acting with "criminal negligence" in failing to approve search warrants under the Foreign Intelligence Service Act (FISA). I believe that the Bureau's seeming inability to tie Nosair and Sphinx to the 9/11 plot can fairly be cited as another example.

In any case, within months of the Sheikh's arrival, Nosair was ready to use the shooting skills Ali Mohamed had taught him, to fire the first shots in al Qaeda's new war against America. His target was Rabbi Meier Kahane, founder of the Jewish Defense League (JDL). Kahane openly advocated the removal of all non-Jews from Israel. His views were considered so extreme that he'd been banned from the Israeli Knesset; and he'd recently returned to New York City.

At this point, we don't know for sure how much of a role Ali Mohamed may have played in designing the plot, but on his frequent New York visits he stayed with Nosair and used his house at 577 Olympia Avenue in Cliffside Park, New Jersey, to store the intelligence that he'd stolen from Fort Bragg. In one manila folder, Mohamed stashed Green Beret manuals marked TOP SECRET FOR TRAINING. He even hid communiqués classified as Secret from the U.S. Joint Chiefs of Staff (JCS).[15]

One of these was a JCS WARNING ORDER, addressed to eight separate U.S. military command centers and support groups, the White House, and the Defense Intelligence Agency, not to mention the U.S. embassies in Cairo, Egypt, Khartoum, Sudan, Mogadishu, Somalia, and Riyadh, Saudi Arabia.

"There were dozens and dozens of documents that were of various classified status found in Nosair's possessions after the search warrant was executed," says Steven Emerson.[16] "From the actual ship docking locations of U.S. warships in the Persian Gulf to training manuals for Special Operations warfare. That would've been of immense value to the holy warriors and to the World Trade Center conspirators back in 1993, as they were trained for carrying out terrorists operations."

Another document, entitled "Location of Selected Units on 05 December 1988," listed the precise positions of Special Operations Forces (SOF) worldwide—including the army's Green Berets and Navy SEAL teams—along with details of their missions. That document, along with the JCS WARNING ORDER, is included—complete with Mohamed's handwritten notes in Arabic—as Appendix I on page 546. That single communiqué could have easily gotten Mohamed indicted on charges of espionage and treason, defying the legal judgment of the JAG officer at Fort Bragg who had spurned Lt. Col. Anderson's request for a court martial.

The cache of intelligence from Nosair's house also contained hints of al Qaeda's most famous New York target. Along with a receipt for 1400 rounds of ammunition and an Arabic manual on improvised explosive devices, there were maps of the World Trade Center, along with audiotapes of Sheikh Rahman exhorting his faithful to "mount steeds of war" for the jihad.

One passage deep inside Nosair's notebook called for the "destruction of the enemies of Allah . . . by . . . exploding . . . their civilized pillars . . . and *their high world buildings*" [*emphasis added*].

Ali Mohamed had schooled Nosair in the tradecraft of secret cells. The "brothers" should always use code, he advised. If they had to write down something, their notebooks should begin in Arabic with passages from the Koran or Islamic poetry so as to throw off any investigators who might seize the material.

Nosair had reason to believe his notebook might be seized.

The First Murder

On the night of November 5, 1990, as Kahane left the podium in the Morgan D Room of Marriott's East Side Hotel, Nosair burst in and began firing the same .357 Magnum photographed by the FBI at Calverton sixteen months before. The rabbi was struck twice, once in the neck.

Nosair rushed from the conference room but was grabbed by Irving Franklin, a 73-year-old Kahane supporter. After a brief scuffle, Nosair shot the old man in the leg and raced toward the hotel's front door, searching for a taxi.

This is where Ali Mohamed's possible role in the assassination comes into play.

The original plot called for two of Mohamed's trainees, Mahmud Abouhalima and Mohammed Salameh, to assist in the getaway. Nosair was to leave his car with Salameh on nearby Park Avenue and then walk to the Marriott a block away. Salameh would then drive Nosair's Oldsmobile back home after the killing. Abouhalima, who had a hack license, was supposed to be waiting outside of the hotel in a cab to speed Nosair away.

But the doorman at the hotel waved Abouhalima away from the entrance, according to Shannon Taylor, a freelance photographer who took a famous shot of Kahane lying *in extremis*. So when the wide-eyed Nosair rushed from the hotel, he mistakenly got into a taxi driven by Franklin Garcia, a New York cabbie. Suddenly, a young follower of Kahane jumped in front of the cab and prevented it from moving. In the back seat, Nosair realized the error and pointed the barrel of the .357 to Garcia's head, whereupon the taxi driver burst from the cab. He later told jurors that he was so terrified that "I almost pee my pants."[17]

Now, exiting the cab and running down Lexington Avenue with the nickel-plated gun, Nosair was spotted by Carlos Acosta, a uniformed U.S. postal inspector who drew his service weapon. Nosair fired first, wounding Acosta in the shoulder just outside the edge of his flak vest, but the heroic officer dropped to his knee and returned fire as Nosair started to run; striking the Egyptian in the neck with a single shot.

A pair of ambulances rushed both the shooter and the victim to Bellevue Hospital's trauma unit. Operated on in parallel stalls, Nosair survived but Kahane expired.

After the killing, Abouhalima and Salameh regrouped at Nosair's home in Cliffside Park, New Jersey. But they were taken into custody by the NYPD later as material witnesses. The house was raided early the next day.

Detectives and FBI agents seized forty-seven boxes in the raid—boxes that included prima facie evidence of an international bombing conspiracy with the World Trade Center as a target.[18] Among the files seized was a potential "hit list" of prominent Jewish figures, among them federal judge Jack B. Weinstein, who would go on to play a prominent role in the suppression of key al Qaeda-related evidence by the FBI and Southern District prosecutors six years later.

Nosair's Oldsmobile was later found on Second Avenue, three blocks away from where it was originally parked, suggesting that it had been moved by somebody *after* the shooting. But later that day, November 6, the NYPD's chief of detectives, Joseph Borelli, concluded that the Kahane murder was a "lone gunman" shooting. The evidence was immediately impounded by the Manhattan District Attorney's office, which ultimately tried the case as a local murder.

The conventional wisdom, as expressed in several books dealing with the Kahane murder, is that Manhattan District Attorney Robert Morgenthau simply acquiesced to Borelli's hasty assessment. The Congressional Joint Inquiry tasked with examining intelligence failures leading up to 9/11 concluded that "The NYPD and the District Attorney's office . . . reportedly wanted the appearance of speedy justice and a quick resolution to a volatile situation. By arresting Nosair, they felt they had accomplished both."[19]

As I noted in *1000 Years for Revenge,* the prosecutors were eager to avoid a "show trial." especially after Nosair lawyered up with celebrated attorney William Kunstler.

New Revelations from the Trial Transcript

At the time I wrote that passage, I didn't have access to the full transcript of the subsequent Nosair trial; so I cited the Joint Inquiry conclusion based on the best evidence I had. While researching that first book in the summer of 2003, no complete copy of the Nosair trial transcript was available. But in this new phase of the investigation, which focused on Nosair's trainer Ali Mohamed, I wanted to examine every aspect of the murder. So in the fall of 2005, I reached out to Sara Stanley and Joyce Fisher, the court reporters who had transcribed most of the 3,000 pages of trial transcript in *People v. El Sayyid Nosair,* Indictment No. 14030-90.

With their help, and assistance from Barbara Thompson, director of public information in D.A. Robert Morgenthau's office, I was able to piece together a complete transcript. It proved to be an eye opener and led me to conduct an extensive follow-up interview with William Greenbaum, the chief prosecutor on the case, who has never before spoken publicly about the trial. What I discovered now alters the historical record of those events. The evidence now shows that, from early on, the Manhattan district attorney's office was pushing the FBI and federal prosecutors toward a broader investigation of the Kahane killing.

"We sensed a much bigger conspiracy," said Greenbaum, "and we were sure that more than one person was involved. . . . When we looked at Nosair's keys, we asked ourselves, *where is his car?* It was a green Olds. We looked for it in Manhattan. The first piece of the puzzle fell into place when a really great detective named Jose Rosario informed us that he had gone down Second Avenue at a certain point looking for the car and it had not appeared and then later it got ticketed and towed from a location he'd already checked. Which means somebody moved it for him.

"It's incredible now, thinking back, how many commands were working that murder: You had the FBI's Newark and New York offices, the Jersey and New York Joint Terrorism Task Forces, the Cliffside Park P.D., the Bergen County [New Jersey] prosecutor's office, the 17th and Midtown North precincts of the NYPD, the U.S. Postal Inspectors, and our office, not to mention NYPD Crime Scene." Greenbaum says that the initial investigation by his office turned up evidence that they were "dealing with something much bigger." But shortly after the killing, "a decision was made to turn the boxes of evidence over to the Feds. They held onto them for several months before we got them back."[20]

At that point, the chain of custody had been broken, and much of the evidence—including the material Ali Mohamed had stolen at Fort Bragg—became tainted and inadmissible.

Soon, says Greenbaum, the D.A.'s office lost the support of other federal agencies for trying the Kahane killing in the context of a far broader conspiracy.

"At first," he says, "we had tons of low-level federal people coming in to us and supporting the idea of a broader inquiry. When we said 'These Islamic guys want to eat us up,' they agreed and I felt that there was a real chance to get to the bottom of the plot. To see who, if anyone, had supported Nosair."

That process would have led the D.A.'s investigators directly to Ali Mohamed via the evidence from Fort Bragg—a full eight years before the FBI finally arrested him.

But Greenbaum says, "the Feds would go back to 26 Federal [the FBI's New York Office] and nothing would come of it."

"We even had army people from Fort Bragg who came up interested in the maps that were found in Nosair's place," he says. "But then they went home and we never heard a word."

Still, that didn't stop Greenbaum from pushing. At a bail hearing for Nosair on December 18, 1990, he declared, that "This is no ordinary crime and an ordinary murder case. It is anything but. It is a planned assassination of a controversial and public figure."[21]

Greenbaum didn't realize it at the time, but one of the discoveries made by investigators for Morgenthau's office would have chilling relevance in years to come.

A "Method for Forcing Entry into an Airplane"

As the bail hearing continued, Greenbaum went on to cite a surprising list of evidence seized both from Nosair's home and his locker in the basement of the court building across the street. It included: "material relating to bomb making," "material . . . to train an individual on the uses and makeup of a hand grenade," and guidelines "for breaking and entering into a building."

Then Greenbaum made a disclosure that went unnoticed in the press coverage of the trial at the time. Also seized in the Nosair house search, he said, was a training manual "in Arabic language" on the "method for forcing entry into an airplane."[22]

Since much of the training material seized from Nosair's Cliffside Park house was furnished by Ali Mohamed, this was early, if circumstantial, proof of Ali's possible connection to the 9/11 plot that would be executed eleven years later. This reference to forced airplane entry tactics was not mentioned in the nineteen-page FBI 302 cataloguing the items seized from Nosair's Olympia Avenue house at the time.[23] Morgenthau's office was conscientious enough to get a translation, demonstrating their willingness to take the case further and underscoring Greenbaum's point that the Kahane murder was no "ordinary" crime.

And there was more evidence to support that opinion. At the bail hearing, Greenbaum cited a security-products price list found in Nosair's house. It advertised "audio jammers, recorder controls, cameras and sentry detectors." Also found were ads clipped from gun magazines hawking "barrel extensions and dummy suppressors," also known as silencers. Later Greenbaum asserted that Nosair had "altered" the .357 Magnum murder weapon, "we believe, to accommodate a silencer."

In perhaps his most shocking revelation, Greenbaum reported that Nosair's locker in the court building contained "a long thin vial" of "sodium cyanide." This didn't seem to ring any bells at the time, but later, after his arrest, Ramzi Yousef told FBI agents that he had considered lacing the 1,500 pound bomb with cyanide so that the deadly vapors would rise up through the elevator shafts of the Twin Towers and kill thousands.[24]

It's impossible to say whether the vial in Nosair's locker might have been tied to that fiendish scheme, but again, the common link between Nosair and the cell that helped Yousef construct the bomb, was Ali Mohamed.

Greenbaum gave other hints that Nosair was more than a "lone gunman." Recovered in those forty-seven boxes of evidence from Cliffside Park were articles on the assassination of Anwar Sadat and the attempted murder of Egyptian foreign minister Zaki Badr,[25] for which Ali Mohamed's leader, Dr. Ayman al-Zawahiri, was later indicted, convicted in absentia, and sentenced to death.[26]

Outside Support for Nosair

At the bail hearing, Greenbaum warned that "individuals . . . outside our country" were concerned about Nosair's welfare. The D.A.'s office had confirmed press reports that Al-Fatah, the terrorist organization, "would be willing to put up any amount of bail."[27]

"It wasn't the kind of offer one would expect in a lone gunman shooting," Greenbaum told me later.

There were plenty of signs that foreign "individuals" were looking out for Nosair.

One of them was Abdel Halim Mandour, a prominent Egyptian lawyer with close ties to Sheikh Rahman's terror group the al Gamma'a Islamiyah (IG). Mandour had shown up at a preliminary hearing for Nosair as an observer. In 1997, Mandour was denied a visa to enter the United Kingdom in what the *Guardian* described as "the Egyptian government's campaign to persuade Britain to crack down on fundamentalists accused of involvement in terrorism."[28] In October 1997, the *Arabic News* reported that Mandour was the "head of the defending body of the leader of the I.G."—that is, Sheikh Rahman.[29] A month later, Mandour spoke in defense of sixty-six defendants accused in the IG's bloody Luxor massacre, in which fifty-eight people were slaughtered by a group calling itself "Omar Abdel Rahman's Squadron of Havoc and Destruction."[30]

Years later, Mandour was cited in a Reuters story on the IG as speaking at a press conference with the blind Sheikh's son.[31] Nosair himself was an IG member and had sworn allegiance to Rahman. So Mandour's presence at the hearing in 1990 was further evidence of the killer's ties to an international terrorist organization. But defense counsel Michael Warren tried to explain away Mandour's visit by claiming that he was merely "sent here under sponsorship by the Egyptian bar."

Judge Alvin Schlesinger accepted that explanation without challenge.

"Odious" Death Threats

Throughout the trial, Schlesinger played a key role in limiting the evidence to the simple shooting itself. At the bail hearings, he admitted that he had received death threats that were "odious in nature."[32]

"I have no idea who these people are or what groups they come from or represent," Schlesinger declared, but he indicated that the calls—which were "marked by hate [the likes of] which I have never experienced"—came from the Nosair camp. Schlesinger, who is Jewish, also chastised defense counsel, Michael Warren, for a statement he'd made to the press suggesting that the judge had been "bought off by Zionist influences."

But William Kunstler, the crusading firebrand, shot back, repeatedly accusing Schlesinger of bias. He went so far as to demand that the judge recuse himself.[33] The motion was denied, but Schlesinger felt compelled to declare his impartiality.

"I have . . . had throughout my lifetime very extended . . . friendships with people of the Moslem faith," he said. "They have been my friends. I have entertained and been entertained by delegates from Egypt. I've been entertained in years past by the chairman of the Arab League who then happened to be an Egyptian. . . . Never in my personal experience has there been any bias for or against any particular people in any religion. . . . There's nothing in my life or anything I have done or said that would manifest any such prejudice."[34]

Greenbaum, for one, felt that the bias accusations led Schlesinger to "bend over backwards" at trial to "favor the other side." "Kunstler did a fantastic job for his client," he says. "He had the judge wrapped around his finger. He was playing him like a violin."[35]

Did Schlesinger cut the defense extra slack? The very fact that he even *considered* granting bail for Nosair suggests as much. With his international ties and only sketchy ties to the community, Nosair was clearly a flight risk. At the December 18 hearing, Greenbaum introduced evidence that Nosair had either lived at or received mail at *six* separate addresses in New York and New Jersey over the previous two years, including two in Brooklyn and three in Jersey City,[36] and that he'd stolen a New York state license plate for his Oldsmobile prior to the murder.

"After murdering his victim," Greenbaum told the judge, "he shot two people, one of whom was a uniformed police officer, and put a gun to the head of an innocent cab driver on the street in order to effect his escape, indicating a desire to escape justice."

Moreover, Greenbaum pointed out, Nosair would have no strong reason to stay behind in the United States. "The defendant began life as an Egyptian national," he told the judge. "He has family in Egypt. He has places to go, he has people who are willing to post whatever amount of bail is set for this defendant, and if he makes any kind of bail, whether it is in the millions or hundreds of thousands, he is gone."

As 1990 came to a close, any hope of connecting Ali Mohamed back to the Kahane murder was lost. But Greenbaum's arguments proved successful. Nosair was never granted bail; he remained in the city jail at Rikers Island until trial began the following year. But this previously unexamined bail hearing reveals how hard—if unsuccessfully—the Manhattan D.A.'s office worked to signal the Egyptian's ties to a much bigger conspiracy.

Meanwhile the FBI-NYPD search of Nosair's house the night after the murder signaled another enormous misstep by the Bureau's New York Office. Shortly after their arrest as material witnesses, Mahmud Abouhalima and Mohammed Salameh were released.[37] Though they had been photographed at the Calverton shooting range in 1989 with the full knowledge of JTTF investigator Tommy Corrigan, he admitted in the summer of 2006 that he had been unaware that the two Ali Mohamed trainees were even in *custody* in connection with the Kahane slaying.

"I don't remember ever seeing Salameh and Abouhalima being brought in," says Corrigan. "I'm not saying that it didn't happen, but I wasn't aware of that until many years later, actually [learning about it] on a news program."[38]

If the FBI had tied Abouhalima and Salemeh to the Calverton surveillance photos, as some authors have suggested,[39] they didn't make the connection soon enough to keep them in custody. Ali Mohamed, who had played a key role in al Qaeda's first murder on U.S. soil, slipped back into the quiet obscurity of Santa Clara, not even close to anybody's suspect list. But months later another violent homicide in New York would take place, and this time the victim would be a man Mohamed had once called a close friend. Would the Feds pick up on al Qaeda's chief spy this time?

DEATH OF A "BAD MUSLIM"

N ext to Sheikh Rahman and Ali Mohamed, the most influential Egyptian in al Qaeda's New York organization was Mustafa Shalabi. A confidant of the slain Abdullah Azzam, Shalabi had been dispatched to New York in 1986 to set up the Alkifah Center. *Newsweek* later called him Azzam's "trusted lieutenant" in the United States.[1]

By the summer of 1990, when he picked up Sheikh Rahman at JFK International Airport, the Brooklyn Alkifah Center was still grossing more than a hundred thousand dollars per month[2] in cash for the "struggle." Shalabi even took it upon himself to raise the money for El Sayyid Nosair's legal fund after William Kunstler had signed on for the defense. By the time Nosair's trial began, $163,000 had poured in.[3] Nosair's cousin Ibrahim El-Gabrowny had even contacted Osama bin Laden himself;[4] and the al Qaeda "Emir" contributed $20,000[5]—another example of al Qaeda's direct connection to the New York cell.

Ali Mohamed had been in constant telephone contact with Shalabi and the Alkifah Center for months before his Calverton training sessions began. In 1990, when bin Laden sought Shalabi's advice on his upcoming move from Afghanistan to the Sudan, Mustafa recommended Mohamed as the man Osama could trust to run the operation.[6]

Shalabi was respectful of al Qaeda, the terror network that had consumed the dead Azzam's MAK, but he remained loyal to his old mentor's wishes. This soon put him in deadly conflict with both bin Laden and the blind Sheikh.

Even though it was Shalabi himself who sponsored Rahman's visa entry into the United States, he balked when the blind cleric demanded half of the Alkifah's monthly income to be used for a fund to help overthrow Hosni Mubarak in Egypt. Like Azzam, Shalabi believed that the funds—from those who still supported the mujahadeen cause—should be used to set up an Islamic regime in Kabul. At stake was well over a million in cash, coming into the Alkifah Center annually.[7]

By the late summer of 1990, tensions were mounting. In the Abu Bakr Mosque, the Sheikh began denouncing Shalabi openly as a "bad Muslim."[8] Rahman even suggested that his fellow Egyptian was embezzling the Alkifah's funds. Handouts were passed out under the Sheikh's name, mini *fatwas* declaring that Shalabi was "no longer a Muslim."

"We should not allow ourselves to be manipulated by his deviousness," the leaflets said. It was a measure of the Sheikh's mercurial ability to sell out a loyal follower if it suited his purpose. Ali Mohamed possessed a similar moral code of convenience. As terrorism expert Steven Emerson says, "Mohamed could be alternately charming or a killer."[9]

Besides bin Laden, Sheikh Rahman had a powerful ally, the Pashtun Afghan warlord Gulbuddin Hekmatyar, who had been the CIA's chief bagman during the supply operation for the rebels. So the tide began to turn against Shalabi.

At the same time, the wily Ali Mohamed appeared to support him. In fact, by early 1991, two months after the Kahane murder, when Shalabi began to fear for his life, he confided in Ali. Mohamed got in contact with Shalabi's family in Egypt.

He actually drove Shalabi's wife to the airport,[10] and made plans to move her husband back home. At least that's how Ali presented himself to the increasingly terrified Alkifah director.[11]

On February 26, the eve of the Gulf War, Shalabi hurriedly packed for a flight to Cairo where his family was waiting. But he never made it to Egypt.

Two Red Curly Hairs

A few days later, a neighbor of Mustafa Shalabi noticed that the door to his Seagate, Brooklyn, apartment building was open. Ali Mohamed's former confidant was sprawled on the floor.[12] "He was knifed, shot, and beaten with a baseball bat," says former JTTF investigator Tommy Corrigan. "This wasn't some . . . genteel thing. He was made an example of."[13]

Detectives from the NYPD's 61st Precinct took control of the crime scene. In the course of their investigation, they discovered that more than $100,000 in Alkifah cash was missing from the apartment.[14] Mahmud Abouhalima, "the Red," came in and identified the body, falsely claiming that he was the victim's brother. Forensic investigators found two red curly hairs clutched in the corpse's hand. At first glance they weren't conclusive; Shalabi himself was a redhead. But the lead didn't go much further. Neither Abouhalima nor the blind Sheikh was ever charged[15] in connection with the murder.[16]

There were other suspects, including Clement Rodney Hampton-El, the American black Muslim trained by Ali Mohamed and photographed by the FBI at Calverton. Hampton-El was associated with the al Fuqra, a radical Islamic African American sect that had been linked to the murder of an Islamic cleric in Arizona.[17]

After the grisly homicide, Steven Emerson believes, Ali Mohamed was enlisted to perform the same kind of role that Harvey Keitel's character played in the film *Pulp Fiction*. "Ali was the cleaner," says Emerson. "He was brought in to clean up the apartment, escort the family back to Egypt, and to make sure that nobody who was involved in the killing could ever be found."

The Arrival of Wadih El-Hage

At this point it's unclear whether Ali Mohamed was ever questioned in the death.[18] But even if he wasn't, another al Qaeda figure arrived in New York at the time of the murder who might have shed some light on Ali's role, if any, in the brutal slaying. His name was Wadih El-Hage.[19] A Lebanese

Christian convert to Islam who frequented the Tucson Islamic Center, El-Hage had multiple contacts with the New York cell. He'd purchased AK-47s for Abouhalima, and he visited El Sayyid Nosair at Rikers Island prison within days of Shalabi's murder. His voice was even heard on Shalabi's answering machine after police had sealed off the crime scene.[20] All of this was happening at a time when Ali Mohamed was "safekeeping" a treasure trove of Alkifah documents removed from Shalabi's apartment prior to the NYPD search.

El-Hage later went on to work as Osama bin Laden's personal secretary in the Sudan, and was a key member of the Nairobi embassy bombing cell where he worked side by side with Ali Mohamed creating false IDs for the coconspirators.[21] A classic al Qaeda "sleeper," El-Hage, who later ran a tire store in Texas, used the United States in the same way Ali Mohamed did: as a safe place to regroup in between acts of terror.[22]

In any case, the brutal slaying of Mustafa Shalabi, on the heels of the killing of Abdullah Azzam, represented the final takeover by Osama bin Laden and his Egyptian cohorts of the MAK network.

"At the time," says retired JTTF investigator Tommy Corrigan, "Nobody realized how important the Alkifah Center was. It was basically a direct link from al Qaeda right into New York."[23]

The proximity of Ali Mohamed to Shalabi before the murder, and his contacts with the slain Egyptian's family immediately *after*, underscore his key role as an operational point man for bin Laden, who took control of the Center after the Egyptian's death.

The murder remains an open cold case, in the files of the 61st Precinct. NYPD detectives still had the case file until 2002, when the FBI requested the evidence. But back in 1991, with their takeover of the Alkifah, bin Laden, al-Zawahiri, and the blind Sheikh had a brick-and-mortar al Qaeda office in New York.

What Did They Know?

When it comes to the story of Ali Mohamed, the central question is as old as Watergate: What did the government know and when did they know it? There's little doubt that the CIA and DIA, two of the Big Five intelligence agencies,* ran interference for him from the mid-1980s at least until his army discharge in late 1989. Ali may have lost his official status as a CIA asset in 1984, but it seems clear that some government agency helped him circumvent the Watch List, to secure his JFK Warfare Center posting, and to operate in the highly secure environment of Fort Bragg for years, despite compelling evidence of his loyalty to radical Islam.

But whichever agency was serving as his guardian angel in those years, the one most responsible for failing to ferret him out as an al Qaeda spy was the FBI.

In 1983, the year of the Beirut embassy and Marine barracks bombings, President Ronald Reagan had first designated the Bureau as the lead agency for stopping terrorism inside the United States.[24] Three years earlier, the nation's first Joint Terrorism Task Force (JTTF) was created in the FBI's New York Office. An outgrowth of a successful NYPD-FBI bank robbery task force, the original JTTF comprised eleven NYPD detectives and eleven FBI special agents.[25] Today that flagship task force consists of nearly 150 investigators from a dozen local and federal agencies,[26] and there are now one hundred more JTTFs around the country.[27]

But the FBI has always been notorious for its redundant divisions,[28] and in the mid-1980s there was also a separate Intelligence Division within the FBI's New York Office that overlapped with the JTTF's responsibilities.

From the bombing of the World Trade Center in February 1993, through the attacks of September 11, the United States fought its nascent "war on terror" against al Qaeda as a series of legal cases, investigated by the FBI's New York Office and prosecuted by assistant U.S. Attorneys in the Southern District of New York.[29] Located less than a football field away from each other across Foley Square in Manhattan, the NYO and the SDNY became the two bin Laden offices of origin, and the clearinghouse for the lion's share of intelligence on al Qaeda within the FBI and the DOJ.

---

*The Federal Bureau of Investigation (FBI), the Central Intelligence Agency (CIA), the Defense Intelligence Agency (DIA), the National Security Agency (NSA) and the U.S. State Department's Bureau of Intelligence and Research (INR).

The Bureau began gathering that evidence with the Calverton surveillance in the summer of 1989. As such, the special agents from the NYO and the AUSAs from the SDNY deserve most of the credit—and most of the blame—for the advances and losses against bin Laden's terror network, from the time Ali Mohamed began training its first New York operatives through the second attack on the Twin Towers.

The squads in the agency's Foreign Counter Intelligence Division (FCI) ran counterespionage investigations, tracking hundreds of foreign agents from the Chinese, Russian, and Eastern bloc missions to the United Nations. But they also tracked state sponsors of terrorism, including Islamic radical groups from the Gamma'a al-Islamyah (Islamic Group) to Hezbollah and the PLO.

The problem was that for years, these two components of the New York Office—the JTTF and FBI Intelligence squads—were acting out of sync.

A Disconnect Inside the FBI's New York Office

"There was always the problem of, How do we coordinate the various activities?" says retired agent Jack Cloonan, who supervised a squad in the Intelligence Division as far back as 1985. "The JTTF evolved out of domestic-type terrorism cases, like the New African Freedom fighters," whereas the Intelligence Division was directed toward a terror threat to New York that had its origins overseas. "A and B weren't talking," he says now. "The Terrorism Task Force didn't really have a whole lot of interest in doing things on the Intelligence side of the house."

After 9/11, a number of senior Justice Department officials, including former Attorney General John Ashcroft, blamed that "dysfunction" on "the wall," a reputed legal barrier separating FBI criminal investigators of past terror cases from those in the FBI's Intelligence squads whose job it was to prevent future acts.[30] This alleged "wall" was embodied in an infamous March 1995 memo by Deputy Attorney General Jamie Gorelick, a document we'll examine in depth in Chapter 17.[31]

Testifying before the 9/11 Commission in 2004, Ashcroft claimed that "the single greatest structural cause for September 11 was the wall that segregated criminal investigators and intelligence agents."[32] Gorelick herself, he alleged, had "built that wall through her March 1995 memo." At the time he made that statement, Gorelick was on the dais facing Ashcroft as one of the ten 9/11 Commissioners.

Five days later, in her own defense, Gorelick wrote a *Washington Post* op-ed piece insisting that she "did not invent the 'wall,' which is not a wall but a series of procedures implementing a 1978 statute."[33] Whatever its origin, by the time the 9/11 Commission Report was published in July 2004, both sides of the debate seemed to agree that "stove piping," or the compartmentalization, of intelligence was a key factor in the breakdown that led to two 767's slicing into the Twin Towers and a 757 ripping a hole in the Pentagon.

Using the term "silos," Jack Cloonan, the FBI's Ali Mohamed expert, agrees. "The JTTF was interested in prosecuting people," he says. "Which was important, and it was good work and they were excellent at it. But there was a disconnect. Many people [in the JTTF] looked at this work on the intelligence side as not really manly-type work. It was the weenies over there who were doing this [intelligence] stuff that was not very important."

Cloonan contends that these dots weren't connected because special agents in the intelligence squads weren't talking to investigators in the JTTF, with the consequence that al Qaeda operatives like Ali Mohamed fell through the cracks.

"We didn't get to Bragg until ten years after he leaves," says Cloonan, whose job it was beginning in 1996 to put together the pieces of the Mohamed puzzle.

A Failure of People, Not Systems

After nearly five years investigating the intelligence failures within the FBI's New York Office, however, I've come to a different conclusion;

namely that "stove piping" or "walls" had little to do with the Bureau's inability to stop Ali Mohamed. The truth is that the universe of Feds who should have been on his trail was extremely small.* Even within the FBI's NYO, the same investigators working in Foreign Counter Intelligence and the JTTF spoke to each other regularly, shared much of the same intelligence, and worked many of the same cases.

If they failed to connect the dots, it wasn't because a legal barrier or "wall" had been erected between them. It was because of management interference, incompetence, or sheer lack of will. As another veteran of the NYO told me, "This wasn't a system failure. It was a *human* failure."

Case in point: the way the JTTF investigators failed to detect Ali Mohamed's presence in the Meier Kahane murder plot.

Within hours of the rabbi's killing on the night of November 5, 1990, two key investigators from the JTTF who would play a central role in the original World Trade Center bombing investigation got interested in the case.

Detective Lou Napoli was a veteran of the NYPD's Narcotics Division who joined the JTTF in 1983. His partner, Special Agent John Anticev, had graduated from the FBI Academy at Quantico, Virginia, four years later. The founding concept of the Task Force was to partner street-smart criminal investigators like Napoli with agents like Anticev, who knew the Bureau protocols. Anticev's younger brother, Michael, was also an agent in the New York Office.

The night after Kahane was gunned down, while the FBI and NYPD detectives were still searching Nosair's house in New Jersey, Napoli and Anticev went over the FBI's surveillance photos from Calverton and spotted the shooter's picture. They had already identified Nosair as a member of the radical Islamic Group, the blind Sheikh's terrorist group, which one of the squads in Jack Cloonan's Intelligence Division was tracking.

"It was obvious that there were a lot more people involved with the Kahane bullshit than the P.D. said," Napoli told me in 2003,[34] "being that Nosair was part of the IG, that there was a cell structure here, and that the

---

* See the list of key Feds and al Qaeda operatives on pages xxix–xxxv.

other individuals were part of the cell. The P.D. was going with the lone gunman [theory], and we were actually looking at the implications for Gamma'a al-Islamaya that Nosair was involved in. There were training camps in upstate New York."

I asked Napoli if he had caught any scent of Ali Mohamed, but he said no. "We didn't have any of that. The NYPD had all the evidence."

Yet Napoli's story differs, in this respect, from the account of assistant D.A. William Greenbaum, who says that the Feds quickly confiscated the forty-seven boxes of evidence seized from Nosair's house.

"The New York City police department had the investigation the first couple of days," said Napoli.[35] "They were hemming and hawing about whether to go federal or state. Then, three or four days in, we got the word that it was going to be given to us and we picked up the evidence. We had [it] for two, possibly three days, and we were starting to photostat it. Then we got the word that things had been changed, that the state was going to do it and we had to bring all the evidence back. We didn't really get a good look at it until after the [Kahane murder] trial."

But another agent who worked the New York Office says that he doesn't buy that excuse. "If you search a guy's house who's just killed a world figure like Kahane and you find top secret files, you ought to pull out all the stops. Since when does the NYPD dictate to the Feds how they should handle a case?"[36]

The Murteza Brothers

Among the evidence seized from Nosair's house, along with Ali Mohamed's Top Secret memos from Fort Bragg, was "a Federal Firearms License number 6-06-005-01-2A."[37] The licensees were listed as Daniel B. and Ray Murteza, gun dealers from Waterbury, Connecticut.[38] Raymond Murteza, an Albanian Muslim and a former Waterbury police officer, was questioned by NYPD detectives five days after the Kahane murder, but when he was asked whether he'd sold Nosair the murder weapon, his answers were evasive.

"He admitted that he knew Nosair," said NYPD Inspector Charles Luisi at the time. "But he also stated that he never sold him any weapons." Later Murteza reportedly conceded that he'd sold a .357 Magnum to a close friend, but minutes later told police he couldn't remember who bought it. "He's not been forthcoming," Luisi said at the time.[39]

In a search of Murteza's home in the Bunker Hill section of Waterbury, police recovered five .357 Magnum rounds and four spent shells said to be manufactured by the same Yugoslavian company that made the bullets found in the Kahane murder weapon. Murteza had reportedly practiced shooting with Nosair at the High Rock firing range in Naugatuck, Connecticut, as James C. McKinley reported in the *New York Times* on November 11, 1990, six days after the Kahane shooting.

Two days later, on November 13, Detective Lou Napoli followed up on the firearms license linking Nosair to Raymond Murteza. Interviewing Joe Norton, a range officer at the High Rock range, Napoli made the extraordinary discovery that every single weekend from 1988 to 1990 a group of "Mid-Eastern" men had fired *thousands* of rounds from AK-47s and other semiautomatic weapons.* This revelation made the four weekend Calverton exercises from July 1989 seem small-time, and hinted at a much broader pattern of paramilitary training by Islamics in the greater New York area as early as 1988, the year al Qaeda was founded. But after the NYPD declared the Kahane murder a "lone gunman" shooting, the FBI apparently terminated the investigation.

Months later after the Shalabi murder, Napoli and his partner, John Anticev, decided to focus on Mahmud Abouhalima, the redheaded would-be getaway driver for Nosair, who had identified Shalabi's bludgeoned body after his February 1991 murder. Informed by the janitor at Abouhalima's Brooklyn apartment building that he was storing blasting caps, they got a warrant.[40] But by the time they returned to conduct a search, posing as utility workers, they came up empty.[41]

In the fall of 1992, Abouhalima, who also trained at High Rock, bragged to an undercover informant that he often led Napoli and Anticev on long car chases into Connecticut.[42]

---

* See FBI 302 memo written by Napoli at Appendix II on page 547.

He was so skilled at eluding the two JTTF investigators that "the Red" soon earned another nickname: "The Teflon Terrorist."[43]

It would be another two years before Southern District prosecutors connected the Murteza brothers to Sheikh Rahman's Ali Mohamed-trained cell. They weren't even cited as "unindicted coconspirators" until 1994. (See Appendix X, pp. 574–75.) But JTTF investigators Napoli and Anticev seemed to miss that link early on. It's impossible to say for sure what would have happened if they had connected the dots to Ali Mohamed in the summer of 1991. Would the Bureau have then "opened" Ali as an informant on the West Coast the following year?

There's little doubt that Mohamed was able to use his bicoastal lifestyle to advantage—interacting with the special agents in San Francisco and San Jose FBI while keeping his distance from the "office of origin" in New York.

But Napoli and Anticev didn't miss him because they were working for the Joint Task Force or because of some "disconnect" with the Intelligence Squads. They missed him because they didn't do a thorough enough examination of the Nosair-Mohamed Fort Bragg intelligence, which ultimately resided with the FBI. This wasn't about "the wall" or competing divisions—it was about two investigators who failed to follow through once they'd connected the Calverton photos to Nosair and his cell.

Why does it matter? Because that failure to zero in on Ali back then would cost the Bureau its first chance to interdict Osama bin Laden when he was most vulnerable. By 1991, he had decided it was time to leave Afghanistan for the Sudan—and the man he trusted to get him there was none other than the former Egyptian army officer now known as "Ali the American."

8

FLIGHT TO
KHARTOUM

For months the Saudi billionaire had contemplated a move to Sudan, where the Islamic fundamentalist government of Sheikh Hassan al-Turabi would offer a safe haven.[1] The presence of U.S. forces in Saudi Arabia as a staging ground for Operation Desert Storm in February had infuriated bin Laden. Their proximity to the holy sites of Mecca and Medina only caused him to move up his timetable for the exit. Once he had cemented a foothold in New York with the takeover of the Alkifah Center, bin Laden intended to use the Sudan as a base where al Qaeda could grow exponentially.

Until now, very little has appeared in the public record about bin Laden's move from the Afghanistan theater of operations. It was a complicated logistical operation and fraught with danger because bin Laden was developing a growing profile in Western intelligence agency databases. Al-Turabi's radical National Islamic Front had seized control of Sudan in a 1989 coup, and a civil war ensued. After terror training camps had been shut down in Libya, al-Turabi allowed his country to play host to a range of groups, from Abu Nidal's Popular Front for the Liberation of Palestine Central Command (PFLPCC) to Lebanon's Hezbollah.[2]

Sheikh Omar Abdel Rahman, Ali Mohamed's mufti, had sought refuge in Sudan after escaping house arrest in Egypt and it was from Khartoum that the CIA appears to have provided his U.S. visa. Now, in the early 1990s, bin Laden saw the Sudanese capital as a potential base from which to elevate al Qaeda to the status of a multinational corporation, exporting franchises worldwide.

He tasked Ali Mohamed specifically to help him make the trip.

As terrorism expert Steven Emerson noted, the move carried enormous risk, since bin Laden had already made more than his share of enemies.[3] But if anyone was up to the job of what spies call "exfil" and "infil," it was Ali Mohamed, a man who would move terrorists in and out of the United States with impunity. When he confessed to his role in the mission in his 2000 plea session, he was explicit about his responsibilities: "I helped transport Osama bin Laden from Afghanistan to the Sudan. When I engaged in these activities, I understood that I was working with al Qaeda."

The ex-intelligence officer decided that a direct flight from Kabul to the Sudanese capital would be too risky, so the trip would be accomplished via Pakistan. Years later, he told the FBI: "He [bin Laden] has his own personal jet . . . we brought it," adding that the "tough part [was] how to take him from Peshawar to Karachi. It's a hundred miles away in very hard terrain. How to disguise him? How to get him outside the country?"[4]

As Simon Reeve reports in his exhaustive *The New Jackals: Ramzi Yousef, Osama bin Laden and the Future of Terrorism,* bin Laden made the flight in his Gulfstream G-8. He was greeted with open arms by al-Turabi, a Sorbonne-educated intellectual. At this point, in his mid-thirties, bin Laden had three wives, a Syrian and two Saudis, who together had born him fifteen children. But Mohamed had more to worry about than bin Laden's immediate entourage. As it turns out, the Saudi billionaire had planned to take along more than two thousand of the most loyal "Holy Warriors." These so-called "Afghan Arabs" were a diverse international group made up of black South Africans, blue-eyed Chechens, Kurds, Yemenis, Uzbekis, and Saudis.

One of bin Laden's most trusted followers in the Afghan "struggle" had been Abdurajak Janjalani, a Libyan-trained Filipino whose nom de guerre was "Abu Sayyaf," literally translated, "father of the sword."[5] He would go on to cofound the Abu Sayyaf Group (ASG), an al Qaeda terror cell in the Philippines that would provide key logistical support years later during the genesis of the 9/11 plot.

Ali Mohamed not only helped to ensure that this core group of two thousand fighters made the trip safely to Khartoum, but his responsibility went beyond mere travel arrangements: He was also tasked with setting up an entire new level of second-tier training camps. In the Sudanese capital, Ali instructed the battle-hardened Afghan fighters on advanced techniques in kidnapping, bomb-making, urban warfare, counter espionage, and cell structure.[6] "Because of his army experience," said one source in the Egyptian weekly *Al-Ahram,* Mohamed "played an important role in providing Jihad members with military training."[7]

To help finance the new Sudanese headquarters of "the base," bin Laden created a series of holding companies, including a construction business called Al Hijra, an agricultural company called al Themar al Mubarak, a pair of investment companies: Ladin International and Taba Investments, and a transport company for smuggling known as Quadarant Transport.[8]

In this new safe haven, bin Laden, Egyptians al-Zawahiri, and Atef, and the leaders of al Qaeda's *shura,* or ruling council, including Abu Ubaidah al-Banshiri, would set the stage for a geometric leap forward in their violent vision of the jihad. In the months to come, they would meet with radicals from Egypt and Pakistan to discuss the creation of an international Islamic front consisting of the "Afghan Arabs" and hundreds of new recruits, all charged with waging war on America and Israel.[9]

By the early 1990s, as British-trained engineer Ramzi Yousef began to design stunning new acts of terror for al Qaeda. It was Ali Mohamed who furnished al Qaeda's leaders with an inside look at how the Americans were tracking them.

The man of many faces, who tricked Linda Sanchez into believing he was a "gentleman," was about to execute a brutal game plan of deception. In the terror manual that he later compiled, his goal was stated explicitly:

> The confrontation that we are calling for with the apostate regimes does not know Socratic debates . . . Platonic ideals . . . nor Aristotelian diplomacy. But it knows the dialogue of bullets, the ideals of assassination, bombing, and destruction, and the diplomacy of the cannon and machine-gun.[10]

Meanwhile, in the early fall of 1991, while Ali Mohamed remained focused in the Sudan protecting bin Laden's interests, the FBI, by chance, opened up a crucial vein that could have unraveled the entire al Qaeda New York cell.

Another Egyptian Inside

In August 1991, six months after the Shalabi homicide, Nancy Floyd, a young FBI special agent from Texas who was working Russian Foreign Counterintelligence (FCI) in the NYO, walked up to the desk of the Hotel Woodward on West 55th Street and Broadway. Working the "hotel asset" program developed by her mentor, Special Agent Len Predtechenskis, Nancy was trolling for intel on any Russian diplomats who might have used the hotel for an "assignation." The man she met, who worked as a combination janitor, elevator operator, and night clerk, would soon give the FBI its next best opportunity to penetrate the cell trained by Ali Mohamed.[11]

Emad Salem was a short, stocky, forty-two-year-old Egyptian. Like Ali Mohamed, he had once been an intelligence officer in the Egyptian army. A moderate Muslim with no terrorist connections and no help from the CIA, Salem had followed a path to New York City that was more arduous than Mohamed's.

Typical of most Middle Eastern immigrants, he came in on a visa and took jobs way below his educational level or pay grade, struggling variously as a cab driver and security guard.[12] When Nancy Floyd found him at the dingy hotel north of Times Square, Salem puffed his résumé and claimed to have met a number of heads of state, from Sadat to Qadaffi. Once she cut through the bluster, however, he proved to be a reliable source of information, and helped the young agent on a number of INS-related cases. He also "outed" an Egyptian at the UN who was working as an illegal CIA plant.[13]

Before long, Salem alerted Floyd to the presence in New York of a man he described as "more dangerous than the worst KGB hood": Sheikh Omar Abdel Rahman. Salem told Floyd that the cleric's New Jersey mosque was "a nest of vipers," and that the word on the street among Egyptian immigrants was that Rahman was plotting a violent jihad in New York City.[14]

Despite the Kahane murder the year before, terrorism was still considered a backwater assignment at the FBI. Floyd was working for the same FCI Division as Jack Cloonan, focusing on Russians. At the time, there was no one in charge of the Terrorism Branch at 26 Federal Plaza that included the JTTF. But the earnest Floyd, a self-starter, was never one to let divisional separations hold her back, and she told her supervisor in FCI that if they paid Salem his weekly $500 salary he'd be willing to risk his life and attempt to infiltrate the Sheikh's inner circle.[15]

Nancy's boss, FBI supervisor Jim Sherman, gave Salem six weeks to get "under," but the remarkable former Egyptian officer, who was anxious to get back into a clandestine intelligence role, did it in two days.

In the fall of 1991, Salem showed up in the crowd of supporters outside the Kahane murder trial at Manhattan Criminal Court. He quickly ingratiated himself with Nosair's uncle, Ibrahim El-Gabrowny, as well as Abouhalima and Salameh, Ali Mohamed's Calverton trainees, who had been Nosair's intended getaway drivers.[16]

The two JTTF investigators assigned to Salem as his official control agents were Special Agent John Anticev and Detective Lou Napoli, who had been tracking Abouhalima for more than a year. The Salem undercover initiative was an operation opened by FCI that had a direct impact on the JTTF—contradicting Jack Cloonan's contention that the two terror branches "weren't talking" and that "the Terrorism Task Force didn't really have a whole lot of interest in doing things on the Intelligence side of the house."[17] There was no "wall" imposed here. The insertion of Emad Salem as an undercover asset was a joint JTTF-FCI operation in every respect, and almost immediately it got results.

Within weeks, Salem was appearing in news photos as the blind Sheikh's new bodyguard. He even drove the cleric to a series of fund-raising speeches in Detroit—in a van provided by the FBI—and was trusted enough by Rahman to be given a "contract" to kill Egyptian president Mubarak.[18]

But part of Salem's deal with the Feds was that he would be a deep cover "asset," as opposed to an informant who was willing to tape conversations and swear to his undercover evidence on the stand. Salem, who had family in Egypt, was deeply wary of the blind Sheikh's deadly reach. So the Bureau promised him that he'd never have to wear a wire or testify in open court.[19] Salem's job was to provide undercover intelligence and to help the Bureau gauge the threat. If he sensed a crime about to be committed, Salem would inform Floyd or his JTTF control agents; the Bureau would then endeavor to get probable cause for a search warrant, or insert an undercover informant who could corroborate Salem's intelligence.

The Visitors from Sudan

The jury in the trial of El Sayyid Nosair was sworn in on November 13, 1991, a year and eight days after the Kahane murder. At that point, the forty-seven boxes of evidence pointing to a broader international conspiracy were languishing in the FBI's New York Office, with nobody in the JTTF apparently willing to mine them and pursue the Ali Mohamed-Fort Bragg connection.

In a courtroom on the thirteen floor of the criminal courts building—across from where Nosair had worked as a janitor, the defense team led by William Kunstler and cocounsel Michael Warren exploited the forensic anomalies in the case and repeatedly played the Jewish card, suggesting that Nosair himself was somehow the victim of a "Zionist" conspiracy. Unfortunately for prosecutor William Greenbaum, the defense was able to score significant points with the jury, in part because of the way the city medical examiner's office handled Kahane's body. Since Orthodox Jewish law forbids the evisceration of bodies post mortem, the medical examiner, pressured by Hasidic leaders, had released the rabbi's remains without an autopsy—mandatory in violent death cases no matter how obvious the cause.[20] "Kunstler had a field day with that issue," prosecutor Greenbaum told me.

But the D.A.'s biggest hurdle was actually proving that Nosair himself had fired the fatal shots. Despite dozens of eyewitnesses present at the time of the murder, no one was willing to take the stand and say for sure that Nosair, who had worn a yarmulke to disguise himself as a Sephardic Jew, was the actual shooter. His prints weren't even on the .357 Magnum. There was conflicting testimony on the actual number of shots fired and even evidence that some Jewish Defense League members present that night were armed.

"Even though there was a smoking gun, it was not positively identifiable," said one alternate juror after the verdict.[21]

All of this might have been moot if the jurors had been able to hear about the Top Secret manuals stored in Nosair's house, or the memos from the Joint Chiefs purloined by Mohamed. Yet Judge Alvin Schlesinger seemed unwilling to entertain *any* suggestion that outside Islamic elements might have played a role in the Kahane murder.

Then an event occurred, out of the jury's presence, that offered proof positive that "outside forces" had a keen interest in this local New York murder trial. On December 10, 1991, Kunstler announced the arrival of "three visitors; three Arab lawyers from Sudan."[22] By that time, bin Laden had made his flight from Afghanistan to Khartoum, where Ali Mohamed was helping him set up offices and training camps. The Saudi billionaire was virtually unknown at the time in the United States, and the press failed to pick up on the importance of the attorneys from Khartoum.

Eager to appear unbiased, Judge Schlesinger announced from the bench that he would be "very pleased" to meet the Sudanese attorneys, and halted the proceedings for a private seven-minute session with them in his robing room.[23] Then the jurors were led into the courtroom, with no reason to suspect that anyone outside of New York City had taken any interest in the case. The trial continued and they were left to focus on the conflicting forensic evidence, with Kunstler and Warren exploiting the special treatment afforded Kahane's remains.

Victory over Slaughtered Lamb

At 8:15 P.M. on the night of Saturday, December 21, 1991, after twelve days of trial, the verdict came in. El Sayyid Nosair was acquitted of the primary homicide count; convicted only on lesser gun-related charges. After the verdict, a near-riot broke out on Centre Street in front of the Manhattan Criminal Court building. Police had to erect barricades to separate pro-Kahane Jewish Defense League members—who were brandishing a mock electric chair and screaming "Death to Nosair"—from Islamic onlookers who chanted *"Allah-u-Akhbar!"—God is great!*—in celebration of the limited verdict.[24] Mahmud Abouhalima, the big red-head, hoisted Kunstler on his shoulders alongside Emad Salem, the FBI's own asset, who was shaking his fist at Jewish demonstrators demanding a new Federal trial. Also on hand were Mohammed Salameh, Ibrahim El-Gabrowny (Nosair's cousin), and other members of Ali Mohamed's trained crew.

The next day, Nosair's supporters filled the second-floor function room of the Abu Bakr Mosque in Brooklyn. They slaughtered a lamb and listened to defense attorney Michael Warren pledge to file an appeal. A home video of the feast captured Mohammed Salameh, sporting a green sweater and picking his nose; Mahmud Abouhalima and his almost identical six-foot-two-inch, redheaded brother Mohammed, along with Siddig Siddig Ali, a Sudanese member of the cell, who would later lead a plot to blow up the UN building for Sheikh Rahman.[25]

Dressed in a red plaid shirt and jeans, Emad Salem, the FBI's asset, not only attended the dinner, but he borrowed a video camera and took most of the key surveillance footage himself, later slipping a copy of the tape to the FBI. The cell around the Sheikh trusted Salem so much that he regularly visited Nosair at Attica State Prison after Judge Schlesinger handed down the maximum sentence on the lesser charges: seven and a half to twenty-two years.

As effective as Ali Mohamed would be as an al Qaeda agent posing as an FBI informant, Emad Salem, a fellow Egyptian army veteran, would prove loyal to the Bureau, repeatedly risking his life in the "nest of vipers" for $500 a week. Lou Napoli, who nicknamed Salem "the Colonel," described him as "an incredibly valuable asset." According to Napoli, "he was an individual who saw an opportunity for fame; for glory. . . . But he went at it with that fervor. That's what he wanted to do. And it was easy to run him. . . . We directed him, but he was easy to direct because he [knew] what he wanted. He wanted the glory of being the man who took down an individual [Sheikh Rahman] who was a terrorist in his own country."

But since Salem wasn't recording his undercover meetings with the blind Sheikh and others, he had to be debriefed each night—and this turned into a serious problem when Napoli and Anticev, who were assigned to process Salem's intelligence, often proved unavailable.[26]

"John and Louie were supposed to be meeting him," said one FBI source. Salem "wasn't wearing a wire and he needed to get rid of this information quickly. It was all in his head. But he could never get hold of Anticev or Napoli. Their idea was to meet him every week or ten days."

Nancy Floyd, the agent who had found Salem in the first place, recognized the problem, and tried to fix it herself. "Nancy was working double duty," said Len Predtechenskis, her mentor in FCI. "Working all hours, debriefing Salem, driving home to Stamford [Connecticut] where she lived, then back in the morning where she'd put in a full day." Eventually, Predtechenskis says, her supervisor got impatient: "Nancy was spending too much time working something that had nothing to do with the Russians."[27]

Jack Cloonan contends that agents from FCI and the JTTF were "disconnected" on intelligence, but in this case the two terror divisions in the FBI's NYO were working the *identical* asset; the problem was that conflicts arose over their responsibilities.

There was no "wall" separating Nancy Floyd from Napoli or Anticev. Rather, Floyd was compelled to work extra hours when the evidence suggests that other investigators simply failed to carry their weight.

Floyd finally complained to Napoli. "You have got to start writing this stuff up. Emad is telling me he couldn't get with you." Napoli denied any negligence, later insisting to me that Salem only reached out to Floyd because he "felt he wasn't getting anywhere with us, [He] wanted to do things his way." Napoli said,[28] "So he appealed to Floyd."[29]

Whatever petty personal squabbles may have been stirring in the NYO, by the spring of 1992, Emad Salem presented the FBI with its best chance of interdicting Sheikh Rahman's "urban jihad" before any more blood could be shed.

Repeatedly visiting Nosair at Attica, Salem was encouraged to hit "twelve Jewish locations," a plot that included bombing a series of synagogues and the Manhattan Diamond District and assassinating the very judge who had sentenced him. Like any good undercover asset, Salem played for time, buying fuses for the purported bomb and milking Nosair and other cell members for intelligence so that the FBI could develop probable cause for search warrants and arrests.

Then a management conflict developed inside the NYO over how best to run Salem—and within months, both the JTTF and the Intelligence Division of the New York Office would lose their eyes and ears inside the terror cell Ali Mohamed had trained.

Blinding the Bureau

By June 1992, Carson Dunbar, the assistant special agent in charge (ASAC) of the FBI's NYO—the Bureau's chief administrative deskman in New York—was appointed head of the Terrorism Branch. His deputy was an outspoken supervisor named John Crouthamel.

Neither man had any affection for the straight-shooting Nancy Floyd, especially since she had been critical of Napoli and Anticev.[30] Floyd was debriefing Salem on a nightly basis at a TGI Friday's restaurant near 26 Federal Plaza, returning to the office afterward to type up the "serial" reports on his progress.[31]

Around the time Dunbar took over, Crouthamel met in a midtown hotel with Anticev, Napoli, and Salem, and reportedly tried to induce the Egyptian to sever ties with Floyd, who had effectively taken the reins as his principal handler. "We've got to get that bitch off this case," he said.[32] This made Salem, who trusted Nancy implicitly, even more nervous.

The situation grew more acute when Salem, still undercover, was summoned by Dunbar to his office at 26 Federal Plaza. According to FBI sources who spoke to Salem immediately after that meeting, Dunbar demanded that Salem take additional polygraphs to prove his reliability.[33] But Salem balked. For months he'd been supplying the FBI with probative intelligence, at great risk to himself, and he saw no reason to have to prove himself now.

The breaking point came when Dunbar insisted that Salem wear a wire and testify openly against the Sheikh. That was the final straw: Dunbar had changed the rules of engagement, and Salem withdrew, depriving the FBI of its key asset inside the Sheikh's cell.[34]

"The withdrawal of Emad really hurt us a lot," says JTTF veteran Tommy Corrigan.[35]

Now, for its next best effort at penetrating al Qaeda's American-based cells, the FBI was forced to turn to another former Egyptian intelligence officer.

Ali Mohamed was on the West Coast, but he was only too anxious to become the Bureau's new "informant" inside bin Laden's terror network. To make matters worse, the Bureau assigned an agent to "control" him who would soon become the alibi witness in a grisly triple homicide case that would distract his attention for years.

From using Emad Salem to go undercover and sting al Qaeda, the roles were now reversed.

With Ali Mohamed, the FBI itself was about to get stung.

9

IN COLD BLOOD

On Easter Sunday 1992, in the affluent Sunnyside neighborhood of Fresno, California, an intruder wielding a silenced AT-9 semiautomatic pistol entered the single-story ranch-style house at 5663 E. Park Circle Drive. He'd been given the alarm code, so there was no sign of forced entry. After ransacking the house to make it look like a burglary, the intruder waited in the dark for Dale Ewell, a wealthy airplane sales executive; his wife, Glee; and their pretty blonde twenty-four-year-old daughter, Tiffany, to return from their beach house.

Two days later, detectives from the Fresno County sheriff's office found their bodies. Mrs. Ewell had been shot four times from the front, point blank. Her husband and daughter lay in thickened pools of blood nearby, both shot from behind with single "taps" to the head.[1] The local paper called it "Fresno's murder case of the decade, perhaps of the century."[2]

Determining motive is the key to solving most murders, and lead detective John P. Souza and his partner, Chris Curtice, soon suspected the one person who would benefit most from the $8 million estate left by the Ewells: their twenty-year-old son Dana, a student at nearby Santa Clara University.

But Dana had an ironclad alibi for the time of the triple homicide: He was celebrating Easter with his fiancée, Monica Zent, and her father, John, a veteran special agent from the San Francisco office of the FBI.

Days after the killings, Zent, a slim, blond forty-six-year-old agent who'd worked a number of terrorism cases for the Bureau, accompanied Ewell to his first interview with the sheriff's detectives. To Detective Souza, the special agent's demeanor at that session was "pompous."

"The first thing he did," says Souza, "he threw his business card down and flashed his ID announcing, 'I'm John Zent—FBI.'"[3]

Souza and his fellow detectives were unimpressed. "We said, 'Okaaay, and what do you have to offer, Mr. Zent?'" At that point, Zent followed Dana into an interrogation room, but the detectives asked him to step outside. ""I think we'll need to talk to Dana alone," they said.[4]

"It was like Zent was running interference for Dana," remembers Souza.[5]

In the weeks that followed, Souza and Curtice began discovering anomalies in Dana Ewell's conduct. In several media stories, Dana had lied about running his father's airplane dealership. He'd also falsely boasted about being a "young successful millionaire investor/entrepreneur." Relying on his embellished self-descriptions, the *San Jose Mercury News* ran a piece that began, "It's easy to pick Dana Ewell out of a crowd. . . . Ewell is a self-made millionaire who amassed his fortune playing the stock market, running two companies and selling mutual funds."

As Kraig Hanadel describes in *Catch Me If You Can*, his compelling book on the case, the evidence began to point to a murder-for-hire plot:

> Dana had a history, Souza had learned . . . of hiring others to do his dirty work, So if the road continued to lead to Dana, Souza had to find the hit man and maybe the hit man would bring down Dana.[6]

Souza, who saw Dana as "a habitual liar" and a "sociopath,"[7] soon learned from college friends that Ewell had partied shortly after his family's funeral. More chilling, he'd even showed off the blood-splatter residue at the crime scene before the death house could be cleaned.[8]

Souza and Curtice also found evidence that Dana was looting his grandmother's $400,000 trust account, and making payments to Joel Radovcich, an unemployed dropout from the San Fernando Valley, who had recently begun taking helicopter pilot lessons at $500 an hour. In addition to covering the flying lessons, to the tune of $11,320,

Dana had arranged for his fiancée, Monica Zent, to receive $17,014 from the trust account in payment of her tuition at the University of San Diego Law School,[9] plus additional cash and gifts totaling almost $40,000.[10]

Monica, who reportedly transformed herself from a "mousy" brunette to a stunning "bottle blonde" after the murders, continued to live with Dana. She reportedly used one of Ewell's credit cards to buy an H&K SP89 nine-millimeter semiautomatic handgun. She even lived for a time with Dana in a Los Angeles "safe house" where he hid out from police, and reportedly used a series of bank accounts with him.[11]

No evidence ever surfaced that linked Monica as a coconspirator in the murders or even suggested that she had any prior knowledge of the deaths. But along with her father, Monica continued to profess Dana's innocence.[12]

Zent Takes On the Fresno Sheriff's Office

In an open letter to the *Fresno Bee,* on November 25, 1992, more than seven months after the still-unsolved triple murder, Zent cited his FBI experience in a published attack on the Fresno County Sheriff's detectives while proclaiming his family's "love" for Dana. It is virtually unprecedented that an active duty FBI agent would comment on a homicide investigation—especially one in which he has a personal interest. But the letter, reproduced here, offers a real insight into the man that the FBI had depended on to monitor Ali Mohamed:

> In response to your recent article concerning Dana Ewell, my family believes that both the *Fresno Bee* and the Sheriff's office have, without validity, tried to link Dana with the death of his family. It is well know[n] to the Sheriff's office that Dana was with our daughter having dinner in our Morgan Hill home when this crime occurred. Evidence along with witness statements including my own full[y] support Dana's whereabouts. The concept that Dana hired someone to do this crime is really grasping for straws. Perhaps it isn't apparent, but Dana is a victim, he has lost in one crime all of his immediate family.
>
> During that Easter weekend on Saturday, my family spent a long and enjoyable dinner with Dale, Glee, Tiffany and Dana at their Pajaro Beach home. . . . Dana's

love for his family, his respect for his parent[s], was mirrored in their love for him—that pride parents have in realizing their children are doing well.

I've been in Federal law enforcement working complex, criminal investigations for over 21 years. In my opinion there have been a number of improper procedures coupled with a lack of professionalism and objectivity within this case. . . .

Some have taken note that Dana has a nice car, clothes and goes to an expensive college. Having spoken with Dale and Glee, I know they very happily provided the best for both Dana and Tiffany. The fact that the Ewells had significant financial resources simply made it easier for them to give the best to their children. This is an action any parent would do if money wasn't the issue.

Without question, Dana has suffered a great loss compounded by those who would link him to his crime without any factual basis. Eventually someone will be caught who will explain the events surrounding this sad crime, usually after getting off the hook for some other crime. Until then, the idle speculation or unfounded implications should be avoided by all. Put yourself in Dana's shoes; he would gladly forgo all the money to simply again be with his family.

Our family loves and supports Dana as one of our own. Before this crime and since, he had been a very welcomed guest in our home. The harm that has been done to him within Fresno and at Santa Clara University will pass, but none of it has been beneficial to solving this crime. The challenge is to solve every aspect of the crime—to then identify the perpetrator—not to simply take aim at Dana in light of one's own limitations or inabilities.

—John Zent, Morgan Hills

If Zent thought his letter accusing the sheriff's detectives of "lack of professionalism" would put them off, he was wrong. In fact, after his office was challenged in the paper, Sheriff Steve Margarian, an elected official whose own mother lived in the Sunnyside neighborhood where the crime occurred, made it his personal mission to clear the case.[13]

Over the next twenty-four months, Margarian's office spent more than $1.5 million on the Ewell case—an almost unheard-of sum for a local law enforcement department.

In a multicountry, multistate probe worthy of any federal investigation, the detectives began following Joel Radovcich's black Honda CRX as he crisscrossed Los Angeles, Orange, and Riverside counties, responding to pages and making cryptic calls from pay phones, many of them located outside 7-Elevens.

"We had up to fifteen undercover cars at one point," recalls Detective Souza. "We weren't gonna lose him."

The detectives went so far as to clone Joel's pager. Eavesdropping on one pay-phone conversation, they overheard Joel order a sophisticated $431 electronic lock-picking device.

That led them to Ernest "Jack" Ponce, a bartender from San Bernadino who had purchased the missing AT-9 assault pistol suspected as the murder weapon. Detectives had already traced books on silencer making to another of Joel's mail drops. And when they caught up with Ponce's father, a doctor, he admitted that Joel's brother, Peter, had "gotten involved in . . . a Menendez type deal," referencing the two Beverly Hills brothers who killed their parents.[14]

Linking the murder weapon to Joel was crucial, since 9mm slugs found at the crime scene bore unusual markings suggesting that they had been fired from a gun that had been "ported"—a crude method of silencing a weapon by drilling holes in the barrel.

At this point in the investigation, Detectives Souza and Curtice went so far as to collect a series of barrels from AT-9s manufactured at the same time as the suspected murder weapon bought by Ponce for Joel. After a series of test firings, the FSO's forensics tech got a virtual perfect match to the fatal slugs.

Tightening the noose, Detective Curtice confronted Dana at the dormitory where he lived with Monica Zent. One night, more than a year after the killings, he stood in the doorway of Ewell's room as Monica sat on a bed nearby. In the presence of a campus police officer, Det. Curtice looked at Dana and announced point blank, "the information we have leads us to believe that Joel Radovcich killed your family."[15]

As Curtice later told Kraig Hanadel, "it looked like someone punched Dana in the gut. I mean, he was fish-belly white. And for once he was speechless."

Curtice and another detective then hung back as Dana and Monica rushed out of the dorm and into Dana's Mercedes. A high-speed chased ensued. When they reached the freeway, the Mercedes raced for an exit ramp, cutting diagonally across three lanes of traffic, and the detectives lost them. But via the cloned pager, they quickly learned that Dana had signaled Joel. They traced the call to a Pac Bell pay phone, and in a scene worthy of an episode of *CSI*, Curtice sped to the location and caught Dana red-handed talking to the man he'd hired to shoot his family.

"When you confront a suspect with the name of a man you say killed his family, and then he bolts out to call that person, it's fairly probative of a guilty mind," says Souza.[16]

Yet the case soon stalled when Jack Ponce repeatedly refused to submit to a polygraph. Without the murder weapon, Souza and Curtice had a compelling but essentially circumstantial case, and the investigation hit a wall.

Finally, after two years, the detectives presented their "murder book" on the case to an FBI-Department of Justice profiling team that was visiting Fresno. When they learned of Special Agent John Zent's involvement, and reviewed the case file, the investigators reportedly "displayed shock." They encouraged the sheriff's detectives to contact Zent's superiors in the FBI's San Francisco office.[17]

Sheriff Margarian then wrote to Zent's regional supervisor, listing a series of actions, including the *Fresno Bee* letter, that he felt suggested an effort on Zent's part "to interfere/obstruct our investigation," including flashing his FBI ID to gain access to the murder scene on the day the bodies were discovered, and reportedly instructing his daughter not to cooperate in the investigation.[18] The sheriff also reportedly cited "strong indications" that Zent was "advising Dana Ewell on how to handle investigators."

It's unknown whether the Bureau opened an OPR (Office of Professional Responsibility) internal affairs investigation on Zent, but he later told reporters that the FBI had instructed him to stop discussing his views on the case.[19]

In the late spring of 2006, I contacted Detective John Souza, now semi-retired, at the small ten-acre farm where he grows onions and tends a few grapevines. After sending him a short history on Ali Mohamed, I asked what he thought of Special Agent Zent's capabilities.

He paused a few moments, and then said, "I would equate them to his performance with Dana Ewell. With Dana, [Zent] just totally ignored the signals, the flags. If he couldn't see the guilt of this kid, who was an absolute sociopath, after two years—when we had built an airtight forensic case with a coconspirator who flipped—how was he going to sniff out an al Qaeda spy? In my judgment, John Zent lacks the capacity to admit he's wrong and that is not a good quality for an investigator."

When I spoke to Souza's partner, Chris Curtice, who remains on active duty, he put it another way: "If this guy Mohamed was a terrorist sleeper agent who wanted to infiltrate this country and find out what the FBI had on al Qaeda, he could not have encountered a better special agent to 'control' him—quote unquote—than John Zent."[20]

As we'll learn later, Curtice and Souza were dead right about Dana's complicity in the murders, and Special Agent John Zent was dead wrong.

10

INCIDENT
IN ROME

Zent's judgment notwithstanding, it was in 1992, around the time of the Ewell murders, that Ali Mohamed again came to the attention of the FBI—the result of an incident in Rome following the summer Olympic games in Barcelona.

Ali was on a TWA flight that landed in Leonardo Da Vinci–Fiumicino Airport. One published account has maintained that he was returning from Afghanistan where he was training al Qaeda operatives when he got stopped by airport officials.[1] But new evidence in this investigation suggests that Mohamed was on his *way* to the training camps after he and his wife had been in Spain.

"I left for the USA from Barcelona and AM took the train to Rome on his way back to the Middle East," Linda Sanchez told me by e-mail.[2]

The incident in Italy was the result of an effort by Mohamed to smuggle a hidden storage device onto the plane. As retired Special Agent Jack Cloonan tells it, "Ali has on his person a Coke can, [the kind] in which you hide things. It came to the attention of the security person in Fiumicino who happened to be a woman." Cloonan says that the security agent notified her superior, who was a former CIA officer. "And they question

Ali and Ali tells them that he's working on a special program that has to do with the Olympics."[3]

Linda Sanchez told me that Ali "was detained until the last minute and was told that if anything happened to the flight, he would be held responsible." Brushing it off as innocent, she says, "It was just a Coke can that he picked up at the Spy Shop in San Francisco and thought his friends would get a kick out of it. Nothing more."[4]

One can only imagine how Ali might have instructed his jihadi "brothers" on how to put such a storage container to use as a smuggling device. As we'll see later, after 9/11 he confessed to Cloonan that he'd tutored terrorists on how to sneak weapons aboard airliners.

In any case, Linda, who remains in denial about Ali's real intentions, confirms that "the Rome incident was reported by TWA to the FBI." Months later, "it was that incident that caused the [Bureau] to get involved [with Ali] in the first place."

Informant Without Polygraph

Jack Cloonan says that in 1992 Ali was first "opened" by the Bureau as a "134" Foreign Counter Intelligence agent, tasked with gaining intelligence on a local area mosque. But Cloonan admitted that Mohamed was assigned to a rookie agent who didn't polygraph him. And Linda Sanchez confirmed that.

"One of the most unbelievable aspects of the Ali Mohamed story is that the Bureau could be dealing with this guy and they didn't put him on the box," says retired Special Agent Joseph F. O'Brien, who worked organized crime for years in the New York Office. "The first thing you do with any kind of asset or informant is you polygraph him and if the relationship continues, you make him submit to continued polygraphs down the line. That is a basic principal of running informants."[5]

By "opening Ali up as a 134" informant, says Cloonan, the Bureau was "tasking him to get information to support a FISA application on a wire tap" monitoring a series of suspects at the mosque. "And then, for one reason or another," says Cloonan, "the kid that's running the case transfers to something else and John Zent ends up on it. But John Zent doesn't open Ali up as a 134. He opens him as a 237, which is a criminal informant."

It was another case where "the wall" didn't seem to exist. Criminal investigations and FCI cases were being handled by the same agents in the same office using the same informants, as happened in New York with Emad Salem. Cloonan, who only began to examine Ali's status four years later, now insists that Mohamed was "only an informant for a very short period of time," and that John Zent "targeted" him "with mosques down in San Jose—essentially trying to get information about false documents." Cloonan maintains that the investigation was "focused and it really [wasn't about] terrorism. It [involved] low-level criminal activity." He also says that Ali was never paid by the Bureau—but admits that he was reimbursed for "expenses."

However, in my brief dialogue with Special Agent Zent, he seemed to suggest that Ali played a more important role as a source.

The FBI has different rules for various types of informants. There are "informational" assets, who simply provide intelligence, and "operational" assets like Emad Salem, who are tasked to accomplish a mission. The rules governing them are contained in the Bureau's Manual of Administration and Operation (MAOP).

"The classified version of it," says Cloonan, "outlines what you have to do to support a 134 case. Under the 134 informant program, you have an IA, or an Informative Asset, which essentially is a person that's kind of a listening post. And then you have an OA, for Operational Asset, who is receiving tasking. And there is a fundamental difference between the two. The roads can overlap." As Cloonan explains it, "an OA is a guy that you are directing. He's operational. He's probably getting money and you've got more stringent oversight on behalf of the Informant Unit back in Washington."

Cloonan, who was based in the New York Office, insists that Ali Mohamed "never made it to the OA status." But John Zent, who "controlled" Ali on the West Coast, hinted to me that his relationship with Mohamed ran far longer and was much more involved than Cloonan alleged. When I told Zent that I had done a lengthy interview on Mohamed with Jack Cloonan, Zent flashed a hint of arrogance and wrote me via e-mail that

"Jack spoke with Ali [when he was] in *custody*, [a] much different man than the *free* one that I met and developed as a potential resource."[6] That was on May 15, 2006.

Indemnification and Compensation

I had already overnighted copies of my two 9/11 books to Zent and followed up with several voice-mail messages and e-mails imploring him to tell his side of Ali's story.

Three days later, Zent, who retired from the Bureau and now works as an executive in Risk Management for Yahoo, e-mailed me back. His daughter Monica eventually got her J.D. and was admitted to practice law in California. In the first of several e-mails on May 18, Zent deferred to his daughter and set some rather unprecedented terms for the interview:

> Peter
>
> I've copied our daughter Monica who is the family counsel. The advantage of children is hopefully they achieve higher levels of success, thus I defer to her good counsel. I do feel that there are elements of the Ali story that are somewhat haunting and represent lost opportunities of huge dimension, having said that. Here . . . are the issues:
>
> 1. possibility of classified information
> 2. indemnity from legal actions
> 3. family security concerns
> 4. compensation
> 5. Is 15 seconds of fame worth those potential downsides?
>
> John Zent[7]

In thirty-five years as an investigative reporter, this was the first time I had ever been asked for either payment or legal indemnification by a potential interviewee. My first thought was, *What does he have to hide?*

And yet there was one phrase in his e-mail, delivered almost offhand, that piqued my interest. Zent's interaction with Ali Mohamed, he suggested, represented "lost opportunities of huge dimensions." To see where he was going with this, I wrote back:

John, does this mean you are considering the interview? If so, what kind of compensation did you have in mind?

He responded the same day:

Peter talk with Le Alligator*

Money isn't the driver here but again it's always nice if the other areas can be resolved primarily indemnity and the issue of security levels as I would like to see the significant issues missed fixed moving forward.

johnz[8]

Finally, after one more exchange, Zent got cold feet.

Peter

I applaud their efforts and for well over 30 years that['s] what I did too, but now I have, thanks to some years in private industry, some reasonable net worth that would be at stake if the government took exception to my statements and thoughts having signed agreements upon retiring that a[re], in fact, legally binding. I think enough is said and totally understand your position. . . . I'm not going i[n] without protections in place and not doing [i]t as a confidential source either.

Sorry johnz[9]

Det. John Souza wonders to this day "why would a law enforcement officer with twenty plus years (like Zent) interfere with a homicide investigation?"[10] When you are dealing with a guy like Ali Mohamed, says Souza, "the key quality in an investigator is 'character assessment,' the ability to read your source. Dana Ewell snowed Zent and now he's got this terrorist guy who's snowing him, And that says to me that he's got poor people judgment qualities."[11]

Given retired Special Agent Zent's unwillingness to talk, we can only draw inferences from his handling of the Ewell case to shed light on how he may have "handled" Ali Mohamed. Det. Souza describes Zent as "arrogant" with a "big ego" who "is never wrong." As we'll see later in this book, Zent remained completely loyal to Dana Ewell despite a devastating body of evidence that he planned and financed the death of his parents and sister with malice aforethought.

---

*I wasn't sure if this was a reference to his daughter.

"I'm not surprised," Souza said, "that a trained terrorist was able to dupe John Zent because he'd been duped by a 21-year-old kid."[12]

At this point in the story one thing is clear: if Det. Lou Napoli and Special Agent John Anticev had problems "controlling" Emad Salem, a *legitimate* FBI asset who had burrowed into al Qaeda's New York cell, John Zent, the agent assigned to monitor Ali Mohamed would have been challenged in the *best* of circumstances. His unwillingness to talk notwithstanding, it's clear that his personal involvement in the Ewell murder case and the months of his time it consumed, made Zent particularly vulnerable to exploitation by the real al Qaeda spy.

Al Qaeda Establishes a Chicago Base

The fact that Zent may have been "distracted" at best by the murder probe and at worst entirely snookered by Mohamed is particularly troublesome coming in 1992 because in late March of that year, Osama bin Laden and Dr. Ayman al-Zawahiri made another major inroad in their effort to penetrate the United States. They incorporated Benevolence International Foundation (BIF), one of many purported al Qaeda "charities" or NGOs (nongovernmental organizations) that were a front for their terror network.[13]

With offices in Khartoum, Bosnia, and Palos Hills, Illinois, BIF became a vast "cut out" for smuggling al Qaeda money, arms, explosives, and military hardware worldwide. Years later, its associated list of board members and contributors would become a road map for the FBI in understanding the full depth of the al Qaeda "sleeper" presence in the United States. Together with the cell Ali Mohamed had set up on the West Coast, and the New York cell operating out of the Alkifah Center at the Al Farooq Mosque in Brooklyn, bin Laden's operation now had footholds at strategic spots across the country.

And the FBI's two best hopes for infiltrating the organization—Emad Salem on the East Coast, and Ali Mohamed on the West—were dead ends. With the lost opportunity to penetrate al Qaeda's New York cell, and its "control" of the triple agent Ali Mohamed in the hands of the trusting and distracted John Zent, the FBI had let its guard down.

It was the perfect moment for the blind Sheikh to place a call to Pakistan. With Emad Salem, their prospective "bomb maker," out of commission, Rahman called in reinforcements, and in early September 1992 Ramzi Ahmed Yousef, a brilliant engineer trained in the United Kingdom, flew into JFK.[14] In the weeks ahead, under the direction of this world-class bomb maker, Ali Mohamed's trained cell members would revive El Sayyid Nosair's "twelve Jewish locations" plot—only to transform it into something far more ambitious.

The night after the Kahane killing, during their search of Nosair's house, the Feds had found a notebook in Arabic that threatened the "destruction of the enemies of Allah . . . by means of destroying exploding, the structure of their civilized pillars . . . and their high world buildings . . ."[15] Ali Mohamed's cell members now set their sights on the two 110-story towers of the World Trade Center. It was the first step in a decade-long al Queda mission to take down those towers.

But JTTF investigators didn't get that message translated until it was far too late.

11

THE GREAT ONE

As effective as Ali Mohamed was as an intelligence strategist and spy, Ramzi Ahmed Yousef was his equal as a bomb maker and engineer whose métier was conceiving spectacular acts of terror. Like Ali, Yousef was a man of many faces—a shape-shifter who once impersonated an Italian member of parliament, a chemical engineer from Morocco, and a British industrial technician all within the space of several days.[1] In fact, Ramzi Yousef wasn't even his real name.

The man who bombed the World Trade Center was born Abdul Basit Mahmud Abdul Karim. The son of an oil worker from Baluchistan, Yousef grew up in Kuwait. His uncle Khalid Shaikh Mohammed (KSM) was closely tied to the Muslim Brotherhood,[2] the precursor to Ali Mohamed's terror group, the Egyptian Islamic Jihad, Yousef repeatedly risked his life on behalf of Islamic fundamentalists, yet he was a study in contradiction. Trolling the karaoke bars of Manila, he dated B-girls but expressed devotion to his wife and two daughters back in Quetta, his Baluchi hometown.[3] He told FBI agents that he felt guilty for those who died from his bombs, but in the same interrogation cited Hiroshima and Nagasaki as models in one plot he'd designed to kill a quarter of a million people.[4] He represented himself at the first of his two federal trials, and did a remarkably professional job for a nonlawyer, yet in two of his biggest bombings he miscalculated the location where the devices were planted, killing far fewer victims than he'd intended.

Once called the most wanted man on earth,[5] Yousef created his own fake IDs and routinely changed his appearance to avoid capture.[6] He dyed his hair, used contact lenses, and even dyed his skin to appear more Western. But cosmetics could never hide the scars from his years as a bomb maker. His fingers were disfigured, the bottoms of his feet bore burn marks, and he was partially blind in his right eye.[7] The men who hunted him over the years variously described him as "cold-blooded," "diabolical" and "an evil genius."[8] A Sunni Muslim, he owned a multivolume collection of the Koran,[9] yet he rarely attended Friday prayers at a mosque in Pakistan, and never fasted during Ramadan.[10]

But Yousef was terror's first real outside-the-box thinker. He went from creating huge explosive payloads, designed to be moved to their targets by truck,[11] to ingenious little "bomb triggers" to be planted aboard commercial airliners with the intent of turning them into flying bombs.[12] Unlike Ali Mohamed, who moved in the shadows, Yousef eventually became a celebrity in the world of radical Islam, "a killer afforded rock star status," as one writer put it;[13] In one trial, a young jihadi who had met him referred to Yousef as "the Great One." One of his lawyers called him "extremely polished and cosmopolitan."[14] Even a member of his own defense team noted that Yousef "had ice water in his veins."[15]

That was the profile of the man al Qaeda sent to New York in late summer of 1992 to replace Emad Salem.

On the night of September 1, Yousef arrived at JFK International Airport on Pakistan Airlines Flight 7803 from Karachi. Seated next to him in first class was Mohamed Ajaj, a twenty-two-year-old Palestinian member of the al-Fatah terrorist group, who was carrying bomb manuals, fake passports, and tapes of suicide bombers.[16]

Feigning outrage when INS agents grabbed him, Ajaj provided a diversion as Yousef, posing as an Iraqi refugee from Saddam Hussein's prisons, requested asylum. Though an alert female INS agent noted the links between Ajaj and Yousef and sought to detain him, she was overruled by her boss. So after being assigned a hearing date, Ramzi Yousef was allowed to exit the airport and enter New York City as a free man.

That story has been told before. In *1000 Years for Revenge*, I told it my-self in detail.[17] But until now the link between Ramzi Yousef, Ajaj, and Ali Mohamed has never been firmly established. Is it possible that al Qaeda's master spy and al Qaeda's chief bomb maker collaborated on the plot that escalated the "twelve Jewish locations" plot into the World Trade Center bombing conspiracy? The evidence is circumstantial but compelling.

First, among the materials carried by Ajaj and seized the night of his ar-rest at JFK was a blue manual on improvised munitions. It contained pages from Fort Bragg military manuals.[18] Although such manuals were also available at gun shows in the early 1990s, they are another hint to the Yousef-Ali connection. Among the materials in Ajaj's luggage was a letter of introduction to the Khalden al Qaeda training camp in Afghanistan, where Ajaj was said to have met Yousef.[19] Khalden is located just outside the al Qaeda camp at Khost where Ali Mohamed was training terrorists in bomb building in late August and early September of 1992.

How do we know this? The intelligence comes from the sworn testi-mony of Khalid Ibrahim, an al Qaeda operative in 1995.[20] Further, a sworn FBI affidavit on Mohamed from 1998 puts him inside the Khost camp "for at least 4 weeks"[21] during this period. Ali himself later admitted that "in 1992 I conducted military and basic explosives training for al Qaeda in Afghanistan."[22] And that timing dovetails with when his wife, Linda, told me that he'd been stopped on the TWA flight in Rome. The 9/11 Commission would later conclude that the Twin Towers bombing "plot or plots were hatched at or near . . . Khalden . . . a terrorist training camp on the Afghanistan-Pakistan border."[23] And one need not forget that one of Ali Mohamed's main disciples was El Sayyid Nosair, whose notebook with threats to the "high world buildings" was found in his house along with training manual excerpts from Fort Bragg similar, if not identical to the one's Ajaj carried that night into JFK.

As we'll see later in this book, there is other probative evidence tying Ali Mohamed not only the first attack on the WTC but the sec-ond planes-as-missiles plot that Yousef conceived in Lahore, Pakistan, in September 1994—a plot that was carried out by his uncle KSM. In fact, within hours of leaving JFK on the night of September 1, 1992, Yousef took a cab to the Alkifah Center, the so-called "jihad office," from which Ali Mohamed had trained Nosair, Salameh, and Abouhalima back in 1989. This was the center where Ali had been a regular, run by Mustafa Shalabi, who had begged Ali for help when he'd been threatened in the winter of 1991. The web of tightly knit al Qaeda operatives was relatively small, and Ali Mohamed was the common thread.

Now in the early fall of 1992, using the alias "Rashed," Yousef soon set up shop across the Hudson River in Jersey City. He rented a storage locker with the help of Ali's other trainee Nidal Ayyad and began working almost daily for the next five and a half months with Abouhalima and Salameh who helped him construct the urea nitrate-fuel oil bomb.[24]

Training the Brothers in bin Laden's Own House

Since August, Ali himself had been in the Khost camp, which had been built in the 1980s with CIA help.[25] Khalid Ibrahim, whom Ali had trained at Nosair's apartment back in 1989 spotted him there using the alias "Abu Osama," perhaps in deference to his beloved "Emir."[26] The training itself actually took place in the house bin Laden had vacated in the Hyatabad neighborhood of Peshawar, Pakistan.[27] A teeming Casablanca-like town near the Afghan border, Peshawar was the staging area for the CIA's covert aid to the mujahadeen during the war against the Soviets.

Two of the students Mohamed trained would go on to play key roles in the plot to blow up the U.S. embassy in Nairobi, Kenya, in 1998 and it's a measure of al Qaeda's long-range planning that their tutelage began six years earlier. One of them was Anas Al-Liby, a twenty-eight-year-old member of the Libyan al Qaeda cell known as al-Muqatila. A man who would go on to become "the computer wizard of al Qaeda's hierarchy,"[28] Al-Liby was later linked, along with his cell, to a 1996 plot to assassinate Libyan dictator Mu'ammar al-Qadaffi.[29] Alleging that MI-6, Britain's equivalent to the CIA may have helped finance that plot, the London *Observer* noted that "Astonishingly, despite suspicions that he was a high-level al Qaeda operative, Al-Liby was given political asylum in

Britain and lived in Manchester until May of 2000 when he eluded a police raid on his house and fled abroad."

It was during that raid when British authorities uncovered the infamous al Qaeda terror manual "Military Studies in the Jihad Against the Tyrants," which was largely written and translated by Ali Mohamed.[30] After putting together this "encyclopedia of jihad," Jack Cloonan says, Ali used it to tutor the men who were about to rewrite the history of terror.

"Ali amasses all of this data on how to train people in assassinations, how to do surveillances," Cloonan remembers.[31] "He puts together this training syllabus—and who is in his first training class? Bin Laden, Abu Ubaidah, al Qaeda's number three, who subsequently drowns in Lake Victoria, Mohammed Atef, and others in the leadership. So once al Qaeda is conceived, here's Ali doing this training."

In Peshawar in the fall of 1992, Al-Liby proved to be one of Ali's quickest studies, along with his brother Saif Al-Liby and L'Houssaine Kerchtou, later known to the Feds as "Joe the Moroccan." Kerchtou ultimately abandoned al Qaeda and became one of the star witnesses in *United States v. bin Laden,* the embassy bombing trial in the spring of 2001. His detailed description of the training that he received from Ali Mohamed, known by the aliases Bakhbola, Bili Bili, Haydara, and Abu Mohamed al Amiriki, is worth examining in depth. It demonstrates how an experienced military officer like Ali Mohamed was able to turn undisciplined young men into spies and killers.[32]

Through his experience working for the FBI, the CIA, Egyptair, and the JFK Special Warfare Center, "Ali the American" knew Western counterterrorism tradecraft like he knew the back streets of Kafr El Sheikh. During his sessions at Khost, and later in bin Laden's former home, Ali instructed the trainees in how to do surveillance on a bombing target, how to take covert photos, how to develop the negatives (when film was still the only option), and how to put the intelligence into a report for submission to al Qaeda's leadership. It was a cruder version of the spy training young CIA case officers got at Camp Perry, Virginia, but under Ali Mohamed these young jihadis became the entry-level agents in a four-tiered protocol of attack that included intelligence, analysis, logistics, and operations.

In Cloonan's judgment, Mohamed would have been "an excellent trainer," but "probably not an easy teacher to deal with. He was very demanding of his students. He didn't suffer fools, and if you weren't serious and really dedicated he wouldn't waste his time. . . . Just looking at his innate capabilities I would say he would have been a great teacher."

And that seems to have been the case. Before enrolling in Mohamed's training program, "Joe" Kerchtou was warned by Mohammed Atef, al Qaeda's military commander, that his new teacher would be "a severe man." Examining his testimony in *United States vs. bin Laden* on February 23, 2001, it's clear that Ali Mohamed could be as tough and profane as any drill sergeant from Fort Jackson. He was questioned by an assistant U.S. attorney:

KERCHTOU: He is very very strict. . . . I mean he is not a good practitioner of Islam. You could hear from him some bad words. . . . At the beginning he started checking our intelligence. After that, he explained how to make surveillance of targets and how to collect information.

AUSA: Can you describe what it was you were told to do?

KERCHTOU: We use different techniques, like, you take pictures of that target, then locate the target on a map, then you can go in the target to see how many people are working there. We trained how to use different cameras, especially small cameras—Olympus and Canon—and how to take pictures in the guesthouse in which we were living. You take your camera without using the camera straight in your eyes. You just take it like this [at waist level]. Another guy came behind us to see if you are taking the target very well or not. Then he will say go down or up, until you [got] used to tak[ing] the picture very well without using your eyes.

AUSA: Tell us about what you were instructed to write in the reports when you did a surveillance.

KERCHTOU: Normally, on the top of the paper you say how secret it is, and the date, and the time you started your work, and the name of the target, and you start describing the target and putting [down] all the information on the target. You draw the pictures, a map, and some addresses.

AUSA: Did your group do any practical surveillances of places other than the building where you were working?

KERCHTOU: Yes. We started with small things, like a bridge, like a stadium, normal places where nobody was, and then in the second stage we went to police stations, and in my group we were trained to go into the Iranian consulate and the Iranian cultural center in Peshawar.

AUSA: Did you know what happened to the report—who it would go to, whether there was any other group involved?

KERCHTOU: During the training, [Ali] Mohamed explained to us that this job is the first part of military part. You collect the information about this certain target, and whenever you finish your work, you send your reports to your bosses and leave. Our bosses are number two. They go through the report and read all the information, and they decide how to attack that target, then they send another group who supply everything to attack that target. When third group finishes the job, [they] leave. Then the fourth group come[s] in to do the final job.

AUSA: After the training was over, were you told where Haydara, or Abu Mohamed the American [i.e., Ali Mohamed], was going next?

KERCHTOU: Abu Mohamed, or Haydara, told me that he is going to Jihad Wal camp so as to give another military course to the trainers there.

Six years after training with Mohamed, Kerchtou would use what he'd learned to bomb a target slightly bigger than the consulate of Iran—the U.S. embassy in Nairobi. Long before that, however, another group of Mohamed's trainees was helping Yousef in a plot to take down the tallest pair of buildings on the East Coast.

The Hiroshima Event

In the early fall of 1992, using the key members of Mohamed's cell, Yousef began to assemble the components necessary to build a device capable of what he would later call "a Hiroshima-like event."[33] His goal was to place the bomb at the base of the Trade Center's North Tower and have it collapse into the South Tower, killing 250,000 people.

An engineer, Yousef had read *Hawley's Condensed Chemical Dictionary* cover to cover multiple times and memorized the contents.[34] He enlisted Nidal Ayyad, the Kuwaiti from Calverton, to requisition chemicals. Abouhalima, the Red, used his cab for surveillance and logistical support. Mohammed Salameh lived in the bomb factory helping Yousef construct the device.[35] In an epic story littered with lost FBI opportunities, the fall of 1992 was a period when the FBI had its next best chance to stop not just the *first* attack on the World Trade Center, but the *second* as well. Evidence gathered by the Philippines National Police (PNP) in 1995 would cement the link between Yousef and the 9/11 attacks. But having lost Emad Salem as their key "asset" inside the cell, JTTF investigators Napoli and Anticev were at a point of desperation.

In truth, all they would have had to do to crack the plot was follow the men in those Calverton photos. Instead, two weeks after Yousef's arrival they *subpoenaed* them, ordering twenty-six members of the Abu Bakr and al-Salaam Mosques down to the FBI office for questioning.

Among the Egyptians in the group were Mahmud Abouhalima and Ibrahim El-Gabrowny, Nosair's cousin, along with Ahmed Abdel Sattar, a naturalized citizen who worked as a mailman on Staten Island. Sattar would come to play a key role in support of Sheikh Rahman, the shadowy figure behind the cell. Once again, underscoring the importance of Egyptians in al Qaeda's leadership and operational base, several dozen of the émigrés from Cairo and Alexandria met first at a mosque in Lower Manhattan and decided to stonewall the JTTF agents. When they reached the lobby at 26 Federal Plaza, the brazen postal worker Sattar used his federal ID at the door to get the group into the lobby.[36]

Upstairs Napoli and Anticev tried to get tough. They had the Egyptians fingerprinted. Next they showed them pictures of the Calverton surveillance and demanded details of the Kahane and Shalabi homicides, asking them if they knew Nosair or the blind Sheikh. Anticev told Sattar that eventually the Feds would get Sheikh Rahman, the same way they'd gotten John Gotti.[37] But the cocky Egyptians were unfazed. They all left without being charged and the JTTF was back at square one.

Then, a few weeks later, the FBI's onetime star informant, Emad Salem, offered them another chance to break the bombing plot that was now afoot. In October, he met Nancy Floyd at a Subway sandwich shop near the FBI's New York Office to get his last cash payment of $500. During the brief encounter Salem tried to warn her. He'd caught wind that something was being planned and he begged her to follow Nosair's two getaway drivers, Abouhalima and Salameh.

But Floyd's hands were tied. She told Salem that in the weeks since he'd left, she'd been frozen out of the terrorism investigation by ASAC Carson Dunbar. She would try and pass on the word and encourage the surveillance, but there was little else she could do.

Still, insistent that something terrible was about to happen, Salem issued a chilling warning. If the FBI wouldn't follow "the Red and Salameh," as he'd warned, then they shouldn't "bother to call" him "when the bombs go off."[38]

12

GROUND ZERO
PART ONE

Confident that they had a world-class bomb maker to execute the New York plot, bin Laden and al-Zawahiri left their primary U.S. asset, Ali Mohamed, in Afghanistan training rebel commanders in map reading, surveillance, grenade throwing, and the construction of improvised explosive devices (IEDs).

Soon, funded by money wired from al Qaeda-related accounts in Germany and the Mideast, Yousef began working with Mahmud Abouhalima, Mohammed Salameh, and Nidal Ayyad to assemble the components of a 1,500-pound bomb. Ironically, among the boxes of evidence seized from the house of El Sayyid Nosair the night of the Kahane murder was a formula for a urea nitrate device, but it languished in the files still unprocessed by the FBI's New York Office.[1] Abouhalima, Salameh, and Ayyad (who worked for a New Jersey chemical company) were all known to the NYO, having been photographed in the Calverton surveillance in 1989. They were frequent visitors to Nosair's trial in 1991. They'd all been subpoenaed by Anticev and Napoli weeks before, but after thumbing their noses at the Feds they'd simply driven back to Jersey City, where Yousef was working on the bomb design.[2]

As I reported in *1000 Years for Revenge,* the FBI could have easily uncovered Yousef's Jersey City bomb factory on Pamrapo Avenue. All they had to do was follow Emad Salem's suggestion and tail Salameh, who was interacting daily with Yousef.

Salameh was actually living in the bomb factory and during the IED's construction Yousef's temper often flared as the semi-competent terrorist mixed the wrong chemical combinations for the urea nitrate slurry that would give the device its blasting radius.[3]

Originally, the slightly built Palestinian was scheduled to be the wheel man for the rented yellow Ryder truck that would deliver the device. But by the fall of 1992 Salameh was involved in no less than three separate traffic accidents. In one, Yousef was injured and hospitalized. Still, showing audacity worthy of Ali Mohamed, he used a stolen phone credit card to order chemicals from his hospital room.[4]

In November 1992, Yousef actually showed up at a Jersey City police station to report a lost passport. He was laying the groundwork for a cover story that he later used at the Pakistani Embassy in New York City where he applied for a new passport under his real name, Abdul Basit. Although he missed his asylum hearing in December, the Feds made no effort to locate him, even though he'd entered the country with Mohammed Ajaj, now jailed at the U.S. penitentiary in Otisville, New York.[5]

If the FBI had obtained simple Title III wiretap warrants on Abouhalima, "The Red," they could have traced calls from his home phone to the pay phone outside the bomb factory. Yousef was repeatedly seen by witnesses using the phone near the Pamrapo Avenue apartment.[6] The phone bill for all of Yousef's calls during this period was in excess of eighteen thousand dollars as he telephoned contacts in the Middle East, Pakistan, Turkey, and Yugoslavia.[7] If the Feds had merely installed a trap to monitor Abouhalima's calls, they would have discovered at least eight from the Pamrapo Avenue[8] pay phone and four calls on February 3, 1993, from the Trade Center itself, where Abouhalima went on surveillance runs. Earlier Napoli and Anticev had enough probable cause to obtain a search warrant on the redheaded cab driver. Why didn't they follow Salem's advice and investigate him now?

If the Justice Department had examined transcripts of the Otisville prison phone calls of Mohammed Ajaj, they would have discovered that he was talking in code to Yousef, who had asked him to retrieve his bomb manuals.[9] The calls between them were patched by Southwestern Bell through Big Five Hamburgers, a restaurant in Texas owned by Ajaj's uncle.[10] But just as the Feds had failed to translate Nosair's notebook with the musings about taking down the "high world buildings," any transcripts of these calls weren't reviewed by the FBI (if at all) until after the Trade Center bombing.

Demonstrating new levels of boldness, Ajaj actually petitioned federal Judge Reena Raggi to allow him to get the contents of his suitcase from JFK, which included: "books and manuals on how to use hand grenades, how to commit sabotage, how to make poisons and Molotov cocktails, how to place land mines, instructional materials on how to kill with a knife, diagrams depicting how to make silencers, videotapes about suicide car bombings and how to make TNT."[11]

Incredibly, Judge Raggi granted Ajaj's motion and directed that the terrorist kit be returned. But the suitcase was held in the FBI's New York Office, and Ajaj wisely decided that "Rashed" should not attempt to retrieve it. Reena Raggi would show up two more times on the timeline of federal negligence on the road to 9/11.

Yousef was so audacious during this period that he even allowed himself to be captured by an ATM camera withdrawing cash while he made a call using another person's phone card.[12] After his escape to Pakistan following the bombing, Yousef's parents were reportedly *harassed* by phone company reps seeking to collect on the fortune in phone bills that he owed. Once Ramzi's name had shown up in the press along with his birth name, Abdul Basit, the dunning notices went out. The *phone company* managed to locate Yousef's parents. But the FBI was still looking for him.[13]

A Lost Chance to Stop the WTC Bombing

Another stunning opportunity to stop the first WTC bombing came on December 19, 1992. As the Feds later learned, Mahmud Abouhalima had placed a call to Emad Salem.[14] But since the former Egyptian intelligence officer had been forced out as an undercover asset by ASAC

Dunbar, Salem never returned the call. It wasn't his job any more to risk his life for five hundred dollars a week—especially if he wasn't appreciated.

In the checkered history of the FBI's New York Joint Terrorism Task Force (JTTF)—a history littered with what-ifs—it's safe to say that if Salem had answered that call, he could have put the Feds right at Ramzi Yousef's doorstep. By then Abouhalima was interacting with the bomb maker almost daily. But even without Salem, all the Feds had to do was take his advice given to Nancy Floyd at that Subway sandwich shop and follow "the Red and Salameh." By January 1993, Abouhalima had moved with his German wife and their five children to a New Jersey apartment complex, where they lived openly in the adjacent apartment to Mahmud's six-foot, two-inch brother Mohammed, who was almost his twin.

Ten years later, when I interviewed Det. Louis Napoli of the JTTF, I asked him why the Bureau had so much trouble locating this highly visible red-headed Egyptian. Napoli told me that the JTTF had lost track of Abouhalima because he'd gone to . . . New Jersey.

"Abouhalima beat feet on us," said Napoli. "We were trying to locate him but he went to Jersey. You've got to remember, there are boundaries. The Hudson River separates New York and New Jersey."[15] But an agent in the New York Office flatly disagreed: "I worked numerous cases [out of the New York Office] where the subjects lived in New Jersey. The idea that they couldn't have followed Abouhalima across state lines . . . is ridiculous."[16]

Another veteran agent from the NYO, Julian Stackhouse, told me that the main reason the Feds failed to locate Abouhalima and Salameh was that Carson Dunbar wouldn't approve the surveillance. "Mr. Dunbar didn't believe anything Salem said, so why would he give his approval to go after these two on his [Salem's] recommendation?"[17] Dunbar has denied that claim, but no better explanation has surfaced.

Al Qaeda Strikes Again

Two months after Abouhalima's last call to Salem, Yousef and his cell, trained by Ali Mohamed, finished their 1,500-pound device. They delivered it to the

B-2 parking level below the North Tower of the World Trade Center around lunchtime on the morning of February 26, 1993[18]—two years to the day after Mustafa Shalabi's disappearance.

Ramzi himself lit the fuses, fashioned with cloth and black powder provided by Abouhalima. This time, Yousef trusted Salameh to drive the red Corsica getaway car.

Moments after they sped out of the World Trade Center garage, the device detonated with the force of 150,000 pounds per square inch, obliterating the van and blowing through four floors of eleven-inch-thick rebarred concrete. Monica Smith, a pregnant thirty-five-year-old Ecuadorian immigrant who worked as a secretary in an office on the B-2 level, was killed, along with five others.[19] A thousand people were injured.

Under the direction of Ramzi Yousef, Ali Mohamed's cell had brought bin Laden's thousand-year war against the Crusaders to New York City. It would prove to be Yousef's first of two dates with the Twin Towers.

"That was a wakeup call," says retired FDNY fire marshal Robert McLoughlin. "It was unfathomable to think—in the greatest city in the world, with what you think is the best protection—that someone would have the audacity to try and topple those two towers. It was just unthinkable at the time."[20]

McLoughlin, a veteran fire investigator, had no idea back in 1993 that the FBI had any prior warnings that a bomb or bombs would go off in New York City. Neither did most people in law enforcement, outside of the FBI. One of the problems was that some journalists who examined the years leading up to the 1993 bombing were willing to give the Bureau a pass.

For example, after Mahmud Abouhalima fled to Egypt in the wake of the bombing, it was Emad Salem who went back to the Al Farooq Mosque and discovered his whereabouts. But Neal Herman, the supervisory special agent in the FBI's New York Office who ran the JTTF at the time, suggested that the Red had been brought to ground by FBI investigative work: "By the middle of the first week, we were beginning to fan out with names on ticket manifests of people who had fled," Herman said. "We traced [Abouhalima] through a series of investigative leads and tickets and people he had worked with at his car service."[21]

The press obliged by lionizing Herman. In *The Cell,* by former ABC News correspondent John Miller with Michael Stone and Chris Mitchell, the JTTF was celebrated as a crack team: "Beginning in 1990 Neal Herman's domestic terrorism unit at the JTTF represented the best hope America had of preventing a new international form of Islamic militarism from metastasizing into a potentially implacable threat."[22] Much of the book is told from the perspective of Detective Lou Napoli; it never even mentions Nancy Floyd by name.

Yet while Floyd had recruited Salem, it was Napoli and John Anticev, Herman's JTTF investigators, who'd long since lost the trail of Ali Mohamed's New York cell, and who failed to follow up on Salem's plea to track "the Red and Salameh."

Miller once worked as a press aide to NYPD commissioner Bill Bratton. He later followed Bratton to Los Angeles as his "Chief for Counter-Terrorism."[23] In *The Cell* he simply spun his account of the road to 9/11 in favor of the FBI.

As we'll see later, much of ABC's highly controversial miniseries *The Path to 9/11* was told from Miller's point of view. The docudrama minimized the role of Special Agent Nancy Floyd and portrayed Lou Napoli as the principal JTTF investigator attempting to solve the Trade Center bombing case, which they dubbed TRADEBOMB. *The Cell* was listed in opening credits for the miniseries; Miller's coauthor Stone was cited as a consultant; and an actor portraying Miller was seen throughout the five-hour film that was presented without commercial interruption. Airing over two nights beginning September 10, 2006, the miniseries drew heavy fire from alumni of the Clinton administration.[24]

Today John Miller works as assistant director of public affairs for the FBI. In effect, he's their chief public relations man.

Promising a Return to Take Down the Towers

As Ramzi Yousef watched the North Tower smoldering, disappointed that the device hadn't snapped the building at its base,[25] he vowed to return and finish the job.

That night, as he plotted his exit while sitting in the first-class lounge of Pakistani Airlines at JFK, Yousef heard an FBI report crediting "Serbian terrorists" for the bombing. Flashing jealousy, he called Nidal Ayyad. The former Rutgers student had used his computer at a New Jersey chemical company to type the letter taking credit for the blast on behalf of "The Fifth Battalion of the Liberation Army," Yousef's name for his al Qaeda funded cell.[26] Five of the letters had been mailed as the Corsica roared out of the garage, but now Yousef wanted Nidal to type a new ending to the letters and resend them. In fact, he dictated a chilling prediction:

> Our calculations were not very accurate this time. However we promise you that next time it will be very precise and the Trade Center will be one of our targets.[27]

The FBI found that early warning of the 9/11 attacks on Ayyad's computer within *one week* of the Trade Center bombing in 1993. Why didn't they pick up on it? Why did senior FBI and DOJ officials continue to deny al Qaeda's involvement and insist for years that the bombing was the result of a "loosely organized group" of Sunni extremists—a position that would persist right through the 9/11 Commission, which endorsed the same conclusion?[28]

Excluding the FDNY from Tradebomb

One courageous investigator who learned the truth was FDNY Fire Marshal Ronnie Bucca. Kevin Shea, his best friend from Rescue One, was among the first to respond that Friday to what was first called in as a "transformer fire" at the WTC. Minutes after the blast, edging along the B-2 ramp in pitch black smoke with his partner Gary Geidel, Shea unknowingly reached the fractured edge of the ramp and went over, falling down into the fiery pit. When he hit bottom, his thigh got impaled on a piece of rebar. His legs were broken, but he was alive.

Shea was a lucky survivor of al Qaeda's first major terrorist attack on the U.S. homeland, and that night in his room at Beekman Downtown Hospital, Ronnie Bucca promised that he'd track down the people responsible for planting the bomb that almost killed him. But in an exercise of class bias that led to hundreds of pieces of evidence remaining disconnected on the road to 9/11, the FBI *excluded* the FDNY from the TRADEBOMB investigation. Even though Yousef's bombing created arguably the biggest arson fire in New York history, the fire investigators from the FDNY were intentionally removed by the Bureau from the subsequent investigation.

"We were basically told by the FBI 'You can go in,'" said McLoughlin.[29] "'But you will enter the scene under the auspices and guidance of an FBI agent. You will not determine anything. The Bureau of Fire Investigation is shut down.'" McLoughlin said that the word had come down to the marshals from FDNY headquarters.

Other men might have given up, but not Ronnie Bucca, the "Flying Firefighter" who had come back to the job after breaking his back. "What Ronnie did was work mutuals, which are tours where you do twenty-four hours straight," says the FDNY's chief fire marshal, Louis F. Garcia, who had also worked in Rescue One.[30] "He would go to the library and read everything he could about terrorism, to the point where he had become a self-taught expert. Then he put in for an assignment in the army reserve, where he'd been a Green Beret, so that he could go down to Washington and get access to the hard intelligence."

As a member of the 3413th Military Intelligence Detachment, a special unit tasked to support the Defense Intelligence Analysis Center at Bolling Air Force Base, Bucca had a TOP SECRET security clearance. He worked weekends during his reserve duty in the seven-story building at Bolling that DIA spooks dubbed the "Death Star." After reading the intel, Bucca soon came to understand how the FBI had blown the first WTC bombing investigation; how they'd actually had a man inside the cell of radical Sheikh Omar Abdel Rahman; and how this "asset," an Egyptian named Emad Salem, had been recruited by Special Agent Nancy Floyd, a tenacious, female "brick agent." But Carson Dunbar, an FBI Assistant Special Agent in Charge, had so enraged Salem that the Egyptian withdrew from the cell months before the bombing—cutting off the FBI's eyes and ears inside what had become a lethal Osama bin Laden–funded al Qaeda conspiracy developing in New York City.

"After that," says Garcia, "Ronnie began warning people that these guys were going to come back and hit the Trade Center again."

"He's Probably Gonna Want—A Million Dollars"

On the night of the bombing, Mary Jo White, who was about to become the U.S. Attorney for the Southern District of New York, was pacing back and forth across the office of Jim Fox, the assistant director in charge of the FBI's New York Office. Determined to break the case, she quizzed Lou Napoli and John Anticev for details about the cell. At some point Napoli let it slip that they'd had an asset "that was very close to these people."

"Asset? What asset?" snapped White. When told of Emad Salem, she immediately demanded that Napoli and Anticev "get him in here."

"Well," said Lou, "We were paying him, like, five hundred a week. This time, you know, considering what's happened, he's probably gonna want—a million dollars."

"I don't give a damn what he wants," she shot back. "If he can deliver, give it to him."

Within days, the prosecutors at the SDNY coaxed Salem into going back under, this time wearing a wire. Over the next three months, he uncovered a new plot by the Sheikh's followers. The plan called for setting off bombs at the midpoints of the Holland and Lincoln Tunnels, the UN General Assembly Building, the George Washington Bridge, and 26 Federal Plaza, the building that housed the FBI's New York Office.[31] The Feds would later name this the Day of Terror plot.

In contact almost nightly with Nancy, Salem worked with the conspirators in a Queens warehouse that the Feds had wired for video and sound. But he was so distrustful of Carson Dunbar that the Egyptian made a second set of undercover audiotapes.[32] Fearing the Bureau would betray him, he bugged the FBI agents as well as the cell members. On one of the tapes, FBI brass later heard Nancy Floyd declare that her bosses were a bunch of "chickenshits."[33] Meanwhile, ASAC Carson Dunbar continued to doubt Salem. At one point he demanded that the Egyptian replace a live timer he had put into the warehouse.[34] In truth, the device posed zero danger under the 24/7 surveillance, and fearing that the removal of the device might blow his cover, Salem told Floyd that he was ready to bail on the entire sting operation.

But Floyd kept him active, and when the Feds finally busted the cell, on June 24, 1993, ultimately indicting Sheikh Rahman, Nosair, and ten others, Salem became the government's linchpin witness.

This time, however, he didn't come cheap. The man who could have helped the FBI wrap up Ali Mohamed's al Qaeda cell for five hundred dollars a week during the first Bush presidency would now earn $1.5 million for his work . . . on Bill Clinton's watch.[35]

13

BIN LADEN'S COPILOT

One of the central questions we'll answer in this book is how much prior knowledge Ali Mohamed may have had about the planes-as-missiles plot executed on September 11, 2001. He was the primary U.S. intelligence agent for Ayman al-Zawahiri and Osama bin Laden, and as we examine the origins of the plot, which they directed and funded, Mohamed's connections will become clear.

As demonstrated in Chapter 18, the specific targeting and staffing for the plot began with Ramzi Yousef in Pakistan in the fall of 1994. But his lifelong partner, Abdul Hakim Murad, had begun training in U.S. flight schools three years before that.

Murad first met Yousef in the early 1980s at a mosque in Fuhayil, the Kuwaiti city on the Persian Gulf where they both grew up.[1]

By 1991, Murad had attended the Emirates Flying School in Dubai, where he got his single-engine private pilot's license but he was anxious to qualify on multiengine commercial planes. On November 19 of that year, as El Sayyid Nosair's trial got underway, Murad flew to Washington's Dulles Airport via Heathrow in England. Over the next eight months, he attended four separate U.S. flight schools: Alpha Tango in Bern Stages,

Texas;[2] the Richmore Flying School in Schenectady, New York; Coastal Aviation in New Bern, North Carolina, where he got his multiengine license on June 6, 1992; and the California Aeronautical Institute in Red Bluff, California.[3]

When he passed through Manhattan in 1992, Murad performed a visual inspection of the World Trade Center.[4] Later, he would boast to a Philippines interrogator that *he* had chosen the Towers as a target for Yousef.[5]

On July 27, 1992, Murad flew to Bahrain. A month later he got a call from his old friend Ramzi. Drawing on a code Murad clearly didn't understand or remember, Yousef told him that he'd just completed "chocolate training." When Murad seemed puzzled, Yousef said *"boom."* This was during the same period when Ali Mohamed was training jihadis at the Khost camp, near the Khalden camp where Yousef was enrolled. The bomb maker told Murad that he was about to travel to New York to find "employment." A few weeks later, on September 1, Yousef landed at JFK.

It's clear from this investigation that Ali Mohamed also appreciated the importance of pilot training early on. As it turns out, one of Ali's key U.S. sleeper agents was trained at the same flight school associated with two of the 9/11 hijackers and Zacarias Moussaoui, who was originally accused by the Justice Department of being the "twentieth hijacker" on September 11.

Mohamed's Airman Sleeper

Ihab Mohammed Ali settled in Orlando, Florida, in 1979 after his family had emigrated from Egypt.[6] But as Chuck Murphy reported in a remarkable profile for the *St. Petersburg Times,* Ihab never quite adjusted to American life. Though one of his sisters enrolled in the junior ROTC program at Oak Ridge High School in Orlando, Ihab didn't seem to fit in. He refused to join a single club at school and never even posed for his high school class photo.[7]

In 1989, Ihab left for Pakistan, where he worked for the Muslim World League (MWL),[8] a Saudi-based nongovernmental organization (NGO) with direct ties to bin Laden and al Qaeda.[9] The MWL is believed to be the parent organization of the International Islamic Relief Organization (IIRO), another NGO with links to bin Laden through his brother-in-law Mohammed Jamal Khalifa, the former head of IIRO in the Philippines.

By 1991, Ihab Ali had connected with Ali Mohamed, who had come to trust him enough that he enlisted Ihab to help him move bin Laden's entourage from Afghanistan to the Sudan. At that point, Ihab chose the code name "Nawawi," after a thirteenth-century Syrian Muslim cleric.

By 1993, the newly radicalized Ihab Ali Nawawi was back in the States, and enrolled in the Airman Flight School in Norman, Oklahoma. After earning a commercial pilot's license there, he approached another local flight school.[10] Though hijacker/pilots Mohammed Atta and Marwan al Shehhi later visited, Airman Ihab's initial goal was *not* to become a suicide pilot like the 9/11 hijackers. His mission was to copilot a Sabre-40 aircraft, a military version of a corporate jet. Months earlier, al Qaeda had purchased a Sabre-40 from the Aerospace Maintenance and Regeneration Center at Davis-Monthan Air Force Base in Tucson, Arizona.[11] Ihab was tasked to serve as copilot.

Known as "the boneyard," Davis-Monthan maintains thousands of decommissioned military planes in a fleet that stretches across hundreds of acres in the Arizona desert. How a terrorist organization was able to buy a former U.S. military plane for a mere $210,000 has never been fully explored.

Essam al Ridi, the Egyptian pilot who purchased the plane for bin Laden, later testified about his efforts to restore the aircraft.

"I bought it [and] refurbished it completely," al Ridi testified. He "updated the version of avionics" and gave it a paint job. "We took off from Dallas-Fort Worth to Khartoum."[12]

There, bin Laden threw a dinner party for al Ridi, surrounded by bodyguards wielding AK-47 assault rifles. "We just had dinner and chatted," he said. "I gave the keys to the airplane to bin Laden."[13]

Al Ridi, who had trained at the Ed Boardman Aviation School in Fort Worth, later testified that bin Laden asked him to use the Sabre-40 to transport Stinger missiles from his former base in Afghanistan to the new Khartoum training camps that Ali Mohamed had established. Eventually, on a return flight to Khartoum with Ihab Ali in the second seat, al Ridi lost control of the aircraft and crash-landed into a sand berm at fifty miles an hour.[14] Al Ridi crawled out of the cockpit and abandoned his position in al Qaeda, but Ihab Ali remained loyal to the terror network.

In fact, as late as 1998 Ihab was close enough to Ali Mohamed that he tipped him off that the FBI might have connected him to Wadih El-Hage, one of the embassy bomb plot's leaders.

Ihab Mohammed Ali Nawawi was another Egyptian naturalized U.S. citizen working as an al Qaeda sleeper whom the FBI failed to detect until it was too late. As we'll see, he wasn't arrested by Bureau agents until 1999, the year *after* the embassy bombings, even though two years *before* that, in 1997, FBI agents traced a call from Ihab's sister's phone in Orlando to an al Qaeda safe house used by the Nairobi bomb cell.[15] In May 2001, four months before 9/11, SDNY prosecutor Ken Karas admitted that Ihab Ali was "another person who lurks in the background. . . . He is somebody who is an al Qaeda member . . . who ends up in Florida."[16]

The question is, why didn't the Feds get onto him earlier if Ali Mohamed, one of Ihab's key U.S. contacts, had been working as an informant for the FBI since 1992?

Despite retired agent Jack Cloonan's assertion that Ali was "only an informant for a very short period of time," it's clear that by the spring of 1993 Special Agent John Zent was still in contact with him. In fact, Zent intervened with law enforcement agents north of the border who were questioning Ali about his ties to another major al Qaeda operative.

Escaping the Mounties

Essam Hafez Marzouk, an active member of the Islamic Jihad's Vanguards of Conquest cell, was yet another Egyptian with close ties to bin Laden and Dr. al-Zawahiri. Ali Mohamed first met Marzouk in 1988.[17] They reconnected again in Afghanistan in 1991, when Marzouk was running one of al Qaeda's training camps.[18] Mohamed used Marzouk, along with Ihab Ali, to help move bin Laden to Khartoum that same year. At that point, Mohamed gave Marzouk his U.S. driver's license, knowing that he might need it to prove to immigration officials that he had contacts in America.

Two years later, in 1993, Marzouk arrived at Vancouver International Airport from Damascus, Syria, via Frankfort. The thirty-three-year-old Egyptian claimed refugee status on his arrival, but his plan was for Ali Mohamed to pick him up after he'd cleared customs in Vancouver and drive him across the border into the United States. Canadian immigration officials detained him, however, after finding two false Saudi passports among his belongings.[19]

"Marzouk is a very valuable person to Ayman Zawahiri," says Jack Cloonan. "He is essentially a logistics expert. He wants to come into the United States, for what purpose? We now know that there was an EIJ cell operating in the San Francisco area. So you could extrapolate from that and say that Marzouk was coming in to be part of that network."[20]

When Marzouk didn't show, the brazen Ali Mohamed went to the Vancouver airport customs office looking for him. That proved to be a mistake, since the Royal Canadian Mounted Police decided to question him as well.

The interrogation went on for hours. Finally, Mohamed began to get concerned. He had made applications to become a translator at the FBI offices in both San Francisco and Charlotte, North Carolina, and he didn't want this encounter with the RCMP to blow either chance to examine Bureau files from the inside.[21]

Ali checked his watch. It was getting close to midnight. Finally he gave the Mounties a phone number and told them to call it. He hadn't just applied to the FBI, he told them now, he was actively *working* with the Bureau. If they called that number, the agent on the other end of the line would vouch for him.

The Canadians placed the call. The special agent who picked up was John Zent. Whatever he said, caused the Mounties to let Mohamed go.

"Ali Mohamed was in the Americans' good books," says Phil Rankin, the lawyer who represented Marzouk.[22] "He got away from the RCMP by telling them, 'phone this FBI agent in the U.S. and he'll vouch for me.'"

"The people of the RCMP told me, by midnight, that I can go now," Mohamed later admitted. He promised to return to their office the next day.

Sure enough, he came back and reportedly brought enough cash with him to pay attorney Rankin, according to a statement later given by Mohamed's Santa Clara protégé Khalid Dahab.[23] But Rankin denies that, claiming that Marzouk paid his own fees and his bail with $20,000 he had on him. Mohamed "never gave me one penny, period," says Rankin.[24]

Of course, it would be in the interest of Rankin's client not to have any such money traceable back to al Qaeda. But the issue remains clouded, since Rankin admits that Ali may have slipped the money to Marzouk.

"Whether he gave Marzouk money is a different issue—I don't know," Rankin says. Whoever supplied it, that amount of cash is indicative of the resources al Qaeda operatives had at their disposal as early as 1993.

The Mounties questioned Mohamed further that second day, and also searched his car. "They found nothing. . . . I left Canada [at] 4:30 P.M. for the States," Ali later recalled.

Thanks to Special Agent John Zent, al Qaeda's master spy was free.

Even Jack Cloonan, who was defensive of Zent during a taped interview for this book, later admitted that it was a "huge" mistake for Zent to vouch for Mohamed.[25]

"I don't think you have to be an agent who has worked terrorism all [his] life to realize something is terribly amiss here," Cloonan says. "What was the follow-up? It just sort of seems like [this incident] dies. I can understand how [Zent] would like to get this [RCMP seizure] to go away if Ali were a real valuable source and was giving [him] all kinds of information and maybe [he] would throw him a bone to help him out because [he's] not paying him. Maybe that's the way it was approached [by Zent] but it begs more questions than [it] answers."

During this period, Ali was feeding Zent "intelligence" on Mexican smugglers who were moving illegal immigrants into the United States from the South.[26] "This gave Mohamed a *de facto* shield effectively insulating him from FBI scrutiny for his ties to bin Laden," says terrorism expert Stephen Emerson.[27]

Later in 1993, strangely enough, Mohamed *would* give Zent legitimate intelligence on bin Laden and al Qaeda—intel alarming enough that it should have shaken the walls of the FBI's New York Office. At the time, however, the Feds had their hands full with another Egyptian central to al Qaeda's brewing war against America.

Dog Day Siege for the Sheikh

By the summer of 1993, the Justice Department and the FBI were in a desperate worldwide manhunt for Ramzi Yousef. For a while, however, the search was eclipsed by the thorny political question of how to handle Sheikh Omar Abdel Rahman. The blind cleric had been named as a co-conspirator in the bridge-and-tunnel plot broken by Emad Salem,[28] but he was avoiding arrest by holing up in the Abu Bakr Mosque in Brooklyn, protected by hundreds of his followers.

Months earlier, the Sheikh's forces had staged a kind of coup d'état, taking over the Mosque's board. The congregation lost three quarters of its members as less militant Islamics withdrew. Soon the mosque was offering martial arts classes for children and paramilitary training for adults. When one of the few remaining moderates questioned the new regime, a member close to Mahmud Abouhalima warned him, "Be quiet or you'll end up like Shalabi."[29]

By early July, dozens of NYPD uniforms and detectives, along with agents from the FBI, INS, and lawyers from the U.S. attorney's office set up a command post at 250 Engine, a firehouse across from the mosque. Fire marshals Ronnie Bucca and Robert McLoughlin listened in as negotiations between lawyers for the Sheikh and the Feds dragged on.

"It was kind of eerie," says McLoughlin. "There was a tremendous police presence."[30]

Members of the Sheikh's inner circle included Egyptian naturalized U.S. citizens Ahmed Abdel Sattar, the U.S. postal worker, and Ahmed Amin Refai, an accountant for the FDNY. Both men would later show up in the FBI's files as potential terror threats in the years leading up to 9/11.

With tensions mounting, Rahman's followers put sirens on the mosque roof and blared recorded speeches by the Sheikh, which could be heard for blocks. The neighborhood was close to the area where Rabbi Meier Kahane had lived, so dozens of angry Jewish Defense League supporters flocked to the site, holding placards with pictures of the slain rabbi and demanding the Sheikh's surrender.

Barricades were lined up to clear a path into the mosque; on one side JDL members screamed "Kahane lives" in Hebrew, while the Sheikh's followers yelled *"Allah-u Ahkbar"* on the other. In the muggy New York summer of 1993, it was a volatile situation—and the hunt for Ramzi Yousef languished until the Feds could defuse the powder keg in Brooklyn.

Attorney General Janet Reno had recently been stung by criticism that she had moved too quickly against the Branch Davidian sect in the siege that ended with the fiery deaths of seventy-five followers in Waco, Texas. She was therefore loath to arrest the Sheikh, who had a hold over his zealous followers akin to that of Davidian leader David Koresh.

One night, during the mosque standoff, it appeared that the Sheikh had been whisked into a van by his followers. The NYPD and FBI gave chase, only to discover that they'd been thrown off by a Sheikh look-alike.[31] The scene was starting to take on the black comic drama of *Dog Day Afternoon* and the Feds were losing patience.

Finally, in early July, negotiators on both sides reached an agreement. Sheikh Rahman would not be formally arrested, but taken into "protective custody" pending an INS hearing on his immigration status.[32]

Earlier that year, visiting New York, Egyptian President Hosni Mubarak had declared that the United States might have prevented the World Trade Center bombing if the Feds had listened to his warnings about the Sheikh.[33] He also told an Egyptian newspaper that Rahman had worked with the CIA. Under pressure from the State Department, however, the paper retracted the story a few days later.[34] Now, after looking the other way as Rahman slipped *into* the United States, some elements in the U.S. government were eager to deport him. The "protective custody" cover was a way of averting a potential riot on the Brooklyn streets.

While all of this was playing out, the FBI and Justice Department lawyers seemed to have no idea how important the blind cleric was to al-Zawahiri, bin Laden, or their network of jihadis worldwide. But as time passed, they would be almost overwhelmed by evidence that Sheikh Rahman was a reverential figure for al Qaeda.

As we'll see, beginning in December 1996, the FBI received the first of three warnings that bin Laden would attempt to hijack a plane to free the Sheikh.[35] When al Qaeda–related terrorists took credit for the African embassy bombing in 1998, the Sheikh's release was one of their demands.[36]

Weeks before the bombing of the U.S.S. *Cole* in October 2000, al-Zawahiri and bin Laden appeared in a video *fatwa,* demanding that the Sheikh be set free.[37] Days before the 9/11 attacks, the Taliban government in Kabul offered to swap a group of U.S. missionaries for the blind Sheikh. As recently as April 22, 2005, in entering a plea, Zacarias Moussaoui, the French Moroccan initially identified by Khalid Shaikh Mohammed as part of a "second wave" of al Qaeda suicide airline attacks after 9/11, declared that his goal in hijacking a plane to fly into the White House was to free the blind Sheikh.[38]

But on July 3, 1993, the crisis finally ended. Abdel Rahman was transported up to the U.S. penitentiary at Otisville, New York, where Ramzi Yousef's traveling companion, Mohammed Ajaj, was being held. Later that summer, the Sheikh was formally charged in the Day of Terror plot, which had been broken by Nancy Floyd's asset Emad Salem. Beginning in 1995, Rahman would stand trial with ten others, including Kahane killer El Sayyid Nosair.

With the blind Sheikh out of the way, the FBI's New York office finally turned its focus back to the Yousef hunt. Did their obsession to find the mastermind of the World Trade Center bombing cause them to miss what can only be described as an intelligence gift from Ali Mohamed?

Confessing His al Qaeda Connection

Within months of the Sheikh's siege, Ali Mohamed sat down with John Zent and another agent from the San Francisco office and opened an astonishing window for them into what al Qaeda was planning.

According to a sworn affidavit filed in Federal court in 1998, Mohamed admitted that "Osama bin Laden ran an organization called al Qaeda and was building an army which may be used to overthrow the Saudi government. Mohamed further stated that bin Laden was operating camps in the Sudan and that Mohamed himself was training people" there. "Mohamed also advised the FBI that he had provided antihijacking and intelligence training in Afghanistan" to Essam Marzouk, who had now made bail in Canada.

This "confession" seems startling. Ali Mohamed had volunteered to the U.S. government that he was conspiring with bin Laden and al Qaeda. What could have possessed him to blow his cover this way?

Terrorism expert Steven Emerson believes that this was no more than a tactic to pique the interest of the Feds—part of Mohamed's modus operandi.

"Mohamed was injecting himself into a position where he could provide enough information that they would look at him as an asset," says Emerson.[39] "And once somebody is considered an asset, it insulates them from being investigated as a suspect or a defendant. He was protected that way, not maliciously, because he would provide tidbits about human smuggling. He'd provide tidbits about bin Laden's organization—and remember that OBL was not on the radar screen nationally, really, until 9/11. During those years prior to 9/11, investigators were collecting intel on OBL, but he was not considered a strategic threat to the United States."

Years later, Patrick Fitzgerald, who was head of Organized Crime and Terrorism in the Southern District—and effectively directing the FBI's Squad I-49, the bin Laden unit—claimed that the first time he ever heard the term "al Qaeda" was in 1996, when bin Laden turncoat Jamal al-Fadl walked into a U.S. embassy in Eritrea and surrendered to the Feds.

"I didn't know the word al Qaeda when we were prosecuting people in '93, '94, and '95." Fitzgerald declared in a 2005 interview.[40]

Yet the affidavit describing Ali Mohamed's 1993 description of al Qaeda was written by none other than Special Agent Daniel Coleman, who worked closely with Fitzgerald and Special Agent Cloonan in I-49. It was Coleman who actually accompanied Fitzgerald to a debriefing of al-Fadl in Germany in the fall of 1996.

If Coleman's sworn affidavit is accurate, then Ali Mohamed gave the FBI chapter and verse on bin Laden and al Qaeda *two years* before Fitzgerald says he ever heard the name of the terror network. To use Jack Cloonan's term, where was the "disconnect?" How could the man considered to be the Justice Department's bin Laden expert, not have picked up on Mohamed's astonishing admission years earlier?

"It may be that Ali was the source of a series of dots, that the FBI just didn't *want* to connect," says terrorism analyst Paul Thompson. "It's pretty much a given that they'd failed to prevent the first Trade Center attack. If they'd listened to Emad Salem, their informant, they probably could have stopped Yousef before he built that bomb. So my guess is, the Bureau went into CYA mode."[41]

As we'll see later, the Justice Department went out of its way to keep the FBI's dealings with Mohamed a secret. But now, back in May 1993, confident in his position as the real "Teflon Terrorist,"[42] Ali Mohamed began to come clean to John Zent and his fellow agents in the San Francisco office.

"John realizes that Ali is talking about all these training camps in Afghanistan," says Jack Cloonan. "And [he] starts talking about this guy named bin Laden. So John calls the local rep from army intelligence and says, 'Listen, this guy is talking about all this stuff going on over in training camps and bin Laden, and I don't know anything about this. Maybe you guys should talk.' Well, who shows up in San Jose but a special team? At the San Jose RA [resident office] Ali's a numbered source at this point."

Cloonan says the army investigators were from Fort Meade, Virginia, which is the home of the National Security Agency. "They bring maps with them and they bring evidence," he says. "There's also what's known as a PEBBLE request that comes into the FBI from the DOD. If the military wants to interview the subject of an FBI case, they have to issue this request. PEBBLE is the code name for this program. And so they debrief Ali, and he lays out all these training camps."

Cloonan says that he's still not certain about Ali's motivation at the time. Was he arrogant? Did he think he could drop hints of his true loyalty as an Islamic radical and get away with it, as he had with his superiors at Fort Bragg? Or was he playing both sides of the fence?

"I think there's a little bit of both there, frankly," says Cloonan. "Although I still think he's extremely dangerous. But he nevertheless gives us [the information]."

The File Is "Probably Destroyed"

What is crucial at this juncture in the story is that apparently nothing happened. Two major intelligence entities (the FBI and the DOD) were now on notice that Osama bin Laden was running terror camps with the goal of overthrowing the government of Saudi Arabia, a key U.S. ally and that he ran a network called al Qaeda. Yet even with this astonishing confession as far back as 1993, neither the FBI nor the Pentagon saw Ali Mohamed or Osama bin Laden as significant enough threats to take any aggressive action.

Keep in mind that the interview took place within months of the World Trade Center bombing, an act of terror committed by a cell that Ali had trained.

Why weren't the dots being connected? Why didn't the West Coast agents issue an alert to the NYO? Why weren't JTTF agents like Anticev and Napoli consulted on the significance of Ali's confession? Or were they? We don't know.

At that point, in 1993, JTTF boss Neal Herman was conducting a worldwide manhunt for Ramzi Yousef, whose cell had been funded by bin Laden and trained by Ali Mohamed, the FBI's own West Coast informant.

By now the Pentagon, whose investigators had talked to ADA William Greenbaum about Nosair's belongings, had to know that the Top Secret files had included memos from Fort Bragg—files most likely lifted during Ali Mohamed's tenure there. They had been found as part of a homicide investigation into the murder of a world figure like Meier Kahane.

"Even with the benefit of 20/20 hindsight," says retired FBI NYO agent Joe O'Brien. "You have to ask yourself, 'Who in the government was running this show? Why didn't the Bureau bring the hammer down on this guy Mohamed then and there?"

Jack Cloonan, who learned about the Pentagon investigators years later, made an attempt to locate their report. "It would've been very helpful" in completing the file on Ali Mohamed, he says. "But we were never able to find it. We were told that the report was probably destroyed in a reorganization of intelligence components within the Department of Defense."[43]

As we'll see in Chapter 33, it wouldn't be the last time that sensitive data pertaining to al Qaeda was destroyed by the DOD.

For the moment, however, it must have been obvious to Ali Mohamed that he was enjoying some kind of extraordinary protection. And so he left for Africa on the orders of Mohammed Atef, bin Laden's military commander—assigned to begin surveillance work for al Qaeda's most spectacular act of terror yet.

PART II

14

ANOTHER ALIAS

In May 1993, Ali Mohamed, a man who operated with more than a dozen aliases, added yet another name to his list—and he actually went to an American court to get it done. On May 14, he filed an Order to Show Cause for Change of Name with the Santa Clara County Superior Court. The caption in the case was entitled "In the Matter of the Application of Ali Abouelseoud Mohamed."[1]

A hearing date was set for nine o'clock on the morning of July 6, 1993, in Department 14, one of the courtrooms at San Jose's First Street courthouse. In his petition, Ali requested that his name be changed to "Ali Nasser Mohamed Taymour." Under "reason for proposed name change" he wrote in small block letters:

ETHNIC PROBLEM IN EGYPT BETWEEN OUR TRIBES
"TRIBAL FEUDS." IT ENDANGERS MY LIFE

Though he was suddenly presenting himself as a member of a tribe, the only relative Mohamed listed was Linda Sanchez, his wife. He also added Linda's address: Apartment 2 at 720 Harvard Avenue in Santa Clara. Adding his date and place of birth as "06-03 1952 Egypt," he signed the document with his name reversed: "Mohamed Ali":

Mohamed Ali

Signature of Petitioner

‧‧A‧L‧I‧‧A‧B‧O‧U‧E‧L‧S‧E‧O‧U‧D‧‧M‧O‧H‧A‧M‧E‧D‧‧
(Type or Print Name)

As required by law, Mohamed published the proposed name change in the legal notices section of the _San Jose Post-Record_. It was an opportunity for "all people interested in this matter" to appear before the court and show cause "why this application for change of name should not be granted." The notice listed the hearing date.

On June 14, a month after his initial application, Mohamed returned to file the public notice with Judge Donald L. Clark. Apparently there were no objections: On July 6, Judge Clark granted the request, and Ali Mohamed became Ali Nasser Mohamed Taymour.

Why did Ali Mohamed, who operated for years under the fictitious names Omar, Haydara, Osama, Ahmed Bahaa, and Adam, feel the need at this point to assume another new persona? Could it have been to avoid detection? That's hard to believe at this point. By the spring of 1993, Ali had been "hiding" in plain sight for years.

Might it have had something to do with Mohamed's newest career goal—his ongoing effort to get translator jobs with the FBI offices in San Francisco and Charlotte, North Carolina? To answer that question, I consulted an authority who would appreciate the significance of an al Qaeda spy getting access to FBI documents for translation.

Sibel Edmonds is the now-celebrated U.S. naturalized citizen of Turkish descent who tried to blow the whistle on security leaks and mismanagement relating to terrorism in the Bureau's own translation unit at the Washington field office.[2] After being fired in the spring of 2002, she petitioned to get her job back, only to be slapped with an unprecedented gag order. Championed by the American Civil Liberties Union, her case was eventually tossed out of federal court after the Justice Department invoked the "state secrets privilege." Rarely utilized until the Edmonds case, the current Bush administration has used it to quash eighteen more cases brought by whistleblowers and other victims of alleged government abuse in the "war on terror." The privilege has now been invoked more times under George W. Bush than any of his predecessors.[3] In 2004, Sibel founded the National Security Whistleblowers Coalition. In March 2006, she won the distinguished Newman's Own First Amendment Award, bestowed by the PEN American Center.

After briefing her on the Ali Mohamed story and sending her a copy of Daniel Coleman's ten-page affidavit describing John Zent's 1993 meeting with Mohamed, I asked Sibel to comment.

"You can see why Ali Mohamed would want to get into the FBI" as a translator, she said.[4] "Language specialists are the front line of gathering intelligence. This is where all the raw intel comes into these agencies, be it wire taps or documents or e-mails." But Edmonds adds that translators require a security clearance of TOP SECRET and, despite his ability to fool the Bureau as an informant, it's unlikely that even a spy as clever as Ali Mohamed would have survived the FBI's vetting process.

Still as Steven Emerson observed, "A translator is going to have access to intelligence and thereby provide an opportunity for the enemy to get inside our most trusted secrets." If Ali Mohamed had succeeded in penetrating either FBI office, he says, it "would've been an incredible compromise to U.S. national security."[5]

In any case, one FBI agent who worked in the San Jose office noted that Ali's determination to get these jobs speaks for itself. "You've got to give this guy points for sheer audacity," he said. "Mohamed had to have iron balls to think he could pull off a translator's job on either coast."[6]

Or, having interfaced with John Zent at this point, was Ali so sure that he could beat the Bureau that he took a chance of getting an inside track on raw intelligence?

"A Fair Amount of Ineptness"

Retired FBI agent Jack Cloonan supplied yet another potential explanation for Mohamed's name-change petition. "He was getting false passports from the Egyptian consulate in San Francisco," Cloonan told me.[7]

False passports? That was another tantalizing admission by the FBI agent charged in 1996 with building a file on Ali. The question is, did the FBI know about these false passports at the time Ali was working for them as an informant? Or did Cloonan discover the passport story only after Ali's arrest in 1998?

In a May 4, 2006, face-to-face interview with Cloonan in New York, I noted the earlier reports that Mohamed was "giving crumbs" to West Coast agents regarding "Mexican Coyote" human smugglers.

Cloonan responded this way: "What you have is a fair amount of ineptness on the Bureau's behalf, and it goes back to the very same thing that I was talking about earlier in our conversation and that was intel vs. criminal. That is the overarching theory here that leads to the dysfunction."

Yet Cloonan had already told me that after the World Trade Center bombing in February 1993 "the FCI end of it, which covers the Middle East, [got] molded into the JTTF." In effect, the Bureau had broken down the structural wall between criminal investigators on the Joint Terrorism Task Force and Foreign Counter Intelligence agents attempting to ward of future acts of terror.

With a united terrorism branch in the NYO, the bin Laden office of origin, why didn't the FBI see Ali Mohamed for the spy that he was—especially after he'd given John Zent such a detailed briefing on al Qaeda in May 1993?

As *Wall Street Journal* reporters Peter Waldman, Gerald F. Seib, and Jerry Markon later wrote, "even though that interview occurred after the World Trade Center blast, and after Mr. Mohamed's U.S. training manuals already had been found in Mr. Nosair's possession, Mr. Mohamed was let go without further investigation. Investigators on the case say the FBI was flummoxed by its first al Qaeda insider."[8] According to the WSJ reporters, Mohamed even "flunked a lie detector test administered by the U.S. government."

So again the question is why? Why didn't the FBI put the puzzle pieces together on Ali? Was it because John Zent wasn't talking to the agents in the New York JTTF? If not, the Bureau was missing a key opportunity to tie Mohamed to new revelations being unearthed in the summer of 1993 by the New York Office. They were finally beginning to make some headway against the blind Sheikh and his cell.

Sheikh Rahman and bin Laden's Brother-in-Law

In August, the FBI searched Sheikh Rahman's residence in New Jersey and found a business card from Mohammed Jamal Khalifa, the brother-in-law of Osama bin Laden. As reported, Khalifa had run the Philippines office of the International Islamic Relief Organization (IIRO), an al Qaeda-associated charity front. One of his aliases, "Abu Baraa," was found written on one of the manuals seized from Ramzi Yousef's' al Fatah traveling companion, Mohamed Ajaj, the night he got busted at JFK.[9] Pages from that manual contained material from Fort Bragg that may have been supplied by Ali Mohamed, effectively completing the chain of evidence—if anyone in the FBI cared to connect it.

Also found in a briefcase of the blind Sheikh during that 1993 search was sixty-two thousand dollars in cash, giving some hint of the resources available to al Qaeda's New York cell. David Frasca, one of the FBI agents involved in that search, would go on to make two titanic errors in the summer of 2001 at the clock ticked down to 9/11. The universe of key Feds responsible for connecting the dots on al Qaeda's U.S. presence was small indeed.

As we'll see later, by late 1994 Khalifa would come to the attention of the agents of the FBI's San Francisco office after he was arrested in John Zent's home town of Morgan Hills, California. Steven Emerson believes that Khalifa was interacting with Ali Mohamed. Why weren't the two FBI offices on either coast sharing the intel on Ali, the man who had trained Sheikh Rahman's cell? If they had done a full court press on Ali at this point in 1993—if they had simply followed him from Santa Clara back to Khartoum—the FBI would have been able to monitor an historic meeting and grab two of the world's most lethal terrorists at the same time.

The Terror Summit

Earlier in this book we talked about how, as far back as 1984, Ali had made contact with members of the Iranian Hezbollah, the terrorist group known as the "Party of God." As noted, the CIA later claimed that Ali blew his Agency cover with them in Hamburg and, as a result, they cut him loose. But Ali clearly maintained his contacts with Imad Fayez Mugniyah, the head of Hezbollah's military wing, because now in 1993 he brokered an historic meeting between the Shiite leader and Osama bin Laden.[10]

Mugniyah was the man behind the string of 1980s terror plots from the Beirut embassy and marine barracks bombings in 1983 to the 1985 hijacking of TWA Flight 847. He was also the point man who directed a series of notorious kidnappings beginning with the torture-murder of the CIA's chief of station and culminating in the capture of A.P. Beirut bureau chief Terry Anderson.

"Hezbollah is the A-team of terrorism," says former Senator Bob Graham, who cochaired the Congressional Joint Inquiry into the 9/11 attacks.[11] It's a testimony to Ali Mohamed's credibility and charisma that he was able to guarantee security for both leaders at the meeting—the terror equivalent of a sit-down between the Capulets and the Montagues.

Bin Laden and Mugniyah could not have been more different in their personal style. While bin Laden granted multiple interviews and routinely appeared in video fatwas, Mugniyah shunned the spotlight. There was only one known picture of him and he reportedly underwent plastic surgery to alter his appearance. Yet there is increasing evidence that as a result of that 1993 meeting in Khartoum, Hezbollah and al Qaeda formed a working alliance.

For example, fourteen members of the Iranian branch of Hezbollah were indicted for the June 1996 attack on the Khobar Towers complex in Saudi Arabia, in which nineteen U.S. servicemen were killed.[12] But new evidence uncovered in this investigation suggests that al Qaeda was a partner in the plot. In 1996, the FBI obtained intelligence that Ramzi Yousef had been tapped initially to locate the truck for the Khobar suicide bomb. With a Bureau informant in the cell next to him, Yousef discussed repeated al Qaeda contacts with Iran where Mugniyah was believed to be hiding.[13]

Meanwhile, six years after they had first begun to use Ali as an informant, the FBI finally acknowledged that "bin Laden and other ranking members of al Qaeda stated privately to other members of al Qaeda that: al Qaeda should put aside its differences with Shiite Muslim terrorists organizations, including the government of Iran and its affiliated terrorist group Hezbollah, to cooperate against the perceived common enemy, the United States and its allies."[14]

That Sunni-Shiite alliance first brokered by Ali Mohamed in 1993 takes on terrifying new dimensions when one considers that with the "liberation" of Iraq, al Qaeda-related Sunni terrorists joined forces with Shiite radicals and Baath Party alumni of Saddam's regime to fuel the insurgency that has brought the country to the edge of civil war. Why did it take the U.S. government so long to recognize the lethal potential of that alliance? That's the broader strategic question. But there is also a more practical one: Why weren't FBI agents on Ali's tail in 1993, *after* the World Trade Center bombing, which was executed by his trained cell members, and *after* he had confessed to FBI agents his ties to bin Laden and al Qaeda?

"We can only imagine what acts of terror might have been prevented down the line if the FBI had followed Mohamed to Khartoum in 1993," says Congressman Curt Weldon (R-PA), who recently began to fully appreciate the role of Ali in the years leading up to the September 11 attacks.[15]

Steven Emerson calls the terror summit a watershed in the growth of al Qaeda. "This was the first time that there was a divide that was going to be bridged between the Sunni extremists and the Shiite extremists as represented by Hezbollah, a phenomenally important bridge that would provide an incredible opportunity for bin Laden to enlarge his scope of operations."[16]

From Sudan to Somalia to "Black Hawk Down"

The best evidence of a solid link between al Qaeda and Hezbollah is Saif al Masry. Captured by Georgian special forces in October 2002,[17] al Masry was identified during the African embassy bombing trial in 2001 as a member of al Qaeda's *shura,* or military committee.[18] In 1993, al Masry, another Egyptian trained by Hezbollah, was part of the al Qaeda cell that fought against U.S. forces in Somalia and led to the incident that took the lives of eighteen army rangers and Delta Force commandos, as chronicled in Mark Bowden's remarkable book *Black Hawk Down.*[19]

The *Black Hawk Down* incident is another al Qaeda operation that bears Ali Mohamed's fingerprints—one that takes our story to the east coast of Africa, where Osama bin Laden had established a beachhead.

After leaving Afghanistan in 1991, with Ali's help, bin Laden had set up shop in Khartoum, directly across the Red Sea from Saudi Arabia. To the southeast was Eritrea, where a thirty-year struggle for independence from Ethiopia had resulted in an unstable, rebel-led government by 1991. Below that, at the strategic mouth of the Red Sea, was Djibouti, where Ali Mohamed would later create terror cells. And directly south of Djibouti, wrapped around the horn of East Africa, was Somalia.

Following a civil war that broke out in January 1991, Somalia had been wracked by massive famine. The UN moved in the following year, but their mission was undermined by Islamic fundamentalist warlord Mohamed Farrah Adid, whose paramilitary forces stole much of the food and supplies.[20] President George Herbert Walker Bush sent in U.S. rangers to support the food effort, but they encountered heavy resistance from Adid's followers—among them a number of battle-trained commanders who had fought the Soviets in Afghanistan.[21]

Sensing that the U.S. presence could thwart Adid's efforts to install an Islamic "republic" in the capital and worried that the United States might destabilize the pro-al Qaeda government in Sudan, bin Laden dispatched five groups of al Qaeda operatives, some of them trained by Ali Mohamed, to Mogadishu in late September 1993.[22]

Mohamed himself later admitted that he had entered the war-torn country, and bin Laden confirmed that "my colleagues fought with Farah Adid's forces in Somalia."[23] Bin Laden also insisted that one hundred Americans died in the attack, not eighteen. What he never disclosed was the role played in the operation by his chief security agent and spy.

One of Mohamed's cohorts involved in the mission was Mohammed Saddig Odeh, who would be indicted with Ali for the African embassy bombings. A key member of one of the Kenyan cells, Odeh later boasted that he'd provided the rocket launchers and rifles that brought down the helicopter gunships.[24] Another indictee in the embassy bombings, linked to the Black Hawk incident, was Abdullah Ahmed Abdullah, an al Qaeda terrorist still at large.[25]

An Inspiration for the Embassy Bombings?

We may never know every detail of what occurred at that historic summit in Khartoum brokered by Ali Mohamed, but circumstances suggest that it may have been the birthplace of the African embassy-bombing plot. Bin Laden was a great admirer of Mugniyah's "work" in Beirut; and he is believed to have instructed Ali Mohamed to pattern the African embassy destruction after the Hezbollah truck bomb that took down the U.S. diplomatic headquarters in Beirut.

As payback for America's intervention in Somalia, bin Laden had envisioned an attack on U.S. interests in Africa. By the late fall of 1993, with the success of the Khartoum terror summit behind him, Ali Mohamed left for Nairobi to set the plot in motion. It was a cruel irony that Ali Mohamed, who had spent years at Fort Bragg, where Delta Force trains, helped support the Kenya al Qaeda cell members who contributed to the murder of eighteen Army Rangers and Delta commandos in Mogadishu. But it was symbolic of his cold-blooded devotion to al Qaeda.

It's often difficult for Westerners to understand how jihadis, with loved ones of their own, can support the commission of mass murder in the name of God—especially the murder of civilians.

When Mahmud Abouhalima, a father of five, was in federal jail awaiting trial for his role in the World Trade Center bombing, a former aide to Harlem heroin czar Leroy Nick Barnes (convicted of beating a man to death with a bat) was shocked at the terrorist's indifference to human life. Ramzi Yousef attempted to justify his mass casualty plots by identifying his cell in military terms, and arguing that any noncombatants who supported a nation that committed acts against his view of Islamic law were liable under a doctrine of "collective punishment."[26]

Jack Cloonan, whom Ali Mohamed called "Mr. Jack," says he only saw Mohamed show emotion twice—including once when he was allowed to call his younger sister.

"I don't know that much about his personal life," says Cloonan.[27] "He was not inclined to talk about his parents, other than [to say that] he was close to them. He talked most about his siblings, their struggle in Alexandria, and how they lived, and some of the discrimination that he thought they faced. He was very close to his brothers and sisters, and very close to his younger sister. If you ever wanted to see a [human] side of Ali, ask him about his younger sister and ask him about what he did for his nieces. He was always buying them something, just like any uncle would for his special nieces. He talked about them and it was kind of refreshing to listen to him. Ali would talk about his younger sister with some real remorse and real tears in his eyes, but his eyes would always light up when he talked about his nieces."

Always Operational

But in his professional life, Cloonan admits that Mohamed was "always operational." There wasn't a moment when he let down his guard. To Mohamed, the attack on those Army Rangers in Somalia was just another military mission. And within weeks, bin Laden and the al Qaeda hierarchy were dispatching him on a new assignment that would take him back into Kenya.

In the early 1990s, while commuting from his wife Linda's home in Santa Clara, Mohamed had helped Khalid al Fawwaz set up al Qaeda's office in Nairobi.[28] The cell was being run by Abu Ubaidah al-Banshiri, bin Laden's military commander. Mohamed established a car business in Nairobi as a cover for their activities[29] and worked closely with Wadih El-Hage, the terrorist who had arrived in New York City around the time Mustafa Shalabi's body was found back in 1991. The two of them set up a phony NGO that provided al Qaeda operatives with false IDs. Ali also went into the precious gem business, brokering African diamonds and

Tanzanite.[30] He met with Ubaidah and Atef, at Wadih's home to plot strategy. Their code names were almost comical: Mohamed was "Jeff"; El-Hage was "Norman."[31]

Now, in the fall of 1993, Mohammed Atef sent Ali Mohamed back into Kenya to scout out potential targets, including U.S., British, French, and Israeli installations.[32] Like the experienced intelligence officer he was, Mohamed took 35mm photographs and sketched elaborate diagrams of his targets, which included the U.S. embassy and the U.S. AID building, along with the French embassy and cultural center.

"The stuff is put on a first-generation Apple laptop computer," says Jack Cloonan, who was later briefed by Mohamed on the details. "He does it with Anas Al-Liby," the twenty-eight-year-old Libyan al Qaeda operative who later became the so-called "computer wizard" of the terror network.[33] By December, Al-Liby and Mohamed had photographed a dozen targets.[34]

A stickler for details, Ali even developed and enlarged his own pictures. The work was done in the apartment of L'Houssaine Kherchtou, the bombing conspirator-turned-government witness whom the U.S. Feds dubbed "Joe the Moroccan." Kerchtou later testified that Mohamed and Al-Liby created a makeshift darkroom in the apartment by closing off the sitting room with blankets.[35] The photo equipment and his expenses for the trip were paid for by al Fawwaz, the London-based Saudi who became a bin Laden spokesman and financier to the African cells.[36]

In another solid link between al Qaeda and the WTC bombing cell trained by Ali Mohamed, a search of Fawwaz's London apartment later found bomb manuals virtually *identical* to those that Mohammed Ajaj attempted to smuggle into JFK in September 1992. One of Ajaj's manuals had the words "al Qaeda" on the cover. But according to a detailed analysis by Stephen Engelberg in the *New York Times,* the Feds mistakenly translated those words to mean "the basic rule," not "the base," *and the significance was initially missed.*[37]

Early in 1994, Ali completed the embassy surveillance and presented his report to bin Laden and his commanders back in Khartoum.

"My surveillance files and photographs were reviewed by Osama bin Laden, Abu Hafs [Atef], Abu Ubaidah, and others," Ali later admitted.

"Bin Laden looked at the picture of the American embassy and pointed to where a truck could go as a suicide bomber."[38]

Cloonan now says that the FBI had no idea at the time that Mohamed was playing such a critical intelligence role for al Qaeda: "Nobody realized the extent which Ali was involved in these issues and they clearly had no inkling at that point that he was close to Zawahiri, that he had been to the training camps to the extent that he had and that he's been tasked by Mohammed Atef to do the surveillance."

But keep in mind that Mohamed's targeting of the Nairobi embassy came just months *after* he'd confessed to Special Agent John Zent that he had personally trained al Qaeda operatives in camps run by Osama bin Laden in the Sudan. Why did it take the Bureau so long to understand the full significance of having an al Qaeda spy as their West Coast informant?

From the time of his initial surveillance to the time the bomb detonated in 1998, killing 213 and injuring thousands,[39] the FBI would have more than four years to uncover the plot. Cloonan even noted al Qaeda's philosophy of long-range planning. He called it "the sleeping dog theory." "You don't attack the dog when he's awake," he said. "You attack the dog when [he's] asleep. Very simple."

For another four years, the FBI was a dog asleep. The Kenya cell, which Ali Mohamed helped establish and train, would operate despite FBI surveillance, multiple wiretaps on cell members, and a raid of a key cell leader's home a year before the bombing, which revealed direct evidence of Ali Mohamed's connection to the plot.

Until now, no one in the U.S. media has connected the dots to fully appreciate the cruel irony of all this.

If the Canadian Mounties had had their way, Ali Mohamed might have been locked up in 1993—but they cut him loose on the word of Special Agent John Zent and Mohamed went on to become the key surveillance agent on one of the worst al Qaeda attacks on U.S. interests before 9/11. How much longer would it take before the FBI understood the true depth of Ali's loyalty to al Qaeda, and his betrayal of the new country he had sworn allegiance to: America?

15

THE SECOND
FRONT

After his surveillance operation in Kenya, Ali Mohamed was dispatched by al-Zawahiri east to Djibouti to photograph the U.S. embassy and a series of French Foreign Legion bases.[1] Later, serving both an intelligence and operational role for al Qaeda, Mohamed was tasked to monitor a home in Marbella, Spain, owned by a member of the Saudi royal family. He also accepted an assignment to blow up a BBC transmission tower in Cyprus,[2] and personally carried money from bin Laden to Algeria to bribe an official in order to spring an al Qaeda operative from jail.[3] Ten years after swearing *bayat* to "the Doctor," al-Zawahiri, and the EIJ, Mohamed had developed into an all-purpose courier, commando, and espionage agent. He accomplished all of this while commuting back and forth between his safe haven in California and Africa, his primary theater of operation.

Meanwhile, with that continent, seemingly covered, bin Laden decided to open up a second front in Asia, with Ramzi Yousef and his uncle Khalid Shaikh Mohammed (KSM) as point men.

With a massive IQ and an ego to match, Yousef was the only al Qaeda operative who approached Ali Mohamed's intelligence and audacity. But while Ali operated in the open with seeming impunity, Yousef thrived as a fugitive, conjuring more and more spectacular acts of mass murder. He seemed to covet the title *Newsweek* bestowed on him: the "Most Wanted" man on earth.[4] After his escape from New York on the night of the World Trade Center bombing, Yousef was sighted everywhere from Gaza to Colombia to the United States and Canada.[5]

Actually he was tucked away with his wife and first-born daughter at a safe house in Quetta, the regional capital[6] of Baluchistan, 375 miles from Karachi, Pakistan. A former staging area during the CIA's secret supply operation for the mujahadeen, Quetta had since become a lawless third-world haven for heroin traffickers, arms dealers, and al Qaeda killers. At one point, Pakistan's Federal Investigation Agency (FIA) sent a C-130 transport into Quetta searching for Yousef, but he always seemed a step ahead of them and slipped away.

On April 2, 1993, Yousef made the FBI's Ten Most Wanted List, and became the object of a worldwide manhunt. The State Department issued a $2 million reward for his capture, and Interpol tagged him with a "red notice," indicating his status as a fugitive.

Back in New York, Neal Herman assembled a team of JTTF agents for the Yousef hunt, which included Special Agents Chuck Stern and Frank Pellegrino, Brian Parr from the Secret Service, and Detective Lou Napoli, who seemed anxious to make up for his failure to track Abouhalima and Salameh to Yousef in the fall of 1992.

Given Baluchistan's porous borders, and the shelter afforded by his extended family, Yousef had a thousand places to hide. At this point in his career, scarred and disfigured, a celebrity in the world of radical Islam, he could easily have retired. Yet the bomb maker missed the luxury of first-class travel and the feel of a well-cut Italian silk suit, and by the summer of 1993 he was spoiling for another mission.

The Bhutto Hit

Driven by a combination of greed and revenge, that summer Yousef accepted a contract from the Army of the Companions of the Prophet

(Sipah-e-Sahaba), a sect of Sunni Muslim extremists, to assassinate the most famous woman in Pakistan.

At the time, Benazir Bhutto, the glamorous, Oxford-educated daughter of the former prime minister, was campaigning for the office once held by her father, Zulfiqar Ali Bhutto. In the 1970s, the elder Bhutto had suppressed an uprising of Baluchistanis that reportedly led to as many as ten thousand deaths. The senior Bhutto was overthrown in a coup by General Mohammad Zia-ul-Haq who was backed by Islamic extremists. The elder Bhutto was hanged by Zia's regime in 1979, but Yousef never forgot the attack, and by August he accepted three million Pakistani rupees—roughly sixty-eight thousand U.S. dollars—to make the hit.

With the help of his old friend Abdul Hakim Murad, the commercial pilot who had trained in four U.S. flight schools, Yousef attempted to plant an improvised explosive device in a storm drain outside Bhutto's residence in the Clifton district of Karachi.[7] But when it exploded prematurely, the bomb maker was almost killed and he suffered permanent eye damage.[8] Despite his wounds, within weeks the ever-ambitious Yousef was plotting to shoot Bhutto with a high-powered rifle, Manchurian Candidate-style. But that plan too was thwarted.[9]

The following June, demonstrating his willingness to challenge the al Qaeda leadership, which had recently brokered a détente with Hezbollah, Yousef planted a bomb at the Mashed Reza Shiite mosque in his home province. It killed twenty-six worshippers, most of them women.

In the late summer of 1994, even as Yousef was recuperating from the Bhutto blast, bin Laden, al-Zawahiri, and the rest of the al Qaeda leadership decided to use him to carry the jihad to new levels of terror. The bomb maker was called on to establish a cell with his uncle Khalid Shaikh Mohammed, Murad, and Wali Khan Amin Shah, a thirty-eight-year-old Uzbeki hero of the Afghan campaign, whom bin Laden revered and referred to by the nickname "the Lion."

It was decided that Manila, the capital of the Philippines, would be their staging area.[10] A third-world nation exploited for decades by corrupt Catholic leaders like Ferdinand Marcos, the Philippines had a growing Islamic population and harbored two al Qaeda related groups, the paramilitary Moro National Liberation Front (MNLF) and the Abu Sayyaf Group

(ASG), founded by Abdurajak Janjalani, one of the so-called Afghan Arabs who had fought with bin Laden against the Soviets.

The Big Noise

In September 1994, in preparation for three Manila-based plots, Yousef withdrew with Murad to the slums of Lahore, Pakistan, for a new round of "chocolate" training. There, Yousef developed an ingenious "undetectable" improvised explosive device (IED) using a Casio Databank DBC-61 watch, a tiny circuit, and the high-explosive nitrocellulose, also known as gun cotton.

The alarm on the Casio watch, which could be set up to a year in advance, would be connected to a circuit powered by two nine-volt batteries with a broken bulb "initiator." When the alarm went off, a C106D semiconductor[11] soldered inside would send a charge across the circuit that would produce a spark in a "pig's tail" filament inside the broken bulb—which, in turn, would detonate the liquid-based explosive.

Yousef dubbed the plot "Bojinka."

For years terrorism analysts, reporters, and historians have reported that "Bojinka" was a Serbo-Croatian word used variously to mean "explosion," "big noise," or "loud bang"; an allegation that a number of ethnic Serbs have since challenged.[12] But the Croatian word *bocnica* translates as "boom,"[13] and there is a wide body of evidence suggesting that al Qaeda had made deep inroads into the mid-1990s wars across the former Yugoslav Republic. Whatever the origin of the operational name, it's clear that by the fall of 1994, Yousef, KSM, Murad, and Wali Khan Amin Shah planned to create a series of "explosions" and "loud bangs," on multiple fronts, both in the streets of Manila and in the air over the Pacific.

Thirty-eight-year-old Shah was macho and athletic. Like Yousef and his uncle, he was a man of many aliases with passports under his own name from Pakistan and Afghanistan, even Norway.[14] He raced through the Manila streets on a red Honda dirt bike, and seduced a shapely bar girl named Catherine Brioso whom he'd met at the Manila Bay Club. Shah moved in with the sexy Filipina, who went by the name Carol Santiago.

He gave her cash for a pager and rented a series of rooms with her at the Dona Josefa Apartments, a six-story building at 711 President Quirino Boulevard.[15]

48 Hours of Terror

There, in Room 603 on the top left corner, Yousef established the bomb factory where he would launch three of the most audacious terror plots ever conceived. The first was Bojinka, a nonsuicide scenario in which Yousef and his conspirators would smuggle components for his Casio-nitro bomb triggers on board the first legs of a series of one-stop U.S.-bound jumbo jet flights originating in Asia. Once they were on board, the plotters would assemble the bomb (using diluted nitroglycerine) and plant it under a seat directly above the fuel tank, then leave the aircraft at the end of the first leg. The bombs would detonate on the second leg of the flight, as the planes headed home full of tourists. The cell members would then go on to plant additional devices on up to a dozen successive flights over the course of two days.

The Feds later dubbed the plot "48 Hours of Terror,"[16] estimating that if it was carried out, up to four thousand people, mostly Americans, would have been killed.[17] But the actual intent was to have the aircraft blow up days, weeks, or even months later as the jumbo jets crossed the Pacific, idled at U.S. airport terminals, or approached cities like Los Angeles, San Francisco, and Chicago.[18] "Just imagine if they had pulled this off," says Frank Gonzalez, a former U.S. postal inspector who later worked on Yousef's defense team.[19] "It could have interdicted world airline travel for months and caused economic chaos."

As a shocking reminder of al Qaeda's resilience and undying willingness to perfect its terror plots, a reconfigured version of Bojinka was uncovered by British intelligence in August of 2006[20]—this time with the liquid-based bombs designed to blow up planes over the Atlantic.

But back in 1994, for the first incarnation of Bojinka, it was Wali Khan's job to help funnel the money to the Manila cell from bin Laden's brother-in-law Mohammed Khalifa. The conduit was an NGO "cutout" called Konsonjaya; a front company set up in Kuala Lumpur, Malaysia.[21] Another indicator of bin Laden's long-range planning was the presence in the Manila cell of Riduan Isamuddin, aka Hambali, an Indonesian cleric who sat with Wali Khan on the board of Konsonjaya in 1994;. He would go on to help plot the Bali nightclub bombing of October 2002, which left 202 dead and 209 injured.[22]

The first test of the Casio-nitro IED came the night of December 1, 1994, when Yousef dispatched Wali Khan to place a small prototype under a seat in Manila's Greenbelt Theater. The multiplex's "Cinema C" was virtually empty when the Uzbeki terrorist entered and looked around, but he waited for a night scene to come onto the screen, darkening the theater, before he moved up and placed the bomb under a fourth row seat. Shah left the theater and mounted the Honda, kick-starting it and revving the motor as he checked his watch and counted down the seconds. Yousef had synched Shah's Casio to the bomb timer, which was set to go off at 10:35:00.

As soon as Shah heard the blast inside, people began running out, coughing and bleeding. Although the device caused only minor injuries, Yousef was now confident enough in the configuration to perform what he called a "wet test" on a Philippine Airlines Boeing 747.

The Second Bomb to Go Off on a 747

At 5:35 on the morning of December 11, 1994, Yousef approached a security checkpoint at Benino Acquino International Airport in Manila. He was posing as an Italian national named Arnaldo Forlani, a variation on the name of an Italian politician whom Yousef had found in the Windows software on his Toshiba laptop.[23] The Catholic religious medals around his neck were designed to deflect suspicion if he set off the metal detector. Yousef had seen a CNN report that suggested such scanners began monitoring for metal objects one inch above the ground, so he had hidden the two nine-volt batteries that would power the device in the heels of his shoes.

A U.K.-trained engineer, Yousef had soldered the C106D semiconductor (or switch) into a Casio DBC-61 and wired it to a small "female" connector that he tucked under the watchband. The rest of the IED's components appeared innocuous: a penlight flash, what looked liked a bottle of contact lens cleaner, some wires with snap connectors, and a bag of cotton balls. All were packed neatly into a shaving kit along with a few other toiletries.

Also carrying his Toshiba laptop, Yousef sailed through the security check and boarded PAL Flight 434, bound first for Cebu City in the southern Philippines and then to Narita Airport in Japan. He sat in seat 35F, toward the back of the 747-100. In the early morning hours, the big jumbo jet was almost deserted.

Once the plane had reached cruising altitude, Yousef put his laptop in the empty seat next to him, unzipped the side pocket, and pulled out the wires he'd prepared in advance.

Making sure that he wasn't being watched, Yousef worked quickly in moves he had rehearsed in advance. He snapped the batteries into the connectors in the circuit, then took out the contact lens cleaning bottle, which he'd filled with diluted nitroglycerine. He shoved the cotton balls, which he'd soaked in nitric acid, into the bottle. The mixture created nitrocellulose or gun cotton—the same explosive used in dynamite.[24] Yousef then inserted the broken bulb into the bottle and capped it, making sure the circuit was protected. He set the Casio's alarm four and a half hours ahead and zipped the IED back into the shaving kit.

Until that morning, only one other bomb had ever exploded on a 747, considered by pilots one of the most reliable aircraft ever built. On December 21, 1988, Libyan terrorists had hidden a Toshiba boom box packed with twelve to sixteen ounces of Semtex, a Czech form of plastic C-4 explosive, in a suitcase stowed in the forward cargo hold of Pan Am Flight 103. As it flew over Lockerbie, Scotland, en route from London's Heathrow Airport to JFK in New York, the device exploded, shattering the plane and leaving a debris trail eighty-one miles long. The death toll was 270, including eleven people on the ground.

But airport security worldwide had been greatly enhanced since the Pan Am 103 crash, and Yousef, had reasoned that the same type of aircraft could be brought down without having to risk smuggling a high explosive like Semtex or C-4 on board.

By creating what amounted to a Casio-nitroglycerine "blasting cap," out of components that could pass easily through a security checkpoint, Yousef theorized that if properly positioned over the center wing fuel tank, the tiny watch-powered bomb would blow downward, shattering the tank and turning the 747 into a kind of "flying bomb."

Now, with his Casio-nitro device hidden in the shaving kit, Yousef moved up to the twenty-sixth row. Seat 26K was empty, so Yousef sat down. Looking left, then right, to make sure he wasn't observed, he then reached down and pulled out the life jacket beneath the seat, quickly replacing it with the bomb. He had chosen the twenty-sixth row based on his calculation that the aft end of the center wing fuel tank on the 747 was located beneath it.

In Cebu City, Yousef disembarked and quickly approached the terminal counter, paying cash for a one-way ticket back to Manila to establish his alibi. He would arrive before noon, sneaking up the back stairs of the Dona Josefa to Room 603, and emerge after lunch, making sure to pass the lobby security guard, who kept a log of the tenants' comings and goings. The log would later show that Yousef (under the alias Naji Owaidah Haddad) had come in around 9:40 the night before, and hadn't left since.[25]

Meanwhile, back in Cebu City, as the second leg of Flight 434 was boarding, a twenty-four-year-old Japanese engineer name Haruki Ikegami sat down in Seat 26K. He had no idea that he had just a few hours to live.

By the time the flight took off for Japan it was three-quarters full, with 273 passengers and a crew of 20. Just after 10:44 A.M., heading north over the Philippines Sea at 33,000 feet, Flight 434 approached the small island of Minamidaito, forty nautical miles south of Okinawa.[26]

Captain Eduardo Reyes was about to radio Naha Airport on the southern tip of the island to report his bearings when suddenly, the alarm on Yousef's Casio went off. A low-voltage charge shot along the circuit, enhanced by the nine-volt batteries. The filament in the broken bulb sparked, setting off the high explosive. The IED blew downward into the fuselage with such force that the crew members in the cockpit were jolted from their seats and the enormous aircraft suddenly banked to the right.

Captain Reyes sounded an immediate "Mayday," but when he disengaged the autopilot, he discovered that the blast had severed some of the plane's hydraulics and now he was unable to turn. Suddenly, the purser burst into the cockpit to announce that Haruki Ikegami had been killed, his body literally cut in half by the blast. Captain Reyes put the plane back on autopilot while he ran through the options in his mind. He had no idea if the blast had damaged the structural integrity of the 747 or if the landing gear had been affected. He wasn't sure if it was leaking fuel. Requesting emergency landing permission on Okinawa, he held his breath and disengaged the autopilot once again. This time he was able to maneuver the plane. It took the captain forty-five minutes to ease the jumbo jet onto a proper approach to the airport. Steward Fernando Bayot later called it "the longest forty-five minutes in my life."[27]

At Naha, the controllers couldn't tell if the gear had been damaged as the huge jumbo jet flew low over the tower for a visual inspection, so a Lear jet made two passes below the 747 and confirmed that the gear was down and locked. Moments later, a cheer went up from the surviving passengers in the cabin as the huge tires screeched across the tarmac and the plane landed safely.

The "Undetectable" Bomb

That night, in the XO karaoke bar in Manila's Malate district, Yousef, KSM, Murad, and Wali Khan toasted what they began to call "the undetectable device." All they had to do on future flights was move the IED forward a few rows where it would blow down and detonate the fuel tank on any jumbo jet they targeted. Yousef and each of his Manila cell members now intended to plant three devices over a forty-eight-hour period aboard U.S. flag carriers leaving Asia for the United States—up to a dozen in all.

But "Bojinka" was only one of three murderous plots that Yousef and KSM had in the advanced planning stages in Room 603 of the Dona

Josefa. Along with Murad and Wali Khan, they were also planning to murder Pope John Paul II, who would be arriving in Manila on January 12, 1995. After hiding pipe bombs along the parade route, which would take the pontiff right past the Dona Josefa, Yousef would detonate the devices by remote control. With onlookers expected to be packed along the motorcade route ten to twenty deep, the casualties might be in the thousands, and this time (unlike New York) Yousef could observe the carnage himself first hand from the Dona Josefa's corner sixth-floor window.

But the Bojinka and Pope plots were merely a rehearsal for a much more devastating attack on U.S. soil. Sometime in the months or years ahead, once they had trained enough pilots and "muscle hijackers," Abdul Hakim Murad would fly the lead aircraft in an audacious bicoastal plot to hijack a series of commercial airliners and fly them into buildings in the United States—including the White House; the Pentagon; CIA headquarters in Langley, Virginia; a nuclear facility; and two of America's tallest skyscrapers, the Sears Tower in Chicago, and the Transamerica Tower in San Francisco.

By that point, in late 1994, Yousef and KSM had up to ten Islamic "brothers" training in U.S. flight schools.[28] They would go on to execute the terror plot that Yousef had envisioned after he failed to topple the North Tower of the WTC into the South Tower. It was the plot he'd warned the FBI about on the night of the February 1993 bombing, when he'd had Nidal Ayyad type an addendum to the Liberation Army credit letter: "our calculations were not very accurate this time. However we promise you that next time it will be very precise and the Trade Center will be one of our targets." The next time Ramzi Yousef attacked the Twin Towers it would be from *above*, not below, and this time he would not fail. As they clicked glasses that night at the XO bar, Yousef exclaimed, "As Allah commands it, so it will be done."

16

LOSING THE AL QAEDA KEY

On December 16, 1994, five days after Yousef's successful wet test aboard PAL 434, the agents in the FBI's San Francisco office made an extraordinary seizure. Mohammed Jamal Khalifa (MJK), Osama bin Laden's best friend and former roommate, was captured at a Holiday Inn just twenty-six miles from Ali Mohamed's house in Santa Clara, California. The arrest took place in Morgan Hills, the very Silicon Valley town where Special Agent John Zent lived. If this arrest had been properly followed up by the FBI and the Justice Department, it could have led to the seizure of both Ramzi Yousef and his uncle Khalid Shaikh Mohammed, and stopped the 9/11 plot dead in its tracks. But what followed was a series of missteps and bad decisions at the highest levels of the State and Justice Departments that would have a catastrophic impact on America's ability to end bin Laden's jihad against America.

Khalifa, thirty-seven, was born in Medina, Saudi Arabia. A short, wiry man with a close-cropped beard.[1] His aliases included Abdul Bara, Abu Baraa, and Jimmy Jack.[2] Khalifa was so close to the Saudi billionaire that he'd married bin Laden's sister. From 1983 to 1991, he had been trusted by al Qaeda with running the Philippines branch of the International Islamic

Relief Organization (IIRO),[3] one of their key NGO's with links to the Hamas terrorist organization.[4] The Philippines National Police (PNP) believed that Khalifa was bankrolling the Yousef-KSM-Murad-Wali Khan Manila cell via Konsonjaya, the cutout company in Malaysia.[5]

The PNP also suspected Khalifa of having "contacts with Islamic extremist and fundamentalist groups . . . in Iraq, Jordan, Turkey, Russia, Malaysia, United Arab Emirates, Romania, Lebanon, Syria, Pakistan, Albania, the Netherlands, and Morocco."[6]

More significant, he also had ties to al Gamma'a Islamyah (IG), Sheikh Rahman's Egyptian-based terror group. Khalifa's business card was discovered in a search of the blind Sheikh's residence the year before, and he was one of 172 unindicted coconspirators named by prosecutors Patrick Fitzgerald and Andrew McCarthy in the Day of Terror case, which was about to get underway in the SDNY in early 1995.

At the time of his arrest in Morgan Hills, Khalifa was traveling with Mohammed Loay Bayazid, aka Abu Rida al-Suri, a naturalized U.S. citizen who worked in the Chicago office of the Benevolence International Foundation, the al Qaeda NGO. In the early 1990s, Bayazid had attempted to obtain uranium for Osama bin Laden.[7] Further, although Khalifa was carrying a Saudi passport, he'd flown into the Bay area from London carrying a Philippines Special Return Certificate indicating that he was heading back to Manila.[8]

With his direct connections to bin Laden, the blind Sheikh, and Ramzi Yousef, Mohammed Jamal Khalifa was the biggest al Qaeda fish the Feds had caught since Rahman himself in July 1993.

"It's difficult to express just how many dots the FBI and Justice Department prosecutors could have connected with Khalifa, at the time of his arrest, given the contacts he had," says Paul Thompson, terrorist researcher and author of *The Terror Timeline,* who has compiled a database of more than 10,000 open-source al Qaeda–related articles and court pleadings on the nonprofit website www.cooperativeresearch.org.

After serving a search warrant on Khalifa, the Feds found files in his Newton PDA that listed one of his aliases as Abu Baraa.[9] That same name had been scrawled inside one of the bomb manuals carried by Yousef's traveling partner Mohammed Ajaj, who had been convicted earlier in

1994 for the World Trade Center bombing. Searching Khalifa's belongings, the FBI and INS discovered Islamic literature tying him to IIRO.[10] Also in the PDA were Wali Khan's beeper number and a number in Pakistan that Yousef had used to call Manila. Encrypted phone numbers tied to Khalifa's NGO were later found on Yousef's Toshiba laptop, and when Wali Khan was finally arrested, he was found to be carrying multiple numbers for MJK.[11]

Given his links to Yousef's cells in New York and Manila, Khalifa was the human linchpin who could have furnished the FBI with proof of Yousef's *two* planned attacks on the World Trade Center: his 1993 bombing, executed with the help of Ali Mohamed's trained jihadis, and the planes-as-missiles operation, conceived in Manila, that Yousef's uncle KSM would ultimately carry out on 9/11.

Moreover, Khalifa was motivated to talk. At the time of his arrest in Morgan Hills, he was wanted in Jordan for a series of al Qaeda related bombings. As a State Department cable after his arrest stated: "FYI, Osama bin Laden's brother-in-law, Muhammad Jamal Khalifah [sic], was arrested in California on 12/16. REFTEL (reference telegram) refers to Khalifa as a known financier of terrorist operations and an officer of an Islamic NGO in the Philippines that is a known Hamas front. He is under indictment in Jordan in connection with a series of cinema bombings earlier this year."[12]

On the day of his arrest in mid-December, the State Department designated Khalifa a "Deportable Alien." A deputy assistant secretary of state issued a certification of revocation for Khalifa's visa for having "engaged in terrorist activity."[13]

A week later, on December 23, Philip C. Wilcox Jr., the State Department's coordinator for counterterrorism, wrote to advise an immigration judge that Khalifa had "engaged in serious terrorist offenses" and that his release "would endanger U.S. national security"[14] (Appendix III on page 548).

He noted that "in the last two days there has been a significant additional development in this matter. On December 21 the State Security Court in Jordan found Mohammed Jamal Khalifa guilty of the charges for which he was indicted and imposed a capital sentence."

After a four-month trial involving twenty-five suspected terrorists, the Jordanians had condemned Khalifa.[15] Now in the safety of U.S. custody, he was facing execution if he returned to Amman.

The details in Khalifa's Newton address book should have led the FBI directly to Ramzi Yousef, the world's most wanted man—who, unbeknownst to the Feds, was responsible for the PAL bomb plot that went down just five days before Khalifa's seizure, and who was now contemplating three mass-casualty terrorist attacks. Further, for the two bin Laden offices of origin in New York, Khalifa's web of associations should have underscored al Qaeda direct command and control of Yousef's New York and Philippines operations. As to what the Feds could expect to get out of MJK, his death sentence in Jordan meant that he was motivated to talk, rather than risk extradition.

But the Feds never got a chance to question him. On January 5, 1995, a decision was made by Secretary of State Warren Christopher, and supported by Deputy Attorney General Jamie Gorelick, that ranks as one of the most profound intelligence errors committed by any U.S. official in the years leading up to 9/11.

"Jordan is aware of Mr. Khalifa's presence in the United States," Christopher wrote to Attorney General Janet Reno, "and has asked for our assistance in sending him to Jordan so that he may be brought to justice. To permit Mr. Khalifa to remain in the United States in these circumstances would potentially be seen as an affront to Jordan and at odds with many of the basic elements of our cooperative bilateral relationship [and] potentially undermine our longstanding and successful policy of international legal cooperation to bring about the prosecution of terrorists."[16] Christopher's legal theory seemed part of a determined effort by top officials at Justice and State to craft an exit for Khalifa (Appendix III on page 548).

Philip Wilcox's letter of just two weeks before, and the certificate revoking MJK's visa had cited him for "terrorist activity." But according to Khalifa's lawyer Marc Van Der Hout, "They dropped that halfway through his bond hearing. Then they [substituted] a charge that hadn't been used before—enacted in 1990—that a person can be deported if the Secretary of State has reasons to believe the alien's presence or activities could have potentially serious adverse foreign policy consequences. This is the first time they ever tried to use that statute."[17]

Christopher's letter made no mention of Khalifa's crucial value to the United States in *its own* terror fight. Keep in mind that the FBI found evidence in his PDA linking MJK directly to Yousef, the mastermind of the WTC bombing, who was *at that very moment* the object of a worldwide manhunt. That discovery alone should far have outweighed Jordan's desire to punish Khalifa for a series of movie theater bombings.

Nonetheless, the very next day, Jamie Gorelick—serving in Janet Reno's absence as acting attorney general—sent an "expedite" letter in support of Christopher's deportation request. Strangely, Gorelick began the letter by noting that, pursuant to federal law, "the deportation of an alien in the United States . . . shall be directed by the Attorney General to a country promptly designated by the alien if that country is willing to accept him into its territory *unless the Attorney General in his discretion concludes that deportation to such country would be prejudicial to the interests of the United States*" [emphasis added].[18]

It's difficult to fathom how it could have been in the interests of the United States to allow the deportation of Osama bin Laden's brother-in-law; a man the State Department had just named as "a terrorist." But Gorelick went on record personally as supporting Christopher's recommendation, concluding that "should deportation be ordered, deporting Mohammed Khalifa to any country other than Jordan would be prejudicial to the interests of the United States and that he should be deported to Jordan pursuant to Section 243 (a) of the Immigration and Nationality Act (INA)."

Rather than keeping him in the United States so that he could be debriefed by FBI agents, Gorelick was signing off on a decision first pressed by Warren Christopher who was feeling pressured from the Jordanians to extradite the accused terrorist financier.

"I remember people at CIA who were ripshit at the time" over the decision, says Jacob L. Boesen, an Energy Department analyst then working at the CIA's Counter Terrorism Center. "Not even speaking in retrospect, but contemporaneous with what the intelligence community knew about bin Laden, Khalifa's deportation was unreal."[19]

From the time of his arrest, Khalifa maintained his innocence, contending that he was a legitimate businessman and philanthropist who had visited the Bay Area merely to meet with seed brokers as part of his import-export business. He categorically denied being a terrorist and claimed that his conviction in Amman was the result of perjured testimony by a witness who had been tortured.[20]

Khalifa was initially housed in the relatively low-security Santa Rita Jail in Alameda County.[21] Then, over the next few months, a curious series of events began to unfold. Rather than cooperating with the Feds, Khalifa initially fought his extradition to Jordan.[22] He also filed a civil suit to get back the contents of his luggage, which included the coveted PDA and other computer files.

Astonishingly, the Feds complied. On March 23, in a response to Khalifa's motion for return of property and an order unsealing his search warrant, assistant U.S. Attorney Stephen R. Freccero stated that "The United States has no objection to the unsealing of the search warrant [and] the return of the property seized."

So the treasure trove of al Qaeda related intelligence went back to MJK.

The Oklahoma City Reversal

Then, on April 19, 1995, an event occurred in Oklahoma City that caused a significant change in Khalifa's status as a U.S. detainee. A five-thousand-pound urea-nitrate nitro-methane bomb similar in design to Yousef's WTC device and delivered in a similar yellow Ryder Truck, exploded outside the Murrah Federal Building killing 168 people, including 19 children.

Two separate federal juries and an Oklahoma state jury would eventually conclude that disgruntled army buddies Timothy McVeigh and Terry Lynn Nichols were the sole perpetrators of the blast. But questions about the potential "others unknown" who may have been involved sprang up within hours of the bombing, based initially on eyewitness accounts and the FBI's months-long search for a "John Doe No. 2," an alleged accomplice with a dark, Middle Eastern complexion.[23]

In *1000 Years for Revenge,* I devoted an entire chapter to the extraordinary circumstantial links suggesting a possible connection between Ramzi Yousef and Terry Nichols, who happened to be in Cebu City, the same relatively obscure town in the Philippines, at the same time.[24] McVeigh's attorney, Stephen Jones,[25] told me he believed that his client had been instructed in bomb building by Yousef via Nichols, whom Edwin Angeles, a former leader of the Abu Sayyaf Group, swore he'd seen in another southern Philippines city with Yousef and Abdul Hakim Murad. Angeles had referred to Nichols as "the farmer."[26]

As to McVeigh's bomb-making capabilities, his only test of an ammonium-nitrate fuel oil device before the April 1995 bombing occurred in the fall of 1994, when, according to key government witness Michael Fortier, McVeigh tried to detonate a metal milk jug and it failed.[27] Then, after Nichols returned from the Philippines, the two ex-army suspects, who had no other bomb training, somehow managed to build a weapon of mass destruction strong enough to take down a federal office building.

There were other intriguing facts. Yousef and Manila coconspirator Wali Khan had applied for their Philippine visas on November 3, 1994.[28] The very next day, Nichols—who'd made four trips to the Philippines since 1992—got his visa in Chicago.[29] A phone card in the name of Darryl Bridges, which Nichols and McVeigh used, showed multiple phone calls after Nichols left the Philippines in early January 1995 to the same guesthouse in Cebu City where Nichols's Filipina wife, Marife, was staying.[30] Her uncle, who owned the guesthouse, had worked in Saudi Arabia, and the lodging was reportedly frequented by fundamentalist Islamic students from a nearby college. There were twenty-two attempts to get through to the guesthouse on February 14 alone. Were Nichols and McVeigh dialing back to Yousef's Abu Sayyaf associates for help in designing their bomb?

But the most intriguing piece of evidence linking the Yousef cell to the Oklahoma City bombing was an FBI 302 memo[31] that I discovered dated April 20, 1995, the day *after* the explosion. When Yousef's cohort Abdul Hakim Murad, who had been arrested in Manila on January 6 and rendered back to New York to await trial, heard of the Murrah Building bombing, he immediately took credit for it in the name of Yousef's cell, the so-called "Liberation Army."

That 302 was filed by FBI agent Frank Pellegrino and Secret Service Agent Brian Parr, two of the key JTTF agents from the New York Office assigned to the Yousef hunt. It was Parr who'd extracted a confession from Yousef on his return flight from Pakistan after his arrest in February 1995. Another FBI 302 from that interrogation had confirmed Yousef's links to Mohammed Jamal Khalifa through Wali Khan. So the circle of evidence was tightening.

The suspicion raised in Stephen Jones's memoir that "others unknown" had been involved in the Oklahoma City bombing,[32] and that it had been a conspiracy with al Qaeda connections, would persist for years. As recently as June 2006, Congressman Dana Rohrabacher (R-CA), chairman of the House International Relations Oversight Committee, announced a hearing into whether there might be a Yousef-Nichols connection to the Murrah Building bombing.[33]

Even former White House terrorism czar Richard Clarke admitted in his 9/11 memoir, *Against All Enemies,* that it was possible that al Qaeda operatives in the Philippines had "taught Terry Nichols how to blow up the Oklahoma Federal Building."[34] As Clarke noted, "We do know that Nichols' bombs did not work before his Philippine stay, and were deadly when he returned."

Khalifa's Status Changes Dramatically

Then, on April 19, the very same day as the Murrah Building bombing, Mohammed Jamal Khalifa's situation changed significantly. As terrorism analyst John Berger, who maintains the website www.intelwire.com first discovered, Khalifa was abruptly shifted from the low-security Santa Rita jail to the maximum security Federal Correctional Institution in Dublin, California.[35]

Then, a week after insisting that he remain in the United States, Khalifa did an abrupt 180-degree turn and now asked to be *deported* to Jordan after all.[36]

According to a *San Francisco Examiner* story, Khalifa wept before a federal judge as he denied his guilt, exclaiming, "I really don't see any sign that I can protect myself here."[37]

Quoting Khalifa's attorney, Marc van Der Hout, Eric Brazil wrote in the *Examiner* story that "the current 'anti-alien climate' and extreme sensitivity to terrorist allegations in the wake of the Oklahoma City bombing made the United States a less promising field than Jordan on which to fight his legal battles."[38]

In return for Khalifa's acceptance of the deportation order, the Feds now dropped the initial terrorism allegations and asserted a broader charge that his presence in the United States constituted a foreign policy hazard.[39] Curiously, his case merited such special treatment that he went before the federal magistrate in San Francisco's federal district courthouse rather than the immigration courtroom on Kearny Street, which was typical in such matters.[40]

"There's no doubt that this case was being given high-level treatment by the Justice Department and State," says terrorism researcher Paul Thompson.

When Did Khalifa Leave?

On May 5, 1995, the story took an even more mysterious turn. In a UPI story entitled "Alleged Terrorist Deported to Jordan," Thomas J. Schiltgen, the INS director for Northern California, was quoted as saying that Khalifa had been returned to Jordan two days before, on May 3.[41] The Associated Press ran a similar story, datelined Amman, quoting Khalifa's lawyer, who declared that "has been deported from the United States for retrial here."[42]

Yet according to Bureau of Prison records, on that date Khalifa was merely "admitted to an in-transit facility" of the BOP. John Berger, who obtained the BOP records, wrote this analysis on March 20, 2006:

> At approximately 8:37 A.M., MJK was transferred out of Dublin FCI and out of BOP custody. He was designated 4-I on the data record. According to BOP, this designation indicates that he was removed from the custody of the BOP and placed

in the custody of *another government agency.* BOP officials would not disclose the agency to which he was remanded.[43] [*emphasis added*]

The question is whether that "government agency" kept Khalifa in custody here in the United States, or in a remote facility overseas because, according to his BOP inmate data sheet, "Khalifa remained in 4-I status for almost another four months until August 31, 1995."[44]

Why is the date of Khalifa's actual deportation from the United States important? Because in July 1995 a witness in his Jordanian murder case reportedly recanted, and Khalifa's death sentence was rescinded. If he returned to the Jordanian capital *after* that date, he would be a free man. Thus, if MJK was still in U.S. custody as late as August, the initial reason for his extradition would have been eliminated. If Khalifa was no longer a wanted fugitive in need of extradition, then keeping him in this country would result in no "serious adverse foreign policy consequences," as Warren Christopher had alleged earlier. And the FBI would have had a potential seminal witness against bin Laden.

Greeted by the Saudis

Whether it was in May or August 1995, eventually Mohammed Jamal Khalifa, the brother-in-law of the man who would declare war on America, was ultimately extradited to Jordan and set free.

"The day he flew back to Saudi Arabia, he was greeted by a limo and a high-ranking official of the government embraced him," said Mike Scheuer, former head of Alec Station, the bid Laden unit at CIA.[45]

The *San Francisco Chronicle* quoted Vincent Cannistraro, a former CIA counterterrorism chief, as alleging that right after his return Khalifa went on to help establish the Islamic Army of Aden in Yemen; the al Qaeda related group that later claimed credit for the bombing of the U.S.S. *Cole* in October 2000.[46]

"He should never have been allowed to leave U.S. custody," Cannistraro said.

In April 2004, in a declaration pursuant to a lawsuit filed on behalf of thousands of 9/11 victims by the South Carolina law firm of Motley-Rice,

Khalifa swore under oath that he had "never supported the loss of inno-cent life" and believed that there is "no justification for the tragic attacks of September 11, 2001. I have never supported any person or organization that I have known to participate in terrorist activities," he declared.[47]

More recently, Khalifa was said to be "running a seafood restaurant in Jedda," Saudi Arabia, according to Terry McDermott, who interviewed MJK for his acclaimed book on the 9/11 hijackers, *Perfect Soldiers.*[48]

"The road to 9/11 is paved with thousands of missed opportunities," says terror expert Steven Emerson.[49] "Along with each missed opportunity, we can go back and kick ourselves in the shin and one of those [instances] would've been holding onto Mohammad Jamal Khalifa and following up on what he was doing for the Osama bin Laden organization."

Given Khalifa's seizure in Morgan Hills, California, where John Zent, Ali Mohamed's control agent lived, and given that he was picked up by the Feds at a Holiday Inn just twenty-six miles from Ali's own home in Santa Clara, one of the biggest unanswered questions is whether MJK was en route to a meeting with Ali before he was arrested.

We don't have any hard proof of any intended meeting, but Emerson says that his gut tells him, the two top-tier al Qaeda operatives were talk-ing: "It seems to me that they probably were in contact," he says. "I'm basing that only intuitively on the fact that they were in the same area, they were close to bin Laden, and they would've had an incentive to stay together."[50]

Covering for an Act of Negligence

The Khalifa case is worth studying in detail, though, not just because of the massive security loss that it represented for America, but because it may have led to the infamous March 1995 memo from Deputy Attorney General Jamie Gorelick who sought to define how the FBI and Justice De-partment would investigate terrorism for years to come.

In that memo, promulgated two months after her letter acquiescing to Khalifa's deportation, Gorelick issued the Justice Department policy creat-ing the infamous "wall."[51] She instructed FBI agents and DOJ prosecutors to separate *past* criminal investigations, "including the bombing of the World Trade Center" and "the indicted case of *United States v. Rahman, et al.*" from Foreign Counter Intelligence (FCI) investigations of *future* terrorist acts. In effect, Gorelick was ordering the breakup the Justice Department's war on terror into two separate camps.

"Because the counterintelligence investigation will involve the use of surveillance techniques authorized under the Foreign Intelligence Surveillance Act (FISA) against targets that, in some instances, had been subject to surveillance under Title III, and because it will involve some of the same sources and targets as the criminal investigation, we believe that it is prudent to establish a set of instructions that will clearly separate the counterintelligence investigation from the more limited, but continued, criminal investigations," Gorelick wrote.

Since most of the Justice Department's body of knowledge on al Qaeda, Yousef, and the blind Sheikh's plots was contained in the files of FBI agents and SDNY prosecutors who worked those criminal cases, Gorelick's extraordinary edict had the potential legal effect of isolating them from the FCI agents trying to stop the next al Qaeda bomb from detonating.

Gorelick's memo also had a more personal effect: It may well have helped to obscure her support for Khalifa's extradition at a time when prosecutors in the SDNY had recently commenced the epic case they were mounting against the blind Sheikh and his cohorts.[52]

Beyond What Is Legally Required

What makes Gorelick's memo even more astonishing is that it wasn't legally necessary. She even admitted in her order that these new "procedures . . . go beyond what is legally required."

As mentioned earlier, the 2004 disclosure of that memo by Attorney General John Ashcroft, in his testimony before the 9/11 Commission, set off a firestorm of criticism since Gorelick was serving as one of the ten commissioners. After Ashcroft's revelation, F. James Sensenbrenner Jr. (R-WI), chairman of the House Judiciary Committee, accused Gore-

lick of having "an inherent conflict of interest" and called for her immediate resignation.[53] But the "wall memo" debate quickly degenerated
into partisan finger-pointing after Ashcroft was forced to admit that his
own deputy attorney general Larry Thompson had renewed the terms of
the Gorelick memo in August 2001, weeks before 9/11.[54]

As retired FBI special agent Joe O'Brien sees it, "The wall memo was a
disastrous move. Because, as it turned out, all of these cases were related.
This was a bin Laden–New York show from start to finish."

In years to come, Gorelick would play a key role in a decision that
buried evidence linking Ramzi Yousef to the notorious crash of TWA
Flight 800. As one of the 9/11 commissioners, Gorelick would also support a decision that limited the scope of the commission's investigation
"with regard to the Department of Justice" to the "period 1998 forward."[55] That narrower field of inquiry ensured that the commission
wouldn't look back at the disastrous Khalifa deportation, which Gorelick
supported, or question whether she had used "the wall" memo to keep
prosecutors from connecting the dots on her negligence.

"There's no doubt that the commission should have gone back at least
as far as the first Bush administration in order to effectively measure the
intelligence failures that led to the attacks," says Monica Gabrielle, a
member of the core group of 9/11 victim families that campaigned for the
creation of the commission. "But Gorelick was one of those who wanted
to concentrate only on the last few years."

Apparently she got her way. In the entire 604-page authorized edition
of *The 9/11 Commission Report,* there isn't a word about Gorelick's role in
supporting the exit of Mohammed Jamal Khalifa, or about the "wall
memo"—two of the most damaging moves the U.S. justice system took
on the road to 9/11.[56]

17

HIDING BEHIND THE WALL

O ne of the most bitter critics of Gorelick, and the "wall" she raised with her memo, was a former prosecutor in the SDNY who once technically worked under Gorelick. Andrew C. McCarthy was a street-smart AUSA who put himself through Columbia College by working as a U.S. marshal. The day after Gorelick sought to defend herself in a *Washington Post* Op-Ed piece entitled "The Truth About the Wall," McCarthy wrote a scathing critique for the conservative *National Review Online* asserting that Gorelick "belongs in the witness chair, not on the commissioner's bench."

Pointing out accurately that the "wall memo" was completely unnecessary, McCarthy branded Gorelick "a key participant" in the government's "pre-9/11 intelligence failure."[1] As it turns out, however, in December 1994—the very same moment when Gorelick and Secretary of State Christopher were pushing to extradite Khalifa—McCarthy himself was engaging in his own disconnection of the dots.

At the center of his attention was Ali Mohamed.

After years of missing the connections between Ali Mohamed's trained cell members, from Nosair to Abouhalima and Salameh, the Feds of the Southern District had assembled an extraordinary body of evidence linking Sheikh Rahman and his eleven codefendants in what they called a "jihad army" bent on waging a war of urban terrorism in the streets of New York.[2]

In late December 1994, McCarthy and his coprosecutors Patrick Fitzgerald and Robert Khuzami were gearing up for the Day of Terror trial, in which they would seek to convict the blind Sheikh and his cell for the "bridge and tunnel plot," which Emad Salem had helped to break. This was the Feds' way of mopping up for their failure to see the conspiracy in the Kahane murder in 1990, and the FBI's inability to stop Yousef in 1992 before he planted the World Trade Center bomb.

The months-long trial, grounded in a seldom-used Civil War era law prohibiting seditious conspiracy, would allow the SDNY to connect the al Qaeda links going back to the rabbi's killing. Nosair himself would be charged along with the Sheikh; and this time the Feds would nail him for the Kahane murder—not just the low-level gun charge the Manhattan D.A. had been forced to accept in 1991.

For this second trial, Nosair would be represented by Roger Stavis, a brilliant criminal defense attorney who avoided the theatrics of William Kunstler. As Stavis prepped for trial, he was shocked to find, among the documents seized from Nosair's house, those TOP SECRET training manuals from Fort Bragg. This caused him to start asking questions about the mysterious "Ali Mohamed," the U.S. Army sergeant who seemed to have played some role in training Nosair and his cohorts.

Stavis immediately began investigating Mohamed himself.

"I got down to Bragg months before the FBI ever thought to show up," recalls Stavis. "You would have thought that those documents the FBI recovered on the Joint Chiefs and those TOP SECRET manuals would have prompted the Bureau to figure out who Ali Mohamed was, long before this trial."

His defense for the Prozac-popping Egyptian was that Nosair was trained by Ali Mohamed, who had been an "asset" variously of the CIA and the U.S. Army, and thus the U.S. government itself should share culpability for Nosair's shooting spree. The Kahane murder, in Stavis's argument was "blowback" from America's covert support for the mujahadeen and Ali Mohamed was a merely an expeditor.

In the course of his investigation, Stavis connected more dots about Mohamed than the government itself had ever managed.

"I have him in Fort Bragg," recalls Stavis.[3] "I have him here [in New York] training these people. And then I have him in Afghanistan, because one of the witnesses who trained with him in New Jersey went to Afghanistan, saw him there, and also saw him in New Jersey. And he stayed at Nosair's house. I refer to that as completing the triangle."

So Stavis wrote up a subpoena for Ali Mohamed and started looking for him.

A Defense Lawyer's Search for Ali Mohamed

"This was late '94," says Stavis. "I wanted him. And I tried everything to find him." But Mohamed, it seemed, had disappeared. "Even his wife hadn't seen him out in California," Stavis says. "I invoked the Classified Information Procedures Act [CIPA]," a special set of legal procedures for getting witness testimony in potentially classified matters. "I think a lot of bells went off in Langley," the CIA headquarters. "People went running around."

Finally some bells went off in the New York Office of the FBI and the SDNY.

At the time, Ali Mohamed was in Africa, staying in a Nairobi safe house and interacting daily with Wadih El-Hage, one of the leaders of the embassy-bombing cell. Earlier that year Mohamed had been in Khartoum, staying in Osama bin Laden's own house. After surviving an assassination attempt, bin Laden had personally asked Ali to train his bodyguards.[4]

Now, with Stavis seeking Mohamed's testimony, prosecutor Andrew McCarthy was worried. At that point, no one outside the Bureau or the SDNY knew that Ali had been an FBI informant. McCarthy could only guess what the former army sergeant might say if he got on the stand under oath in open court.

"If Ali would have been put on [the stand] at that point in time, [he] would have been viewed as an agent provocateur," says retired special agent Jack Cloonan. "Maybe there would have been an issue of entrapment raised. It wouldn't have helped the government's case."[5] That subpoena became "a huge, huge issue for Ali" as well, says Cloonan.

As an al Qaeda spy who was playing two FBI offices off each other at that point, Mohamed had reason to be concerned. If he was compelled to testify in federal court with the national media covering the trial, the truth about his espionage career from Fort Bragg onward would have been exposed by defense attorneys like Roger Stavis. "That would have effectively blown his cover as an FBI informant," says Stavis, and "shut him down as a spy then and there." And Ali had more work for the jihad to do.

By the first week in December 1994, al Qaeda's military commander, Mohammed Atef, met with Ali at El-Hage's house and ordered him to do surveillance of U.S., British, French, and Israeli targets in Senegal.[6]

Helping Ali Avoid a Subpoena?

According to Cloonan, prosecutor Andrew McCarthy was so desperate to get to Mohamed that he contacted the FBI's San Francisco office, and Ali's control agent, John Zent, called Ali's wife, Linda Sanchez, to find out where he was. Nairobi bombing cell member L'Houssaine "Joe" Kerchtou later testified that Mohamed "received a call from the United States from a friend of his saying that he had some problem and he should come back."[7]

The "friend" was Khalid Dahab, the Egyptian who was running Mohamed's Santa Clara cell in his absence. Dahab placed the call to El-Hage's house after Linda told him that the Feds wanted an audience with her husband.

Mohamed later confirmed that after receiving a phone call in late 1994 from "an FBI agent who wanted to speak to me about the upcoming trial of *United States v. Abdel Rahman*,"[8] he abruptly canceled the Senegal surveillance and headed back to the United States.[9] As Jack Cloonan recalls, he even expressed anger when the Feds failed to reimburse him for his airfare.

By that point, however, McCarthy was so worried about Stavis's subpoena that he actually flew to California with New York FBI agent Harlan

Bell to interview Mohamed.[10] True to form, Ali shined them on. A master at spinning lies that seemed odd enough to be credible, Ali told them that he was working in Kenya in the *scuba diving* business. He admitted that he'd made two prior trips to Pakistan, but claimed that the first in 1988 was as an "observer," and the second in 1991 was in response to a request by the late Mustafa Shalabi to move Osama bin Laden out of Afghanistan.[11]

It was the second time in two years that Mohamed had revealed his association with the al Qaeda leader.

Keep in mind that during his treasonous support for the terror network, Mohamed was a U.S. citizen. As recently as August 1994, he had been in the U.S. Army Reserve. His enlistment oath bound Ali to "support and defend the Constitution of the United States against all enemies, foreign and domestic" and "bear true faith and allegiance to the same . . . so help me God."[12] When he was sworn in as an assistant U.S. attorney, McCarthy had taken a similar oath. Given the extraordinary case he'd built against the Sheikh and his cohorts, McCarthy knew full well who Mustafa Shalabi was. In fact, McCarthy had even named the dead Egyptian as an unindicted coconspirator in the upcoming case, along with 171 others, from Osama bin Laden to the Murteza brothers, the Connecticut gun dealers who dealt with Nosair. Even the murdered Abdullah Azzam was on the list, along with Mohammed Jamal Khalifa, whom Jamie Gorelick was about to help extradite from U.S. custody. (Appendix X, page 574–575).

McCarthy and coprosecutors Fitzgerald and Khuzami were about to argue in front of a jury that the Sheikh's cell (which Ali had trained) was part of a "jihad army" fighting a war against America in a series of battles.[13] The Kahane murder was one battle. The Trade Center bombing another and the Day of Terror plot represented just the latest outbreak in that war.

Having read the Nosair files, McCarthy knew that Mohamed had commuted up from Fort Bragg to train what his colleague Robert Khuzami would call the "soldiers in this army." As lead prosecutor on the case, McCarthy must have realized that Ali played a key role in that "military" hierarchy. In fact, he'd even named Ali himself as an unindicted coconspirator. And yet now, on December 9 in Santa Clara, McCarthy sat listening with Special Agent Bell, as Ali handed them a story about going off to Africa to run a diving business.

"I didn't disclose everything I knew," Mohamed said later, in a master-piece of understatement.[14]

From what we know on the public record, after McCarthy and Bell left that meeting and returned to New York, there were no immediate repercussions for Mohamed, short of his name turning up on that unindicted coconspirators list. But at this point in the story, the question is, why? Why did McCarthy and Bell fly more than 3,000 miles to speak to the al Qaeda spy? Were they after the truth? Did they really want to know just how deep his roots ran with al Qaeda and the EIJ? Were they hoping to get enough on Ali to convert him from an unindicted coconspirator to a full-blown defendant in the Day of Terror trial? Or was the meeting really about damage control?

Nosair's Cousin Accuses McCarthy

The answer may lie in a hand-scrawled letter from El Sayyid Nosair's cousin Ibrahim El-Gabrowny, which he wrote as part of his appeal after being convicted in the Day of Terror plot. In it he contends that in October 1999, four years after his conviction, he found himself in the Metropolitan Correctional Center (MCC), the federal jail in lower Manhattan. In the cell next to his on the Nine South tier, where all terror suspects are housed, was Ali Mohamed (whom the Feds finally arrested in September 1998).

Referring to himself in the third person, El-Gabrowny described his interactions with Mohamed:

> El Gabrowny and Ali Mohamed engaged in several conversations. . . . At one time El Gabrowny asked Ali Mohamed whether or not he ever received the subpoena that Nosair's lawyer sent to him [and] further if he did received the subpoena, why he did not come to testify.

El-Gabrowny then makes a shocking allegation:

> Ali Mohamed . . . added that regarding the subpoena that was sent to him by Nosair's lawyer, he actually received it and was prepared to abide with the order and come to testify on Nosair's behalf. But . . . Mr. Andy McCarthy, the AUSA on El-Gabrowny and Nosair's case, came accompanied with an FBI agent and paid him a visit. Ali Mohamed further added, during this visit Mr. McCarthy told him that he

(i.e., Mr. McCarthy) knew about the subpoena. . . . Then Mr. McCarthy advised Ali Mohamed to ignore the subpoena's order and not to go to testify on Nosair's behalf and that Mr. McCarthy will cover up for him regarding that.

In his appeal, El-Gabrowny—who by then had become something of a jailhouse lawyer—argued that "Ali Mohamed's testimony was crucial to refute a major part of the Government's allegation, and that would substantially effect the case for Nosair, El-Gabrowny and the rest of the codefendants. Accordingly, if El-Gabrowny's claim is true, this will represent a sever[e] Brady violation, since the Government through it's representative Mr. Andy McCarthy acted maliciously to destroy evidence and withhold exculpatory information from the defense, that if they were revealed—they would substantially effect the jury's mind and change the whole outcome of the trial."[15]

Here El-Gabrowny refers to a federal rule promulgated after the historic 1963 U.S. Supreme Court case *Brady vs. Maryland*, which held that "the suppression by prosecutors of evidence favorable to an accused upon request violates due process where the evidence is material either to guilt or punishment, irrespective of the good faith or bad faith of the prosecution."[16]

Bin Laden's Phantom Spy

Later at trial, when defense attorney Roger Stavis sought to question Norvell De Atkine, the Fort Bragg officer who used Ali Mohamed in the training videos, Andrew McCarthy objected on grounds of "competence," arguing to the judge that "This witness is being proffered so that they don't have to put Ali Mohamed on the stand to ask him about it himself."[17] In short, McCarthy was attempting to use Mohamed's absence from the trial to his advantage.

Later that day, after Stavis tried to enter Mohamed's army service record into evidence, McCarthy objected: "He [Stavis] wants to put in pages of stuff, detailed minutia about the guy's career in the army which is not relevant to the case."

But the army career of Ali Mohamed couldn't have been *more* relevant to that case. He had infiltrated the army as a phantom spy for bin Laden, as surely as he had infiltrated the FBI—and trained the key cell members of the very "jihad army" that was currently on trial for waging war against the United States.

In legal terms, El-Gabrowny's note amounted to double hearsay. But was it nonetheless an accurate account of a conversation he had with Ali Mohamed? Clearly the allegation was serious enough to warrant further investigation. If a federal prosecutor like McCarthy had actually intervened with Mohamed to keep him from honoring a federal subpoena, that might constitute a violation of the Brady rules.

On June 9, 2006, I contacted McCarthy by e-mail, sending him a copy of El-Gabrowny's note and asking him for a comment. He never responded.

When I interviewed Roger Stavis on March 17, 2006, he said he'd never heard the charge that McCarthy had encouraged Mohamed not to testify. But he emphasized that "we couldn't find Mohamed," and suggested a reason: "You have to understand, the Feds didn't want Afghanistan in the case at all. It undermined the entire theory of their prosecution."[18]

In any case, as the Day of Terror trial commenced on January 30, 1995, Ali Mohamed ignored Stavis's subpoena and never showed up at court. Even if we dismiss El-Gabrowny's hearsay allegation that McCarthy told him to stay away, McCarthy was certainly aware that Stavis wanted him on the stand. He'd been in contact with Mohamed as late as December 9, and could have acted to facilitate his appearance at trial. But he didn't.

"They didn't want him to testify for the same reasons that I *did*," says Stavis. "I'm telling you that I would have done anything to get him on the witness stand."

Ali might have been protected by the Feds that December 1994, but he certainly wasn't loyal to them. Immediately after his meeting with McCarthy and Special Agent Bell, Mohamed informed on them to Mohammed Atef, al Qaeda's military commander. Perhaps fearing that the FBI was getting too close, Atef told Mohamed not to return to Nairobi.[19]

McCarthy Stays in Touch with Ali

Still, to maintain his cover as an FBI informant, Mohamed continued talking to the Feds. On December 22, an hour and twenty minutes after talking to Wadih El-Hage in Kenya, he called Andrew McCarthy.[20] If the Bureau had been vigilant enough to monitor that single phone call, it might have led them to Osama bin Laden.

Why? Because as they eventually learned, the cell phone Mohamed used to call McCarthy was later used by El-Hage just before he went to see bin Laden.[21]

But Mohamed continued to snooker McCarthy. On February 2, 1995, just after the start of the trial, McCarthy sent the list of unindicted coconspirators to various defense attorneys in the Day of Terror case. Somehow Ali Mohamed got a copy of it. Did McCarthy give it to him? We don't know, but a copy was found in Mohamed's house when the Feds searched it more than three years later.[22] Ali later admitted that "I obtained a copy of the coconspirator list for the Abdel Rahman trial. I sent the list to El-Hage in Kenya expecting that it would be forwarded to bin Laden in Khartoum."[23] Using the code words of the tradecraft he knew so well, Ali addressed the list to "the Supervisor" (bin Laden), and signed it "Haydara," one of his many aliases.[24] Thus, while pretending to cooperate with the Feds, he was betraying their most confidential communiqués.

Throughout his dealings with Andrew McCarthy, Mohamed remained loyal to al Qaeda. And yet McCarthy, who fully understood the deadly power of the "jihad army," seemed almost protective of him. Why? Why would an ex-U.S. marshal and savvy federal prosecutor like McCarthy, so willing to criticize Jamie Gorelick for raising the "wall," fail to connect the dots on Mohamed himself after meeting with him face-to-face at the end of 1994?

Whatever the reason, Mohamed would thrive for another four years before his espionage career came to an end.

Ramzi Yousef wouldn't be so lucky.

The Bomb Factory "Fire"

The planes-as-missiles plot hatched in the brilliant but twisted mind of Ramzi Yousef in the fall of 1994 might have been executed sooner but for an incident that occurred in Room 603 of the Dona Josefa on the night of January 6, 1995—the very same night that Jamie Gorelick sent her "expedite" letter supporting Mohammed Jamal Khalifa's release.

Yousef and Murad were working away in their underwear on that hot night, assembling components for a series of Casio-nitro bomb triggers. The stuffy room was filled with chemicals, pipe bombs in various stages of completion, and religious garments, including cassocks and crucifixes that Yousef and his cell intended to use as camouflage while planting the devices along the Pontiff's motorcade route.[25]

Yousef and Murad had spent the New Years' holiday in the southern Philippines, drilling with members of Abu Sayyaf, an al Qaeda related group.[26] They planned to execute the Bojinka plot right after assassinating the Holy Father, during the week of January 12.

At around ten o'clock in the evening, as they mixed a series of chemicals, there was an unintended chemical reaction.[27] Smoke began billowing out of the room.[28] Neighbors called the fire department, and the small blaze was extinguished as soon as they arrived.

A rookie patrolman named Fernandez, from the local PNP Malati District Station, accepted Yousef's cover story that he and Murad had merely been playing with "firecrackers" left over from a New Year's celebration.[29]

While the smoke cleared, Yousef rendezvoused at a nearby 7–Eleven with Murad and Wali Khan, planning a possible exit strategy in case the police returned. He then sent Murad back to the apartment house to retrieve his Toshiba laptop, which contained details of all three plots the cell had set in motion. But when he entered the building's lobby, Murad was arrested by Aida Fariscal,[30] an alert PNP captain who didn't believe the firecracker story.[31]

Then, as he was leaving the Dona Josefa's lobby with Fariscal, Fernandez, and a PNP sergeant named Tizon, Murad suddenly took off running. The cops gave chase, and as Murad turned left at the building's entrance, Fernandez dropped to his knees and fired. The bullet whizzed past Murad's ear, but he tripped on the root of a tree, and the police were able to grab him, shoving him against a building. "We'll shoot you if you move," said Fernandez.

Desperate, Murad turned to Fariscal, and tried to bribe her with $2,000 in American Express checks he'd hidden in his sock.

"Hmmmm," Fariscal replied. "Two thousand dollars is two year's pay for most in this country. I think maybe it is too big a bribe for just fire-crackers."[32] Moments later, when she entered Room 603, Fariscal was shocked to find that the one-bedroom apartment was littered with chemi-cals and bombs in various stages of assembly.

As all of this played out, Ramzi Yousef was watching from across Quirino Boulevard. He actually considered sneaking up the back stairs to retrieve his Toshiba laptop, but when he heard the siren as a bomb-disposal truck arrived, he backed away.

Early the next morning, January 7, Yousef and his uncle, Khalid Shaikh Mohammed, slipped away, en route to Islamabad, Pakistan. The world's most wanted man had escaped again.

18

THE THIRD PLOT

I n the hours after the fire, as Room 603 at the Dona Josefa filled with PNP intelligence officers and army brass, fingerprint evidence from the bomb factory was still being analyzed. Nobody yet in Manila had connected Naji Owaidah Haddad, Yousef's Moroccan alias, with the prime suspect in the World Trade Center bombing. Certainly nobody back at FBI Headquarters in Washington had a clue.

The revelation of Yousef's identity would eventually come from Abdul Hakim Murad, who was handcuffed, blindfolded, and shipped across the Pasig River to Camp Crame, the headquarters of the Philippines Intelligence Group. Held in the empty office of a single-story bungalow, Murad was subjected to sleep and food deprivation in those first few hours. His lawyer would later allege that he was tortured by electric shock and force-fed liquids, a method of torture known as "water boarding."[1] Yet these techniques only caused Murad to stonewall. So several days after his arrest, the interrogation was turned over to Colonel Rodolfo B. "Boogie" Mendoza, the baby-faced commander of the PNP's Special Investigations Group. An authority on Islamic terror, Mendoza had been running Blue Marlin, an operation that had identified a number of radical fundamentalists associated with Abu Sayyaf, the al Qaeda spin-off cofounded by Afghan war veteran Abdurajak Janjalani.[2]

Soon, using a combination of trickery, food deprivation, and guile, Mendoza began to peel back the layers and get the full story from Murad, who had initially identified himself as Saeed Ahmed.[3]

Mendoza specifically ordered that Murad not be placed in a cell. Seeking to earn the terrorist's confidence, he had him cuffed to a metal bed in a room that contained only a small table and a chair. Instructing Murad's handlers to keep him hungry and blindfolded, Mendoza waited until he knew the prisoner was famished; then he had his assistant, Major Alberto Ferro, lift him up so that Murad was sitting in front of the table. A McDonald's hamburger, fries, and a Coke were then placed in front of him.

When his blindfold was removed, the starving Murad lunged for the Big Mac. But Mendoza demanded that the terrorist give him some piece of intelligence before he could eat. When Murad balked, Mendoza removed the burger and started to leave.

"If you want it, you have to give me something first," he said.

"Like what?" asked Murad wearily. "I have told the others everything."

At that point, Mendoza told Murad that he was his "last best hope." If he didn't talk *immediately,* the PNP would turn him over to the Mossad, the feared Israeli intelligence service. Mendoza said that the PNP had captured Wali Khan, who had been carrying Murad's passport. They knew Murad had made a trip to America in 1992. What was he doing in the United States? The colonel wanted details.

Salivating now, Murad eyed the food. Mendoza assured the Muslim that it was "one hundred percent beef. No pork." Murad hesitated. He didn't want to betray Yousef, but the prospect of being shipped to Tel Aviv troubled him even more. Finally, he blurted out some details about the World Trade Center bombing.

"I'm involved in it," said Murad. "The ones who did it—Salameh, Abouhalima—I know them."

Those were names he easily could have read in a newspaper. Mendoza started to leave again when Murad exclaimed, "I am *telling* you. . . . They are using fuel oil and nitric acid. It is ignited with an improvised det cord—gunpowder rolled in cloth. They cover it in plastic to keep down the smoke."

These were details known to few outside the FBI or the bombing cell itself. But Mendoza wasn't satisfied. He demanded the name of "the one who lit the fuses." He wanted the mastermind.

Murad had suffered several days of torture to protect his lifelong friend from Kuwait. But his options were running out. Finally he blurted out Yousef's real name: "Abdul Basit."

Mendoza didn't recognize it and pushed for the bomb maker's *nom de guerre*. Finally, in a muffled voice, Murad hung his head. "Ramzi Yousef."

Now Mendoza was impressed. "Yousef?" he said wide-eyed. "The terrorist the Americans are after?"

Murad nodded sadly and turned away.

"We were really shocked," Mendoza told me later. "Remember, at this time Yousef [was] one of the biggest fugitives in the world. After some time, Murad told me that he will cooperate, provided that he not be brought to Israel and we untie his handcuffs and blindfold."

That day Murad got his Value Meal. Then, over the next sixty days, in admission after admission, he opened up to Mendoza, ultimately revealing the precise details of the plot to kill the Pope and Bojinka. Early on he also gave up a "third plot," which involved flying a small single-engine plane full of explosives into CIA headquarters.

But Mendoza wasn't satisfied. Why would Murad have gone to four U.S. flight schools and spent thousands of dollars to earn his multiengine commercial pilot's license for a plot like that? He suspected that Murad was hiding something much bigger.

"One day, he is kind of cocky," Mendoza told me.[4] "Murad is saying, 'You don't know something that I do.' And I asked him what it was, and he started discussing the plan to hijack commercial airliners. He told me *airliners,* not airplanes." The targets he revealed initially were the Pentagon and a nuclear facility.

"Murad is talking about a plan that is separate from Bojinka," Mendoza said. "Murad is talking about pilot training in the U.S., and . . . Murad is talking . . . about the expertise of Yousef. Not only was this a parallel plot to Bojinka, but what is the motive of Murad to have flight training in the U.S. And who are the other pilots met by Murad in the U.S.? That is an enormous question."[5]

Later, Philippines secretary Rigoberto "Bobby" Tiglao told CNN Manila bureau chief Maria Ressa that in addition to the CIA, Pentagon, and the nuclear facility, the other targets revealed by Murad included the Transamerica Tower in San Francisco, the Sears Tower in Chicago . . . and the World Trade Center.[6]

The Seventh Target

All of this was reported in print for the first time in *1000 Years for Revenge*. In that book, published in 2003, I cited the six targets, and reported from other sources that at the time of the Dona Josefa fire, Yousef and KSM had up to ten Islamic pilots training in U.S. flight schools.[7] But then I got wind that there had been a *seventh* target in the initial plot. So I started digging and soon tracked down the very Philippine investigator who had been tasked by the country's National Bureau of Investigation (NBI) to retrieve the files from Yousef's encrypted laptop. He confirmed for me that the seventh original target had been the White House.

This was yet another fact withheld by SDNY prosecutors after the breakup of the Manila cell that might have led the world community to the planes-as-missiles plot five and a half years before 9/11.

Major Alberto Ferro, who conducted the interrogation of Murad with Colonel Mendoza, later testified at the 1996 Bojinka trial in Manhattan federal court that on January 7, 1995, he put Yousef's laptop in a locker at Camp Crame.[8] Mary Horvath, an FBI computer specialist, testified that the Toshiba was given to the FBI by the PNP the following April.[9] The computer's hard drive was then sent to the Microsoft Corporation in Redmond, Washington, for analysis. David Swartzendruber, a Microsoft investigator, examined the drive, and concluded that Yousef began entering data into the laptop regarding the Bojinka plot as early as mid-September 1994.[10]

At the 1996 Bojinka trial of Yousef, Murad, and Wali Khan in the Southern District, the Feds restricted their disclosure of the laptop's contents to the nonsuicide Bojinka plot and to the initial plan to pilot a

Cessna-like plane into CIA headquarters. But a blueprint for virtually the entire 9/11 plot was also contained on that laptop and the Philippines National Police got the details in *early January 1995*.

"We told the Americans about the plans to turn planes into flying bombs as far back as 1995," said Avelino "Sonny" Razon, the former colonel from the Presidential Security Group (PSG) who ran the Bojinka investigation. "Why didn't they pay attention?"[11]

What Was Really On That Laptop?

Mistrustful of U.S. intelligence operatives, especially the CIA, the PNP had decided to copy the Toshiba's hard drive *before* they turned it over to U.S. authorities. The presence of a radical Islamic cell in this heavily Catholic country—especially one that had threatened the Pope himself—was considered a threat to the government of President Fidel Ramos, a former general. So the NBI called in Rafael "Raffy" Garcia III, president of Mega Data, one of Manila's largest information technology companies. Shortly after 9/11, Garcia spoke to Luis F. Francia from the *Village Voice* on condition that his name not be used.[12] In the *Voice* piece, one of the best accounts of the Feds' prior warnings about the 9/11 plot, Garcia told much of the story—but not all of it.

Realizing that the Toshiba was a key puzzle piece, I kept searching, and ultimately uncovered an obscure confession Garcia had written for a Philippines magazine not available in the States. So I contacted him just before Easter in 2005.

Garcia told me he owned a condo in the San Francisco Bay area and would be willing to meet on an upcoming trip to Los Angeles. He'd just bought a new Mercedes SL65 roadster and was anxious to test drive it. On March 27, 2005, we had the first of two face-to-face meetings. Sitting with me in my Santa Barbara office, Garcia confirmed precisely what he had written in the Philippines publication:

Decoding Yousef's computer was not difficult.[13] I bypassed the passwords and immediately accessed the files. This was how we found out about the various plots being hatched by the cell of Ramzi Yousef. First, there was the plot to assassinate Pope John Paul II. Then, we discovered a second, even more sinister plot: Project Bojinka. The planes would have come from Seoul, Hong Kong, Taipei, Tokyo, Bangkok, Singapore, and Manila. Even the airlines and the specific flight numbers had been chosen. There was a document where calculations had been made on how to set the timers on the bomb to be placed on each flight so that they would explode within a set time.

But Garcia was even more surprised to discover the audacious third plot. "We found another document that discussed a second alternative to crash the eleven planes into selected targets in the United States instead of just blowing them up in the air. These included the CIA headquarters in Langley, Virginia; the World Trade Center in New York; the Sears Tower in Chicago; the Transamerica Tower in San Francisco; and the White House in Washington, DC. Murad himself was to fly the plane that would be crashed into the CIA headquarters."[14]

During our second meeting, in May, Garcia told me he was worried.

"I got a lot of threats after that story came out," he said.[15] "There were people in the U.S. intelligence community that didn't want to admit that the full-blown 9/11 plot had been uncovered by the PNP in 1995 and turned over to the FBI." To protect himself, Garcia said, he kept a copy of the hard drive in a safe location.

Garcia wanted to emphasize that he didn't blame the Bureau LEGAT (Legal Attaché) at the U.S. embassy in Manila. "The heat was coming from Washington," he said. "You have to understand that Boogie Mendoza, Sonny [Razon],[16] and other PNP officials took tremendous flak following these disclosures when people across the world began to wonder why the U.S. FBI hadn't followed up on this intelligence."[17]

What's important to the broader story that leads to 9/11 is that Garcia's account jibes precisely with what Colonel Mendoza learned from Murad. Moreover, both men told me that the details of the planes-as-missiles plot were among the materials they turned over to the U.S. embassy in Manila—as early as January 1995, according to Garcia. Mendoza said that he sent the files no later than May.

A year after I first interviewed Garcia in March 2005, another key player in the laptop chain of evidence contacted me via my website: www.peterlance.com.

Sam Karmilowicz had retired in December 2005 after a distinguished twenty-one-year career as an agent in the Diplomatic Security Service, the State Department agency responsible for protecting embassies abroad. Karmilowicz was assistant regional security officer (RSO) at the U.S. embassy in Manila at the time of the Dona Josefa fire. He e-mailed me in March 2006, after reading *1000 Years for Revenge,* and in a series of phone conversations he confirmed a story he first related to investigative reporter Alexander Cockburn for a piece in *Counterpunch,* the online political newsletter.[18]

Before the rendition of Abdul Hakim Murad back to the States for trial, Karmilowicz says, he was sent to Camp Crame by embassy officials to pick up an envelope containing the evidence that Colonel Mendoza and the PNP had extracted from Murad. As Cockburn described it, "Karmilowicz was instructed to transcribe the chain of evidence and to express mail the materials to a U.S. Justice Department Office in New York City. Mike Garcia and Dietrich Snell, the Assistant U.S. Attorneys who prosecuted Murad, almost certainly had access to the materials that Agent Karmilowicz sent to the Justice Department, although it is unknown what, if anything, was done with the evidence."[19]

That makes three credible witnesses—Rodolfo Mendoza, Rafael Garcia, and Sam Karmilowicz, a retired federal agent—who have now confirmed that the FBI or SDNY prosecutors had evidence from Mendoza's interrogation and the Toshiba laptop.

The Genesis of the 9/11 Plot

There was other evidence to corroborate this "third plot" in the FBI's files. The Bureau lab report listing evidence seized from Room 603 shows that Yousef was in possession of a January 1995 edition of *Time* magazine featuring a cover story detailing the recent hijacking of an Air France A-300 airbus from Hourari-Boumiediene Airport in Algiers.[20] It was an event many terrorism analysts believe was an intended test mission for Yousef's U.S.-directed third plot.

The hijackers, members of the bin Laden–funded Armed Islamic Group (GIA), boarded Flight 8969 on Christmas Eve 1994, storming the cockpit and wiring the airliner with explosives. After a hostage standoff, they flew to Marseilles and demanded that the Airbus be fully fueled. When the GIA terrorists killed two hostages, the plane was stormed by France's elite GIGN "super gendarmes" and the crisis ended.[21] Passengers later told police that the hijackers intended to fly the Airbus into the Eiffel Tower.[22]

From other sources in the Philippines, I uncovered a once-secret FBI NO/FORN memo[23] proving that the FBI in Washington had received the intelligence of the planes-as-missiles plot from the PNP. It acknowledged that "Yousef and Murad . . . discussed future attacks in the U.S. including possibly flying a plane loaded with explosive into the CIA building," and possibly attacking "a U.S. nuclear facility" (Appendix XI, page 576).

But as we'll see, the prosecutors in the SDNY and their representatives on the 9/11 Commission would soon construct a fictional narrative of the plot's conception, removing Ramzi Yousef and al Qaeda from the scenario and pushing the date of origin forward two years from Manila to Afghanistan.

With no corroborative evidence beyond the word of Khalid Shaikh Mohammed, himself, the 9/11 Commission would conclude that KSM had merely *pitched* the idea of the plot to bin Laden in 1996, and that he "was not . . . an al Qaeda member at the time of the Manila plot."[24] Despite the PNP's overwhelming evidence identifying Mohammed Jamal Khalifa, bin Laden's brother-in-law, as funder of the Manila cell, Murad's confession of a planes-as-missiles plot *separate* from Bojinka, and proof from the SDNY's own Day of Terror trial of al Qaeda's ties to the 1993 World Trade Center bombing cell trained by Ali Mohamed, the 9/11 Commission somehow concluded that Yousef's uncle KSM "apparently did not begin working with al Qaeda until after the 1998 East Africa embassy bombings."[25]

Relying on the Word of KSM for the Plot's Origin

That same fiction would be introduced into the penalty phase of Zacarias Moussaoui's trial as late as March 2006. Both accounts would be based *solely* on the alleged confession of KSM to U.S. authorities after his capture in March 2003.[26]

As we'll see later, the reliability of Khalid Shaikh Mohammed, himself subjected to heavy torture and water boarding, is highly suspect. But the Feds were quick to use him to take sole credit for the 9/11 plot.

Why did the FBI and the Justice Department choose to promote Khalid Shaikh Mohammed's account, ignoring the trail of conflicting evidence? The logic was simple. If Ramzi Yousef had nothing to do with planes-as-missiles operation, then the Bureau's two bin Laden "offices of origin" couldn't be held accountable for their failure to stop Yousef in the fall of 1992 when he plotted his first attack on the Trade Center. Further, if bin Laden and al Qaeda weren't associated with the September 11 plot until 1998, then the Feds could never be blamed for the years they failed to detect the al Qaeda threat even though a triple agent like Ali Mohamed was working as one of their informants.

Mohamed was arrested on September 10, 1998, three years before AA Flight 11 hit the World Trade Center's North Tower. If the plot had not coalesced until *after* he was put away, the Feds could argue that Mohamed was out of the loop. Thus they couldn't be held accountable for failing to get the plot details out of him as he sat in the MCC.

The Feds' contention that the Dona Josefa fire merely revealed Operation Bojinka, and a plot to fly a small plane into the CIA, would allow officials like Condoleezza Rice to sit before the 9/11 Commission and swear that she could not have envisioned Islamic pilots hijacking airliners and using them as missiles. In testimony before the commission on April 8, 2004, Rice attempted to explain a widely criticized statement she had made in May 2002 that "I don't think anybody could have predicted that these people would take an airplane and slam it into the World Trade Center, take another one and slam it into the Pentagon; that they would use an airplane as a missile."[27]

Under oath before the commission, Secretary Rice back-pedaled on that statement, saying "I probably should have said, '*I* could not have imagined.'"[28]

Yet nine months before she appeared before the commission as National Security Advisor, Rice had access to the Final Declassified Report of the Joint Inquiry, the first congressional investigation into the 9/11 attacks.

That document notes *twelve* separate reports in the seven years before 9/11 suggesting that terrorists might use airplanes as weapons:[29]

• In December 1994, Algerian Armed Islamic Group terrorists hijacked an Air France flight in Algiers and threatened to crash it into the Eiffel Tower. French authorities deceived the terrorists into thinking the plane did not have enough fuel to reach Paris and diverted it to Marseilles. A French antiterrorist force stormed the plane and killed all four terrorists.

• In January 1995, a Philippine National Police raid turned up material in a Manila apartment suggesting that Ramzi Yousef, Abdul Murad, and Khalid Shaikh Mohammed planned, among other things, to crash an airplane into CIA Headquarters. The police said that the same group was responsible for the bombing of a Philippine airliner on December 11, 1994. Information on the threat was passed to the FAA, which briefed U.S. and major foreign carriers.

• In January 1996, the Intelligence Community obtained information concerning a planned suicide attack by persons associated with Shaykh al-Rahman and a key al Qaeda operative to fly to the United States from Afghanistan and attack the White House.

• In October 1996, the Intelligence Community obtained information regarding an Iranian plot to hijack a Japanese plane over Israel and crash it into Tel Aviv. A passenger would board the plane in the Far East, commandeer the aircraft, order it to fly over Tel Aviv, and crash the plane into the city.

• In 1997, an FBI Headquarters unit became concerned about the possibility that an unmanned aerial vehicle (UAV) would be used in terrorist attacks. The FBI and CIA became aware of reports that a group had purchased a UAV and concluded that the group might use the plane for reconnaissance or attack. The possibility of an attack outside the United States was thought to be more likely, for example, by flying a UAV into a U.S. embassy or a U.S. delegation.

• In August 1998, the intelligence community obtained information that a group, since linked to al Qaeda, planned to fly an explosive-laden plane from a foreign country into the World Trade Center. As explained earlier, the FAA found the plot to be highly unlikely given the state of the foreign country's aviation program. Moreover, the agencies concluded that a flight originating outside the United States would be detected before it reached its target. The FBI's New York Office took no action on the information.

• In September 1998, the intelligence community obtained information that bin Laden's next operation might involve flying an explosives-laden aircraft into a U.S. airport and detonating it. This information was provided to senior government officials in late 1998.

• In November 1998, the intelligence community obtained information that the Turkish Kaplancilar, an Islamic extremist group, had planned a suicide attack to coincide with celebrations marking the death of Ataturk, the founder of modern Turkey. The conspirators, who were arrested, planned to crash an airplane packed with explosives into Ataturk's tomb during a ceremony. The Turkish press said the group had cooperated with bin Laden, and the FBI's New York Office included this incident in a bin Laden database.

• In February 1999, the intelligence community obtained information that Iraq had formed a suicide pilot unit that it planned to use against British and U.S. forces in the Persian Gulf. The CIA commented that this was highly unlikely and probably disinformation.

• In April 2000, the intelligence community obtained information regarding an alleged bin Laden plot to hijack a Boeing 747. The source, a "walk-in" to the FBI's Newark office, claimed that he had learned hijacking techniques and received arms training in a Pakistani camp. He also claimed that he was to meet five or six persons in the United States. Some of these persons would be pilots who had been instructed to take over a plane, fly to Afghanistan, or, if they could not make it there, blow the plane up. Although the source passed a polygraph, the Bureau was unable to verify any aspect of his story or identify his contacts in the United States.

• In August 2001, the intelligence community obtained information about a plot to bomb the U.S. embassy in Nairobi from an airplane or crash the airplane into it. The intelligence community learned that two people who were reportedly acting on instructions from bin Laden met in October 2000 to discuss this plot.

• In March 1999, the intelligence community obtained information regarding plans by an al Qaeda member, who was a U.S. citizen, to fly a hang glider into the Egyptian Presidential Palace and detonate explosives. The person, who received hang-glider training in the United States, brought a hang glider to Afghanistan. However, various problems arose during the testing of the glider. He was subsequently arrested and is in custody abroad.

That last account refers to Ali Mohamed's number two in Santa Clara, Khalid Dahab, who had taken hang-gliding lessons. The details of that plot were revealed after Dahab's seizure and confession during that 1999 terror trial in Egypt.[30]

In any case, far apart from any *general* warnings about aircraft as weapons, between the evidence furnished by Colonel Mendoza and the hard copy downloaded from Yousef's laptop, the Feds of the Southern District had the full-blown details of the planes-as-missiles plot by *the spring of 1995.* Why didn't they pick up on it? Why wasn't a public hue and cry sounded in 1995 for Khalid Shaikh Mohammed, the fourth member of the Manila cell, who was now on the loose and beginning to construct a plan to execute his nephew's plot? Why did the SDNY Feds keep KSM's identity secret for three more years, until the hijacking suicide plot was well in motion?

The answer is that, by the time of Jamie Gorelick's "wall memo" in the spring of 1995, the Feds were beginning to lay the groundwork for a cover-up designed to protect the Justice Department from blame for failing to interdict the Ali Mohamed–trained cell years before the *first*

World Trade Center attack. Despite a number of earnest and tenacious FBI special agents and assistant U.S. attorneys pushing for the truth, there were officials within the two bin Laden "offices of origin" who were now affirmatively moving to disconnect the dots.

Meanwhile, on the West Coast, after getting a pass from AUSA McCarthy and Special Agent Bell, Ali Mohamed began to execute his most impressive smuggling operation yet. It would reunite him with al Qaeda's number two, the murderous doctor who had sent him into the United States as al Qaeda's primary sleeper ten years before.

19

RED CRESCENT TOUR

I f there was any figure in the jihad for whom Ali Mohamed would give up his life, it was the forty-four-year-old surgeon he'd sworn an oath to in 1984. Dr. Ayman al-Zawahiri had picked Mohamed out of a cadre of special forces commandos purged from the Egyptian army, and from the moment he began his infiltration of America with the in-flight seduction of Linda Sanchez, Mohamed had taken orders directly from the man he called Abu Moab.[1]

Born in 1951, al-Zawahiri was the progeny of two important Egyptian families. His father, Rabie, was a prominent pharmacology professor at Ain Shams University in Cairo. al-Zawahiri's paternal grandfather was Grand Imam of Al Azhar,[2] the thousand-year-old university in Cairo where Omar Abdel Rahman was educated. His maternal grandfather, Dr. Abd al-Wahab Azzam, was the president of Cairo University, a founder and director of King Saud University in Riyadh, Saudi Arabia, and the former Egyptian ambassador to Pakistan, Saudi Arabia, and Yemen. His uncle was the first secretary general of the Arab League.[3] There's even a street in Cairo named for the al-Zawahiri family.[4]

Young Ayman's Islamic nationalist views were cemented early on. He was arrested at fifteen for his membership in the outlawed Muslim

Brotherhood, the oldest militant group in the Arab world. Sixteen years later, after helping to found the ultra-radical Egyptian Islamic Jihad, he went on to become a surgeon.

Jailed for three years after EIJ members murdered Sadat, al-Zawahiri became an instant celebrity in Egypt when, as one of the few English-speaking suspects among three hundred seized, he gave press briefings through the bars of his jail cell. Screaming at the top of his lungs during one interview, the young doctor exclaimed, "We want to say to the whole world. Who are we? Who are we? Why did they bring us here? We are Muslims who believe in our religion."[5]

After being personally cleared in the Sadat assassination, al-Zawahiri was released in 1984. He found his way to Afghanistan where he served as medic with the mujahadeen. There, in 1987, he met Osama bin Laden.[6] In his seminal al-Zawahiri profile in the *New Yorker,* Lawrence Wright notes that the young surgeon helped to forge the Saudi billionaire's operational and political worldview.

"When Ayman met bin Laden, he created a revolution inside him," Montasser al-Zayat, a prominent Islamic lawyer, told Wright.

With his bushy beard and Coke-bottle thick glasses, al-Zawahiri projected the look of an elder mullah. Prematurely grey, he appeared years older than the spectacularly fit Ali Mohamed, who was just a year younger.

But behind his avuncular exterior, al-Zawahiri was known for his cruelty and lack of mercy. He once ordered the murder of a fifteen-year-old boy in Sudan after a report that he was collaborating with Egyptian intelligence officers.[7]

Ali Mohamed had smuggled al-Zawahiri into California once in the early 1990s, just after the formation of al Qaeda, but that was long before U.S. law enforcement had bin Laden on the radar screen. Now, in 1995, he did it again.

"Zawahiri called Ali in the United States any number of times," says retired special agent Jack Cloonan, who vetted Mohamed after 9/11. "He brought Zawahiri to the United States twice. Now let's think about that for a moment."

Using a forged passport obtained by Mohamed, al-Zawahiri traveled under the alias of Abd-al-Mu'izz.[8] When he arrived in Santa Clara, "the doctor" was hosted by Dr. Ali Zaki, the obstetrician-gynecologist from San Jose whom Linda Sanchez described in her interview with me as "a wonderful person."[9]

The Other Egyptian Doctor

According to Health Grades, an online reference service for medical professionals, Dr. Zaki is Board Certified in obstetrics and gynecology. His full name is Aly Atef Abdel Rahman Ahneo Zaki, and he graduated from Kasr El Aini Medical School in Cairo in 1971. Kasr Al Ainy bills itself as "the oldest and largest faculty for medical education in the Middle East."[10] Dr. Zaki's own website states that he "graduated from Cairo University in 1971 and did his postgraduate training in the U.K. until 1997 at which point he moved to the U.S. to continue training until 1980. He served as an assistant professor in the medical college of Ohio from 1980 to 1983. From that point on he has operated his private practice in the heart of Silicon Valley, San Jose, CA."[11]

According to his Health Grades rating, Dr. Zaki was "reprimanded" on October 31, 2001, in California, after being "charged with purchase and subsequent resale of a dangerous drug for overseas distribution and sale."[12]

I made multiple attempts to interview Dr. Zaki for this book, but he refused to talk to me. He was quoted, however, in a series of articles on the al-Zawahiri tour by reporters for the *Wall Street Journal* and the *San Francisco Chronicle*.

As Lance Williams and Erin McCormick wrote in the *Chronicle,* "Zaki said he had been introduced to 'Dr. Mu'izz,' al-Zawahiri's fake name, by [Ali] Mohamed and [Khalid] Dahab, whom Zaki said he knew because both worshipped at the same mosque."[13] Zaki insisted that he had provided limited help for what he believed was a charitable cause. He also claimed that the Feds had thoroughly probed his association with Ali Mohamed and al-Zawahiri.

"I have been investigated by the FBI, and I testified before the grand jury for the bin Laden case, and I explained to them, [al-Zawahiri] might have been [here] in the mid-'90s, but the only time I met Mr. Zawahiri was in 1989 or 1990, and he came with a different name as a representative of the Red Crescent, which is equivalent to the Red Cross."

Perhaps concerned about the scrutiny that would follow from his association with al Qaeda's second in command, Dr. Zaki hired former U.S. congressman and presidential candidate Pete McCloskey to help him respond to the press. McCloskey told Williams and McCormick that Zaki had "fully cooperated with FBI agents and a U.S. grand jury that questioned him about al-Zawahiri, [Ali] Mohamed," and Ali's protégé Khalid Dahab. McCloskey described Zaki to the *Chronicle* reporters as "a law abiding and religious man who would never knowingly support terrorism and who had done nothing wrong." McCloskey emphasized that Zaki was "not a man of violence. . . . This is not a man who would jeopardize an American future," he said.[14]

In a second interview, this one with *Wall Street Journal* reporters Peter Waldman, Gerald F. Seib, and Jerry Markon, Dr. Zaki said that he didn't know al-Zawahiri's real identity at the time of his California visits, describing him as "a physician who was taking care of over one million people in Afghanistan."[15] Yet, given al-Zawahiri's prominence as the son of Egypt's ambassador to three countries, and his notoriety in connection with the Sadat murder, it is difficult to believe that a fellow Egyptian like Zaki wouldn't have recognized the bearded man behind the glasses as the head of the Egyptian Islamic Jihad. Still, when talking to the *Journal* Dr. Zaki claimed ignorance: "I was asked to escort him while he did fund-raising for the Kuwaiti Red Crescent," he remembers. "Was that a crime?"[16]

Testimony in that 1999 Egyptian terror trial suggested that the tour had been bicoastal, with Ali Mohamed escorting al-Zawahiri to a series of mosques in North Carolina[17] as well as California. A key witness at the 1999 trial where al-Zawahiri was convicted in absentia, testified that most of the $500,000 raised on this trip went to the EIJ. Khalid Dahab, Ali Mohamed's assistant in Silicon Valley, who turned state's evidence at the trial, confessed that part of the half million went to finance the bombing of the Egyptian embassy in Pakistan.[18]

As for Mohamed's wife, Linda, she says she didn't get to meet al-Zawahiri on either trip. In her interview with me, she concluded that her husband had shielded her from such an important visitor because "I'm not Muslim, I'm Christian."[19]

Escorting bin Laden's right-hand man onto U.S. shores was another stunning testament to Ali Mohamed's skill and bravado as an espionage agent for the jihad. It's as though a German spy had managed to smuggle Heinrich Himmler, the head of Hitler's dreaded SS, into the United States at the dawn of World War II for a fund-raising tour of German-American churches.

Imagine if the Bureau had known about Mohamed's sponsorship of the EIJ-al Qaeda leader, who was wanted in Egypt at the time?

The evidence now suggests that they did.

The FBI Has It "Covered"

In 1999, two members of President Clinton's NSC staff, Daniel Benjamin and Steven Simon, met with FBI agents Michael Rolince and Steve Jennings in a White House session aimed at synchronizing agency efforts against the al Qaeda threat.

One of the NSC staffers had discovered intelligence in an old file describing al-Zawahiri's tour of the United States. "I couldn't believe it," he told the two agents. "Did you know about that?"

Rolince and Jennings answered with wary nods.

"Well, if he was *here*, someone was handling his travel and arranging his meetings and someone was giving him money," responded one of the White House aides. "Do you know who these people are? Do you have them *covered*?"

"Yeah, yeah, we know," the agents replied. "Don't worry about it. We got it covered."[20]

Special Agent Rolince would come up again on the timeline of FBI negligence leading up to September 11. In fact, Jack Cloonan, a key player in the NYO's bin Laden unit, told me that Rolince was one of "six people" who might have prevented the 9/11 attacks if they had simply "done their jobs."[21]

As we now know, however, one of the special agents Rolince claimed was "covering" Ali Mohamed was the extraordinarily trusting John Zent.

In my extensive interview with Cloonan, which I recorded with his permission, he asked me to turn the tape off several times as he made disparaging comments about Zent. But all Cloonan would say on the record that was remotely critical was this:

> John believes that Ali is buying rugs over in that part of the world [Africa], and that he runs a diving business, and he thinks he has various other interests. John is interested in Ali buying fake documents in and around San Jose.[22]

When it came to Ali Mohamed, in other words, Special Agent Zent seemed more interested in pursuing petty crimes than terrorism.

Just how well was the FBI "covering" Ali Mohamed by 1995? Clearly not well.

One problem, as discussed, was that FBI agents on the West Coast weren't always talking to the East Coast agents about Mohamed. Further, as Cloonan noted, even *within* the New York office, "A and B"—the JTTF and the intelligence squads—"weren't talking."

Of course, we've also seen that senior Southern District Feds like Andrew McCarthy, and FBI agents like Harlan Bell, were communicating face-to-face with Ali by late 1994. Yet Mohamed was still able to pull off spectacular feats of deception like the "Red Crescent" tour.

Terrorism analyst Steven Emerson says it was the result of Ali's brilliant skill at manipulation. "Ali Mohamed could be alternatively charming or a killer," says Emerson.[23] "He knew how to play off agencies against each other. He knew how to find the bureaucratic crevices in agencies that allowed him to be protected from investigation by offering tidbits of intelligence—just enough to make sure he was protected as an asset so that another agency wouldn't go after him, or another branch of the same agency such as the FBI wouldn't go after him or investigate him. Mohamed was able to exploit that system with murderous efficiency."

The Second Ali Mohammed

Within hours of fleeing Manila early on the morning after the Dona Josefa fire, Ramzi Yousef and his uncle Khalid Shaikh Mohammed were safely tucked away at the Su Casa, a two-story, twenty-room split-level guesthouse

controlled by Osama bin Laden in Islamabad, Pakistan.[24] In an extraordinary bit of irony—or a tongue-in-cheek ploy by Yousef to pay homage
to bin Laden's chief spy—he registered at the Su Casa under the name
"Ali Mohammed."[25]

Days before, Yousef rekindled an acquaintance with Istaique Parker,[26] a
young South African student, and recruited him to help smuggle bombs
hidden in toy cars aboard United and Northwest flights out of Bangkok.[27]

At the time, Yousef's wanted poster was being distributed throughout
the Islamic world as a result of the Rewards for Justice Program, a State
Department initiative that had been denigrated by management at Foggy
Bottom, but pressed by a tenacious Diplomatic Security Service (DSS)
agent named Bradley Smith. Smith, who had survived a terrorist bombing
with his wife years earlier in Turkey, was determined to use the moribund
Rewards program, which carried a $2 million bounty, to bring Yousef to
ground. But he was being hampered both physically and by political forces
inside State.[28]

Shortly after the Trade Center bombing in 1993, Smith was diagnosed
with Lou Gehrig's disease and given a few months to live. Still, he vowed
to stay alive long enough to see Yousef in handcuffs and he did. In fact,
after breaking his leg because the State Department building where he
worked (SA-10) lacked wheelchair access, Smith won a lawsuit and was
granted the right to conduct the Yousef hunt from home, using encrypted
DSS phones and computers.[29]

Smith produced a series of television ads promoting the Rewards program, and printed Yousef's likeness on thousands of matchbooks distributed throughout the Middle East. In early February 1995, Parker learned
of the reward and called the U.S. embassy in Islamabad.[30]

On the morning of February 7, 1995, after Parker met face-to-face
with Yousef at the Su Casa, he left the building, running his fingers
through his hair in a prearranged signal for the Feds. Suddenly, a team of
DSS and DEA agents backed by Pakistani ISI officers stormed Yousef's
room on the third floor of the guesthouse.[31]

Kicking in the door, they confronted the bomb maker lying on his bed.
The Feds found a copy of a July 1994 *Newsweek* nearby, open to the page
that described Yousef as the world's "most wanted" felon. Scattered around

the room were a host of toy cars and baby dolls, which Yousef intended to stuff with nitro-cellulose and turn into bombs.

One of the ISI agents pulled Yousef off the bed, pressing his face against a window and flex-tying his hands behind him. Not noticing the U.S. agents at first, Yousef began speaking to them in Urdu, the national language of Pakistan, assuming this was merely a low-level roust by immigration officials to check his papers.

Then DSS agents Jeff Riner and Bill Miller, an ex-Marine from Georgia, entered the room. Riner flashed a Polaroid snapshot to compare with Yousef's wanted poster. Startled, the bomb maker turned to Miller, who leaned in and drawled, "What's up, Ramzi?" Just then Yousef began to tremble, his eyes went wide, and his knees buckled beneath him. After he'd spent almost twenty-four months as a fugitive, the Americans finally had him.

Losing the "Mastermind" Part One

The arrest had almost nothing to do with the FBI. During the capture, Ralph Horton, the Bureau's LEGAT from Bangkok, reportedly waited outside the guesthouse. Bradley Garrett, an agent from the D.C. field office who had arrived in Islamabad that morning on a completely different case, got to the Su Casa late and missed the takedown.[32]

Although he later claimed on *60 Minutes II* that he had been a part of the Yousef seizure,[33] Garrett apparently failed to canvass the Su Casa. If he had, he might have encountered Yousef's uncle, Khalid Shaikh Mohammed, who was staying in a first-floor room. Following the arrest, KSM actually found the time to give an interview to a stringer for *Time* magazine and the *Los Angeles Times*, in which he offered specific details on the Yousef arrest.

"It was like a hurricane. A big panic," the eyewitness said. "They were dragging him downstairs. He was blindfolded, barefoot, and had his hands and legs bound." According to KSM, Yousef was shouting, "I am innocent. Why are you taking me? Show me your arrest warrant!"[34] KSM even gave his own name, "Khalid Shaikh," identifying himself as a Karachi businessman. By the time Garrett showed up at the guesthouse, Yousef's uncle had fled.

It wouldn't be the last time the FBI let the man they later called the "mastermind" of 9/11 slip through their fingers.[35] Yet the real brains behind the planes-as-missiles operation was his nephew Ramzi, the thin, black-haired bomb maker with the cloudy grey eyes.

Within an hour after his capture, Yousef was in an ISI military station where he was fingerprinted and read his rights. When asked to identify himself, Yousef said, "Ali Baloch," using the word that describes residents of his home province of Baluchistan. When the agents pressed him on his aliases, he admitted, "I have many."[36]

He was dressed at the time in a mustard-colored ISI prisoner's jumpsuit, but when he learned he would be brought back to lower Manhattan, Yousef asked for a suit coat, tie, dress shirt, slacks, and shoes. It had taken Col. Mendoza and the PNP sixty-seven days to unwrap his best friend, Murad, but as he sat across from FBI agents Garrett and Horton and Bill Miller of the DSS, Yousef himself seemed anxious to open up, almost proud of his first attack on the Trade Center.

"I masterminded the explosion," he confirmed.

"The Great One" Confesses

When the Boeing 707 arrived to take him away, Secret Service Agent Brian Parr and FBI agent Chuck Stern were accompanied by the Bureau's elite Hostage Rescue Team, which is routinely used for the extradition of terror suspects from one country to another—a practice known by the now-familiar term "rendition." Once used selectively, for suspects moved to the United States to stand trial with full due process rights, the practice became a favorite tactic of the Bush administration after 9/11. A study by the New York Bar Association estimated that more than 150 so-called "enemy combatants" have been transported this way since 2001—and that many, if not most, were transported to countries that condone torture as an interrogation technique.[37]

But at that time, in February 1995, the Justice Department was still quite scrupulous about due process issues, so much so that after Yousef was led onto the plane, agents Parr and Stern read him his Miranda warnings a *second* time. He was given a medical examination and made to change into an orange Bureau of Prisons-style jumpsuit. Then a makeshift "room" was created in the middle of the plane by hanging a series of blankets around seats.

Once airborne, Yousef signed a rights waiver and began to open up to the agents. He demanded that they not take any notes, in the mistaken belief that they wouldn't be able to use what he said against him in court. But what he didn't realize was that the entire conversation was being broadcast back via satellite to SIOC, the FBI's Strategic Information and Operations Center at Bureau headquarters in Washington.[38]

In the hours that followed, the man one jihadi referred to as "the Great One," began to talk. Though he never implicated the Saudi billionaire by name, Yousef gave the FBI a virtual road map connecting bin Laden and al Qaeda to his first attack on the Twin Towers.

First, Yousef admitted that when he flew into JFK on September 1, 1992, he was carrying an ID card from *Al Bunyan*, a newspaper and Arizona cultural center both controlled by bin Laden.[39] He mentioned that Mahmud Abouhalima, "the Red," was with him in the Pamrapo Avenue bomb factory as he built the World Trade Center bomb—confirming by implication that the Feds could have found him if they'd tracked Abouhalima as Emad Salem had suggested.

Another key piece of intelligence was Yousef's admission that he had learned about Mohammed Jamal Khalifa, bin Laden's brother-in-law, from Wali Khan. Khalifa was still in U.S. custody at the time and here was Yousef, the suspected World Trade Center bomber acknowledging a connection to him. Despite this admission, in the months ahead, Deputy Attorney General Jamie Gorelick would continue to support MJK's extradition to Jordan.

Stern's FBI 302 on the interrogation read, in part, as follows:

> BASIT (YOUSEF) would not elaborate on exactly how the WTC bombing was financed, except to say that he had received money from family and friends. . . . When questioned regarding a business card in the name of MOHAMMED KHALIFA, found in BASIT'S apartment in the Philippines[,] BASIT stated that he did not

personally know KHALIFA, but that KHALIFA's business card had been given to him by WALI SHAH, as a contact in the event BASIT needed aid. BASIT also acknowledged that he was familiar with the name OSAMA BIN LADEN, and knew him to be a relative of KHALIFA's but would not further elaborate.

There it was, in an FBI memo: proof that Khalifa was considered so important to Wali Khan, an intimate of bin Laden, that if Yousef should get into trouble, MJK was the man to call.

It was nighttime when the 707 landed at Stewart Airport in Orange County, New York, a location north of the city chosen by the Feds to avoid the media. Yousef was transferred to a Sikorsky helicopter for a trip to the Metropolitan Correctional Center in lower Manhattan. Heavily shackled and cuffed to a belly belt with leg irons, Yousef's head was covered by a hood as the chopper flew south along the Hudson.

Then, as the Sikorsky approached the Twin Towers, gleaming in the exceptionally clear night, the hood was removed. Though there are three different versions of the story,[40] all parties agree that an agent nodded toward the World Trade Center and said, "See. You didn't get them after all." At that point, by one account, Yousef looked at the Towers he'd failed to topple in 1993, turned back to the agents, and snapped, "Not yet."[41]

20

THE COVER-UP
BEGINS

On the day of Yousef's capture, a week into the Day of Terror trial
back in New York, Assistant U.S. Attorney Andrew McCarthy introduced the photographs that the FBI's Special Operations Group had
taken at the Calverton range in July 1989.[1] Among those identified in the
surveillance shots were El Sayyid Nosair (the Kahane killer), Mohammed
Salameh, and Mahmud Abouhalima, both convicted in 1994 of helping
Yousef build the World Trade Center bomb. But there was no mention by
the government of the former army sergeant who had commuted up from
Fort Bragg to train them.

Still, with defense attorney Roger Stavis's opening statement, Mohamed's name had surfaced for the first time in a major publication. On
February 3, Paul Quinn-Judge and Charles M. Sennot ran their story in
the *Boston Globe* quoting "government sources" who claimed that Ali had
CIA help getting into the United States. "His presence in the country is
the result of an action initiated by Langley, said a senior official referring
to the CIA by its location in suburban, Langley, Virginia."[2]

"This *Globe* story began to focus attention on Ali Mohamed," says terrorism analyst Paul Thompson. "Until then he was virtually unknown
outside of al Qaeda or the U.S. intelligence community."

But if Ali was feeling any heat, he didn't show it. At this point, he was back on the West Coast, having little trouble ducking Stavis's subpoena. After meeting with McCarthy and Special Agent Harlan Bell in December, Mohamed may have felt as if he had an almost unofficial immunity from the Feds. So he decided to ratchet up his espionage efforts for the jihad.

In January 1995, Mohamed had applied for what was later described in an FBI affidavit as "a security clearance to work . . . at a classified area within a facility maintained by a . . . company that did business on behalf of the Department of Defense."[3] As part of a background check, the audacious Ali had to explain why his passport showed so much travel to and from the Middle East and Africa. In the first of three statements to investigators for the Defense Investigative Service (DIS), he said that he was in the import/export business, purchasing vehicles in Saudi Arabia and Kuwait for sale in Tanzania and Kenya, and that during his trips to Africa he bought "leather items" for resale in the Gulf states.

Mohamed had failed to mention the import/export cover on his job application for the security position, so he explained the lapse to DIS investigators by claiming he'd been advised that "recent overseas employment would disqualify him" for the job.[4] That was his way of giving the Feds what Steve Emerson would call "tidbits" of truthful information, to impress them with his apparent candor. But the extent of his travel— much of it to countries that sponsored terrorism—was difficult to get around.

At a second meeting with the DIS vetters, Mohamed admitted to making fifteen trips to Kenya, five to Ethiopia, and ten to Tanzania and Uganda, along with single visits to Niger, Djibouti, Morocco, Kuwait, and the United Arab Emirates. But he carefully omitted mention of his visits to Sudan or Somalia, even though he'd told the Feds about his work in Khartoum two years earlier.[5]

What made Mohamed think he could get away with withholding information he had already given to the FBI? As Emerson points out, "the bureaucratic crevices inside the FBI and certainly between the FBI, the CIA, and the Defense Department were enormous. [Mohamed] could drive truck bombs through them and play off one against the other."[6]

In his next statement to the DOD investigators, however, Mohamed had to resort to a boldfaced lie: "I have never had any contact with [or] been asked to work for anyone representing a non-U.S. intelligence/security service or group, movement or association that advocates or practices violence against the U.S. government, its citizens, or its allies."[7]

He went even further in a third statement made in Santa Clara: "I have never been approached by organizations that could be called terrorist."[8] But here Ali added a qualifier that might have allowed him to pass a polygraph if anyone in the federal government had thought to give him one: "I would prefer to call these organizations 'opposition groups,'" he said, "because they were opposing terrorist governments."

One can only wonder if this was the same logic used by Mohammed Jamal Khalifa when he swore under oath in the Motley-Rice 9/11 case that he had "never supported any person or organization that [he had] known to participate in terrorist activities."[9]

Working as a Guard at a Northrop-Grumman Facility

One would think that Mohamed's final attempt at sleight-of-hand would have pole axed his chances for a security clearance. But according to retired Special Agent Cloonan, Mohamed was able to get himself a job as a guard with Burns Security,[10] working at a facility run by Northrop-Grumman in Sunnyvale, California.[11]

"They were building some components for subs," says Cloonan. "It was a cleared facility. A base that made the triggers for the [Trident] missile. Ali had to get a security clearance because he worked for Burns, and since Burns had the contract at this facility, which is a defense contractor, that's why the DIS interviewed him."

Mohamed "never got the clearance," says Cloonan, but he nonetheless ended up working for Burns inside the gates at the facility. After Mohamed's arrest in 1998, when Cloonan interviewed personnel from Northrop-Grumman to get the full story, he says "their reaction was 'Okay. But he never got access to sensitive information.' However, Ali told Cloonan that "he'd walk around and he had access to a computer. I think it was password-sensitive so the sensitive, classified information he did not have access to. But he was there, nonetheless."[12]

"It's amazing what Ali Mohamed was able to get away with at Fort Bragg even without a security clearance," says Lt. Colonel Anthony Shaffer, who investigated al Qaeda beginning in late 1999 as a DIA liaison to Operation Able Danger.[13] "The intelligence he accessed as a supply sergeant is proof that he didn't need the keys to the front office to do harm to U.S. interests. The very fact that he was at the Special Warfare School meant that he would have access to information on all units at Bragg, no matter how classified it was."[14]

The Missing Witness Part One

Meanwhile, back in New York, El Sayyid Nosair's attorney Roger Stavis was doing his best to keep Mohamed's presence alive in the Day of Terror case. On September 1, 1995,[15] an exasperated Stavis requested a "missing witness instruction [to the jury] with regard to Ali Mohamed."[16] He reminded Judge Michael B. Mukasey that "Mohamed was the person who came from Fort Bragg, North Carolina, who was assigned to the United States Army Special Forces." At that point the judge quipped, "Yes, we saw him on that splendid videotape." But Stavis countered, "When we attempted to find Ali Mohamed, we found a friend at Fort Bragg who knew his wife was in California. His wife hadn't seen him for over a year. We could not bring him in."

Yet Mohamed was clearly in the country during much of the eight-month trial. According to an affidavit filed by the FBI after his 1998 arrest, Mohamed had two meetings with DIS investigators in August 1995 and one on November 8. In each instance, he was home in Santa Clara. In a 2001 profile of Mohamed for the *San Jose Mercury News,* reporters Sean Webby and Rodney Foo noted that he attended the Masjid an-Noor in Santa Clara, and even "occasionally played soccer with other members."[17] Friends remember him scouring local video stores for Arabic-language comedies, "interpreting them into English for others as the films unreeled."

With the heat on in Africa following his December 1994 meeting with McCarthy and Bell, Mohamed seemed to stay pretty close to home during the Day of Terror trial.

"A Sweeping Victory"

By October 1, though, the issue of Mohamed's absence in that trial was rendered moot. Characterized by the *New York Times* as "the biggest terrorism trial in U.S. history," it ended with guilty verdicts for Sheikh Rahman and the nine remaining codefendants. AUSAs McCarthy, Fitzgerald, and Robert Khuzami even succeeded in convicting El Sayyid Nosair for the murder of Meier Kahane.[18] Hailed as a "sweeping victory" for the Feds, the verdict was also a vindication for Emad Salem and the FBI street agent who had first recruited him, Nancy Floyd.

At that point, almost no one outside the confines of 26 Federal Plaza or the SDNY knew the real truth: that Salem had first infiltrated the Sheikh's cell in the fall of 1991, and that ASAC Carson Dunbar had caused his withdrawal, leading Rahman to bring in a professional bomber named Ramzi Yousef.

Few people outside the government knew that in October 1992 Salem had admonished the FBI to "follow" Salameh and Abouhalima, or that his advice had been ignored by the FBI.

Only a handful of Feds in the two "offices of origin" knew that Salem, who was now going to get $1.5 million and a new life in the Witness Protection Program, could have brought Ali Mohamed's cell down in the fall of 1992, when George Herbert Walker Bush was in the White House, and he could have done it for $500 a week.

"Salem was of immense value," says Steven Emerson.[19] "Had higher-ups in the FBI not disqualified him back in '92, he would have retained his connections with those who carried out the February '93 bombing. It might have been able to avert it."

In fact, when defense lawyers got word that the mistrustful Salem had begun recording his own "bootleg tapes" during the Day of Terror investigation—and arranged for portions of the tapes to be played at trial— Nancy Floyd, the only agent he trusted, could be heard describing her bosses as "gutless."[20]

In the days after the stunning verdict, one might have thought that Floyd would be rewarded for recruiting arguably the most important informant to date in the "war on terror." But instead Floyd became the object of an internal affairs investigation opened by the Bureau's Office of

Professional Responsibility (OPR). Embarrassed by her candor as re-vealed on the tapes, someone in the FBI's NYO had leaked a fallacious story to the *New York Post*[21] suggesting that she was having an affair with Salem. The *Post* ran the story under the headline "Temptress and the Spy," and Floyd had a cloud over her head for years, unable to advance in the Bureau or transfer to her Office of Preference (OP), an important perk for brick agents.[22]

The Day of Terror trial represented the second major victory against the Yousef-Rahman cell for the prosecutors of the SDNY and the agents of the JTTF. However, evidence uncovered in this investigation suggests that 1995 was the pivotal year when lawyers and special agents in the two "of-fices of origin" began intentionally disconnecting the dots—obscuring the connections that would have given other agencies a much clearer picture of Osama bin Laden's capacity to wreak havoc on America. The cover-up began, I believe, in March with Gorelick's wall memo. Although Andrew McCarthy would openly attack Gorelick years later for that pronounce-ment, I believe he perpetuated the cover up through the Day of Terror trial in a different way, by thwarting defense attorney Roger Stavis's attempts to document Ali Mohamed's role as a trainer of the "jihad army." While act-ing independently, McCarthy and Gorelick had the same ultimate motive: to save the Justice Department embarrassment if word got out that the FBI had failed to stop the first World Trade Center attack, or that senior officials at Justice like Gorelick had allowed bin Laden's brother-in-law Khalifa to slip out of federal custody. And by the spring of 1995, there was yet another scandal festering in the New York Office of the FBI that threatened to set back the FBI's war on organized crime for years.

The G-Man and the Hit Man

The scandal involved allegations brought by three special agents that their supervisor may have been in a corrupt relationship with a Mafia killer. Ironically, this alleged "unholy alliance" between the G-man and the hit man not only threatened to derail up to seventy-five organized crime cases in the Eastern District (EDNY), it also led to the burial of a treasure trove of al Qaeda-related evidence in 1996, at a time when I-49, the bin Laden squad in the New York Office, was just beginning to get a handle on the al Qaeda threat.

It's a tangled story, which I told first in *Cover Up* in 2004, but the long-suppressed scandal erupted again in a series of murder indictments in the spring of 2006. This new prosecution by the Brooklyn district attorney (detailed in Chapter 40) holds open the prospect that the full truth behind the FBI/DOJ negligence on the road to 9/11 may soon emerge. But to understand the full story, we have to dial back more than four decades to the summer of 1964.

During that long, hot summer, the Justice Department faced a crisis in the state of Mississippi. Three civil rights workers, Andrew Goodman, Michael Schwerner, and James Chaney had disappeared. Their station wagon had been found burned and abandoned after they were released from custody by a local sheriff's deputy who was tied to the Ku Klux Klan.[23] The young men were presumed dead, and Attorney General Robert Kennedy had ordered FBI Director J. Edgar Hoover to break the case at all costs. But after sending dozens of special agents to Neshoba County, the case—labeled MISSBURN by the Bureau—had hit a dead end.

In the story, as retold in the 1988 film *Mississippi Burning,* the FBI dispatched an African American agent down to discover the whereabouts of the victims. But in fact Hoover had sent out an order through FBI ranks for a "special," and Gregory Scarpa, then a young killer with the Colombo crime family in Brooklyn, was sent south to break the case.[24] As W.O. "Chet" Dillard, who served as D.A. after the incident, told me in an interview, "Old J. Edgar figured that if he was gonna break that thing—and he was hurtin' to break it—he was gonna have to go to some extreme measures, and he did."[25]

Gregory Scarpa was a psychopathic killer who would become known years later as "the Killing Machine" and "the Grim Reaper." When he got down to Mississippi, he kidnapped a local mayor and threatened to emasculate him if he didn't give up the location of the three men. Almost immediately the politician, more terrified of the mobster than the Klan, disclosed that Goodman, Schwerner, and Chaney had been buried beneath fifteen feet of red clay under an earthen dam.

As one former lawyer later described him, Greg Sr. was the type who could take a fellow wiseguy to lunch, joke with him over a plate of ziti, and shoot him between the eyes before the check was paid.[26]

By the mid-1970s, Scarpa had risen in the Colombo ranks via bookmaking, loan sharking, and credit card fraud. But his most lethal skill set included an ice-blooded willingness to commit murder. Comparing himself to the fictional James Bond, with his "license to kill," Scarpa demonstrated a macabre side by forwarding the Satanic digits 6-6-6 to the beepers of fellow wiseguys after he'd made a kill. But Greg, who later had a son with the same name, also led a double life. In mob parlance, he was a "rat." Meeting almost weekly with an FBI agent named Anthony Villano, he would give up mob secrets in return for protection. It was the same sort of "deal with the devil" that FBI agents later made with Ali Mohamed, hoping that his value as an informant would outweigh his risk to national security.

But Scarpa Sr. went beyond violence to outright acts of cruelty. He once had a man killed in front of his wife while they were stringing Christmas lights, and had the grave dug for another victim before the date of his execution. Since FBI rules forbid an informant from engaging in violent behavior, Villano was forced to close out Scarpa as a snitch in 1975.

Then, five years later, Roy Lindley DeVecchio, an ambitious young special agent in the FBI's New York Office, spotted Scarpa's name in the files and put him back to work as a source.[27]

Feeding Information to the "Girlfriend"

Scarpa's real ascendancy in the Colombo ranks came after his reengagement with the Feds, as he seemed to capitalize on inside information unavailable to his rivals. DeVecchio, who was known to Scarpa Sr. variously as "Del," "Mr. Dello," and "the girlfriend," also prospered, becoming a supervisory special agent in the NYO and taking control of a joint FBI-NYPD organized crime task force. Scarpa Sr. was ultimately admitted to the coveted ranks of a "top echelon" (T.E.) informant, and the FBI rules requiring at least two agents to work a source were bent, allowing DeVecchio to interact privately with the killer. The killer's previous control agent, Villano, had once likened his relationship with Scarpa to "getting married," and soon DeVecchio seemed to get just as close to the Colombo hit man.

In the early 1990s, two decades after patriarch Joe Colombo was gunned down in public, a war of succession developed between two rival factions of the family: those loyal to "Allie Boy" Persico on one side, and those loyal to acting boss Vic Orena on the other. Always an independent actor, however, Scarpa Sr. killed wiseguys on both sides in his own bid to gain control of the family. This synced perfectly with DeVecchio's suspected goal: If Scarpa Sr. became the family's boss, he would have a seat on the national commission of La Cosa Nostra, giving the Bureau unprecedented access to the upper reaches of organized crime.

"The problem was," says defense attorney Alan Futerfas, "the relationship was deeply corrupt."[28] The evidence, developed in a series of federal trials and the recent investigation by the Brooklyn district attorney, now suggests that DeVecchio actually *helped* the killer eliminate his competition. Among his victims was Nicholas "Nicky Black" Grancio.[29] Larry Mazza, Scarpa Sr.'s protégé, later told investigators that "the girlfriend" had ordered FBI agents and NYPD cops away from a surveillance site so that Scarpa could blow the head off Grancio, one of his chief rivals.[30]

Gregory Scarpa Jr., who kept the books for his father, later testified that DeVecchio was paid more than one hundred thousand dollars over the years in return for this inside help, rewarded with vacations to places like Aspen, Colorado, and treated to call girls in a Staten Island motel.[31] DeVecchio denied the charges vehemently, but he refused to take a polygraph, invoked the Fifth Amendment, and answered "I don't recall" more than forty times even after a grant of immunity, something almost unheard in federal criminal practice.

The FBI Opens a Devecchio OPR

By early 1994, DeVecchio's number two, Special Agent Chris Favo,[32] and two other agents in the Colombo task force, Jeffrey Tomlinson and

Howard Leadbetter II, brought what amounted to charges against De-Vecchio, and the Bureau opened an OPR internal affairs investigation. The immediate problem for the FBI was that the alleged "unholy alliance" between the G-man and the hit man threatened to derail those seventy-five cases brought by federal prosecutors in the EDNY stemming from the Colombo war. Most of those cases would depend on the testimony of DeVecchio, as an expert witness, and Scarpa Sr., who would take the stand for the government under an exception to the hearsay rule for "coconspirator testimony."

But after Futerfas and his partner, Ellen Resnick, caught wind of the alleged corruption between the elder Scarpa and his control agent, they argued that if Greg was actually an FBI *agent provocateur,* then the coconspirator exception should fall. Two federal judges agreed and fourteen Colombo defendants, including underboss William "Wild Bill" Cutolo, were acquitted.[33]

On May 8, 1995, Assistant U.S. Attorney Ellen M. Corcella, the EDNY prosecutor coordinating the Colombo war prosecutions, was forced to send a letter to Futerfas, Resnick, and six other defense attorneys revealing some of "the items that Special Agent R. Lindley DeVecchio may have disclosed to Gregory Scarpa Sr."

The stunning series of admissions was based on information gathered in the Bureau's own internal OPR investigation of DeVecchio. The letter appears on pages 215–216.

"You don't need a law degree to appreciate how this kind of information could have been fatal to some of those members in the Colombo crime family that Scarpa Sr. wanted to eliminate," says defense counsel Flora Edwards. "Those disclosures went far beyond anything a senior FBI supervisory special agent needed to tell his snitch. He's also telling the 'Grim Reaper' where his rivals are so he can rub them out. There is no question that DeVecchio had crossed the line and the Feds had enough to indict *him* as well."[34]

After Futerfas, Resnick, and other lawyers succeeded in getting the first fourteen cases dismissed, "the floodgates were about to open," says Resnick.[35] Sixty more Colombo war cases hung in the balance, and Jack B. Weinstein, one of the senior judges in the Eastern District, predicted that if the trend continued, the remaining cases would "unravel."[36]

U.S Department of Justice

United States Attorney
Eastern District of New York

VC:GAS:EMC
F.#9305994
Devecchi.1t

United States Attorney's Office
225 Cadman Plaza East
Brooklyn, New York 11201

May 2, 1995

Hand
BY ~~TELEFAX ONLY~~

Gerald L. Shargel, Esq.
1585 Broadway, 19th Floor
New York, New York 10036

James M. LaRossa, Esq.
LaRossa, Mitchell & Ross
41 Madison Avenue, 34th Floor
New York, New York 10010

Alan S. Futerfas, Esq.
260 Madison Avenue, 22nd Floor
New York, New York 10016

Steve Zissou, Esq.
42-40 Bell Boulevard
Suite 302
Bayside, New York 11361

James Neville, Esq.
8 West 40th Street,
9th Floor
New York, New York 10018

Emanuel A. Moore, Esq.
89-17 190th Street
Hollis, New York 11423

Bettina Schein, Esq.
41 Madison Avenue,
34th Floor
New York, New York 10010

> Re: United States v. Victor M. Orena, et al.
> Criminal Docket No. 93-1366 (ERK)

Dear Ms. Schein and Messrs. Shargel, LaRossa, Futerfas, Zissou,
Neville and Moore:

In accordance with the ruling of Judge Korman, in lieu
of disclosing an affidavit that had been presented to Judge
Korman ex parte, please be advised that the following constitutes
our knowledge of the items that Special Agent R. Lindley
DeVecchio may have disclosed to Gregory Scarpa, Sr. and the
approximate time of the disclosure:

> a. the planned 1987 arrest by DEA of Gregory
> Scarpa, Jr., and his crew, and that law enforcement
> believed that Cosmo Catanzano was a "weak link," who
> might cooperate with authorities if arrested;

In one of the great ironies in a story with more than its share, Judge
Weinstein's name had appeared on that hit list of prominent Jewish figures
found in the home of El Sayyid Nosair the night after the Kahane murder.[37] But there is an even more compelling connection between this tangled web involving al Qaeda and the mob.

2

b.   on or about February 27, 1992, that Carmine
Imbriale was cooperating with law enforcement;

c.   during the Colombo Family war, information
on at least one member of the Orena faction who had a
hit team that was looking for members of the Persico
faction;

d.   following the arrest of Joseph Ambrosino,
that there were arrest warrants outstanding for
Lawrence Mazza and James DelMasto (two of Scarpa's
closest associates), but that if they stayed away from
their normal "hangouts" they could avoid being
arrested;

e.   in or around January 1992, that it was
believed that Orena was staying at his girlfriend's
house, the location of which (as then known by some in
law enforcement)[1] was also conveyed;

f.   in or around January 1992, the address of the
house in which Salvatore Miciotta was residing; and

g.   in early 1992, subscriber information for
telephone numbers of two of Scarpa's loanshark
customers;

h.   in the mid to late 1980s, that Scarpa's
social club was subject to court-ordered electronic
surveillance and that he would soon be arrested on
charges involving dealing with fraudulent credit cards.

Very truly yours,

ZACHARY W. CARTER
UNITED STATES ATTORNEY

By: *Ellen M. Corcella*
Ellen M. Corcella
Assistant U.S. Attorney

cc: Clerk of Court (ERK)

---

[1]   In January 1992, certain FBI agents had incorrect information on the location of the house of Orena's girlfriend.

Less than a year after Corcella sent that letter to defense lawyers, Greg
Scarpa Jr., the son of the Colombo killer, was in a jail cell on the ninth
floor (south) tier of the Metropolitan Correctional Center, the federal jail
in lower Manhattan. In one cell adjacent to him was none other than
Ramzi Yousef, who had been rendered back to the United States in early
February 1995. In the cell on Scarpa's other side was Abdul Hakim

Murad, Yousef's oldest friend, who had trained in four U.S. flight schools and later boasted to Col. Rodolfo Mendoza that he would "fly the plane in for Allah" when Yousef's planes-as-missiles plot commenced.

Now, in a twist of the story beyond anything a fiction writer could conjure, Greg Scarpa Jr. would extract from Ramzi Yousef a bonanza of al Qaeda-related evidence—information that should have led to the capture of Yousef's uncle, Khalid Shaikh Mohammed, who was already at work developing the 9/11 plot. The intel Scarpa provided could also have connected the Feds to an active al Qaeda cell operating then in New York City and provided the Bureau with evidence connecting Yousef and al Qaeda to one of the great airline crash mysteries of all time.

All they had to do was connect the dots.

21

THE BIN LADEN SQUAD

I n early 1996, almost three years after the World Trade Center bombing, the Clinton administration began to focus its response to the
"jihad army" whose members had been convicted the previous October. In
the middle of the Day of Terror trial, the president had signed Presidential
Decision Directive 39, a secret order designed to "deter, defeat, and respond vigorously to all terrorist attacks."[1] The PDD tasked the CIA to
take "an aggressive program of foreign intelligence collection, analysis,
counterintelligence, and covert action"—authorizing the "return of suspects by force, without the cooperation of host government(s)" if necessary. The FBI was charged as lead U.S. agency to reduce the nation's
security vulnerabilities.

Though the unclassified version of the PDD is heavily redacted, it's
clear that Osama bin Laden soon became a principal target.

Before January was over, the CIA had created "Alec Station," the first
"virtual" office that focused on a specific individual (as opposed to a
country).[2] Formally known as "the bin Laden issue station," it was initially staffed by sixteen analysts and located in an office park a few miles
from the headquarters at Langley.[3] It was run by Michael Scheuer, by
then a fourteen-year veteran of the Agency. Scheuer named the station

"Alec" after his son. The FBI representative from the NYO at the station was Dan Coleman, who soon developed such an expertise on al Qaeda he was nicknamed "the professor."[4] In order to work the station, Coleman had to submit to a polygraph and get a series of new clearances that would allow him to gain access to the CIA's Hercules database system.[5]

At the same time, the two bin Laden "offices of origin" in New York, the SDNY and the FBI's NYO, dedicated an existing unit, Squad I-49, to building a case against the Saudi billionaire. Coleman became a key component, along with Special Agent Jack Cloonan. Patrick Fitzgerald, the AUSA who was the "second seat" to Andrew McCarthy in the Day of Terror trial, had since become chief of the Organized Crime-Terrorism Unit in the SDNY. He was effectively tasked to direct the squad as lead prosecutor.

It would be a career-making position for Fitzgerald, the Harvard-educated son of Irish immigrants. In years to come, he would emerge as the DOJ's leading bin Laden authority, described in a February 2006 *Vanity Fair* profile as a man with "scary smart intelligence," an "uncanny memory," and "a mainframe computer brain."[6] As lead prosecutor in *United States v. bin Laden,* the African embassy bombing case in 2001, Fitzgerald would be rewarded for his conviction of the Saudi billionaire *in absentia* with an appointment as U.S. attorney for the Northern District of Illinois—becoming the top Fed in Chicago, a city infamous for political corruption. With a staff of 161 AUSAs, Fitzgerald, whose close friends called him "Fitzie," would oversee Operation Safe Road, a public corruption case that would result in the conviction of seventy-three defendants, including thirty public employees and officials.

If that wasn't enough to keep him busy, by December 2003 Fitzgerald would be tapped by George W. Bush's Justice Department as special prosecutor in the Valerie Plame CIA leak investigation.[7] It would be his job, in essence, to determine whether presidential aide Karl Rove, one of the most powerful men in Washington, had leaked the name of former CIA covert operative Valerie Plame in an effort to punish her husband for writing an op-ed page piece critical of the Bush White House for using false intelligence to justify the invasion of Iraq.

Tracking Fitzgerald's Awareness of al Qaeda

In any serious investigation of how the FBI and DOJ failed to detect Ali Mohamed as an al Qaeda spy before the embassy bombings he helped to execute, an examination of Fitzgerald's awareness of bin Laden's trajectory is crucial.

Both Coleman and Fitzgerald declined to be interviewed for this book, but Fitzgerald granted an extensive interview in 2005 for the National Geographic Channel's four-hour documentary *Inside 9/11*. I obtained a copy of the interview transcript in which Fitzgerald discussed his first awakening to al Qaeda and its terror chief.

"I didn't know the word al Qaeda when we were prosecuting people in '93, '94, and '95," Fitzgerald said. "And then this elusive figure came to the attention of the American government called Osama bin Laden. And I remember early in 1996 we were all trying to figure out, Was Osama bin Laden as bad as people were saying in the national security community? Because he seemed to be coming up everywhere. He was like Elvis. Every time you read about a terrorist group in a different country carrying out violent action, you heard the name Osama bin Laden and you wondered whether it was just sort of a fictional person. Was he a wealthy benefactor of people who were fighting oppression in different countries, [or] did bin Laden know precisely what these people were doing?"

Desperate to answer those questions, Fitzgerald's bin Laden squad began operating on "two parallel tracks," according to Cloonan. "One [track] was intelligence driven to support the activity that Alec Station was doing . . . which would include disruptions, and in some instances, renditions and working with a number of services overseas. The other [track] was on the criminal side."[8]

That structure indicates that little more than ten months after the issuance of Jamie Gorelick's "wall memo," Fitzgerald and company were apparently disregarding her mandate that criminal investigation should be segregated from intelligence threat prevention. Squad I-49 in the FBI's NYO was actively working both jobs. That reality becomes important as we assess Fitzgerald's performance. Why? Because years later, when investigators began trying to suss out what went wrong, Fitzgerald would pointedly blame "the wall" for the apparent inability of the SDNY and the FBI to prevent the 9/11 attacks.[9]

Despite Fitzgerald's 2005 assertion that he "didn't know the word al Qaeda" in 1995, Special Agent John Zent had conducted the interview with Ali Mohamed in 1993, two years *before* that, in which the spy confessed that "Bin Laden ran an organization called al Qaeda and was building an army which may be used to overthrow the Saudi Government." How do we know that? It was documented in a sworn 1998 affidavit written by Special Agent Dan Coleman, one of Fitzgerald's key operatives.[10]

Even Jack Cloonan admitted to me that "Ali Mohamed was a well-known entity by 1996 because of his involvement with some of the people in the first Trade Center case. He was an unindicted coconspirator."[11]

"The Osama bin Laden case opened up in 1996," he says, "And, out of that case, there were a number of subfiles that were created." One of them was on Ali Mohamed. "This was a classified case, and then the focus of the case changed because [Attorney General] Janet Reno and the U.S. attorney at the time, Mary Jo White, said that the Bureau and the Southern District—on the advice of Justice—were going to build a prosecutable case against bin Laden." Cloonan says that he first became aware of Ali Mohamed *himself* when he began working on the squad in January.

The Case Against bin Laden

One would think that the quickest way for Fitzgerald, Cloonan, and Coleman to get up to speed on bin Laden would have been to summon their informant Ali Mohamed to another face-to-face meeting, but as we'll see, Mohamed had his hands full at that time in Khartoum. The Clinton White House was now putting extreme pressure on the Sudanese government, led by Sheikh Hassan al Turabi, to extradite the al Qaeda chief.

In February, Sudan's defense minister, General Elfatih Erwa, secretly visited the United States to propose a trade: Osama bin Laden's extradition to Saudi Arabia to stand trial in return for an easing of U.S. economic sanctions against Khartoum.[12]

Since bin Laden is the scion of one of the most powerful families in the country, the House of Saud was unwilling to have its potential ties to al Qaeda's leader exposed—especially bin Laden's early relationship with the corrupt Bank of Credit and Commercial International (BCCI), which had links to many members of the Saudi royal family.[13] The Egyptian government of Hosni Mubarak balked as well. The prospect of a trial in Cairo, which might involve Egyptians al-Zawahiri and Atef as coconspirators, was not in the cards—at least not that early.[14] So the Sudanese turned to the United States.

Once again, the Justice Department dropped the ball. In another profound misstep that paved the way for the 9/11 attacks, the White House contacted the FBI's JTTF and the SDNY to see if they had enough evidence on bin Laden to convict him. But they said "no."

The moment was lost.[15]

Clinton Says bin Laden Nonindictable in 1996

In a speech delivered two months after 9/11, President Clinton reiterated that same Justice Department opinion on bin Laden. "We couldn't indict him then because he hadn't killed anybody in America," the former president said. "He hadn't done anything to us."[16]

In fact, he had. Rabbi Meier Kahane was the first victim, and there were six more on February 26, 1993, when Yousef's bomb went off below the North Tower of the World Trade Center. Bin Laden's links to those deaths could have been proven easily by examining his direct ties to El Sayyid Nosair and Sheikh Omar Abdel Rahman. Bin Laden had fronted twenty thousand dollars for El Sayyid's defense[17] and had financed the blind Sheikh's living expenses.[18] Further, prior to his extradition in 1995, the address book of Mohammed Jamal Khalifa had numbers tying bin Laden to Wali Khan and Ramzi Yousef, who were now sitting a few cells apart on the 9 South tier of the MCC in lower Manhattan.

The Philippines National Police had furnished the SDNY Feds with documentary evidence linking bin Laden to Yousef's Manila cell via Khalifa.

Even after Jamie Gorelick's support for his extradition, the Justice Department could have mounted a potent conspiracy case with the connective tissue provided by the indictment of the one man who was tied to all seven murders (Kahane and the WTC six), the FBI informant whom Jack Cloonan was now supposed to make book on: Ali Abdel Saoud Mohamed.

Andrew McCarthy, Fitzgerald's partner, had enough on Ali Mohamed to name him as an unindicted coconspirator in the Day of Terror case. Mohamed was so close to bin Laden that he'd trained his personal bodyguard in Khartoum. But McCarthy and Fitzgerald had kept him out of the Day of Terror trial.

Now as Fitzgerald, Cloonan, and Coleman sought to build a criminal case against bin Laden, no asset would have been more valuable to them than the former Egyptian army officer who had become a U.S. citizen in 1989. But by January 1996 Ali was busy. Bin Laden had summoned him back to Khartoum and he was tasked again with moving the al Qaeda prince and his entourage.[19]

Ali Maintains bin Laden's Trust

There's been some speculation among reporters covering Mohamed's story that he may have fallen out of favor with the al Qaeda leadership at this time. In a *New York Times* piece published November 21, 2001, Susan Sachs cites Khalid Dahab's testimony in the 1999 Egyptian terror trial in support for her conclusion that "Mr. Mohamed ran afoul of the bin Laden organization after 1995 because of a murky dispute involving money and was no longer trusted by bin Laden lieutenants."[20]

During the African embassy bombing trial in 2001, L'Houssaine "Joe the Moroccan" Kerchtou, a bin Laden turncoat, testified that as early as 1994 bin Laden's third in command, Mohammed Atef, didn't want "Abu Mohamed al Amriki [Ali Mohamed] to see his passport or the name he was using, because he was afraid that maybe [Mohamed] is working with [the] United States or other governments."[21] Similarly, Mohamed Rashed Daoud al-'Owali, the Saudi who drove the truck for the embassy bombing, testified in the same trial that he'd been told that by 1997 "an Egyptian man that was trained by the American military was no longer trusted in the bin Laden camps."[22]

But in the spring of 1996, bin Laden's faith in Ali was so strong that he trusted Mohamed to coordinate his move back to Jalalabad, Afghanistan, from Khartoum—a transit fraught with peril, given Osama's increasingly high visibility. Jack Cloonan confirms the kind of faith al Qaeda's leaders had in Mohamed.

"Who did bin Laden and al-Zawahiri and Atef reach out for when there was an assassination attempt on bin Laden and they wanted someone to come in and assess bin Laden's security?" he asks. "Ali Mohamed. Would they have reached out to somebody that wasn't trustworthy? If Ali had been coopted by the FBI or coopted by another intelligence service, he could have provided details on bin Laden's security and what weapons they carry, how many people are on a detail, how they move, whether bin Laden's got a body double, whether bin Laden dresses in disguises. Would they have entrusted that to anybody who they didn't have absolute confidence in?" Cloonan clearly felt the answer was no.

But the true litmus test of Ali's continuing loyalty to the jihad would come two years later, in 1998, when the suicide bomb truck that detonated outside of the U.S. embassy in Nairobi was positioned—per bin Laden's orders—in the *precise* location where Mohamed had taken the surveillance photos in 1993. If the al Qaeda leadership even picked up a hint that Ali had crossed to the other side, they would have radically altered the logistics of the bomb plot. There is little doubt that, up to the point of his arrest in September 1998, Ali remained in bin Laden's "good books."

Flight to Afghanistan by Way of Qatar

In their flight back to Afghanistan, bin Laden's core group—including his twenty-five wives, their children, and 150 close supporters—made the journey on a leased C-130 transport. The trip required a refueling stop, and bin Laden (traveling under the code name the "Haj") chose to land in Doha, the capital of Qatar, in the United Arab Emirates. The ruling al-Thani family had a number of radical Islamists in senior governmental positions, including Abdallah bin Khalid al-Thani, then the minister of religion.[23] At the Doha airport, bin Laden's plane was boarded by a number of government officials, who greeted him warmly.[24]

After the Haj and his entourage arrived safely in Jalalabad, another commercial flight leased from Arian, the Afghan national carrier, took off from Khartoum. It was flown by Sayed Nabi Hashimi. He gave his account of flying a series of close bin Laden associates to Pepe Escobar, a reporter for the *Asia Times:*

> Our plane had two configurations: with 56 passengers and with 79. They wanted 84 passengers. We flew women, children, clothes, rickshaws, old bikes, mattresses, blankets. We finally reached Jalalabad early in the morning. And then I knew we had transported the bodyguards and the families of bin Laden's inner circle. At the airport all sorts of important people came to see them, in six or seven big cars.[25]

Other al Qaeda operatives beyond the inner circle were given $2,400 in cash to purchase tickets on commercial flights.[26]

Chapter 7 for Mohamed's Number Two

While Ali Mohamed was preoccupied with the bin Laden move, his own number two back in Santa Clara was feeling pressured. Khalid Dahab, the Egyptian former medical student, had lost his job as a car salesman. The son of a well-to-do family, Dahab had been reduced to trying to support an American wife and four children on fifteen thousand dollars a year. So on May 2 he filed for bankruptcy, citing thirty-six thousand dollars in outstanding debts.[27]

The legal papers in the Chapter 7 filing show that Dahab had become so enamored with his mentor that he had changed his last name to Mohamed, spelling it as Ali did. Among his creditors were Macy's and the two banks who held his Visa cards, First USA and Wells Fargo. Khalid may have been plotting against his adopted country, but he certainly benefited from its bankruptcy laws. His filing was discharged with extraordinary speed, less than four months after he went into Chapter 7.

The case didn't seem to deter Khalid from his work for the jihad. Since 1990, Dahab had been using his Silicon Valley apartment as a kind of communications hub for al Qaeda. During that period, the government of Hosni Mubarak in Egypt had cut phone ties to governments like Sudan, Yemen, and Afghanistan that harbored terrorists. So relay stations or "switch boards" were set up by al Qaeda in countries like the United States with unrestricted phone access. As terrorism analyst Paul Thompson observes, "a jihadi in Aden, Yemen, for example, would call Dahab in Santa Clara; then, using the three-way calling function, Khalid would patch him through to another operative, say, in Khartoum."[28] In the fall of 1992, Ramzi Yousef and al-Fatah terrorist Mohammed Ajaj had used the very same system to patch Ajaj's calls from prison to the pay phone outside Ramzi's Jersey City bomb factory via Ajaj's uncle's burger restaurant in Texas.

Under Mohamed's direction, Dahab had recruited ten Islamic sleepers who infiltrated into the United States. He translated into Arabic topographical maps and other army manuals supplied by Mohamed for al Qaeda training.[29] And, despite his financial troubles, Dahab was considered so loyal that Ali Mohamed took him to meet bin Laden personally after the move from Khartoum.

During that visit, bin Laden reportedly praised Dahab, but he also tasked him with getting passports. KSM was now in Doha, Qatar, working on his nephew Ramzi's planes-as-missiles plot, which would require smuggling a series of jihadis into the United States for pilot training, and they would need immigration documents.

Yousef, now in a federal jail cell on the ninth floor of the MCC, was also preoccupied with obtaining passports. But by the spring of 1996, the FBI would luck into another chance to interdict the 9/11 plot. It came from the unlikeliest of sources: Greg Scarpa Jr., son of the vicious killer that the FBI had used in the mid-1960s to break the MISSBURN case.

Al Qaeda Meets the Mob

Scarpa Jr. was a relatively low-level wiseguy who had run a marijuana ring in Brooklyn and Staten Island for the Colombo family. But in the world of intelligence, as in business, access is everything, and for the younger Scarpa the proximity to Ramzi Yousef presented him with a unique opportunity. The Feds had decided to try Yousef first for the Bojinka case, and later for his role as mastermind of the World Trade Center bombing. After escaping from the custody of the Philippines National Police in early 1995, Wali Khan Amin Shah had been captured and rendered back to the United States. He would stand trial with Yousef and Abdul Hakim Murad, in a prosecution set to begin jury selection in late May 1996.[30]

As another measure of his self-confidence, Yousef was seeking permission from Federal Judge Kevin Duffy to represent himself. The fatal Bojinka bombing had occurred before the passage of new air piracy statutes that carried the death penalty, but nonetheless, Yousef was facing life in prison for the murder of Haruki Ikegami, cut in half by the Casio-nitro bomb Yousef had planted on PAL Flight 434 with the intent of exploding the 747's center wing fuel tank.[31]

As the trial approached in late winter, the federal prosecutors were obliged under Brady rules to disclose the sum of their case to the defense, so Yousef was well aware that Murad's confession to Colonel Mendoza in the Philippines would almost assure a conviction.[32]

The indictment focused only on the Bojinka plot. Despite the intelligence from Yousef's laptop on the "third plot," there wasn't a single word in any of the pleadings about the planes-as-missiles scenario Mendoza had uncovered. Still, by late March, Yousef must have appreciated the weight of evidence against him. So he began to think about a strategy that would guarantee him a mistrial.

"Yousef believed that Scarpa, being allegedly in the Mafia, was a person who was antigovernment," says Larry Silverman, Scarpa Jr.'s lawyer at the time.[33] "And since Yousef's whole philosophy was anti-U.S. government, they seemed to develop a relationship."

Scarpa Jr. occupied the cell between Yousef and Murad. At some point in March, Yousef broke a bed strut away from the wall of his cell and began passing tiny rolled-up notes, which he called "kites," through Scarpa to Murad, who had broken a hole in the wall that adjoined the other side of Greg Jr.'s cell.[34]

In thirty years of murder and mayhem, Greg Scarpa *Senior* had done only thirty days behind bars, thanks to his status as a Top Echelon informant for the FBI.[35] Scarpa Jr. hoped that if he spied on Yousef for the Feds, he might get the same kind of treatment—if not a reduction in charges, then at minimum some "downward release time" under Rule 5K1.1 of the Federal Rules of Criminal Procedure.[36]

Yousef's strategy was to somehow get word out to his "people" in New York and in the Middle East and cause a bomb to be placed aboard a U.S. airliner identical to his PAL 434 device.[37] If such a 747 should explode after takeoff in the United States while he was in custody, Yousef reasoned, the similarity to his Bojinka scenario might give the unsequestered jurors reasonable doubt about his involvement in the Philippines bombing. After all, those same perpetrators might just as easily have put the bomb on PAL 434 in 1994.

As soon as Greg Scarpa Jr. passed word to the FBI through his lawyer, Larry Silverman, that he was getting notes from al Qaeda's chief bomb maker, the Bureau took him very seriously. "The [FBI] smuggled in to Scarpa a minute camera that Scarpa was able to use to take photographs of the kites," says Silverman. The Bureau even supplied a female FBI agent, posing as a paralegal named "Susan Schwartz," to retrieve the film.[38]

A Cloud over the NYO

While the FBI was beginning to reap a bonanza of al Qaeda related intelligence from Greg Scarpa Jr., the simmering scandal involving his father's alleged corrupt relationship with his handler, Supervisory Special Agent R. Lindley DeVecchio, threatened to boil over. James Kallstrom, the ex-marine who served as assistant director in charge (ADIC) of the FBI's New York Office, was worried. The FBI's OPR probe into the DeVecchio matter had ground on now for almost two years, threatening to derail the sixty remaining Colombo war cases in the Eastern District.

It's impossible to know at this point just how close Kallstrom was to the investigation or to DeVecchio himself. "Lin," as he was called, was also known in the NYO as "Mr. Organized Crime"[39] because his expert testimony had helped to put dozens of wiseguys in jail. If it was now proven that DeVecchio was involved in a corrupt relationship with the elder Scarpa, some of those cases too might fall.

But Kallstrom had a problem. The letter sent by AUSA Ellen Corcella to defense attorneys on May 8, 1995, had cited eight separate instances where DeVecchio may have leaked key FBI intelligence to Scarpa—evidence that the "killing machine" could have used to eliminate his rivals.

"At this point, Kallstrom was between a rock and a hard place," says defense attorney Flora Edwards. "He was faced with compelling evidence of DeVecchio's guilt, but he didn't want the scandal to derail all the O.C. cases pending in the EDNY."[40]

Full disclosure or cover up? By April 10, 1996, Kallstrom had decided which way to go. In a memo to FBI director Louis Freeh, drafted by James J. Roth, his principal legal officer, Kallstrom pushed Freeh to resolve the matter "expeditiously." Ignoring the Corcella letter, which suggested eight affirmative leaks by DeVecchio of key FBI intelligence, Kallstrom denigrated the case against DeVecchio, claiming that there was "insufficient evidence to take prosecutive action" against him (see following letter).

b3 b7/1,

FEDERAL BUREAU OF INVESTIGATION

Precedence: IMMEDIATE   Date: 04/10/1996

To: DIRECTOR, FBI   Attn: ASSISTANT DIRECTOR, INSPECTION
                               DIVISION

From: ADIC, NEW YORK
           Contact: JAMES J. ROTH

Approved By: ROTH JAMES J

Drafted By: ROTH JAMES J:jjr

File Number(s): 263- (Pending)

Title: SUPERVISORY SPECIAL AGENT R. LINDLEY DEL VECCHIO
       OPR MATTER

          NY requests that whatever investigation is to be
conducted as a result of this letter be conducted expeditiously,
with the results provided to DOJ, and that DOJ be strenuously
pressed to provide a prosecutive opinion regarding this matter so
that it may be resolved. NY believes, based on the investigative
results to date and assuming this latest information does not
change the result, that there is insufficient evidence to take
prosecutive action against SSA DelVecchio. The failure of the DOJ
to provide a prosecutive opinion or for the FBI to
administratively resolve this matter continues to have a serious
negative impact on the government's prosecutions of various LCN
figures in the EDNY and casts a cloud over the NYO.

"I absolutely wrote that letter," Kallstrom admitted years later.[41] "What I was saying in that letter was 'Look, the investigation has been going on for years. Let's get it looked at.' It had nothing to do with a whitewash of the investigation. It was, 'Let's get the thing over with. Let's get the fact finders in a room.' It was the type of thing that I wanted to have come to a conclusion."

In the months ahead, Kallstrom and other top Feds, including Patrick Fitzgerald, certainly got the DeVecchio scandal "over with," at least for the time being. But in the process they flushed enough probative evidence on al Qaeda to have interdicted the 9/11 plot.

"They made a decision, in effect," says defense lawyer Edwards, "that these mob cases were more of a threat to public safety in New York than this bin Laden problem. And we now know just how wrong they were."

22

"HOW TO BLOW UP AIRPLANES"

B y mid-May, Yousef began passing notes threatening to have his "people" put a bomb on a plane to get "a mistrial." One kite, which recommended using the high-explosive RDX instead of nitroglycerine in the Casio-powered device, was entitled "How to Smuggle Explosives into an Airplane." It also suggested using "acetone peroxide" as an alternative explosive ingredient—a chilling precursor to the August 2006 al Qaeda related transatlantic airliner bombing plot uncovered by British intelligence.[1] That scenario also envisioned the use of peroxide in liquid-based bombs.[2] (See Appendix VI on page 555).

The Bureau considered the 1996 threats from Yousef so alarming that FBI agents met with Larry Silverman and his client at least once a week to debrief Scarpa. Their interviews were memorialized in a series of FBI 302 memos.* In April 2004, while I was writing *Cover Up,* I received dozens of the 302s and many of Yousef's kites from Angela Clemente, a forty-year-old mother of three who worked as a forensic investigator. Angela had been looking into Scarpa Jr's case *pro bono* in the winter of 2004 when he passed the documents to her during a visit

---

* Most of the key 302s can be accessed via my website at www.peterlance.com.

she made to the ADX Florence, the so-called "Supermax" prison in Florence, Colorado, where the younger Scarpa was serving a sentence for racketeering.

I'd first touched on the Scarpa story in *1000 Years for Revenge,* and after reading it Angela approached me to help her determine the authenticity of intelligence produced during Scarpa's eleven-month cell-to-cell relationship with Yousef. When I reviewed the documents—which included details from Yousef's various Manila plots that had never surfaced in the mainstream press by the spring of 1996—I was soon convinced that Scarpa Jr. had opened up a significant pipeline to Al Qaeda's most deadly bomb maker.

Consider the following excerpts from a 302 written on March 5, 1996:[3]

> YOUSEF told SCARPA I'll teach you how to blow up airplanes and how to make bombs and then you can get the information to your people (meaning Scarpa's people on the outside). YOUSEF told SCARPA I can show you how to get a bomb on an airplane through a metal detector. YOUSEF told SCARPA he would teach him how to make timing devices. . . . YOUSEF told SCARPA that during the trial they had a plan to blow up a plane and hurt a judge or an attorney so a mistrial will be declared.*

In that same 302 memo, FBI agents uncovered evidence of an al Qaeda cell loyal to Yousef that was then active in New York City:

> According to SCARPA, YOUSEF has indicated that he has four people here. SCARPA described these four terrorists already here in the United States. SCARPA advised YOUSEF has not indicated who these four individuals are or if he is in contact with these four people or how he contacts them. SCARPA does not know if YOUSEF receives or sends any messages from contacts overseas.

That revelation alone should have rocked the corridors at 26 Federal Plaza: After the conviction of the blind Sheikh and his "jihad army," the official position of the Feds had been that they had eliminated the Islamic terror threat to New York City.[4]

---

*The entire 302 can be seen on page 557.

Connecting Those Dots to Sphinx Trading

If the Feds had acted on that intelligence and gone into their files from the Kahane murder case, they might have remembered that El Sayyid Nosair had maintained a mailbox at Sphinx Trading, a Jersey City check-cashing store on Kennedy Boulevard, four doors down from the blind Sheikh's mosque.[5] They might have connected that dot to the man who was one of the two incorporators of Sphinx: one Waleed Abdu Al-Noor, who was listed by Patrick Fitzgerald and Andrew McCarthy as one of the 172 unindicted coconspirators in the Day of Terror trial, prosecuted the year before.[6] (See Appendix X, pp. 574–75)

Perhaps the knowledge that Ramzi Yousef maintained an active al Qaeda cell in New York City in 1996 might have caused the FBI to undertake an ongoing surveillance of Sphinx Trading and its mailbox center. If they had, then five years later, in the summer of 2001, Bureau agents could have interdicted two of the 9/11 hijackers who obtained their fake IDs for the planes-as-missiles plot from Mohammed El-Atriss, the Egyptian who cosigned the incorporation papers on Sphinx Trading with Al-Noor. Phone records showed that El-Atriss had also been in regular phone contact that summer with Hani Hanjour, the pilot who flew AA Flight 77 into the Pentagon. It's important to note that the Yousef intelligence gathered by Scarpa Jr., if properly pursued, would have advanced the FBI's knowledge of the al Qaeda threat to New York exponentially.

By late May 1996, Scarpa Jr. had also uncovered Yousef's threats to a federal judge and to Mike Garcia, the AUSA who was coprosecutor in his upcoming Bojinka case.[7] The Feds took these threats seriously enough that they sought protection for both individuals. By April, the quality of the Yousef intel was so good that the FBI decided to take the intelligence initiative to a new level. They actually went to the trouble and expense of setting up a phony Mafia front company, dubbed "Roma Corporation," designed to monitor Yousef's outside calls.

Ostensibly located in the Flatiron Building at Twenty-third Street and Fifth Avenue, in theory Roma Corp. was an ingenious trap. "The idea was to create a fictitious company that was supposedly a Mafia-run organization," says Silverman. "Yousef would make calls to that organization. They would then transfer his telephone calls to parties outside of the United States, and the FBI would be able to listen into those calls, record them, and, of course, make use of the information." Scarpa Jr. gave Yousef the Roma office number, and conned him into believing that the operation was run by Mafiosi, when in fact FBI agents manned the phones. Yousef was allowed to make calls to the front company from the pay phone on the ninth floor tier of the MCC. The Feds would then patch the calls through to his "people"[8] in New York and abroad.[9] Thanks to the FBI, Scarpa Jr. even supplied Yousef with a fax number at Roma.

"It's difficult to describe what a bonanza of intelligence this was for the Bureau," says a former agent now retired from the NYO. "This was raw data, coming directly from bin Laden's chief bomb maker, who we would later learn played a key role in designing the 9/11 plot."[10] The Roma Corp. patch-through would soon hand the agents of the FBI's NYO a second chance to nab Khalid Shaikh Mohammed, Yousef's uncle, who was now working out the details of the 9/11 plot in Doha, Qatar.

Losing "The Mastermind" Again

The Congressional Joint Inquiry[11] would eventually reveal that at least one call from the FBI patch-through went from Yousef to KSM, the fourth Bojinka conspirator still on the loose, who knew how to build the "undetectable" Casio-nitro bomb trigger.

There are several accounts of how Yousef's uncle was located in Qatar: In *Perfect Soldiers*, Terry McDermott's riveting book on KSM and the 9/11 hijackers, which first appeared as a series in the *Los Angeles Times*, he writes that Mohammed's brother had gone to a university in the Qatari capital, where he had formed a network of social clubs. His brother's charitable work "apparently helped Mohammed settle quickly into Qatar society,"[12] McDermott writes, describing KSM as "a kind of happy networker" who lived a "very public lifestyle" that "caught up with him in 1996."

In his book *Ghost Wars*, former *Washington Post* managing editor Steve Coll writes that "The FBI had been on the lookout for Khalid Shaikh

Mohammed, when, after Yousef's arrest, investigators discovered a $660 financial wire transfer by Mohammed from Qatar to New York to aid the World Trade Center bombers." After that, "the CIA received evidence that Mohammed was hiding in Qatar."[13] KSM was reportedly then tracked to the Doha Water Department, where he was working as an engineer.

In *Breakdown,* his account of U.S. failures leading up to 9/11, *Washington Times* reporter Bill Gertz attributes the KSM tip-off to former CIA operative Robert Baer.[14] In his memoir *See No Evil,* Baer notes that during KSM's time in Qatar, he was in a cell that included Shawqi Islambuli, the brother of the EIJ fanatic who assassinated Anwar Sadat—reinforcing the connections between Yousef's uncle and a man tied to the same EIJ cell associated with Ali Mohamed.

While KSM's location might have come from a combination of intelligence sources, it's clear now that the Roma Corp. patch-through allowed the FBI to pinpoint KSM's whereabouts in Doha, a city of 400,000 people.

Accounts differ as to what happened next. According to reporter Seymour Hersh, FBI Director Louis Freeh appealed directly to the Qatari government, sending a series of diplomatic notes, one of which reported that KSM was involved in a conspiracy to "bomb U.S. airliners" and was also believed to be "in the process of manufacturing an explosive device."[15] That account jibes with Yousef's plan to get one of his people to place "a bomb" aboard a U.S. airliner to effect a mistrial in the upcoming Bojinka case.

ABC's Brian Ross reported that "the FBI tracked Mohammed . . . to Doha, and was within hours of capturing him."[16] Ross's source was Jack Cloonan, a central figure in the NYO's bin Laden squad who told Ross that "a specially equipped government executive jet complete with blackout windows, was standing by to transport Mohammed."

"We were prepared to fly the plane in and to take him out," said Cloonan, but "somebody had leaked the information to Khalid Shaikh and he left." Ross identified the alleged collaborator as none other than Abdallah bin Khalid al-Thani, the Qatari Islamic Affairs minister at the time.

Robert Baer told Terry McDermott that up to four passports had been supplied for KSM—the other three being for bin Laden, al-Zawahiri, and Mohammed Atef.[17] Bill Gertz wrote that the FBI's elite Hostage Rescue Team had been dispatched to Doha for the takedown, but were told to cool their heels in a hotel while the Qataris "put the handcuffs on" KSM. Then, a day later, when the agents finally went to a safe house where KSM had been hiding, he had already fled to the Czech Republic, using the alias Mustafa al Nasir.

Al-Thani Proclaims His Innocence

For his part, al-Thani denied any connection to the 9/11 plot, even though in April 2006 a default judgment was entered against him in one of three September 11 cases in which he was a named defendant. On June 8, 2006, al-Thani's lawyers asked a federal judge to vacate the judgment. "He does not know why he is a defendant in this multidistrict litigation," his lawyer said in a story filed by the Associated Press.[18] The lawyer contended that any action against al-Thani should have been dismissed because he was immune from prosecution and because the allegations were "insufficient to show that his actions were aimed at the U.S. or had any connection to the September 11 attacks."

According to the AP story, al-Thani has held multiple key positions in the Qatari government since 1982, including commander of the army from 1984 to 1992. He is currently the Interior Minister. Ironically, for a man alleged to have helped KSM escape, his current position requires him to oversee regulation of immigration and naturalization.

In 2005, I conducted a lengthy interview with Bathiya Coomasuru, a Sri Lankan naturalized U.S. citizen who had served as chief aide to the nephew of the former Qatari Emir, who was deposed by his son, Crown Prince Hamad bin Khalifa al-Thani, in a 1995 bloodless coup.[19] Al Jazeera, the Arab broadcast network that regularly airs al Qaeda's video *fatwas* is located in Doha.[20] Coomasuru told me that a number of high-ranking members of the current Qatari government are al Qaeda sympathizers. Several of them, he said, had boasted that "their sons had trained in al Qaeda camps." Coomasuru told me that he wasn't surprised to learn that on his escape from Khartoum, bin Laden had found safe haven in Doha. "He is revered by many of the al-Thanis," Coomasuru said.[21]

The irony is that Doha, the place where the "mastermind" of 9/11 hid out, is where the United States decided to locate the Forward Headquarters of CENTCOM, the U.S. Central Command, in preparation for the Iraqi invasion.[22]

Three days after U.S. forces took Baghdad in March 2003, the *Los Angeles Times* quoted former CIA case officer Robert Baer as describing Abdullah bin Khalid al-Thani as a potential danger to U.S. troops. When reporters Josh Meyer and John Goetz disclosed that al-Thani had become Qatar's Interior Minister in 1997, thus putting him in charge of state security, Richard Clarke, the former counterterrorism czar in the Clinton and Bush administrations, was stunned.[23]

"I'm shocked to hear [that]," Clarke said. "You're telling me that [al-Thani] is today in charge of security inside Qatar? I hope that's not true."

If Clarke—arguably one of America's keenest assessors of the al Qaeda threat—was surprised by this news *in 2003,* how easy must it have been for Osama bin Laden's terror network to evade detection in Qatar in 1996? And worse, what potential intelligence in the Iraqi campaign may have been leaked to al Qaeda since the invasion?

Even today, "CENTCOM maintains an enormous facility in Doha," says Lt. Col. Anthony Shaffer, the Bronze Star winner who was a key operative in Operation Able Danger, the army's now-famous late-1990s initiative to track the al Qaeda threat.

"There's no question that if key officials of the Qatari government are sympathetic to our enemy, the potential of undermining our fight against the [Iraqi] insurgency could be profound and the intelligence losses could be huge."[24]

The Yousef-Scarpa Jr. Treasure Trove

Despite the loss of Khalid Shaikh Mohammed in Doha back in 1996, as the Bojinka trial got underway against three of his coconspirators, Greg Scarpa Jr. was feeding FBI agents in the New York Office a constant stream of intelligence from Ramzi Yousef that could have proven crucial to

Fitzgerald, Cloonan, and Coleman in their ongoing effort to build a case against Osama bin Laden.

Among the many revelations contained in the FBI 302s was a plot disclosed by Yousef in which bin Laden, whom he code-named "Bojinka" or "Bojinga," would arrange the hijacking of a series of U.S. airliners in order to free the blind Sheikh, Yousef, and his Manila cohorts. That intelligence alone was considered so important that it turned up in Presidential Daily Briefings (PDBs) to Bill Clinton in 1998 and Bush on the eve of the 9/11 attacks in August 2001.

The Yousef-Scarpa relationship also yielded intelligence that was relevant to ongoing al Qaeda operations. On June 25, 1996, nineteen Americans were killed when a truck bomb ripped open the Khobar Towers complex in Saudi Arabia. The perpetrators were later identified by the FBI as Iranian Hezbollah members, but days after the bombing Yousef told Scarpa that "BOJINGA" (that is, bin Laden) was the "mastermind." The bomb maker even boasted that he was originally tasked "to check out the security measures and that a tanker truck [to deliver the bomb] was discussed at the time."[25]

In late June 2004, the 9/11 Commission concluded that "Al Qaeda . . . may . . . have played a 'yet unknown role' in aiding Hezbollah militants in the 1996 bombing of the Khobar Towers."[26] Keep in mind that Ali Mohamed, the FBI's best source on al Qaeda, had first brought together Osama bin Laden and Hezbollah leader Imad Mugniyah for a terror summit in the early 1990s.

"There's little doubt that if the FBI had fully utilized this intelligence that was coming out of Ramzi Yousef through Scarpa Jr. they could have connected major dots on al Qaeda's strength in the summer of 1996," says Lt. Col. Shaffer, who began investigating al Qaeda for the U.S. Special Operations Command in late 1999. "As we found, Yousef and the blind Sheikh's cell in New York were directly connected to bin Laden and the al Qaeda leadership."[27]

But once again, just as they had with Emad Salem's infiltration of Yousef's first bombing cell, the FBI would fail to make the most of Scarpa Jr.'s intelligence. "The people running this [Roma Corp.] operation really didn't have the expertise that was required," says Larry Silverman, Greg

Scarpa Jr.'s attorney. "From what I knew, they had very junior agents who were not very knowledgeable in this type of operation."

The result was that the FBI wasn't able to monitor Yousef's outside calls in real time. The agent posing as a wiseguy who was monitoring the calls spoke Arabic, but Yousef, a master of six languages, was communicating in more obscure languages like Urdu and his native Baluchi.[28] "So while they later on may have learned what was in the conversations, they really didn't learn live-time what was being spoken," says Silverman.

And evidence now suggests that that "flaw" in the Roma Corp. operation led to the second biggest act of terror and mass murder in U.S. history: the crash of TWA Flight 800. The evidence is circumstantial, but compelling: With the unintended help of the FBI in allowing Yousef to make outside calls to his "people," it appears that the Bureau may have paved the way for the legendary airline disaster in the summer of 1996—a crash that immediately looked to FBI investigators like Bojinka fulfilled.

"An Airplane Blew Up"

On July 18, 1996, the most damning evidence against Yousef—the confession of Murad to Col. Mendoza—was about to be admitted in the Bojinka trial. Just thirteen hours before that, on the night of July 17, TWA Flight 800 took off from John F. Kennedy Airport with 230 passengers and crew aboard, bound for Paris. The 747 was identical to the PAL Flight 434 aircraft that Yousef had used for his Bojinka plot "wet test" in 1994.

Moments after clearing Long Island airspace, at 8:31:12 P.M.,[29] an "event" occurred in the area of the center wing fuel tank that caused the tank to explode. The blast decapitated the aircraft, severing the cockpit and front end of the plane from the body, which continued to rise, engines still turning. After the "event," the plane climbed for twenty-four seconds before the entire front end blew away.[30] This created a streak in the sky that may have led onlookers on the ground to think they were watching a missile. Seconds later, the rest of the fuselage broke apart, plummeting to the Atlantic and killing everyone on board.

The cockpit voice and data recorder showed no hint of any mechanical cause for the crash. There had been no "Mayday" from the crew.

A White House Situation Room meeting was convened that night—a rarity in an airplane crash[31]—and within days ADIC James Kallstrom ordered hundreds of agents to the crash scene off East Moriches Point on Long Island. His assumption, at this point, was that Ramzi Yousef had made good on his threat.[32]

The next morning after the crash, on July 18, 1996, just as he had told Greg Scarpa Jr. (as recorded in the FBI 302 of March 5, 1996), Yousef asked Judge Kevin Duffy to declare a mistrial.[33]

Duffy, the tough, Bronx-born Irishman who had presided over the conviction of Abouhalima and Salameh in the first WTC bombing trial in 1994, was on the bench again as the Bojinka trial entered its seventh week. The unsequestered jury had awakened to news reports that a Boeing 747 had come crashing down in the ocean, just as Yousef's Bojinka plot had intended.

The judge felt he had to acknowledge the media coverage. But rather than admonishing the jury to ignore the press reports and remain open to the evidence being entered at trial, Duffy reached the conclusion that the two 747 events were completely unrelated.

"Good morning, ladies and gentlemen," he began. "Last night near Moriches Inlet out in Long Island, an airplane blew up. TWA Flight 800. Now there is going to be . . . all kinds of speculation about what happened. I have no clue what happened, nor do you, nor do any of the people who have been speculating up to this point. All we know is that there was an explosion and the airplane went down. It's a tragedy, there is no two ways about it, but that had nothing to do with this case."[34]

The court transcript didn't reveal whether Assistant U.S. Attorney Mike Garcia, whose life had been threatened by Yousef, exchanged looks with his cocounsel Dietrich Snell. Nor do we know whether Patrick Fitzgerald, the Organized Crime-Terrorism chief, was in the courtroom. But any Fed who had access to Scarpa's warnings, captured for posterity in those FBI 302s, had to know that Judge Duffy was dead wrong—the crash of TWA Flight 800 had *everything* to do with the Bojinka case.

23

BOJINKA FULFILLED

Almost immediately after he learned of the crash, Greg Scarpa Jr. shut down. He was afraid that he might somehow be implicated in the disaster, since he had passed on such specific threat intelligence to the Feds. In the younger mobster's mind, the kites he'd photographed from Yousef, warning of his threat to put a bomb on an airliner, should have given the FBI sufficient prior warning to have prevented the explosion.

But as hundreds of FBI agents converged on the Long Island crash scene, ADIC James Kallstrom felt he needed Scarpa more than ever. "I would have bet my meager paycheck that this was an act of terrorism," Kallstrom told me in a 2004 interview, emphasizing that initially he believed that the crash was the result of an act of sabotage "to the 99th percentile."[1] In fact, he was so impressed by the quality of Scarpa Jr.'s notes and kites from Yousef that he phoned Scarpa's lawyer, Larry Silverman, within days of the crash.

He said "Don't let Scarpa stop now," remembers Silverman.[2] "It was clear to me from the tone of Kallstrom's voice, from the content of what he said, that at that point in time he was convinced that the downing of the plane was an intentional act of terrorism or sabotage. The fact that here was one of the most high-ranking FBI officials calling a defense attorney and asking for his help in convincing his client to continue to cooperate [told me] that he strongly believed that this was not a mechanical failure."[3]

In the weeks that followed, with the help of the U.S. Navy, the FBI dredged up 96 percent of the aircraft[4] and assembled it in an abandoned aircraft hangar in Calverton, Long Island—just a few miles away from where Ali Mohamed's cell members had practiced firing automatic weapons in the summer of 1989.

Almost immediately, investigators for the National Transportation Safety Board (NTSB), not accustomed to finding terrorism as the cause of aircraft disasters, locked horns with federal agents. Even before the plane had been partially assembled, they concluded that the origin of the fuel tank explosion was mechanical.[5] With zero forensic evidence and an unparalleled safety record for the 747, Safety Board investigators nonetheless theorized that an electrical short had ignited vapors in the almost-empty center tank, causing it to explode.

The FBI's chief metallurgist, William Tobin, agreed. With only 10 percent of the wreckage recovered, Tobin declared that neither a missile nor a bomb had brought down the plane.[6] " 'No indicia of high explosive,' was the way he put it," according to Ken Maxwell, the FBI's supervisory special agent who ran the Calverton reassembly site.

Maxwell told me that Tobin "made up his mind early on in the case that it had to be an accident because he didn't see any blatant metal evidence. It was his position that there was no bomb and he was the ruling authority."[7]

But Tobin's model for measuring "indicia" of bomb damage was incomplete. Only two bombs had ever exploded prior to 1996 on a 747: the one aboard Pan Am 103 in 1988, and Yousef's Bojinka wet test device aboard PAL 434 in December 1994. The Pan Am flight had been brought down by a Toshiba boom box packed with almost a pound of Semtex (Czech C-4) explosive—an event that caused enough metallurgical damage to the aircraft's structure to bring it down.

But the criminal genius of Ramzi Yousef was his design of the tiny, undetectable Casio-nitro bomb trigger, which acted as a blasting cap capable of turning the fuel tank of a 747 into the ignition source of the aircraft's destruction. With the Bojinka device, only a small quantity of high explosives was necessary to rupture the fuel tank.

The IED Yousef had planted under seat 26K in the PAL 434 wet test had blown a hole through the passenger cabin floor, killing Haruki Ikegami. If the device had been placed two rows forward, it could have imploded down and detonated the fuel tank. As to how such a device might have gotten on board, there was published speculation that the IED could have been hidden on the fatal aircraft in the Athens airport, where it had been serviced before its departure for JFK. The FBI would later announce that it was gearing up to send agents to the Greek airport, which had been reportedly cited in the past for "lax security."[8]

Any complete evaluation of metallurgical bomb damage aboard TWA 800, should have factored in that second scenario—especially given that Yousef was on trial at that very moment for planting the PAL 434 device, and that he had threatened to explode a device on a U.S. airliner just weeks before the TWA 800 crash. But as I documented in *Cover Up,* FBI metallurgist Tobin admitted that in assessing "indicia" of bomb damage aboard TWA 800, he used *only* the Pan Am 103 model. In fact, he told me that he was completely ignorant of Yousef's Bojinka rehearsal aboard PAL 434.[9]

Explosive Residue Found in the TWA 800 Wreckage

In the weeks following the TWA 800 crash, FBI investigators would find evidence of the high explosives PETN, nitroglycerine, and RDX in the area between rows 17 and 25 in the wreckage.[10] Yousef had recommended the use of RDX in his May 19 kite to Scarpa under the subhead "How to Smuggle Explosives into an Airplane." In fact, within days of the RDX discovery, at Calverton, Steven Burmeister, head of the FBI's lab in Washington, testified at the Bojinka trial that investigators had found methenane, a key component of RDX, in Yousef's Manila bomb factory.[11]

On July 29, FBI agent Joe Cantamessa told reporters that if the FBI received "one more positive result" in its Washington lab, confirming additional high-explosive evidence aboard the wreckage, that would be enough to declare the crash a crime.[12]

By August 22, just over a month after the crash, the FBI was so close to concluding that a bomb was the source of the disaster that *New York Times* reporter Don Van Atta Jr. filed a story that appeared under the headline "Prime Evidence Found That Device Exploded in Cabin of Flight 800."[13] The piece ran in the *Times* the very next day.

Defusing the Bomb Theory

But hours before Van Atta's story went to press, James Kallstrom attended a meeting in Washington, D.C., with FBI Director Louis Freeh and Jamie Gorelick, the same deputy attorney general who had supported Khalifa's extradition to Jordan and written the "wall memo" the year before.[14]

By the time the meeting was over, Kallstrom's thinking had apparently taken a 180-degree turn. Returning to New York, he tried to kill Van Atta's story and began to seek an alternative explanation for how high explosives could get on the flight 800 wreckage *in the absence of* a bomb.[15]

In an interview with me in 2004, Kallstrom denied that he underwent such a "sea change" after the Freeh-Gorelick meeting, insisting that "there might be some other explanation for how that [explosive residue] got there." As to his attempts to kill Van Atta's story, he said, "I was always trying to be honest with all the reporters, including Van Atta, and I told him that it was premature to say that this was caused from a bomb on the plane and I wouldn't go with that."[16]

But Kallstrom's actions at the time suggested a new agenda. On August 24, he declared publicly that "it's not inconceivable that this chemical would be available through some other means other than through an explosive device, and left on the airplane." That statement prompted a senior law enforcement official interviewed by the *New York Times* to "laugh out loud." The *Times* story noted that "investigators did not take such a scenario seriously."[17]

"'For whatever reasons,' says the FBI source, 'the Bureau and Justice were gearing up to spin this thing away from a bombing plot to some kind of mechanical event.'"[18]

Kallstrom first presented a theory that the explosive traces found in the wreckage must have been tracked onto the aircraft by U.S. troops five years earlier, when the downed 747, which carried the tail number N93 17119, had been used to ferry soldiers to the Gulf War. But CNN reporters quickly learned that the aircraft had been completely retrofitted since the Gulf War, so that theory was dead.[19]

The K-9 Theory

In late August, Kallstrom asked an FBI agent who worked directly with Tom Pickard, Louis Freeh's second in command, to check with the FAA. Perhaps the explosives had found their way onto the fatal aircraft via a test involving bomb-sniffing dogs.[20] The confirmation came on September 19, when Kallstrom got word that N93 17119 had been used by a K-9 officer at Lambert International Airport in St. Louis to conduct a test that qualified a bomb-sniffing dog five weeks before the crash.[21]

The Bureau reasoned that the patrolman, Herman Burnett, had spilled explosives from the test aids, and that the chemical residue had somehow lodged in the 747's carpet, only to be picked up after the crash by the FBI lab.[22]

Although the wreckage had been under water for weeks, and had undergone a power cleaning before being tested for explosives, the media went along with the theory.

Three days later, on September 22, the *New York Times* accepted the FBI's explanation. The explosive residue had come from the K-9 test, they reported. The bomb theory was dead. *Newsday,* which later won a Pulitzer Prize for its TWA 800 coverage, also embraced the theory.

No one in the media sent a reporter to St. Louis to interview Officer Burnett. The FBI, which had almost a thousand agents on the case, didn't send anyone from New York. An agent from the local St. Louis office took Officer Burnett's statement. Nonetheless, Kallstrom endorsed the bomb-sniffing dog theory *emphatically* in a September 5, 1997, letter to Congressman James A. Traficante, who was investigating the crash.[23]

As implausible as the K-9 theory was, it held.

Even terrorism czar Richard Clarke accepted the fuel tank ignition theory. "In the days that followed," wrote Clarke in his memoir *Against All Enemies*, "no intelligence surfaced that helped advance [a criminal theory in] the investigation."[24] President Clinton himself was convinced. "On July 17, TWA Flight 800 exploded off Long Island, killing some 230 people." Clinton wrote in his autobiography, *My Life*. "At the time everyone assumed—wrongly, as it turned out—that this was a terrorist act."[25]

In another note of irony, John O'Neill, the FBI's celebrated counterterrorism chief, came to believe that the TWA 800 investigation, with its hundreds of agents, was draining Bureau resources from the war on terror. By the time he transferred from FBI Headquarters to run the National Security Division in New York, O'Neill started talking to ADIC Kallstrom about "an exit strategy."

But Neal Herman, the JTTF boss who believed from the day of the crash that Yousef was responsible, was later quoted as asking "My God, what the hell is an exit strategy? We get out of cases when they're over."[26]

"O'Neill's discussions with Kallstrom and with Washington and the NTSB were putting on a lot of pressure," said Supervisory Special Agent Maxwell. So by mid-November 1997, sixteen months after the crash, Maxwell got a call from Kallstrom. "Shut it down," he said. It was a very direct order. "Shut it down." Within days, on November 15, 1997, the FBI formally accepted the NTSB's unsupported mechanical "spark" theory and the case was effectively closed.[27]

Shattering the K-9 Theory

In May 2004, after receiving copies of the heretofore secret FBI 302 memos documenting Scarpa Jr.'s intelligence from Yousef, I contacted Officer Burnett and flew to St. Louis to meet him. I also obtained a copy of the TWA gate assignment for June 10, 1996, the date of the K-9 test.[28]

TWA's own records, which were in the possession of the FBI back in 1996, showed that Officer Burnett left the aircraft at *noon* on June 10 after completing the test. None of the chemical aids he used included the explosives nitroglycerine or RDX. All of his test aids were in closed containers, with the exception of some old "det" cord, which he nonetheless put in a closed overhead compartment across the passenger cabin from the right side where the fuel tank had exploded. Following protocol, Officer Burnett conducted the test on an empty aircraft.

When he finished the test and left the plane at noon, a few flight attendants were just beginning to arrive.

In 1996, TWA had a rule that its crew members on 747s had to check in at least ninety minutes before a flight's departure. Yet TWA's gate assignment for June 10, 1996, showed that N93 17119, the aircraft that became TWA 800 five weeks later, left Gate 50 at the end of the C Concourse, fully catered, fully crewed with several hundred passengers aboard, just *thirty-five minutes later,* bound for Hawaii.[29] (See Appendix VII on page 567.)

At the same time, an almost *identical* 747, with the tail number N93 17116, was parked at Gate 52 on the opposite side of the C-Course terminus.[30] That aircraft didn't leave until 1:45 P.M., more than enough time for the crew to arrive and prep the plane for departure.

In sum, Officer Burnett told me that he believed he had done the test with the dog on a *different* 747 from the one that exploded in a fireball five weeks later in New York.[31] If he is correct—and the TWA documentation suggests that he is—then the explosive test aids he used could not have leaked onto the wreckage of the aircraft that became TWA 800.

My investigation removed the FBI's linchpin theory for the explanation of how high explosives got on the fatal aircraft *absent* a bomb. The Scarpa 302s demonstrated that Yousef had a motive for getting a bomb on board. The FBI patch-through scheme had inadvertently given him a communication channel to his uncle KSM, the one fugitive Bojinka conspirator who knew how to build the Casio-nitro device. And Athens was an airport where security was lax enough for an al Qaeda operative to place such a device on board.

In the absence of any physical evidence to justify the NTSB's mechanical theory, the weight of circumstantial evidence now supports the argument that the crash of TWA 800 was the second biggest act of terror and mass murder in U.S. history—and that the FBI and DOJ suppressed the evidence that could have proven as much at the time.

The details behind the FBI's motives are set forth in *Cover Up,* but the bottom line was that the Bureau and prosecutors in the Eastern District of

New York (EDNY) were worried that the Colombo war cases might un-ravel if Greg Scarpa Jr. were found to be credible as a witness.

The Ends/Means Decision

In his upcoming trial, Scarpa Jr.'s defense would be that the RICO viola-tions he was charged with were the result of crimes that had effectively been sanctioned by Lin DeVecchio, the senior supervisory special agent whom Greg Jr. contended was passing key FBI intelligence to his father. EDNY prosecutor Ellen Corcella had admitted as much in her May 8, 1995, letter, but James Kallstrom had declared the evidence against DeVecchio "insuffi-cient" a year later in his communiqué to FBI director Louis Freeh.

"At some point, personnel in the Eastern District and the Justice De-partment came to understand the significance of Scarpa Junior's testi-mony," says defense attorney Flora Edwards. She later represented Vic Orena, the Colombo family acting boss, who claimed he'd been framed by DeVecchio. "Greg Junior had to be discredited. Because once he became credible about Ramzi Yousef, then he'd be credible about what he was going to say in my hearing, too."[32]

Kallstrom categorically denies the link between the DeVecchio scandal and the TWA 800 probe. "It doesn't matter if Lin DeVecchio and the fa-ther of this person next to Ramzi Yousef acted properly or improperly," Kallstrom said in a 2005 interview.[33] "It doesn't matter on [the TWA 800] investigation. What does matter is a year and a half worth of forensic work we put into the plane. And the fact that we could not find any evidence of [a terrorist act]."

Scarpa Jr. would later swear under oath that his father was paying Lin DeVecchio for FBI intelligence on his wiseguy rivals, information he used in his campaign to eliminate them one by one.

Also, given the pattern of FBI negligence from the moment al Qaeda established a base in New York City in 1989, it's clear that FBI officials were worried that their Roma Corp. patch-through plan, which Yousef ex-ploited, may have contributed to the crash. That was reason enough for DOJ officials to obscure the true source of the disaster.

Clearing DeVecchio

After two years, the FBI OPR investigation into the allegations that Greg Scarpa Sr. had corrupted Lin DeVecchio was shut down. DeVecchio was allowed to retire in September 1996 with a full pension.

The story might have ended there. But in September 2005, a year after I had laid out the case for the FBI/SDNY ends/means decision in *Cover Up*, investigators from the Rackets Bureau of the Brooklyn D.A.'s office, called me in for a meeting. The investigators asked me if I had uncovered any new evidence in the year since the book was published that would alter my analysis of the alleged Scarpa Jr./DeVecchio cover up. I told them that I stood by my findings.

Then, in January 2006, I learned that, based on the blueprint that I'd laid out in *Cover Up,* together with a series of documents and witnesses provided by forensic investigator Angela Clemente, the Rackets Bureau had determined that there was sufficient probable cause to open a grand jury investigation.[34]

On March 30, 2006, Roy Lindley DeVecchio was arrested and arraigned on four counts of second degree murder stemming from his relationship with Gregory Scarpa Sr.[35] As we'll see, events in the succeeding months have begun to vindicate the evidence against him discovered in the course of my investigation. Further information has emerged that corroborates the Yousef/Scarpa Jr. intelligence. And new evidence has surfaced, from a key source recently retired from the National Security Agency (NSA), that casts new light on the theory that Ramzi Yousef ordered a bomb placed aboard a U.S. airliner to get a mistrial in the Bojinka case.

Claiming Credit for the Crash

Former JTTF detective Tommy Corrigan was one of the lead investigators on the TWA 800 case. Like Kallstrom, he too began by assuming the crash was an act of sabotage, but then changed his mind to side with the NTSB.

During the reassembly process, Corrigan says, "I watched that plane from the earliest part of its assembly in the hangar to the last piece that was hung. . . . And our investigation, without a doubt, determined that it was an accident. It had nothing to do with terrorism.[36] There was never any intelligence or chatter about that aircraft, and that's unusual. If something goes down, even if somebody isn't taking credit for it, [if] there's chatter on the lines, you're gonna pick [it] up. With Flight 800 there was nothing."

But Corrigan, a senior JTTF investigator, appears to have been misinformed on this point, just as he missed the arrest of Abouhalima and Salameh the day after the Kahane murder.

In fact, this investigation has found that several Islamic groups took credit for the crash.

Seven hours before the plane exploded, an Arabic daily in London got a fax from a radical Muslim group, the Islamic Movement for Change. This was the same group that took credit for the 1995 bombing of the U.S. military training mission to the Saudi National Guard in Riyadh, which left five Americans dead. The message warned that "The mujahadeen will deliver the harshest reply to the threats of the foolish American President."[37]

Attorney General Janet Reno later said that after the TWA 800 crash two groups took responsibility. One identifying itself as a fundamentalist Islamic group contacted a Tampa, Florida, television station.[38] But an even more significant claim of responsibility was uncovered on July 31, 1997. When the FBI and NYPD raided the Park Slope, Brooklyn, apartment of two Islamic radicals accused of attempting to bomb New York's subways, they recovered a note that not only took *credit* for the downing of TWA Flight 800, but also demanded the release of Ramzi Yousef.[39] Presiding at the trial of the reputed subway bombers (Ghazi Ibrahim Abu Maizar and Lafi Khalil) was none other than Reena Raggi, She was the same judge who had ordered Mohammed Ajaj's bomb manuals returned before the WTC bombing; and in the fall of 1998, she would also preside in the case of Greg Scarpa Jr.[40]

Now there is new evidence of outside forces taking credit for the downing of TWA 800.

At the end of April 2006, Sibel Edmonds, the former FBI translator who founded the National Security Whistleblowers Coalition, interviewed a recently retired NSA staffer who had joined her organization. The twenty-seven-year veteran of the NSA told her about an intercepted message relating to TWA 800 that was picked up in July 1996, following the crash. The message was in Baluchi, the native dialect of Ramzi Yousef and his uncle KSM. After receiving a classified intercept from the FBI, the NSA sent out the message for translation to the Defense Language Institute (DLI).

In July 2006, Edmonds put me in touch with the NSA source. He was so concerned that his home phone might have been tapped that he drove for an hour one night to call me from a pay phone.

"It was a short time after the 800 crash," he remembered.[41] "I was working around one or two in the afternoon when the translation came back from the DLI of this highly classified FBI intercept that the Bureau had picked up after the plane went down. It was in Baluchi, and we had two translators who could have handled it right away. But for unknown reasons it was sent out to the Language Institute. Anyway, when we got it back I was so shocked at what I read I immediately took it over to one of our Baluchi people and he expressed outright *anger* that he hadn't been able to do the translation right away. If he had, he felt that it might have affected the investigation."

There was a pause on the line. I asked the NSA veteran what the intercept had said.

"You have to understand it was in Ramzi Yousef's native tongue." He paused again.

"Right. Baluchi," I interjected. "Come on. What did it say?"

"The message said . . . 'TWA 800 . . . what had to be done has been done.' There were two more words but they were unintelligible."

24

CROSSING
THE LINE

Documenting the failures by the FBI and Justice Department on the road to 9/11 has always been a matter of two parallel questions: What happened and why? From the shutdown of the Calverton surveillance in 1989 to the Bureau's seeming inability to recognize Ali Mohamed as an al Qaeda spy, through the failure of the FBI's two bin Laden offices of origin to act on the intelligence from Yousef to Greg Scarpa Jr. in 1996, the central question has been one of cause.

Were these mistakes a function of simple negligence, gross negligence, structural impediments like "the wall" that supposedly prevented agencies from sharing intel, or something more insidious? Based on evidence from the fall of 1996, the answer was becoming more clear.

When it came to the reams of kites and FBI 302s documenting the intelligence from Ramzi Yousef—the architect of the World Trade Center attacks in 1993 and 2001—the Feds in the FBI's New York Office and the SDNY had now begun to cross the line from negligence to intent in their disconnection of the dots. At least that's what the evidence suggested to me.

Consider the primary points.

Limiting Evidence at the Bojinka Trial

During the three-month trial, Assistant U.S. Attorneys Mike Garcia and Dietrich Snell presented a riveting, evidence-driven case against Yousef, Murad, and Wali Khan, presenting more than a thousand exhibits over forty-four days.[1] They laid out a chilling examination of Yousef's fatal wet test aboard PAL 434, described the Dona Josefa bomb factory in minute detail, and characterized the material retrieved from Ramzi's Toshiba laptop as "the most devastating evidence of all."[2]

Snell and Garcia called dozens of witnesses, including eleven separate Philippines law enforcement officials. Yet they never called Rodolfo Mendoza, the man who had uncovered the third, planes-as-missiles plot during his interrogation of Murad. When Mendoza's assistant, Major Alberto Ferro, was put on the stand under oath, he said he didn't recall *who* had interrogated Murad,[3] even though he was in the room with Mendoza throughout most of the questioning.[4]

While Yousef's Toshiba laptop, as deencrypted by Rafael Garcia, contained the full details of the plot later executed on 9/11, not a word of that scenario was mentioned during trial. Nor was there any reference to Mohammed Jamal Khalifa, who had bankrolled the Yousef-KSM Manila cell and was now safely in Saudi Arabia, having been flown to Jordan and freedom courtesy of the U.S. Justice Department.[5]

Hiding the Identity of Khalid Shaikh Mohammed

Most surprising, during the entire summer-long trial, the name of the fourth Bojinka conspirator, Khalid Shaikh Mohammed, who had escaped the Feds, was mentioned by name only *once,* in reference to a letter found in Room 603. It was drafted around the same time that Siddiq Ali, one of the Day of Terror plotters, had pleaded guilty and become a government witness in that case.[6]

The letter read, "To: Brother Mohammed Al Siddiq. We are facing a lot of problems because of you. Fear Allah, Mr. Siddiq, there is a day of judgment. You will be asked, if you are very busy with something more important, don't give promises to other people. See you in the day of judgment. Still waiting, Khalid Shaikh, and Bojenka."[7]

Except for one other cryptic reference to his alias (Salem Ali), there was no other mention of KSM at the trial; even though by January 1996 the SDNY had secretly indicted Mohammed. *No one* in the media knew who he was, and certainly no one outside the FBI and other select U.S. intelligence agencies knew that the FBI had lost him for a second time in Doha after the Roma Corp. patch-through had helped to pinpoint his whereabouts.

Keeping the KSM Hunt Secret

"The hunt for Khalid Shaikh was conducted in secret by the FBI," says a former Diplomatic Security Service agent who was involved in the Yousef hunt. "With Ramzi, the search was very public, utilizing the [Rewards] program. His want poster was plastered on matchbook covers from Islamabad to Kabul and it was the money that caused that South African kid [Parker] to drop a dime on him."[8]

Why should the FBI have kept the name of the fourth Bojinka conspirator secret? Could it have been because one of their agents, Bradley Garrett, got to the Su Casa Guesthouse in Islamabad late and failed to stop him before he talked to a *Time* magazine stringer and escaped?[9] Was it because KSM was now developing the planes-as-missile plot, which his nephew conceived in the fall of 1994, and which the FBI had known about as early as 1995, via Yousef's Toshiba laptop and Murad's confession?

Was the Justice Department trying to minimize Yousef's role in the plot because the FBI had failed to stop him before the first WTC bombing, when they failed to heed Emad Salem's warning to follow Abouhalima and Salameh? Was the Justice Department trying to keep secret Jamie Gorelick's catastrophic blunder in supporting Khalifa's extradition at a time when he could have given the FBI bin Laden's entire al Qaeda game plan? Were senior DOJ and FBI officials hoping to hide their possible complicity in the crash of TWA 800, after Yousef used their own patch-through scheme to get word to his uncle in Qatar, where KSM was "in the process of manufacturing an explosive device"—an admission by Louis Freeh as reported by Sy Hersh?

Containing the Truth on Ali Mohamed

And where was the FBI's star al Qaeda informant through all of this? By late spring of 1996, the Bureau had enough probable cause to establish wiretaps on five of the phones used by Nairobi cell members.[10] One of them was Wadih El-Hage, the Lebanese convert who had been Osama bin Laden's personal secretary in the Sudan. El-Hage had been in New York back in 1991 at the time Shalabi was murdered. He was the same operative who had purchased guns for Mahmud Abouhalima, Ali Mohamed's trainee. He'd even visited one of "the Red's" fellow Calverton shooters, Kahane killer El Sayyid Nosair, at Rikers Island.[11]

By 1994, Ali Mohamed was staying with El-Hage in his home in Kenya; and now, two years later, the Feds were tapping Wadih's phone. El-Hage was communicating regularly with Mohamed, who had made multiple trips to Africa using his putative import-export businesses as cover. Ali was so close to bin Laden that he'd lived in his house while he'd trained his bodyguards back in Khartoum. Bin Laden's brother-in-law Khalifa had been arrested twenty-six miles from Mohamed's Santa Clara home in late 1994. The year before that, Ali had admitted to FBI agents that bin Laden's al Qaeda "organization" was building an army to overthrow the Saudi government and that he himself had trained Osama's operatives in Sudanese camps, schooling them in antihijacking and intelligence methods.

Now, as KSM was putting his nephew Yousef's planes-as-missiles plot into motion, where was Ali Mohamed, the informant the FBI was counting on to help them track al Qaeda? Did the Feds *want* to know, or were they afraid to ask?

In 1996, Jack Cloonan, the veteran New York agent in the newly dedicated squad I-49, was just getting up to speed on Mohamed. In fact, Cloonan says, when he was tasked to build a file on the former Egyptian army major, he had no idea that Ali had even worked for the FBI.

"At that point in time, I didn't know that San Francisco had opened Ali as an informant and had that much of a relationship with him," says Cloonan. "I found that out after I started looking into Ali and what he was doing out in California and where he was living."[12]

Cloonan later attributed the Bureau's bicoastal "disconnect" on Ali to "silos," or what the 9/11 Commission later called the "stovepiping" of intelligence between and within agencies. But San Francisco Special Agent John Zent's preoccupation with the Ewell murder case, might also help to explain how the FBI's New York Office could have been so far out of the loop on Ali Mohamed, who had been opened as an informant by Zent and other agents four years earlier.

Still, that doesn't explain the disconnect *within* Cloonan's own bin Laden unit, which was effectively run by Patrick Fitzgerald, by then the head of Organized Crime and Terrorism in the SDNY.

Limiting the Yousef-Scarpa Jr. Intel within Squad I-49

One of the most astonishing revelations at this stage of my investigation was Cloonan's admission that he had only "passing" knowledge of the Yousef-Scarpa intelligence from March 1996 through February 1997. The Yousef-Scarpa initiative had generated dozens of FBI 302s. FBI ADIC James Kallstrom had found the kites from Yousef so compelling that he'd given Scarpa a camera to photograph them and assigned a female FBI agent posing as a paralegal to retrieve the film. He'd then gone to the next step of setting up "Roma Corp," the phony wiseguy front company that allowed them to monitor Yousef's outside calls—if not in real time—and one of them had led to their failed pursuit of KSM in Doha.

Among the evidence that Scarpa had pulled out of Yousef was the presence of four of Yousef's "people" in New York City; evidence of possible al Qaeda involvement in the June 1996 Khobar Towers bombing;[13] and evidence of a bin Laden plot to hijack a U.S. airliner to free Sheikh Omar Abdel Rahman.[14] By ignoring this evidence, the Feds passed up an unprecedented opportunity to penetrate Yousef's cell in New York.

Failing to Connect with Yousef's Cell in New York City

At one point, Yousef had even offered to introduce Greg Jr.'s "people" to his own "people" in New York and abroad. What did Yousef want in return for this opportunity? A contribution of $2,500 to his "commissary account" at the prison. The Feds had initially funneled $500 into the account via Greg Jr. They routinely spent hundreds of thousands of dollars a year on informants and "buy-bust" money in any number of criminal stings. But when they decided to shut down the Yousef-Scarpa intelligence initiative, they decided it wasn't worth $2,500 to connect with the four New York associates of the man who was about to be convicted of trying to blow up a dozen U.S. jumbo jets.

"That information from Greg Jr. was clearly credible," says Larry Silverman, Greg Scarpa Jr.'s attorney, himself a former federal prosecutor. He says that he first heard the name Osama bin Laden from his client, after Yousef told Greg Jr. the actual identity of the person the bomb maker referred to as "Bojinga" in the FBI 302s.

"This information . . . came forth in stages," adds Silverman. "That proves it was credible. If, at any point in any of the stages, the information that he was providing was inaccurate, the government would have pulled the plug."

Yet back in 1996, despite Yousef's offer to connect the FBI posing as wiseguys with his New York "people," the Feds ignored the tip, even though they encouraged Scarpa to keep feeding them Yousef intelligence all the way through February 1997.[15]

We know from multiple 302s that Patrick Fitzgerald met on several occasions with Scarpa Jr. and his attorney, and that he was a party to all of the intel gathered.[16] Fitzgerald was effectively Cloonan's superior in I-49, the bin Laden squad, and the man credited with having the most comprehensive knowledge of al Qaeda in the Justice Department.[17] Yet Cloonan claims to have had little or no knowledge of the Yousef-Scarpa treasure trove. "It was being handled off in another squad," Cloonan told me.[18]

But that claim didn't ring true with other New York FBI agents working organized crime at the time. "What I can't understand," says one, "is how you can have Fitzie, who's the bin Laden brain, [running the show], and yet guys on his own squad aren't getting the full playbook. 'The wall' doesn't explain that. If guys like Jack Cloonan, who was trying to put together a file on [Ali] Mohamed, was in the dark about what Yousef was giving Scarpa, then you have to ask yourself, Why? We're not talking about not sharing with agents in another office across the country, we're talking about right inside 26 Federal."[19]

The Disconnection of the Dots

It now appears that by the late summer and early fall of 1996 the FBI and Justice Department had gone into a containment mode, with key officials deciding to limit the evidence and affirmatively acting to disconnect certain dots. In some cases Gorelick's "wall memo" became the justification;[20] in others, the containment of intel was more subtle, designed to chill special agents who might otherwise have complained to their superiors about the disconnect.

The message wasn't lost on Nancy Floyd, the agent who had recruited Emad Salem, arguably the most important FBI undercover asset in the war on terror. By 1996, Floyd was in the third year of a four-and-a-half-year OPR investigation, one that had already lasted more than a year longer than the Bureau's probe into Lin DeVecchio. In 1998, she would be found guilty of "insubordination" to Carson Dunbar and suspended for two weeks.[21] It was a clear signal from FBI management to other street agents who might consider taking the initiative in terrorism investigations.

"What they were saying with Nancy was, 'See what happens when you think outside the box,'" says her old mentor, retired Special Agent Len Predtechenskis. "Nancy stuck her neck out and went above and beyond and she got put on the bricks for it. What does that say to other agents?"[22]

Whatever the cause, the compartmentalization of intelligence prevented other counterterrorism agencies, and the oversight committees in Congress, from understanding the true depth of the repeated FBI/DOJ losses against al Qaeda.

From the failure to link Ali Mohamed to the WTC bombing cell in 1989—despite the Calverton surveillance—to the failure to stop Yousef in the fall of 1992; to Gorelick's endorsement of Khalifa's release in 1995 and the escape of KSM in Islamabad; to the Bureau's burial of evidence linking Yousef to the TWA 800 crash; to KSM's second escape from Qatar in 1996, officials of the FBI and DOJ had every interest in hording the intel so that these multiple failures in the terror war would not be exposed. But in containing that intelligence, the FBI and Justice prevented other U.S. intelligence agencies from connecting the dots on Osama bin Laden's network, even as KSM was working to execute his nephew's planes-as-missiles plot.

Meanwhile, with control agents like John Zent seemingly outgunned, and an FBI "informant" like Ali Mohamed studying the Bureau's counterterrorism play book, the al Qaeda leadership was able to get a stark appreciation of their enemy's weaknesses.

25

VICTORY
DECLARED

Still, by their own account, at least, the Feds were on a roll. On September 5, 1996, after back-to-back convictions of the original WTC bombing plotters and the Day of Terror cell, Yousef, Murad, and Wali Khan were found guilty by a jury of eight men and four women in the Bojinka case. As the verdicts resounded in the courtroom, Yousef sat quietly in an open-necked shirt and slacks, a change from his customary lawyer's suit.[1] After the verdict, Murad's attorney complained that the crash of TWA 800 "had an impact on the jury," and was a key factor in the convictions.[2]

The word spread quickly among the Feds. FBI special agent Frank Pellegrino, who had been dispatched to the Philippines within days of the Dona Josefa fire, called his boss, Neil Herman, head of the NYO's Joint Terrorism Task Force. When he got the news, Herman was out in the Calverton, Long Island, hangar where the wreckage of TWA 800 had been assembled.

"It's over," said Pellegrino. "We won. He's been convicted on all counts."

But Patrick Fitzgerald was about to get a gift of new evidence that would make it clear the the Bojinka verdict was a temporary victory.

Earlier in the year, Jamal al-Fadl, a thirty-three-year-old Sudanese national born in Khartoum, had entered a U.S. embassy in Africa and turned himself in after embezzling more than $100,000 from a series of bin Laden's companies.[3]

"Jamal walks in to the RSO [Resident Security Officer] in Eritrea and he talks to the Agency station chief who realizes that he's got the real thing," says Jack Cloonan. "This is not a provocation," or false turncoat. By the time the CIA handed al-Fadl over to the FBI in the fall of 1996, his value as a source was so clear that his identity was kept secret.

First labeled CS-1—"confidential source number one"—al-Fadl soon picked up the nickname "Junior." Patrick Fitzgerald and Special Agent Dan Coleman were so anxious to debrief him that they flew to Germany to meet him. Before they were done, al-Fadl had told them a story that should have dispelled any doubts in Fitzgerald's mind about whether al Qaeda was behind the Trade Center bombers and the Day of Terror plotters, whom "Fitzie" himself had coprosecuted.

It soon became clear that al-Fadl had been a kind of Zelig[4] of terror, showing up at many of the benchmark moments in al Qaeda's history and interacting with all the top players. The young Sudanese said that after high school in Khartoum he had lived the life of a pothead until his roommate got arrested and did two years in prison. In 1986, Jamal took off for America. Drifting through the South, he stopped in Georgia and North Carolina to work on his English. And then, as so many young Islamics did, he found his way to the Alkifah Center at the Al Farooq Mosque on Atlantic Avenue in Brooklyn.

Under the strict fundamentalist guidance of his Imam, Mustafa Shalabi, al-Fadl turned his life around. The Brooklyn Alkifah was then the flagship center of the MAK network for the mujahadeen in America, and al-Fadl quickly got caught up in the cash-rich fund-raising efforts. But soon carrying money for the "brothers" wasn't enough of a challenge to keep Jamal interested so in the late-1980s he headed to Afghanistan. At the Khalid Ibn Walid camp, he spent forty-five days training in the use of automatic weapons, small arms—even RPG-7 grenade launchers.[5]

Then, one night at a guesthouse in Afghanistan, al-Fadl met Osama bin Laden. The Saudi billionaire exhorted him personally to show bravery for the jihad and risk his life against the Soviet infidels. At that point, al-Fadl decided it was time to pick up an AK-47.

Once he'd reached the front lines, al-Fadl found himself commanded by a fierce Uzbeki he knew as Osama Asmurai, the man bin Laden called "the Lion." His other alias was Wali Khan Amin Shah. After advanced training at a series of camps where he learned to build bombs, al-Fadl swore an oath in 1989 to the new terror network that bin Laden and the Egyptians had created from the remains of the MAK. Present with him the night he uttered the *bayat* were two top al Qaeda leaders, Abu Ubaidah al-Banshiri and Mohammed Atef.

Once bin Laden moved to Khartoum with Ali Mohamed's help in 1991, al-Fadl was dispatched there as well. As a Sudanese citizen, he could perform functions for the jihad there that were more difficult for foreigners. For example, Dr. Ayman al-Zawahiri gave him enough cash to buy a farmhouse that would be used for al Qaeda training.

In the months that followed, the multilingual Jamal drew closer to bin Laden's inner circle in Khartoum. He was paid $500 a month—a fortune by Sudanese standards—but by 1992, when Wadih El-Hage came to work with bin Laden, al-Fadl grew jealous that the Lebanese-American convert to Islam was earning more. Al-Fadl had been working as bin Laden's paymaster, but by 1993 he lost even that job to El-Hage, who was rising in importance to al Qaeda's inner circle.

Still, Jamal was privy to the dealings of al Qaeda's *shura*, a kind of fundamentalist board of directors where he witnessed bin Laden's hateful diatribes against America. After U.S. troops had landed in Somalia, al-Fadl remembered Osama saying that they had to cut off the "head of the snake." He also saw how bin Laden collaborated with the blind Sheikh, who was then head of the Islamic Group, and al-Zawahiri, who ran the Egyptian Islamic Jihad—two organizations that were clearly becoming al Qaeda surrogates by that point.

Toward the end of 1993, al-Fadl was given a major assignment. A broker was offering uranium to al Qaeda for a price of U.S. $1.5 million. A key al Qaeda operative named Mohamed Loay Bayazid was brought in to examine the deal, and al-Fadl was tasked to "go in and study" whether the offer was genuine. He concluded that it was, but told the Feds that he was later cut out of the deal.

Not sure if the transaction was ever consummated, al-Fadl grew to resent his living conditions, and soon he began skimming commissions from a series of bin Laden-related businesses, using the money to buy property for his sister and a car for himself. Eventually, after embezzling almost $110,000, he was caught. But rather than face death, the practical-minded al Qaeda leaders told him he would have to repay the money—all of it, half up front and the rest in installments. Jamal begged bin Laden himself for forgiveness, but the Saudi billionaire admonished him and said there would be no absolution without repayment in full.

Unable to come up with anything close to the full amount, al-Fadl decided to run. After fleeing to Syria and Jordan, he eventually found his way to Eritrea and the CIA.

Connecting the Dots Back to Brooklyn

In the fall of 1996, as al-Fadl told his story to Fitzgerald and Coleman, he declared that he was willing to testify in open court if the United States would embrace him.

It was an irresistible offer. Al-Fadl's direct and personal contact with bin Laden, his *shura* council, and al Qaeda's network of training camps and front companies made him terrorism's equivalent to Joseph Valachi, the Mafia's first major "stoolie," who testified before Senate racketeering hearings in the early 1960s.

But in Fitzgerald's efforts to build a case against bin Laden, the thirty-three-year-old Sudanese became even more than that. "Junior" was the one man who could connect all of the dots, from Mustafa Shalabi and the Alkifah Center in 1986 to Mohammed Loay Bayazid, the uranium procurer who had flown into the United States with Mohammed Jamal Khalifa in December 1994. His relationship to Wali Khan, bin Laden's beloved "Lion," underscored the significance of Wali as a key member of Yousef's Manila cell. Al-Fadl knew what acts of terror bin Laden had plotted in the past. He knew where the bank accounts were, and what NGOs al Qaeda was hiding behind. Most important, he understood the through line—the chain of dots that ran from the FBI's Calverton surveillance of Ali Mohamed's cell up through the Kahane murder, the World Trade Center bombing, and the Day of Terror plot. He knew that all those violent acts were the product of a hierarchical network controlled by bin Laden and his Egyptian deputies al-Zawahiri, Rahman, and Atef. This was no loosely organized group; it was as tightly run as a Panzer division. Fitzgerald might chose to call that al Qaeda network a "jihad army," but by the fall of 1996 he knew exactly what it was.

Still, if Squad I-49 had connected the dots in full and published a timeline that other intelligence agencies like the CIA and DIA could have accessed, they would have also documented years of FBI and Justice Department negligence from their shutdown of the 1989 Calverton surveillance, through Carson Dunbar's effective dismissal of Emad Salem before the 1993 WTC bombing, and—perhaps worst of all—the FBI's seeming inability to appreciate the threat posed by Ali Mohamed, the Bureau informant who was an al Qaeda spy.

As Jack Cloonan put it to me, in a vast understatement, "Junior's arrival really begins to change the dynamics of this case dramatically. Having a live, walking, talking body; a live, cooperating witnesses is really a great thing."[6]

The Man Who Knew Too Much

Jamal al-Fadl, aka CS-1, should indeed have been "a great thing" for the FBI and the SDNY prosecutors. But he also presented a new problem for Patrick Fitzgerald. Al-Fadl's story proved bin Laden's personal ties to both Shalabi and Wali Khan, Yousef's Manila cohort (now convicted in the Bojinka case). Once those ties were made public, it would be impossible for Fitzgerald to deny that bin Laden was the puppetmaster behind both of Ramzi Yousef's cells. Between his corroboration of the blind Sheikh's importance to al Qaeda and his testimony tying Khalifa's traveling companion Bayazid to the top shelf of al Qaeda operatives, there were just too many tight connections and too few players for any investigator to claim that the New York and Manila cells were "loosely organized" or independent of bin Laden's reach.

Ramzi Yousef was the one operative who united those two cells, and his uncle Khalid Shaikh Mohammed was still on the loose.

By the fall of 1996, Patrick Fitzgerald had a choice. He could continue to ignore the evidence that documented the history of Bureau and DOJ failures, or he could use al-Fadl to string them together in a once-and-for-all honest assessment of al Qaeda's victories against the United States and its threat to America in the future.

But as Patrick Fitzgerald must have known, that would have meant bucking James Kallstrom, Jamie Gorelick, and Valerie Caproni, chief of the EDNY's Criminal Division. Caproni was counting on the denigration of Greg Scarpa Jr. and the exoneration of SSA Lin DeVecchio to keep those sixty Colombo war cases alive. Caproni had been a party to the "Scarpa material," as the Feds would later call it. So had Dietrich Snell, who prosecuted Yousef, and Ellen Corcella, who wrote the May 8, 1995, letter documenting DeVecchio's leaks. Even Howard Leadbetter II, one of the three FBI agents who had first accused DeVecchio, was aware of Scarpa's eleven-month intelligence initiative in the MCC. Fitzgerald, Caproni, Snell, Corcella, and Leadbetter were all present at a session on March 7, 1996, documented in an FBI 302 (see Appendix VI on page 554).

As the head of the SDNY's Organized Crime and Terrorism Unit, Patrick Fitzgerald knew exactly how the wiseguy could rip open the dark underside of the DeVecchio scandal. And that was too great a risk for him to take.

The Company Line

At some point in that fall of 1996, despite getting chapter and verse from al-Fadl on the true connections between al Qaeda and Yousef's two cells, Fitzgerald chose to go with the company line. He would acquiesce to a decision that would soon dismiss the critical Yousef-Scarpa Jr. intelligence cache as a fabrication. He would support the closing of the DeVecchio OPR. Even though AUSA Ellen Corcella had listed eight nuggets of FBI intel that DeVecchio may have leaked to Scarpa Sr., "Mr. Organized Crime" was allowed to retire with a full pension.

Finally, when Greg Jr. came up for trial, the Feds would throw the book at him.

David Kelly, the assistant U.S. attorney who was Fitzgerald's partner in 1995 as chief of the SDNY's Organized Crime and Terrorism Unit, would use a mob snitch to claim that Scarpa Jr. and Yousef had concocted all of that intel. Fitzgerald would go along with that story as well. Even a top bin Laden unit subordinate like Jack Cloonan would claim that he knew of the 302s from Yousef via Scarpa Jr. "only in passing."

It didn't seem to matter that those FBI 302s had documented death threats made by the terrorist to Greg Jr. and his family, or that the wiseguy had risked his life for eleven months to "rat out" Yousef and his "people" in New York.

To make this rewrite of history work, Yousef had to be minimized as well. So Fitzgerald would perpetrate the fiction that al Qaeda wasn't behind Yousef's cell in New York. As late as 2005, for that National Geographic documentary on 9/11, he would deny with a straight face al Qaeda's role in the Trade Center bombing and Day of Terror plot.

"People assume that the World Trade Center bombing was an al Qaeda operation," he said. "I've never assumed that the World Trade Center bombing is an al Qaeda operation. What I would say is, we learned that the World Trade Center bombing and the Day of Terror plots where part of a jihad network. I wouldn't necessarily conclude that that was al Qaeda."[7]

The FBI/DOJ cover story that Fitzgerald endorsed also appears in the 9/11 Commission's final report, which holds that the cell responsible for the Kahane murder and the WTC bombing was part of a "loose network of extremist Sunni Islamists" not directly affiliated with al Qaeda at the time of the 1993 bombing or the Bojinka plot in 1995. That same school of thought also holds that Yousef's uncle Khalid Shaikh Mohammed didn't even join al Qaeda until 1998.[8]

That fiction, which Fitzgerald and other DOJ officials perpetrated through the 9/11 Commission hearings and beyond, allowed the FBI and prosecutors in the SDNY deniability, insulating themselves from the charge that they were negligent in ignoring Emad Salem's advice and not stopping the first attack on the World Trade Center in 1993. Further, by removing Ramzi Yousef from the planes-as-missiles operation, pushing the plot forward several years and making it the exclusive creation of KSM, they removed DOJ officials like Jamie Gorelick—herself a 9/11 Commissioner—from culpability for supporting the extradition of the Manila cell's financier, Mohammed Jamal Khalifa.

As we'll see, the hypocrisy in this practice was particularly pronounced for Fitzgerald, who, as U.S. attorney for the Northern District of Illinois, announced the indictment a year after 9/11 of Enaam M. Arnaout, who was charged with providing "material support for al Qaeda" via the Benevolence International Foundation, a bin Laden-affiliated NGO with offices near Chicago.[9] The thirty-six-page affidavit by FBI agent Robert Walker in support of Arnout's indictment reads like a road map tying bin Laden to Sheikh Rahman and Ramzi Yousef via his brother-in-law, Mohammed Jamal Khalifa.[10] Using Jamal al-Fadl as an unnamed principal witness, the affidavit follows al Qaeda's trail back to the mid-1980s, when Arnaout worked for the MAK/Services Office Network, which morphed into al Qaeda after the death of Abdullah Azzam in November 1999. The affidavit from Fitzgerald's own office offers detailed evidence of the direct links between bin Laden, al Qaeda, and the Yousef cells in both New York and Manila. And yet, three years after issuing that indictment, Fitzgerald refused to tie al Qaeda to the World Trade Center bombing.

But Fitzgerald's deniability was never more pronounced than in his dealings with Ali Mohamed. As we'll see, by ignoring or mishandling key intelligence picked up by their own unit, Fitzgerald and company would miss the next massive attack on U.S. interests—the plot Ali Mohamed had set in motion five years earlier in Kenya.

26

TAPPING
THE CELL

History—even contemporary history—is inherently retrospective. Retracing the steps that led to an act of terror after the fact is a far simpler prospect than the challenge of *preventing* the event in the first instance. Even so, there is a startling body of evidence to suggest that, by 1997, the FBI's elite bin Laden squad knew enough, that it should have prevented the African embassy bombings the following year.

First, consider the fact that it was the FBI's own U.S.-based informant who helped pave the way for bin Laden's East African initiative in the first place. By his own admission, Ali Mohamed had "assisted al Qaeda in creating a presence in Nairobi, Kenya, by the early 1990s"[1]—that according to Ali's own sworn plea session. One of his principal cell members in Nairobi was Wadih El-Hage, who created a charity called Help Africa People as an al Qaeda front.[2] A car business was set up by Ali Mohamed to generate income. At El-Hage's house Ali rendezvoused with the same two al Qaeda leaders who had witnessed Jamal al Fadl's *bayat,* Abu Ubaidah and Mohammed Atef.[3]

By 1992, Ali Mohamed had become an informant for FBI agents on the West Coast.[4] A year later he confessed to them that he was training al Qaeda operatives in the Sudan, and that bin Laden sought the overthrow of the Saudi government.[5] After being captured and detained in 1993 by the Canadian Mounties, Mohamed was freed because Special Agent John Zent vouched for him. Months later he returned to Nairobi, where he and Anas al Liby conducted photographic surveillance of the U.S. embassy.[6]

In 1994, Ali traveled to Khartoum, where he showed the pictures he'd developed himself to bin Laden, Ubaidah, and Atef. By Mohamed's own account, "Bin Laden looked at the picture of the American embassy and pointed to where a truck could go as a suicide bomber."[7] Late in 1994, on another stopover at El-Hage's Nairobi house, Mohamed was summoned back by the Feds to California, where he told Assistant U.S. Attorney Andrew McCarthy and FBI agent Harlan Bell that he was merely running a scuba diving business.[8]

Though he was listed by McCarthy as an unindicted coconspirator in the Day of Terror case, Ali Mohamed never testified—despite the strenuous efforts of defense attorney Roger Stavis, who had subpoenaed him.

In March 1995, Mohamed obtained a copy of the list of 172 unindicted coconspirators, which included the names of bin Laden and his brother-in-law Mohammed Jamal Khalifa, and sent the list to bin Laden via Wadih El-Hage.[9] That connection should have become crucially important to Squad I-49. Why? Because by the late spring of 1996, the Feds had learned of the existence of a Kenya cell tied to bin Laden. Beginning in August, the U.S. intelligence community established wiretaps on the phones of five cell members, including the one El-Hage had used for calls to bin Laden himself.[10] Within months, the U.S. attorney's office for the SDNY had empanelled a grand jury to investigate bin Laden and his involvement with al Qaeda.[11]

Through the phone calls they intercepted, the Feds learned that El-Hage and his deputy, Harun Fazhul, were providing false passports and travel documents to al Qaeda associates in Azerbaijan and Sudan; passing coded messages to al Qaeda members in countries ranging from Afghanistan, Egypt, and Yemen, to Italy, Germany, England, and the United States; and warning associates when they were compromised by the authorities.[12]

Two of the wiretaps were on El-Hage's home and business[13]—during a period in 1996 when Ali Mohamed was in regular contact with El-Hage.

By then the FBI's 134 classified intelligence case, first opened on Ali Mohamed, had long since been converted to a 237 criminal investigative case.[14] By 1996, as a senior investigator in Patrick Fitzgerald's bin Laden squad, Special Agent Jack Cloonan began to "data mine" and "amass information on Ali Mohamed." By his own account, the process took him back to Ali's tenure at Fort Bragg between 1987 and 1989, and documented his training of the cell members responsible for the Kahane assassination and the World Trade Center bombing.

Fitzgerald now began looking at Osama bin Laden in the context of an organized crime investigation, developing what Cloonan calls "a RICO concept" of a "criminal enterprise."

Prosecuting al Qaeda Like the Mob

The Racketeer Influenced and Corrupt Organization Act (RICO), passed by Congress in 1970, allowed federal prosecutors to "combine related offenses" in a prosecution "which would otherwise have to be prosecuted separately in different jurisdictions."[15] For an assistant U.S. attorney like Fitzgerald, who had cut his teeth on mob prosecutions, RICO gave him sufficient reach to go after a worldwide criminal "enterprise"—like al Qaeda.

With al Qaeda, "you've got multiple acts, multiple personalities" all acting in concert, says Cloonan. "So Fitzgerald decided to treat this as if it was an O.C. [organized crime] type of case." That's when Cloonan began to ask the $64,000 question: "When you start going back and piecing this stuff together, you're beginning to say to yourself, 'How is it that Ali, who comes up in these cases—why isn't he off the street someplace?'"

At that juncture in 1996, given Mohamed's 1993 admission that he had trained al Qaeda operatives in Afghanistan and the Sudan, in addition to the evidence that he had trained Nosair, Abouhalima, Salameh, and other members of the WTC bombing cell, the Feds had more than enough probable cause to seek a RICO indictment against him.

Moreover, by the end of 1996, they had debriefed Jamal al-Fadl, who'd strung the al Qaeda dots together all the way back to the death of his murdered boss Mustafa Shalabi and the Alkifah Center. Al-Fadl tied bin Laden's terror network to Yousef's Manila cell through Wali Khan, and to the Kenyan bombing cell through Wadih El-Hage. And the Feds knew that Mohamed was in regular contact with El-Hage, who had taken over for al-Fadl as bin Laden's paymaster in Khartoum.

Why, at this point, didn't Patrick Fitzgerald write up an arrest warrant for Ali Mohamed, who was back in California and subject to arrest?

That's another question I wanted to put to Fitzgerald. But he refused to talk to me for this book, as did Special Agent Dan Coleman, who might know the answer himself. To use an organized crime term, Mohamed was clearly part of the Nairobi "enterprise." Why did Fitzgerald and company allow him to remain at large, where he could continue to "wreak havoc" for the jihad?

New Blood but Old Thinking

The chances of linking al Qaeda to the Yousef-KSM Manila cell theoretically improved with the addition of FBI special agent Frank Pellegrino to the bin Laden squad. Pellegrino was the agent who arrived at Camp Crame in early January 1995 while Abdul Hakim Murad was being interrogated by Col. Rodolfo Mendoza. He was one of the two agents cited in the April 20, 1995, FBI 302 memo documenting how Murad had taken credit for the Oklahoma City bombing on behalf of Yousef's "Liberation Army" cell, and he had specific knowledge of the sealed indictment that had been handed down in January on Khalid Shaikh Mohammed, Yousef's fugitive uncle.

Pellegrino was an agent who could tie Ramzi Yousef to the al Qaeda "enterprise." But he was also the FBI investigator who had made the premature declaration "We won!" after Yousef's Bojinka conviction. During his testimony at the trial in August 1996, the *New York Times* reported that "The government's case . . . experienced a potential setback" due to the notes Pellegrino had kept on his interrogation of Wali Khan.[16] Years later, Pellegrino would fail to connect a key player in the Yousef-KSM Manila cell to a 9/11 planning session attended by two of the hijackers in Malaysia.[17]

In short, Frank Pellegrino's judgment was not unimpeachable.

By February 1997, however, the agents of Squad I-49 didn't need any extra help assessing the case that was unfolding before them. By now they were literally picking up Wadih El-Hage's phone calls to top al Qaeda commanders like Mohammed Atef.[18] The FBI even monitored a call by El-Hage's assistant Harun, who reported that his boss was visiting bin Laden in Afghanistan. During that meeting, the Feds learned, the Saudi billionaire told El-Hage to "militarize" the East African cells.

If the I-49 agents still believed that El-Hage and company were merely selling cars in Kenya, that one intercepted call should have set them straight.[19]

Then they got another Ali Mohamed-related hit.

On February 26, the Feds intercepted a call between El-Hage's mobile phone in Kenya and Ihab Ali, aka Nawawi, the Florida cabdriver Ali Mohamed had trusted to help move bin Laden to Khartoum in 1991. A later intercepted call contained a warning: "Be careful about possible apprehension by American authorities."

This was additional evidence tying Ali Mohamed to the "enterprise," since he had called that same cell phone in 1994.[20]

Nawawi's presence on the FBI's radar should have alerted the Feds that a much bigger al Qaeda plot was looming in the background. Nawawi was the pilot who had trained at the same flight school in Norman, Oklahoma, that two of the 9/11 hijackers would later visit. But in 1996 nobody in the FBI's NYO was looking at flight schools—even though FBI asset Harry Ellen had warned his control agent, Ken Williams, to investigate a suspicious pilot at a training center in Phoenix.[21]

Danger in Nairobi

In the months to come, there would be three specific and very credible warnings that the U.S. embassy in Nairobi was in danger. The first came that summer, when an informant turned over to the CIA warned that operatives in the Nairobi office of the Al-Haramain Foundation (a Saudi-based NGO) were plotting to blow up the U.S. embassy.

According to a riveting account of the investigation by James Risen of the *New York Times,* the Agency took the threat seriously enough to dispatch a counterterrorist team to Kenya, where the local police, to their credit, arrested nine Arabs connected to the Foundation. After examining Al-Haramain's files and finding no evidence of the plot, the team members from Langley asked to question the suspects.[22]

But the CIA station chief, described by Risen as "a career analyst" with a "lack of field experience," refused to ask the Kenyan authorities for access to the arrestees, and CIA headquarters decided not to buck him.

Later, U.S. Ambassador Prudence Bushnell was assured that the threat had ended with the arrests. Not until January 2004, twenty-eight months after 9/11, did the U.S. State Department realize the gravity of the Feds' error and move to block the assets of the Al-Haramain foundation in Kenya because of the group's ties to al Qaeda.[23]

The next warning came in August 1997, when Dan Coleman, the bin Laden squad's man at Alec Station, conducted a search of Wadih El-Hage's house at 1523 Fedha Estates in Nairobi. Coleman was known as "the professor" for his reputed knowledge of al Qaeda. In the course of the search, which was done in the presence of El-Hage, his wife, and children, he seized El-Hage's Macintosh Powerbook 140 computer and various address books. One of them contained Osama bin Laden's satellite phone number, but the eureka moment came when Coleman turned up the home and business contact information for Ali Mohamed.

"Bang. That should have been it," said one former FBI agent from the NYO who has analyzed some of the evidence gathered while researching this book. "What other proof do you need of a nexus between a U.S. citizen who has worked as a Bureau informant and one of the key leaders of the embassy bombing cell? What the hell were they waiting for?"

Ali's Ultimate Confession

By the fall of 1997, despite their penetration of the Nairobi cell, Fitzgerald and his agents in the bin Laden squad still seemed incapable of linking the dots, and their frustration was building. They had to decide whether to bust Mohamed or to try and turn him. Perhaps, as a measure of Fitzgerald's ego, he chose the latter strategy, arranging to meet the al Qaeda spy face-to-face. In October he flew to Sacramento, where Mohamed had moved with his wife Linda Sanchez. With him were Special Agents Jack Cloonan and Harlan Bell.

Rather than handing Ali an arrest warrant, Fitzgerald offered to buy him dinner. Until now, the full details of that extraordinary summit between the Justice Department's top bin Laden hunter and bin Laden's chief protector have never been told.

Cloonan, who was present, describes what happened.

"The purpose in us going to meet Ali at that point in time is that we wanted to gain his cooperation," he says. "We knew of his long history having been connected to al Qaeda, and what we desperately wanted was to convince Ali Mohamed to cooperate with us that night."[24]

When Ali sat down at that table, says Cloonan, "he refused to eat anything. The whole session lasted several hours.[25] Although it started rather cautiously, we started to ask a few questions. At that point we were doing the proverbial kabuki dance about who was going to get over on who, and exactly how far Ali could go, and how we could push him. He was assessing us at the same time."

But Ali Mohamed, the master spy who was confident enough that he'd once told Special Agent John Zent that he was training al Qaeda operatives in antihijacking methods, didn't flinch. In fact, as the dinner went on, he got bolder.

Ali admitted that he had trained bin Laden's bodyguards in the Sudan back in 1994, after assassins tried unsuccessfully to take bin Laden down. While the Sudanese intelligence service, the Mukhabarat, had provided perimeter security for the "Haj," a code name for bin Laden, Mohamed said that *he* had trained the jihadis guarding bin Laden's inner sanctum, and proudly boasted that he lived in Osama's house during this period.

He also confessed that he'd been in Somalia during the intervention by U.S. troops that eventually led to the notorious downing of the two Black Hawk helicopters in 1993. Ali even admitted that "bin Laden's people were responsible" for the killing of U.S. soldiers there.

Seemingly unconcerned about the consequences of his confession, Ali admitted to moving bin Laden from Afghanistan to Khartoum by way of Pakistan and India in 1991—another coconspirator admission that could have provided probable cause for a RICO arrest warrant. Just seven months earlier, in March, bin Laden had told reporter Peter Arnett on CNN that he had "declared jihad against the U.S. government because the U.S. government is unjust, criminal, and tyrannical."[26] Now, FBI informant Ali Mohamed, a naturalized U.S. citizen honorably discharged from the U.S. Army, was telling Patrick Fitzgerald that he "loved" bin Laden and "believe[d] in him."

Then, Ali crossed the line and uttered words that amounted to treason. He told Fitzgerald that he didn't need a *fatwa* or religious edict to make war on the United States, since it was "obvious" that America was "the enemy." With that admission, Mohamed echoed his videotaped statement recorded a decade earlier at Fort Bragg when he said that it was his *duty* as a Muslim "to change *darl ul harp* to *dar ul Islam* and establish Islamic law" in any country he was in.

"It's an obligation. It's not a choice," he'd said.

In 1995, Fitzgerald had convicted Sheikh Omar Abdel Rahman and his "jihad army" on charges of "seditious conspiracy." What further proof did Feds like Fitzgerald, Cloonan, and Bell need than this unqualified endorsement of the terrorist leader who wanted to cut off the "head" of the American "snake?"

The Feds sat there for a moment, stunned. Then, eyeing Fitzgerald across the table, Mohamed made an audacious announcement.

"He said that he was in touch with hundreds of people he could call on in a moment's notice that could be, quote, 'operational.' and wage jihad against the United States," says Cloonan. "Very brazenly, he said, 'I can get out anytime and you'll never find me. I've got a whole network. You'll never find me.'"

That was Mohamed's answer. There was no way he was going to betray the jihad to these hapless Feds. Finally, he got up and left.

"He gave us the impression that he was sitting on potentially a powder keg," says Cloonan who was so shaken that when he got back to his hotel room he actually drew his gun, thinking that Ali might be waiting for him inside.

"I was very, very nervous," he says. "I was thinking, 'Oh my God, Ali is in here or something.' So I literally bladed the door open and I took my gun out and I started to enter the room with my gun pulled out in a defensive position. [Then] lo and behold, I started to open the door and, of course, there was a big mirror on the door and the next thing I know I'm confronted with myself pointing a gun. I jumped about ten feet."[27]

That comic moment, however, didn't last long for Cloonan. That night after his face-to-face encounter with Ali, Patrick Fitzgerald turned to Cloonan and said, "This is the most dangerous man I have ever met. We cannot let this man out on the street."

But that's just what he did. Patrick Fitzgerald allowed Ali Mohamed to go free—although he did hedge his bets. On the off-chance that he couldn't get Mohamed to rat, Fitzgerald had obtained FISA warrants to tap the phone in Ali's Sacramento home and to bug his computer.

"The Sacramento [FBI] office did a wonderful job of getting into his apartment, wiring it up, and exploiting his computer," says Cloonan. "So we were able to download a lot of stuff."

That stunning revelation, published here for the first time in print, raises an even bigger question: If Fitzgerald and the agents in his bin Laden squad now had access to Mohamed's phone and hard disk, why didn't they come to understand his role as a key player in the embassy bombing plot?

After his arrogant rejection of their offer to cooperate, why did they leave him alone? If their motive was to lie in wait—to monitor his phone calls and e-mail traffic—why didn't that surveillance put them right in the middle of the embassy plot? After all, Ali was one of its key operatives.

In the fall of 1997, five years after he first went to work as a sham FBI informant and eight years after he trained the World Trade Center bombing cell, why didn't Fitzgerald and company drop the hammer on Ali Mohamed?

Could Fitzgerald's reluctance have had anything to do with the realization that Ali's arrest and subsequent cross-examination by defense attorneys would expose the FBI to ridicule? Just as coprosecutor Andrew McCarthy wanted to keep Ali off the stand in the Day of Terror trial, Fitzgerald may have reasoned that any indictment of al Qaeda's chief spy would rip the lid off years of gross negligence by three of America's top intelligence agencies, shining a light on the CIA, the DIA, and, in particular the Bureau, whose agents on both coasts seemed to wink at Ali as he ate their lunch for years.

The Southern District Feds like Fitzgerald and Dietrich Snell (who coprosecuted Yousef in the Bojinka case) insisted instead that the terrorists who threatened New York were a "loose" amalgam of "Sunni Islamists,"[28] and, thus, by implication, difficult to track. But in truth, as Jamal al-Fadl had already documented for Fitzgerald and Coleman, the universe of key al Qaeda operatives who had come to wage war against America was very small. In 1997 there were just over two dozen key players on the list—half of them Egyptian:

Mustafa Shalabi	Egyptian	Ramzi Yousef	Baluchi
Omar Abdel Rahman	Egyptian	Khalid Shaikh Mohammed	Baluchi
Ayman al-Zawahiri	Egyptian	Abdul Hakim Murad	Baluchi
Osama bin Laden	Saudi	Wali Khan Amin Shah	Uzbeki
Mohammed Atef	Egyptian	Mohammed Jamal Khalifa	Saudi
Abu Ubaidah	Egyptian	Riduan Isamuddin (Hambali)	Indonesian
El Sayyid Nosair	Egyptian	Wadih El-Hage	Lebanese
Mahmud Abouhalima	Egyptian	Ihab Ali	Egyptian
Mohammed Salameh	Palestinian	Anas Al-Liby	Libyan
Nidal Ayyad	Kuwaiti	Essen Marzouk	Egyptian
Clement Rodney Hampton-El	American	Abdel Sattar	Egyptian
Ibrahim El-Gabrowny	Egyptian	Khalid Dahab	Egyptian
Jamal al-Fadl	Sudanese	Ali Mohamed	Egyptian

Those same figures had shown up on the FBI's radar time and time again since the Calverton surveillance of 1989, and yet they had repeatedly outflanked the best and the brightest in the SDNY and the FBI's NYO. Ali Mohamed was the metaphorical "Kevin Bacon," who enjoyed no more than one or two degrees of separation from any of them. Five years after he became an FBI informant, Squad I-49 had compiled a dossier on Mohamed that would make any spymaster's head spin. Patrick Fitzgerald had a grand jury empanelled; under RICO he could easily have found probable cause for an arrest warrant. But in the fall of 1997 he left Ali on the street, a move that would soon prove fatal in Africa.

The East African "Target"

After the Sacramento dinner, FBI agent Harlan Bell, the Squad I-49 investigator who had met Mohamed in late 1994 with AUSA McCarthy, began recording his phone calls with Ali. Bell didn't make the connection at the time, but later, after the bombing, he replayed one of their taped conversations and his jaw almost hit the ground.

"It became apparent from listening to one of those tapes that Ali was talking about a possible target in East Africa," says Cloonan.[29] "He never specifically said the embassy or that he knew that an attack was imminent, but he was giving this up in a sense *before* the attack took place."

Still, not only did the Feds allow Ali Mohamed to remain free, they permitted El-Hage to exit Kenya—thinking that if they endorsed Wadih's exit to New York, they might induce him to flip. It was a replay of the same kind of naiveté shown by Special Agent John Anticev and Det. Lou Napoli of the JTTF, who thought they could get Abouhalima, Sattar, El-Gabrowny, and that cadre of other Egyptians to turn after they hauled them down to 26 Federal Plaza in the fall of 1992.

Now, five years later, accompanied by his wife and seven children, El-Hage left Nairobi. But when he got in front of a grand jury in Manhattan, he simply lied. Even though his al Qaeda ties to New York dated back to the Shalabi murder and beyond; even though he'd bought guns for one of Ali Mohamed's trainees and visited another one after the Kahane murder; even though he had worked as bin Laden's personal secretary, El-Hage too was allowed to walk at the time. He traveled to Arlington, Texas, where he began operating a tire shop in a middle-class neighborhood and biding his time.

Despite their penetration of the Nairobi cell, Fitzgerald and his agents in the bin Laden squad still seemed incapable of linking the dots.

A Second Conviction for Yousef

But a few weeks later, the Feds were gloating. Ramzi Yousef was found guilty again, this time for masterminding the World Trade Center bombing plot.

A number of agents in the FBI's NYO, the bin Laden office of origin, now believed they had reached a point of closure in the long battle with al Qaeda. But by mid-November the viability of al Qaeda and its affiliate groups would be demonstrated, with fatal results.

Sheikh Rahman, Ali Mohamed's spiritual *mufti,* had been imprisoned since the summer of 1993. But more than four years later, the vicious massacre at the Luxor ruins in Egypt was committed in his name. On November 16, four days after Yousef's conviction, six assassins surrounded fifty-eight tourists at the Luxor site and began shooting and stabbing them. The group responsible was the al Qaeda-related al Gamma'a Islamiyah (IG), which the Sheikh had led for more than a decade. John Anticev and Lou Napoli had discovered that El Sayyid Nosair was an IG member as early as 1991. Abdel Sattar, the Egyptian-American postal worker who was on the Sheikh's arm during the siege of his Brooklyn mosque back in 1993, was a senior IG leader, and passed death pronouncements from the Sheikh to IG operatives in Egypt from his home on Staten Island, using it as a communications hub for al Qaeda just as Khalid Dahab had done in Santa Clara.

Now in Luxor, as horrified forensic investigators combed over the bodies, they came upon three generations of a British family: Katrina Turner, a young British Airways flight attendant, with her mother and five-year-old daughter. Most of the victims' bodies had been slit open—and inserted into the wounds were leaflets calling for the release of Sheikh Rahman.

If the Feds ever needed a reminder of how vicious al Qaeda could be, it was Luxor. Rather than winding down with Yousef's conviction, bin Laden's jihad against the West was now escalating. And despite another specific warning, the Feds couldn't seem to stop the next devastating act of terror to date—the bombings set in motion by Ali Mohamed himself.

27

THIRD AND
FINAL WARNING

B y now, the importance of Egyptians to the al Qaeda hierarchy was
clear. If Sheikh Rahman, Dr. Ayman al-Zawahiri, and Mohammed
Atef hadn't supported bin Laden's takeover of the MAK network after the
murder of Abdullah Azzam in 1989, there might never have *been* an al
Qaeda—at least not in the lethal configuration into which it evolved.
Emad Salem proved to the FBI in 1991 that it took an Egyptian to get inside the cell trained by Ali Mohamed, himself an alumnus of the Cairo
Military Academy. And now, in November 1997, as the clock ticked down
on bin Laden's suicide truck-bombing plot, it was another Egyptian informant who gave the Feds their final warning.

Mustafa Mahmud Said Ahmed was what the security officers at the
U.S. embassy in Nairobi would call a "walk-in." Like Istaique Parker, the
young South African who entered the embassy in Islamabad in 1995 and
handed up Ramzi Yousef, Ahmed had a shocking story to tell. He warned
the CIA officers that a group was planning to detonate a truck bomb inside the embassy's underground parking garage.

Ahmed had already spoken to the Kenyan police and admitted that he
had taken surveillance photos. He predicted that the upcoming attack

would involve several vehicles and stun grenades.[1] The CIA took the confession seriously enough at first to send reports about Ahmed's warnings to two separate government agencies.[2]

But the Agency reportedly received earlier intelligence that Ahmed was a "fabricator," and certain case officers were inclined to dismiss him as "the terrorist who cried wolf." His threat reporting was eventually discounted, and after being detained for a time, Ahmed was deported. He made his way to Tanzania, where he was eventually arrested for his alleged role in the simultaneous truck bombing at the U.S. embassy in Dar es Salaam that was part of the very same plot.

As time passed, Ambassador Prudence Bushnell was growing more worried. On December 15, 1997, she cabled the State Department, warning that the location of the embassy made it "extremely vulnerable to a terrorist attack," and requesting a new building. Two weeks later, another cable warned that "the embassy's security profile . . . is cause for serious concern."[3] As *New York Times* reporter James Risen reported, "Ms. Bushnell's increasingly insistent demands for a new embassy were so far out of step with the State Department's plans that officials at headquarters were beginning to see her as a nuisance who was obsessed by security, according to one official familiar with the matter."

But as it turned out, Bushnell's concerns were dead-on. In early January 1998, the CIA's deputy station chief was mugged near the embassy compound; and officials also uncovered a plot to kill Ambassador Bushnell herself.[4]

General John Zinni, then commander of the U.S. Central Command, had visited Nairobi, and he agreed with Bushnell's assessment. He sent a cable to the State Department warning that the embassy was vulnerable, and offered to send a team of specialists to harden the embassy grounds and make it a more difficult target for terrorists.

State rejected his offer as well.

It's unclear whether Ambassador Bushnell's concern was communicated to Patrick Fitzgerald or the agents of I-49, though clearly Special Agent Dan Coleman, the FBI's man at Alec Station, should have had access to the two prior warnings received by the CIA involving Mustafa Ahmed and Al-Haramain. Given Coleman's search of Wadih El-Hage's computer files, which documented the presence of a cell tied to the "Haj," it's difficult to understand why the possibility of a plot threatening the embassy had not yet reached critical mass in the bin Laden squad.

Meanwhile, on January 18, 1998, Ihab Ali, aka Nawawi, the Egyptian cab driver who had crash-landed Osama bin Laden's Sabre-40 jet in 1994, got wind that the FBI had interviewed Wadih El-Hage. So he sent a warning letter to Ali Mohamed[5] asking him to give his "best regards to your friend Osama."

The letter prompted Ali to call El-Hage in Arlington, Texas.

The Feds had tapped multiple phone calls between Ihab in Orlando and El-Hage's house in Kenya between April 1996 and February 1997.[6] Since the fall of 1997, they'd also had a tap on Ali Mohamed's phone in Sacramento. And yet with all of the traffic between these key al Qaeda operatives—one in California, one in Texas, one in Florida, each a naturalized U.S. citizen—Fitzgerald's squad seemed clueless about what was about to go down in Nairobi.

Then, in the first week in January, Fitzgerald's boss in the SDNY, U.S. Attorney Mary Jo White, had another pressing issue to deal with: how to inform the media about an indictment about to be unsealed involving Khalid Shaikh Mohammed, the al Qaeda leader who had twice eluded the FBI.

The KSM Reveal

By now, Ramzi Yousef had been convicted twice by SDNY prosecutors, but his uncle KSM was still at large and working to perfect the planes-as-missiles plot his nephew had set in motion in 1994.

Unlike Yousef, who was brought to ground via the very public Rewards for Justice program, KSM had become a phantom fugitive. Though the SDNY charged him in January 1996, they kept the indictment sealed from the press and public. Few people, outside the limited confines of the U.S. Justice Department or al Qaeda, knew he was the uncle of Ramzi Yousef, the terrorist who had masterminded the WTC bombing and the Bojinka plot.

On January 8, Yousef was about to be sentenced by Judge Kevin Duffy, who had presided over both of his trials as well as the 1994 proceeding that convicted Abouhalima, Salameh, and Yousef's traveling companion, Mohamed Ajaj.

Naturally, a barrage of publicity would accompany Yousef's last public moments—and it was behind the smokescreen of attention created by that courtroom event, that the SDNY unsealed the indictment of KSM.

Ever conscious of his media image, Yousef appeared for the sentencing in a dark gray suit with a new growth of beard. He had made another motion for a mistrial in the Bojinka case, but Duffy, a tough Bronx Irishman, turned him down. Then he loomed over the bench and delivered a line that is now famous: "You are an apostle of evil," declared the Judge, a devout Catholic.[7] "Your god is not Allah. Our system of justice has not often seen the type of horrendous crimes for which you stand convicted."

Then, announcing that Yousef's "evil" needed to be "quarantined," Judge Duffy slammed down his gavel. He imposed a sentence of 240 years—the combined ages of the six WTC victims. Yousef would serve out the term in solitary confinement at the ADX Florence, the notorious prison in Florence, Colorado, known as Supermax.[8]

But Yousef was defiant to the end. "Yes, I am a terrorist and I am proud of it," he snapped back. "And I support terrorism so long as it was against the United States government and against Israel, because you are more than terrorists. . . . You are butchers, liars, and hypocrites."[9]

That quote, which embodied Yousef's audacity, ran as the lead sentence in a page-one *New York Times* story the next day.[10] Under the headline, "Mastermind Gets Life for Bombing of Trade Center," the story featured celebratory quotes from U.S. Attorney Mary Jo White and Mayor Rudolph W. Giuliani, the ex-SDNY prosecutor who declared that the sentencing "sends a clear message to the world: the United States will vigorously prosecute and punish those who murder and maim the innocent."

But almost buried in the piece, on the inside "jump" page, were these two paragraphs:

TIMELINE
PART I

01 • October 6, 1981 (page 7)

Egyptian president **Anwar Sadat** is assassinated by radical army

Sadat assassination

troops loyal to the Egyptian Islamic Jihad. One EIJ member associated with the unit that killed Sadat is Major **Ali Abdel Saoud Mohamed**. His alibi at the time is that he is on an officer exchange program studying at the JFK Special Warfare Center at Fort Bragg, North Carolina, where Green Beret and Delta Force officers receive advanced training.

Mohamed

02 • 1981 (page 9)

One of more than three hundred radicals jailed for the assassination is young surgeon **Ayman al-Zawahiri**. The English-speaking son of a prominent Egyptian family, al-Zawahiri emerges as the spokesman for the EIJ suspects and becomes a celebrity in the growing ranks of radical Islam.

al-Zawahiri in 1981

03 • April 18, 1983 (page 13)

The U.S. embassy in Beirut is bombed, killing 63, including 17 Americans. On October 23, suicide truck bombers hit the **U.S. Marine barracks** and a French garrison—321 die. Hezbollah takes credit for all three attacks. The following March 16, Hezbollah operatives kidnap the CIA's Beirut station chief, William Buckley. He's tortured and held captive for more than a year before his execution in mid-1985.

Marine barracks

04 • 1984 (page 16)

Forced out of the Egyptian army for his radical views, **Ali Mohamed** is assigned by al-Zawahiri to learn how to hijack airliners for the EIJ. He takes a job as "security advisor" with Egyptair, the state airline. After Buckley's kidnapping, desperate to get human intelligence (HUMINT) inside Hezbollah, the CIA's Hamburg station recruits Mohamed to infiltrate a Shiite mosque. Later, the Agency alleges that Mohamed blows his cover, causing CIA to cut their ties with him. But some analysts believe Mohamed maintains his CIA ties.

Mohamed

05 • September 6, 1985 (page 23)

Flying TWA from Athens to JFK airport in New York, Mohamed slips past a State Department Watch List, a fact that will later bolster suspicions about ongoing links to the CIA. On the flight he meets Linda Lee Sanchez, a 43-year-old medical technician from Santa Clara, California. Six weeks later they're married at the **Chapel of the Bells** in Reno, Nevada.

Chapel of the Bells

06 • 1986 (page xvi)

FDNY firefighter **Ronnie Bucca** falls five stories during a rescue attempt at a burning West Side tenement. He breaks his back and is not expected to live, but Bucca, an ex-Green Beret paratrooper, vows to return to Rescue One, the "special forces" of the FDNY. A year later, he qualifies back into the company.

Ronnie Bucca

07 • 1986 (page 30)

Ali Mohamed moves into Linda Sanchez's home in **Santa Clara,** California. From there he recruits **Khalid Dahab**, a former Egyptian medical student who enters the U.S. on a student visa. Together they set up a "sleeper cell" of at least ten Islamic radicals. Dahab uses his one-bedroom apartment as an al Qaeda communications hub. His al Qaeda brothers refer to Mohamed as Ali Amiriki, "Ali the American."

Santa Clara home

Dahab

08 • August 15, 1986 (page 34)

Ali Mohamed enlists in the U.S. Army at Oakland, California. After basic training he is transferred to the JFK Special Warfare Center at Fort Bragg. **Lt. Col. Robert Anderson,** his commanding officer, later likens the odds of a radical ex-Egyptian army officer with EIJ ties getting posted at the highly secure SWC to winning the lottery.

Anderson

09 • 1987 (page 18)

In Afghanistan, the Islamic mujahadeen have been battling the Soviets since 1979. The CIA sends more than $3 billion in covert aid to the rebels. Saudi billionaire **Osama bin Laden** arrives to support the struggle, soon joined by EIJ leader **Ayman al-Zawahiri.** They forge an alliance with **Abdullah Azzam,** who runs a worldwide fundraising network for the Muj called the Services Office for the mujahadeen, aka the MAK. The flagship MAK base in the U.S. is at the Alkifah Center in the al Farooq Mosque in Brooklyn, New York.

Azzam

bin Laden & al-Zawahiri

10 • 1987–89 (page 39, 55)

At Fort Bragg, **Ali Mohamed** works as a supply sergeant, with no formal security clearance, but he is able to obtain top secret records and other key intelligence, including a list of the locations of Special Forces and Navy SEAL units worldwide and a JCS Warning Order, a top secret communiqué from the Joint Chiefs of Staff to all strategic Pentagon commands. (See Appendix I, pages 546–47.)

Mohamed

11 • 1988 (page 41)

During Operation Bright Star, a semi-annual U.S.-Egyptian war games exercise, **Ali Mohamed** is identified as a radical Islamic sympathizer by Egyptian military officers. The discovery almost forces a shutdown of the exercise before he is ordered sent home to Fort Bragg. Despite his known sympathy for Islamic extremists, Mohamed is thereafter used to make training videos at the JFK SWC.

Mohamed

12 • 1988 (page 43)

Ali Mohamed informs his commanding officer at Fort Bragg that he intends to use his annual leave to fight with the mujahadeen against the Soviets in Afghanistan—an action that could be a disaster if he is caught or killed during the CIA-supported covert war. Although Lt. Col. Anderson balks, Mohamed makes the trip anyway. He returns with war trophies: the belts of two elite **Soviet Spetsnaz commandos** he claims he killed.

Spetsnaz commandos

13 • July 1989 (page 47)

Ali Mohamed travels from Fort Bragg to train the al Qaeda cell that will later execute the 1993 World Trade Center bombing and the Day of Terror plot to blow up the U.N., the FBI's New York office, and the bridges and tunnels into Manhattan. Over four weekends, an FBI surveillance team follows Ali's trainees **Mahmud Abouhalima, Mohammed Salameh, El Sayyid Nosair, Nidal Ayyad,** and Clement Rodney Hampton-El from the Al Farooq Mosque to a shooting range in **Calverton, Long Island.** They are photographed by the FBI firing thousands of rounds from automatic weapons.

Calverton FBI photo

Abouhalima

Salameh

Nosair

Ayyad

14 • 1989

At an Islamic conference in Oklahoma City, Mahmud Abouhalima meets Wadih El-Hage, a Lebanese Christian convert associated with the Al Bunyan Islamic Center in Tucson, another Services Office outpost. El-Hage agrees to supply AK-47s to Abouhalima.

15 • November 1989 (page 46)

As the Soviets leave Afghanistan, a dispute breaks out among the "Afghan Arabs" over the best use of the fortune that continues to pour in. **Azzam** wants to use the money to set up an Islamic regime in Kabul. **Osama bin Laden** wants to use it for a worldwide jihad against the West. Mysteriously, Azzam and his two sons are murdered in a car bombing. Though bin Laden professes grief, intelligence analysts believe he was responsible. Within months, with the support of his Egyptian allies **Dr. Ayman al-Zawahiri, Mohammed Atef,** and **Sheikh Omar Abdel Rahman,** bin Laden takes over Azzam's Services Office network, using it as a grid for his new terror network, al Qaeda.

Azzam

bin Laden

al-Zawahiri

Atef

Rahman

16 • 1990 (page 101)

Abdul Basit, a Baluchistani who grew up in Kuwait, graduates from a U.K. engineering school. He enrolls at the University of Dawa and Jihad, an al Qaeda training camp in Pakistan. Adopting the name **Ramzi Yousef,** he begins studying bomb making.

Yousef

17 • July 1990 (page 53)

The CIA helps **Sheikh Rahman** enter the United States by approving his visa in Sudan even though he is on a U.S. Watch List. When he arrives at JFK airport he's picked up by Mustafa Shalabi and **Mahmud Abouhalima**, who becomes his chauffeur and aide.

Rahman   Abouhalima

18 • November 5, 1990 (page 56)

Rabbi Meier Kahane is murdered by **El Sayyid Nosair,** another Ali Mohamed trainee. **Abouhalima,** known as "the Red," is slated to drive the getaway car.

Kahane   Nosair   Abouhalima

19 • November 6, 1990 (page 58)

Later, at Nosair's New Jersey house, FBI agents and NYPD detectives seize 47 boxes of evidence, including bomb recipes, Arabic writings threatening the WTC, and Ali Mohamed's top secret memos stolen from Fort Bragg. **Abouhalima** and **Salameh** are seized as material witnesses but later set free. (See Appendix I, pages 545–46.)

Abouhalima   Salameh

20 • November 13, 1990 (page 74)

A week after the Kahane killing, Detective Lou Napoli of the FBI-NYPD Joint Terrorist Task Force (JTTF) follows up on a document seized at Nosair's house linking him to Raymond Murteza, an ex-cop who engaged in weapons training with Ali Mohamed's cell members at a Connecticut gun range. Napoli learns that on successive weekends from 1988 to 1990, the "Mid-Eastern" men fired thousands of rounds from AK-47s and other semiautomatic weapons. But when the NYPD declares the Kahane murder a "lone gunman" shooting, the FBI terminates the investigation. (See Appendix II, page 547.)

21 • 1990 (page 54)

The FBI discovers that **El Sayyid Nosair**, the killer of Rabbi Meier Kahane, has a mailbox at **Sphinx Trading**, a Jersey City check-cashing store four doors away from the **al-Salaam Mosque,** where Sheikh Omar Abdel Rahman holds court and where **Ali Mohamed** showed videos from Fort Bragg to the cell members behind the 1993 WTC bombing.

Nosair   Mohamed

Sphinx mailboxes   Sphinx business card   Sheikh's mosque

A power struggle breaks out between Sheikh Rahman and **Mustafa Shalabi,** Abdullah Azzam's hand-picked imam, who runs the Alkifah Center. Shalabi appeals to **Ali Mohamed** for help. Ali drives Shalabi's wife to the airport as Mustafa plans to escape home to Cairo. But he never makes it. Shalabi is later found shot, stabbed, and bludgeoned with a baseball bat at his Seagate, Brooklyn, home. Abouhalima IDs the body for the NYPD, but is never charged. The voice of **Wadih El-Hage,** a Lebanese Christian convert to Islam, is heard on Shalabi's answering machine. Thousands of dollars in Alkifah funds are missing from the crime scene. Ali Mohamed has secreted away most of the Alkifah's most incriminating documents. The murder in the NYPD's 61st Precinct remains unsolved.

El-Hage

Mohamed

Shalabi's home in Brooklyn

Osama bin Laden chooses **Ali Mohamed** to handle security as he makes the treacherous move from Afghanistan to the Sudan with his twenty-five wives and children. **Ayman al-Zawahiri, Mohammed Atef,** and the al Qaeda Shura Council make the move under Ali's supervision, along with two thousand "Afghan Arabs" loyal to al Qaeda.

bin Laden

Mohamed

Atef

al-Zawahiri

Nosair's cousin **Ibrahim El-Gabrowny** gets $20,000 from **bin Laden** for Nosair's defense. The FBI later admits that this is the first time bin Laden's name comes up in association with the New York cell members around the blind Sheikh.

El-Gabrowny

bin Laden

FBI Special Agent **Nancy Floyd** recruits **Emad Salem,** an ex–Egyptian Army major, to infiltrate the blind Sheikh's cell. He's paid $500 a week by the Bureau. The agreement with the FBI is that Salem will act as a pure intelligence "asset." He will not have to wear a wire or testify.

Floyd

Salem

While living in Santa Clara and commuting to Khartoum to assist bin Laden and al Qaeda, **Ali Mohamed** is opened as an informant by the FBI's San Francisco office. His control agent is John Zent, a twenty-one-year Bureau veteran.

Mohamed   Souza, Ewell, Curtice

But within months of taking on Mohamed as a source, Zent is embroiled in a grisly triple murder case. He becomes the primary alibi witness for **Dana Ewell**, a young Santa Clara University student suspected by Fresno County Sheriff's office of conspiring to kill his father, **Dale**, his sister **Tiffany** and his mother, **Glee**, in a scheme to inherit the Ewell's $8 million estate. Special Agent Zent's daughter **Monica** is Dana's fiancée.

Monica Zent   Ewell family

 Detectives **John Souza** and **Chris Curtice** begin a two-year investigation of the crime, but Special Agent Zent is openly critical of the detectives and declares that **Dana Ewell** is innocent. While the detectives find no evidence connecting **Monica Zent** to the murders, she receives up to $40,000 from Dana via his grandmother's trust fund. Monica continues to live with Dana, sharing bank accounts with him and proclaiming his innocence even though police later find a yearbook picture of Monica with her eyes shot out at a secret Los Angeles apartment the couple shared. The multi-year investigation consumes much of John Zent's attention—at a time when he is responsible for monitoring al Qaeda spy Ali Mohamed.

From November 1991 to July 1992, Yousef's oldest friend, fellow Baluchistani **Abdul Hakim Murad**, trains at U.S. flight schools in Texas, New York, North Carolina, and California. He obtains his commercial pilot's license and surveys the World Trade Center as a possible target.

Murad

Nosair is convicted in the Kahane shooting and sent to Attica. Meanwhile, Nancy Floyd's asset **Salem** has burrowed deep into the cell and is getting close to **Sheikh Rahman**. On a trip to Detroit, the cleric asks Salem to murder

Nosair   Salem, Rahman

Egyptian president Hosni Mubarak. Salem learns that Rahman is the leader of al Gamma'a Islimaya (IG), an Egyptian terror group that tried to assassinate Mubarak in 1990. Soon the FBI discovers that Nosair is also an IG member.

During renovations in the old inspection section of the FDNY, **Ahmed Amin Refai**, an Egyptian who works as an FDNY accountant, obtains the blueprints for the **World Trade Center**. Refai worships at the Al Farooq and Al Salaam mosques, where Rahman preaches.

Refai   WTC

Operating undercover without a wire, Salem complains to **Nancy Floyd** that he can't reach Special Agent **John Anticev** or his partner on the Joint Terrorist Task Force NYPD, Detective **Lou Napoli**. So Floyd, an agent in the Russian (GRU) branch of the FBI's NY office, works double time to debrief the Egyptian.

Floyd

Anticev

Napoli

As Salem gets deeper into the bombing plot, **Carson Dunbar**, an ex–NJ State Trooper—and now FBI Asst. Special Agent in Charge of the NY office—takes over the Terrorism branch. In a meeting with Anticev, Napoli, and Salem, Dunbar's subordinate, Supervisor John Crouthamel, calls Nancy Floyd "a bitch" and says he wants her off the Salem investigation.

Dunbar

As **Salem** gets closer to the bombing cell, Carson Dunbar demands that he wear a wire and testify in open court. Angry that the FBI is changing the terms of his undercover agreement, Salem withdraws. The FBI agrees to pay him $500 for the next three months, and Nancy Floyd continues to meet with him. But by late July, Salem withdraws from the Sheikh's cell. The FBI now has no asset inside the bomb conspiracy.

Salem

Ronnie Bucca is sworn in as a fire marshal with the FDNY's Bureau of Fire Investigation. From his military intelligence detachment in the Army Reserves, he hears that the FBI had a mole inside a bombing plot, but cut him loose.

Bucca

After Salem leaves the bomb plot, **Sheikh Rahman** calls Pakistan, and **Ramzi Yousef** arrives at JFK. With him is **Mohammed Ajaj**, carrying multiple passports and bomb books. He's arrested and gets the last INS cell. But Yousef is given an asylum hearing and set free.

Rahman

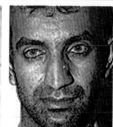
Yousef

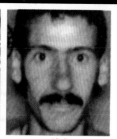
Ajaj

35 • Fall 1992 (page 108)

With the help of Ali Mohamed's trainees, **Yousef** builds the bomb in Jersey City. **Nidal Ayyad** supplies the chemicals. **Mohammed Salameh** helps construct the device, and **Mahmud Abouhalima** does reconnaissance runs to the WTC. Ayyad and Salameh set up bank accounts. Thousands of dollars are wired from the Mideast and Europe. During this period, the FBI misses multiple chances to interdict the plot.

Yousef   Ayyad

Salameh   Abouhalima

Floyd   Salem

36 • Fall 1992 (page 109)

In his last meeting with **Nancy Floyd**, **Salem** pleads with her to make sure Anticev and Napoli follow Abouhalima and Salameh. But Floyd has effectively been removed from any terrorism investigative work by Dunbar. Salem's parting words: "Don't call me when the bombs go off."

37 • Fall 1992 (page 112)

From November 1992 up until the bombing in February 1993, **Yousef** and his cell are highly visible. **Salameh** is in three car accidents. Yousef is hospitalized and uses a stolen phone card to order chemicals. He runs up $18,000 in phone charges and is recorded by an ATM camera. He talks regularly to **Ajaj** in federal prison, using three-way calling via a Texas burger restaurant, but the Feds fail to monitor the calls in time. Yousef

Salameh   Ajaj

reports his passport stolen to police and obtains a new one from the Pakistani Embassy in New York. Though he missed his asylum hearing, neither the INS nor the FBI discovers his presence as he builds the 1,500-pound bomb in an apartment on Pamrapo Avenue in Jersey City.

Yousef

38 • February 1993 (page 113)

During this period Anticev and Napoli lose track of **Abouhalima** and **Salameh**. Napoli later says they weren't able to follow them because they fled to New Jersey. But the redheaded Egyptian is living openly with his German wife and four

Abouhalima   Salameh

kids. The Feds know her name (Weber). In fact, they searched Abouhalima's house in 1992 after tracing calls to Weber from Nosair. But as Yousef builds the bomb, they fail to obtain wiretap or search warrants; nor do they use the FBI's Special Operations Group to follow the Red effectively. If the FBI had sat on Abouhalima, he would have led them straight to Yousef and the bomb.

In the early morning hours of February 26, **Yousef, Abouhalima, Salameh,** and **Ismoil** load the bomb into the Ryder truck. A three-car convoy heads to Brooklyn, where Yousef spends the night with Salameh.

Yousef

Abouhalima

Salameh

Ismoil

Just after noon, Yousef parks the Ryder van outside Room 107 on the B-2 level between the **Twin Towers.** At 12:17:37 the bomb detonates, blowing a four-story crater down to the B-4 level. Monica Smith, a pregnant secretary in Room 107, is instantly killed along with her unborn child. The blast kills 5 others, injures 1,000, and causes half a billion dollars in damage.

Bomb damage at the WTC

Kevin Shea, a close friend of Ronnie Bucca's from Rescue One, is almost killed after falling into the four-story crater. Early the next morning, after visiting Shea in the hospital, Ronnie goes down to the B-2 level to photograph the edge of the ramp from which Kevin had fallen.

Shea

Within months of the World Trade Center bombing, **Ali Mohamed** is captured by the Royal Canadian Mounted Police while trying to smuggle al Qaeda terrorist **Essam Marzouk** into the U.S. During his interrogation by the Mounties, Mohamed says that he's working with the FBI and gives them John Zent's number. Zent vouches for Mohamed, securing his release. Months later, Mohamed is in **Nairobi** doing surveillance for the bombing of the **U.S. embassy** there. Bin Laden himself will use Mohamed's photos to target the suicide bomb that will kill 213 and injure thousands in 1998.

Ali Mohamed

Essem Marzouk

Nairobi Embassy

PART II

01 • February 27, 1993 (page 117)

Ronnie Bucca is determined to investigate the bombing, but the FDNY is effectively shut out of the probe by the FBI. So Bucca begins his own investigation, which leads him to the discovery of an unpublished warning from the bombers: They know what they did wrong in failing to topple the WTC, they say, and they pledge to return and finish the job.

Bucca

02 • February 27, 1993 (page 116)

The morning after the blast, **Yousef** escapes to Pakistan. He is disappointed that the North Tower didn't snap at its base and crash into the South Tower; he had expected 250,000 deaths. A fragment of the unpublished threat letter later discovered by Bucca reads: "Our calculations were not very accurate this time. However we promise you that next time it will be very precise and the Trade Center will be one of our targets."

Yousef

03 • February 28, 1993 (page 114)

Immediately after the bombing, **Emad Salem** contacts **Nancy Floyd**. He tells her the FBI could have prevented the blast if they had just listened to him and followed Abouhalima and Salameh. He soon tips the Feds that Abouhalima has fled to Egypt, and the Red is captured.

Salem   **Floyd**

04 • March 4, 1993

A VIN number discovered in the rubble leads the FBI to the Ryder agency, where **Salameh** is arrested after demanding a refund of his $400 deposit. He and **Abouhalima**, whom the FBI had under surveillance as far back as 1989, are now charged as coconspirators in the bombing.

Salameh   **Abhouhalima**

05 • 1993 (page 140)

Ali Mohamed brokers an historic summit in Khartoum between terror leaders from the two warring sects of radical Islam: **Osama bin Laden,** representing the al Qaeda Sunnis, and **Imad Mugniyah,** representing the Shiite "Party of God," Hezbollah. Known as the "faceless terrorist," Mugniyah is believed to be the mastermind behind 1983 Beirut bombings and the Buckley abduction, along with infamous acts of terror including the 1985 hijacking of **TWA Flight 847.**

As a measure of Ali Mohamed's clout, the summit produces a détente between Hezbollah and al Qaeda that some analysts believe resulted in the **Khobar Towers bombing** in 1996. It may have paved the way for the initial Sunni-Shiite alliance in the Iraqi insurgency beginning in 2003.

Imad Mugniyah

TWA #847 hijacking   **Mohamed**   **bin Laden**   **Khobar bombing**

10

06 • **1993** (page 117)

FDNY Fire Marshal **Ronnie Bucca** educates himself on the recent history of Islamic terror. With a TOP SECRET security clearance and operational experience as a Green Beret and decorated firefighter, Bucca wants to contribute to the Yousef hunt, but his application to the NYPD-FBI Joint Terrorist Task Force is rejected. The JTTF effectively excludes the FDNY.

Bucca

07 • **1993** (page 128)

Ali Mohamed meets with his FBI control agent, John Zent, and reveals that **Osama bin Laden** is running an organization called al Qaeda that is dedicated to overthrowing the government in Saudi Arabia. Incredibly, Mohamed even confesses that he himself has been giving hijacking and intelligence training to al Qaeda operatives at

Mohamed   **bin Laden**

camps in the Sudan. Zent contacts the Pentagon, and a group of investigators from Fort Meade, home of the National Security Agency (NSA), fly out to interview Mohamed. But nothing comes of the investigation, and the FBI later finds out that reports of the interview have been destroyed.

08 • **June 1993** (page 119)

The FBI raids a bomb factory set up by Salem, exposing the plot to blow up a series of NYC landmarks including the UN, George Washington Bridge, and two tunnels into the city.

09 • **June 1993** (page 209)

In the course of the sting **Salem** nets **Siddig Siddig Ali** (a Sudanese), **Clement Rodney Hampton-El**, and **Rahman** himself, plus nine others. Salem becomes the linchpin witness in the Feds' case.

Salem   **Ali**   **Hampton-El**   **Rahman**

10 • **June 1993** (page 209)

But after the bomb factory takedown, **Salem**, now in Witness Protection, admits that in addition to the "bad guy tapes" he recorded his own "bootleg tapes" because he didn't trust FBI superiors. Carson Dunbar and the FBI's top NY lawyer order **Nancy Floyd** to go to Salem's apartment to retrieve the tapes. Knowing nothing about the unautho-

Salem   **Floyd**

rized tapes, which include her own criticism of FBI superiors, Floyd visits the apartment and gets into an argument with FBI attorney Jim Roth over which tapes Salem has consented to release. The attorney takes them all, and Floyd is later heard discussing with Salem how FBI supervisors might have prevented the original WTC bombing if they had let him do his job the first time. She's also heard on tape calling her FBI bosses "gutless" and "chickenshits." In apparent retribution for her candor, the FBI opens up an OPR internal affairs investigation of Floyd. Rather than being rewarded as the heroine who recruited the FBI's key Day of Terror asset, Agent Floyd is isolated and chastised.

11 • July 3, 1993 (page 127)

After a siege outside a Brooklyn mosque the Feds take Sheikh Rahman into custody. Two of his loyal followers are Egyptian naturalized citizens and government employees: **Ahmed Amin Refai**, the FDNY accountant, and **Ahmed Abdel Sattar**, a U.S. postal worker.

Refai   **Sattar**

12 • 1994 (page 210)

The FBI's New York office opens an internal affairs investigation (OPR) on **Roy Lindley DeVecchio**, a senior supervisory special agent known in the Bureau as "Mr. Organized Crime" for his success at getting Mafia convictions. Three agents under DeVecchio have presented evidence suggesting that he may have leaked key FBI intelligence to **Gregory Scarpa Sr.**, an underboss for the Colombo crime family during a two-year war between rival

War victim

factions in which twelve people have died. Lawyers later contend that the Colombo war may have resulted from an "unholy alliance" between the G-Man and the hitman.

The investigation is complicated by the fact that **Scarpa Sr.**, a vicious killer nicknamed the "Grim Reaper," has been a Top Echelon (TE) FBI informant for many years. As early as 1964, FBI director **J. Edgar Hoover** recruited him to help solve the infamous "MISSBURN" case after **three civil rights workers** were kidnapped and murdered by the Ku Klux Klan. In thirty years of crime, Scarpa Sr. has spent only thirty days behind bars, leading some to suggest that the FBI has rewarded him with a de facto license to kill. By 1996 this growing scandal inside the FBI's New York office will intersect with the Bureau's probe of al Qaeda, leading to a cover-up of key intelligence that could have helped the FBI and CIA interdict the 9/11 plot.

DeVecchio   **Scarpa Sr.**   **Hoover**   **Goodman, Chaney,
& Schwerner**

White

13 • March 4, 1994 (page 209)

Abouhalima, **Salameh**, **Ayyad**, and **Ajaj** are convicted in the World Trade Center bombing. But Yousef and Ismoil are still at large. The U.S. Attorney for the Southern District of New York, **Mary Jo White**, declares that the verdict should send "an unmistakable message that we will not tolerate terrorism in this country."

Abouhalima   **Salameh**   **Ayyad**   **Ajaj**

14 • March 11, 1994 (page 210)

Agent **Nancy Floyd** becomes the object of a story leaked to the *New York Post* suggesting that she is being investigated by the FBI for an alleged affair with Emad Salem. Later, under oath, Floyd vehemently denies the charge, and the bootleg tapes exonerate her. An ongoing OPR investigation finds no evidence to support the charge.

Floyd

By July 1994, **Ramzi Yousef** is the world's most wanted terrorist. **Brad Smith**, a Diplomatic Security Service Agent at the U.S. State Department, runs Rewards for Justice, a program that offers $2 million for Yousef's capture. Diagnosed with Lou Gehrig's disease, Smith is given just months to live, but he vows to stay alive until Yousef is arrested.

Smith

Yousef Wanted Poster

Working out of the Philippines, **Yousef** conceives three plots. (1) He will kill **Pope John Paul II** on a visit to Manila in January 1995. (2) He will create an undetectable liquid-based bomb to be smuggled on board eleven U.S. jumbo jets entering the United States from Asia. Yousef names this plot Bojinka, after the Serbo-Croatian term for "big noise." (3) With **Abdul Hakim Murad**, the pilot trained at four U.S. flight schools, Yousef will coordinate the training of Islamic pilots at U.S. schools who will then commandeer airliners and fly them into buildings in America. This third plot becomes the blueprint for the 9/11 attacks.

Yousef

Pope John Paul II

Murad

On Christmas Eve, in what may have been a dress rehearsal for Yousef's "third plot," Algerian Islamic terrorists with ties to Osama bin Laden hijack an Air France jumbo jet laden with fuel. According to witnesses, the suicidal hijackers intended to fly the plane to Paris to take down the **Eiffel Tower.**

Eiffel Tower

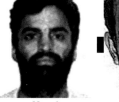
Murad

Yousef

To help execute his three plots, which he and **Murad** will stage from Manila, **Yousef** calls on his uncle **Khalid Shaikh Mohammed**. The fourth conspirator is **Wali Khan Amin Shah**, an Uzbeki veteran of the Afghan war whom Osama bin Laden calls "the lion." Wali sets up a front company in Malaysia called Konsonjaya to fund the three plots. On the board is an Indonesian cleric named **Riduan Isamuddin** (aka **Hambali**), who will later be linked to the 2002 Bali bombing. The money for the three plots will come from bin Laden's brother-in-law **Mohammed Jamal Khalifa**.

Mohammed   **Shah**   **Hambali**   **Khalifa**

Using his Filipina girlfriend as a front, Shah rents a safe house at the Dona Josefa Apartments along the pope's parade route in Manila. Yousef later checks in to Room 603.

20 • December 11, 1994 (page 152)

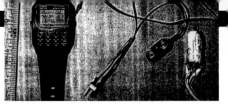

Creating a series of false IDs, **Yousef** mimics the identity of **Arnaldo Forlani**, an Italian government official. He buys a ticket from Manila to Cebu on PAL Flight 434, with ongoing service to Japan.

Using apparently innocuous parts consisting of a Casio DBC-61 watch as a timer and diluted nitroglycerin in a contact lens cleanser bottle, Yousef boards PAL Flight 434 and builds the

Exclusive photo of Yousef's undetectable bomb trigger

bomb on the first leg of the two-leg flight. He puts the assembled device in the life jacket pouch under seat 26K by the center fuel tank of the 747, then deplanes in Cebu.

When PAL Flight 434, bound for Japan, reaches cruising altitude, the Casio alarm ignites the filament of a broken bulb Yousef has embedded in the nitrocellulose explosive. The bomb detonates—

killing the passenger in seat 26K and narrowly missing the center fuel tank. The 747 is forced to make an emergency landing on Okinawa.

Yousef

As Forlani

21 • December 11, 1994 (page 156)

That night in a Manila karaoke bar, Yousef celebrates his successful "wet test" of the undetectable Casio bomb with **Wali Khan Amin Shah** and his uncle **Khalid Shaikh Mohammed**.

Shah   **Mohammed**

Bucca

22 • December 1994 (page 149)

Since the 1993 WTC bombing, **Ronnie Bucca** has developed a database of Islamic terror groups. One of them is the Abu Sayyaf Group (ASG), which operates out of the Philippines. When they take credit for the PAL bombing, Bucca becomes convinced Yousef is involved.

23 • December 16, 1994 (page 157)

In Morgan Hill, California, the hometown of Special Agent John Zent, Osama bin Laden's brother-in-law Mohamed Jamal Khalifa is arrested by INS agents. At the time, evidence from the Philippines National Police suggests that Khalifa is bankrolling the Ramzi Yousef-Khalid Shaikh Mohammed Manila cell. Khalifa's PDA contains evidence linking bin Laden to the two Yousef cells (in New York and Manila). Facing a death sentence in Jordan, Khalifa is motivated to talk and might make an extraordinary witness if the Feds push for his interrogation. A senior State Department official describes Khalifa as "engaged in serious terrorist offenses," and predicts that his release will "endanger U.S. national security." But Secretary of State **Warren Christopher** and Deputy Attorney General **Jamie Gorelick** soon advocate Khalifa's extradition to Jordan, thus losing a key potential witness against al Qaeda.

Christopher

Gorelick

24 • January 6, 1995 (page 178)

On the night of January 6, while mixing chemicals in his Dona Josefa bomb factory, Yousef accidentally ignites a small fire that fills the room with smoke. The Manila police are called. Yousef and Murad tell a rookie cop that they are just playing with firecrackers. He buys the story and leaves.

25 • January 6, 1995 (page 179)

But when the cop reports the firecracker story, veteran PNP Captain **Aida Fariscal** becomes suspicious and orders the young cop and a sergeant back to the Dona Josefa. There they confront Abdul Hakim Murad.

26 • January 7, 1995 (page180)

As the police escort Murad out of the Dona Josefa lobby, he takes off running. The patrolman pulls his gun and fires a shot that zings past the terrorist's ear. Murad suddenly trips and goes down, whereupon the cops arrest him. He tries to bribe **Fariscal** with $2,000 in American Express checks,

Fariscal

but she demands to see Room 603, where he's been staying. When she enters the room, Fariscal is shocked to find a picture of the pope, priest's cassocks, a map of the pontiff's parade route, and a laboratory of chemicals and bombs in various stages of construction. She also finds Yousef's Toshiba laptop, which lays out the entire Bojinka plot to blow up 11 U.S. jumbo jets. By playing a hunch, this local Filipina police captain has found the lair of Ramzi Yousef, the world's most wanted man.

27 • January 7, 1995 (page 180)

But as Murad is led away by the police, **Ramzi Yousef** watches from across the street. Early the next morning he takes a flight to Pakistan, where he is joined by his uncle **Khalid Shaikh Mohammed**. The Mozart of Terror escapes. Both men will go on to plan the 9/11 attacks.

Yousef   **Mohammed**

28 • January 7, 1995 (page 182)

Telling PNP officials his name is Saeed Ahmed, **Murad** is taken to Camp Crame in Manila for questioning. Allegedly tortured, he refuses to talk until he is turned over to Col. **Rodolfo Mendoza**, an expert on Islamic terror groups. Murad soon confesses details of the WTC bombing. He also admits his role in the pope and Bojinka plots.

Murad   **Mendoza**

29 • January 20, 1995 (page 183)

Two weeks after his capture, Murad confesses to a plan to fly a small single-engine plane into CIA headquarters in Langley, Virginia, but says the plot is just in the early planning stages.

30 • February 1995 (page 184)

Finally, after Mendoza threatens to turn him over to the Israeli Mossad, Murad admits to Yousef's third plot, which is well into the planning stages. He tells Mendoza that ten Islamic terrorists are currently training in U.S. flight schools. The ultimate targets will be the **CIA**, the **Pentagon**, the **World Trade Center**, the **Sears Tower** in Chicago, the **Transamerica Tower** in San Francisco, and a U.S. nuclear facility.

CIA Headquarters

Pentagon   **World Trade Center**   **Sears Tower**   **Transamerica Tower**

Meanwhile, as the hunt for Ramzi Yousef intensifies, DSS agent Brad Smith amps up the Rewards program with **posters** and matchbooks with Yousef's image promising a $2 million reward.

But the master bomber remains undaunted. From hiding in Pakistan, Yousef recruits a young Islamic South African, Istaique Parker, and induces him to plant **nitrocellulose bombs** hidden in toy cars inside luggage to be checked onto United and Delta flights in Bangkok. Yousef's laptop seized at the Dona Josefa contains details of the Bojinka plot. Within hours after the Room 603 search, Delta and United Airlines are put on high alert. A number of flights are aborted, and some are forced to land.

But at the last minute, Parker gets cold feet. He returns to Islamabad and calls the U.S. Embassy. DSS agents debriefing him learn that Yousef will be returning to Islamabad in a few days. When Yousef calls Parker from the Su Casa, a guest house controlled by Osama bin Laden, DSS agents raid it with Pakistani authorities. The bomb maker is arrested. But his uncle Khalid Shaikh Mohammed, staying downstairs, escapes. Astonishingly, Mohammed gives an innocent-bystander press interview and is later quoted in *Time* magazine.

Exclusive photo of toy cars and nitrocellulose seized in a raid on Yousef's Islamabad lair

On a 707 bound for the United States, **Yousef** confesses to FBI agents his role in the pope and Bojinka plots. He also gives minute details of the WTC bombing. But on his arrival back in New York, as he's being flown by helicopter past the WTC, Yousef delivers a chilling warning. An FBI agent eyes the Twin Towers and says, "You didn't get them after all." Yousef replies, "Not yet!"

Yousef

A week before Yousef's capture, the Day of Terror trial begins. The Feds accuse **Sheikh Rahman** of leading a "jihad army" dating back to the first firing range sessions at Calverton, L.I., in 1989. Included in the ongoing plot are the slaying of Rabbi Kahane by **Nosair** (whose defense was funded by **Ibrahim El-Gabrowny**) and the WTC bombing. **Siddig Ali** admits to being the operational leader who chose the UN and the Lincoln and Holland tunnels as targets. He admits that he and **Clement Rodney Hampton-El** attended training sessions in Pennsylvania where Yousef's bomb was tested with the help of **Mohammed Abouhalima**.

This demonstrates further that the FBI could have stopped Yousef if they had followed Mohammed's brother **Mahmud**, "the Red," who was working directly with Yousef as he built the WTC device.

Rahman

Nosair

El-Gabrowny

Ali

Hampton-El

Mohammed Abouhalima

Mahmud Abouhalima

35 • February 1995 (page 172)

Ali Mohamed is listed by assistant U.S. attorneys **Andrew C. McCarthy** and **Patrick Fitzgerald** as one of the 172 unindicted coconspirators in the Day of Terror trial, in which the lead defendant is Sheikh Rahman. The attorney for **El Sayyid Nosair** subpoenas Mohamed to testify, but McCarthy flies

McCarthy   **Fitzgerald**

to California to meet with Mohamed and reportedly discourages him from taking the stand. To make the California meeting, Mohamed has to fly back to Santa Clara from Nairobi, Kenya, where he is working with embassy bombing cell operative **Wadih El-Hage.** Later, the audacious Mohamed fumes because he expected the Feds to pay for his airfare back from Africa.

Rahman   **Nosair**   **Mohamed**   **El-Hage**

36 • 1995 (page 209)

Emad Salem, Nancy Floyd's recruit, is the Fed's linchpin witness. At one point in testimony he admits that the Day of Terror plot was almost foiled when Carson Dunbar ordered him to remove a timer from the safe house. Called as a defense witness, Floyd is heard on Salem's bootleg tapes pointedly criticizing FBI supervisors for undermining the first WTC bombing investigation. Meanwhile her OPR investigation continues. A fellow agent speculates that Floyd is being punished by her FBI superiors for telling the truth about the failure of the New York office to stop the first bombing.

37 • March, 1995 (page 167)

Deputy Attorney General **Jamie Gorelick** signs the infamous "wall memo," in which she calls for a separation of intelligence between FBI investigators probing *past* terror crimes and agents seeking to prevent *future* acts of terror. Gorelick admits that the memo goes "beyond what is legally required." Some analysts see the memo as a legal justification for the disconnection of dots by DOJ officials, who may be seeking to hide past acts of negligence by the FBI and DOJ on the road to 9/11. (See memo at Appendix IV, page 549.)

Gorelick

38 • April 1995 (page 186)

Col. Rodolfo Mendoza turns over the details of Murad's confession to the U.S. Embassy in Manila, including a list of Yousef's six targets in the airline hijack plot, among them the WTC and the Pentagon.

39 • 1995 (page 196)

Ali Mohamed smuggles **Ayman al-Zawahiri** into the U.S. for his second fund-raising tour of U.S. mosques. Up to half a million dollars is reportedly raised on both coasts by the team, fraudulently using the name of the Red Crescent. Traveling incognito, al-Zawahiri is accompanied on one of the U.S. trips by San Jose obstetrician Ali Zaki, another Egyptian émigré, who later claims he didn't know the infamous al-Zawahiri was a terrorist.

Mohamed   **al-Zawahiri**

According to later testimony from Mohamed's protégé **Khalid Dahab,** some of the money from the U.S. tour goes to finance the bombing of the **Egyptian Embassy** in Pakistan, an act of terror linked directly to al-Zawahiri. Working as Ali Mohamed's protégé, Dahab helps set up a sleeper cell in Santa Clara in the middle of California's high-tech heartland.

Egyptian Embassy   **Dahab**

The FBI acknowledges Mendoza's evidence in a memo classified as SECRET/NOFORN. The memo warns of potential "future attacks" by Yousef against the CIA and a nuclear facility. Later the FBI investigates two of **Murad's** U.S. flight schools. But the Bureau makes no other mention of Yousef's third plot, and, for unknown reasons, further investigation of the airliner hijacking scenario is dropped.

Even more surprising, while the FBI memo's author suspects Yousef of having links to Osama bin Laden, it describes his WTC bombing cell and the Day of Terror bombers as "a loose group of politically committed Muslims." The memo concludes that they do "not belong to a single cohesive organization." This finding conflicts with the U.S. attorney's allegation in the ongoing Day of Terror trial that Yousef and Sheikh Rahman are part of a "jihad army" wreaking a war of urban terror in New York.

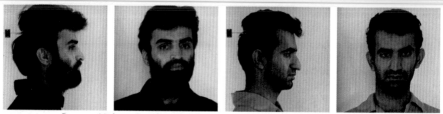

Bureau of Prisons booking mug shots of Abdul Hakim Murad and Ramzi Yousef

Perhaps most incredible is an admission made by Murad to FBI agents during their flight to New York. As Special Agents Frank Pellegino and Thomas Donlon later record in an FBI 302 form, Murad advises them that "Yousef wanted to return to the United States . . . to bomb the World Trade Center a second time."

At 9:00 A.M. on April 19, a 5,600-pound bomb made of ammonium nitrate and nitromethane detonates in a yellow Ryder truck parked outside the **Murrah Federal Building** in Oklahoma City, killing 168 people, including 19 children. Eyewitnesses describe several suspects exiting the area, including a Middle Eastern man.

Murrah Federal Building

Police sketches are released for a **Robert Kling,** described as a 180-pound, 5'10" white man, and **John Doe No. 2,** described as 5'9" with olive skin, a thick neck, and slicked-back hair.

Kling   **John Doe No. 2**

45 • April 19, 1995 (page 163)

Within hours of the blast, **Timothy McVeigh** is in police custody; **Terry Nichols** later surrenders. While McVeigh bears a striking resemblance to the eyewitness sketch, Nichols looks nothing like the swarthy John Doe No. 2. Yet within months the FBI drops its worldwide manhunt for the third suspect.

McVeigh **Nichols**

46 • April 19, 1995 (page 164)

Hours after the Oklahoma City bombing, Abdul Hakim Murad (now in federal jail in New York) takes credit for the blast in the name of Ramzi Yousef's Liberation Army. FBI agent Frank Pellegrino, who interrogated Murad on his trip from Manila, reports the terrorist's declaration in an FBI 302 later admitted at trial.

47 • April 1995 (page 163)

A growing body of circumstantial evidence suggests that Ramzi Yousef may have designed the Oklahoma City device for Terry Nichols when he was in Cebu, Philippines, in 1994–95. Nichols's passport shows four trips to the Philippines since 1990; **Edwin Angeles**, a former leader of the Abu Sayyaf terror group, swears to police that Nichols, aka "The Farmer," met Yousef in the Philippines in the early 1990s.

Angeles

48 • 1995 (page 163)

Passport records show that on November 3, 1994, Wali Khan Amin Shah and Ramzi Yousef applied for Philippines visas while in Singapore. On November 4, Terry Nichols applied for his Philippines visa in Chicago.

49 • 1995 (page 164)

The most curious circumstantial evidence comes from Michael Fortier, the government's star witness in *U.S. v. Timothy McVeigh*. Fortier swears under oath that the only ammonium nitrate–fuel oil device McVeigh ever built was a dud. Then, after Nichols was in Cebu City at the same time as **Ramzi Yousef**, Nichols and McVeigh built the 5,600-pound ammonium nitrate–nitromethane bomb that destroyed the Murrah Building.

Yousef

50 • May 8, 1995 (page 214)

The investigation of **Lin DeVecchio** threatens to undermine the prosecution of seventy-five Mafia cases stemming from the Colombo war. **Valerie Caproni**, head of the criminal division in the Eastern District of New York (EDNY), expresses concern that key intelligence has leaked. **Ellen Corcella**, the AUSA prosecuting many of the cases, is forced to disclose to defense attorneys eight instances in which DeVecchio may have revealed key intelligence, including the location of **Scarpa Sr.'s** chief rival, **Victor Orena Sr**. As a result, fourteen of the cases are dismissed. (See Corcella's letter at Appendix V, pages 551–52.)

Caproni

Corcella **DeVecchio** **Scarpa Sr.** **Orena**

Sheikh Rahman is sentenced to life in prison for his role in the Day of Terror plot. But in a precursor of things to come, Egyptian U.S. postal worker **Ahmed Abdel Sattar** vows that "the man will never be silenced," and the al Gamma'a Islamiya (IG)— the Egyptian terrorist group that the Sheikh heads—threatens to attack U.S. civilian targets.

Rahman   Sattar

Patrick Fitzgerald, the head of Organized Crime and Terrorism in the SDNY, tasks FBI Squad I-49 in the New York office with building a criminal case against Osama bin Laden. Special Agent **Jack Cloonan** has the job of investigating bin Laden's chief U.S. spy, Ali Mohamed. Meanwhile the CIA forms Alec Station, a dedicated bin Laden unit headed by analyst **Mike Scheuer.** Squad I-49 agent **Dan Coleman** is seconded there as the FBI's man inside. As his knowledge of al Qaeda grows, Coleman earns the nickname "the professor."

Fitzgerald   Cloonan   Coleman   Scheuer

Meanwhile, **Jamal Ahmad al-Fadl**, a young Sudanese who worked as an aide to the murdered Mustafa Shalabi at the **Alkifah Center**, walks into a U.S. Embassy and becomes CS-1, a secret informant for the Feds. In extraordinary testimony he confirms the existence of al Qaeda, describes how **Osama bin Laden** runs training camps for the worldwide jihad, and tells the FBI that one of bin Laden's closest associates is Assad, aka "the lion," the nom de guerre of Ramzi Yousef's Manila coconspirator **Wali Khan Amin Shah.**

al-Fadl   Alkifah Center   bin Laden   Shah

For the New York office of the FBI, this intelligence completes a circle of evidence dating back to the surveillance photos of the Calverton shooting sessions in 1989—proving a direct link between al Qaeda, bin Laden, and WTC coconspirators **Abouhalima, Salameh, Nosair,** and **Ayyad,** as well as Day of Terror defendant **Hampton-El.** The revelation comes five years before 9/11, but the public doesn't get a hint of the link until February 2001, and the FBI itself doesn't understand the connection between Special Forces Sgt. **Ali Mohammed** and bin Laden until 1998, following two more al Qaeda bombings.

Abouhalima   Salameh

Nosair   Ayyad   Hampton-El   Mohammed

55 • March 1996 (page 226)

While awaiting trial in federal jail in lower Manhattan, Colombo crime family wiseguy **Gregory Scarpa Jr.,** son of the "Grim Reaper," finds himself in a cell between **Ramzi Yousef** and **Abdul Hakim Murad.** Believing he can trust the mafioso, Yousef begins passing notes through Greg Jr. to Murad via holes in their cell walls. The notes include threats to a federal judge and prosecutor, and a prediction that Yousef's people will put a bomb on a plane to get a mistrial in the upcoming Bojinka trial, in which Yousef will represent himself. The notes also include detailed schematics for Yousef's Casio-nitro bomb trigger used on PAL Flight 434 in 1994. The FBI takes the intel so seriously they give Greg Jr. a camera to photograph Yousef's notes and memorialize them in dozens of official FBI 302 memos. (See Appendix VI, page 556.)

| Yousef | Scarpa Jr. | Murad |

56 • April 10, 1996 (page 229)

While Scarpa Jr. is providing the FBI with key al Qaeda intelligence from Yousef, the FBI's New York Office grows concerned that the widening scandal of alleged corruption between Supervisory Special Agent **Lin DeVecchio** and **Scarpa Sr.** could derail the sixty remaining Colombo war cases in the EDNY. So **James Kallstrom,** ADIC of the NYO, sends a memo to FBI director **Louis Freeh** suggesting that there is: "insufficient evidence to take prosecutive action" against DeVecchio. This despite the Corcella letter from a year earlier citing eight suspected leaks to Scarpa Sr. Pushing for a resolution of the OPR investigation, Kallstrom writes that the scandal is having a "negative impact" on LCN [La Cosa Nostra] prosecutions and "casts a cloud over the NYO." (See Appendix V, page 553.)

   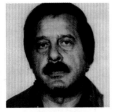

| Kallstrom | Freeh | DeVecchio | Scarpa Sr. |

57 • 1996 (page 223)

The Feds are so impressed by the quality of **Scarpa Jr.**'s intelligence on Yousef that they set up a phony Mafia front company, called the Roma Corp., and allow **Yousef** to make outside calls from jail. While Yousef believes that his calls to al Qaeda members in the U.S. and the Mideast are being patched through by Scarpa's wiseguys, the phones are actually manned by FBI agents. But they only speak Arabic, and Yousef is talking in Baluchi and Urdu. At least one call goes to **Khalid Shaikh Mohammed,** hiding out in Doha, Qatar, while perfecting his nephew Yousef's planes-as-missiles plot. The FBI sends its HRT team to arrest KSM, but he escapes. Meanwhile, Yousef renews his threat to have his people put a bomb on a U.S. airliner to get a mistrial.

One of the notes Yousef passes to Scarpa Jr. is entitled "How to Smuggle Explosives Onto An Airliner." It cites the explosive RDX and acetone peroxide, an ingredient that will show up in a reincarnation of the Bojinka plot by al Qaeda in 2006.

| Yousef | Scarpa Jr. | Khalid Shaikh Mohammed |

58 • May 29, 1996 (page 227)

In the first of two prosecutions, **Yousef** goes on trial in U.S. Federal Court in Manhattan for the Bojinka plot and the murder of the passenger on PAL Flight 434. Judge Kevin T. Duffy allows Yousef to represent himself, with the assistance of attorney Roy Kulcsar. In his opening statement the bomb maker claims he was imprisoned in Pakistan at the time the Bojinka and pope plots were set in motion in Manila. There isn't a word, from federal prosecutors or Yousef, however, about his third plot—the plan to hijack airliners.

Yousef at trial

59 • June 1996 (page 253)

Although eleven Philippine National Police officials testify, Rodolfo Mendoza, who elicited the 9/11 plot confession from **Murad,** is never mentioned. His own assistant, Maj. Alberto Ferro, testifies that he "cannot really recall" who questioned Murad. Though Murad's training in four U.S. flight schools is mentioned, there isn't a word in the nearly 6,000-page transcript of **Yousef**'s plan to fly airliners into the WTC, the Pentagon, and other U.S. buildings. But the forensic evidence against Yousef is overwhelming. On July 18, 1996, the Feds are about to introduce part of Murad's confession giving details of the Bojinka plot, but then . . .

The defendants

60 • July 17, 1996 (page 239)

On the night of July 17, **TWA Flight 800** bound from JFK to Paris crashes near Long Island, killing 230 people. The explosion takes place near row 26, adjacent to the center fuel tank—an area identical to the detonation point aboard PAL Flight 434. When the wreckage is assembled in a hangar, the high explosives RDX, PETN, and nitroglycerine are found near row 26. The explosion mimics the Bojinka plot; Yousef's attorney, Kulcsar, argues that the news event will prejudice the jury.

TWA 800 wreckage

61 • July 17, 1996 (page 240)

James Kallstrom, ADIC of the FBI's NYO, immediately suspects terrorism, and Yousef is at the top of his list of suspects. Because of the multiple FBI 302s documenting Yousef's threat to bomb an airliner, Kallstrom deploys a thousand FBI agents to the crash site off Long Island. After the crash, the FBI picks up a message in Baluchi. It reads "TWA #800 . . . What had to be done has been done." As 96 percent of the aircraft (N 93-17119) is re-assembled, the FBI finds the high explosives RDX, nitroglycerine, and PETN in the area between the seventeenth and twenty-fifth rows near the center wing fuel tank. FBI chief metallurgist William Tobin declares "no indicia" of bomb damage, but he fails to consider Yousef's PAL 434 bomb damage as a precedent.

Kallstrom

62 • August 22, 1996 (page 244)

The *New York Times* is about to run a story entitled "Prime Evidence Found That Device Exploded In Cabin of Flight 800," when Kallstrom is summoned to a D.C. meeting with Deputy AG **Jamie Gorelick** and FBI director **Louis Freeh.**

Freeh   **Gorelick**

Whatever is discussed at the August 22 meeting causes Kallstrom to do a 180-degree turn and seek an explanation for the presence of high explosives in the wreckage *that does not involve a bomb.* He tries to kill the *Times* story, and later accepts a specious theory that the explosive residue was spilled by a K-9 officer conducting a bomb sniffing dog test aboard the plane six weeks earlier. But the officer, Herman Burnett, later produces evidence that he did the test on a *different* aircraft (N 93-17116), negating the FBI's linchpin theory for how explosive residue got on TWA 800.

64 • September 5, 1996 (page 260)

The question of whether **Yousef**'s cell had a hand in the downing of TWA 800 becomes moot by Sept. 5, however, when he's convicted with Murad and Shah for the Bojinka plot. FBI Agent Frank Pellegrino, who interrogated Murad, calls his FBI supervisor to say, "It's over. We won." But even from federal lockup, Yousef continues to plot further terrorist acts.

Yousef

Kallstrom

65 • 1996 (page 265)

Half a dozen senior DOJ and FBI officials are a party to the treasure trove of al Qaeda intelligence from Yousef from March 1996 through February 1997, including **James Kallstrom, Patrick Fitzgerald**, and AUSAs **Dietrich Snell, Valerie Caproni**, and **Ellen Corcella**. Contained in dozens of FBI 302s, the intel demonstrates proof of an active al Qaeda cell in NYC, and a threat by bin Laden to hijack a plane to free Sheikh Rahman.

But within months, reputedly on the word of a Mafia informant named John Napoli, the Feds label the "Scarpa Materials" a "hoax" and "scam."

A key agent in Fitzgerald's Squad I-49 claims that he never sees this intel on al Qaeda's active presence in NYC.

FEDERAL BUREAU OF INVESTIGATION

Date of transcription   3/7/96

At the request of GREGORY SCARPA, JR., Date of Birth: August 3, 1951, he was interviewed at the Office of the United States Attorney, Eastern District of New York, Brooklyn, New York. Present at this interview was SCARPA'S Attorney, Lawrence Silverman, Assistant United States Attorneys (AUSA) DEITRICH SNELL and PATRICK FITZGERALD, Southern District of New York and EVELYN CORCELLA, and VALERIE CAPRONI, Chief of the Criminal Division, Eastern District of New York; and Special Agents PAMELA M. McDAID and HOWARD LEADBETTER II (FBI); and RICHARD CORAGGIO

FBI 302 on Fitzgerald's meeting with Scarpa

Fitzgerald

Snell

Caproni

Corcella

66 • September 1996 (page 249)

The Feds close the **DeVecchio** OPR, allowing him to retire on a full pension even though he took the Fifth Amendment and answered "I don't recall" more than forty times *after* a grant of immunity. **Greg Scarpa Sr.** dies of AIDS in prison; his son **Greg Jr.** is ultimately sentenced to forty years for RICO violations. But at what cost? The ends/means decision by the Feds to preserve the Colombo war cases and bury the DeVecchio scandal results in U.S. intelligence agencies being walled off from crucial evidence of al Qaeda's active links in 1996 to New York City, the blind Sheikh and Ramzi Yousef.

DeVecchio

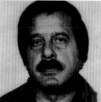

Scarpa Sr.

Scarpa Jr.

PART III

Since his surveillance for the embassy bombing plot in late 1993, **Ali Mohamed** has been in constant touch with **Wadih El-Hage,** one of the key

Mohamed

El-Hage

Nairobi cell members, who had been in Brooklyn as far back as 1991 at the time of the Shalabi murder. The Feds have had a wiretap on El-Hage's phone since 1996, and in August 1997 Special Agent **Dan Coleman** from Squad I-49 finds contact information for Mohamed in a search of El-Hage's house. El-Hage is allowed to leave Nairobi even though al Qaeda turncoat Jamal al-Fadl had told **Fitzgerald** and Coleman in 1996 that El-Hage was **bin Laden's** personal secretary. El-Hage lies to a grand jury in New York, but the FBI lets him go.

bin Laden   **Coleman**   **Fitzgerald**

Patrick Fitzgerald meets face-to-face with Ali Mohamed, who has moved with his wife, Linda Sanchez, to Sacramento, California. Fitzgerald hopes to convince the al Qaeda spy to "turn." But in the company of Squad I-49 agent **Jack Cloonan,** Mohamed audaciously tells Fitzgerald that he is in touch with hundreds of people who are prepared to go "operational" on a moment's notice.

Mohamed also tells the Feds that he can disappear anytime, and spurns them. He admits that

Fitzgerald   **Cloonan**

he trained bin Laden's personal bodyguard in Sudan in 1994. In fact he lived in the Saudi billionaire's house at the time. Ali even tells the Feds that he "loves" bin Laden, that he believes in him, and that he doesn't need a *fatwa* or Islamic degree to attack the U.S. Since bin Laden had told CNN seven months earlier that he had "declared jihad" against America, Mohamed's words amount to sedition—the same charge Fitzgerald used in 1995 to convict Sheikh Rahman. Yet again Fitzgerald allows Mohamed to remain free.

After the meeting, Fitzgerald tells Cloonan, "This is the most dangerous man I have ever met. We cannot let this man out on the street." They bug his computer and tap his home phone, but the Feds leave Ali Mohamed free.

Calling Yousef "an apostle of evil," Judge Duffy sentences him to 240 years in solitary—one year for the combined ages of his WTC victims. Defiant to the end, the bomb maker says, "I am a terrorist and I am proud of it." The same day, the Feds unseal a secret indictment of Khalid Shaikh Mohammed dating back to 1996. For unknown reasons, the Justice Department has kept the hunt for Mohammed quiet for almost two years—in contrast to the well-publicized Yousef hunt, which helped trigger his capture.

Now, as with his nephew, the announced reward is $2 million. But by 1998 **Mohammed** is in the advanced stages of executing Yousef's third plot. As Islamic pilots train in U.S. flight schools, Mohammed prepares to establish a cell in Hamburg, Germany. **Mohammed Atta,** an Egyptian, will take the place of Murad as chief hijacker-pilot in what Mohammed will later call "Holy Tuesday."

Mohammed   **Atta**

05 • January 1998 (page 326)

Despite Yousef's imprisonment, **Ronnie Bucca** believes the threat from the bomb maker's al Qaeda associates is ongoing. Now serving with the Army Reserve's 3413th Military Intelligence Detachment of the 800th MPs at the Defense Intelligence Analysis Center in Washington, Bucca studies **declassified DIAC link charts** that show a direct connection between Ramzi Yousef and Osama bin Laden. He warns his colleagues and superiors in the FDNY of an ongoing threat to New York in general, and the WTC in particular. (See Appendix VIII, pages 568–69.)

Bucca

DIAC link chart

06 • February 5, 1998 (page 286)

Testifying before Congress, **Dale Watson**, the FBI's assistant director for counterterrorism, says, "Although we should not allow ourselves to be lulled into a false sense of security, I believe it is important to note that in the five years since the Trade Center bombing, no significant act of foreign-directed terrorism has occurred on American soil."

Watson

07 • April 1998 (page 289)

Dana Ewell and **Joel Radovich,** the dropout he hired to kill his family, go to trial. Despite overwhelming forensic and eyewitness evidence of their guilt, including the barrel of the AT-9 murder weapon and the testimony of a coconspirator, Ali Mohamed's control agent John Zent testifies as a character witness for Ewell. Still, the pair is found guilty and barely escape the death penalty.

Ewell

Radovcich

Zent's efforts to defend Dana Ewell occur even as an al Qaeda cell is preparing to execute Mohamed's plan to blow up the U.S. embassy in Nairobi. It was on Zent's word that Mohamed was released from the RCMP in 1993 and went on to do the surveillance for the upcoming bombing plot.

08 • 1998 (page 282)

In the months before August 1998, the U.S. receives three significant warnings of a possible attack on the Nairobi embassy. U.S. Ambassador **Prudence Bushnell** makes multiple appeals to the State Department to harden the embassy, but little is done. As late as November 1997, an Egyptian informant tells the CIA that a group is planning to detonate a truck bomb. **Ali Mohamed** even tells an FBI agent in Squad I-49 that a "target" in Africa is vulnerable.

Bushnell

Mohamed

9 • August 1998 (page 292)

The most shocking dot comes on August 7, when the FAA and the Bureau pick up intelligence that unidentified Arabs are planning to fly "an explosive-laden plane" from an unnamed country into the World Trade Center. The FAA reportedly finds the plot "highly unlikely, given the state of the foreign country's aviation program." The FBI's New York office files the intel away without taking action.

10 • 1998 (page 292)

More than two years after the FBI finds evidence of an al Qaeda bombing plot, the U.S. embassies in Kenya and Tanzania are simultaneously bombed. The suicide truck is located precisely where Ali Mohamed took the surveillance photos in 1993, and where bin Laden himself instructed the bomb to be placed. Two hundred and twenty-four people are killed and thousands injured. After the bombing, al Qaeda again demands the release of blind Sheikh Rahman.

Days after the bombing, **Ali Mohamed** confesses to the Feds what should have been obvious to them for years: that he knows who did the bombings. But the Feds don't search his house for several weeks. Finally, on September 10, the FBI arrests him after he lies to a grand jury. But for the next nine months he's held in secrecy on a "John Doe" warrant. The Feds are terrified that word of Ali's duplicity will get out and that the FBI's New York Office and the SDNY will be held accountable for the years they allowed al Qaeda's chief spy to remain free.

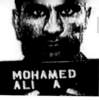

MOHAMED
ALI A

By now, **Mohammed Atta** and **Ramzi Binalshibh** have set up a safe house at 54 Marienstrasse in Hamburg. Over the months to come it will serve as a combination crash pad and flight training center for the suicidal jihadis who will perfect Ramzi Yousef's third plot.

Atta   Binalshibh

At trial, **Greg Scarpa Jr.** testifies about the eleven-month intelligence initiative in which he risked his life to provide the Feds with evidence of an al Qaeda presence in New York City. But **Judge Reena Raggi** believes **Patrick Fitzgerald**'s contention that the Yousef/Scarpa evidence, contained in dozens of FBI 302s, was a "part of a scam." She sentences Scarpa Jr. to forty years for RICO violations; he is to be housed in the Supermax prison, along with convicted terrorists including Ramzi Yousef and **Terry Nichols.**

Raggi   Fitzgerald   Scarpa Jr.   Nichols

Assigned to work on terrorism issues full-time for the FDNY, **Ronnie Bucca** learns that **Ahmed Amin Refai**, the Egyptian-American accountant with the FDNY, has submitted a false report for a lost ID. The second ID would have allowed access to fire department headquarters. After learning that Refai has told multiple lies to law enforcement officers relating to the "lost" ID, Bucca begins investigating. He learns that Refai has made frequent trips to Egypt (on a $35,000 salary) and had obtained the blueprints of the WTC prior to the bombing in 1993.

Bucca   Refai

Bucca, who believes **Refai** may be an al Qaeda mole inside the FDNY, later discovers TV news footage showing Refai acting as blind **Sheikh Rahman**'s personal bodyguard. Bucca turns over the file on the accountant to the FBI's Joint Terrorism Task force, but Detective Lou Napoli dismisses the evidence. He's the same JTTF investigator who missed multiple meetings with Emad Salem in 1992, ended his probe of Islamic militant AK-47 training in Connecticut in 1998–90, and failed to follow Abouhalima and Salameh before the first WTC bombing.

Refai *(l.)* with Rahman

Operation Able Danger commences. It's a secret data mining operation ordered by Joint Chiefs chairman **Hugh Shelton** and General **Pete Schoomaker,** the head of the army's Special Operations Command (SOCOM). The Army's Land Information Warfare Facility (LIWA) searches the Internet for open-source intelligence on al Qaeda. The liaison to the DIA is Lt. Col. Anthony Shaffer, a decorated counterintelligence officer. The goal: identify al Qaeda targets for elimination.

Shelton   **Schoomaker**

During a summit meeting in Kuala Lumpur, Malaysia, al Qaeda operations are planned by representatives from seven countries. Later dubbed the "9/11 planning session," the attendees include **Nawaf al-Hazmi** and **Khalid Al-Midhar,** two al Qaeda veterans who will later serve as "muscle hijackers" aboard AA Flight 77 on 9/11. Al-Midhar has been tracked to the meeting by CIA (via an FBI tip). The Agency asks the Malaysian Special Branch to photograph the attendees. Though **Khalid Shaikh Mohammed** is reportedly absent, his No. 2 on the planes-as-missiles plot, **Ramzi bin al-Shibh,** is there.

Al-Hazmi   **Al-Midhar**   **Mohammed**   **bin Atash**

Hambali   **Sufaat**   **al-Shibh**   **al-Quso**

Another top al Qaeda operative at the summit is **Khallad bin Atash,** who played a key role in the embassy bombings and will later direct the attack on the U.S.S. *Cole* with Yemeni **Fahad al-Quso.** Also present is **Riduan Isamuddin**, aka Hambali, an Indonesian cleric who is the link to the Yousef-KSM Manila cell, since he served with Wali Khan Amin Shah on the board of Konsonjaya, the front company that funded the cell.

The conference takes place at the condo of Yazid Sufaat, who later entertains **Zacarias Moussaoui,** the alleged twentieth hijacker. After 9/11, FBI agents will accuse the CIA of withholding pictures of the summit attendees, thus preventing the FBI from capturing al-Midhar and al-Hazmi, who slip into the U.S. on January 15, 2000, when the CIA fails to get their names on a Watch List. But a key FBI agent in Squad I-49, **Patrick Fitzgerald's** bin Laden squad, is reportedly shown the surveillance photos in 2000, and at that point the two muscle hijackers are living openly in San Diego.

Moussaoui   **Fitzgerald**

19 • February 2000 (page 332)

Atta

al-Shehhi

After several data runs, the Able Danger operation at LIWA gets four extraordinary hits that, if acted upon by the FBI, could have interdicted the 9/11 plot. The data harvest reveals the identity of lead hijacker **Mohammed Atta**, **Marwan al-Shehhi** (who will pilot UA Flight 175) and AA Flight 77 hijackers **al-Midhar** and **al-Hazmi**.

The operation also finds an active link between al Qaeda and the Brooklyn cell of **Sheikh Rahman.** This confirms al Qaeda's link (via **Ramzi Yousef**) to both attacks on the WTC (1993 and 2001) and vindicates the intelligence uncovered by Col. Rodolfo Mendoza of the PNP.

al-Hazmi

al-Midhar

Rahman

Yousef

20 • March 21, 2000 (page 342)

Jacob L. Boesen, a contract employee with Orion Scientific, which produces many of the link charts visually representing the Able Danger data, builds a declassified chart on the two Yousef cells showing links to the WTC bombing.

Mohamed

bin Laden

The chart, which represents the most active intelligence known to the DIA and the Able Danger unit at that time, shows **Ali Mohamed** within al Qaeda's inner circle, along with **Osama bin Laden, Ayman al-Zawahiri, Mohammed Atef, Wadih El-Hage,** and **Mohammed Jamal Khalifa,** bin Laden's brother-in-law—the funder of the Yousef-KSM Manila cell, extradited to Jordan in 1995 with the support of Deputy A.G. Jamie Gorelick. (See Appendix VIII, pages 568–69.)

al-Zawahiri

Atef

El-Hage

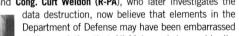

Khalifa

21 • April 2000 (page 346)

Weeks after Boesen's chart is declassified, the 2.5 terabytes of data gathered by the Able Danger operation are ordered destroyed by the Pentagon. **Lt. Col Anthony Shaffer** and **Cong. Curt Weldon (R-PA)**, who later investigates the data destruction, now believe that elements in the Department of Defense may have been embarrassed at the revelation that Ali Mohamed, honorably discharged as a U.S. Army sergeant after his service at the JFK SWC on Fort Bragg, was also a top-tier al Qaeda spy. Between April and September 2000, three separate meetings in which Shaffer seeks to brief the FBI on the Able Danger findings are cancelled by lawyers for the Defense Intelligence Agency (DIA).

Shaffer

Weldon

22 • September 2000 (page 355)

On the 20th anniversary of the JTTF, U.S. Attorney Mary Jo White celebrates with Task Force members at Windows on the World, the restaurant atop the WTC's North Tower. Citing "the close to absolutely perfect record of successful investigations and convictions," White notes that in her seven years in the Southern District of New York she has put away twenty-five Islamic terrorists, including Ramzi Yousef and Sheikh Rahman. But in treating Osama bin Laden's jihad as a series of legal cases rather than a global threat to U.S. security, the Feds have made a serious miscalculation. Now, as they party, Ramzi Yousef's extended family of Islamic radicals begins finalizing a plot to take down the very building where the JTTF members are celebrating.

If the Feds ever needed a reminder of al Qaeda's ongoing threat and the importance of **Sheikh Rahman** to **Osama bin Laden**, they get it a few days later, when the Saudi billionaire issues another video *fatwa*.

Rahman   **bin Laden**

Wearing a dagger, surrounded by al Qaeda's Egyptian leaders **Mohammed Atef** and **Dr. Ayman al-Zawahiri** as well as **Refa'i Taha Musa**, the head of the IG, bin Laden sits next to Rahman's son, who calls on jihadis to "avenge your Sheikh" and "go to the spilling of blood." Bin Laden also tells his followers to remember **El Sayyid Nosair**, the man who spilled al Qaeda's first blood in New York in 1990 with the murder of Rabbi Kahane.

While many intelligence analysts continue to link Iraq with the WTC bombing, it is clear by now that al Qaeda's leadership under bin Laden is dominated by Egyptian radicals. Expelled from Sudan since 1996, the Saudi billionaire now operates from Afghanistan. As is often the case, his *fatwa* is a precursor of violence to come.

Atef   **al-Zawahiri**   **Taha Musa**   **Nosair**

In a data run in the late summer of 2000, a new configuration of the Able Danger unit finds an al Qaeda "hot spot" in Aden, Yemen. **Shaffer** alerts SOCOM, which reportedly alerts the U.S. Central Command. But the threat intelligence reportedly doesn't get to the skipper of the U.S.S. *Cole,* who docks his ship for refueling in Aden harbor.

Shaffer

On the morning of October 12, two al Qaeda suicide bombers load a device made of C-4 explosive into a small skiff and take off across the harbor in Aden, Yemen. **The U.S.S. *Cole,*** an advanced guided missile destroyer, is at the refueling dock. As the skiff approaches the ship, the jihadis smile and wave at *Cole* crew members, who wave back. Then, when the white fiberglass boat pulls alongside, the bomb detonates, blowing a four-story hole in the side of the ship. The two bombers and seventeen U.S. sailors are killed.

The U.S.S. *Cole*

Khallad bin-Atash, a coconspirator in the bombing, had attended the January 5, 2000, Kuala Lumpur meeting where the 9/11 attacks were planned.

John O'Neill, the FBI's chief bin Laden specialist, arrives in Yemen with three hundred agents determined to break the case, but he runs afoul of U.S. Ambassador **Barbara Bodine**, who demands a much lower Bureau profile. The career diplomat goes so far as to block O'Neill's return visa to Yemen after he flies to the United States.

O'Neill   **Bodine**

Assistant FBI Director **Dale Watson**, the man who downplayed the U.S. al Qaeda presence before Congress, later tells the *Washington Post* that "sustained cooperation" with the Yemeni government "has enabled the FBI to further reduce its in-country presence." The same day, Yemen's prime minister tells the *Post* that no link has been established between the *Cole* bombers and al Qaeda.

Watson

After almost two years of protracted negotiations with the Feds, **Ali Mohamed** finally pleads guilty and admits his role as al Qaeda's top U.S. spy. Though he confesses to planning and supporting the embassy bombing plot, he is spared the death penalty. His plea deal, which remains under heavy seal, allows him to enter witness protection. Though he has separately been sentenced in absentia to death in Egypt, Mohamed manages not to give up the 9/11 plot to the Feds. The media speculates that he'll be the star witness in *United States v. bin Laden,* the embassy bombing trial Patrick Fitzgerald will prosecute in February 2001. But Mohamed never takes the stand, and the Feds are spared the embarrassment of a defense cross-examination in which Mohamed could have exposed years of negligence by the CIA, DIA, and FBI.

MOHAMED
ALI A

Muscle hijackers **Nawaf al-Hazmi** and **Khalid al-Midhar** move into rooms rented to them by **Abdussattar Shaykh**, a San Diego Muslim leader who happens to be a "tested" undercover "asset "of the FBI. Al-Hazmi even lists his real name in the San Diego phone book, but the FBI seems powerless to detect the pair. (For phone book listings, see Chapter 32, page 349.)

al-Hazmi   al-Midhar   Shaykh

In Phoenix, FBI Special Agent **Ken Williams** is embroiled in a dispute with **Harry Ellen**, a convert to Islam who worked as an FBI asset in Gaza. As a Phoenix newspaper prepares a series of stories regarding the dispute, Ellen claims that as early as 1996 he met with Williams at **a location near a field in Phoenix** (below) and told him to be wary of Islamic flight students. Shortly thereafter, **Hani Hanjour**, who will fly AA Flight 77 into the Pentagon on 9/11, begins taking pilot lessons at a Scottsdale, Arizona, flight school. Ellen later claims that Williams spurned his 1996 advice to monitor flight schools. By 2001 Hanjour is staying with **al-Midhar** and **al-Hazmi**.

Williams   Ellen

'96 meeting place   Hanjour   al-Hazmi   al-Midhar

Terrorism czar Richard Clarke calls a White House meeting with officials from the FBI, FAA, Coast Guard, Secret Service, and INS warning that "something really spectacular is going to happen here, and it's going to happen soon." The next day, Clarke chairs a meeting of the National Security Council's Counterterrorism Security Group (CSG) and orders a suspension of all nonessential travel by the staff.

FBI agent **Ken Williams** sends a memo to FBI Headquarters. He reportedly identifies eight Middle Eastern men studying at Arizona flight schools and urges the Bureau to do background checks. The communiqué, which will go down in history as the "Phoenix memo," is also sent to agents in the FBI's New York office, the Bureau's office of origin for all bin Laden–related terrorism cases. At least three people in the office see the memo, but no action is taken.

Williams

Khalid al-Midhar and another of the nineteen 9/11 hijackers are sold fake IDs by Mohammed El-Atriss, an Egyptian who was co-incorporator of Sphinx Trading, the check-cashing store in Jersey City, located four doors from the blind Sheikh's al Salaam Mosque. El-Atriss's partner was Waleed al-Noor, one of Patrick Fitzgerald's unindicted co-conspirators in the Day of Terror trial with Sheikh Rahman. Sphinx is the same location where El Sayyid Nosair, one of Ali Mohamed's trainees, kept a mailbox discovered by the FBI in 1990. El-Atriss makes up to seven phone calls to Hani Hanjour as well. The Bureau could have seized al-Midhar, a

El-Atriss

al-Midhar's fake ID

Sphinx Trading

Mohamed

key 9/11 hijacker, if they'd been monitoring Sphinx, but once again they fail to detect al-Midhar's presence, despite his move from San Diego to New Jersey, where he continues to live openly while the weeks count down toward the execution of Ramzi Yousef's return engagement with the WTC.

A Presidential Daily Briefing to George W. Bush on vacation in Crawford, Texas, is entitled "Bin Laden Determined to Attack In the U.S." The PDB not only references a threat to hijack a plane to free blind Sheikh Rahman—a plan to which Greg Scarpa Jr. had alerted the Feds in 1996 after learning of it from Ramzi Yousef—but also cites "a senior EIJ member" living in California, a reference to Ali Mohamed. But the repeated references to the blind Sheikh and a hijack threat are ignored, even though by the first week in September the Taliban government in Afghanistan offers to exchange eight Christian missionaries in exchange for Sheikh Rahman. Ali Mohamed, now in witness protection, remains silent about Yousef's plot to hijack airliners and use them as missiles; only after 9/11 does he confess to Special Agent Jack Cloonan that he trained hijackers in the use of box cutters.

Bush in Crawford

Mohamed

Rahman

Yousef

Using box cutters and other short-bladed knives, nineteen hijackers seize control of four U.S. airliners. Mohammed Atta pilots AA 11 into the WTC's North Tower. Marwan Al-Shehhi flies UA 175 into the South Tower. Hani Hanjour, aided by al-Midhar and al-Hazmi, crashes AA 77 into the Pentagon—despite months of prior warnings to the FBI, CIA, and DIA via the Able Danger operation. FDNY fire marshal Ronnie Bucca, who warned for years that Yousef would attack the WTC again, dies on the seventy-eighth floor of the South Tower as he tries to beat back the flames, one of 343 heroic firefighters lost that day.

Bucca on 9/11

Atta

al-Shehhi

Hanjour

al-Midhar

al-Hazmi

34 • Spring 2004 (page 397)

After briefing the 9/11 Commission about the Able Danger unit's 2000 report on the four hijackers and al Qaeda's ties to the blind Sheikh, **Lt. Col. Anthony Shaffer's** testimony is ignored by **Dietrich Snell,** the former SDNY AUSA who is now a senior counsel to the commission. In the commission's final report, Snell pushes the origin of the plot forward two years and alleges

Shaffer

that Ramzi Yousef was not involved—relying *solely* on the word of **Khalid Shaikh Mohammed,** who has been tortured. Testifying before the Commission, **Patrick Fitzgerald** calls **Ali Mohamed** "one of the most chilling examples of al Qaeda's espionage," but says nothing about how Mohamed outgunned the FBI for years. Meanwhile, after talking openly about the Able Danger cover up, Shaffer has his security clearance pulled, and the Bronze Star winner becomes the target of a DOD witchhunt.

Snell

Mohamed

KSM captured

Fitzgerald

35 • February 2005 (page 415)

In the Supermax prison, **Greg Scarpa Jr.** learns from Oklahoma City bomber **Terry Nichols** about an undiscovered cache of explosives from the Oklahoma City bombing hidden in Nichols's former home in Kansas. Forensic investigator **Angela Clemente** alerts Congress, and the FBI recovers the explosives precisely where Scarpa said they would be. Meanwhile, Brooklyn D.A. **Charles "Joe" Hynes**'s Rackets Bureau begins to examine evidence on SSA Lin DeVecchio, investigated by Clemente.

Scarpa Jr.

Nichols

Clemente

Hynes

36 • September 2005 (page 430)

Hynes empanels a grand jury to review the evidence on **Lin DeVecchio.** On March 30, 2006, DeVecchio is indicted on four counts of homicide relating to the murders of **Mary Bari,** Larry Lampesi, Joe DeDomenico, and **Patrick Porco,** all killed on the word of DeVecchio's Top Echelon informant **Greg Scarpa Sr.**

DeVecchio

Scarpa Sr.

Bari

Porco

37 • September 11, 2006 (page 463)

All roads lead back to Brooklyn. On the fifth anniversary of the biggest unsolved mass murder in U.S. history, the Brooklyn D.A.'s case holds out the last best hope that a probe of the DeVecchio scandal will shed new light on the key al Qaeda intelligence from Ramzi Yousef to Scarpa Jr. in 1996. If congressional investigators take that line of inquiry seriously, it could lead to a new investigation into possible obstruction of justice by senior FBI and DOJ officials on the road to 9/11.

Afterward, Ms. White and Lewis D. Schiliro, the acting assistant director of the New York Office of the Federal Bureau of Investigation, announced the unsealing of an indictment that charged another defendant in the Manila bombing conspiracy.

"The defendant, Khaled Shaikh Mohammad, whom prosecutors described as a possible relative of Mr. Yousef, who helped him finance and develop the airline bomb plot, is a fugitive. Officials said the Government has offered a reward of up to $2 million for information that assists in the arrest or conviction of the fugitive, who is said to be in his 30's."

Nearly three years after his 1995 escape from the Su Casa guesthouse in Islamabad, and two years after the FBI helped Yousef contact him— only to lose him again in Doha, Qatar—the Feds were finally alerting the world that there was another major al Qaeda "fugitive" loose with a price on his head.

In one sense, Khalid Shaikh Mohammed had been the ultimate "sleeper," an agent who operates in the shadows, lying low for years until he's activated. He'd been a college student in North Carolina, and though he was an early member of the Muslim Brotherhood,[11] terrorism analysts had little sense of him until he showed up in Manila with his nephew in 1994.[12] Even then, as he frequented karaoke bars and used "B-girls" as fronts to open bank accounts and buy mobile phones for the cell, KSM behaved more like a lounge lizard than a terrorist.[13] The FBI had known about him since early 1995; his picture was even contained on Yousef's Toshiba laptop,[14] and the Philippines National Police had identified him as the mysterious figure with the alias "Salem Ali."

But by now, in January 1998, as his first public wanted poster was issued, KSM had risen to the position of senior al Qaeda military commander and was actively involved in executing the planes-into-buildings plot his nephew had conceived.

"You just have to ask," says terrorism analyst Paul Thompson, "what possible reason could the SDNY have had for keeping KSM's indictment a secret? Why weren't they all over the worldwide media for him, the same way they had been for Ramzi? During those years, from 1995 to 1998, Khalid Shaikh was able to [develop] the suicide-hijacking plot."

It was clear now that there were some dots that the Justice Department didn't want people on the outside—especially the media—to connect.

Louis Freeh's Right-Hand Man on Terrorism

In early February, testifying before Congress, Dale Watson, the FBI's assistant director for counter terrorism, gave a cautionary but confident assessment.

"Although we should not allow ourselves to be lulled into a false sense of security, I believe it is important to note that in the five years since the Trade Center bombing, no significant act of foreign directed terrorism has occurred on American soil."[15]

Without disclosing the FBI's knowledge of Ramzi Yousef's possible connection to the crash of TWA 800, Watson later told Congress that he knew of only three al Qaeda suspects in the United States prior to August 1998.[16] Apparently he hadn't seen the FBI 302s documenting Yousef's declaration to Greg Scarpa Jr., that he had an active cell in New York in the spring of 1996. Further, in making that statement before a congressional oversight committee, Watson was reinforcing the FBI myth that Osama bin Laden had no connection to al Qaeda's 1993 Trade Center bombing cell, whose members were trained by Ali Mohamed, bin Laden's personal security consultant.

In his 2005 memoir, *My FBI*, then-director Louis Freeh lavished praise on Watson. "Dale ran our counterterrorism (or CT) section and later the newly formed CT Division and was my right hand in the most important FBI cases of the decade," wrote Freeh, who called Watson "the single best qualified and knowledgeable CT leader and expert we had. None of the FBI's progress in this area would have happened without him."[17]

Apparently that opinion was not universally shared in the bin Laden office of origin. In the spring of 2006, retired Special Agent Jack Cloonan told me that when Watson "was in the New York Office he was referred to as 'a rube.'" Cloonan added that "every time Watson walked by" his FBI boss, the supervisor would take "a can of 'bullshit spray' and spray it at him."

The contempt of elite agents like Cloonan for Headquarters-based "suits" like Watson was nothing new in the FBI. In fact, the bifurcated Bureau culture seemed to pit street or "brick" agents like Cloonan against their bosses, known collectively as "management."[18]

But in the early months of 1998, Cloonan and I-49 squad agents like Dan Coleman and Frank Pellegrino seemed no closer to unraveling the embassy-bombing plot than they'd been before their encounter with Ali Mohamed in October. And it wasn't as if they hadn't been warned. In fact, the namesake of their unit was about to offer a major clue as to his intentions.

The Jews and the Crusaders

On February 22, 1998, Osama bin Laden issued his most aggressive *fatwa* to date. Under the banner of the "International Islamic Front for Jihad on the Jews and Crusaders," his edict, published in *Al-Quds al-Arabi,* stated that "Muslims should kill Americans—including civilians—anywhere in the world where they can be found."[19] The *fatwa* was endorsed by Dr. Ayman al-Zawahiri's Egyptian Islamic Jihad, the group Ali Mohamed had embraced since the Sadat assassination in 1981. In fact, it contained language that sounded strikingly similar to Ali Mohamed's videotaped warning made at Fort Bragg years before: "The ruling to kill the Americans and their allies," wrote bin Laden, "is an individual duty for every Muslim who can do it in any country in which it is possible to do it."

Patrick Fitzgerald was certainly aware of that Fort Bragg tape. As coprosecutor in the Day of Terror trial, he had listened as Roger Stavis played it for the jury on the afternoon of July 13, 1995. During that session, Fitzgerald sat listening as Khalid Ibrahim spoke in great detail about the training he and other "brothers" had received from "Abu Osama"—the man Fitzgerald knew to be Ali Mohamed.

Fitzgerald's squad was in the best position inside the Justice Department to stop the disaster that was about to unfold in Africa, but he wasn't the only Fed who didn't seem to appreciate the warnings.

In February 1998, six months before the bombings, Sudan's intelligence chief once more offered to share terrorism data with the FBI in a letter addressed to David Williams, Special Agent in Charge (SAC) of the Middle East and North Africa.[20]

Keep in mind that the Sudanese, who had played host to bin Laden for five years, were in possession of extraordinary intelligence about the way he did business. Further, the government in Khartoum was highly motivated to cooperate, because it wanted its assets in U.S. banks unfrozen.

But SAC Williams replied to the Sudanese on June 24 that he was "not in a position to accept your kind offer"—and another opportunity to interdict bin Laden months before the embassy bombings, was lost.

The Clock Ticks Down

By March, in response to Ambassador Bushnell's urgent request for an assessment of the U.S. embassy's vulnerability, the State Department sent a team to Nairobi to update their 1994 threat assessment. They recommended $500,000 in security improvements, including new fences, enhanced perimeter surveillance, and a roll-down garage door for the underground parking garage.

At that point, the bombing coconspirators were assembling the components for the device that would explode in Dar es Salaam, Tanzania. Khalfan Khamis Mohamed bought a white Suzuki to be used to transport the bomb that was to be built using TNT, gas cylinders, and detonators.[21] In Ramzi Yousef's 1993 World Trade urea-nitrate device, he had used hydrogen cylinders to enhance the blasting radius.

In April and May, Ambassador Bushnell attempted to bypass a State Department official and communicate her urgent concern directly to Secretary of State Madeleine Albright. She noted that she had been fighting for months for a more secure embassy in the face of mounting terrorist threats, and reported that she herself was the target of an assassination plot. The State Department had repeatedly refused to grant her requests, citing a lack of money, but in Bushnell's view that kind of response was "endangering the lives of embassy personnel."

Albright reportedly took no immediate action.[22]

Witness for a Killer

In April, six years after the grisly triple murder at the Ewell house in California, son Dana Ewell and his paid accomplice, Joel Radovcich, were about to go on trial. The Fresno County sheriff's detectives had put together an ironclad case against them: They had the murder weapon, purchased for Joel by Jack Ponce, tied directly to slugs found at the crime scene; Ponce's testimony linking Joel and Dana to the murder-for-hire plot; and indisputable proof that Dana had milked a trust fund from his grandmother to help support the daughter of his alibi witness, Special Agent John Zent— the man the Bureau had relied on to monitor Ali Mohamed.[23]

Despite a meticulous investigation by Detectives John Souza, Chris Curtice, and their team, Zent and his daughter continued to visit Dana in prison and maintain his innocence.[24] In fact, when the trial began, Zent was even called as a character witness by Dana's lawyers. As he approached the witness stand on the day of his testimony, the former FBI agent greeted the accused murder conspirator with a "Hi, Dana" and wished him "good luck" when he'd finished.[25]

Zent's testimony was troubling, especially given that he was a veteran federal agent. He admitted that he'd helped to establish Dana's alibi, days after the murders, by rummaging through the trash at his Morgan Hills house to retrieve two receipts for purchases Ewell had made around the time Radovcich was executing his family.[26] Moreover, despite the overwhelming evidence of Dana's guilt, Zent used part of his time on the stand to challenge the professionalism of the Fresno sheriff's detectives—whom he admitted he began calling "Bert and Ernie," after the Sesame Street characters.

A week later, prosecutor James Oppliger mounted a rebuttal case, using most of his witnesses to counter the statements Zent had made under oath. As Steve Elliott reported in the *Fresno Bee*, "Zent's credibility was clearly the target from the start . . . as witness after witness testified that events happened differently from how Zent claimed they did. . . . Altogether, 11 of the 15 witnesses who testified Tuesday disputed parts of Zent's account of the events. Ewell's lawyers and Radovcich's attorney had the opportunity to call their own witnesses to counter the prosecutor's rebuttal case, but neither side did."[27]

On May 12, 1998, Dana Ewell was found guilty of the murder of his mother, father, and sister. The jury noted the "special circumstances" of "multiple murder, murder for financial gain, and murder by lying in wait," each of which made the young man eligible for the death penalty.[28] The jury was so appalled by the crime, and certain of Dana's guilt, that during the penalty phase 11 of the 12 voted that he should die by lethal injection.[29] If not for one holdout, the young man who might have become John Zent's son-in-law would have met the executioner.

"You have got to wonder, what kind of agent did the FBI trust to watch this al Qaeda killer Mohamed, when six years after this incredibly violent triple murder, he's testifying for Dana as a character witness?" says Detective John Souza. "What does it say, not just about his skill at judging character, but at his own ability to admit he was wrong?"

It was on the word of John Zent that Ali Mohamed had been sprung from the custody of the Royal Canadian Mounted Police in 1993. Once on the street, he'd gone on to train the al Qaeda operatives who helped bring down two U.S. Blackhawk helicopters in Somalia. He'd brokered that summit between bin Laden and the chief of Hezbollah and he'd photographed the U.S. embassy in Nairobi for the suicide truck-bomb plot. Now, in the spring of 1998, the clock was ticking down on that plot. And Patrick Fitzgerald's elite bin Laden squad—despite multiple warnings—was somehow unable to detect it.

Moving the Jihad to "U.S. Soil"

In May 1998, Osama bin Laden granted his notorious "interview" with John Miller, then a correspondent for ABC News. The word "interview" is in quotes because, as Miller later admitted, he was forced to submit his questions in advance, and since he didn't speak Arabic, he had no idea how bin Laden was responding. But during the videotaped encounter in a hideout in Afghanistan, bin Laden gave another signal to Fitzgerald and his squad members about bin Laden's links to Yousef's Manila cell.

While the Saudi billionaire denied knowing Yousef before the World Trade Center bombing, he talked warmly about Wali Khan Amin Shah, who planted the bomb in the Greenbelt Theater in Manila as a precursor to Ramzi's wet test aboard PAL 434.

"His nickname in Afghanistan was 'the Lion,'" said bin Laden. "He was among the most courageous Muslim young men. He was a close friend and we used to fight from the same trenches in Afghanistan."[30]

Then, with a nod to his chief bomb maker, who had already designed the planes-as-missiles operation that his uncle was developing, bin Laden made a prediction that should have caused heads to turn at 26 Federal Plaza.

"We say to the Americans as people and to American mothers, if they cherish their lives and if they cherish their sons, they must elect an American patriotic government that caters to their interests not the interests of the Jews. If the present injustice continues with the wave of national consciousness, it will inevitably move the battle to American soil, just as Ramzi Yousef and others have done."

In the FBI's own files they had a record of the addendum Ramzi Yousef had called in to Nidal Ayyad the night of his escape from New York after failing to knock the North Tower of the WTC into the South Tower: "our calculations were not very accurate this time." declared Yousef. "However we promise you that next time it will be very precise and the Trade Center will be one of our targets."[31]

Fourteen months later, in 1995, as Special Agent Frank Pellegrino interrogated Abdul Hakim Murad on his rendition back to the United States, Yousef's oldest friend made a similar prediction, which Pellegrino memorialized in a 302 memo: "Murad advised that Ramzi wanted to return to the United States in the future to bomb the World Trade Center a second time."[32] Pellegrino was now a key operative in I-49, Fitzgerald's bin Laden squad.

Taken in isolation, bin Laden's threat to strike "U.S. soil" might have been seen as mere posturing. But if Fitzgerald's squad had been honest about connecting all the dots, they would have admitted that al Qaeda had already attacked the World Trade Center towers once, and they would have alerted other U.S. intelligence agencies that Yousef's uncle was now working on a plot to hit them again. That failure to join all those dots, by selectively editing out intelligence to remove "al Qaeda" from the Kahane murder and the WTC bombing, would have fatal consequences on September 11, 2001—especially in light of a report that was received in August 1998 by the FAA and the FBI.

Startling intelligence had come in that unidentified Arabs were planning to fly "an explosive-laden plane," from an unnamed country into the World Trade Center.[33] It was the most specific of a dozen planes-as-missiles warnings picked up by U.S. intelligence agencies in the years leading to 9/11. The Bureau's NYO filed the intelligence away at the time without taking action.

But if they needed any reminder of al Qaeda's viability, it came on August 6, when the Egyptian Islamic Jihad, Ali Mohamed's old group, warned that they would soon deliver "a message to the U.S. which we hope they read with care, because we will write it, with God's help, in a language they will understand."[34]

Ali Mohamed knew exactly what was about to happen. In fact, he had done the surveillance five years earlier and worked directly with the cell.

Ground Zero Nairobi and Dar es Salaam

The next morning, eight years to the day after U.S. troops were first sent into Saudi Arabia,[35] a suicide truck bomb detonated outside the U.S. embassy in Nairobi, Kenya, on the precise spot where Ali Mohamed had taken the pictures. Within minutes, a similar bomb exploded in Dar es Salaam, Tanzania.

In Kenya, just as Mustafa Ahmed had predicted, the fiendish plot began when the bombers set off a stun grenade, bringing embassy workers to the glass windows just before they shattered. Ambassador Prudence Bushnell, who had valiantly tried to warn the State Department, narrowly escaped death.[36] Between the two bombings, 224 were killed and four thousand were injured.

Again, the question is, "What did the FBI know about the planning for those bombings and when did they know it?" Until this analysis of the Ali Mohamed case, the true depth of the FBI's negligence prior to the embassy bombings has never been revealed. The fault lies with the Bureau in general and the New York Office in particular, but the lion's share of culpability belongs to I-49, the bin Laden squad, and its boss, Patrick Fitzgerald.

By August 1998, he knew chapter and verse on Ali Mohamed: how he'd been working as an informant or asset for the Bureau since 1992; how his "control" agent, John Zent, had helped him give the Mounties the slip in Canada—a favor that had freed him up to initiate the embassy bombing plot; how Andrew McCarthy, Fitzgerald's partner in the Day of Terror case, had spoken directly to Ali in late 1994 and cited him as an unindicted coconspirator; how the FBI had wiretaps on the home of Ali's close associate Wadih El-Hage from 1996 on; how Fitzgerald had secured FISA warrants so that his squad could monitor Ali's home phone and computer; how agent Bell had recorded Ali's prediction that a "target" in East Africa was at risk; how the following August, a year before the bombings, Special Agent Dan Coleman had searched El-Hage's house, only to find the phone number of their own informant, Ali Amiriki (Ali the American); and then, finally, how Fitzgerald, Cloonan, and Bell had taken a pass at Mohamed in October—only to hear him declare that he "loved" Osama bin Laden and didn't need a religious edict to attack the United States.

"There is zero doubt," says one former agent who worked in the FBI's NYO, that "if Ali Mohamed ha[d] been properly vetted, his inside knowledge of the embassy-bombing plot, coupled with the intel the Bureau had, could have interdicted that event."[37]

Unable to Stop the Train Wreck

The day after the bombing, the Feds were suddenly desperate to get a hold of Mohamed, their "man" inside al Qaeda. "It was like a replay of the catch-up scene after World Trade One," says that same agent. "The way Anticev and Napoli scrambled to find Salem. The only difference was that Emad had been working for *us,* and it was patently clear by now that Ali Mohamed was working for *them.*"

Two days later, a group calling itself the "Islamic Army for the Liberation of the Holy Places" took credit for the bombing. The name, with its echo of Ramzi Yousef's "Fifth Battalion of the Liberation Army," was another reminder of how tightly woven this al Qaeda family of terrorists really was.

On the ninth floor tier of the MCC in December 1996, Yousef had told Greg Scarpa Jr. that Osama bin Laden (aka "Bojinga") was planning to hijack planes to free the blind Sheikh. Now, as they listed their demands, the al Qaeda murderers insisted on "the release of . . . the Muslims detained in the United State[s?] . . . first and foremost Sheikh Omar Abdel Rahman (the spiritual guide of the al Gamma'a Islamya) who is jailed in the United States."

If anybody in squad I-49 had taken the time to go back and read Special Agent Nancy Floyd's reports on her early meetings with Emad Salem in 1991 they might have found a reference to the "nest of vipers" the Sheikh maintained at the al Salaam mosque on Kennedy Boulevard in Jersey City. That was the mosque that Nosair had attended, the same location as the "Jersey Jihad Office" where Ali Mohamed had proudly screened his training tapes from Fort Bragg for his Egyptian trainees back in 1989—nine years earlier.

If Fitzgerald had analyzed the Kahane assassination evidence, he would have been reminded that El Sayyid Nosair had maintained a mailbox at Sphinx Trading Company, the Jersey City check-cashing store four doors down from that mosque. Sphinx had been coincorporated by Waleed al-Noor, one of the unindicted coconspirators Fitzgerald and McCarthy had named in the Day of Terror case. In the same location, three years later, two of the 9/11 hijackers would pick up their fake IDs for the execution of Ramzi Yousef's planes-as-missiles plot on September 11.

By now, there were so many al Qaeda dots on the chart in the bin Laden squad that they were resolving into a straight line, and it led from the Calverton surveillance right through the embassy bombings to Ali Mohamed.

If Patrick Fitzgerald had sat for an interview with me, I would have asked him how he felt after he first got word that those suicide truck bombs had erupted in East Africa. Did he have any regrets that he had tried to *turn* Ali rather than busting him? Court records would later show that the Feds were intercepting the phone conversations and faxes of the Kenya cell members right up to the day of the attacks.[38] With all the wiretaps and all the warnings, how did Fitzgerald miss that oncoming train wreck in Africa?

Ali Mohamed had enjoyed an extraordinary *fourteen-year run*, deceiving one intelligence agency after another. He'd stung the CIA, the Green Berets, and then the FBI. But given their ability to go back and access his earlier damage with Nosair and the WTC bombing cell, the FBI had the most to explain. How had the best and the brightest in the NYO and the SDNY failed?

For Fitzgerald and company, it was time for damage control. Time, once and for all, to stop trusting Ali and bring him in.

As terrorism expert Steve Emerson put it: "Ali Mohamed is one of the most frightening examples of the infiltration of terrorists into the infrastructure of the United States. Like a [character in a] John Le Carré thriller, he played the role of a triple agent and nearly got away with it."[39]

28

THE SPY WHO
WASN'T THERE

It took the Feds two days after the bombing to reach Ali Mohamed by phone. During that first call and a subsequent conversation, he told FBI agents that he knew who had carried out the bombings, but would not give the government the names.[1] He also tried backpedaling, disassociating himself from the plot. He told the agents that he had lived in Kenya in 1994, running truck-importing and diamond-selling businesses for bin Laden, but that when he was "shown a file concerning a plan to attack the U.S. embassy in Nairobi," he had "discouraged" the cell members from carrying out the attack.

Considering that Mohamed had told Fitzgerald at their dinner meeting in the fall of 1997 that he had fake passports and the means to leave the country quickly, it's mind-boggling how long it took the Feds to search his home: They didn't arrive at 7233 Pepperwood Knoll Lane in Sacramento, California, until August 24, more than two weeks after the Nairobi bombing.[2] Apparently the SDNY prosecutors had let their FISA warrant on Ali's phone tap lapse, because they didn't begin monitoring his calls again until August 11.[3]

On the day of the search, the Feds got a key to the two-bedroom apartment from the manager of Ali's building, a single-story complex with three other units.

The ten-member team, comprised of computer specialists, photographers, and an English-Arabic translator, entered when Mohamed wasn't home.[4] Right away the agents found a desktop computer and a laptop. They cloned both hard drives and removed a series of CD-ROM and floppy disks. A trove of original documents was photocopied, and then returned to Mohamed's files: Clearly, the Bureau didn't want Ali to know they'd been there.

Among the papers recovered were a series of training documents, and a passport with a new alias: Ahmed Baha'a El-din Mohamed Adam. In a file marked "Cocktail," the agents discovered what appeared to be a draft manual on sleeper cell structure, created as recently as May 30, 1998. For those analysts who believed that Mohamed had somehow turned, this was proof positive that he'd remained loyal to al Qaeda.

The file on cell structure read in part:

> Every member knows how to do everything.
> Every member has a legal job as a cover (Student, worker, trade).
> Safety is the main concern, so the contingency plan is very important. Before working on the target you have (to) specify a rally point to meet in case of separation for any reason.
> The communications between the different groups are conducted through the dead mail drop only.
> Each group does not know anything about the other group, even Majmouat.* Al-qeyada does not know how many group[s] under its leadership. Only the one group know each other because the members of one group only working with each other.

This was prima facie evidence that Mohamed, who had links to the New York cell dating back to 1989, was an operative of al Qaeda.

The agents also found what they later described as "a coded letter from a coconspirator advising of Wadih El-Hage's 1997 trip to visit Osama Bin Laden and his subsequent interview by American authorities"—proof that Ali knew the Feds were watching El-Hage. The computer also contained

---

* *Majmu'at* in Arabic means "the collected" or "the collection." "Al-qeyada" is Ali's spelling for the terror network he was working for.

an account of the 1996 ferry accident on Lake Victoria in Africa in which al Qaeda leader Abu Ubaidah reportedly drowned.

It's unclear whether Mohamed returned to the apartment after the Feds had been through it, or if he'd detected their search. But at some point that month he got a warning call from Anas Al-Liby, the al Qaeda computer hacker who had helped him do the embassy surveillance back in 1993. Mohamed Rashed Daoud al-'Owali, the Saudi who had driven the bombing truck, had been arrested and revealed the substance of the call. As Jack Cloonan remembers, "Anas says to him, 'Do you know that brother [meaning al-'Owali]? 'Cause if you do, get the fuck out of there.'"

"After the bombing," Mohamed later admitted, "I made plans to go to Egypt and later to Afghanistan to meet bin Laden. But before I could leave, I was subpoenaed to testify before the grand jury in the Southern District of New York."[5]

With his cover now blown, the smart thing for Ali Mohamed to do would have been to run—to bring the curtain down on his fourteen-year career as al Qaeda's top American spy and withdraw to the safety of bin Laden's Afghan redoubt.

Ali Rolls the Dice

But like many of the characters who change history, Ali Abdel Saoud Mohamed had a fatal flaw: pride, one of the seven deadly Christian sins. He had stood eyeball to eyeball with Patrick Fitzgerald, the Justice Department's bin Laden brain, and he had faced him down. He'd seen how his brother Wadih El-Hage had lied with impunity before a grand jury in New York and escaped to sell tires in Texas. He himself had admitted treasonous crimes to the Feds and yet he was still on the loose. So Ali Mohamed reasoned that he could brass it out.

"He figures, 'I'll roll my dice and I'll walk,'" says Cloonan. "'I really didn't put the bomb down, you know? Maybe I can get away with this. I can bullshit.' He figures he'll go before the grand jury and commit perjury."[6]

But by now Patrick Fitzgerald, who'd been played like a fool by Ali, had run out of patience. On September 10, 1998, almost three years to the day before the attacks of 9/11, Mohamed flew back to New York and entered a grand jury room.

As bin Laden's trusted security adviser, and the protégé of Dr. al-Zawahiri, al Qaeda's second in command, Mohamed almost certainly knew of the planes-as-missiles operation that Khalid Shaikh Mohammed was now executing. Yousef had conceived the plot in Manila in 1994, when his cell was financed by Mohammed Jamal Khalifa. At that point, Ali Mohamed was living in Kenya with Wadih El-Hage, who was bin Laden's personal secretary. Mohamed had stayed in bin Laden's own house in 1994 as he trained his bodyguards. His close friend Ihab Ali had earned his pilot's license after studying at the Norman Flight School in Oklahoma, where two of the 9/11 hijackers would be spotted. Later, after 9/11, Ali would give the Feds a chilling account of how he had trained jihadis on how to hijack planes. The number of secrets Ali Mohamed knew could have unraveled the top leadership of al Qaeda, if only the Feds could turn him. And now he was walking right through the door of a secret grand jury room.

Patrick Fitzgerald himself described what happened next: "Ali Mohamed lied in that grand jury proceeding and left the courthouse to go to his hotel, followed by FBI agents, but not under arrest. He had imminent plans to fly to Egypt. It was believed at the time that Mohamed lied and that he was involved with the al Qaeda network."[7]

That statement was delivered by Fitzgerald to the Senate Judiciary Committee on October 21, 2003, more than two years after 9/11. He would go on to blame "the wall" for the FBI's reluctance to arrest Mohamed on the spot, and attribute his ultimate seizure to "luck," falsely claiming that "Mohammed had not by then been tied to the bombings." But Fitzgerald neglected to tell the senators that SDNY prosecutors and FBI agents had been monitoring the bombing cell members for two years, or that they'd had multiple face-to-face meetings with Mohamed himself.

He continued:

The decision had to be made at that moment whether to charge Mohamed with false statements. If not, Mohamed would leave the country. That difficult decision had to be made without knowing or reviewing the intelligence information on the other side of the "wall." It was ultimately decided to arrest Mohamed that night in his hotel room. The team got lucky but we never should have had to rely on luck. The prosecution team later obtained access to the intelligence information, including documents obtained from an earlier search of Mohamed's home by the intelligence team on the other side of "the wall." Those documents included direct written communications with al Qaeda members and a library of al Qaeda training materials that would have made the decision far less difficult. (We could only obtain that access after the arrest with the specific permission of the Attorney General of the United States, based upon the fact that we had obligations to provide the defendant with discovery materials and because the intelligence investigation of Mohamed had effectively ended.)

Fitzgerald was attempting to use Jamie Gorelick's 1995 memo ordering agents to separate criminal investigations from intelligence probes, as an excuse for not having grabbed Ali sooner. But in fact, as we've demonstrated time and again, with respect to I-49, his bin Laden Squad, there was no "wall." No barrier divided Fitzgerald, the prosecutor, from Agents Bell or Cloonan when they sat across that table from Ali Mohamed in Sacramento. They were attempting to gather both raw intelligence and evidence of an indictable crime. They had gone through the proper FISA channel to obtain search warrants on Mohamed's phone and computer months before the embassy bombing. They'd searched El-Hage's house in August 1997, a year before the truck bomb erupted in Nairobi. No wall had prevented them from connecting the dots on Ali's links to Nosair, Yousef's WTC bombing cell, or the blind Sheikh's "jihad army," which Fitzgerald himself had prosecuted.

Patrick Fitzgerald, it seemed, suffered from a fatal flaw of his own: trust. Somehow this son of an Irish immigrant doorman seemed to lack the street smarts to perceive how Ali Mohamed was shining him on. The only "luck" he experienced on September 10, 1998, was in Ali's mistaken decision to return to New York.

But even in their attempt to put the handcuffs on Mohamed, the agents of Squad I-49 underestimated him. After cornering Ali in his hotel room following his grand jury appearance, they allowed him to go into a bathroom, where he immediately destroyed key evidence. The incident was another stunning embarrassment for the Bureau, but Jack Cloonan was willing to confess the details:

> While he was under guard in the hotel room, [Ali] asked to go to the bathroom. He went into the bathroom and he had an address book with him, and he ripped a page out of that [book] that had a telephone number and a safe house address for al-Zawahiri in Bern, Switzerland.

After flushing the evidence, Cloonan says, Mohammed went through the address book looking for other incriminating information before the Feds finally realized what was happening and put him under arrest.[8]

"Police work 101 is that when you are bringing a suspect into custody, you immediately search his person," says an agent who worked organized crime in the FBI's New York Office. "Given what they had to know about Mohamed at this point, it boggles the mind to think that they let him out of their sight for a second once they'd decided to grab him."

Ali Mohamed AKA John Doe

Once he was out of the bathroom, the Feds finally put the handcuffs on Ali. But to shield itself from the embarrassment of arresting an al Qaeda spy who had been one of their own informants, he was charged on a "John Doe" warrant. His case was sealed and he was locked away in the MCC. Mohamed soon became the spy who wasn't there. He had been brought to ground, but the potential scandal the Feds faced if word got out about the years that he'd played them, meant that Ali still controlled the play.

Despite all the murder and mayhem he had wreaked for the jihad, he knew how valuable he could be to SDNY prosecutors as they continued to fight the war on terror from courtrooms in Lower Manhattan. And so, as Benjamin Weiser of the *New York Times* put it, Mohamed was buried "under a cloak of secrecy rarely seen in the public courts."[9]

Later, the Justice Department would issue what it called an "information" to the public on the East African embassy bombings. It laid out the names of the principal players in the twin bombings planned by al Qaeda:

> On August 7, 1998, at approximately 10:30 A.M. local time, two Embassies of the United States of America, located in the East African cities of Nairobi, Kenya, and Dar es Salaam, Tanzania, were attacked in coordinated truck bombings, later determined to have occurred approximately four minutes apart. In Nairobi, 213 people were killed in the blast, while 11 individuals died in the bombing at Dar es Salaam. The bombings were carried out by members and associates of Usama Bin Ladin's organization, known by the Arabic word "al-Qaeda," literally, "the base". . . .
>
> Within hours of the bombings, FBI personnel were dispatched to East Africa to assist the Kenyan Criminal Investigative Division (CID) and Tanzanian CID in conducting crime scene forensic examinations, as well as investigative interviews,

searches and arrests. The information detailed herein was primarily developed as a result of these investigations, still ongoing, at Nairobi and Dar es Salaam.

Sometime in 1993 to early 1994, individuals associated with al-Qaeda, a terrorist organization founded by Usama Bin Ladin and Muhammed Atef, began to locate to Kenya, primarily to the Nairobi and Mombassa areas.

One of the first Osama bin Laden associates and former mujahidin to move to Kenya was Wadih El-Hage (hereafter referred to as El-Hage), a Lebanese Christian by birth, who later became a naturalized American citizen and converted to Islam. At this time, Abu Ubaidah al-Banshiri (hereafter referred to as Abu Ubaidah), a powerful member of Usama Bin Ladin's leadership, was also in Tanzania. Until his death in a ferry accident on Lake Victoria in May 1996, Abu Ubaidah was believed to have been one of Usama Bin Ladin's two most influential military commanders.

Initial planning of the attacks against the US embassy at Nairobi seems to have begun in Spring 1998, with the movement of key personnel into East Africa.

There were two problems with this official account by the Feds. First, as they should have known, the planning had begun in the late fall of *1993*, five years earlier. Second, the photographs that showed bin Laden where to place the truck bomb were taken by a man who had been released from Canadian custody just before the surveillance on the word of an FBI agent. And, in perhaps the worst lapse in its "information," the Justice Department left out the man's whereabouts: he was sitting in a New York federal jail under a fictitious name, courtesy of the U.S. government.

Son of "The Killing Machine"

A few weeks later, in another Federal courthouse across the East River in Brooklyn, the Feds would seek to rewrite history again—excising from the public record a major intelligence initiative from 1996 that had revealed the existence of an active al Qaeda cell in New York City. Once again, Patrick Fitzgerald was directly involved.

Greg Scarpa Jr. had been indicted on multiple RICO counts of illegal gambling, loan sharking, racketeering, and tax fraud. The charges against him also included five counts of homicide. Assistant U.S. Attorney Sung-Hee Suh told Jerry Capeci, then writing his "Gangland" column for the New York *Daily News* that "Junior was ready and willing to follow his father's lead."[10]

The judge in the case, Reena Raggi, was no stranger to terrorism issues. In December 1992, she was the magistrate who had granted Mohammed

Ajaj's[11] request to get back his suitcase of manuals and tapes seized by the INS the night he flew into JFK with Ramzi Yousef[12]—materials that included "books and manuals on how to use hand grenades, how to commit sabotage, how to make poisons and Molotov cocktails, how to place land mines, instructional materials on how to kill with a knife, diagrams depicting how to make silencers, videotapes about suicide car bombings and how to make TNT."[13] Ajaj was identified by an Assistant U.S. Attorney as a member of the Al-Fatah terrorist group. And even though the material never found its way back to him, Raggi had granted his motion.

Judge Raggi was also a former AUSA in the Eastern District, the very office that was seeking to put Greg Jr. away. Now she was back on the bench in U.S. District Court as Scarpa Jr. took the stand in his own defense. On October 13, 1998, lawyer Larry Silverman questioned his client about the work he'd done to pass Yousef's secrets on to the Feds.

Greg Jr. described the two-inch camera that the warden of the MCC had given him to photograph Yousef's "kites." "It was a spy camera," said Greg.[14]

The younger Scarpa then told the court how he'd been trained for his undercover role by an FBI agent named Pat White. White, he said, "had told me to show [Yousef] that [I'm] the boss of a crew and [I'm] a tough guy and that [I'm] in a wing of the Cosa Nostra, the Mafia. And he says, 'You got to tell him that you're willing to . . . do things that he wants to do. You know, go along with him.' I was pretending that I was a big mob guy."

Silverman then asked Greg about the bomb formula Yousef had passed to him in one of his kites. "It was very complicated," said the wiseguy, who had only a high-school education. "I wouldn't understand it at all." He then told how Yousef had described to him a scenario almost identical to his wet test aboard PAL 434: "I found out the way that they would smuggle the equipment for the bomb itself, through the metal detector and onto the airplane without being detected. I would take pictures of timing devices. . . . Anything that I could grab a picture of—a kite—that was important to give to the government—I would."

Scarpa Jr. also described the genesis of Roma Corp. "I was able to hook Ramsey Yousef straight up with the FBI without me involved. I was told to tell Ramsey that it was my crew outside, that I'll be able to give him a three-way call to overseas, you know, where his people are."

Silverman asked him who he understood would be patching through these three-way calls. "The national security," said Greg. "The FBI."

The discussion of Greg Scarpa Jr.'s eleven-month spy mission for the Feds ended after less than an hour of testimony. The government declined to cross-examine him.[15]

On October 23, the jury returned a series of guilty verdicts on the RICO charges, but Greg Jr. was acquitted in all five homicides.

In a letter to Judge Raggi on April 7, 1999, Larry Silverman noted that "Mr. Scarpa's cooperation with the government was substantial and the government, in good faith, ought to move for a downward departure pursuant to U.S.S.G Section 5K1.1."

But at that point, as Silverman noted, the Feds were disputing the validity of Scarpa's intelligence. So Silverman moved for an order compelling the Feds to produce "any and all documents, recordings, photographs, relating to Mr. Scarpa's cooperation."

If Silverman had been able to get copies of the kites at the time, he'd have obtained prima facie evidence that Scarpa had valuable intelligence that could only have come from Ramzi Yousef.

For example, in May 1996, Scarpa Jr. obtained this schematic of Yousef's Casio-nitro watch and passed it to the FBI:

The Following diagram is an example of Connecting SCR C1060 To The Back of a Digital Clock

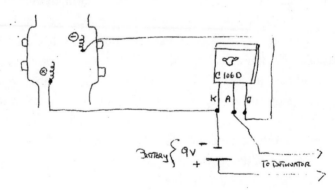

④ To Test The Circuit, Connect a 6 or 9 V Bulb To The Two wires going To The Detonator, The Bulb Should only operate. Whenever The Alarm Of The Clock Sets Off

It contained a detail that only the bomb maker could have known about at that time: the C106D semiconductor that Yousef had soldered into each of his "bomb triggers." During testimony in the Bojinka trial, the Feds would later describe that as Yousef's unique "signature."[16] But that information wasn't disclosed by the Feds until August 26.

Any doubt as to the quality of the intelligence could be dispelled by comparing that schematic to the following photograph. It was taken from the FBI lab report on items seized in a search of Room 603 at the Dona Josefa apartments in Manila—Yousef's bomb factory. The systems are virtually identical:

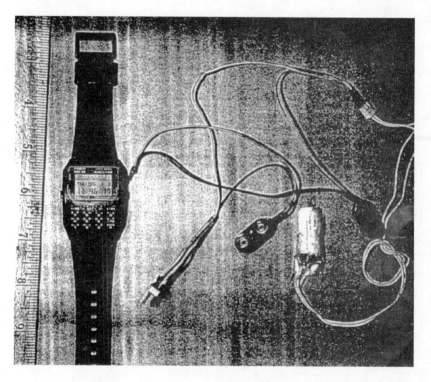

The Feds were so desperate to keep that picture secret that in September 2002, when Associated Press reporter Jim Gomez express-couriered a copy of the lab report to John Solomon, the AP's deputy bureau chief in Washington, the U.S. Customs Service, acting on a tip from the FBI, took the almost unprecedented step of seizing the package from a FedEx facility in the Midwest.[17]

"The interception was improper and clandestine," complained AP president and CEO Louis D. Boccardi at the time.[18] Only when Sen. Chuck Grassley (R-IA) pushed for an FBI OPR to be opened on the seizure, did the Bureau withdraw its objection and apologize. But the incident pointed up just how much the Feds wanted to keep secret any evidence that might prove the validity of the Yousef-Scarpa intelligence initiative.

The reams of detailed intel Greg Scarpa Jr. extracted from the bomb maker from March 1996 through February 1997 were not only genuine, they were unique to Yousef, and of such complexity that no Mafia wiseguy with Greg's limited education could ever have fabricated them. Moreover, Yousef could hardly have benefited by leaking such secrets if he'd known that Scarpa was in league with the Feds. The specific details he let slip—the existence of his four cell members in New York, the bin Laden (Bojinga) plot to hijack planes to free the blind Sheikh, and the evidence tying him to the downing of TWA 800—could only have worked against Yousef if the FBI had been willing to connect the dots.

Nonetheless, by the late summer of 1996—after ADIC Kallstrom, FBI Director Freeh, and Deputy A.G. Gorelick had all met in Washington—the Feds sought a way to explain that bonanza of intelligence *without* lending credibility to Greg Scarpa Jr.—a witness whose testimony could decimate the sixty remaining Colombo war prosecutions in the Eastern District of New York.

Since the evidence, now memorialized in dozens of FBI 302 memos, couldn't be ignored or hidden, they concocted a story that it wasn't really *evidence*—that, in effect, Yousef and Scarpa had made it all up.

29

THE "HOAX"
AND THE "SCAM"

O nce the Feds had decided to abandon the Yousef/Scarpa intel, they worried that any outside information confirming its authenticity might raise questions—particularly when attorneys like Larry Silverman were pushing for release of the kites and the FBI 302s. And then Silverman went further. He asked Judge Raggi that the government "be required to produce any recorded conversations made by the terrorists over the 'Roma' telephone line, which was secured by the government with the assistance of Mr. Scarpa."

"That would have been proof positive," Silverman told me, "that they had derived a benefit from Greg's work." It might also have exposed the possible negligence of the FBI in failing to translate Yousef's outside calls in real time, as was alleged.

The Feds were so worried about the 302s and kites getting out that they sought two protective orders in 1997 to keep them sealed.[1] Yet by the time Judge Raggi got around to sentencing Scarpa, the government had come up with its fabrication theory to explain the treasure trove of 302s documenting Scarpa's eleven-month initiative. It was likely "part of a scam," declared Judge Raggi.[2]

That scam story was cited by a federal court ruling later denying Ramzi Yousef's appeal of the Bojinka case. "In late 1996," wrote the Court, "the government learned from two sources that Scarpa was, in fact, colluding with Yousef and others to deceive it."[3]

Now, for the first time, we'll produce evidence that the Feds *themselves* actually concocted the "hoax" and "scam" story and that their principal source denies ever telling prosecutors that Yousef's intelligence provided by Greg Jr. wasn't genuine.

This revelation requires some additional background.

Greg B. Smith, the veteran reporter for the New York *Daily News* who first revealed the details behind the Scarpa intelligence initiative in September 2000, confirmed that the Roma Corp. patch-through had "been personally approved by Patrick Fitzgerald himself."[4] He cited a June 25, 1999, sealed affirmation by Fitzgerald in which a follow-up investigation of Scarpa Jr.'s intel "appeared to corroborate Scarpa's information."

In the course of researching this book, I obtained a copy of that seven-page affirmation. It stands as a kind of smoking gun, offering new insights into the selective way that the Feds decided to connect the dots on al Qaeda beginning in 1996.

Fitzgerald's Sealed Affirmation

"I became familiar with Scarpa in or about March, 1996," wrote Fitzgerald, who admitted that he "met with Scarpa on a number of occasions during 1996 and also spoke regularly with Special Agents of the FBI who debriefed Scarpa on other occasions. . . . During the debriefings Scarpa alleged that Ramzi Yousef and others were planning terrorist activity from within the Metropolitan Correctional Center." Fitzgerald cited a number of Scarpa Jr.'s allegations, including his report that "Yousef was planning to blow up airplanes and/or kidnap . . . high officials of the United States Government to disrupt his imminent trials."[5]

Fitzgerald admitted that "While Scarpa's apparent criminal history made the Government skeptical of his information at first, the Government could not fail to follow up on the information provided, given the past criminal behavior of the incarcerated terrorists and the grave consequences if any of the allegedly contemplated conduct was carried out.

"The follow up investigation appeared to corroborate Scarpa's information. In particular Scarpa provided 'kites' (notes exchanged between inmates in the MCC) which bore Yousef's handwriting and whose contents were consistent with Scarpa's account of terrorist machinations."

At this point in the affirmation, Fitzgerald confirmed his initial belief in the legitimacy of the Scarpa materials.

"Some details provided by Scarpa of Yousef's impending plans were consistent with information we had earlier received from a confidential source whose information was not in the public domain. In addition to the information provided about terrorist plots, Scarpa also provided information concerning the fact that Yousef tampered with some trial exhibits, by among other things, causing himself to bleed and then placing his blood on certain exhibits seized at or about the time of his arrests in order to create the impression that he had been tortured during post arrest questioning in Pakistan. While this information appears to be accurate, the SDNY did not call Scarpa as a witness at Yousef's trial or otherwise put such evidence before the jury."

Then, after endorsing the quality of Scarpa Jr.'s intel, Fitzgerald made a stunning admission: "By late summer 1996, the Government made an investigative decision that it no longer wished to pursue the investigation of Yousef using the 'patch through' telephone."

Keep in mind that it was on August 22, 1996, that the FBI'S New York ADIC, James Kallstrom, flew down to Washington for a meeting with Deputy Attorney General Jamie Gorelick and FBI Director Louis Freeh. Whatever was discussed at that meeting appears to have caused Kallstrom to reverse course on the TWA 800 investigation.

"There are a number of unanswered questions relating to that meeting," says forensic investigator Angela Clemente, who first uncovered the Yousef-Scarpa Jr. 302s.

"Did they talk about the growing scandal involving Lindley DeVecchio?" she asks. "It's not such a stretch to think that came up [at the meeting], since Kallstrom had sent that memo to Director Freeh in April saying that the DeVecchio OPR was 'casting a cloud' over the FBI's New York Office."

Could that August 22 meeting, which produced such a profound turn-around in the TWA 800 probe, have also led to that "investigative decision" by the government cited in Fitzgerald's affirmation—that it would no longer pursue the Roma Corp. patch-through?

What would have been the Justice Department's motivation for that? Remember that Greg Scarpa Jr. intended to testify that his father had paid more than $100,000 to DeVecchio in return for the kind of intelligence cited in AUSA Ellen Corcella's letter of May 8, 1995. If the Feds decided to indict Ramzi Yousef for the crash of TWA 800, Greg Jr. would have necessarily been their star witness. If he'd been rendered credible in *that* trial, he would have been credible later, in 1998, when he would testify that his father had been bribing DeVecchio for years. And that testimony might have derailed those sixty Colombo war cases in Corcella's Eastern District.

Citing John Napoli as Source of the "Hoax" Story

After describing the discontinuation of the Yousef patch-through in his June 1999 sealed affirmation, Patrick Fitzgerald went on to declare that he had "since learned information which convinced me that Scarpa's effort at 'cooperation' was a scam in collusion with Yousef and others. . . . In the latter part of 1996, Scarpa . . . told the Government that an inmate, John Napoli, had even better access to Yousef and his colleagues than Scarpa himself."[6]

Napoli, another reputed wiseguy who had been convicted of money-laundering, arrived on the ninth floor tier next to Scarpa on December 17, 1996, more than nine months after Yousef started slipping kites through the cell wall to Scarpa Jr. Now the Feds were claiming that Scarpa Jr. had confessed to Napoli that his work informing on Yousef was a "hoax" and a "scam."

Judge Kevin Duffy used those very words in denying a motion by Yousef's codefendant Eyad Ismoil in the second World Trade Center bombing case. Ismoil had moved for Judge Duffy to recuse himself from the case because one of Scarpa Jr.'s reports, documented in an FBI 302, was that Yousef had made a death threat against the judge. "It is now clear that Scarpa's claims were actually a hoax concocted by Scarpa and the Defendants,"[7] wrote Duffy, adding that "Judge Reena Raggi properly denied Scarpa's claims of cooperation." Duffy concluded that "Scarpa's allegations of Yousef's threats were merely part of a ruse without any substance behind them."

In *United States v. Yousef*, an appeal in the SDNY, the prosecution's related pleadings describe Napoli as "the first of two sources for this information." The government's motion opposing a new trial for Yousef states, "Napoli understood that Yousef was aware of and a willing participant in [Scarpa's] fraud on the government."[8]

"They may have used Napoli," says Silverman, "but I can tell you that this material from Greg Jr. was absolutely genuine."[9] In a subsequent interview, Silverman noted that "it couldn't possibly be a hoax . . . because this information that [Greg Jr.] provided came forth in stages. And if at any point in any of the stages, the information that he was providing was inaccurate or a hoax, the government would have pulled the plug at that time. They would not have given him a camera to use in an institution, which is a highly unusual event. They would not have provided monies to put in Yousef's account on Scarpa's behalf to give him the credibility. They would not have allowed Scarpa to have Yousef make telephone calls through an FBI source. All of these things . . . occurred in sequence; they all didn't occur on one day. To say that all those things were a hoax really does injustice to what information he provided."

Napoli's Denial

Because the quality of the Yousef/Scarpa intelligence is a crucial issue in determining whether senior federal prosecutors like Patrick Fitzgerald intentionally buried probative evidence, I sought out John Napoli. He's currently serving a term at the Big Spring Federal Correctional Institution, a minimum security prison located between El Paso and Dallas, Texas.

On February 11, 2006, I arranged for Napoli to call me while I was in the office of his attorney, Gerald LaBush in New York City. With Napoli's permission, I recorded the conversation.

For years, the Feds had cited Napoli as the primary source for their allegation that Greg Scarpa Jr.'s Yousef intel was fraudulent, but what he told me was startling.

He said that while Scarpa had asked him to testify for him in his upcoming RICO case, and offered to cut him in on the Yousef intel in return—as a means of a currying favor with the Feds—the actual intelligence initiative itself was completely *genuine*. As a measure of his credibility, Napoli even cited Yousef's Toshiba laptop, which the Feds knew contained cryptic references to Osama bin Laden, whom Yousef had code-named "Bojinga" in his communiqués to Scarpa.

My interview with Napoli, transcribed verbatim below, reads like a scene from *The Sopranos*, complete with references to "Bojangles" (for "Bojinga") and "Saddam" (for "Osama"). But the content of his account is extremely credible:

LANCE: John, when they concluded at Greg's trial that the material was a hoax and a scam, they claim that you and one other witness corroborated that.

NAPOLI: What happened was this: When I got there (to the MCC), Scarpa approached me. We became kind of friends, and he started telling me what he was doing about cooperating with Yousef. And he had this great plan that I could testify for him, and in return that he would give me information to bring to the Southern District about Yousef. I said, "What information would that be?" And he said, "Well, they found a computer with Bojangles and they don't know the name. I never gave it to the Feds." And he told me who Bojangles was and it was Saddam bin Laden. So I called [Assistant U.S. Attorney David] Kelly.

I never said anything [to Kelly] about [Greg Jr.] giving false information. I never spoke to Ramzi. I never spoke to Ismoil. I never spoke to none of them. Zero. No conversations. Not one. And they [the Feds] said, after this is all done, that *I* came to them and I said that I was gonna go along with Scarpa's plan. At no point did [Greg Jr.] have a deal with Yousef to give false information. Yousef had no clue what Greg was doin'.

As far as my personal[ly] being there, hearing it, seeing it—anything that Yousef gave Greg *wasn't* a scam. It *wasn't* a hoax. He [Greg] wasn't trying to do *anything* with Ramzi against the government. He was legitimately trying to help them. He was giving them information.

A timeline put together by Napoli's attorney indicates that he met with AUSA David Kelly early in 1997, around the time Scarpa Jr. ended his intelligence initiative with Yousef. Kelly, who was Fitzgerald's partner as head of the Organized Crime and Terrorism Unit in the SDNY, would go on to become the U.S. attorney for the SDNY—the top federal prosecutor in New York City.

If Napoli's account is accurate, it appears that two senior federal prosecutors, Fitzgerald and Kelly, went along with a government story that characterized the Yousef-Scarpa Jr. intelligence as fraudulent. If, as per Fitzgerald's affidavit, that occurred in conjunction with the late summer decision by the Feds to pardon DeVecchio and destroy Greg Jr. as a potential witness against him, then the creation of the "hoax" and "scam" story by the Feds could, in my opinion, amount to a serious obstruction of justice.

Fitzgerald was asked to answer a series of detailed questions raised by this investigation, but through his spokesperson in Chicago, Randall Samborn, he declined.

Four Decades in the "Max"

Whatever Fitzgerald's explanation may be, one thing is clear: it wasn't just intelligence that got buried when the Feds came up with the "hoax" story: Greg Scarpa Jr. got buried as well. Although he was convicted only of RICO violations and not a single homicide, when he came up for sentencing on May 8, 1999, Judge Raggi gave him forty years. By comparison, John Gotti's chief executioner, Sammy "The Bull" Gravano, who killed nineteen people, got five years after initially cooperating with the Feds.

And what prison did Judge Raggi send Greg to? The same prison where Yousef ended up: the Florence, Colorado Supermax, a maximum security facility that houses more than four hundred of the nation's most dangerous prisoners.[10] In the last several years, the Supermax has played host to Oklahoma City bombers Nichols and McVeigh, Unabomber Ted Kaczynski, and Olympic Park bomber Eric Rudolph.

Greg Scarpa Jr., if allowed to testify freely and under oath, could authenticate the pile of al Qaeda-related intelligence he had received over eleven months from the bomb maker who was the architect of both attacks on the World Trade Center.

Further, he could furnish key insights into the relationship between his father and DeVecchio, now under indictment for four counts of second-degree homicide. Scarpa Jr., like Ali Mohamed, is another living witness to the negligence of key FBI and SDNY officials in the years leading up to September 11.

Testimony from Scarpa Jr. would present no threat to the security of a hardened subterranean prison like the Supermax, but it might shake the walls of the Justice Department and the J. Edgar Hoover Building, the FBI's headquarters in Washington. Similar testimony from Ali Mohamed could do much more. But as we'll see, after his arrest on September 10, 1998, Federal officials became so concerned about the dots that *he* might connect that he soon became the best-kept secret in the Justice Department.

PART III

30

THE TEN-MONTH DANCE

Two months after Ali Mohamed's arrest, on November 4, 1998, the Feds charged Osama bin Laden, Mohammed Atef, and eleven others with the embassy bombings. The 238-count indictment cited the terrorist leader and his al Qaeda associates for "plotting and carrying out the most heinous acts of international terrorism and murder."[1] At a press conference announcing the indictment, Mary Jo White, U.S. attorney for the SDNY, declared that bin Laden's villainy extended far beyond the terror at the twin bombing sites in Africa: "All of the citizens of the world are also victims," she said, "wherever and whenever the cruel and cowardly acts of international terrorism strike." Bin Laden, Atef, and seven others were charged *in absentia,* along with the four bombing conspirators the Feds had in custody: Wadih El-Hage, Fazul Abdullah Mohammed, Mohamed Sadeek Odeh, and Mohamed Rashed Daoud Al-'Owali.

But the name of the al Qaeda operative most responsible for the bombing's planning was missing. Ali Mohamed was a precious commodity for the Justice Department—not just because of the intelligence he could give up, but for the embarrassment he could save the Feds if he cooperated under the right conditions. So Patrick Fitzgerald and his boss, U.S. Attorney

Mary Jo White, did everything they could to keep him a secret while they tried to cut a deal with him.

"This guy had stolen the FBI's lunch for five years," said a former agent in the NYO. "It was a gigantic scandal and they were in circle-the-wagons mode, praying they could keep it from the media."[2]

But by late October word of this phantom prisoner was beginning to leak out.[3] Terrorism expert Steven Emerson was among the first to catch wind of Mohamed's arrest.

"My first reaction when I discovered that Ali Mohamed had played this duplicitous role was of absolute disbelief," says Emerson.[4] "This man had played the U.S. government perfectly to evade any type of restrictions or extra scrutiny, and his interrogators at the Department of Justice were livid [at] the fact that he had been protected as an asset in previous years."

But outrage was soon followed by panic among the senior DOJ lawyers, who were terrified about what would happen if reporters began to piece together the story of how Ali had snookered the FBI. So when a reporter confronted White with a rumor about Mohamed at the November 4 press conference on the indictment, she begged off.

"Ms. White, we understand there is also another sealed indictment against Mr. Ali Mohamed, who is a former U.S. Army sergeant also linked to the terrorist network in some fashion."

"I've read what you've read," White shot back. "But I can't comment."[5]

For the next ten months, as Mohamed cooled his heels in the MCC, the Feds engaged in a dance with his lawyers, trying to negotiate an exit that would allow the Bureau and the Justice Department to save face.[6] Whenever Ali was brought into the courtroom for any proceeding, the room was sealed. All pleadings referred to him as "John Doe."[7] As a potential defendant he was a cipher—a legal black hole.

The Long, Tortuous Charade

The negotiations took place in a series of meetings known as "proffer sessions," held in a room at the old Federal Courthouse on Foley Square in lower Manhattan. Patrick Fitzgerald was usually in attendance, along with one or more AUSAs and Jack Cloonan or Dan Coleman from the bin Laden squad. Mohamed was represented by defense attorneys James Michael Roth—no relation to the James J. Roth who had been James Kallstrom's top lawyer in the FBI's NYO—and Lloyd Epstein, his cocounsel. Both have steadfastly refused to discuss his case, which remains under seal. But retired special agent Cloonan paints a vivid portrait of the proffer sessions, which began in November 1998.

When "we walked into the session," says Cloonan, "that meant that Ali had signed a letter with the advice of his counsel, that whatever he told us during those proffer sessions, we would not charge him with. However, if we found out that he had *lied* to us, then that information was chargeable."

"For the first six to ten months" of the sessions, Cloonan recalls, what Mohamed told them was "all contrived."

"It's all false," he says. "It's all just Ali spinning a story."[8] As a measure of Mohamed's cockiness during those sessions, Cloonan describes an incident in which the terrorist-spy actually advised the Feds that their computer system had been improperly wired.

"We ushered Ali out of the lockup," says Cloonan, "and made sure nobody saw him as we took him out. We walked into a room, and on the wall, exposed, were color-coded wires, for a computer system." According to Cloonan, "there was [a] breakdown in the computer. Out on the West Coast, Ali [had] got himself trained on computers. So he looked at it and said, 'I don't know who hooked up your [computer] system, but this is not right.'"

The assembled Feds exchanged double takes. "So, we're looking at each other," says Cloonan, "and by this time, we're [saying], 'Okay. We trust you to the extent that you can troubleshoot this.' So Ali says, 'Well, this is not hooked up and this wire represents *this* and this color represents *that*.' He quickly diagnoses [the problem], and he says 'It's not very good work.' And then he says to us, 'You know, if you want me to get on the computer, I'd be very happy to [fix it]. I probably can crack the password and get into it.'"

At that point Cloonan and company said, "Thank you very much, but no."

That's the kind of confidence from Ali that the Feds confronted in these sessions, and as the weeks turned into months and the SDNY prosecutors attempted to bargain with him, he steadfastly resisted a deal.

"Ali did not tell us the truth from the very outset," admits Cloonan. Instead, "he went through this long torturous charade of providing us with information, none of which panned out, none of which made sense. And all this time I think he's assessing us, we're assessing him. Where is this going to go?"[9]

Cloonan says that some of the sessions lasted as long as six hours. But they were never videotaped or recorded. Benjamin Weiser, the veteran *New York Times* reporter who covers the Southern District, notes that the SDNY "is known to have a strict policy of requiring that potential cooperating witnesses disclose all they know, even topics of which the government may not yet be aware."[10] But when it came to Ali Mohamed, the Feds didn't have a lot of bargaining leverage.

"You have to understand, that this was not somebody that the Southern District prosecutors were anxious to have show up in court," says defense attorney Roger Stavis, who had tried in vain to get Mohamed to appear at the Day of Terror trial. "Ali knew that, so he kind of had them over a barrel."

The four embassy bombing suspects in custody were facing the death penalty. Mohamed wanted to ensure that he wouldn't be subject to the same fate. Further, if he was ultimately forced to betray bin Laden, al-Zawahiri, and al Qaeda, he wanted a guarantee that he might someday see the light of day.

The Feds Get Tough. The Egyptians Get Tougher

Though the content of the negotiations remains secret, it's clear that by early spring of 1999 Mohamed had dug in his heels. So Mary Jo White decided to play hardball. On May 19 she formally added his name to the embassy bombing indictment, thinking it might shake him.[11]

It didn't work.

At the same time, however, the U.S. prosecutors found themselves with a new club to use against Mohamed: That spring, the state of Egypt put him on trial *in absentia*—as part of a roundup of Egyptian Islamic Jihad associates. Ultimately they sentenced him to death.

Mohamed was convicted of various terrorism-related charges, largely on the testimony of his Santa Clara protégé Khalid Dahab. The young ex-medical student, who had so worshipped Ali that he changed his last name to Mohamed, had been growing increasingly unhappy in California, trying to support his third wife and five children. Dahab had told a San Jose family law judge that he intended to move his family home to Egypt. He happened to be there when the embassy bombings erupted.[12] After getting word of his impending arrest, Dahab was minutes away from leaving the country when police seized him from an outbound flight.

After a harsh interrogation by Egyptian authorities, Dahab made a shocking confession. At Ali Mohamed's orders, he said, he'd taken hang-glider lessons with the intent of attacking Lima Turra Prison near Cairo in an effort to free EIJ leaders, some of whom had been locked up since the Sadat assassination.[13]

As described by Lance Williams and Erin McCormick in the *San Francisco Chronicle,* the plot was right out of a B-movie. Jihad hang-gliders would swoop off a nearby mountain into the prison grounds, setting off explosives and causing a panic to effect the jailbreak.

This was one of the dozen scenarios cited by the congressional Joint Inquiry in which Islamic radicals had planned to use aircraft as weapons. While it paled in comparison to Ramzi Yousef's planes-as-missiles plot, it was another fragment of evidence that Ali Mohamed was conversant with al Qaeda's more ambitious airborne attack plans.

The sweeping Egyptian terror trial was held at the Haekstep military camp.[14] Of the 107 defendants, thirty-five were condemned to death. Among them: Mohamed's beloved Ayman al-Zawahiri, also convicted *in absentia.*

Al-Ahram, the Arabic weekly, noted that the condemned also included "the Islamist Ali Abdul-Saoud Mustafa, a former Egyptian Army officer"—a reference to Ali Mohamed. "Mustafa, 45, resigned from the Egyptian Army in 1984 before moving to the U.S where he has been living and from where he made several visits to Afghanistan,"[15] the paper noted.

Well-known Egyptian lawyer Montasser El-Zayat told *Al-Ahram* that the sentences metered out were "very harsh," describing them as "a sword hanging on the necks of those condemned to death. If any of them is extradited to Egypt, he will be hanged on the spot," El-Zayat said.[16]

In the face of such a death sentence, one would think that Ali Mohamed might finally have been induced to cooperate with Patrick Fitzgerald and other Southern District prosecutors. But it didn't seem to faze him in the least. "He knew the Feds would never extradite him," says a defense attorney with knowledge of the case who asked not to be identified.[17] "Why? Because the Justice Department would never risk that Ali might tell the world how he had deceived the FBI for so long."

The Negotiations Break Down

Still, Mohamed remained aloof from the other defendants in custody, including his old Nairobi "brother" Wadih El-Hage.[18] A fifth coconspirator, a Tanzanian named Khalfan Khanis Mohamed, was arrested on December 16, 1998, and rendered back to New York. His court-appointed attorney, David Ruhnke, argued that he was a bit player in comparison to Ali Mohamed.

"Khalfan represented somebody who was recruited into the bombing plot maybe three or four months before it actually took place," says Ruhnke.[19] "He was expendable. He kind of came and went, whereas Ali Mohamed was the person who set up the Nairobi cell. He knew exactly what was taking place in Nairobi. He knew that the bombing would take place. When the former head of the Nairobi cell [Abu Ubaidah] drowned in a ferry accident, Ali Mohamed is the one who installed Wadih El-Hage as the titular head of the cell in Kenya—if you believe the government's evidence."

There's little doubt that Ali's lawyers used his position of strength to gain as much leverage in the proffer sessions as possible. By the summer of 1999, they had already begun to disassociate him from the other defendants.

"The government was willing to agree and make a deal with Ali Mohamed that did not expose him to the death penalty," says Ruhnke. "As time went on, we developed a sense that Ali Mohamed was making overtures toward cooperating with the government. A classic clue was that his attorneys stopped attending the cocounsel meetings that we were having on a regular basis."

At the time Fitzgerald, or his FBI agent surrogates, were doing everything they could—short of releasing Ali—to get him to talk. During the sessions, Jack Cloonan, whom Ali fawningly called "Mr. Jack," became the "good cop."

"When I could, I joked with him," remembers Cloonan. "I did my level best to respect his dignity. If he wanted to pray, he could pray. Could I help him make phone calls to his sister in Egypt? Yes. It was important for his family to know that he was being well taken care of, and that he was not being abused, because in their world, if you're in custody of the authorities, you're obviously being tortured."[20]

But far from using the cattle prod or the water board, Fitzgerald, Cloonan, and Coleman treated al Qaeda's master spy with kid gloves. They even brought female FBI agents in during some sessions, hoping that would loosen him up, although Cloonan admitted that to some Muslims "that would have been just the ultimate humiliation." In any case, the ploy didn't work. By the late summer of 1999—almost a year after the embassy bombings—the Feds were no closer to a deal than when they locked up Mohamed.

But they were about to get lucky one more time. By late August 1999, across the East River in Brooklyn, an incident involving another Egyptian would open up another door into al Qaeda's New York cell. All the FBI had to do was walk through it.

The Other Sleeper?

As early as 1997, FBI documents later showed, Ali Mohamed had warned his FBI handlers about "networks of terrorists known as sleepers, who lie low for years but do not need to be told what to do." In another briefing session, he called them "submarines."[21] Mohamed himself was the ultimate sleeper, of course—except that he had audaciously presented himself to agents of three separate U.S. intelligence agencies. Abdel Sattar, the Staten Island postman who operated the IG's New York Office, wasn't formally indicted by the Feds until 2002,[22] and not convicted until 2005.[23] Yet for years he brazenly and sometimes openly did the blind Sheikh's bidding.

But it wasn't until August 1999, a year after Ali Mohamed's arrest, that evidence surfaced of another possible Egyptian-American al Qaeda sleeper, who had been positioned for years inside the city's largest emergency response department: the FDNY. His exposure was the work of Ronnie Bucca, the tenacious FDNY fire marshal who tried repeatedly to get the FBI to consider his evidence. If the Feds had focused on this intimate of the blind Sheikh, they might have had another significant opportunity to derail the 9/11 plot.

In a way, Ronnie Bucca was to public service what Ali Mohamed was to espionage: a triple threat. A former Green Beret paratrooper, Bucca was a veteran of the FDNY's storied Rescue One, the oldest and most demanding heavy rescue company in the world.[24] He'd also become an experienced fire marshal with the FDNY's Bureau of Fire Investigation—the equivalent of an NYPD detective, with the operational know-how of a veteran firefighter. Bucca maintained an active presence in an army reserve military intelligence detachment, and was serving at the Defense Intelligence Analysis Center at Bolling Air Force Base in Washington.

As early as 1993, Bucca became aware of how the FBI had dropped the ball prior to the WTC bombing. He applied for a position with the FBI/NYPD Joint Terrorism Task Force, but they turned him down. The class bias between the "reds" of the FDNY and the "blues" of the NYPD rendered him *persona non grata* on the JTTF. It didn't seem to matter that Bucca had extensive operational experience with the Special Forces and a security clearance of TOP SECRET.

For nine months, beginning in early 1999, Bucca was assigned to work out of Metrotech, the FDNY's new headquarters in Brooklyn. Then, one afternoon in late August, he made a startling discovery: Ahmed Amin Refai, a fifty-nine-year-old Egyptian naturalized citizen, who had worked for more than twenty-five years as an FDNY accountant, was caught lying in an attempt to obtain a second ID to the highly secure headquarters.[25] The building contained the blueprints of some of the city's most important high-rise structures—including the World Trade Center complex.

Well aware of the Egyptian presence in bin Laden's camp, Bucca pressed Refai's boss, a deputy commissioner, and discovered that in 1992, before the first bombing, the accountant had obtained from FDNY files an early set of blueprints for the WTC, along with plans for some of the city's bridges and tunnels.[26]

Ronnie was shocked to learn from FDNY staffers that Refai had been seen in news footage walking arm-in-arm with Sheikh Omar Abdel Rahman before his arrest.[27] He got a copy of a 1993 *ABC News* story that showed Refai accompanying the Sheikh to an immigration hearing, where he acted as Rahman's personal translator.[28] In the video, Refai can be seen clutching the blind cleric's arm and moving him through a crowd as if he were the Sheikh's personal bodyguard. (Timeline segment 15, page 26.)

"Bucca knew that nobody got that close to a terrorist like Rahman without being an intimate," said former special agent Joe O'Brien, who worked organized crime in the New York Office. "The Sheikh had to trust him with his life."[29]

After running an immigration check on Refai and determining that he had lied to fire marshals about both his date and place of birth, Bucca went to the FBI.

"He took the file down to the JTTF," said Fire Marshal Mel Hazel, who worked the case with Bucca. "Ronnie and I knew that this guy Refai was wrong. He'd called in sick the day of the Trade Center bombing in '93, and Ronnie found out that the FBI had interviewed him back in 1994."

One of the JTTF members who looked at Bucca's file on Refai was Lou Napoli, the same senior JTTF investigator who'd failed to follow Abouhalima and Salameh in the months leading to the WTC blast. It was Napoli who identified El Sayyid Nosair as a member of the ultra-violent Islamic Group, which the Sheikh had led. But when he got the information on Refai from Bucca, he rejected it.

"I vaguely recall an incident [with] some plans . . ." says Napoli. "But sources that we had . . . never put this guy [Refai] anywhere in, what you'd call the inside cell. . . . He was peripheral at best."[30]

Retired special agent O'Brien disagrees. "The fact that Napoli, one of the chief FBI terrorism investigators in New York, would call the man who translated for Sheik Omar 'peripheral,' tells you *everything* about the Bureau's capability of stopping the al Qaeda threat," he says. "The blind Sheikh is one of the keys to this whole story, and if the JTTF had fully understood how important he was to bin Laden, they never would have blown Bucca off."

Data Mining for Terrorists

But at precisely that moment, in the late summer of 1999, another of the Big Five intelligence agencies was finally beginning to take the al Qaeda threat seriously. The Defense Intelligence Analysis Center, where Bucca worked weekends, had begun to investigate bin Laden's network via a process called "data mining." Specialized search bots (often called "spiders") would scour the Internet around the clock, searching open-source material for linkages relating to al Qaeda.[31] Sourcing everything from Islamic chat rooms to news stories, utility bills, visa applications, and financial records, the system harvested vast amounts of data quickly. Then, using sophisticated programs such as Starlight, Parentage, and Spire, it was pared down, separating out unrelated figures while honing in on linkages that tracked back directly to al Qaeda and its associated groups.[32]

The data was then represented visually in "link charts," using a high-end graphics program called Analyst Notebook. Jacob L. Boesen was a link chart analyst working for Orion Scientific Systems, a private contractor assigned to DIAC. I got in contact with him in 2002 because he'd worked closely with Ronnie Bucca.[33]

By August 10, 1999, Boesen had constructed a chart based on some of the research that DIAC had done at that point. The declassified version of the chart, which I published in both *1000 Years for Revenge* and *Cover Up,* vindicated what Col. Rodolfo Mendoza had discovered during his interrogation of Abdul Hakim Murad in the Philippines. It showed a *direct* connection between al Qaeda's leadership and the Ali Mohamed-trained cell responsible for the Kahane murder, the WTC bombing, and the Day of Terror plot. The threat to America was not coming from a "loose" series of Sunni cells, but a tightly integrated network with Sheikh Rahman and Ramzi Yousef as key operatives.

Reproduced at the end of this chapter, the chart draws direct lines between bin Laden and Ayman al-Zawahiri (on the right) and Sheikh

Rahman, whose cell is on the left. Within the Sheikh's cell is the World Trade Center bombing cell of Ramzi Yousef, whose picture is located directly below that of Mahmud Abouhalima, "the Red." In that same box are two more of Ali Mohamed's trainees, Mohammed Salameh and Nidal Ayyad. Directly to Abouhalima's right is Ali Mohamed himself (located below Wadih El-Hage).

This chart represents the best intelligence the Pentagon had by the late summer of 1999 on al Qaeda's growing threat to the United States. Keep in mind that El-Hage's voice had been found on the answering machine of the slain Mustafa Shalabi as early as February 1991. Ali Mohamed had stayed with him in Nairobi in 1994. The FBI had maintained a tap on Wadih El-Hage's Nairobi house phone from the spring of 1996. Jamal al-Fadl had told both the CIA and the FBI how El-Hage has worked as bin Laden's personal secretary. Now DIA was confirming the Lebanese convert to Islam's key position in the al Qaeda hierarchy.

"Data mining is incredibly important," says terrorism authority Steven Emerson. "The more sophisticated the organization, the [greater] the number of players, the more impossible it is to do regular human computing, so it really requires a sophisticated relational database software that can spit out the connections based on addresses, phone numbers, corporate connections, or even familiar relationships."[34]

By the end of the year, General Hugh Shelton, chairman of the Joint Chiefs of Staff, and General Pete Schoomaker, head of the Special Operations Command (SOCOM), which included the Green Berets, would undertake a much more detailed and formal data-mining program designed to pinpoint al Qaeda operatives worldwide. They called it Operation Able Danger.[35]

At a time when the Justice Department was doing everything it could to keep Ali Mohamed's identity a *secret,* this new operation, run by the U.S. Army and the Defense Intelligence Agency, would soon turn up evidence that he was the linchpin between al Qaeda and the New York cell Patrick Fitzgerald had chosen to call the "jihad army." That data-mining initiative would also represent one of the last, best chances to derail the oncoming al Qaeda onslaught on America.

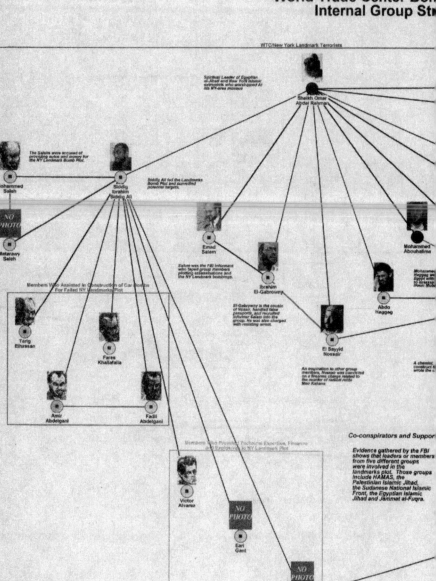

WTC/New York Landmark Terrorists

Spiritual Leader of Egyptian al-Jihad and New York Islamic extremists who worshiped At his NY-area mosque

Sheikh Omar
Abdel Rahman

The Salehs were accused of extorting autos and money for the NY Landmark Bomb Plot.

Mohammed
Saleh

Siddig
Ibrahim
Siddig Ali

Siddig Ali led the Landmarks Bomb Plot and surveilled potential targets.

Matarawy
Saleh

Emad
Salem

Salem was the FBI informant who taped group members plotting assassinations and the NY Landmark bombings.

Ibrahim
El-Gabrowny

El-Gabrowny is the cousin of Nosair, handled false passports, and recruited informer Salem into the group. He was also charged with resisting arrest.

Mohammed
Abouhalima

Mohammed Hagag was Egypt and to assassi Hosni Muba

Abdo
Haggag

Members Who Assisted in Construction of Car Bombs For Failed NY Landmarks Plot

Tariq
Elhassan

Fares
Khallafalla

Amir
Abdelgani

Fadil
Abdelgani

El Sayyid
Nosair

An inspiration to other group members, Nosair was convicted on a firearms charge related to the murder of radical rabbi Meir Kahane.

A chemist construed wrote the c

Members Who Provided Technical Expertise, Finance and Explosives to NY Landmark Plot

Victor
Alvarez

NO
PHOTO

Earl
Gant

NO
PHOTO

Clement Rodney
Hampton-el

Co-conspirators and Suppor

Evidence gathered by the FBI shows that leaders or members from five different groups were involved in the landmarks plot. Those groups include HAMAS, the Palestinian Islamic Jihad, the Sudanese National Islamic Front, the Egyptian Islamic Jihad and Jammat al-Fuqra.

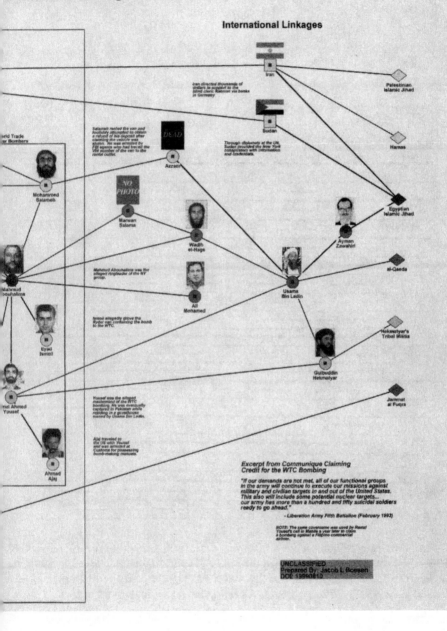

International Linkages

31

OPERATION
ABLE DANGER

If Ali Mohamed was Osama bin Laden's operational spy, a man who combined the double threats of intelligence officer and on-the-ground commando, one of the soldiers who embodied that same skill set for America was a Bronze Star winner named Anthony Shaffer.

Commissioned as an officer in the Ohio National Guard in 1983, Shaffer was selected early in his career to train at "the Farm," the CIA's legendary school for clandestine operatives at Camp Perry, Virginia. Over twenty-three years in the military, Tony Shaffer worked a series of active duty secret ops and task force assignments, alternating between roles as an intelligence officer with the Pentagon's J2 Directorate and as a clandestine operative with the J3. In September 1999, now a major, Tony Shaffer was running a top-secret operation called Stratus Ivy, supporting various DOD "black" operations, when he was assigned to brief four-star general Pete Schoomaker, then head of SOCOM.

"With my unit's permission," says Shaffer, "I was able to brief General Schoomaker at a level that was beyond TOP SECRET. After the briefing he said to me, 'I need you for a special project.' He looked over at the STO Chief, the head of Special Technical Operations, and said, 'I want Shaffer read into the project ASAP.' 'The next day I was read into Able Danger.'"[1]

In the months that followed, Tony would serve as a liaison between the Defense Intelligence Agency (DIA), the army, and SOCOM.

"Able Danger had a dual purpose," says Shaffer. "[After the] African embassy bombings, it was clear to the Pentagon that al Qaeda was our new enemy, and that eventually we would have boots on the ground against them. So the idea was to identify their members and to take them out. The operation wasn't called Able Fun or Able Picnic. It was Able Danger, because the sense within the military community was that we needed to get these guys before they could get us again."[2]

Over the decades, among the thousands of code names chosen by the Pentagon to describe secret and open-source military operations, the prefix "Able" had traditionally been used in conjunction with NATO and nuclear weapons-related exercises.[3] The fact that it was now being affixed to a secret operation relating to terrorism, suggests how seriously the army and the DIA took the al Qaeda threat.

Shaffer says that Able Danger was "the military version of Alec Station," the CIA's unit tasked with collecting al Qaeda-related intelligence. The operation's data-mining center was located at the Land Information Warfare Activity (LIWA) at Fort Belvoir, Virginia. Known as "spook central," Fort Belvoir housed the Information Dominance Center—a building full of army intelligence "geeks," whose bullpen area was designed to look like the bridge of the Starship Enterprise from *Star Trek*.[4]

The lead LIWA analyst running the data mine was Dr. Eileen Priesser, a double Ph.D.[5] The operations officer was a decorated U.S. Navy captain named Scott Phillpott. Army Major Eric Kleinsmith was LIWA's intelligence chief.[6] J.D. Smith and Jacob L. Boesen, working as contract analysts from Orion Scientific, designed many of the link charts in which the "deep data points" connecting the key al Qaeda players were represented graphically.

"You would ask them, for example, to look at Khalid Shaikh Mohammed," says Shaffer, "and these search engines would scour the Internet 24/7 looking at any number of open-source databases, from credit reporting agencies to court records and news stories to Lloyd's of London insurance records. You name it. Once a known associate of KSM was found, they would go through the same process for that individual."

One IDC analyst I spoke to described it as "Six Degrees of Kevin Bacon on steroids."[7]

Told to "Start with the words 'Al Qaeda' and go,"[8] the LIWA data crunchers began an initial harvest in December 1999. The data grew fast and exponentially, and before long it amounted to two terabytes—equal to about 9 percent of the pages in the Library of Congress. "It was a mile wide and an inch deep," says Kleinsmith. "Naturally only a small percentage of the data related to terrorism," says Tony, "So we would have to neck it down—cull it—until we had some substantive hits."

Within months, Operation Able Danger had uncovered some astonishing intelligence.

Discovering the Hijackers

"We found an active al Qaeda cell in the U.S linked to radical Sheikh Omar Abdel Rahman," says Shaffer, now a lieutenant colonel. "That was most frightening—that as late as early 2000 we detected that kind of al Qaeda presence here."[9]

Examining Sheikh Rahman's Brooklyn cell—which operated out of Ali Mohamed's old stomping grounds, the Al Farooq Mosque[10]—the LIWA analysts made another alarming discovery. "We identified lead 9/11 hijacker Mohammed Atta, Marwan al-Shehhi, who flew UA 175 into the South Tower of the Trade Center, and two of the muscle hijackers aboard AA 77, which hit the Pentagon," says Shaffer. That linkage was made months before any of the other Big Five intelligence agencies would trip to their presence.

Coming as it did in early 2000, the identification of Khalid al-Midhar and Nawaf al-Hazmi was a crucial find for the SOCOM operation.

Of all the 9/11 hijackers, these two Saudis had the longest records of al Qaeda involvement,[11] and beginning in January 2000, they soon became the most visible of the nineteen operatives. In fact, the two failed pilots appeared on the radar of the NSA, the CIA, and the FBI so many times in the eighteen months before 9/11 that the U.S. intelligence community had *multiple* opportunities to thwart the plot.

Al-Midhar and al-Hazmi were the poster boys who came to symbolize the "stovepiping" between U.S. agencies in their failure to share intelligence before 9/11.

Until now, most of the blame for failure to track the two Saudis has been leveled at the Central Intelligence Agency. As recently as August 2006, in his 9/11 book *The Looming Tower*,[12] *New Yorker* writer Lawrence Wright charged that the CIA's hoarding of intelligence on al-Midhar, al-Hazmi, and another key al Qaeda operative "may, in effect, have allowed the September 11 plot to proceed."[13]

But even if the FBI had received no help from any other agency, we've uncovered compelling evidence that the agents of Squad I-49 should have tripped to the presence of the two hijackers in the United States *months* before they flew AA Flight 77 into the Pentagon.

After his capture following the embassy bombings in 1998, Mohamed Rashed Daoud al-'Owali,[14] the Saudi who drove the truck, gave FBI agents the number of a safe house in Sana'a Yemen maintained by Sameer Mohammed Ahmed al-Hada, the brother-in-law[15] of Khalid al-Midhar.[16]

"We got the number from a confession from Al-'Owali," says Jack Cloonan. "We gave the information to the [CIA] Chief of Station in Nairobi."[17]

The house was being used as an al Qaeda "logistics center" or switchboard in much the same way Khalid Dahab had used his one-room apartment in Santa Clara—to patch through phone calls from bin Laden operatives worldwide. In fact, it was later revealed that the Saudi billionaire himself called the Yemen house multiple times between 1996 and 1998.[18]

As a result, the NSA and the CIA planted bugs inside the house, installed phone taps, and even went so far as to monitor visitors coming in and out of the dwelling using spy satellites.[19]

"The NSA and the Agency were monitoring it for two years," says Cloonan.

It was the phone line in that Yemeni safe house that led the CIA to the discovery of the single most important al Qaeda planning session prior to the 9/11 attacks. It was scheduled for January 5–8, 2000, in Kuala Lumpur, Malaysia, known to intelligence analysts as "K.L."

The 9/11 Summit

As early as 1998, the NSA had picked up references to al-Midhar Nawaf al-Hazmi and his brother Salem, who would also become a suicide hijacker on 9/11.[20]

When al-Midahr left the Yemeni safe house in early 2000, agents from *eight* CIA offices and *six* allied intelligence services were reportedly asked to track him.[21] Officials in the United Arab Emirates even made copies of al-Midhar's passport when he traveled through Dubai, so that by the time he reached Kuala Lumpur, the CIA knew his full name and the fact that he was carrying a U.S. multiple-entry visa.[22] The attendees at the summit were later photographed by the Malaysian Special Branch, and the pictures were shared with the CIA.

By January 4, a CIA operative made an extraordinary mistake that ignited one of the great interagency disputes on the road to 9/11. After receiving a copy of al-Midhar's picture, the Agency failed to add him to the Watch List. Worse yet, deliberate steps were taken to prevent the FBI from getting the information.

As the 9/11 Commission's final report told the story: "An FBI agent detailed to the Bin Ladin unit at CIA attempted to share this information with colleagues at FBI headquarters. A CIA desk officer instructed him not to send the cable with this information. Several hours later, this same desk officer drafted a cable distributed solely within CIA alleging that the visa documents had been shared with the FBI. She admitted she did not personally share the information and cannot identify who told her they had been shared. We were unable to locate anyone who claimed to have shared the information. Contemporaneous documents contradict the claim that they were shared."[23]

Later, the FBI would claim that their agents weren't informed of al-Midhar's al Qaeda ties until he was back in the United States and within weeks of boarding AA Flight 77. But back in January 2000, while the Malaysian meeting was still in progress, a CIA officer assigned to the FBI's Strategic Information Operations Center (SIOC) at the Bureau's Washington headquarters reportedly briefed two separate FBI agents on al-Midhar's activities.[24]

As terrorism analyst Paul Thompson reports in his detailed review of the al-Midhar incident for cooperativeresearch.org: "This agent then sends an e-mail to another CIA agent describing 'exactly' what he told the two FBI agents. One section reads, 'This continues to be an [intelligence] operation. Thus far, a lot of suspicious activity has been observed, but nothing that would indicate evidence of an impending attack or criminal enterprise. [The first FBI agent was] told that as soon as something concrete is developed leading us to the criminal arena or to known FBI cases, we will immediately bring FBI into the loop. Like [the first FBI agent] yesterday, [the second FBI agent] stated that this was a fine approach, and thanked me for keeping him in the loop.' The two FBI agents are not told about al-Midhar's U.S. visa."

The fact that a key CIA representative at the FBI felt that nothing observed at the Malaysian summit suggested "evidence of an impending attack" is stunning when one considers who was in attendance at the three-day session, which took place at a condominium overlooking a Jack Nicklaus-designed golf course. The condo was owned by Yazid Sufaat, a Malaysian who traveled to Afghanistan in the summer of 2000 and later acknowledged his al Qaeda ties.[25]

Participants in the January 2000 Malaysian meeting, in person or by phone. Top: Nawaf al-Hazmi, Khalid Al-Midhar, Khalid Shaikh Mohammed, Khallad bin Atash. Bottom: Riduan Isamuddin (aka Hambali), Yazid Sufaat, Ramzi bin al-Shibh, Fahad al-Quso.

Details of the Malaysian terror summit have been a matter of public record for some time, but of the eight attendees initially reported, the one most disputed by scholars and reporters is Khalid Shaikh Mohammed, who by then was in the late stages of perfecting his nephew Ramzi's planes operation.

A number of mainstream media accounts, from CNN to the *Los Angeles Times,* initially put KSM at the summit.[26] Singapore-based terror expert Ronan Gunarata later testified before the 9/11 Commission that he had seen interrogation reports in which KSM admitted running the summit,[27] and in a 2003 study of radical Islam in Southeast Asia,[28] Dr. Zachary Abuza, a U.S. terrorism scholar, reported that KSM was at the conference.

But Khalid Shaikh's attendance in Kuala Lumpur was later denied by U.S. officials, and some researchers like Dr. Abuza are now backtracking on whether he was *physically* in at the K.L. condo.[29] As Michael Isikoff and Mark Hosenball reported in *Newsweek,* KSM's presence at the meeting "would make the intelligence failure of the CIA even greater. It would mean the agency literally watched as the 9/11 scheme was hatched—and had photographs of the attack's mastermind . . . doing the plotting."[30]

In any case, KSM's number two in the planes-as-missiles plot, Ramzi bin al-Shibh, *was* there, along with Khallad bin Atash, a senior al Qaeda operative who played a key role in executing the African embassy bombings. Atash, who lost a leg reportedly fighting in Afghanistan and now wore a metal prosthesis, would go on to mastermind the attack on the U.S.S. *Cole* later in 2000. One of his operatives from the *Cole* plot, Fahad al-Quso, was also present at the K.L. summit,[31] along with Riduan Isamuddin, aka Hambali, the head of Jemaah Islamiya, the Indonesian wing of al Qaeda. It was Hambali who served with his wife on the board of Konsonjaya, the Malaysian front company that funded the Yousef-KSM Manila cell where the 9/11 plot was born.

To use a metaphor Patrick Fitzgerald would understand from his mob-busting days, the K.L. summit was the equivalent of the infamous Mafia conference in 1957 at Appalachin, New York, which finally alerted the FBI to the presence of the national organized crime syndicate J. Edgar Hoover later identified as "La Cosa Nostra."

"Arguably it was like the commission meeting," Jack Cloonan concurs.

The Malaysian summit was so high-profile, according to intelligence scholar James Bamford, that it was monitored, as it took place, at the highest levels of the intelligence community—even at the White House. "Updates were circulated to senior officials on January 3 and 5," wrote Bamford in his compelling study *A Pretext for War*.[32] Included on the list, per Bamford, was Alec Station at CIA, where Squad I-49 had a representative. White House national security advisor Sandy Berger was reportedly kept up to speed on the conference, and according to Bamford, FBI director Louis Freeh himself was briefed on January 6.[33]

Attended by a who's-who of top al Qaeda operational killers, that meeting set the stage for not only the *Cole* bombing and the 9/11 attacks, but also the October 2002 Bali bombings, to which Hambali was later linked. Even if KSM wasn't there physically, the presence of his deputy bin al-Shibh, Hambali, and Khallad bin Atash should have set off flashing red lights throughout the U.S. intelligence community—especially at the CIA and the FBI, which was now investigating the African embassy bombings *ex post facto*.

Linking the K.L. Summit to the African Bombings

We now know, from the testimony during the March 2006 penalty phase at the trial of accused "twentieth hijacker" Zacarias Moussaoui, that the one-legged Khallad was also an operational leader of the embassy bombing plot. After his capture, Mohamed Rashed Daoud al-'Owali admitted that before the August 1998 bombing he was instructed to go to Pakistan. There he met bin Atash, who told him to prepare for a "martyrdom mission" in which he would drive a truck full of explosives into a target.[34]

"That information came to the FBI on or about September 9, 1998," says a source close to Moussaoui's defense team. "Later al-'Owali gives up the Sana'a Yemen safe house of al-Midhar's brother-in-law Ahmed al-Hada. That intelligence led to the NSA and CIA wiretaps. So you have to ask yourself, why wasn't the FBI *all over* that K.L. meeting? Why wait for the CIA to give them photographs? Why didn't they have their *own* wiretaps on the Sana'a safe house and track al-Midhar on their own? Clearly they had criminal jurisdiction to pursue the leads as a result of Khallad's ties to the embassy bombing."

David Kaplan and Kevin Whitelaw reported in *U.S. News & World Report* that "The content of some of [al-Midhar's] conversations, in fact, was reported to the FBI at the time, but neither the FBI nor the NSA investigated much further, officials now say."[35]

In *The Looming Tower,* Lawrence Wright reports that they even had a link chart up "on the wall of the bullpen" in Squad I-49 "showing the connections between Ahmed al-Hada's phone and other phones around the world."[36]

"Had the line been drawn from the Hada household in Yemen to Hazmi and Mihdar's San Diego apartment," Wright notes, "al-Qaeda's presence in America would have been glaringly obvious."

But whose fault was it that the line wasn't drawn? In his account, Wright puts most of the blame on the CIA, but clearly in its investigation of the African embassy bombings, and what we now know to be its awareness of the importance of al-Midhar and that Sana'a (al Hada) safehouse, Squad I-49 of the FBI's NYO ought to be held equally accountable for not connecting the dots.

Remember, by now, after keeping his name secret for two years, the FBI was pressing a worldwide manhunt for Khalid Shaikh Mohammed. The FBI had lost him twice, once at the Su Casa guest house in Islamabad the day Yousef was busted in February 1995, and then in 1996 after Greg Scarpa Jr.'s patch-through had led the Feds to Doha, Qatar. But by 1999 KSM was in close contact with lead hijacker Mohammed Atta and two of the other 9/11 pilots: Marwan al-Shehhi (identified by the Able Danger operation) and Ziad Jarrah, who went on to commandeer the cockpit of UA Flight 93 that crashed in Pennsylvania. They were all living in an apartment together at 54 Marienstrasse in Hamburg, Germany, with KSM's number two, Ramzi bin al-Shibh.

Described by the 9/11 Commission as the Hamburg "core group,"[37] Atta, bin al-Shibh, al-Shehhi, and Jarrah met with bin Laden and Mohammed Atef in Afghanistan in late 1999, and two of them (bin al-Shibh and Atta) linked up with KSM in Karachi within weeks of the Kuala Lumpur summit.

The fact that the CIA had photographic evidence of the K.L. meeting's attendees and didn't share that with the FBI became an interagency flashpoint after 9/11. In *The Cell*, which he cowrote with ABC correspondent-turned-FBI spokesman John Miller, reporter Michael Stone even claimed that a June 11, 2001, meeting at the JTTF in New York, in which CIA agents refused to disclose details from the Malaysian meeting relating to the *Cole* bombing, ended up in a "shouting match."[38]

One of Stone's key sources was none other than retired FBI special agent Jack Cloonan.

When I interviewed Cloonan, who learned the details of the meeting immediately after it ended, he got much more specific, noting that Steve Bongardt, a veteran of the FBI's TWA 800 investigation, had attended the meeting along with two other FBI agents.

"Dina Corsi, an FBI analyst from Headquarters comes up [to New York] with a CIA officer," says Cloonan, "and they show three pictures of this meeting in Kuala Lumpur that CIA has known the significance of for months and they say they can't share it with us." Then "they ask, 'Do you know anybody in these photographs?' And Steve says, 'Are these from the surveillance in Malaysia?' But they won't answer the question: 'Can't tell you.' We're talking about the so-called 'wall' now. Because the *Cole* investigation is a criminal investigation, ergo [according to Corsi], 'We can't share this information with you.'"

But Cloonan insists that there was no reason for Corsi, one of their own, to keep the contents of the photos secret. "Why are they there," he wonders, if not to share the intelligence? "What sensitive sources and methods [would they be] compromising?" The so-called shouting match nearly turned into something more, as Cloonan tells it: "Bongardt gets so angry he almost goes over the table" at Corsi and the CIA officer. That meeting ultimately led Bongardt to write one of the most chilling and ironic e-mails in FBI history.

Addressing the management at FBI Headquarters, he predicted that "Someday somebody will die—and, 'wall' or not, the public will not understand why we were not more effective."

Proof That the FBI Had Access to the K.L. Photos

In our extensive interview on May 4, 2006, Cloonan gave me a stunning new piece of information that puts the alleged failure of the CIA to share the intelligence on the K.L. meeting in a whole new light. As it turns out, one of the key FBI agents in the FBI's squad I-49 had seen some of the Malaysian summit pictures months before.

"Frank Pellegrino was in Kuala Lumpur" sometime after the summit, Cloonan admitted. "And the CIA chief of station said, 'I'm not supposed to show these photographs, but here. Take a look at these photographs. Know any of these guys?' "

But as Cloonan described it, "Frank doesn't know. He's working Khalid Shaikh Mohammed," and thus would not have recognized any of the faces.

When I suggested that Khalid Shaikh Mohammed may have been at the summit, Cloonan denied it, but then admitted that he wasn't sure. Still, keep in mind—even if KSM, the man the FBI calls the 9/11 "mastermind," did not attend this key planning session prior to the attacks, there was *another* significant al Qaeda face in the crowd that Pellegrino should have recognized immediately: Riduan Isamuddin, aka Hambali.

As chronicled by former CNN Manila bureau chief Maria Ressa in her compelling investigative book *Seeds of Terror,* "Khalid Shaikh Mohammed began visiting Malaysia starting in 1994 and tapped Hambali, whom he first met in Afghanistan, as his operative. He gave the seed money of about 95,000 ringgits, or $33,000, to Hambali to launch Jemaah Islamiya's operations there."[39]

Pellegrino had arrived in Manila within weeks of the Dona Josefa fire in 1995. He was present at Camp Crame for most of Col. Mendoza's interrogation of Abdul Hakim Murad. Mendoza and the PNP had documented Hambali's importance as a key member of the al Qaeda cutout Konsonjaya. How was it possible that a top FBI agent who was now in Patrick Fitzgerald's elite squad I-49 couldn't connect the dots on Hambali, even after seeing the photographs of the K.L. summit from the CIA?

I wanted to ask Pellegrino that question, but he too refused to talk to me.

In any case, one lesson that the FBI should have learned from the Malaysian summit was just how well coordinated al Qaeda was. Far from the "loosely organized group" of Sunni Muslims somehow disconnected from the World Trade Center bombing, as Patrick Fitzgerald suggested in 2005,* al Qaeda was a tightly integrated network with directions coming from the top down directly via bin Laden and Dr. al-Zawahiri. It was an international network capable of staging a summit conference, with operatives from half a dozen countries working together to plan acts of terror on three continents.

In its data-mining initiative, the Able Danger team at Fort Belvoir was making that same kind of connection with many of the same players. Eventually they would identify Aden Yemen as a key al Qaeda "hotspot" within weeks of the *Cole* bombing. In harvesting what eventually grew to 2.5 terabytes of data, they found linkages that corroborated my findings precisely: namely, that the New York cell of Sheikh Omar Abdel Rahman, trained by Ali Mohamed, was directly tied to al Qaeda's leadership. The Able Danger findings corroborated what I had laid out in my last two books: that both attacks on the WTC, the 1993 bombing and the September 11 planes-as-missiles operation, were designed, funded, and directly controlled by al Qaeda's leadership. In fact, the LIWA/DIA data miners went even further—putting Ali Mohamed and bin Laden's brother-in-law Mohammed Jamal Khalifa in the al Qaeda inner circle.

The Smoking Gun Link Chart

How do we know this? The connections were documented in a declassified link chart sent to me by Jacob L. Boesen who worked on many of the Able Danger charts. Declassified on March 21, 2000, the chart showed Ali Mohamed (with his photo from the Fort Bragg video) inside a box with bin Laden, al-Zawahiri, Atef, Wadih El-Hage, and Mohammed Jamal Khalifa. That box linked to the Sheikh Rahman-Ramzi Yousef New York cell via the Egyptian Islamic Jihad and the Abu Sayyaf Group in the

*During his on-camera interview for the National Geographic Channel documentary *Inside 9/11*.

Philippines, which was also linked to the Yousef-KSM-Murad-Wali Khan Manila cell responsible for the 9/11 attacks.

The chart not only vindicates my findings, but defies the conclusion later reached by Fitzgerald and Dietrich Snell, his SDNY colleague, who determined the "origin of the plot" for the 9/11 Commission and pushed it forward two years to Afghanistan in 1996, removing Yousef from the plot and suggesting that at the time KSM was not even a member of al Qaeda—a conclusion that is almost comical in light of the documented evidence of al Qaeda's control of the suicide-hijack plot.

That March 21, 2000, link chart, reproduced on page 343, is the smoking gun document proving that the government understood both Ramzi Yousef and Ali Mohamed were involved with the multiple acts of mass murder and terror perpetrated by bin Laden's network, from the killing of Rabbi Meier Kahane in 1990 forward. It's a graphic representation of the FBI's failures to contain all that horror, and it confirms my contention that Fitzgerald, Snell, Gorelick, and other key DOJ officials sought to hide the full truth behind the Justice Department's failures. (See Appendix VIII, pages 570–571.)

But within days of that chart's declassification, the FBI and Justice were joined by another of the Big Five intelligence agencies in a cover up that kept this key al Qaeda intelligence from the American people. By April 2000, officials of the Pentagon ordered that the 2.5 terabytes of al Qaeda gold mined by the Able Danger unit at LIWA should be *destroyed*. When that happened, a year and a half before the 9/11 attacks, the dots weren't just disconnected, they were obliterated.

WORLD TRADE CENTER BOMBING LINKS

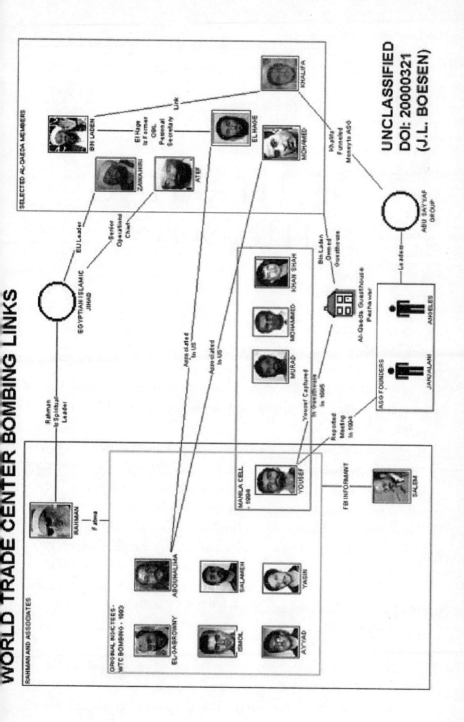

SELECTED AL-QAEDA MEMBERS

BIN LADEN

ZAWAHIRI — EIJ Leader

ATEF — Senior Operational Chief

El Hage, Is Former OBL Personal Secretary

EL HAGE

MOHAMED

KHALIFA

UNK

Khalifa Funded Moayris ASG

ABU SAYYAF GROUP — Leades

EGYPTIAN ISLAMIC JIHAD

Rahman Is Spiritual Leader

Associated in US

Associated in US

MANILA CELL - 1994

MURAD

MOHAMMED

ISHAN SHAH

Bin Laden Owned Guesthouse

Al-Qaeda Guesthouse Peshawar

Yousef Captured In Guesthouse In 1995

Reported Meeting In 1994

YOUSEF

ASG FOUNDERS

JANJALANI

ANSELES

FBI INFORMANT

SALEM

RAHMAN AND ASSOCIATES

RAHMAN — Fatwa

ORIGINAL INDICTEES-WTC BOMBING - 1993

ABOUHALIMA

SALAMEH

YASIN

EL-GABROWNY

ISMOIL

AYYAD

UNCLASSIFIED
DOI: 20000321
(J.L. BOESEN)

32

OBLITERATING
THE DOTS

"The Ali Mohamed link chart opens a whole new series of questions that have to be answered," says Congressman Curt Weldon (R-PA) one of the original backers of the LIWA unit at Fort Belvoir, and the man who first disclosed the story of the Able Danger operation to the *New York Times* in August 2005.

Vice chairman of both the House Armed Services and the Homeland Security committees, Weldon says he was "blown away" by the data-mining capabilities of the Information Dominance Center as early as 1997, when he tapped the LIWA analysts for intelligence in preparation for a meeting in Vienna. At the height of the conflict in the former Yugoslavia, Weldon had heard that a certain Serb named Dragomir Kric had a back channel to Serbian dictator Slobodan Milosevic, who was then holding three U.S. pilots as POWs in Belgrade. Weldon was about to chair a congressional delegation (CODEL) of Democrats and Republicans who would fly to Austria and meet with Russian leaders to try and broker a way out of the crisis.

"Before we left on that trip I wanted to know something about Kric, so I called [CIA director] George Tenet," Weldon told me.[1] "I said, 'The Russians are convinced that this guy Kric can give us information that will allow us to get Milosevic to free those pilots. As the CIA director, can you tell me something about him?' Tenet called me back and gave me 2 or 3 sentences about Kric: that he was from a very influential family; that they had a bank; and that he was tied in with the Communists in Russia. But the Agency didn't know much else about him."

Weldon then approached his contacts at Fort Belvoir, who did a quick data-mining run on the Serb. "They came back to me with ten pages of information about this man," says Weldon. "The fact that he owns the apartment building where Milosovic lives. The fact that their wives are very close. An incredibly detailed profile that I got almost overnight from this tiny under-funded operation on an army base, when our own CIA didn't seem to have a clue who Kric was."

Weldon says that after he returned from meeting the Russians he got phone calls from both the FBI and the CIA. So many members of his congressional delegation had raved about the LIWA report on Kric that the Agency and the Bureau both asked where he was getting his intelligence.

"I met with them on a Monday afternoon," says Weldon. "One FBI agent and a CIA case officer in my office on the Hill, and they were both stunned. Neither of them had even *heard* about LIWA or this type of data-mining capability."

Years later, when he heard that LIWA had been enlisted by the Special Operations Command to harvest intelligence on al Qaeda—and that they'd made the startling links to the blind Sheikh and the four 9/11 hijackers—Weldon says he wasn't surprised.

"This was intelligence that the Able Danger operation got in early 2000 that absolutely, if properly acted upon, could have stopped the 9/11 plot cold," he says.

Maj. Eric Kleinsmith, the former chief of intelligence at LIWA, seemed to agree. "We were able to collect an immense amount of data for analysis that allowed us to map al Qaeda as a worldwide threat with a surprisingly significant presence within the United States." he said at a 2005 Senate hearing.[2]

But by April 2000, Kleinsmith and other LIWA personnel on the Able Danger project were told by DOD lawyers that this vast amount of open-source data may have violated Executive Order 12333, an intelligence directive signed in 1981 by President Ronald Reagan after the Senate and House hearings into CIA domestic spying abuses in the late 1970s.[3]

"The EO," as it's known, was designed to prevent the Pentagon from storing data indefinitely on "U.S. persons," a term defined to include American citizens, U.S. corporations; even permanent resident aliens.

"'U.S. person' information is something that we are skittish about in the Defense Department," said William Dugan, assistant secretary of defense in the current Bush administration, in testimony before that same Senate hearing. "We follow the rules strictly on it."[4]

As a result of the Pentagon's alleged concerns about the 2.5 terabytes of Able Danger data containing information on "U.S. persons" along side al Qaeda terrorists, Kleinsmith says that he and his deputy got a direct order.

"I, along with CW3 Terri Stephens, were forced to destroy all the data, charts, and other analytical products that we had not already passed on to SOCOM related to Able Danger."[5]

"Imagine," says Weldon. "You've got this embarrassment of riches with probative al Qaeda intelligence—the names of four of the September 11th hijackers in the spring of 2000, almost a year and a half before the attacks. You've got Atta, the lead hijacker on the American flight that hits the North Tower of the Trade Center; al-Shehhi, who sends UA 175 into the South Tower; and al-Midhar and al-Hazmi, who hit the Pentagon. They're identified in open-source data and then, under the guise of conforming to this EO, it gets destroyed. Well, guess what? There was no legal justification for it whatsoever."[6]

Indeed, EO 12333 has ten provisions allowing for the retention of data[7] including "Information that is publicly available" and "Information obtained in the course of a lawful foreign intelligence, counterintelligence . . . or international terrorism investigation."

"All of the initial Able Danger data runs involved open-source, nonclassified data," says Lt. Col. Anthony Shaffer, the DIA liaison to the Able Danger operation, "and clearly we were dealing with terrorism. So the excuse that came down from DOD, that this data had to be destroyed in order to protect so-called 'U.S. persons,' just doesn't wash."

"That's what makes what happened in April 2000 all the more outrageous," says Cong. Weldon. "And as we've looked into this, it has turned into a cover-up that's bigger than Watergate. Richard Nixon lost the presidency over a third-rate burglary. This was an affirmative destruction of data that could have helped save the lives of 3,000 people."

The Muscle Hijackers and the One-Legged Terrorist

It's not particularly surprising that the Able Danger data sweep of open-source information would have picked up the soon-to-be muscle hijackers al-Midhar and al-Hazmi. Their visibility in the United States was so high in the eighteen months prior to their airborne assault on the Pentagon that the FBI's failure to detect them seems to border on gross negligence—even with the CIA's refusal to share the intel.

As early as 1999, while monitoring phone calls at the Sana'a Yemen safe house, the NSA picked up references to Khalid al-Midhar, Nawaf al-Hazmi, and his brother Salem, who would also become one of the suicide hijackers on 9/11.[8] The FBI knew about that safe house. In fact, the location was the result of a lead uncovered by their *own* criminal investigation of the embassy bombings. And yet the Bureau seemed in no hurry to establish their own wiretaps on the Sana'a residence or to insist on copies of NSA or CIA intercepts—cooperation one would expect the FBI to demand in the investigation of 224 murders in East Africa.

That wiretap of the home of Khalid al-Midhar's brother-in-law led the CIA to monitor the summit in Kuala Lumpur, but even before that there is evidence that al-Midhar and al-Hazmi had entered the United States.

In a Pulitzer Prize-winning story for the *Washington Post* in late September 2001, Amy Goldstein reported that the two hijackers actually showed up at the Parkwood Apartments, a townhouse complex in San Diego, in late 1999.[9] This San Diego connection would prove key, because after the two hijackers returned to the United States and slipped past a Watch List in January 2000, they ended up living in rooms rented to them by a San Diego *FBI informant.*

Tracked to the K.L. summit, al-Midhar's passport was copied in Dubai and sent to the CIA's Alec Station (where the FBI had an agent in residence). Al-Midhar was later photographed at the K.L. summit by the

Malaysian Special Branch. On January 8, when the conference ended, al-Midhar flew with al-Hazmi to Bangkok, Thailand—both of them using their own names on the flight manifests. Sitting next to them in a three-seat configuration was Khallad bin Atash, the one-legged Saudi who had sent al-'Owali to his intended death in Nairobi. Atash had recently attempted to blow up an Aegis-class guided missile destroyer, the U.S.S. *The Sullivans*—a failed al Qaeda action that was a precursor to the *Cole* bombing.[10]

At that point, the FBI was doing a full-court press on the embassy-bombing investigation. Al-'Owali's tip on the Sana'a safe house had led to the discovery of al-Midhar by the Malaysians. The fact that Special Agent Frank Pellegrino of Squad I-49 had seen pictures of the K.L. summit meant that the Bureau was in the loop. And yet following the January 8 flight, both the FBI and the CIA reportedly lost all three terrorists in the Thai capital. Worse, despite having identified al-Midhar as an al Qaeda associate, and realizing that he had a U.S. multientry visa, the CIA never added his name to the TIPOFF Watch List of some 70,000 suspected terrorists.[11]

As such, using their own names, al-Midhar and al-Hazmi jetted from Bangkok to Los Angeles on January 15. There they were met by Omar al-Bayoumi, a Saudi suspected of being an intelligence officer, who had visited the Saudi consulate in Los Angeles the same day.[12] After three weeks, the two would-be hijackers moved to San Diego, where they lived openly for the next five months.[13] During that period, al-Bayoumi helped them get settled, finding them an apartment across from where he lived.[14] It was later reported by *Newsweek* and the *Washington Times* that al-Bayoumi may have been the recipient of funds sent to his wife *indirectly* from Princess Haifa bin Faisal, wife of Saudi Arabia's then-ambassador to the United States, Prince Bandar. On www.cooperativeresearch.org, Paul Thompson has summarized a series of news reports noting that Princess Haifa began sending cashier's checks to Majeda Dwiekat, the Jordanian wife of one Osama Basnan, a Saudi living in San Diego. Basnan's wife then reportedly signed many of the checks over to the wife of Omar al-Bayoumi.[15] Prince Bandar, who later stepped down as U.S. ambassador, emphatically denied any impropriety at the time the check scandal broke. But according to Thompson:

> Within days of bringing them from Los Angeles, al-Bayoumi throws a welcoming party that introduces them to the local Muslim community.[16] One associate later says that al-Bayoumi's party "was a big deal . . . it meant that everyone accepted them without question."[17] He also introduces hijacker Hani Hanjour to the community a short time later.[18] He tasks an acquaintance, Modhar Abdallah, to serve as their translator and help them get driver's licenses, Social Security cards, information on flight schools, and more.[19]

The High Visibility of "Dumb and Dumber"

During their early months in San Diego, al-Midhar and al-Hazmi proved to be the antithesis of low-profile sleepers. They took flight lessons at the Sorbi Flying Club, bought season passes to Sea World, played soccer in a local park, and interacted with many members of the Muslim community. Al-Midhar bought a 1998 Toyota Corolla for $3,000 and registered it with the California DMV.[20] After moving into a two-story town home at 6401 Mount Ada Road, al-Hazmi got a telephone. He even had his full name listed in the phone directory:[21]

But the two Saudis showed little talent for flying. Announcing that they wanted to learn to fly Boeing jumbo jets, they trained on twin-engine

Cessnas, and demonstrated so little aptitude in the cockpit that their flight instructor, Rick Garza, nicknamed them "Dumb and Dumber."[22]

Throughout the spring and summer of 2000, the National Security Agency, which began monitoring al-Midhar's brother-in-law's home in Yemen in 1998, picked up multiple intercepts between San Diego and the safe house. As it turned out, al-Midhar's wife was about to give birth in the year 2000. But the NSA later claimed that it didn't know that the calls from al-Midhar *originated in the United States.*[23] It wasn't until *after* 9/11 that the Feds realized that Ramzi bin al-Shibh, KSM's number two on the entire planes-as-missiles operation, was al-Midhar's cousin.[24]

On June 3, 2000, lead hijacker Mohammed Atta arrived in the United States, and rented a room in Brooklyn, New York. He listed the same address in Hamburg, Germany: 54 Marienstrasse, where he'd been living with hijacker pilots al-Shehhi and Ziad Jarrah. In San Diego, neighbors of al-Midhar and al-Hazmi claimed that Atta and Hani Hanjour, the pilot of AA 77, visited them. There was a report that Hanjour actually roomed with them for a time, but didn't stay.[25]

"Later, the Pentagon denied that the Able Danger data mining had uncovered Atta, al-Shehhi, and the two San Diego hijackers in early 2000," says Cong. Weldon. "But you can see how visible they were at this time. We're not talking needles in haystacks here. With al-Midhar you've got a terrorist with known al Qaeda connections through the Yemeni safe house. Atta shows up in Brooklyn, and the LIWA people find out he's linked to the Al Farooq Mosque, where the blind Sheikh ran his New York cell. This isn't rocket science. These killers in our midst were *highly* visible."[26]

The FBI Blows Its Best Chance

Despite the FBI's ongoing complaint that they were consistently blindsided by the CIA on the presence of al-Midhar and al-Hazmi, both at the K.L. meeting and in their U.S. entry, the Bureau deserves *equal* criticism for its failure to locate the two muscle hijackers. Why? Because by the summer of 2000 they moved into the Lemon Grove section of San Diego, renting rooms from Abdussattar Shaykh, a local Muslim leader who was also an

FBI *informant*. In fact, Shaykh was considered so important to the Bureau that he was later described as a "tested" undercover "asset."[27] *Newsweek*'s Michael Isikoff first broke that story after 9/11, and terrorism researcher Paul Thompson has advanced it on his website, cooperativeresearch.org. Citing Isikoff's groundbreaking reporting, Thompson completed the mosaic of what must go down as one of the most profound FBI failures in the years leading up to 9/11. Because of the significance of the lapse, we are reproducing Thompson's account in full:

> While hijackers Nawaf al-Hazmi and Khalid al-Midhar live in the house of an FBI asset, Abdussattar Shaykh, the asset continues to have contact with his FBI handler. The handler, Steven Butler, later claims that during the summer Shaykh mentions the names "Nawaf" and "Khalid" in passing and that they are renting rooms from him.[28] On one occasion, Shaykh tells Butler on the phone he cannot talk because Khalid is in the room.[29] Shaykh tells Butler they are good, religious Muslims who are legally in the U.S. to visit and attend school. Butler asks Shaykh for their last names, but Shaykh refuses to provide them. Butler is not told that they are pursuing flight training. Shaykh tells Butler that they are apolitical and have done nothing to arouse suspicion. However, according to the 9/11 Congressional Joint Inquiry, he later admits that al-Hazmi has "contacts with at least four individuals [he] knew were of interest to the FBI and about whom [he] had previously reported to the FBI." Three of these four people are being actively investigated at the time the hijackers are there.[30] The report mentions Osama Mustafa as one, and Shaykh admits that suspected Saudi agent Omar al-Bayoumi was a friend.[31] The FBI later concludes that Shaykh is not involved in the 9/11 plot, but they have serious doubts about his credibility. After 9/11 he gives inaccurate information and has an "inconclusive" polygraph examination about his foreknowledge of the 9/11 attack. The FBI believes he has contact with hijacker Hani Hanjour, but he claims not to recognize him. There are other "significant inconsistencies" in Shaykh's statements about the hijackers, including when he first met them and later meetings with them. The 9/11 Congressional Inquiry later concludes that had the asset's contacts with the hijackers been capitalized upon, it "would have given the San Diego FBI field office perhaps the U.S. intelligence community's best chance to unravel the September 11 plot."[32]

After 9/11, when the Congressional Joint Inquiry discovered Shaykh's identity and issued a subpoena for him to testify, Attorney General John Ashcroft refused to allow his agents to serve it.[33] Sen. Bob Graham, the Democrat who cochaired the Joint Inquiry, used the term "cover up" to describe the stonewalling by Justice in refusing to disclose the depth of Shaykh's apparent duplicity.[34]

33

ABLE DANGER
PART TWO

In the summer of 2000, there was another significant opportunity for the U.S. intelligence community to interdict Ramzi Yousef's suicide-hijacking plot. Although the Able Danger unit's initial data run was ordered destroyed, the army's Special Operations Command set up a follow-up unit. Contracted out to Raytheon's Intelligence and Information Systems facility at Garland, Texas, several of the key LIWA data miners were brought over to do a new "harvest" of open-source material on al Qaeda. Among them were Dr. Ellen Preisser and Jacob L. "Jay" Boesen, who continued to produce link charts for the operation.[1]

"By late summer, that second Able Danger configuration had reconfirmed the previous hits on Atta, al-Midhar, al-Hazmi and al-Shehhi," says Lt. Col. Anthony Shaffer, "but they also identified Aden Yemen as one of the top three al Qaeda hot spots in the world."[2]

Again, this connection wasn't surprising, since the CIA had earlier tracked Khallad bin Atash, the one-legged Embassy bombing plotter with heavy Yemeni ties. Also, another attendee of the Malaysian summit, Fahad al-Quso, was based in Aden.

At this point, Shaffer, the DIA's liaison to the Able Danger operation, was asked by Special Operations Command to contact the FBI.

"We had been working a parallel operation to the FBI looking at The 17th of November, a terrorist organization in Athens," says Shaffer. "The FBI had asked us for help in preparation for the Olympics and we were actually tasked to use the same basic data-mining methodology. It was because of that link that SOCOM came to me and said, 'Would you please broker meetings between us and the FBI regarding passing some of the al Qaeda information?' So I went to my FBI contact on The 17th of November and asked to meet with the agents in the WFO [Washington Field Office] who worked bin Laden."

Shaffer says that three separate meetings with Bureau agents were scheduled between the summer and September 2000. But each meeting was cancelled "on the advice of SOCOM attorneys." The reason? "SOCOM lawyers would not permit the sharing of the 'U.S. person' information regarding terrorists located domestically, due to 'fear of potential blowback,' should the FBI do something with the information and something should go wrong." That's what Shaffer ultimately reported to a House committee investigating the Able Danger data destruction.[3]

Until recently, both Shaffer and Congressman Weldon believed that Pentagon officials had ordered the FBI meetings cancelled for the same reason they gave to explain the destruction of the 2.5 terabytes of data: concern that EO 12333 might have been violated. But in light of my discovery of J.L. Boesen's March 21, 2000, link chart showing Ali Mohamed in the al Qaeda inner circle, both Weldon and Shaffer have come to suspect another reason for the data destruction.

"I can tell you that right after the story broke on Able Danger," says Shaffer, "people from the army came to me and said, 'We don't want to be blamed for 9/11.' And I couldn't understand that position back then, because why would the *army* be blamed? If anything, with the LIWA data mining, we had been ahead of the curve, and we had done our best to sound the alarm. But then, seeing this link chart with Ali Mohamed's picture coming a week or so before the data was destroyed, gave me a sense that there could be another explanation."

Weldon concurs. "Imagine if you are a high-ranking general in SOCOM," he says.[4] "And you have authorized this extraordinary data-mining operation which turns up amazing evidence of an al Qaeda presence in the U.S. in the spring of 2000. Then the LIWA people show you a link chart with a picture of this fellow Ali Mohamed so close to bin Laden. And then you ask who he is, and you find out straightaway that he was an al Qaeda *spy* who was active-duty army, and that he had infiltrated the JFK Special Warfare School at Fort Bragg back in 1987. Not only that, but he stole classified documents on SOCOM troop locations. He may have even trained al Qaeda cell members in Somalia who helped take down those two Blackhawks in 1993. He definitely took the pictures of the Nairobi embassy and precisely targeted the suicide truck bomb that killed hundreds of people in '98. He was bin Laden's personal security adviser. That is the ultimate example of blowback. How do you think an army general would react to that kind of news? That the Green Berets had let an al Qaeda spy into their midst when the senior Bush was in the White House. It is entirely possible that the Pentagon did a damage assessment in April of 2000 and hit the panic button. They just used EO 12333 as the excuse."

Weldon, a loyal conservative, now believes that the suppression of intelligence on al Qaeda is a scandal that transcends political administrations, parties, and agencies.

"From the FBI to the DIA and the CIA there has been an affirmative attempt to cover up the mistakes of the past—of which Ali Mohamed was perhaps one of the most egregious examples," he says. "The consequence was that as we got closer to 9/11 we weren't getting *smarter* about the al Qaeda threat, we were having blinders put on. Key dots were being hidden for the oldest excuse inside the Beltway: CYA—the avoidance of embarrassment."

The situation got so bad that at one point Tony Shaffer says he saw a series of link charts from the original LIWA data runs in which "yellow stickies" had been pasted over the pictures of key al Qaeda operatives like Mohammed Atta, on the orders of SOCOM lawyers.[5]

"The Close-to-Absolutely-Perfect Record"

In September 2000, on the twentieth anniversary of the NYO's Joint Terrorism Task Force, representatives of the seventeen federal, state, and local law enforcement agencies that made up the JTTF assembled for a celebration. In the course of the party, SDNY U.S. Attorney Mary Jo White praised the FBI's flagship task force for what she called a "close-to-absolutely-perfect record of successful investigations and convictions."[6] Later, White wrote an essay calling the JTTF members the "true heroes of the city."

"For twenty years," wrote White, "the JTTF has been a huge success story, measured both in terms of arrests and convictions of terrorists that the public knows about and (even more important) in the mostly unseen work of the JTTF, in detecting and preventing terrorist acts that do not result in prosecutions or publicity."[7]

Naturally, in assessing the JTTF's "next to perfect record," White avoided certain details, such as how the JTTF's boss, Carson Dunbar, had thwarted the FBI's best chance of stopping the first attack on the Twin Towers by alienating Emad Salem and failing to authorize the surveillance he pleaded for on two of Ali Mohamed's trained cell members Abouhalima and Salameh. She left out the fact that her star prosecutor Patrick Fitzgerald and his elite Squad I-49 had years of advance warning of the African embassy bombings, including wiretaps on the key cell members, and the fact that Ali Mohamed, one of the cell's ring leaders, had worked as the FBI's own West Coast informant. She skipped over the fact that Special Agent Frank Pellegrino had seen the surveillance photos of the 9/11 Malaysian summit and failed to recognize either Hambali or Khallad bin Atash, who were weeks away from wreaking bin Laden's next act of "havoc" for the jihad.

With the same arrogance Special Agent John Zent had shown in flashing his Bureau I.D. to intimidate those Fresno sheriff's detectives in 1992, White was trading on the myth—often stoked by the media—that "the best and the brightest"[8] in the FBI's two bin Laden offices of origin would keep New Yorkers safe from Osama bin Laden's terror war. There was even a hint of irony in the location of the JTTF's anniversary party, the same place where Neal Herman's retirement party had been held on September 11, 1999: the spectacular 50,000 square foot restaurant Windows on the World, located on the top floor of the World Trade Center's North Tower.

As the Feds partied on, bin Laden's jihadis were working day and night from Afghanistan to San Diego to Brooklyn to bring those Towers down. None of the revelers seemed to remember Ramzi Yousef's 1993 warning, found on Nidal Ayyad's computer, that his "calculations were not very accurate" but that the Trade Center would again be a target. Or Murad's warning to SA Frank Pellegrino that: "Ramzi wanted to return to the U.S." to attack the Towers a second time. Or even Yousef's chilling warning during that late night flyby of the WTC in 1995 that the Trade Center might still be vulnerable.

Bin Laden's Next Warning

Perhaps sensing how persistently U.S. intelligence agencies underestimated their resolve, the terrorists of al Qaeda were very good about telegraphing their moves. Within weeks of that JTTF party, SOCOM lawyers had cancelled Lt. Col. Tony Shaffer's last chance to share the Able Danger intelligence with the FBI. But while the Pentagon seemed unwilling to have the FBI connect the dots, Osama bin Laden himself was using the world media to call his next play.

On September 21, 2000, he issued another *fatwa,* this one released to Al Jazeera, the Arabic television network, on videotape. As a hint of al Qaeda's next flash point, the Saudi terror leader brandished a jewel-encrusted Yemeni dagger. He also reminded the Feds of al Qaeda's loyalty to the spiritual leader of the New York cell—blind Sheikh Omar Abdel Rahman, whom the Able Danger data miners had clearly linked to al Qaeda just months before.

Bin Laden's last major *fatwa* in 1998, the "Jihad against Jews and Crusaders,"[9] had been signed by Ayman al-Zawahiri and Abu-Yasir Refai Taha, who had taken over for the jailed blind Sheikh as head of the al Gamma'a Islamiyah. Now, on this tape, bin Laden was flanked by Taha and al-Zawahiri again; next to them stood Mohammed Abdel Rahman, one of the blind Sheikh's sons.[10]

After a rambling speech, the younger Rahman urged their followers to "avenge your Sheikh" and "go to the spilling of blood." Then, almost as if to thumb his nose at the New York FBI, bin Laden himself told the faithful to remember *El Sayyid Nosair*. For those in the Bureau who continued to insist that there was no connection between the two attacks on the Trade Center, this video should have been proof positive that they were wrong. Osama bin Laden was personally invoking the name of the very al Qaeda operative—trained by Ali Mohamed—who had spilled the first al Qaeda blood on U.S. soil with the murder of Rabbi Kahane almost a decade earlier.

Yet a number of top U.S. intelligence analysts, including former CIA director James R. Woolsey, continued to insist that Saddam Hussein had been the primary force behind the 1993 World Trade Center attack, and that Ramzi Yousef had been an Iraqi agent. It was a completely specious theory, but one that many in the Bush administration would seize on to help justify the invasion of Iraq in March 2003.[11]

In any case, bin Laden's video *fatwa* with the Yemeni dagger should have been another profound warning to the Feds. "Here he was flaunting his U.S. indictment, saying we will get you," recalls a former FBI agent who worked terrorism. "And a few weeks later he did."

On October 12, al Qaeda suicide bombers, piloting a small inflatable dinghy, drove it into the side of the U.S.S. *Cole,* an advanced guided missile destroyer docked for refueling in Aden, Yemen. The blast blew a four-story hole in the ship and killed seventeen U.S. sailors.[12]

"We had data just days before the *Cole* bombing," says Lt. Col. Shaffer, "that Aden was a hot spot. I communicated this information to SOCOM and they reportedly passed it on to CENTCOM, but for unknown reasons the threat assessment was not communicated to Commander Lippold, the skipper of the *Cole*."

"I met with Kirk Lippold, whose career has basically ended," said Weldon in a February 2006 speech.[13] "He said to me, 'I had three choices that day. I could have refueled at sea. I could have refueled at a different city. If I would have known there was any potential problem in Aden, I would not have gone into port. But no one told me.' Seventeen sailors came home in body bags."

In another sad irony on the lead up to 9/11, it turned out that the National Security Agency's tap on the Sana'a Yemen safe house of Khalid al-Midhar's brother-in-law had yielded up to half a dozen calls to the United States even *after* the Cole bombing. But according to Josh Meyer in the *Los Angeles Times*, "the NSA didn't disclose the existence of the calls until after Sept. 11."[14]

Finally, the Contrite Spy

Eight days after the *Cole* bombing, Ali Mohamed stood stoop-shouldered before Judge Leonard B. Sand in that Southern District courtroom. Patrick Fitzgerald stood at his side with four other assistant AUSAs, including Michael Garcia, who convicted Ramzi Yousef for the Bojinka plot, and Andrew McCarthy who had worked with Fitzgerald to put the blind Sheikh away. The record does not reflect whether Dietrich Snell, who coprosecuted the Bojinka case, was also present, but Mary Jo White was on hand, along with Jack Cloonan, who now says that Ali finally confessed to the embassy bombings eighteen months after his arrest in September 1998.

But the "confession" came only after the Feds agreed to give Ali the "exit strategy" he'd been angling for all along. "Ali paints himself into a corner," says Cloonan, "and he just basically runs out of room.[15] His frustration level is increasing and it is weighing on him physically and mentally. On the day in question when he ultimately admits to what his role was, it is Pat [Fitzgerald who] brings him up to the precipice. I know at one point that day I said to Ali words to this effect: 'I'm not going to look at you as any less of a human being. You deserve some peace, because ultimately that's what we all want, isn't it? Because you may have done some things that I don't particularly agree with, or that frankly might have been deadly or in violation of the law, [but that] doesn't mean that I'm going to treat you any different. You have to find a way out and we're giving you a way out. Do you understand that? We're giving you a way out. We can literally lift this 900-pound gorilla off of your shoulders. What you need is an exit strategy. You need to feel as though you're not being an apostate, that you're a traitor to the cause, that you've disgraced yourself, that you've disgraced Islam. Think long and hard about what we said. This man over here, Mr. Fitzgerald, has treated you very, very fairly. You know that. Do you know that he's a powerful man? My colleague Dan [Coleman] here has done similarly. He's talked to you about his family. He's talked to you about the importance of family and how they're going to help you. I think what you need to do is sit with your attorney and you need a private moment to pray. We're going to go outside, and when I come back in, and we all come back in, things are going to be different.'"

Cloonan says that Mohamed then consulted with his lawyer, James Roth.

"About ten minutes into this, Jim Roth came outside and said, 'He's ready. He did it.'"

"We walked in and sat down. Ali was physically shaken. He slumped in his chair, head down, literally a shell of the man that we sort of knew, tears in his eyes. He said, 'This is what I did.' Then, I remember writing down the notes. He was saying, 'Yes, Mohammed Atef asked me with Zawahiri and bin Laden's blessing to do the surveillance on the U.S. embassy in Nairobi.'"

"'I had to make sure I heard that right,'" says Cloonan, quoting Ali. "'This is what I did, this is who I did it with, this is how I did it, and I did other things. Everything that I've told you up to this point has been a lie. I am telling you the truth from here on out.'"

"I think we had to stop at that point." says Cloonan, "because I think we were all—Ali, Jim, Pat, Dan, and myself—I think we were in mixed emotions. We knew the significance of [the confession] in our world. It may not have meant much to everybody else, but the system worked. We were successful. Slow, maybe, but successful."

Fitzgerald and the agents of Squad I-49 may have been successful in finally pulling the truth out of Mohamed *with respect to the embassy bombing*. But it had come years too late. They had been outflanked by the al Qaeda spy for years, seemingly incapable of detecting his agenda when he was "fully operational."

Ali Mohamed was living proof that the FBI, under three presidential administrations, had been deceived by an asset expert at playing one intelligence agency off against another, even as he betrayed his adopted country for the jihad. Worse, the price the Feds paid for Ali's so called "cooperation" was a plea deal that allowed him to avoid execution and life behind bars. In an echo of Cloonan's reference to "an exit strategy," Judge Sand actually discussed the possibility that if Ali Mohamed did not get the maximum sentence, he would one day be granted "supervised release."[16]

> THE COURT: Your offer is to plead guilty to five counts charging you with conspiracy to kill nationals of the United States, conspiracy to murder, kidnap and maim at places outside of the United States, conspiracy to murder, conspiracy to destroy buildings and property of the United States, and conspiracy to destroy national-defense utilities of the United States. Do you understand that pursuant to the relevant statutes, conviction on those five counts would subject you to a total maximum sentence of incarceration of life imprisonment plus any term of years. Do you understand that you would be subject to that potential sentence?
>
> MOHAMED: Yes, your honor.
>
> THE COURT: Do you understand that in addition to that, you would be subject to a term of supervised release of five years on Counts One, Two, Three and Five and three years' supervised release on Count Six? Do you understand that?
>
> MOHAMED: Yes, your honor.

The details of Ali Mohamed's deal remain secret to this day. But at least one knowledgeable attorney—David Runhke, who represented another of the embassy bombing defendants—has concluded that his arrangement with the Feds was clearly in Ali's favor.

"Mohamed has made some kind of deal with the government," Ruhnke believes, "that will surely have him out of prison on some date certain that he knows about."[17]

The Undiscovered Sleepers

With Ali Mohamed's plea, the curtain fell on the career of one of world history's most audacious and accomplished spies. But the story was far from over. Having failed, before the fact, to extract from Mohamed the details of the embassy-bombing plot he had planned and helped to supervise, Patrick Fitzgerald and his Southern District colleagues now had the potential of exposing hundreds of al Qaeda agents who had burrowed into the United States—many with Ali's help.

In the year 2000, Benjamin Weiser, the *New York Times* reporter who has done perhaps the most extensive newspaper reporting on Mohamed, sought to unseal a series of summaries that shed additional light on what the Egyptian agent was willing to tell the Feds. In one of the proffer sessions, according to Weiser, an FBI report stated that Ali "knows, for example, that there are hundreds of 'sleepers' or 'submarines' in place who don't fit neatly into the terrorist profile. These individuals don't wear the traditional beards and they don't pray at the mosques."[18]

In his 1999 confession to Egyptian authorities, Ali's Santa Clara protégé Khalid Dahab had admitted that he and Mohamed had recruited at least ten sleepers in Santa Clara alone.[19] Now, after Ali's deal with the Feds, the question was just how many other al Qaeda agents there were in this country and when he would give them up.

So far, the evidence suggests that he hasn't.

As this investigation has revealed for the first time, almost six years after entering that guilty plea, Ali Mohamed has yet to be sentenced. His own wife, Linda Sanchez, told me that directly, and it was confirmed by Jack Cloonan. Yet we can say for certain that even today, as he remains in witness protection somewhere in the New York area, Ali Mohamed has never fully betrayed Ayman al-Zawahiri, Osama bin Laden, or the jihad that he was willing to kill for.

How do we know this? Because if Ali had ever given the Feds the name or location of a *single* one of those sleepers, they would have been arrested or indicted by now.

"You might argue that in the beginning, the Bureau might have kept some of the names secret, if they *had* them, for intelligence purposes—to get a sense of the larger network that might be operational here," says a former agent in the NYO. "But they certainly wouldn't have held off on arrests after 9/11, and certainly not now, six years after Ali's confession."

"The fact that he knows where tens, maybe hundreds of al Qaeda agents or sympathizers are, burrowed into America like moles, just goes to show you that we still don't have the full truth from Ali Mohamed,"[20] says the agent. "Keep in mind that he was finally arrested *three* years before 9/11. If he'd given up a single one of those sleepers, it might have helped interdict the plot."

But in the high-stakes poker game between captured terrorist and an FBI anxious for him to sell out in return for leniency, Ali Mohamed got much more than he was ever willing to give.

"His hold card, and the reason he's still not been sentenced," says a defense lawyer close to the embassy-bombing case, "is the sheer embarrassment that the Justice Department would face if somebody like me ever got a crack at Mohamed on the stand."[21]

As the embassy-bombing trial approached, would Ali Mohamed, the Feds' star witness, take the stand? Some senior reporters who covered the Justice Department suggested he would. But, as always, Ali Mohamed possessed an infinite capacity for surprise.

34

THE SECRET
WITNESS

As the year 2000 ended, Patrick Fitzgerald prepped for *United States v. bin Laden,* the trial that would cap off what the Associated Press called "the largest terrorist investigation ever undertaken by the U.S. government."[1] At the time, reporters for the *Wall Street Journal* speculated that Ali Mohamed, the al Qaeda spy who actually executed the surveillance for the bombing, would prove to be Fitzgerald's secret weapon.

"One factor in Mr. Fitzgerald's favor is that bin Laden associate Ali Mohamed is expected to testify for the government after pleading guilty in October to conspiracy charges," the *Journal* reported. "At that time, Mr. Mohamed said in court that Mr. bin Laden asked him to conduct surveillance of targets in Nairobi and pointed to a spot on a photograph of the U.S. embassy where a truck bomb could do the most damage."[2]

Even Ben Weiser at the *New York Times,* an authority on Mohamed, raised the possibility that he would testify: "When four men go on trial in 12 days in New York on charges they conspired with Osama bin Laden in the deadly bombings of two United States Embassies in East Africa in 1998, one of the government's central witnesses could be a former American Army sergeant who pleaded guilty in October to assisting in the terrorist conspiracy. The former sergeant, Ali A. Mohamed, served in one of the Army's most sensitive units at Fort Bragg, N.C., in the 1980s. In 1993, five years before the embassy attacks, he began talking to the FBI about Mr. bin Laden and his role."[3]

The *Journal* story was full of high praise for Fitzgerald, who by then had earned the reputation of being the most knowledgeable SDNY terrorism litigator.

"According to Dietrich Snell, a former assistant U.S. attorney who worked with Mr. Fitzgerald, the prosecutor is a master of jury communication: 'He spends an enormous amount of time mastering the details so he can distill it down for the jury, get them to understand it in ways that resonate with their own lives.' "[4]

But by February 5, 2001, as the trial commenced, there was a key name missing from Fitzgerald's witness list. Though he would soon call Jamal al-Fadl as the lead witness—proving once and for all the direct connection between bin Laden and the original WTC bombing cell—Fitzgerald did *not* call Ali Mohamed.[5] The former Egyptian Army officer turned spy was the one man in custody who could *personally* identify bin Laden as the one who had fingered the position of the suicide truck bomb. Under an exception to the hearsay rule for coconspirator testimony, Ali's eyewitness testimony would have been both admissible and highly probative. Yet in the trial against Osama bin Laden, the man who was arguably the most important single adversary to the United State since Adolf Hitler, Fitzgerald risked losing the case rather than using Mohamed, his best witness.

His motivation in hiding Ali from public view may have been similar to that of his cocounsel Andrew McCarthy, who had sought to keep Mohamed off the stand in the Day of Terror trial. "Mohamed would have been opened up by defense lawyers and told the whole sad tale of how he'd used the Bureau and the CIA and the DIA for years," says retired special agent Joseph F. O'Brien. "The Bureau couldn't risk that kind of embarrassment."[6]

But U.S. Attorney Mary Jo White disagrees. "Embarrassment or fear of embarrassment was totally irrelevant in our thinking throughout," she says.[7] "Totally irrelevant. I mean, we had dangerous defendants guilty of crimes and terrorist crimes. You can take a lot of embarrassment. Embarrassment didn't enter our minds in any of the decisions we made as to who was to testify or not or who to prosecute or not."

Nevertheless, in Fitzgerald's second al Qaeda trial, he had even more to hide. In 1997, he himself had met with Ali Mohamed in Sacramento. He'd sat there while Mohamed declared that he "loved" bin Laden and didn't need a *fatwa* to attack America. Yet despite the multiple wiretaps monitoring conversations and faxes to the Nairobi cell right up to the day of the bombings on August 7, 1998,[8] and despite the evidence from Squad I-49's search of El-Hage's house a year earlier that Mohamed was involved in the plot, Fitzgerald and the agents of his elite unit had been unable to stop it.

That's not a story that Fitzgerald would have wanted to see exposed by defense lawyers during *United States v. bin Laden.*

Training the Hijackers

Still, their eleventh-hour jailing of Ali Mohamed could have helped the Feds cut their losses. As the final months counted down to the 9/11 attacks, the al Qaeda master spy could have helped the Feds piece the puzzle together. After the attacks, he would tell Jack Cloonan that he had trained al Qaeda operatives on how to hijack planes.[9]

On September 11, 2001, the hijackers who flew AA Flight 77 into the Pentagon were reported to have used box cutters.[10] Three of the muscle hijackers who stormed the cockpit and took that plane were Khalid al-Midhar and the al-Hazmi brothers, Nawaf and Salem. Further, Khallad bin Atash, who had flown with them from Kuala Lumpur to Bangkok on January 8, 2000, took a flight to Hong Kong the next day and carried a box cutter in his carry on bag in order to test security.[11]

Right after the embassy bombing in August 1998, Mohamed al-'Owali confessed to FBI agent Stephen Gaudin that the cell leader of the Nairobi plot had told him that al Qaeda had targets *in America.* "Things are not ready yet," the cell leader told the bomber. "We don't have everything prepared."[12] But clearly relatively low level members of the same embassy bombing conspiracy that Ali Mohamed had helped put in motion and maintain were aware of an operation that was going to take place in the United States.

Terrorism analyst Paul Thompson noted that the 9/11 Commission had cited as "alarming information" intelligence from a source contained in a June 12, 2001, CIA report that someone named "Khaled," whom the Agency presumed to be Khalid Shaikh Mohammed, was "actively recruiting people" to travel outside Afghanistan to the United States to carry out "terrorist related activities for bin Laden."[ii]

In an end note to the Report, the commission buried the astonishing fact that "KSM himself was regularly traveling to the U.S."[iii] The source of the CIA report actually picked a photograph of KSM out of a list of other pictures in July 2001. According to the *9/11 Commission Report,* the source's information on KSM's U.S. visits was "current as of the summer of 1998." At that point, Ali Mohamed was still free. Who in the U.S. would the 9/11 "mastermind" have been visiting?

It was almost inconceivable that Ali Mohamed—bin Laden's chief intel officer, who had played such a key role in so many al Qaeda missions—could *not* have been involved in the planes-as-missiles plot. The "planes operation" had originated with Ramzi Yousef as early as the fall of 1994, and Ali had been free for the next four years. He'd trained the cell that made the first attack on the World Trade Center. And yet, even while Mohamed sat in a federal jail cell, with a death sentence in Egypt hanging over his head, the Feds had been unable to get him to give up the 9/11 plot. He revealed nothing that helped tip them to the coming assaults on the World Trade Center and the Pentagon.

But by May 30, 2001, Fitzgerald and the Southern District Feds had achieved another victory. The four al Qaeda embassy-bombing plotters were found guilty of all 302 counts against them.[13] Convicted of conspiring to kill Americans were Mohamed Rashed Daoud Al-'Owali, twenty-four, of Saudi Arabia, the young driver of the bomb truck who had given up the Yemeni safe house; Khalfan Khamis Mohamed, twenty-seven, of Tanzania; Mohamed Sadeek Odeh, thirty-six, of Jordan; and Wadih El-Hage, the naturalized U.S. citizen who had served as bin Laden's personal secretary and played host to Ali Mohamed in Kenya.

Some of the most dramatic testimony at the four-month trial came from former ambassador Prudence Bushnell, who had tried so many times to alert the State Department to the Nairobi embassy's vulnerability. The day of the blast, she was in a building around the corner from the embassy compound. As she descended a stairwell in the building, she said, she was sure she was going to die. "There was blood everywhere on the banister. I could feel the person behind me bleeding onto me. I thought to myself the building was going to collapse." When she got outside, Bushnell said, she saw a burning vehicle and "the charred remains of what was once a human being."[14]

Failing to Stop the Bombings

Because of the secrecy surrounding terror prosecutions in the SDNY, nobody in the mainstream media had a clue at the time of the convictions that Fitzgerald's Squad I-49 had years of advance warning of the plot, or that Ali Mohamed, the spy whom they'd agreed to plead out, had played such a prominent role in its execution. It wasn't until October 2003, more than two years *after* the verdict, that Robert Windrem of NBC News filed this report: "Newly disclosed documents in the East Africa embassy bombings case show that U.S. intelligence was aware of Osama bin Laden's terrorist cell in Kenya two years before the August 1998 bombings that killed 224 people, including 12 Americans. As early as August 1996, the intelligence community bugged the Nairobi phones of bin Laden's personal secretary, Wadih El-Hage, and others in the Kenyan capital, according to court records."[15]

But back in the spring of 2001, Mary Jo White celebrated the win as the latest in a string of legal victories for the SDNY: "These verdicts are a triumph for world justice and for world unity in combating international terrorism," declared White.

As she offered that latest victory speech, three months before "Black Tuesday," the American public had no idea just how vulnerable they were. Since 1981, the FBI had been responsible for protecting Americans from terrorism on U.S. soil—that is, with *preventing* acts of terror in the homeland. But the Bureau continued to think of itself as being in the crime *solution* business. They came in *after* the metaphorical chalk outline was on the ground and there was blood in the street. Time after time, the

FBI had failed in the job of threat *prevention*. But the U.S. public was largely in the dark about that, and now, in the spring and early summer of 2001, as the signals of a major al Qaeda action put all the U.S. intelligence agencies on a heightened state of alert, the average U.S. citizen had no clue that Osama bin Laden's most vicious plot was about to hit.

"The system was blinking red," as former CIA director George Tenet later put it.[16]

If the CIA knew by June 2001 that Khalid Shaikh Mohammed had been visiting the United States, why wasn't Ali Mohamed questioned about this? Or was he? We don't know.

By July 5, 2001, National Security Advisor Condoleezza Rice reported that, while "nonspecific," the intelligence was "sufficiently robust" that President George W. Bush asked her "to go back and to see what was being done about all of the chatter."[17] But White House terrorism adviser Richard Clarke had a more urgent view. In a meeting that same day with a series of agencies including the FBI, FAA, and INS, he warned that "something really spectacular is going to happen here, and it's going to happen soon."[18]

The next day, chairing a meeting of the NSC's Counterterrorism Security Group (CSG), Clarke ordered his staff to suspend all nonessential travel. The drums were beginning to pound.

The Memo from Phoenix Three Years Late

Four days later, on July 10, Special Agent Ken Williams of the FBI's Squad Five in Phoenix issued the now-famous "Phoenix Memo," warning of "the possibility of a coordinated effort by Osama bin Laden to send students to the United States to attend civil aviation universities and colleges." The memo, titled "Zakaria Mustapha Soubra," suggested that the FBI should "accumulate a listing of civil aviation universities/colleges around the country" and "consider" seeking the authority to search visa records of Islamic students attending the flight schools.

The communiqué, sent to FBI headquarters, was also addressed to investigators in the FBI's New York Office. One of them was Jack Cloo-

nan, the man charged with putting together the pieces of the Ali Mohamed puzzle.

Speaking in the spring of 2006, Cloonan was defensive about the
memo and downplayed its significance.

"In the communication that comes in from Phoenix," says Cloonan,
"they open up a preliminary inquiry on this guy Soubra, who's walking
around Embry-Riddle [Aeronautical] university handing out leaflets to
this meeting for an Islamic Association. So Ken Williams advances this
theory that the Bureau [should] take a look at people from Middle East
countries who are here in the United States taking flight training. There
were so many factual errors in that communication, it was sad. But
[Williams] was [later] being held up as the soothsayer; as [being in a position of] preventing 9/11. It was completely erroneous. What he did was
advance a theory and it stuck."

Cloonan admitted to me that his response sounded "a bit defensive."

"But what Phoenix didn't tell you in the communication," he says,
"was that they had gone and opened up preliminary inquiries on every one
of those kids that attended the meeting that this guy Soubra organized.
They interviewed them and nothing panned out. Phoenix didn't tell the
FBI headquarters in that communication that they had done that. So the
same theory that they had advanced, they debunked."

Cloonan may be right about the specifics of the memo, but by the
summer of 2001, the FBI had had a decade to appreciate the threat from
Islamic radicals seeking flight school training. Ramzi Yousef's partner
Abdul Hakim Murad had gotten his commercial pilot's license after studying at schools in New York, North Carolina, Texas, and California in 1991
and 1992. Ali Mohamed's Florida sleeper, Ihab Ali Nawawi, the young
Egyptian who had been trusted to move bin Laden to Khartoum, had
studied at the Airman Flight School in Norman, Oklahoma in 1993. In
1998, FBI agents had even gone to the school to question instructors there
about him.[19] Essam al Ridi, the Egyptian pilot who trained at the Ed
Boardman Aviation School in Fort Worth, was in the cockpit with
Nawawi when they crash-landed Osama bin Laden's Sabre-40 jet in the
Sudan back in 1994. And this investigation has uncovered evidence that
Ken Williams himself had been alerted as early as the fall of 1996 that

Squad 5, the FBI's counterintelligence unit in Phoenix, should be watching flight schools.

As first reported in *1000 Years for Revenge,* Williams had been warned of suspicious Islamic pilots by his late asset Harry Ellen. A native-born U.S. citizen and convert to Islam who used the name Abu Yousef, Ellen went on to provide extremely reliable intelligence to the FBI on activities in Gaza where he had gained the confidence of Palestinian officials.[20]

In a face-to-face meeting on a country road outside Phoenix* in October 1996,[21] Ellen told Williams that he should be "very concerned about air schools."[22] Later Ellen said that he'd identified an Algerian flight instructor for Williams that he'd seen talking to a New Jersey émigré from the al-Salaam Mosque where the blind Sheikh had preached. Al-Salaam was the mosque located a few doors from Sphinx Trading, where Ali Mohamed's trained killer, El Sayyid Nosair, had a mailbox.

"I said, 'This guy is either a good guy or a bad guy,'" recalled Ellen. "'If he's a good guy, he's somebody you should know, and if he's a bad guy he's somebody you should be watching.'" But in a 2003 interview, Ellen told me that Williams "blew him off." Later he had a falling out with Ellen over a Chinese national whom Williams suspected of being a spy.

That dispute took place out of public view, but in June 2001, Mark Flatten, a reporter for the Phoenix area *East Valley Tribune,* got wind of the breakup and was planning to publish a two-part series in which Ellen's warning to Williams about flight schools would be mentioned.[23]

Ellen, who died of heart complications in 2005, told me that he believed Williams was worried that if their dispute went public, the question of whether the FBI had monitored Arizona flight schools might subject the Bureau to criticism. "Ken had known about Islamic pilots and flight training in Arizona for years," Ellen said in that 2003 interview. "But his big memo warning everybody was never sent until he found out that the articles on me and our problems were going to go."

Could Williams's early attention to the flight school threat have given the Bureau a leg up on the planes-as-missiles operation? One thing is clear: Hani Hanjour, who piloted American Airlines Flight 77 into the Pentagon

*See pictures in Timeline segment 28, page 30.

on September 11, had enrolled at CRM Airline Training Center in Scotts-dale, Arizona, as early as 1996.[24] Al-Midhar and al-Hazmi, the two muscle hijackers rooming with FBI informant Abdussattar Shaykh, had washed out of flight lessons in San Diego by the year 2000, and on or about De-cember 12, 2000, al-Hazmi moved with Hanjour to Mesa, Arizona, just outside Phoenix, where Hani enrolled in the Arizona Aviation School.[25]

If Ken Williams had only followed his own advice in the Phoenix memo, years or even months earlier, he too could have been onto the 9/11 hijackers.

According to one official count, there were thirty-three separate terror warnings in 2001; and after the 9/11 Commission issued its final report, we learned of another fifty-two alerts from the FAA that they had some-how neglected to include.[26] Five of the security warnings mentioned al Qaeda's training for hijackers; and two reports actually dealt with suicide operations unrelated to aviation.

The American public had no idea about the threat intelligence that was bombarding U.S. agencies that summer. Still, in July 2001, after years of gross negligence on the road to 9/11, the FBI would have another extraor-dinary chance to interdict the 9/11 plot. All they had to do was go into their own files and examine a discovery they had made as far back as 1991. Of all the revelations uncovered in my five-year investigation, the Sphinx Trading story is perhaps the most compelling example of the FBI's failure to connect the dots.

35

SECOND TO LAST CHANCE

While investigating the murder of Rabbi Meier Kahane, the Feds had discovered that El Sayyid Nosair, Ali Mohamed's trainee, had kept a mailbox in Jersey City on the premises of Sphinx Trading, that check-cashing business at 2828 Kennedy Boulevard. Sphinx, which each year moved millions of dollars in funds between Islamic residents of northern New Jersey and the Middle East, was incorporated on December 15, 1987. The original incorporators were Mohammed El-Atriss, a forty-six-year-old Egyptian, and Waleed al-Noor.[1] Al-Noor, an unindicted co-conspirator in the Day of Terror trial in 1995, was thus well known to both Andrew McCarthy and Patrick Fitzgerald, the prosecutors.

While El-Atriss later claimed he had nothing to do with Sphinx after the incorporation, he admitted under oath in a New Jersey state hearing after 9/11 that he had sold fake IDs to two of the 9/11 hijackers through his company All Services Plus, including the one to Khalid al-Midhar: It lists a fictitious address on Lexington Avenue in Manhattan:

Testimony at that same hearing suggested that El-Atriss may have been in contact with another senior hijacker in addition to the ones to whom he sold the IDs.[2] Fred Ernst, a detective with the Passiac, New Jersey, sheriff's department who investigated El-Atriss, said under oath: "The FBI . . . provided information that indicates [that] Hani Hanjour had contacted All Services Plus prior to the events of September 11th. It's not indicated what those conversations contained, only that phone records between a prepaid cellular phone owned by Mr. Hanjour, had contacted Mr. El-Atriss on *seven* occasions."[3]

The fake credentials were sent to mailboxes the hijackers maintained on the premises of Sphinx Trading—located four doors down from the blind Sheikh's al-Salaam Mosque at 2824 Kennedy Boulevard. This was also the location of the "Jersey Jihad" office where Ali Mohamed had screened his Fort Bragg training tapes for Nosair and the other World Trade Center bombing cell trainees back in the summer of 1989.

"The fact that this same location was where al-Midhar, in particular, got his bogus credentials, is not only shocking, it makes me angry," says a former agent with the FBI's New York Office. "The JTTF in the NYO had this location back in 1991. In the mid-'90s they listed al-Noor, the coowner, as a coconspirator, unindicted in the plot to blow up the bridges and tunnels. And now we find out that this was the precise location where the most visible of all the hijackers in the U.S. got his ID? Incredible. All the Bureau's New York Office had to do was sit on that place over the years and they would have broken right into the 9/11 plot."[4]

El-Atriss, who maintains dual U.S.-Egyptian citizenship, denied any prior knowledge of the 9/11 plot and served six months in jail in 2002 after the Passaic County Sheriff's Department arrested him.

Although held at the time on a half million dollars bail—the equivalent of $5 million in a traditional 10 percent bond—El-Atriss pleaded guilty to the minor charge of selling fake documents, was sentenced to time served, and was released.[5] The U.S. attorney's office in Newark reported that he had taken a polygraph test that cleared him of any involvement in the 9/11 plot.

But in testimony at that bail hearing, Detective Ernst indicated that the U.S. attorney's office in Newark had been openly hostile to the sheriff's investigation. In fact, on the day Ernst and fellow detectives had obtained search warrants and were planning to raid El-Atriss's home and business, Christopher Christie, the Newark U.S. attorney telephoned Ernst's boss, Passiac County sheriff Jerry Speziale, and threatened that if he held a press conference attendant to the raids, he "would be arrested and the U.S. Attorney would . . . shut down the Sheriff's department."[6]

Was this another attempt by the Feds to cover up an earlier embarrassment—their failure to connect the dots on Sphinx and thus uncover the hijackers? We don't know.

But as the clock ticked away in the late summer of 2001, the FBI would get one last opportunity to prevent the attacks of September 11.

Ali Mohamed and the PDB

On August 6, the FBI got another reminder of Ali Mohamed's importance to al Qaeda and the terror that was to come. The CIA's controversial Presidential Daily Briefing, which the Bush administration tried to keep from the 9/11 Commission, was titled "Bin Laden Determined to Strike in U.S."[7] (See Appendix IX, page 573).

The PDB, which President Bush received while on vacation at his Crawford, Texas, ranch, contained an observation that should have reminded Patrick Fitzgerald that his plea deal with Ali Mohamed may have been premature.

"Al-Qa'ida members—including some who are US citizens—have resided in or traveled to the US for years, and the group apparently maintains a support structure that could aid attacks. Two al-Qa'ida members found guilty in the conspiracy to bomb our Embassies in East

Africa were US citizens, and a senior EIJ member lived in California in the mid-1990's."

The PDB failed to inform the president that the two U.S. citizens cited were Wadih El-Hage and Ali Mohamed; or that Mohamed was that senior EIJ member referred to as having lived in the Golden State.

But given the discovery by the Able Danger unit of al Qaeda's direct links to the New York cell of Sheikh Rahman, the next lines in the PDB should have rung the cherries at Bush's Texas ranch: "A clandestine source said in 1998 that a bin Ladin cell in New York was recruiting Muslim-American youth for attacks." The PDB then cited a 1998 report from an undisclosed intelligence service that "Bin Ladin wanted to hijack a U.S. aircraft to gain the release of 'Blind Shaykh' 'Umar' 'Abd al-Rahman' and other US-held extremists."

Ramzi Yousef had made an *identical* prediction to mobster Greg Scarpa Jr. in 1996 and it was contained in a December 30 302 memo in FBI files.* President Clinton had been warned of a hijack-to-free-the-Sheikh plot in 1998. The importance of Sheikh Rahman to al Qaeda had been underscored time and time again, from the moment El Sayyid Nosair shot Rabbi Kahane and the FBI's NYO learned that he was a member of the Sheikh's Islamic Group; through the Day of Terror plot, inspired by the Sheikh; up through the 1997 Luxor massacre, the 1998 embassy bombings, and the *Cole* bombing of 2000—a "spilling of blood" that had been committed in the Sheikh's name.

Still, nobody in the FBI seemed to recognize the significance of the offer that came in a week before September 11, when the Taliban government in Kabul offered to exchange the eight Christian Aid workers being held hostage for Sheikh Rahman.[8]

All of this might be explained away by a combination of incompetence and "stovepiping," but the sheer number of dots on the FBI's chart associated with Rahman, Yousef, and their Ali Mohamed-trained cell raises the question of whether or not by 2001 certain officials in the Justice Department were seeking "plausible deniability" for what one agent would soon describe as the "criminal negligence" of the FBI. That charge came in an

---

*The most significant FBI 302s from the 1996 Yousef-Scarpa Jr. intelligence initiative can be seen at www.peterlance.com.

internal Bureau memo following the arrest, in mid-August, of Zacarias Moussaoui.[9]

The Last Chance

Moussaoui was a French Islamic national of Moroccan ancestry who had recently been to Saudi Arabia, Pakistan, and Malaysia. In fact, on his trip to Kuala Lumpur he stayed at Yazid Sufaat's condo—the very place where the 9/11 summit had been held in January 2000.

After arriving in Oklahoma, Moussaoui deposited $32,000 in the Arvest Bank and enrolled at the Airman Flight School.[10] This was the same school where Ali Mohamed's Florida sleeper Ihab Ali had trained—the same school the FBI had visited in 1998, and, as it turned out, the school where two of the 9/11 hijackers had visited prior to the attacks. Moussaoui had trained on the Cessna 150 at Airman, but failed his written test and decided not to return for the practical exam. The angry Frenchman later blamed his washout on the "inexperience" of the instructors at Airman, but clearly he had a more ambitious agenda and he was anxious to accelerate his learning curve. So Moussaoui contacted the Pan Am International Flight Academy in Eagan, Minnesota, and later paid $8,300 (in $100 bills)[11] for training on a slightly bigger aircraft than the Cessna. This time he wanted to learn how to fly the Boeing 747-400, the biggest jumbo jet in the sky.

Moussaoui, who went by the name "Shaqil," arrived in Eagan in mid-August 2001. He checked in to the Residence Inn and started simulator training, but quickly raised concerns among his instructors after asking how much damage a fully loaded 747 could do.[12] An alert manager at Pan Am called the Bureau's Minneapolis field office, and luckily the call was vectored to Harry Samit, a decorated former navy Top Gun pilot. Though Samit had been out of Quantico for only two years, he had flown everything from single-engine Pipers to F-14s, and he quickly sensed that something was wrong with Moussaoui. Thirty minutes after hanging up with Pan Am, he opened an intelligence investigation.

On August 15, accompanied by an INS agent, Samit interviewed the cocky Moussaoui, who told him that he was taking the expensive advanced jumbo jet training for enjoyment and "his own personal ego." A consensual search of Moussaoui's immediate belongings revealed the $32,000 bank statement and his passport, which proved that the French national was months past his visa limit and thus an illegal alien subject to arrest.

Suddenly, the intelligence case looked like it could have criminal implications—and Jamie Gorelick's now-famous "wall memo" kicked in. Fortunately, there was an easy way for Samit to get over the wall: he could simply make an application for a search warrant under the Foreign Intelligence Surveillance Act (FISA).[13] Given the threat intelligence raining down on Washington that summer, approval for a FISA application should have been a foregone conclusion.

But Samit's application for the FISA warrant, sent to David Frasca, the agent in charge of the FBI's Radical Fundamentalist Unit (RFU) in Washington, was rejected.

Michael Rolince, then chief of the Bureau's international terrorism section, later testified that Agent Samit's "suppositions, hunches, and suspicions were one thing, and what we knew" was a different matter. But under oath, during Moussaoui's penalty phase, Rolince admitted that he never actually read Samit's warrant request.[14] A thirty-one-year Bureau veteran, Rolince was the same FBI official who'd earlier told two astonished NSC staffers that the FBI had Ayman al-Zawahiri's 1995 trip into the United States "covered."

Meanwhile, Michael Maltbie, a supervisor in the RFU, told Samit that FISA warrant applications were troublesome for the Bureau and that seeking one "was just the kind of thing that would get FBI agents in trouble."[15] When Maltbie complained that Samit was getting "spun up" over Moussaoui, the former Navy Lieutenant Commander and intelligence officer responded by firing off a chillingly prescient twenty-five-page memo insisting that he was *trying* to get Headquarters "spun up," to make sure that Moussaoui "did not take control of a plane and fly it into the World Trade Center."[16]

At the time of Samit's urgent warrant request, Rolince admitted to having a twenty-second hallway conversation with David Frasca, who briefed him on an alternate plan in which Moussaoui would be extradited home where French authorities would search him. In other words, Headquarters FBI supervisors were so loath to approve a FISA search warrant that a Rube Goldberg-like scenario was concocted in which Moussaoui would have to first *leave* the United States before his belongings could be effectively examined.

That new plan was to go into effect on September 11.

The failure of FBI Headquarters to endorse Samit's FISA warrant was another stunning lapse, given Moussaoui's April 2005 admission that one of his key motivations in seeking to fly a jumbo jet was that he wanted to crash one into the White House in order to free Sheikh Rahman from a U.S. prison.[17]

Frasca, another official to whom the Phoenix memo was addressed, should have been aware of the Sheikh's significance. In 1993, he'd been one of the agents who'd found the name of Mohammed Jamal Khalifa, bin Laden's brother-in-law, in a briefcase belonging to Rahman.

Special Agent Samit, a lowly "brick agent" in Minneapolis, wasn't expected to know all of that, but his superiors at FBI Headquarters in Washington should have. And, as it turned out, the former navy pilot's suspicions about Moussaoui were dead on.

Under questioning in 2006 at the Moussaoui penalty phase, Samit confirmed that in his report he attributed the FBI's turndown of the FISA request to "obstructionism, criminal negligence, and careerism."

Meanwhile, as the clock ticked down toward September 11, Moussaoui's case was generating attention at the highest levels. CIA director George Tenet later admitted that he had been alerted to Moussaoui's unorthodox flight training requests, and that he knew of the Frenchman's al Qaeda connections. But at the now famous September 4, 2001, "principals meeting" of White House intelligence officials, a week before 9/11, Tenet never even mentioned Moussaoui's name.

And what of those administration officials, like National Security Director Rice, who claimed that there was no "actionable intelligence" of a planes-as-missiles plot?

If senior Bureau agents had simply gone back and looked at the evidence from Col. Mendoza of the PNP in 1995, or reexamined the contents of Yousef's laptop, they would have encountered the very blueprint for the "planes operation."

Despite Ken Williams' Phoenix alert in July 2001; the Sphinx Trading link to al-Midhar weeks later; Moussaoui's arrest in August; their own informant Abdussattar Shaykh, who was renting rooms to two of the hijackers in San Diego; and Ali Mohamed, who had lived in bin Laden's house and who was now in witness protection, the FBI seemed utterly powerless to process the intelligence and interdict the attacks.

The Morning Of

By the morning of September 11, FDNY fire marshal Ronnie Bucca had long since given up trying to alert the FBI to the dangers of al Qaeda. After his brief nine-month assignment as a terrorism adviser to the FDNY had run its course, he returned to the Bureau of Fire Investigation full-time. He had recently told his wife Eve and two children, Ronnie and Jessica, that he was thinking of returning to a rescue company, where saving lives was a daily routine.

That morning he'd arrived to work early at Manhattan Base, the fire marshal's headquarters, located above Ladder 20, a firehouse on Lafayette Street in Soho. Then, at 8:46 A.M. when Mohammed Atta crashed American Airlines Flight 11 into the North Tower of the World Trade Center, Ronnie heard a noise that another marshal later described as "the sound of a dumpster hitting a pot hole."[18] He ran to the window and asked firefighters in the street down below what it was. One of them yelled up, "The Trade Center's on fire."

Moments later, Bucca and his boss, Supervising Fire Marshal Jimmy Devery, were roaring south in Ronnie's Chevy, "lights and sirens" toward the Twin Towers.

"Christ, you called it," said Devery, but Ronnie didn't respond. He just stayed focused and pushed the pedal to the floor.

Apart from warning his firefighter "brothers" throughout the city for years that the Trade Center was "vulnerable," Ronnie had also made regular visits to "Ten and Ten" (Engine #10 and Ladder #10), the firehouse on Liberty Street at the southern perimeter of the WTC complex. On an almost monthly basis he talked to security people at the Towers, asking if there were any new means of entrance or egress that might make the Towers vulnerable. Mindful of the blueprints that Egyptian accountant Ahmed Amin Refai had taken from the FDNY before the first bombing in 1993, Bucca figured that the next attack would come from below.

But just after he and Devery screeched up to the firehouse on Liberty Street, and they pulled on their turnout coats and Cairns helmets, they heard an enormous explosion above them. UA Flight 175, piloted by Marwan al-Shehhi, had just sliced through the South Tower.[19]

Ronnie Bucca wasn't a member of a fire suppression unit. He had no responsibility to enter the complex. But Bucca knew the Towers better than he knew the FDNY headquarters at Metrotech in Brooklyn. So he and Devery strapped on their Scott's airpacks and headed up a side stairwell. A five-mile-a-day runner, Bucca soon outdistanced Devery, who was a heavy smoker. By the fiftieth floor, the supervisor was ready to collapse, but just then a woman in her mid-forties came down the stairs, badly burned. Her name was Ling Young. "She practically fell into my arms," Devery told me later. "So I yelled up to Ronnie, 'I'm gonna take her out.'"

Bucca yelled back that he was going to try and make it to the "fire floor" on seventy-eight, where the 767 had hit. "I hear people screaming," he said, and that was the last that Jimmy Devery saw of him.

Barely able to get Ms. Young out to safety, as bodies dropped into the Plaza around them, Devery looked back up toward the smoke billowing from the South Tower. Radio broadcasts later recovered from that day showed that Ronnie Bucca had made it up to the seventy-eighth floor. There he linked with a battalion chief named Oreo Palmer.

As it turned out, the two men had climbed higher than any other firefighters in either tower. Together, Bucca and Palmer raced against time to help those trapped on the seventy-eighth floor lobby, but the flames were so intense that the tower's structural steel began to melt. Fifty-five minutes after UA 175 had pierced the building, the 110-story tower began to collapse.

Days later, the depth of Bucca's heroism was underscored when his remains were discovered. He had taken off his fire retardant Nomex turnout coat and used it to shield some of the office workers who had huddled amid the flames.

In perhaps the cruelest of all the 9/11 ironies, Ronnie Bucca, the fire marshal who had tried to warn the FBI's JTTF about al Qaeda's threat to the Trade Center, had now himself gone down in Yousef's second attack, executed by Khalid Shaikh Mohammed.

Patrick Fitzgerald had arrived in Chicago that day. Promoted to U.S. attorney for the Northern District of Illinois after his successes in New York's Southern District, he was being shown around town by an SDNY alumnus when he got the news[20] that America was under attack.

One can only imagine how Fitzgerald, the Justice Department's bin Laden expert must have felt. He knew that back east, in some federal detention facility, sat a man who could have warned him that this latest attack in Osama bin Laden's thousand-year war had been coming.

What would Fitzgerald, the man *Vanity Fair* later anointed "the best prosecutor in the United States," say now to Ali Mohamed?

36

FINALLY, MOHAMED SPEAKS

J ack Cloonan had been in Yemen on 9/11, but a week later, as soon as he could get a flight back, he flew to New York. If there was one person who might know how bin Laden had pulled off the attacks, it was Ali Mohamed. He had been held in the witness-protection section of a prison in Florida, and the Feds had him brought back to the MCC. Cloonan didn't want to waste any time. He got to the prison around 11:00 at night. Although today the former special agent insists that Ali wasn't "privy to all the details," he admits that what Mohamed told him was "eerie."[1]

"I walked in and I had him pulled out," Cloonan says. "I said, 'How'd they do it?' and he wrote the whole thing out—the attack, as if he knew every detail of it. He [had] conducted training for al Qaeda on how to hijack a plane. He ran practical exercises in Pakistan and he said, 'This is how you get a box cutter on board. You take the knife, you remove the blade and you wrap it in [redacted] and put it in your carry-on luggage.' They'd read the FAA regulations. They knew four inches wouldn't go through. 'This is how you position yourself,' he said. 'I taught people how to sit in first class. You sit here and some sit here.' He wrote the whole thing out."

"We were amazed at how quickly the FBI produced the names and pictures of all 19 hijackers," says Lt. Col. Anthony Shaffer. "But then again, we were surprised at how quickly they'd made the arrests after the *first* World Trade Center bombing. Only later did we find out that the FBI had been watching some of these people for months prior to both incidents."

Those 1993 arrests and the instant appearance of those 9/11 pictures—was that great police work, or was the Bureau playing catch-up again?

With a $40 billion annual intelligence budget, how did our defense and intel agencies get caught so off guard—or had they? The rescue workers had barely begun to shift through the rubble at Ground Zero when counterterrorism officials began reciting a mantra later made famous by Condoleezza Rice: "I don't think that anybody could have predicted that these . . . people would take an airplane and slam it into the World Trade Center . . . that they would try to use an airplane as a missile."[2]

One of them was Michael Sheehan, the former counterterrorism coordinator at the State Department, who professed surprise as the planes-as-missiles plot.

"The extent of the attack has clearly shocked me," he said in an interview for *Frontline*. "We didn't expect an organization to have such ties within the continental United States, to have such cells operating. We knew that there were sleeper cells in the U.S. But this attack, and the audacity of it, and the use of hijacked aircraft in this manner, clearly was something we did not expect."[3]

Sheehan went on to become the NYPD's deputy commissioner for counterterrorism. He was the same ex-Green Beret Lt. Colonel who had discounted the significance of Ali Mohamed's infiltration of Fort Bragg as late as January 2006.

Like many in the intelligence community, after 9/11 Sheehan clung to the old saw that the only prior warning government officials could have had was the small-plane-into-the-CIA-building scenario first described by Abdul Hakim Murad to Col. Rodolfo Mendoza.

"One of my nightmares as a coordinator for counterterrorism was the use of small aircraft, perhaps packed with explosives, perhaps a Cessna," said Sheehan. "But the use of a hijacked aircraft full of jet fuel was not one that I personally had contemplated and was, indeed, shocking."[4]

As late as May 2002, eight months after 9/11, that same story was repeated by Larry C. Johnson,[5] the former State Department counterterrorism official (under Bush 41 and Clinton) infamous for his July 2001 *New York Times* quote minimizing the importance of Osama bin Laden and al Qaeda: "To listen to some of the news reports a year or two ago, you would think bin Laden was running a top Fortune 500 multinational company," said Johnson, "people everywhere, links everywhere."[6] He then compounded that mistaken assessment five weeks later with a *Times* op-ed piece entitled "The Declining Terrorist Threat," describing al Qaeda as a "a loose amalgam of people with a shared ideology, but a very limited direction."[7] Johnson's piece ran on July 10, 2001, the day the Phoenix Memo arrived.

But Johnson and Sheehan, both noted talking heads who appear regularly on cable news networks from Fox News to MSNBC, told only part of the story. The transcript of Col. Mendoza's January 20, 1995, interrogation session with Murad, which showed up as part of the evidence in the 1996 Bojinka trial of Yousef, Murad, and Shah, created a misconception within the U.S. intelligence community that continued for years.[8] Not only did the Congressional Joint Inquiry repeat the small-plane-into-the-CIA story, concluding that "the plans to crash a plane into CIA headquarters and to assassinate the Pope were only at the 'discussion' stage,"[9] but the 9/11 Commission staff also gave it credence: "Two of the [Bojinka] perpetrators had also discussed the possibility of flying a small plane into the headquarters of the CIA."[10]

As noted in *1000 Years for Revenge,* the almost casual uncertainty of Col. Mendoza's briefing memo left the public impression that Murad had said little that would be a precursor to the September 11 attacks. After 9/11, a former intelligence official was quoted in the *Washington Post* as insisting that it was a far cry from "stealing a Cessna to commandeering a 767."[11]

But as Col. Mendoza revealed in our March 19, 2002, interview, by the end of his sixty-seven-day interrogation Murad had ultimately given up the full-blown hijack-airliners-suicide plot.

"He discussed with me," said Mendoza, "even without me mentioning [it], that there is really formal training [going on] of suicide bombers. He said that there were other Middle Eastern pilots training and he discussed to me the names and flight training schools they went to. This is in February of 1995." And in our interview Col. Mendoza insisted that Murad's plan—conceived by Ramzi Yousef—was "to hijack airliners," not merely use a small plane.

Promotions for Those Who Didn't See It Coming

The advancement of counterterrorism officials who had failed to detect the 9/11 plot was typical of the official reaction in the weeks following the attack. James Kallstrom, the former ADIC of the FBI's New York Office, who had acquiesced in the closure of the DeVecchio OPR and flipped sides in the TWA 800 investigation, was appointed head of New York State's newly created Office of Public Security on October 10, 2001. "Jim Kallstrom is a leader who is widely respected throughout the law enforcement community for his extraordinary expertise, ability, and judgment," said Governor George Pataki in making the announcement. "He is the ideal person to help us do our part here in New York State to face down the challenges that terrorism presents."[12]

"It was the intelligence guys who failed to stop 9/11 that moved up the food chain, after the attacks," said a former agent in the FBI's New York Office who had worked organized crime. "It was the same problem the United States faced in Germany after World War II. The guys who knew how to make the trains run on time were the ex-Nazis we'd just beaten. But we needed them to restart the European economy. After 9/11, who are the ones with the credentials and the right security clearances to find out what happened? The same guys who couldn't see it coming."[13]

Michael Maltbie, who fought FBI agent Harry Samit's request for a search warrant on Zacarias Moussaoui, was advanced to field supervisor.[14] Marion "Spike" Bowman, who had been head of the FBI's National Security Law Unit and the top Headquarters legal official to nix the Moussaoui search warrant, was later awarded a Presidential Citation and a cash bonus equal to 25 percent of his salary by FBI director Robert Mueller.

Seven months after 9/11, Mueller insisted that "the hijackers left no paper trail. In our investigation, we have not uncovered a single piece of paper—either here in the U.S. or in the treasure trove of information that has turned up in Afghanistan and elsewhere—that mentioned any aspect of the September 11th plot."[15]

This, of course, turned out to be patently untrue. The contents of Yousef's own laptop contained the very blueprint of the 9/11 plot, and the FBI LEGAT in Manila had received that intelligence in the winter of 1995. The "treasure trove" of FBI 302s from Scarpa Jr.'s sting of Ramzi Yousef revealed a plot to hijack planes to free Sheikh Rahman in 1996, the identical warning that showed up in the PDB of August 6, 2001, weeks before 9/11. But Mueller continued to circle the wagons.

He went on to reward Pasquale "Pat" D'Amuro, the FBI counterterrorism chief in the New York Office in the months before 9/11, by putting him in charge of terrorism for the entire Bureau.

Later, John Solomon, deputy chief of the Associated Press Washington bureau, reported that a Justice Department investigation collected testimony that, after the collapse of the Twin Towers, D'Amuro "asked a supervisory agent to 'obtain a half dozen items from the WTC debris so the items could be given to dignitaries.'"[16]

According to Solomon's piece, "Six items—none needed as evidence— were gathered and sent to D'Amuro," who reportedly told investigators that "he asked for a piece of the building as a memento," but denied asking for items for dignitaries. After his retirement from the Bureau in 2005, D'Amuro was hired by former mayor Rudolph Giuliani's company to head its "Security and Safety" division.[17] The twenty-six-year Bureau veteran comments regularly on terrorism for CNN.

"They have basically promoted the exact same people who have presided over the . . . failure," says a former Justice Department official, "and those individuals took the same thinking with them."[18]

The Widows Who Demanded the Truth

Within months of the 9/11 attack, Congress announced that a joint panel combining the House and Senate Intelligence Committees would investigate the biggest mass murder in U.S. history. Known as the "Joint Inquiry," the committees spent ten months covering thirty years of intelligence failures. They left out whole sections of the government—including the executive branch—and issued an 858-page report in July 2003 that was heavily redacted. An entire twenty-eight-page section on the Saudis and their possible participation in the attacks was left blank.[19]

One congressional investigator called the report "a scathing indictment of the FBI . . . an agency that doesn't have a clue about terrorism."[20] The report, which the Bush White House had resisted releasing for months, was so incomplete that the cochairman of the joint committee, then Congressman Porter Goss (R-FL), admitted that "I don't know exactly how the plot was hatched. I don't know the where, the when, and the why and the who and that's after two years of trying."[21]

After making that admission, Goss was appointed CIA director by President Bush in September 2004. He succeeded CIA director Tenet, who got the Presidential Medal of Freedom as a reward for his performance in the years leading up to 9/11.

The limited investigation by the Joint Inquiry was one of the reasons that a number of victims' family members started pushing for a more complete and open investigation.

"We simply wanted to know why our husbands were killed," says Kristen Breitweiser, a lawyer whose husband died on 9/11. "Why they went to work one day and didn't come back."[22]

Breitweiser became part of a core group of four New Jersey widows who were the primary advocates for a new independent commission. Dubbed the "Jersey Girls," Breitweiser, Mindy Kleinberg, Lorie van Auken, and Patty Casazza had never met before 9/11. But along with Monica Gabrielle and Sally Regenhard, whose son Christian was one of the 343 FDNY victims of the attacks, they began an assault on Washington with other family members that resulted in H.R. 4628, the Intelligence Authorization Act for Fiscal Year 2003. That bill, signed reluctantly into law by President Bush on November 27, 2002, authorized what was formally called the National Commission on Terrorist Attacks upon the United States, It soon became known as the 9/11 Commission.

"But almost from the beginning, it was clear," says Sally Regenhard, "that this administration was going to fight this panel tooth and nail."[23]

After an embarrassing false start in which President Bush chose Henry Kissinger, Richard Nixon's former secretary of state, as chairman—only to have him quickly withdraw under pressure from the widows—the White House balked at the commission's budget and fought over whether it would have full access to all classified documents from the executive branch in the years leading up to the attacks.[24]

Initially funded with only $3 million, compared to $50 million that had been earmarked for the Columbia Space Shuttle crash investigation in which seven people died, the commission was stymied further when the Bush administration stalled on approving the $11 million necessary to underwrite the investigation through its original slated completion date of May 27, 2004. Later, the *Wall Street Journal* reported that the commission staff was only getting a small fraction of the documents requested from the White House.[25]

There was an additional furor over the appointment of Philip Zelikow as executive director. A former protégé of then-national security advisor Condoleezza Rice, Zelikow had worked on the Bush 43 transition. "Zelikow was the fox guarding the chicken coop," says Monica Gabrielle, "but he was only part of the problem. At least half of the commission's staff were from the very same agencies they were supposed to investigate: CIA, FBI, the White House, the FAA, or . . . from the congressional committees that had failed to do the proper oversight job in the years that preceded the attacks."[26]

Both the list of ten commissioners and the support staff was skewed heavily in favor of the Justice Department on both sides of the aisle. Two of the commissioners, former Illinois Republican governor James Thompson and Watergate investigator Richard Ben-Veniste, had been federal prosecutors. Jamie Gorelick was the former Clinton deputy attorney general who had sent Mohammed Jamal Khalifa packing and penned the infamous "wall memo." Gorelick and Zelikow were the *only* two commission officials who were allowed full access to all of the secret documents.

Another key staff appointment was Dietrich "Dieter" Snell, the former AUSA in the SDNY who had coprosecuted Ramzi Yousef in the Bojinka case and was present at a March 7, 1996, meeting with Greg Scarpa Jr. detailing intelligence from Yousef.

"There's little doubt that Gorelick and Snell should have been *witnesses* before the commission," says Congressman Curt Weldon, who was vice chairman of the House Armed Services and Homeland Security committees in the last congressional session. "Snell, in particular, was appointed a senior counsel in charge of determining the origin of the plot, the most important single question the commission had to answer, and yet he had a built-in conflict of interest that caused him to skew the truth on when the plot was really hatched."[27]

"How do they do an objective review of intelligence failures, when the investigative staff and the commissioners themselves are so close to the agencies or interests they're supposed to audit?" asked Monica Gabrielle.

The chairman and cochairman of the commission, the former New Jersey Republican governor Tom Kean and retired congressman Lee Hamilton, an Indiana Democrat, were generally accepted by the media as being fair and balanced.

Kean read my first book, *1000 Years for Revenge,* over Christmas 2003, and after reviewing my findings about Col. Mendoza's intelligence on the 1994 origin of the plot in the Philippines, he sent me a letter recommending that I testify before the commission.[28]

But in the fall of 2003, I had developed a source on the commission staff, a former law enforcement officer who met with me regularly in New York City, and he gave me an early warning that the commission had already begun to follow a predetermined "script" of events. Democrats and Republicans, he suggested, had gotten together and agreed up front to follow a limited investigation of the events, which would focus on the few years from 1998 forward.

Frustrated at the glacial pace of the investigation, this source told me that by late 2003, only one of the eight teams set up to probe various aspects of the attack had issued subpoenas. "The other teams are completely controlled by Zelikow down in D.C.," he said.[29] The source insisted that evidence was being "cherry-picked" in order to fit the limited story the commission staff was prepared to tell. It was a story that left no room for Ramzi Yousef or the cell surrounding Sheikh Omar Abdel Rahman in the 9/11 plot.

Then, in October 2003, a meeting took place in Afghanistan that threatened to upset that scenario. Lt. Col Anthony Shaffer was on a clandestine mission to hunt down members of the Taliban when he got word that Philip Zelikow would be at Bagram Air Base, in the Parvan province, and was interested in talking to any military personnel with knowledge of al Qaeda in the years before 9/11. After getting permission from his commanding general, Shaffer gave Zelikow a briefing.[30] It would prove to be the defining moment of his military career, and touch off a scandal that would challenge the very credibility of the 9/11 Commission itself.

37

THE BRIEFING
IN BAGRAM

That October in 2003, Shaffer, then an army major, was aboard an army UH 60 Blackhawk helicopter snaking along the Kabul River toward Asadabad, a small firebase in Northeast Afghanistan eight clicks from the Pakistani Border. Wearing forty pounds of body armor and brandishing an M-4 carbine and an M-11 pistol, Tony was attached to Task Force 180, whose mission was to "deter and defeat the re-emergence of terrorism" after 9/11 by hunting down and eliminating members of the fugitive Taliban.[1] As a clandestine officer with the DIA, he was assigned to work in unison with the other "three-letter" agencies, including the FBI and the CIA, in what was a hoped-for reintegration of the intel services that had become so fragmented and stovepiped in the years before 9/11. While he got along well with the FBI agents who were engaged in the Taliban hunt, Tony and other DIA operatives still regarded the CIA as independents, nicknaming them the "Klingons" after the *Star Trek* aliens, who were reluctant members of "the Federation."

"They remained insular," Tony wrote later in a journal he kept, "with their own separate fleet of warships, their own separate way of doing things, refusing to be 'integrated' into the rest of 'Starfleet.'"

As the DIA liaison to Operation Able Danger, Tony had pushed hard in the year 2000 to share the intel that the LIWA data miners had gathered on the four hijackers and on al Qaeda's ties to Sheikh Rahman. Back then, lawyers from the Special Operations Command had cancelled three scheduled meetings he'd set up with the Bureau. And as a "good soldier," he was anxious to share his experience with the 9/11 Commission so that "what was broken in the system might be fixed."

When he met the commission's executive director, Philip Zelikow, at Bagram Air Base, twenty-seven miles north of Kabul, Tony gave him a full account of the groundbreaking data-mining initiative. "I talked for a little over an hour," recalls Shaffer, "going through bullet by bullet, point by point about what Able Danger was: who was involved, how we executed it, our intent to talk to the FBI about the cells we thought were located in the United States, the destruction of the data in April 2000, and the ultimate shutdown of the project.[2] After I got done with the briefing, there was stunned silence in the room. It was pretty clear that these 9/11 investigators had never heard about Able Danger."

At the time, Shaffer told Zelikow and company that the operation had identified "two of the three cells which conducted 9/11" and they included lead hijacker Mohammed Atta.[3] The Atta reference would prove explosive, since by then, the commission was well on its way toward concluding that no U.S. intelligence service had detected Atta's presence until *after* the 9/11 attacks.[4]

After the briefing, though, Shaffer says that Zelikow told him, "What you've said today is very important and it's important that we continue the dialogue upon your return to the United States." He gave Tony his business card and urged him to contact the commission staff for a follow-up briefing once he got back stateside.

Shaffer says that as soon as his leave ended in early January 2004, he called the commission's Washington office and was told that someone from the staff would contact him.[5]

"But he doesn't get a call back," says Congressman Curt Weldon, who has confirmed Shaffer's account. "So Tony calls a week later.[6] The staffer on the other end says, 'Well, we've looked into this and we've decided that we don't need to talk to you.' So they closed the door, even though they had been excited previously."

"Strange Vibes"

According to Tony, at the point when the staffer told him that they had "looked into" his Able Danger allegations, the 9/11 Commission had not yet received *any* documentation on the data-mining project. "I talked to the person who brought it over to them," says Shaffer. "She's an army major. The documents were in two briefcase-sized satchels. She didn't even bring that material to the commission until February 2004. But they shut down their inquiry into what *I* had told them the month before."

Weldon says he now believes that between Shaffer's Bagram briefing to Zelikow in October and the January rejection, "either DIA told the commission *you don't want to go there,* or DIA, in concert [with] a key official on the commission staff, made the decision that we don't want to go down that route."

"Keep in mind," says Weldon, "that the LIWA data miners had already proven that they could outshine the CIA. Now here was confirmation by an officer with the DIA that Able Danger had been able to do what the FBI later claimed they couldn't do—namely identify Atta more than a year before the 9/11 Commission said he was on the radar screen."[7]

Among the documentary evidence Shaffer had offered to share with the commission was a series of link charts from the summer of 2000, one of which, he contends, contained a picture of Mohammed Atta.[8] "I had them in my office in a DIA facility [in] Clarendon, Virginia, under lock and key," says Shaffer, who had a TOP SECRET security clearance that allowed him to sequester the data.[9]

Shaffer was eventually redeployed back to Afghanistan. Then, in the spring of 2004, he suddenly began hearing rumors that he was in trouble. "I'm getting all these strange vibes from my leadership," says Tony.[10] "Not thinking it had anything to do with the fact that I got blown off by the 9/11 Commission."

"Meanwhile," says Weldon, "he's talking to people in the DIA back home who are telling him that material is being removed from his office. Files are being destroyed."

In the summer of 2000, the reconstituted Able Danger unit prepared a large link chart. Shaffer says that it contained not just the names but the *pictures* of Atta and the two new San Diego residents, al-Midhar and al-Hazmi. Again, since Atta had arrived in the United States from Prague on June 3, 2000,[11] and the two muscle hijackers were living openly, it's not that difficult to imagine how an operation that swept vast amounts of worldwide open-source data might have gotten those hits.

Perhaps equally important was Shaffer's allegation that the hijackers were linked to a New York-based cell connected to Sheikh Omar Abdel Rahman.

"The software put them all together, in Brooklyn," Shaffer told *New York Times* reporter Douglas Jehl, who first broke the story nationally[12] after Weldon spoke with a reporter for the *Norristown Times Herald,* a small newspaper in Pennsylvania.[13] Later, Shaffer confirmed that Atta, an Egyptian, had been linked to the Al Farooq Mosque—the same location where bin Laden had taken over the Alkifah Center with the death of Mustafa Shalabi in 1991.

These findings synced precisely with what I had uncovered in researching *1000 Years for Revenge*—evidence that the two attacks on the WTC were linked through Ramzi Yousef and that the blind Sheikh played a central role in both.

The First "Ground Zero"

But that was not the conclusion that the 9/11 Commission was closing in on in the winter of 2004 as it raced to finish its investigation. And that was no surprise: The SDNY was well-represented on the commission staff, and the senior counsel charged with determining the "origin of the plot," Dietrich Snell, was the same man who had convicted Yousef in the Bojinka case. During that trial, Snell failed to introduce any evidence of the planes-as-missiles operation that had been extracted from Yousef's laptop or supplied by Col. Mendoza of the PNP.

After cochairman Kean asked Philip Zelikow to arrange for me to present my findings to the 9/11 Commission, the man Zelikow chose to hear my testimony was Dietrich Snell. So on March 15, 2004, as I headed to the commission's New York Office, I wasn't sure what to expect. Snell knew the answers to a number of the questions that were still dogging me after I'd finished my first book. Among them:

- Why was the evidence that Yousef hatched the 9/11 plot as far back as 1994 ignored by the FBI and the SDNY during the Bojinka trial?

- Why did Snell and his cocounsel Mike Garcia narrow the scope of the trial of Yousef and two other al Qaeda cohorts in 1996—so that the name of the bomb maker's uncle, Khalid Shaikh Mohammed, "the mastermind of 9/11," was barely referenced in more than three months of testimony?

- Why did the FBI and Justice Department keep the hunt for KSM—a top al Qaeda operative with direct access to Osama bin Laden—secret for years? Why had they failed to reach out to the public via want posters and the Rewards program in the same way they had brought KSM's nephew, Ramzi Yousef, to ground?

The Windowless Room

The Ides of March 2004 was a grey day in New York City. After entering the lobby of 26 Federal Plaza, the same building where the FBI's New York Office was located, I was ushered into a windowless conference room on an upper floor by Snell and an FBI agent named Marco Cordero. I had been warned by my commission source that more than 90 percent of the witness intake had been anecdotal and unrecorded. So I had prepared my "testimony" ahead of time.[14]

Snell sat across from me at a conference table. There was no stenographer or recording equipment present. The sandy-haired former AUSA took out a small spiral notebook and began to take notes as I read my statement.

As Congressman Curt Weldon has noted, Snell should have been a *witness* before the commission, instead of one of its principal investigators. So, as the session went on, I stopped periodically to question *him*.

"Why did you limit the Bojinka evidence at the trial?" I asked. "Did you know about Col. Mendoza's revelations? Why did Agent [Frank] Pellegrino testify that he didn't know Yousef's partner Murad was being questioned at Camp Crame in Manila until late March of '95, when he'd been at the base for two months?"

Each time I asked a question, Snell would smile and say, "That's classified," or "I can't discuss that." He was polite and cordial. At the end of my testimony, he said that he would send me a "document" request asking for additional research material. In particular I told him I would send along the transcript of my March 19, 2002, interview with Col. Rodolfo Mendoza, which documented Yousef's creation of the planes-as-missiles plot.

But as it turned out, that was evidence that Snell, as an alumnus of the SDNY, did not want to see. Why? Because it corroborated the findings of the PNP that Ramzi Yousef was the architect of the 9/11 attacks, and in the months ahead Snell and other key commission investigators would remove Yousef from the plot itself.

Given Snell's apparent bias, I decided to send all of the additional backup research (including the Mendoza transcript) directly to commission cochairman Kean. In a cover letter, I asked him to make sure that it was a part of the permanent commission record. But when the commission's final report was published, that evidence was represented in a single footnote, which didn't even mention Col. Mendoza by name—even though he was the investigator who had first uncovered Yousef's suicide-hijack plot:

33. After 9/11, some Philippine government officials claimed that while in Philippine custody in February 1995, KSM's Manila air plot coconspirator Abdul Hakim Murad had confessed having discussed with Yousef the idea of attacking targets, including the World Trade Center, with hijacked commercial airliners flown by U.S.-trained Middle Eastern pilots.

See Peter Lance, *1000 Years for Revenge: International Terrorism and the FBI— The Untold Story* (ReganBooks, 2003), pp. 278–280. In Murad's initial taped confession, he referred to an idea of crashing a plane into CIA headquarters. Lance gave us his copy of an apparent 1995 Philippine National Police document on an interrogation of Murad.

That document reports Murad describing his idea of crashing a plane into CIA headquarters, but in this report Murad claims he was thinking of hijacking a commercial aircraft to do it, saying the idea had come up in a casual conversation with Yousef with no specific plan for its execution.

We have seen no pre-9/11 evidence that Murad referred in interrogations to the training of other pilots, or referred in this casual conversation to targets other than the CIA. According to Lance, the Philippine police officer, who after 9/11 offered the much more elaborate account of Murad's statements reported in Lance's book, claims to have passed this added information to U.S. officials.

But Lance states the Philippine officer declined to identify these officials. Peter Lance interview (Mar. 15, 2004). If such information was provided to a U.S. official, we have seen no indication that it was written down or disseminated within the U.S. government. Incidentally, KSM says he never discussed his idea for the planes operation with Murad, a person KSM regarded as a minor figure. Intelligence report, interrogation of KSM, Apr. 2, 2004.[15]

The footnote mentioned the January 20, 1995, briefing and the small-plane-into-the-CIA scenario that was an early Yousef-Murad concept. But it failed to mention that I had supplied the verbatim of my interview with Mendoza, the "Philippine officer" cited, who had uncovered the full-blown plot involving not a small plane but a series of airliners.

As I left 26 Federal Plaza that day, I had no idea that a group of army investigators in the year 2000 had been on a parallel investigative track. But Snell would soon reject their evidence as well.

Capt. Phillpott Comes Forward

In the late spring of 2004, as Tony Shaffer was beginning to feel the heat, Capt. Scott Phillpott, an Annapolis graduate and twenty-two-year navy veteran who was operations officer for Able Danger, came forward to corroborate what Shaffer had told the commission.

"Capt. Phillpott was a commander of three ships," says Weldon. "He goes to the general who had been in charge of SOCOM, Pete Schoomaker; he's now army chief of staff. And he asks 'General, can I go and volunteer to talk to the 9/11 Commission?' And Schoomaker says yes."

Phillpott's meeting was scheduled for July 12, 2004.

At that point, the 9/11 Commission had already issued the seventeen major Staff Statements that would form the basis of their final report.

Statement No. 16, authored by Dietrich Snell's "team," removed Ramzi Yousef from the planes-as-missiles operation altogether, pushing the origin of the plot forward two years from Manila in 1994 to Afghanistan in 1996, and alleging that KSM alone had come up with the plot.

Like Tony Shaffer's account, Capt. Phillpott's input about the al Qaeda connections to the New York cell of Sheikh Rahman would have defied the spin that the commission had decided to sell. It was a rewrite of history designed to explain how the FBI and Justice Department had failed to detect the 9/11 plot despite multiple warnings.

"So when Scott Phillpott went into that meeting with the commission, who do you suppose they put him with?" asks Congressman Weldon. "Dietrich Snell. Naturally, nothing about what Able Danger found showed up in the commission's report."

In August 2005, when Douglas Jehl and Phil Shenon began reporting the Able Danger story for the *New York Times*, Kean and his cochair, Lee Hamilton, denigrated Phillpott's evidence.

"The commission staff concluded that the officer's account was not sufficiently reliable to warrant revision of the report or further investigation."

Weldon contends that Snell flushed Capt. Phillpott's evidence because the commission was rushing to publish its own contrived version of the 9/11 plot's origin, one that wouldn't accommodate the Yousef-Rahman connection.

"Snell makes [a] famous statement to Scott," says Weldon: " 'Look, we're a week away from publishing. What do you expect me to do with this stuff?' Those were Dieter Snell's own words. I have them from Scott. Snell basically killed the story."

Other 9/11 commissioners, like former navy secretary John Lehman, claimed they were never even briefed on the Able Danger intelligence.

"I think it's a big deal," Lehman told Shenon and Jehl in an August 10, 2005, story for the *Times*. "The issue is whether there was, in fact, surveillance before 9/11 of Atta and, if so, why weren't we told about it? Who made the decision not to brief the Commission's staff or the commissioners?"[16]

Since the commission formally disbanded after its final report in July 2004, Lehman suggested that "Congress, possibly . . . the House and Senate Intelligence Committees" commence an investigation. But Congressman Weldon was growing concerned that, beyond the 9/11 Commission spurning the input of distinguished military officers, efforts were in the works by forces in the Pentagon to target anyone connected with the Able Danger operation willing to come forward and tell the truth.

The first man in the crosshairs appeared to be Tony Shaffer.

Targeting a Whistleblower

"As soon as I got back from Afghanistan in 2004 I intended to go into my office to gather up the Able Danger evidence," says Tony. "That's when I found out that DIA had suspended my security clearance. So I couldn't get access. The next thing they did was come up with the three allegations."

First, the DIA alleged that Shaffer, who had been secretly awarded a Bronze Star in Afghanistan for his heroic service against the Taliban, had unduly received a Defense Meritorious Service medal for the Able Danger operation, among other work.

"The second allegation," says Shaffer, "was that I misused a government phone to the tune of sixty-seven dollars and some odd cents. This was incurred over eighteen months. I would forward my government calls to my personal phone because I have unlimited minutes. Because of that, I incurred a twenty-five-cent charge per call. But I was commander of the unit, and the use of the phone was within my authority."

The third charge seems even more specious. "They alleged that I filed a false voucher claiming local mileage to go to a staff college course at Fort Dix, New Jersey. But the records showed that I *did* go to the course and I graduated," says Shaffer. "The total cost was $180. Still, they were saying that it shouldn't have been expensed to the government, therefore when I filed a voucher it was fraudulent. But keep in mind that this was for a government course that I had to go to, and it went through two levels of review after I filed the voucher."

"After those three allegations, the DIA suspended my clearance when I came off active duty, the first of June 2004," says Tony. "It was that summer that DIA sent those allegations over to the Army to look at for potential punitive action and at the same time they destroyed all of my remaining Able Danger documents."

The source of the smear campaign against Shaffer seems to have been the Defense Intelligence Agency and not the army, because in October 2004, when he was eligible to go to his next rank, the army promoted him to Lt. Colonel. He was later cleared of all three allegations by the army but the DIA put him on extended leave. In the last few months, Shaffer has gone back into uniform, working on several national security-related projects for the army.

An Ali Mohamed Connection?

"Again," says Congressman Weldon, "when this first broke in August of 2005 I was shocked that people in the Pentagon, in the current Bush administration, would work to cover up a scandal on Bill Clinton's watch—the destruction of that [Able Danger] data. But when I got a look at that March 21, 2000, link chart with Ali Mohamed's picture cheek to jowl with bin Laden, that's when it hit me: Nobody in the DIA wanted to be reminded in the year 2000 that down at Fort Bragg they let an al Qaeda spy into the JFK Special Warfare School. The question is: When is the cover up ever going to end?"

In the fall of 2005, Weldon got half the members of the U.S. House of Representatives to sign a letter asking for a full and open hearing on the Able Danger issue. A hearing before the Armed Services Committee finally commenced on February 15, 2006.

One of the key witnesses that Weldon had hoped to call was Dietrich Snell, now working as deputy attorney general in the office of New York A.G. Eliot Spitzer. But Snell never showed up at the hearing. According to a story filed by Niles Lathem and Fredric U. Dicker in the *New York Post*, Spitzer, then a candidate for governor of New York, personally intervened with the committee staff to get Snell exempted from having to testify.[17]

In the months to come, Dietrich Snell would emerge as a potential witness to another cover-up on the road to 9/11—the suppression of the evidence from Ramzi Yousef to Greg Scarpa Jr. in 1996. An independent investigation by the Brooklyn D.A. would result in murder charges being filed against former FBI supervisory special agent Lin DeVecchio. The ensuing criminal investigation could prove to be the last official opportunity to uncover the full truth behind the FBI's negligence in the years leading up to 9/11.

But on October 16, 2006, a little more than three weeks before the midterm elections, the U.S. Justice Department sent a signal that it wouldn't roll over without a fight.

In a move that seemed timed to destroy his chances of reelection, the FBI raided four homes and two offices associated with Congressman Curt Weldon.[18] The eleventh-hour raids in Florida and Pennsylvania stemmed from charges that first surfaced in a *Los Angeles Times* story in February 2004 alleging that Weldon's daughter Karen, a lobbyist, had received lucrative contracts from Dragomir Kric, the very Serbian from whom Weldon had sought data mining intelligence on back in 1997.[19]

Such public raids so close to election day by the Bush Justice Department into the family affairs of a twenty-year veteran GOP Congressman seemed almost without precedent.

"These charges have been floating around for thirty-two months," said Weldon. "The timing simply cannot be coincidental. The fear inside the Beltway that we will uncover the real truth behind 9/11 via Able Danger and the DeVecchio investigation is palpable."[20]

38

THE PUBLIC WHITEWASH

There might have been a faint hope that one of the 9/11 commissioners would get the truth from Snell when he testified before the first session of the last public hearing on June 16, 2004. But it soon became clear that the commission was going to give the FBI and the Justice Department a pass. Before Snell sat before the cameras, the hearing kicked off with a valentine to the two bin Laden offices of origin. Up on the dais, the ten commissioners sat without question as Special Agent Mary Deborah Doran celebrated the counterterrorism achievements of the FBI's New York Office:

> Let me begin by telling you that I am proud to be an agent of the FBI and I am particularly proud of the work done by the Counterterrorism Division in New York. Prior to 9/11, it was primarily the New York Office, together with the U.S. Attorney's Office in the Southern District of New York, supported by dedicated analysts at FBI headquarters and in conjunction with our colleagues at CTC, that constituted the majority of the United States government's institutional knowledge about al Qaeda and the threat it posed to the United States. The dedication and sacrifices made in this cause by these people is incalculable. I hope today that we who sit before you can do justice to their efforts.[1]

"This is the Bureau attempting to rewrite history," says Frank Gonzalez, a former U.S. postal inspector who worked on Ramzi Yousef's defense team. "Their track record on terrorism was frankly abysmal. Understand that this was . . . the office with the greatest concentration of intelligence on al Qaeda and the most expertise in terms of knowing who was who. If any office of the FBI had a shot at getting a fix on Ramzi, it was New York."

The question is: Where was the FBI's New York JTTF when Ali Mohamed's trainees showed up in those Calverton surveillance photos in 1989? Where were they when one of those trainees shot Meier Kahane, and top secret Fort Bragg memos from Mohamed turned up in the killer's house? Where was Ali Mohamed's FBI handler, John Zent, in the late fall of 1993 as Mohamed took pictures of the Nairobi U.S. embassy? Where was he in 1994, when Ali returned to Khartoum and presented his reconnaissance files to bin Laden? Where did Zent think he'd gone when he left the Bay area for such long stretches? Did Zent or anyone else in the Bureau think to trace his movements via the INS, the CIA, or the State Department? Why didn't they force him to submit to regular polygraphs? Why didn't Mohamed shock the FBI as far back as 1993, when he described the existence of "al Qaeda" and told Zent that this terror network intended to overthrow the Saudi government? When AUSA Andrew McCarthy met with Mohamed in late 1994, after he'd named him as an unindicted coconspirator in the Day of Terror case, what did he *say* to him? Did he warn him away from honoring a subpoena and testifying in New York? Why hadn't he indicted Mohamed as a full-blown coconspirator, since the former Egyptian army commando had trained several of the plotters?

Three years later, in 1997, as the embassy-bombing plot ticked away, why hadn't the FBI arrested Mohamed when he leaked to Special Agent Bell that a "target" was going to be bombed in East Africa, and Special Agent Coleman found Ali's name and number in a search of Wadih El-Hage's house in Nairobi? After all, El-Hage was one of the key bombing cell members. The FBI had been monitoring his calls since 1996, and by 1997 they knew, via Jamal al-Fadl, that Wadih had been bin Laden's personal assistant in Khartoum. The al Qaeda East African bombing plot had been designed by their own informant, Ali Mohamed, and yet the Feds failed to stop it. Why?

Most important, where was Patrick Fitzgerald on all of this? He had met Mohamed face-to-face in 1997, ten months before the embassy bombing. He had heard the spy say that he "loved" bin Laden, and didn't need a *fatwa* to attack America. Fitzgerald himself had described Mohamed as "the most dangerous man" he had ever met and admitted that he "could not let [him] out on the street." Why did he let the key architect of the embassy-bombing plot remain free until 224 people died on August 7, 1998? Finally, how was it that Fitzgerald, Cloonan, and Coleman had failed to extract the 9/11 plot from Ali when they'd put him in custody almost three years to the day before AA 11 hit the North Tower?

The 9/11 commissioners could have asked Fitzgerald those questions; after all, he was seated next to Special Agent Doran that very day at the hearing. But they didn't. Instead they allowed Fitzgerald to deliver *his* version of events, virtually unchallenged.

He began by reading a 2800-word statement on what his office had accomplished in the years leading up to 9/11.

Perhaps out of a Catholic sense of guilt, he devoted 10 percent of that statement to Ali Mohamed:

> One of the more chilling examples of al Qaeda's espionage was Ali Mohamed. Mohamed did not pledge *bayat* to al Qaeda but he trained most of al Qaeda's top leadership—including Bin Laden and Zawahiri—and most of al Qaeda's top trainers. Mohamed taught surveillance, countersurveillance, assassinations, kidnapping, codes, ciphers, and other intelligence techniques. Mohamed surveilled the American embassy in Nairobi in 1993. And he was well trained to do it: Mohamed spent 17 years in the Egyptian military (with commando training and experience in embassy security). He left the Egyptian army to join the United States Army and was stationed at the Special Warfare School at Fort Bragg from 1986 to 1989, when he became a United States citizen.
>
> He gave some training to persons who would later carry out the 1993 World Trade Center bombing, he arranged bin Laden's security in the Sudan in 1994 after an attempt on bin Laden's life, and he visited the al Qaeda cell in Kenya. From 1994 until his arrest in 1998, he lived as an American citizen in California, applying for jobs as an FBI translator and working as a security guard for a defense contractor. When he was interviewed as a potential witness in a terrorism trial in December 1994, telephone records showed that he called to the Kenyan al Qaeda cell to let people know—and we now know he was told by al Qaeda not to come

back. He had otherwise been scheduled at the time to conduct surveillance of American and others targets in West Africa. Mohamed is proof that al Qaeda members often hide in plain sight.[2]

But Fitzgerald, the man reputed to know more about al Qaeda than anyone else in the Justice Department, had left out some crucial details of the Ali Mohamed story. He failed to mention how his elite bin Laden squad had allowed Mohamed to remain loose for years, or how, on the word of FBI agent John Zent, Ali had been released from Canadian custody, only to go on and plan the very embassy bombings for which Fitzgerald himself would later prosecute bin Laden.

In the last appearance by a DOJ official before the last official body to examine the biggest mass murder in U.S. history, the Fed who knew Ali Mohamed better than anyone gave the commissioners just *fragments* of the truth. But even his sanitized version of the story failed to stir them.

"You'd think that hearing about this guy who'd infiltrated Fort Bragg, trained the Trade Center bombing cell and protected bin Laden himself, would have sent the commissioners into a battery of questions," says one former agent in the FBI's New York Office.[3]

"Sadly, the only public commission discussion of Mohamed came from Timothy Roemer," complains former Canadian diplomat Peter Dale Scott.[4] But even then, Roemer, a former Democratic congressman considered one of the most aggressive on the commission, merely "repeated Fitzgerald's statement and went no further."[5]

Rewriting History on the Real 9/11 "Mastermind"

As soon as Fitzgerald and Doran left the witness table, Staff Director Philip Zelikow began reading a statement from Dietrich Snell's team on the origin of the plot. Ignoring Col. Mendoza's evidence, he asserted that "The idea for the September 11th attacks appears to have originated with a veteran jihadist named Khalid Shaikh Mohammed, or KSM."[6]

While conceding that KSM was Yousef's uncle and had "provided a small amount of funding" for the first WTC attack, Zelikow delivered the key points of Staff Statement No. 16, which pushed the plot to "the middle of 1996," when KSM was "back in Afghanistan." The statement noted that KSM had met bin Laden there in the 1980s, but mentioned nothing about his role as a key al Qaeda operative since at least 1994. In fact, a previous staff statement actually concluded that "whether [KSM] was then or later became a member of al Qaeda remains a matter of debate."[7]

Jumping forward a year after Yousef had been arrested in 1995, Zelikow contended that in 1996 Khalid Shaikh merely "sought to renew" his old acquaintance with bin Laden. At an Afghan meeting, Zelikow alleged that KSM had merely "pitched" a "scaled up version of what would become the attacks of September 11." Even though Col. Mendoza and other Philippines officials had reported that by 1994 Yousef and KSM had up to *ten* Islamic pilots training in U.S. flight schools, and even though Abdul Hakim Murad had told Mendoza that he himself would be the lead hijacker "flying the plane in for Allah," Zelikow—relying on the research from Snell's team—contended that "bin Laden listened" to KSM's pitch "but failed to commit at that time."

By removing Ramzi Yousef from the plot, Snell, the former SDNY prosecutor, had managed to relieve the Feds from any culpability for the 9/11 attacks when they failed to apprehend Yousef in the fall of 1992 as he prepped the first WTC attack.

In order to make that conclusion stick, it was necessary for Snell and company to ignore the evidence from the Philippines National Police and jettison the Able Danger intel, which reinforced the direct links between al Qaeda and the Brooklyn cell of blind Sheikh Rahman and Yousef. Now at the hearing, Zelikow turned the microphone over to Snell, who began describing a take on the 9/11 plot that focused on the last few years, beginning in 1998, when lead hijacker Mohammed Atta moved into the Hamburg apartment at 54 Marienstrasse with Ramzi bin al-Shibh, KSM's number two.

Snell went on to describe the next members of the Hamburg "core group," Marwan al-Shehhi and Ziad Jarrah. He then noted that while the Hamburg operatives were just joining the 9/11 plot, Nawaf al-Hazmi and Khalid al-Midhar were already living in the United States, having arrived in Los Angeles on January 15, 2000. But he failed to mention that the two muscle hijackers had lived in San Diego as early as November 1999, or that they had later moved into quarters provided to them by the FBI informant Abdussattar Shaykh.

"It was like telling the story of Paul Revere's ride without the horse," says a former agent in the FBI's New York Office, "a rewriting of history that left out all of the Bureau's mistakes." But then Dietrich Snell went even further.

Relying Entirely on the Word of KSM

Only in the footnotes of the commission's final report was it made clear that Snell's entire authority for moving the origin of the 9/11 plot two years forward was the word of Khalid Shaikh Mohammed himself, who had been tortured after his capture on March 1, 2003. KSM's "testimony," if it can be called that, was elicited via an extreme interrogation technique called "waterboarding,"[8] It's a method used to extract information from a suspect after which he is strapped down, dunked under water and made to believe that he might be drowned.[9]

The reliability of intelligence extracted from prisoners via extreme interrogation techniques has come under great scrutiny since the revelations that torture was used routinely at detention facilities like Abu Ghraib prison in Baghdad and Guantanamo Bay in Cuba in the years after 9/11. In December 2005, Douglas Jehl reported in the *New York Times* that the Bush administration had based a false assertion linking Iraq and al Qaeda on the word of a prisoner who had been tortured in Egypt and fabricated the intel to escape harsh treatment.[10]

Meanwhile, Khalid Shaikh Mohammed's "testimony" was considered so unreliable by the CIA that an April 2003 agency report on KSM refers in its title to Winston Churchill's famous phrase "A Bodyguard of Lies."[11]

Still, there are more than one hundred footnoted references to KSM's tortured "testimony" in the 9/11 Commission's final report.

In a series of interrogations that reportedly began twelve days after his capture and continued through the winter and early spring of 2004, KSM allegedly provided details on not only the embassy bombing plot but al Qaeda's inner workings. The Feds have relied so heavily on it that the same material was entered into evidence during the penalty phase of Zacarias Moussaoui's trial in March 2006.[12] That questionable testimony has served to define the official record on the origin of the 9/11 plot—even though Dietrich Snell himself admitted under oath at the March 2005 German trial of an al Qaeda suspect that he himself had never met KSM or bin al-Shibh, that he had merely submitted questions to their interrogators, and that he had no control over how or even *whether* questions were asked.[13]

Perhaps most revealing was this interview Snell gave to producers for *Inside 9/11*, a four-hour documentary on the attacks that aired on the National Geographic Channel in late August 2005. In the interview Snell discusses just how unreliable KSM and bin al-Shibh were:

> We know that [Ramzi] Bin al-Shibh and KSM had lied in various places—after 9/11 interrogations and in interviews with the journalist Yousi Foudra of al Jazeera. They lied to him. So it is definitely an area that is fraught with peril from a credibility standpoint. You have to be very careful about what you go with, and, in the end, all you can do is say, "Here's the evidence. This is what these guys are said to have said. Here's how it fits with the rest of the evidence and the other things that we know or we think we know." There were definitely efforts made by al Qaeda generally and these terrorists in particular to enhance their stature; to exploit the propaganda opportunities that being interviewed by journalists presented. They were no fools about that, and one has to be careful anytime hearing something that is attributed to someone who is willing to fabricate a story and present a certain image that might not at all be true.

Yet in establishing the historical record on the most significant act of terror in world history and in defining the origin of the plot, Snell was willing to rely *entirely* on the word of KSM, Yousef's uncle, who had every reason to distort the truth.

Taking the word of Khalid Shaikh Mohammed for when the 9/11 plot commenced is akin to taking the word of serial killer David Berkowitz for when he committed the first Son of Sam murder.

"It calls into question the most basic conclusions of the 9/11 Commission itself," says Congressman Curt Weldon. "Why? Because if the origin of the plot can't be pinpointed, you can't properly assess accountability. And it's clear now that people like Dieter Snell went out of their way to remove the FBI and Justice Department from accountability in the years leading up to those attacks."

Like Patrick Fitzgerald, Mary Jo White, Andrew McCarthy, Daniel Coleman, and a number of other Feds tied to the two bin Laden offices of origin, Snell turned down my requests for an interview.

Missing the Full Truth on "The Day Of"

On June 17, 2004, the day after Snell's testimony, the 9/11 Commission conducted its last hearing session, which covered the events of the morning of 9/11 itself. Former secretary of state Henry Kissinger, the man President Bush first chose to chair the commission, had earlier compared the intelligence failures leading up to the attacks with Pearl Harbor.[14] But the multiple missteps by the FAA and NORAD on that fateful morning also represented arguably the greatest homeland defense failure in American history.

One of the most important questions that the commission left unanswered was the impact, if any, of at least three war games that were being conducted on that morning, from the Pacific Northwest to the Northeast Air Defense Sector (NEADS) of the North American Aerospace Defense Command, commonly known as NORAD.

At 6:30 A.M. on September 11, Lt. Col. Dawne Deskins, the regional mission crew chief at NEADS facility in Rome, New York, was monitoring Vigilant Guardian, a semi-annual war game involving fighter jets. NEADS protects the entire northeast corridor of the United States, including the Washington, D.C., New York, and Boston, metropolitan areas. At the time of the exercise, the NORAD chain of command was in a state of readiness, but the timing of the 9/11 attacks in the midst of the exercise raised questions.

There were at least two more mock-war exercises ongoing that day.

The second, involving fighter aircraft, was a joint U.S.-Canadian exercise called Northern Vigilance.[15] The third, and perhaps most ironic, was being conducted by, the National Reconnaissance Office (NRO), which manages the nation's network of spy satellites. That exercise was designed to test the NRO's response in the event that an aircraft crashed into its facility.[16] To add to the confusion, the building was located four miles from Dulles Airport in Washington, the departure point for one of the hijacked flights.

At 8:37 A.M., the FAA's Boston flight control contacted NEADS and informed them that American Flight 11 had been hijacked. Lt. Col. Deskins, who originally thought the report was part of the war game, soon made it clear to her boss, Colonel Robert Marr, the head of NEADS, that the United States was under attack. Marr then contacted Major General Larry Arnold at NORAD's command center in Tyndall Air Force Base in Florida, saying, "Boss, I need to scramble [fighters at] Otis [Air National Guard Base]." Arnold authorized the scramble.[17]

That base was on Cape Cod, 188 miles from New York City. Pilots Maj. Daniel Nash and Lt. Col. Timothy Duffy didn't get into the air until 8:52 A.M., twelve minutes after the base was officially notified.[18] Though those F-15s had airspeeds of up to 1,875 mph[19] they apparently flew to the city at speeds ranging from 500 to 900 mph.[20]

Even then, through no fault of their own, the two pilots were vectored toward military-controlled airspace off Long Island, where they remained in a holding pattern from 9:08 until 9:13 A.M. Only then were they ordered into Lower Manhattan. But by that time Mohammed Atta had long since flown AA 11 into the North Tower.

Had Duffy and Nash been allowed to fly at even 1,200 mph, they could have reached New York in nine minutes and forty seconds and intercepted UA 175 before it hit the South Tower at 9:02. But neither pilot was given a shoot-down order to destroy the hijacked plane[21]—which could only have come from the president.[22]

F-16s Eight Minutes Away

In the days following 9/11, many Americans expressed shock that New York City, the cultural and financial capital of the United States, was forced to rely for its defense on fighters from a base in New England, almost two hundred miles away. New Yorkers, in particular, wondered why they had been left so unprotected.

But as he sought to answer that question, reporter Mike Kelly of New Jersey's *Bergen Record* made an extraordinary discovery. Kelly learned that at the very moment when UA 175 was bearing down on Manhattan, two F-16s from the 177th Fighter Wing, based at Atlantic City International Airport in Pomona, were commencing bombing sortie exercises over the Pine Barrens in southern New Jersey.[23] Though not armed with missiles, the planes were eight minutes from lower Manhattan.

Lt. Luz Aponte, a spokeswoman for the 177th, told Kelly that the Wing Commander was unaware at the time that the two fighters were so badly needed. "Isn't that something?" she mused. Kelly even interviewed 9/11 Commission team leader John Farmer, a former New Jersey attorney general who was responsible for Staff Statement No. 17, which covered the day of the attacks. "We want to know why the jets at Pomona were decommissioned," Farmer said, citing an even larger concern—why other Air Force bases closer to New York than Cape Cod didn't order jets to scramble. "That's a big question," commission cochairman Tom Kean told Kelly for the story, which ran in the *Record* on December 5, 2003.

Now, on June 17, 2004, as the second session of the final public hearings got underway, Executive Director Philip Zelikow narrated a dramatic rendering of the events from the morning of 9/11, intercut with video interviews of key participants in the events. But the only reference to the 177th Fighter Wing in his description of Staff Statement No. 17 was as follows:

> In addition to making notifications within the FAA, Boston Center took the initiative, at 8:34, to contact the military through the FAA's Cape Cod facility. They also tried to obtain assistance from a former alert site in Atlantic City, unaware that it had been phased out. At 8:37 and 52 seconds, Boston Center reached NEADS. This was the first notification received by the military at any level that American 11 had been hijacked.

What Zelikow *didn't* tell the commissioners was that, while the Atlantic City base had been phased out as a NORAD facility, it was now a fully operational Air National Guard base on the same state of readiness as Otis, 188 miles away.

Later, the commissioners heard testimony from General Ralph E. Eberhardt, the head of NORAD, who actually managed to see a silver lining in the stunning defense failure by NORAD, which had left both New York and Washington unprotected:

> The good news is that we had the airplanes on alert that day and we were able to be flexible and put more aircraft on alert. The bad news is that we only had fourteen airplanes on alert, seven alert sites. Atlantic City is the only alert site that we had in the vicinity of the threat, during the height of the Cold War, that we did not have that day. And Atlantic City, given the timelines we have, would not have been able to get there on time.

But not a single person present in the hearing room asked General Eberhart about the 177th Fighter Wing from that very same airbase in New Jersey—an Air National Guard facility with fighters that *could* have reached Manhattan in time to intercept UA 175. John Farmer and Tom Kean had acknowledged to Mike Kelly in the *Bergen Record* that they were going to find out how F-16s from their home state had not been called in to defend the Towers. But as the commission was in its waning hours, neither of them said a word about the 177th. Instead they sat on their hands as the commission concluded its "investigation" without holding a single person in the U.S. intelligence community responsible for failing to stop Ramzi Yousef's monstrous planes-as-missiles operation.

"I'm frankly stunned by this," says Lorie van Auken, one of the "Jersey Girls," whose husband Ken died in the North Tower. "If two fighters were only eight minutes away, the commission should have done an exhaustive study on why they didn't get called. To leave them out of the official hearing record is unbelievable to me."

A Runaway Bestseller

Executive Director Philip Zelikow had brokered a deal to publish the commission's "final report" through W.W. Norton, his own publisher.[24] Released on July 22, 2004, the 604-page book became a runaway bestseller, and later a finalist for the National Book Award.[25] The commission staff had reportedly interviewed more than 1,200 people in ten countries, and reviewed more than two and one half million pages of documents. Yet the final report had some glaring omissions—among them its utter failure to tell the story of Ali Mohamed.

It has taken nearly 500 pages of text and 1,500 end notes to document Mohamed's story in *Triple Cross*. But even this rendering, the most thorough account yet, is far from complete. Yet the final report of the last official body to probe the cause of death for 2,973 people sums up Ali Mohamed's extraordinary fourteen-year espionage run in less than a hundred words:

> As early as December 1993, a team of al Qaeda operatives had begun casing targets in Nairobi for future attacks. It was led by Ali Mohamed, a former Egyptian army officer who had moved to the United States in the mid-1980s, enlisted in the U.S. Army, and became an instructor at Fort Bragg. He had provided guidance and training to extremists at the Farooq mosque in Brooklyn, including some who were subsequently convicted in the February 1993 attack on the World Trade Center. The casing team also included a computer expert whose write-ups were reviewed by al Qaeda leaders.

There isn't *a single word* in the commission report about the Able Danger investigation or the 2.5 terabytes of data it generated, which identified four of the hijackers in the year 2000, and linked them to the Brooklyn cell of Sheikh Omar Abdel Rahman and Ramzi Yousef. The testimony of a Bronze Star winner like Lt. Col. Anthony Shaffer and a decorated navy skipper like Capt. Scott Phillpott was ignored. The man who flushed Phillpott's evidence was the same ex-SDNY prosecutor who seemingly ignored the evidence of the planes-as-missiles plot from the PNP in 1995. He had helped keep the identity of KSM secret for two years, and was a party to the burial of the evidence from Greg Scarpa Jr. in 1996: the 9/11 Commission's senior counsel, Dietrich Snell.

Along with Patrick Fitzgerald and Valerie Caproni, who is now the FBI's top lawyer, Snell sat in a proffer session with Scarpa Jr. on March 7, 1996,[26] and was a witness to the intelligence the former Colombo wiseguy was getting from Ramzi Yousef—the architect of both WTC attacks.* Another key participant in that meeting was former EDNY assistant U.S. attorney Ellen Corcella, who had issued that letter to defense lawyers on

---

*See FBI 302 in Appendix VI on page 554.

May 8, 1995, citing eight possible leaks by SSA Lin DeVecchio to Scarpa's murderous father. Also present was Howard Leadbetter II, one of the three FBI agents who had blown the whistle on the alleged corrupt relationship between Scarpa Sr. and DeVecchio, his "control" agent.

The eleven-month Yousef-Scarpa intelligence initiative in 1996–1997 gave the Feds their best chance to interdict an active al Qaeda cell in New York and capture Khalid Shaikh Mohammed, the secret fugitive who was then perpetrating his nephew's 9/11 plot.

But some Justice Department officials had buried that intel, the evidence now suggests, in order to save those sixty remaining Colombo war cases in the EDNY. Not a word about that ends/means decision appeared in Snell's testimony, or in the 9/11 Commission's final report.

Meanwhile, DeVecchio had long-since retired with a full pension, and Greg Scarpa Jr. had been "buried," along with his evidence, in the Super-max prison.

But by 2005, the dormant Yousef-Scarpa story would take a curious turn. The renowned Supreme Court justice Learned Hand, late of the Second Circuit Court of Appeals, once said that the truth comes "from a multitude of tongues," and it was a chance conversation Greg Scarpa Jr. had in the bowels of that prison that set in motion a chain of events that would reopen the DeVecchio investigation. Of all the inmates the wiseguy would choose to talk to, the man who reignited that new line of inquiry was none other than Terry Lynn Nichols, twice convicted of conspiring with Timothy McVeigh in the deadly Murrah Federal Building bombing of 1995.

In this investigation, it seemed that all roads led back to Brooklyn. But first they would take a detour through Oklahoma City.

39

EXPLOSIVES
THE FBI MISSED

B y February 2005, Gregory Scarpa Jr., the Colombo family wiseguy
who had risked his life for eleven months ratting out the true mastermind of both WTC attacks, was in the middle of the seventh year of a
forty-year sentence. Confined to a seven-by-twelve-foot cell in the prison
known as "The Alcatraz of the Rockies,"[1] the U.S. Penitentiary Administrative Facility (ADX) in Florence, Colorado, he slept on a thin mattress
atop a concrete slab. Subject to special administrative measures (SAMs)
that limited his number of visitors and phone calls, Scarpa Jr. was literally
walled off from the outside world, unable to receive any newspapers or pe-
riodicals that would give him a hint of conditions on the other side of the
prison's twelve-foot razor-wire fences. Along with a number of lone-wolf
bombers housed there—such as Unabomber Ted Kaczynski and Olympic
bomber Eric Rudolph—his fellow inmates now included many of the al
Qaeda terrorists who had been convicted in the SDNY and imprisoned on
multiple life sentences, including Ramzi Yousef, Abdul Hakim Murad,
Eyad Ismoil, and Nidal Ayyad.

Despite his solitary confinement, which allowed him only one to two
hours outside of his cell each day, Greg Jr. learned in early 2005 that
homegrown terrorists might be planning to use a cache of undiscovered

explosives from America's second biggest adjudicated act of terror: the Oklahoma City bombing.

The tip came from Terry Nichols, the disgruntled army veteran who was convicted with Timothy McVeigh of planting the bomb on April 19, 1995, that killed 168 people at the Murrah Federal Building. McVeigh himself had been housed at the Supermax until his execution in 2001.[2] Now, during their limited contact, which included the exchange of "kites" similar to those that Yousef had passed to Scarpa, Nichols was warning that a cache of nitromethane buried at Terry's old home in Herrington, Kansas, might be retrieved and used to mark the tenth anniversary of the Oklahoma City blast in 2005.[3] According to Nichols, the explosive was buried with an ammunition can under a pile of rocks in a crawl space beneath the house where the FBI had supposedly done a thorough search following his arrest ten years earlier.

As soon as he got the word from Nichols, Scarpa Jr. contacted Angela Clemente, the forensic investigator who had been working to get him a lawyer for the past several years. With her partner, a Yale-educated Ph.D. named Stephen Dresch, Clemente contacted staff members in the offices of two congressmen she had dealt with on government reform issues: William Delahunt, a Democrat from Massachusetts, and Dana Rohrabacher, a Republican from California.

The most significant revelation from Scarpa Jr., according to Clemente, was Nichols's alleged admission that "others unknown" *were* involved in the original Murrah Building plot—despite Timothy McVeigh's insistence up until his execution that he and Nichols had acted alone.[4]

Another startling new allegation Scarpa learned from Nichols was that Roger Moore, an Arkansas gun dealer whose girlfriend testified against Nichols and McVeigh, may have been an FBI informant.[5] Nichols alleged that it was Moore who supplied the tubes of the high explosive that were buried in the crawl space.

Moore has always vigorously denied any involvement.

"Terry was anxious to have somebody test the boxes the explosive had come in for fingerprints," says Clemente, "and that's why he let word of the explosives slip to Greg."[6]

During McVeigh's trial, the government had argued that Nichols and McVeigh had financed the Oklahoma City bombing by using the proceeds from a gunpoint robbery at Moore's home on November 4, 1994. But evidence later showed that on the day of the robbery McVeigh was at a gun show in Kent, Ohio, hundreds of miles away. Moore alleged that he had been accosted outside of his house at 9:00 or 9:30 A.M. that day by a man wearing a black ski mask and wielding a gun. Moore said that the man then took him inside the house and singlehandedly tied him up with rope and duct tape before robbing a series of guns, ammunition, coins, and other valuables.

In his book *Others Unknown: The Oklahoma City Bombing Case and Conspiracy,* McVeigh's lawyer, Stephen Jones, wondered how Nichols, who "saw poorly" without his glasses and didn't own contact lenses, could have effected the robbery. As Jones noted, Moore was never called by the government as a witness at McVeigh's trial, but at Nichols's trial, when Moore's girlfriend and/or business associate listed one of the guns as stolen, Nichols's attorney demonstrated that Terry had purchased that same weapon at a gun show two years before—a revelation described by Jones as "a stunning blow to the prosecution."[7]

Impeaching Greg Jr. Again

Now, on March 4, 2005, to test Scarpa Jr.'s credibility on the Nichols tip, the FBI reportedly sent a polygraph tech to the Supermax. After a brief examination, he reportedly concluded that Scarpa Jr. had failed.[8] But forensic investigator Clemente insists that the lie detector test was flawed.

"First of all," says Clemente, "the polygraph specialist sent from D.C. was belligerent to Greg Jr., which violates the protocol. Second of all, he asked about four questions, then abruptly left the test, went into another room and returned, but he didn't reinflate the cuff used to measure the subject's responses. Finally, this man abruptly ended the test, and told Greg Jr. he wasn't credible."[9]

And yet, just as he had with Yousef in 1996, Scarpa offered the FBI details of the explosives and their location that only Terry Nichols himself could have known. Clemente and Dr. Dresch reduced Scarpa's verbatim recitation of Nichols's account to a memo and sent it to an aide to Congressman Rohrabacher. In it they predicted that if the FBI searched the crawl space they would find:

a cardboard box [approx. equal to] 18″ × 18″ × 18″ wrapped securely in clear plastic wrap containing a full case of the nitro methane (red tinted) liquid portion (component) of the 2-part binary explosive component known as kine-stik (aka kine-pak). [The liquid is in small clear plastic tubes.] This box is the original box the product came in when delivered to [Roger] Moore's home at Royal, Arkansas. Thus this is the box which would have his fingerprints on the outside or on the inside flaps. . . . There is a 2nd box that's also a brown cardboard similar in size to the first, possibly a bit larger. It too is wrapped securely in clear plastic and is sitting right next to the first box. This second box contains numerous (a couple hundred) electric blasting caps. And nearby these 2 boxes is a .50 caliber military ammo can ([approximately] 6″W × 8″H × 12″L). It contains at least one non-electric blasting cap, a 16 oz. can of black powder, 2 instructional booklets and some other miscellaneous items.

The details of the location of the explosive were even more specific. According to Scarpa, Nichols even suggested that in locating the kine-stiks the investigator should bring a flashlight and wear coveralls:

Find north basement stairway near bathroom. Near bottom step is a square hole about 2 ft. by 2 ft. through the cement wall to left (east). This leads to the crawl space under most of the house. As soon as you enter into the crawl space both to the right which is south and left north are two piles of rocks. These are up against the wall you just went through.

Note: The two rock piles were part of the foundation wall which was torn down to make other access holes for other parts of the house.

Under the south pile is my ammo can.

Under the north pile are two cardboard boxes wrapped in plastic. Simply remove the rocks. The north pile probably has some dirt covering the two boxes but not much. There is little light so a drop cord or flashlight would be helpful. And coveralls—the crawl space area is a dirt floor. The box to be fingerprinted, etc., is the one with the little tubes of reddish clear liquid.

Despite the Bureau's claim that Scarpa had failed his polygraph, enough pressure was brought to bear by congressional staffers that the FBI finally agreed to a search. A team of agents entered the empty Herrington, Kansas, house on March 31.

Two days later, John Solomon, the Associated Press's Washington deputy bureau chief, filed this story on the AP's national wire:

> WASHINGTON (AP) The FBI is facing the possibility it made an embarrassing oversight in the Oklahoma City bombing case a decade ago after new information led agents to explosive materials hidden in Terry Nichols' former home, which they had searched several times before. FBI officials said the material was found Thursday night and Friday in a crawl space of the house in Herrington, Kan. They believe agents failed to check that space during the numerous searches of the property during the original investigation of Nichols and Timothy McVeigh.
>
> "The information so far indicates the items have been there since prior to the Oklahoma City bombing," Agent Gary Johnson said in a telephone interview from Oklahoma City.[10]

Solomon reported that McVeigh's attorney, Stephen Jones, "knew that some materials gathered for the attack were never found by the FBI and this discovery could answer some of those questions. But he added that it could also prove to be another black eye for the FBI, which was criticized for causing a delay in McVeigh's execution after it found new documents in the case."

"I think it is clearly embarrassing if it turns out to be true," Jones said in Solomon's story. "We've gone from not producing everything for the defendants to failing to recover from one of the conspirator's homes evidence that clearly is material."

In a follow-up story on April 14, 2005, the AP's Mark Sherman reported that "While the FBI found no evidence supporting the idea that an attack is in the works for Tuesday's 10th anniversary [of the Oklahoma City bombing,] the information that explosives had been hidden in Nichols former home in Herrington Kansas turned out to be true."[11]

Steven Schwadron, Congressman Delahunt's chief of staff, confirmed in the piece that the congressman's staff had forwarded the warning to the FBI after receiving a letter about the hidden cache from Clemente and Dr. Dresch in early March. According to Sherman, the Bureau refused to comment on why it took weeks between the initial warning and the search to find the explosives, which had been buried beneath a home in a residential neighborhood.

"Clearly the FBI—particularly Valerie Caproni, the general counsel—has every interest in discrediting Gregory Scarpa Jr.," says Clemente, who first supplied me with Scarpa Jr.'s trove of intel from Yousef back in 2004. "Keep in mind that Caproni was one of the top Feds who went along with the story that Greg Jr.'s material from Yousef was a 'hoax' and a 'scam,' and supported the four-decade sentence they gave him, even though Greg Jr. hadn't been convicted of a single homicide. She thought he would be buried forever and they would throw away the key and now, here he was in March of 2005 tipping the FBI to another major embarrassment connected to a massive act of terror."

Burying the Marijuana King

Caproni, the former head of the criminal division in the EDNY, whose career was tied to the successful prosecution of those sixty remaining Colombo war cases, reportedly considers Scarpa's conviction "one of her proudest accomplishments." Or so she told Robert Vosper, who wrote a flattering profile of Caproni in the October 2004 issue of *Corporate Legal Times.*

"The younger Scarpa ran a lucrative marijuana operation in Brooklyn and Staten Island for the Colombo family," Caproni told Vosper. "Not only was his crew dealing, but also forcing just about every drug dealer in Bensonhurst to pay a 'street tax.' When one dealer couldn't pay off his $20,000 debt to Scarpa, the crew broke his cheekbone and both arms."

"The police said that when they took him to the hospital he looked like a fly," Caproni told Vosper. "Both of his eyes were black and blood-shot, and his arms were broken. They beat the stuffing out of him."[12]

It's true that Greg Jr. was known as "the marijuana king" of Staten Island and that he kept the records on his father's lucrative book-making operation. "But he has never been convicted of a single homicide," says his former lawyer Larry Silverman.[13] "So when Caproni and the other prosecutors in the EDNY supported that forty-year sentence, it had nothing to do with anything remotely resembling fairness or justice."

"It was about the cover-up," insists Clemente, who pushed to reopen the DeVecchio investigation along with Andrew Orena, the son of Vic

Orena, the reputed head of the Colombo crime family, who got a life sentence in 1992. It was Orena's faction, allegedly pitted against a faction of the family controlled by Alphonse "Allie Boy" Persico, that DeVecchio claimed had led to the infamous Colombo war between 1991 and 1992.

Back then, when Orena and his capo, Pasquale Amato, were sentenced to life, their attorneys had no idea that Greg Scarpa Sr. had not only instigated the war, but that he'd killed a third of the victims himself—and done so with the alleged support and encouragement of R. Lindley DeVecchio, the FBI's top New York agent on organized crime.

By early 1992, Christopher Favo, DeVecchio's number two in squad C-10 of the FBI's New York Office, had become concerned that key intelligence on the location of witnesses in the Colombo war was finding its way to Scarpa Sr.[14] In January of that year, Favo gave DeVecchio what was thought to be the address of Orena's girlfriend where he was believed to be hiding out. He also furnished a mistaken address for one of Vic's soldiers.[15] Later, a cooperating member of Scarpa's crew admitted that he'd tried to kill both men by hunting them at the faulty addresses, which Greg Sr. had supplied to him from his "law enforcement" source.[16]

It was that mistake on the hideout address that was one of the eight possible "disclosures" by DeVecchio to the "Grim Reaper" contained in EDNY prosecutor Ellen Corcella's letter to defense lawyers on May 8, 1995.* Corcella worked directly under Caproni, who was found to have withheld a key piece of exculpatory evidence from defense attorneys documenting the alleged corrupt relationship between the hit man and DeVecchio whom the killer referred to in code as his "girlfriend."

Withholding the "Girlfriend 302"

Known as the "girlfriend 302," the memo documented a confession by Scarpa Sr.'s protégé, Larry Mazza, admitting that Greg Sr. had a law enforcement source who "supplied information on a regular basis." According to the 302, "The information that SCARPA SR. received through his

* See Corcella letter in Appendix V on pages 551–552.

source(s) included, but was not limited to, the address of VICTOR ORENA'S girlfriend's home."

Ellen Resnick, the defense lawyer who, with her partner, Alan Futerfas, was the first to get wind of the alleged "unholy alliance" between DeVecchio and Scarpa Sr., explained the significance of the "girlfriend 302."

"It's evidence that Scarpa Sr., while acting with the advice and consent of a senior FBI agent, is getting the addresses of his rivals so that he can go off and kill them," she says. "The production of that 302 to defense attorneys at a critical time would have been devastating."

But Caproni herself later admitted that she had kept the 302 in her desk.[17] Further, as the FBI geared up to conduct its OPR internal affairs probe on DeVecchio, she called the investigating agent and asked him to hold off. "Caproni advised that no FBI interviews of La Cosa Nostra (LCN) members expected to testify in an upcoming trial should be conducted," wrote OPR special agent Thomas Fuentes, "because of the potential adverse impact on the prosecution."[18]

"In other words," says defense attorney Flora Edwards, "further corroboration by the Colombo turncoats of the Scarpa-DeVecchio 'marriage' could result in an acquittal."

Caproni's request for a slowdown in the OPR on DeVecchio couldn't have been because she thought DeVecchio was innocent. The very next day, after that phone call to Fuentes, the OPR special agent interviewed her again. In a five-page 302, Caproni admitted that as far back as 1987 she knew that Scarpa Sr. was an FBI informant. She admitted that the information she got from DeVecchio on Scarpa's crew was "little prosecutive value," and that DeVecchio had threatened to "get" Agent Chris Favo if an OPR was opened on him.[19]

Futerfas and Resnick later filed a twenty-page memorandum effectively accusing the U.S. attorney's office of obstructing justice. Finally, after months of litigation, Federal judge Charles P. Sifton issued a sweeping decision, reversing the conviction of the initial series of Colombo war defendants.

After that, Chris Favo, who had first accused DeVecchio, began to regret coming forward. He concluded that informing on DeVecchio with the other two agents "was a mistake that would follow us for [the rest of] our careers."[20]

In May 1995, Vic Orena Jr., his brother John, and five other defendants went on trial for murder conspiracy charges relating to the Colombo war. Before the jury, AUSA Ellen Corcella admitted that DeVecchio and Scarpa Jr. had an unusual relationship. Later, a document surfaced at the trial that convinced jurors that it was the FBI, and *not* the Orena or Persico factions, that had instigated the two-year war. After acquitting all seven of the defendants on all charges, some of the jurors reportedly asked prosecutors why DeVecchio hadn't been indicted for murder.

Juror 186 told Greg Smith of the New York *Daily News,* "Something like this really knocks the credibility out of the FBI!" Juror Nancy Wenz stated, "If the FBI's like this, society's really in trouble."[21]

But although Orena Jr. was set free, Vic Senior remains in prison for life on the 1992 conviction. His son Andrew contends that it was based on the same tainted evidence from DeVecchio and Scarpa Sr. that resulted in his brother's acquittal.

"My father did a lot of questionable things," says Orena. "But he's innocent of the crime he's doing life for."

Andrew Orena also appealed to Congressman Delahunt's office, and the renewed allegations—which we documented in *Cover Up,* published in September 2004—found their way by February 2005 to the office of Brooklyn district attorney Charles "Joe" Hynes.

The Boys from Brooklyn

Now in his fourth elected term as district attorney of King's County, encompassing the borough of Brooklyn, Hynes is a salt-of-the-earth Irish-American. A former FDNY commissioner, Hynes rose to fame in the mid-1970s when he was appointed special prosecutor to investigate a notorious nursing home fraud scandal. In 1987, he made national headlines after being chosen by then-governor Mario Cuomo to investigate a racially motivated murder in the Howard Beach neighborhood of Queens.

In 2004, Hynes' office first developed what became known as the "Mafia Cops" case, in which two retired NYPD detectives, Louis Eppolito and Steven Caracappa, were accused of participating in a series of eight murders-for-hire on behalf of Anthony "Gaspipe" Casso, the convicted underboss of the Lucchese crime family.[22]

Veteran organized crime reporter J.R. de Szigethy compared the detectives to Perry Smith and Richard Hickock, who committed the *In Cold Blood* murders.[23] As Ed Bradley noted in the *60 Minutes* piece that first exposed the Mafia Cops story nationally, Casso had made allegations against Eppolito and Caracappa as early as 1998, but the case languished until Thomas Dades, a detective who had worked with the NYPD's Intelligence Division, came out of retirement and began working the cold case for Hynes's office.[24]

Then, after the Rackets Bureau developed the case, it was removed to Federal Court in the EDNY—because the RICO statute would allow prosecutors to use uncorroborated testimony to convict the ex-cops. But the case was assigned to Judge Jack B. Weinstein, the same judge who had rejected Vic Orena's habeas petition in 2004 and called Greg Scarpa Jr.'s evidence "unpersuasive."[25] Almost from the start, Weinstein expressed concerns that the five-year statute of limitations on RICO "enterprises" might have run out. "You've already been informed on a number of occasions that this court views the statute of limitations issue as a critical issue," Judge Weinstein told federal prosecutors.[26]

Now in 2005, having lost the prosecution of the Mafia Cops, Assistant D.A. Mike Vecchione and his deputy, Noel Downey of the D.A.'s Rackets Bureau, took the referral from Congressman Delahunt's office on DeVecchio very seriously.

In September, Downey and veteran NYPD detective George Terra, his chief investigator, invited me to meet with them in their Brooklyn offices. They had digested *Cover Up* and told me that it provided a great "blueprint" or overview of the Scarpa/DeVecchio matter. Months earlier they had met with Angela Clemente, and had begun to examine the phonebook-sized OPR file on DeVecchio, which the Feds had closed in September 1996.

In discussing the possibility that senior officials of the FBI's New York Office or prosecutors in the EDNY and SDNY might have turned their heads to evidence that DeVecchio was a coconspirator to homicide, I reminded Downey and Terra of the way Eastern District prosecutors had treated Joe Simone, an NYPD detective who, with his partner, Pat Maggiore, had made a third of the collars in the two-year Colombo war probe.

The Grancio Hit

Working directly under Chris Favo in Squad C-10, Simone and Maggiore had been tailing Nicholas "Nicky Black" Grancio, a Colombo capo loyal to Vic Orena, at a time when Greg Scarpa Sr. was gunning for him back in 1992. Grancio "had a new white Toyota Land Cruiser," Simone recalled in a 2004 interview with me. "My partner Pat and I followed him to outside a social club he had on McDonald Avenue near Avenue U and Graves Neck Road in Brooklyn." The date was Monday, January 6, 1992.

Using a surveillance post designated as "Plant 26" on the second story of a building overlooking the site, the Colombo task force was keeping almost round-the-clock surveillance on Grancio. What Simone and Maggiore didn't realize at the time was that Greg Scarpa Sr. was looking all over Brooklyn for Nicky Black.

His protégé Larry Mazza later testified that while the cops were watching Grancio, he drove past the Land Cruiser in a van. At the wheel was Jimmy Del Masto, a member of Scarpa's crew. Greg Sr. was in the back with a shotgun.[27]

"They wanted to kill Grancio," says defense attorney Flora Edwards, "but they couldn't get a clear shot at him because the cops were all over him."[28] So Scarpa Sr. borrowed Mazza's cell phone and called somebody named "Del." He said, "What the fuck is going on here? The whole world's here. Do something."

Moments later, at 2:00 P.M., the two cops and the other Feds watching Grancio got a call. "Out of the clear blue," as Simone remembers, "Favo calls and tells us all to come back to Federal Plaza for a Team Meeting. Now this is unusual, since it's two in the afternoon and we normally meet at the end of the day."[29]

"About ten minutes after they left for 26 Federal, there wasn't a cop in sight," says Edwards. "All the surveillance was gone. So Larry told me that he and Scarpa Sr. pulled up next to the SUV where Grancio was sitting and blew his head off."

Later, the meeting at the FBI's New York Office was interrupted with word that Grancio had been murdered. "So we take off and rush back there," says Joe. "At the crime scene, we find that the back of Nicky's head's been blown away."

If the call from Scarpa Sr. did go to DeVecchio, and he was responsible for Favo's "unusual" request to pull back the team, that could make DeVecchio an accessory to homicide. On May 6, 1993, at a sentencing hearing before Judge Weinstein in the Eastern District, Greg Scarpa Sr. pleaded guilty to the Grancio murder.[30] Later, Larry Mazza pleaded guilty as an accomplice.

But in 1996, when the Feds decided to close the DeVecchio investigation, they found themselves in a difficult position. "How could they justify all those leaks going to Scarpa Sr. and his people?" asks Edwards.

"So what they decided to do," says Clemente, "was put it on Joseph Simone, a hero cop."

The Fabricated Deli Phone

On December 8, 1993, as Det. Simone got ready to retire from the NYPD, a series of police and FBI vehicles pulled up outside the modest home in Staten Island where he'd lived for thirteen years with his wife, Eileen, a nurse, and their five children. Within hours he was under arrest for bribery.

"DETECTIVE STUNG BY FEDS" was the banner headline in the New York *Daily News*. "Detective Joseph Simone, who worked on the NYPD-FBI Organized Crime Task Force for seven years, was charged with selling information to the Orena faction of the warring Colombo family for two years, earning at least $2,000," the article read.

The author of the piece was Jerry Capeci, the *Daily News* columnist who was later cited in FBI 302s as the recipient of FBI intelligence leaked by Lin DeVecchio. But the public didn't know that.

In an FBI 302 memo dated June 1–2, 1994, "Del's" deputy, Special Agent Christopher Favo, confessed that "on several occasions, SSA DeVecchio approached me or another agent with specific questions about the investigation of the war or the Colombo family and our answers to the questions appeared in Capece's [sic] column the following day with an attribution to a law enforcement source.[31] On several occasions I mentioned this to SSA DeVecchio, and he blamed the leaks on the prosecutors in the EDNY. I began withholding information from SSA DeVecchio on Monday mornings to prevent its appearance in Tuesday's column."

"Initially they had sixty counts against me," says Simone. "Everybody was trying to dump what went bad in the Colombo wars on me—like wires . . . giving up CIs. . . . Everything. They ended up coming down to four counts: two attempted alleged bribery and two attempted alleged conspiracies."

Overnight, Joseph Simone went from a hero in his Staten Island community to a tabloid disgrace. "The roof caved in on my life," said Simone. "I never saw it coming."

"What was really incredible," says Simone's former attorney, John Patton, "was that the 'evidence' against Joe, if you could call it that, was either supplied by a known mob fabricator or entirely manufactured by the Feds."

At Joe's trial in Brooklyn Federal Court, Patton was able to prove that Simone had been out of the office, on vacation three hours away, at a time when prosecutors were claiming that he'd used his phone to signal wiseguys. He also shattered the purported testimony of Salvatore "Big Sal" Miciotta, a Colombo killer who was later tossed from the Witness Protection Program for his lack of credibility.[32] As the primary "witness" the Feds were using to prove that Simone had accepted the $2,000 "bribe," Miciotta had switched off a tape recorder before meeting Simone, after one of his cohorts was heard to say of Simone "He don't want nothin."

"It's clear from the transcript of this tape, in which Miciotta is wired, that he believes that Detective Simone would not take a bribe," says Angela Clemente.

"Later, they said I was using a pay phone outside a deli to tip off the wiseguys and they claimed to have a female FBI agent on an adjacent phone listening in," says Simone. "But as it turned out, there was only one phone there. We had the deli owner who was prepared to testify that there was only one phone on the side of the building that I used and there never had been two phones by the front door where this agent said she'd been."

At trial, FBI special agent Lynn Smith testified that on September 23, 1993, she was part of an *eight*-person FBI surveillance team following Simone. Under oath she alleged that they had tracked him to a deli-superette on the corner of Arthur Kill Road and Elverton Avenue, and that she had overheard him talking on a phone "located outside [the] door of the superette." Asked by Joe's defense lawyer, John Patton, if there was one phone or two, she replied, "One on the left and one on the right, on each side of the door."[33]

"Understand the significance of this," says Angela Clemente. "The FBI is so intent on nailing this poor cop, that they put eight agents on him. A female agent testifies under oath to a phone that doesn't exist so they can make it look like Joe is calling to tip off wiseguys. The truth is, he used to stop at that deli before coming home to call his wife and ask if she wanted him to bring home cold cuts for dinner. But the Bureau goes to all this trouble to make it look like he's caught up in some major leak to the Colombos."

In the face of the nonexistent evidence, Simone was acquitted on all counts. But later, based on the *identical* evidence, an NYPD hearing officer named Rae Downes Koshetz decided that Simone should not have been associating "with known criminals," even though it was part of his job with the Colombo Task Force. As a result, Joe lost his NYPD pension, a decision upheld by then-NYPD commissioner Howard Safir, a former Fed who had run the Witness Protection Program for the U.S. Marshals service and had worked with many of the same Bureau officials who seemed bent on targeting Simone. "This astonishing decision, in which Det. Simone was found guilty and stripped of his pension, suggested one of two things," said Patton. "Either the hearing officer was incredibly naïve with respect to the fact that Joe was working in an O.C. squad and expected to mix with wiseguys as part of his job, or she was doing the bidding of the Feds."

When I read the transcripts of Simone's federal trial and his NYPD hearing, as well as the FBI 302 from the date of his arrest, I was convinced he'd been set up by federal prosecutors to explain the leaks to Scarpa Sr.

But I was also stunned that in September 1993, seven months after the World Trade Center bombing—even as Ali Mohamed was deceiving FBI agents on both coasts—the FBI had assigned up to eight agents in an effort to discredit a decorated cop.

At that September 2005 meeting with Downey and Terra in the Brooklyn D.A.'s office, I encouraged them to empanel a grand jury so that they could fully investigate the DeVecchio case.

Seven months later, on March 30, 2006, D.A. Hynes stood before a podium at a press conference and made a stunning announcement: He was unsealing indictments that morning charging Roy Lindley DeVecchio with four counts of second-degree murder.

40

FOUR COUNTS OF HOMICIDE

The indictment charged that DeVecchio "did solicit, request, command, importune and intentionally aid in the death[s]" of Mary Bari, the beautiful girlfriend of Allie Boy Persico whom Scarpa Sr. shot on September 24, 1984; Joseph DeDomenico, 44, known as "Joe Brewster," slain on September 17, 1987, after DeVecchio allegedly leaked that he might become a turncoat; Patrick Porco, the seventeen-year-old friend of Scarpa Sr.'s second son, Joey, murdered on Memorial Day weekend in 1990; and Lorenzo "Larry" Lampesi, a mob rival shotgunned to death by Scarpa Sr. during the Colombo war on May 22, 1992.[1]

When Special Agent Chris Favo reported the Lampesi hit to DeVecchio, he reportedly laughed, slapped his desk with his open hand, and exclaimed "We're going to *win* this thing."[2] Favo testified later that DeVecchio "seemed to be a cheerleader for the Persico faction" in the war, and that "a line had been blurred. . . . He was compromised. He had lost track of who he was."[3]

"This is the most stunning example of official corruption that I have ever seen," said D.A. Hynes at the press conference announcing the indictments. "Four people were murdered with the help of a federal law en-

forcement agent who was charged with keeping them safe. Lindley De-
Vecchio deserves the maximum sentence of 25 years to life for each of
these killings."[4] Hynes gave a hint as to the former supervisory special
agent's possible motivation for allegedly selling out the Bureau.

"In exchange for this confidential law enforcement information and
protection supplied by DeVecchio," Hynes said, "it is alleged that he received weekly payments from Scarpa from 1980 to 1992. Significantly,
during the twelve years that Scarpa was considered a paid informant assigned to DeVecchio, FBI records indicate that DeVecchio received
$66,598 from FBI headquarters in Washington, D.C., and somehow re-
ceived clearance from Washington to transfer the funds to Scarpa without
having Scarpa sign a receipt. That clearance was in direct violation of standard FBI procedure. Accordingly, there is no evidence that Mr. DeVecchio
ever transferred any of these funds to Scarpa."

Later that day, at DeVecchio's arraignment, the sixty-five-year-old retired SSA, who had spent thirty-three years in the Bureau, seemed fright-
ened and fatigued, a far cry from the swaggering curly-haired Colombo
task force boss the Feds called "Mr. Organized Crime." Back then, DeVecchio had favored Rolex watches, European silk suits with pocket squares,
monogrammed shirts, and diamond cufflinks. Now his dark hair had gone
grey, and he faced the federal judge in a simple grey open-collar buttoned-
down shirt and dark slacks.

Ordered held on $1 million bail, DeVecchio was released only after a
lengthy bargaining session in which he was able to post $100,000 in cash
and five former FBI agents agreed to cosign for the remaining $900,000,
making them jointly and severally liable if DeVecchio ever fails to appear.[5]

The new indictments spared DeVecchio from charges in the Nicky
Black murder case, but there was little consolation in that.

Months earlier, an attorney for Grancio's family had filed a wrongful
death suit against DeVecchio and his first deputy in the Colombo task
force, Chris Favo. The suit alleged that the Feds had called off that January
6, 1992, surveillance of Grancio by Det. Joe Simone and his partner, allowing Scarpa Sr. an opening to gun down his victim.

The court papers held that the case was "about the corrupt and unlaw-
ful relationship between law enforcement and a ruthless killer and career

criminal that went unchecked for years and led to the cold blooded murder of a man."[6]

During the same week in January when word of the D.A.'s grand jury first surfaced in the press, DeVecchio's lawyer, Douglas Grover, called the allegations "nonsense"[7] and "laughable,"[8] and insisted his client had done nothing wrong.[9] At the arraignment in March, Grover criticized Rackets Bureau chief Mike Vecchione, alleging that he was unaccustomed to making organized crime cases, a charge Vecchione disputed sharply.

The Friends of Lin

After the arraignment, DeVecchio was surrounded by a group of more than forty retired FBI agents who walked him out of court along Jay Street in Brooklyn, literally shoving aside bystanders and reporters as they beat an exit.

One of the agents was Chris Mattiace, who had worked with DeVecchio for years. He told reporters later, "We believe in him. We believe that the charges are frivolous."[10]

Mattiace was one of the early organizers of the Friends of Lin DeVecchio Trust, a fund-raising committee designed to counter the charges against DeVecchio in the media, while raising money for his defense. The Trust's board contains an impressive list of FBI alumni, including James Kallstrom, the former ADIC of the FBI's New York Office. After the arraignment, Kallstrom went so far as to declare DeVecchio innocent—an endorsement rarely given by a federal agent, retired or not, in the face of official charges.

"Lin DeVecchio is not guilty and did not partake in what he's being charged with," Kallstrom told Angela Mosconi, a reporter for the New York *Daily News*. "It's as simple as that. His work went a long way toward the success of the FBI task force break up of La Cosa Nostra as we knew it." Of course, Kallstrom's own credibility could be negatively affected if the charges against DeVecchio are proven. It was his April 10, 1996, memo to Louis Freeh suggesting that there was "insufficient evidence to take prosecutive action against" DeVecchio that cleared Scarpa Sr.'s "girlfriend" the first time.

Kallstrom and former FBI officials like Jim Roth, who drafted the Freeh memo, are circling the wagons now in defense of DeVecchio, some out of loyalty for a fellow agent. But others are concerned that if a full-blown corruption inquiry rips open the FBI's New York Office, other agents could be next. On January 7, within days of word surfacing about the DeVecchio grand jury, Mattiace, who is chairman of the Hudson Valley Chapter of the Society of Former Special Agents, sent a confidential e-mail to other retired SAs. "I am hopeful that the Society will speak out on this issue which any one of us could have found ourselves in," Mattiace wrote, "There but for the grace of God go I."[11]

Sparing the Bureau Embarrassment

There are some other celebrated ex-Feds who might feel some heat if Hynes's investigation opens up new veins of official corruption; on April 15, 2006, *New York Times* reporter Alan Feuer disclosed that former SDNY U.S. attorney and New York mayor Rudolph W. Giuliani had given DeVecchio a pass way back in 1976, when agents of the Bureau of Alcohol Tobacco and Firearms wanted to indict him for selling handguns in Pennsylvania.[12]

According to an affidavit filed in the appeal of Pasquale Amato, the guns were worth $60,000.[13] Feuer tracked down the former AUSA who wanted to bring charges against DeVecchio for the sale, and he alleged that while serving as deputy attorney general in the Justice Department, Guiliani refused to go forward. "Rudy expressed no other reason not to prosecute the guy except the guy was a cop," said Daniel M. Clements, the former assistant U.S. attorney, who is now in private practice. "He didn't want to embarrass the Bureau."[14]

Meanwhile, just days before Feuer's story appeared in the *Times,* DeVecchio's attorney, Douglas Grover, filed a motion in the EDNY to get the cases transferred to Federal Court, arguing that DeVecchio should be immune from prosecution because he dealt with Scarpa Sr. in the course and furtherance of his federal duties. Announcing that DeVecchio's legal team planned to use "federal statutes and witnesses including federal agents and people now under federal protection," the motion was assigned to Judge Frederic Brock.[15]

"I find no basis in fact or law for such an application," D.A. Hynes said in a prepared statement.[16] But others who are watching the DeVecchio case closely expressed concern. "What could happen here is another repeat of the Mafia Cops debacle," says Andrew Orena, son of Vic Sr., who is hoping that a full vetting of the DeVecchio corruption charges could clear his father.[17]

A Stunning Reversal

On April 6, 2006, after a month-long trial, the accused Mafia Cops, Lou Eppolito and Steven Caracappa, were convicted on seventy counts tied to eight separate murders, in what was hailed by the press as "one of the most spectacular police corruption scandals in the city's history."[18]

It was a rollercoaster ride of a case, which included testimony that Eppolito was fond of snakes, and that after a bit part in the movie *Goodfellas* his head shot hung on the wall of a Chinese restaurant. After the verdicts, U.S. Attorney Ros Mauskopf declared that "today, twenty years after the death of Israel Greenwald [one of the victims] justice has finally been done."

But her victory declaration turned out to be premature.

First, the two ex-cops went after their celebrated defense lawyers, Bruce Cutler and Edward Hayes, alleging that they had failed to properly represent them. Cutler, who had successfully defended John Gotti multiple times, and Hayes, who inspired a character in Tom Wolfe's novel *The Bonfire of the Vanities*, were cleared by Judge Weinstein, who denied the motion. But then Weinstein, the same man who had predicted that the Colombo war cases would "unravel"[19] if the DeVecchio scandal continued, dropped a bombshell.

The banner headlines across two pages of the New York *Daily News* said it all: JUDGE RUBS OUT MOB COP VERDICT.

As John Marzulli reported, "Despite having murdered, maimed and sold out informants to blood-thirsty mobsters, the Mafia Cops' racketeering conviction was stunningly overturned yesterday—all because they apparently steered clear of the mob for the last five years."[20]

In a 102-page ruling, Weinstein tossed out the guilty verdicts, concluding that the five-year statute of limitation for RICO cases had effectively made the convicted killer detectives ineligible for punishment in a federal courtroom.[21]

"I never heard of anything so stupid," said Betty Hydell, whose son Jimmy was reportedly kidnapped, thrown in the trunk of a car by Eppolito and Caracappa, and delivered to his execution site in 1986. "I thought this was all over."

Defense attorney Cutler called Weinstein's ruling "courageous," but some wondered why, if the case turned on the statute of limitations issue, Weinstein hadn't tossed it out of federal court months *before* trial—especially since he had repeatedly warned prosecutors about the very issue as early as September 2005.[22]

"This incredible waste of the taxpayers money will give you an idea of what could easily happen if the DeVecchio case goes federal," says Andrew Orena. "The fact that the Feds *cleared* DeVecchio, when there was overwhelming evidence of corruption, tells you that these murder charges finally brought by the Brooklyn D.A. never could have developed in Federal Court. I'm concerned that if the case is transferred to the Feds it will die. After all, what's DeVecchio's main argument? That he was sanctioned in doing what he did by some higher-ups in the FBI and Justice Department. If this case goes all the way, a lot of major heads could roll, from New York to Washington."

The Deep, Dark Pit

Meanwhile, the support team around DeVecchio has decided to fight the charges against him by attacking the credibility of some of the investigators who have attempted to document the corruption charges. The Friends of Lin DeVecchio website alleges that Hynes's indictment was motivated by "lucrative book and movie deals" tied to the Mafia Cops case, which the Rackets Bureau initiated. Alleging that Dades and Vecchione are working on a book for HarperCollins (which happens to be my publisher) citing my book *Cover Up* and referring to me as a "conspiracy theorist," the

DeVecchio "Friends" have concluded that "Publicity and money are the reasons for the prosecution of Lin DeVecchio."[23]

Andy Kurins, a former agent now working DeVecchio's case as a private investigator, has been sending me regular e-mails attempting to attack the credibility of Angela Clemente, the forensic investigator who provided me with the FBI 302s from Scarpa Jr. Kurins alleges that "Angela Clemente is being paid by Vic Orena." He ended one recent e-mail to me with this rather ominous plea: "I hope that you have not been sucked into this vortex of lies and self serving agendas against Lin and have time to extricate yourself from a pit which will only get deeper and darker."[24]

I told Kurins that I stand by my reporting in *Cover Up* and urged him to read the DeVecchio OPR. I also sent him a copy of Ellen Corcella's May 1995 letter listing eight possible leaks from DeVecchio to Scarpa Sr., which included the address where Salvatore Micciotta was living. Back in the 1990s, faced with a choice between life in prison or death at the hands of Scarpa Sr., "Big Sal" might well have been motivated to turn "rat" for the Feds and falsely accuse Joe Simone of bribery.

As to Angela Clemente, the consequences of continuing her investigation of the DeVecchio corruption case became chillingly clear on June 16, 2006, when she kept a late-night appointment with an alleged "informant" and nearly ended up dead.

Tipster Slay Try on G-Mom

That was the headline in the *New York Post* the day after the meeting, when Clemente was rushed to Brooklyn's Lutheran Medical Center.[25] Earlier that morning, responding to a 911 call at 5:45 A.M. police had reportedly found her sprawled halfway out of the front seat of her car near the Caesar's Bay strip mall in Bensonhurst, Brooklyn. Clemente, known for meeting mob-related sources at all hours, had gone there late the night before to meet a source.

"I thought the meeting would be safe," she told me, "because he had indicated to me that he was a former police officer."

For days before the encounter, working on an investigation of the 1992 murders of Colombo soldiers John Minerva and bodyguard Michael

Imbergamo, Clemente had been finding notes on her car window suggesting that this source had new information on the case.

"I went to meet him," she told me, "and almost as soon as I got out of my car he asked me if I was going to keep pushing on this case. When I said I was, he started beating and choking me. Then I passed out."[26] Witnesses confirmed that Clemente had a heavy contusion on her back when she was admitted to the ER. The *New York Post* reported that she'd suffered a seizure.

Near her heavily guarded hospital bed, Rackets Bureau chief Vecchione said "We consider this very serious. She was working on a case not unrelated" to DeVecchio.[27] The *Daily News* quoted Vecchione as saying that Clemente had "a large ugly welt on her stomach; cuts and bruises on her neck, head, legs, and lip; and choking marks on her neck."

Yet within weeks, Jerry Capeci, a primary beneficiary of DeVecchio's leaks according to the OPR file, had run several pieces in the *New York Sun* questioning the assault. In a column on June 29 headlined "Cops Probing Sleuth's Beating Story," Capeci alleged that "cops are wondering whether Angela Clemente was spinning tales about a mysterious beating she suffered in the parking lot of a Brooklyn shopping center.

"There are 'gaping holes' in Clemente's story, said one law enforcement source. Another said detectives have 'serious doubts' about her account of the beating."[28]

Capeci claimed that Angela had "missed two scheduled follow up sessions with police sketch artists" at the 62nd precinct, which is investigating the assault. But in fact one of those sessions was canceled by the detectives themselves, and Angela had to miss the second after her mother reportedly had a stroke.

In another column, filed on July 20, 2006, Capeci insisted that Angela "still hasn't sat down with police sketch artists to create a likeness of the suspect she claims assaulted her during a bizarre early morning confrontation at a Bensonhurst, Brooklyn shopping center five weeks ago."[29]

"That's just completely false," Angela told me in an interview on July 21. "I've met with investigators for the D.A.'s office and they have a full description of my assailant. There are also significant new leads on how I was tracked in the days leading up to the attack."[30]

After her attack, the *New York Post* suggested that Clemente would be dropping her interest in the DeVecchio matter.[31] But in an interview with me in late July she said that she was more determined than ever to get at the truth behind the Feds' decision to bury the evidence from Ramzi Yousef to Greg Scarpa Jr. in 1996, and their apparent attempt to silence him again in 2005, when he produced evidence of the undiscovered Oklahoma City explosives.

"All of this is connected," says Clemente. "The Lin DeVecchio investigation is the key that can unlock a scandal involving years of misconduct at the highest levels of the Justice Department and the FBI. Why would I give up on that?"

What Lies Beneath

I got a sense of what the stakes are myself back in the summer of 2004, when I was finishing my reporting for *Cover Up*. After receiving a packet of what the Feds later called the "Scarpa materials" from Angela, including Yousef's "kites" and the FBI 302s, I contacted Greg Jr. at the Supermax prison. On July 6, he wrote me back and consented to an interview. I then phoned Warden Robert A. Hood at the prison, requesting a face-to-face meeting with Greg Jr. That same day I received an astonishing response from the warden in the form of a letter, reproduced as Appendix VI on page 566. In that letter, Warden Hood concluded, based on what he called his "sound correctional judgment," that to grant my request for an interview would "pose a risk to the internal security of this institution and to the safety of staff, inmates and members of the public."

When I first reported on that letter in *Cover Up*, I raised the question, "What do they have to hide?" Now, after spending a year and a half documenting the cover up of the Ali Mohamed story—and seeing my reporting on DeVecchio vindicated by the D.A.'s indictments—I have my answer.

41

WHY ANY OF THIS MATTERS

On August 10, 2006, officers from Scotland Yard and MI5, Britain's domestic security service, swept through the United Kingdom, raiding up to fifty locations from East London to Birmingham. Seizing more than 400 computers, 200 cell phones, and 8,000 other pieces of evidence from paper files to memory sticks,[1] they uncovered what soon became known as the "trans-Atlantic airline bombing plot." Twenty-four men, all U.K.-born Muslims, were arrested. The British authorities said that their intent was to smuggle a series of "liquid-based" improvised explosive devices (IEDs) aboard up to nine flights between Europe and the United States. The plot, described by U.S. Homeland Security Secretary Michael Chertoff as "quite close to the execution stage,"[2] was to involve four carriers: British Airways, Continental, United, and American. The conspirators intended to explode the IEDs in flight—possibly over U.S. cities. If the plot had been carried out, the airborne death toll alone could have been as high as 2,700.[3]

Raiding what British authorities called a "bomb factory" in the heavily Pakistani Walthamstow neighborhood of East London, agents seized quantities of hexamethylene triperoxide diamine (HMTD), a highly volatile peroxide-based explosive in the same family as triacetone triperoxide (TATP), the chemical linked to both the al Qaeda London bombings of July 2005 and a series of suicide bombings in Israel.[4] FBI director Robert Mueller III said the undertaking had "all the earmarks of an al Qaeda plot."[5] And with good reason: The British authorities had originally been tipped to the plot after Pakistani officials arrested Rashid Rauf, a British-born al Qaeda associate described as a "hardened Islamic militant," in the eastern city of Bahawalpur.[6] It was Rauf's seizure, and the fear that it would send the U.K. coconspirators underground, that prompted the British to act.

"There is definitely an al Qaeda connection to this," declared Pakistan's ambassador to the United States, Mahmud Ali Durani.[7]

Recovered in the searches were a series of so called of "martyr videos" similar to those taped by the nineteen 9/11 hijackers prior to their airliner-suicide plot. One U.K. suspect's video was reportedly inspired by a November 2002 *fatwa* issued by Osama bin Laden admonishing jihadis to "kill as they kill."[8]

There were other significant al Qaeda signatures in the plot.

TATP was the chemical used by Richard Reid, the so-called "shoe bomber" who was captured aboard American Airlines Flight 63 en route from Paris to Miami on December 22, 2001. An alert flight attendant smelled what she thought was a burnt match when Reid had tried to ignite explosive devices in his shoes, but he was subdued by other passengers and arrested. The FBI later confirmed that there were two TATP-based IEDs hidden in his shoes, prompting airlines worldwide to force passengers to remove footwear as they passed through airport screening devices. Mohammed Mansour Jabarah, an al Qaeda operative captured and interrogated in Oman in 2002, reportedly said that Reid had been sent on the bombing mission by Khalid Sheikh Mohammed himself.[9]

HMTD and the explosive RDX were found in the car of Algerian al Qaeda-funded "Millennium bomber" Ahmed Ressam, who was seized on December 14, 1999, while planning an attack at Los Angeles International Airport.

As evidence that the August U.K. plot was directed from al Qaeda's top echelons, just two weeks before the operation was broken, Dr. Ayman al-

Zawahiri was seen in a video *fatwa* warning of another "spectacular" attack on the United States.[10]

In the hours after the British plot's exposure, air travelers across the globe were forced to remove all liquid, gels, and creams from their carry-on luggage, causing flight cancellations and massive delays.[11] For many in airline security, it was a terrifying déjà vu.

As reported in *1000 Years for Revenge,* shortly after components of Ramzi Yousef's liquid-based Casio-nitro IEDs were discovered at the Dona Josefa Apartments on the night of January 6, 1995, the FAA had called U.S. airline officials to issue an alert. The threat was considered so imminent that the communiqués went out on unsecured "open" phone lines.

Dick Doubrava, a security official at Delta, told me that he immediately ordered all airliners halted on the ground in Bangkok and other Asian cities. "We were looking for small amounts of liquid that could be easily concealed," said Doubrava.[12] For weeks, airline passengers throughout Asia were prevented from boarding commercial jets carrying any liquids.

"If you talk to anybody in the business who traveled the Pacific right after this, everything went," said Glen Winn, then corporate security manager at United Airlines.[13] "I don't care if you had after shave, expensive perfume, or a five hundred dollar bottle of wine, it went into a bucket at the gate."

Bojinka Part Two

"There's little doubt that this latest plot was an attempt to execute a modern-day version of Ramzi Yousef's Bojinka plot," says terrorism analyst Paul Thompson.[14] "And that shouldn't be surprising. As we saw with both 9/11 and the *Cole* bombing, al Qaeda has a habit of seeing earlier thwarted plots carried through."

Indeed, both the *New York Times* and the *Los Angeles Times* ran sidebar stories on August 11 referencing Yousef.[15] Carrying strikingly similar headlines on how the trans-Atlantic plot bore "Echoes" of operation Bojinka, both pieces cited Yousef's wet test aboard PAL Flight 434 in 1994.

But on that same day, the *Los Angeles Times* also ran a piece entitled "Al Qaeda Imprint Debated," citing an unnamed U.S. intelligence official who claimed "some ambiguity" as to "whether this is al Qaeda central or not."[16]

The suggestion that the terror network was now "fragmented," and that "homegrown" terrorists independent of bin Laden and al-Zawahiri were behind this latest plot, was reminiscent of the spin embraced by the 9/11 Commission and pronouncements from a number of U.S. Feds since then, who have sought to portray al Qaeda in 2006 as "loosely organized."

"We can't say that this points back to al Qaeda central," the *Los Angeles Times*'s source insisted.

This argument echoed the line the Justice Department had been following for a decade, in its longstanding effort to distance later al Qaeda plots from Ramzi Yousef. But the paper trail created on May 19, 1996, when Yousef slipped a kite to Greg Scarpa Jr. advising that "acetone peroxide" and RDX were two "explosive substances" that "can be easily smuggled" aboard "an airplane" (Appendix VI on page 555), clearly suggests a direct line of succession between the plots. However, after the Feds decided to bury the "Scarpa materials" and clear Supervisory Special Agent Lin DeVecchio, that particular "dot" on the chart documenting al Qaeda's terror war against America was disconnected by Patrick Fitzgerald, FBI general counsel Valerie Caproni, and James Kallstrom, the terrorism adviser to New York State.

"Nothing stays buried forever,"[17] notes forensic investigator Angela Clemente, who first retrieved that kite from Scarpa Jr. as she sat with him in the Supermax prison in 2004. "Only now Greg's in danger." In a call to me on September 15, 2006, Clemente reported that Scarpa Jr. had now been moved out of solitary into the general prison population at the Supermax, "where he's received death threats."[18]

As late as September 20, 2006, officials at the ADX Florence continued to refuse my requests to talk to Scarpa Jr. I wanted to interview him now more than ever, especially after he'd learned of the hidden explosives in Oklahoma City bomber Terry Nichols's former house in Herrington, Kansas. According to Clemente, Nichols had suggested to Scarpa that "others unknown" may have been involved in the Murrah Building bombing, and I wanted to ask him about that, as well as the Justice Department's allegations—now repudiated by former inmate John Napoli—that he had fabricated Yousef's kites as memorialized in those dozens of FBI 302s. I also wanted to question the younger Scarpa about Yousef himself, who is housed in the Supermax, especially after Yousef's former attorney told me in August that nobody in the government seemed anxious to talk to him.

"After 9/11 we made a number of offers to the Justice Department to make him available," says Bernard V. Kleinman. "And we were repeatedly ignored."[19]

Except for a botched effort by FBI agents from the Colorado Springs office to shake the truth out of Yousef on the morning of 9/11, Kleinman is aware of no other attempts by federal authorities to question the man most responsible for the planes-as-missiles plot.

Rewriting History on TWA 800

And what of the intelligence generated by Scarpa Jr. connecting Yousef to the crash of TWA 800? On the tenth anniversary of the 747's explosion, Yousef's name never came up in the media. Even *Newsday*, which won a Pulitzer Prize for its coverage of the disaster and published multiple articles in the summer of 1996 on the discovery of explosive residue aboard the wreckage,[20] ignored the FBI 302s suggesting an al Qaeda nexus to the crash.

The special multipage supplement *Newsday* published on the anniversary did carry a two-page story on alternative theories, headlined: "Conspiracy Theorists Still See It Differently."[21] The piece, by Bill Bleyer, discounted two versions of the missile theory, and even discussed the possibility of a "meteor downing" the 747. Bleyer went into detail about Nelson DeMille's novel *Night Fall*,[22] which debunks the "frayed wire" theory of the NTSB. But the piece devoted not a word to the possibility that the crash of Flight 800 was "Bojinka fulfilled."

There were other clues to the government's real feelings about TWA 800. Two weeks after the anniversary, on August 1, *Newsday* ran a story under the headline "Federal Agencies Disagree over Need to Eliminate Vapors from All Airliner Fuel Tanks," noting that "the National Transportation Safety Board is mightily frustrated with the lack of progress in efforts to improve fuel tank safety."[23]

"That should tell you something," says Jack Cashill, an investigative journalist whose book *First Strike* (coauthored with James Sanders) first uncovered the fraud behind the FBI/NTSB K-9 theory used to explain the presence of high explosive residue in the TWA 800 wreckage.[24] "If there had been an actual threat to the safety of passengers aboard Boeing 747s from those fuel tanks, the FAA would have issued an immediate air worthiness directive and they would have been retrofitted by now. But the truth is there was *never* a threat, because a spark in the vapors did not cause that center wing fuel tank aboard Flight 800 to explode. Never in the history of American commercial aviation has a plane spontaneously blown up in mid-air, not in the seventy-five years before TWA Flight 800's demise, and not in the ten years since."[25]

"If the exposure of the British airliner bomb plot has taught us anything," says Angela Clemente, "it's that we need to go back and revisit the evidence Greg Scarpa Jr. extracted from Ramzi Yousef in 1996. The similarities to Yousef's Bojinka plot are just too compelling—especially in light of that Yousef kite mentioning 'acetone peroxide.' If that evidence had been properly examined by the Justice Department ten years ago, they could have made significant inroads against al Qaeda and maybe there wouldn't have been a U.K. plot in 2006."[26]

Are We Safer? The FBI Litmus Test

In a series of speeches marking the fifth anniversary of the 9/11 attacks, President George W. Bush repeatedly asserted that the United States was more protected from the threat of Islamic terror than it had been on September 11, 2001. "Five years after 9/11, are we safer?" Mr. Bush asked in a speech before an audience of conservative intellectuals on September 7. "The answer is yes, America is safer. We are safer because we've taken action to protect the homeland."[27]

Clearly, any definition of "safer" must include an analysis of the reforms made by all five of the major U.S. intelligence agencies since 9/11, along with an examination of the military progress made against Islamic radicals in Afghanistan and Iraq. But an assessment of the FBI's counterterrorism record in the last five years can provide perhaps the best litmus test of whether the homeland is more secure. After all, the Bureau is the principal agency charged with protecting America against domestic terror threats—and in the years since 9/11 there have been a number of significant benchmarks allowing us to judge whether or not the FBI has undergone sufficient reform to thwart the next attack.

Director Robert Mueller acknowledged the need for Bureau reform in testimony before Congress on May 8, 2002: "We must refocus our missions and priorities. New technologies must be put in place to support new and different operational practices. And we must improve how we hire, manage, and train our workforce; collaborate with others; and manage, analyze, share, and protect information. All will be necessary if we are to successfully evolve post-9/11. Most would have been necessary even absent 9/11."[28]

It was significant that Mueller put "new technologies" at the top of his reform list, because at that very hearing, he uttered a statement that would haunt him for years:

> The [9/11] hijackers also apparently left no paper trail. In our investigation, we have not yet uncovered a single piece of paper—either here in the U.S. or in the treasure trove of information that has turned up in Afghanistan and elsewhere—that mentioned any aspect of the September 11th plot.

And yet, as this book has documented, the paper trail was significant—from Ramzi Yousef's 1993 pledge to return to hit the Towers, to the detailed evidence of the "planes operation" on Yousef's Toshiba laptop, which had been in federal custody since 1995.

What was it that caused the "disconnect" in the Bureau between the West and East Coast offices in their seeming inability to put the puzzle pieces together on Ali Mohamed? What caused the "stovepiping" later asserted by Jack Cloonan? Surely the FBI had a computer system in place that would have connected the dots on Yousef and Mohamed, stringing them together in a matrix that documented al Qaeda's threat to America?

The answer is no.

To this day, despite hundreds of millions of dollars spent to upgrade its information-sharing capabilities, the FBI has yet to install a computer database system that would allow agents to effectively connect al Qaeda operatives worldwide.

In 2002, beginning with a story by reporters Eric Lichtblau and Charles Piller, the *Los Angeles Times* published a series of articles documenting the Bureau's "paper-driven culture."[29] As the *Times* reported, the FBI's system was so antiquated that, immediately after 9/11, frustrated agents in Tampa were unable even to e-mail photos of the nineteen hijackers to the Bureau's regional offices. They had to resort to overnight mail.[30] The 1980s-era technology at the Bureau lacked even the capacity to search and link words like "flight" and "schools."[31]

The Bureau had pledged to upgrade its information systems via a project called Trilogy, described by the 9/11 Commission as "a 36 month plan for improving its networks, systems and software." Former IBM executive Robert Dies, who was brought in by former director Louis Freeh to consult, told the commission that his goal was merely "to get the car out of the garage." The only other reference to Trilogy by the commission was its admission that "the project was underway, but by no means fully implemented" at the time of 9/11.[32]

That turned out to be a broad misstatement of fact. By May 2004, a review of Trilogy by the National Research Council (NRC) found that the system failed to support the Bureau's new counterterrorism mission and should be "redesigned." At that point, the project, launched in November 2000 with a $380 million price tag, had grown into a $626 million white elephant.

Director Mueller repeatedly cited Trilogy as an essential component in the FBI's reform strategy, designed to improve its ability to thwart terrorism.[33] But the NRC concluded that Trilogy was "not likely to be an adequate tool for counterterrorism analysis" and should be rebuilt "from scratch."[34]

In 2005, the FBI scrapped the final phase of Trilogy, known as the Virtual Case File system, at a cost of $170 million.[35] In testimony before the Senate Judiciary Committee, Mueller predicted that the system would not be fully operating until *2009,* eight years after the 9/11 attacks.[36] By March 2006, Eric Lichtblau, now covering the Bureau for the *New York Times,* cited a report by the Justice Department's inspector general predicting that it could cost another half billion dollars to complete the Virtual Case File overhaul.[37]

No E-Mail for Some FBI Agents in New York

Perhaps the most jaw-dropping revelation came that same month, when the Associated Press reported that "budget constraints are forcing some local FBI agents to operate without e-mail accounts, according to the agency's top officials in New York."

"As ridiculous as this might sound, we have real money issues right now and the government is reluctant to give all agents and analysts dot-gov accounts," said Mark Merson, the ADIC of the New York Office.[38]

Retired special agent James Whalen, a veteran of the NYO, calls the Bureau's failure to get the Virtual Case File system on line five years after 9/11 "frightening."

"Look at the number of times Abouhalima, that red-headed Egyptian cab driver, showed up in the Bureau's files in the years before he helped bomb the Trade Center," says Whalen. "If a JTTF agent could have hit a button and gotten a print-out on that guy back in '93, lives might have been saved. Well, guess what? They still can't do that today thirteen years later."[39]

The most primitive tool any desk-bound investigator can use is the "knowledge-discovery database," a system that allows for searches of large data volumes so that patterns and associations can be established.

As noted, it's now believed that the very name "al Qaeda" referred to an initial database of Afghan Arabs and other Islamic "Holy Warriors," compiled by bin Laden and al-Zawahiri after the war against the Soviets. What better way for the FBI to track the relationships in that terror network than a viable search engine that could combine both open source documents—like those searched by the Able Danger analysts—and classified FBI files.

The findings in this book, and my two previous 9/11 investigations, were the product of a data-mining "harvest" that was modest in comparison to the 2.5 terabyte retrieval accomplished by the Able Danger team. Nonetheless, using a conventional computer and Internet search engines, I was able to build a database on al Qaeda that included evidence from thousands of open-source news articles, more than one hundred books or government reports, and dozens of interviews with active duty and retired intelligence community sources. In addition, the file has grown to include more than 45,000 pages of court transcripts from the 1991 trial of El Sayyid Nosair through the penalty phase of the Zacarias Moussaoui trial in 2006.

My database was enhanced by accessing research done by terrorism analysts Paul Thompson, who maintains www.cooperativeresearch.org, and John Berger, who operates www.intelwire.com. After assisting me with some of the research for *Triple Cross,* Berger began publishing his own series of Ali Mohamed articles on his site beginning September 11, 2006. Thompson has been covering the Ali Mohamed story for years.

The Sphinx Trading discovery came as the result of linkages in my master database. Inputting data into an off-the-shelf version of Filemaker Pro software revealed the fact of Nosair's Sphinx mailbox, which emerged during the Nosair trial in 1991. Combined with published newspaper accounts, a search of corporate records for the Jersey City-based company, and the appearance of coincorporator Waleed al-Noor as one of the unindicted coconspirators in the Day of Terror case, a Google search turned up the 2003 arrest of Mohammed El-Atriss, al-Noor's partner in the original incorporation. That led to the discovery that El-Atriss had provided fake IDs to two of the 9/11 hijackers in 2001.

I then visited the physical premises of Sphinx in February 2006, and spoke to staffers who confirmed al-Noor's continuing involvement in the operation.

Any high school or college student could have made the same linkages with a Mac or a PC and broadband Internet access.

We can only wonder why the Sphinx connection wasn't made by investigators for the Joint Terrorism Task Force or Squad I-49 looking backward from 1996. Was it the lack of an adequate computer system, a "failure of imagination"[40] (as the 9/11 Commission concluded), or simply a desire to disconnect certain linkages intentionally in an effort to spare the Bureau from embarrassment for its earlier failures?

The broader question is this: Even if the Bureau ever gets an adequate searchable database up and running, will it have the organizational mindset or competence to keep the nation safe from terrorists? The answer lies in a series of other benchmarks on Bureau performance over the past five years. The first indication actually came months *before* the 9/11 attacks.

The FBI Since 9/11

June 9, 2001   FBI special agent Robert Wright, a veteran terrorism investigator who had probed Hamas, presents a mission statement to the Bureau in which he writes: "Knowing what I know, I can confidently say that until the investigative responsibilities for terrorism are removed from the FBI, I will not feel safe. The FBI has proven for the past decade it cannot identify and prevent acts of terrorism against the United States and its citizens at home and abroad. Even worse, there is virtually no effort on the part of the FBI's International Terrorism Unit to neutralize known and suspected terrorists residing within the United States. Unfortunately, more terrorist attacks against American interests, coupled with the loss of American lives, will have to occur before those in power give this matter the urgent attention it deserves." Wright asks for Bureau permission to make the statement public, but he's prevented from discussing it with the media and the statement isn't disseminated until May 2002, nine months *after* 9/11.[41]

September 2002   FBI agent Mike German becomes concerned that a Tampa, Florida-based terrorism investigation will fail due to "grave violations of FBI policy and possibly even grave violations of the law."[42] He complains to the Justice Department's inspector general that FBI managers falsified records, falsely discredited witnesses, and failed to adhere to regulations governing electronic surveillance. After German attempts to contact Director Mueller, he's removed from the case. "The phone just stopped ringing, and I became persona non grata," he says. In frustration, he retires from the FBI in 2004 and it isn't until December 2005 that the IG's report effectively vindicates his allegations. The *New York Times* calls the FBI's actions a "cover-up," and cites German as "the latest in a series of whistleblowers at the FBI who said they had been punished and effectively silenced for voicing concerns about the handling of terror investigations and other matters since Sept. 11, 2001."[43]

January 14, 2005   The DOJ inspector general vindicates FBI whistle-blower Sibel Edmonds, concluding in a report that the Bureau had failed to aggressively investigate charges of espionage she'd brought against a coworker whom she'd accused of minimizing key al Qaeda-related intelligence after 9/11. The report also concludes that Edmonds's attempt to point out deficiencies in the FBI's translation section was "the most significant fact" in her firing in 2002. The American Civil Liberties Union (ACLU) agrees to join Edmond's appeal of a 2004 Federal Court decision dismissing her whistleblower lawsuit against the government, after Attorney General Ashcroft invoked the rarely used "state secret" privilege and the Justice Department retroactively classified a 2002 congressional briefing on Edmonds's allegations.[44]

March 28, 2005   *U.S. News & World Report* publishes a cover story about Mueller's attempts to reform the Bureau. Insiders say that the senior leadership tends to withhold bad news from Mueller. One anonymous FBI official admits that "[Mueller] is . . . isolated and shielded." Regarding the failure of the Virtual Case File system, the official notes that "There's no way . . . the top guys around him . . . were going to tell him the bad news because VCF . . . was his baby and no one was going to say, 'Your baby's ugly.'" The article reports that the Feds' counterterrorism ranks had seen a "head-spinning exodus of top-tier executives—five officials have held the top counterterrorism job since 9/11; five others held the top computer job in 2002–2003 alone."[45]

May 5, 2005   The Justice Department's inspector general reports that the FBI fell "significantly short" of its goal for hiring intelligence analysts in 2004 and faces a surge of analysts leaving in the next five years. In addition, the report says that the Bureau lacks a formal strategy for retaining analysts, and hasn't even determined how many it needs to meet its mission. The 190-page report, which covers the period from October 2001 through July 2004, notes that the FBI ended 2004 with about one-third of its analyst positions still unfilled. After retirement, the most common reasons cited for the analysts' exodus are low pay, poor advancement, unfulfilling work assignments, and the lack of respect they felt from within the Bureau.[46]

June 7, 2005   The ten former 9/11 commissioners hold a hearing as part of a follow-up to the commission report. They are heavily critical of the FBI's reform efforts. According a *Washington Post* account of the hearing, "The problems are so acute that members of the influential Commission may want to reconsider whether the United States needs a separate agency to handle domestic intelligence, one Democratic member said." Former commissioner Jamie Gorelick, who pushed for the extradition of bin Laden's brother-in-law, says that she is "taken aback" by a string of recent FBI failures. High turnover, poor training, and a continued inability to build a modern computer system are cited as major problems.[47]

June 10, 2005   The Justice Department inspector general issues another report, described by the *New York Times* as "blistering," citing at least five instances in the months before 9/11 when the FBI blew chances to locate muscle hijackers Khalid al-Midhar and Nawaf al-Hazmi. The report is made public after being kept secret for a year, but large portions are blacked-out, including a 115-page section on one terror suspect. In attempting to explain FBI Headquarters' failure to follow up on the "Phoenix Memo," the report cites a so-called fear of "racial profiling" among agents.[48]

June 12, 2005   The *Washington Post* reports that many cases on the government's terrorism list have nothing to do with terrorism. They cite as examples one pre-9/11 case in which three Arab grocers were convicted of stealing Kellogg's cornflakes; another in which a Sudanese actor was released after his name was confused with that of Khalid Shaikh Mohammed; and a third case involving Jordanians convicted in a Florida immigrant-marriage scam.[49] The prosecutor who investigated the New Jersey grocers was U.S. Attorney Christopher Christie, the same Fed who was so critical of the Passaic County Sheriff's Department for jailing Mohammed El-Atriss—the man who sold two of the 9/11 hijackers their fake IDs via Sphinx Trading.

June 20, 2005   Attorney Stephen M. Kohn, who has interviewed a number of the FBI's top counterterrorism officials, writes a letter to the Senate Judiciary Committee alleging that "the FBI has been led by managers without counterterrorism experience . . . especially in Middle Eastern terrorism and their testimony under oath is that they are learning about counterterrorism on the job."[50] Kohn notes that, in a sworn deposition, Mueller was unsure of the relationship between Osama bin Laden and Sheikh Omar Abdel Rahman, and that Dale Watson, the FBI's counterterrorism chief for two years after 9/11, was unable to differentiate between Shiites and Sunnis, the two principal sects of Islam. The current and former FBI officials gave sworn depositions pursuant to a lawsuit brought by Bassem Youssef, one of the few Arab-speaking Bureau agents. While instrumental in breaking the 1996 Khobar Towers bombing case, after 9/11 Youssef alleged that he was repeatedly passed over for a top-level Headquarters job in terrorism.[51]

June 29, 2005   William Odom, the retired army lieutenant general who ran the National Security Agency (NSA) from 1985 to 1988, writes an op-ed page piece entitled "Why the FBI Can't Be Reformed," declaring that "The problem is systemic. No one can turn a law enforcement agency into an effective intelligence agency. Police work and intelligence work don't mix. The skills and organizational incentives for each are antithetical." He concludes, "The only hope for improvement is the creation of a separate agency, equal to the CIA and under the new Director of National Intelligence."[52]

July 27, 2005   The DOJ inspector general releases a new audit of the FBI's translation program. Noting that it takes an average of sixteen months to hire a contract linguist, mostly due to bureaucratic slowdowns, the report reveals that the Bureau has met its translator hiring targets in fewer than *half* of the languages examined, and that the quantity of unreviewed counterterrorism audio is increasing, from 4,000 hours in April 2004 to 8,000 hours in March 2005. FBI field offices are still failing to review high priority intelligence data within twenty-four hours. Worse, there is no nationwide system in place to monitor the quality of translations.[53] The *New York Times* reports that seven months after the Directorate of Intelligence was created, the manager who runs the information sharing office linking federal, state, and local anti-terrorism offices says that he has only one full-time employee and two contractors working for him.[54]

September 12, 2005   In another report, the DOJ inspector general concludes that the FBI frequently violates its own internal guidelines in handling confidential informants (CIs). In nearly nine out of every ten cases reviewed, guidelines on the handling of CIs were broken in ways that risked compromising investigations. In a conclusion that mirrors the allegations against former FBI SSA Lin DeVecchio, the report notes that FBI agents sometimes allowed informants to engage in criminal activities without getting necessary approval from supervisors or lawyers, that they failed to report unauthorized illegal activity, and/or that such activity was often approved only retroactively.[55]

November 28, 2005   The Supreme Court refuses to hear an appeal by former FBI translator Sibel Edmonds. Two lower courts had accepted the federal government's argument that her case could not proceed without revealing state secrets.[56]

December 19, 2005   Newly released documents obtained by the ACLU indicate that the FBI has conducted many investigations involving activist groups with no ties to terrorism. One document indicates an FBI plan to monitor a "Vegan Community Project." Another document talks of the Catholic Workers group's "semi-communistic ideology." Other groups monitored include PETA (People for the Ethical Treatment of Animals) and the international environmental organization Greenpeace. An ACLU official says, "You look at these documents and you think, wow, we have really returned to the days of J. Edgar Hoover."[57]

January 7, 2006   Yet another Justice Department IG's report blames overconfidence in fingerprint identification technology and sloppy paperwork in explaining why the FBI falsely accused a man in the 2004 Madrid train bombings. Brandon Mayfield, a lawyer in Portland, Oregon, was jailed for two weeks in May 2004 before being cleared. The report concludes that there was no misconduct by the FBI or abuse of the Patriot Act in the case.[58]

March 2006 During the penalty phase of the trial against Zacarias Moussaoui, the FBI agent presented as the Bureau's leading al Qaeda authority exhibits a stunning ignorance of key players in the terror network. On the stand, Michael Anticev, brother of the New York JTTF's John Anticev, testifies that he'd never heard the allegation that Abdul Hakim Murad intended to fly a plane into the CIA building. Anticev first denies that the FBI ever had a chance to arrest Khalid Shaikh Mohammed after his 1996 indictment, then when pressed, admits that KSM had been "tipped off" to the FBI's arrest attempts. He then claims that he "only heard from the media" in 2003 that KSM had been captured. Anticev also admits that he was "unaware" of any training of al Qaeda hijackers prior to 1998 and didn't know that Ihab Ali (Ali Mohamed's Florida sleeper) had gone to the same Oklahoma flight school as Moussaoui. The *Los Angeles Times* reports that Anticev sometimes responded "in faltering speech," and either "did not know many central facts about al Qaeda or did not want to publicly reveal them."[59]

April 19, 2006 The FBI seeks to search the files of Jack Anderson, the late newspaper columnist, in an effort to remove any classified material he may have collected in more than forty years of investigative reporting. Anderson had a long feud with the FBI and exposed many cases of government wrongdoing. "I'm not aware of any previous government attempt to retrieve such material," says Lucy Dalglish, executive director of the Reporter's Committee for Freedom of the Press. "Librarians and historians are having a fit and I can't imagine a bigger chill to journalists."[60]

May 2, 2006 FBI Director Mueller is grilled at a Senate Judiciary hearing when Sen. Patrick Leahy (D-VT) cites evidence of more than one hundred cases in which FBI agents have improperly surveilled antiwar groups, including the Quakers.[61] Sen. Chuck Grassley (R-IA) declares that "The barriers to the transformation of the FBI go far beyond its troubled efforts to upgrade its computers." After only eight months on the job, says Grassley, "the FBI announced that the head of the newly created National

Security Branch is retiring. The previous Director of Intelligence at the FBI stayed for less than two years."[62] Then, noting the March 30, 2006, indictment of SSA DeVecchio, Grassley openly criticizes the Friends of Lin DeVecchio Trust. According to their website, he says, "More than forty agents appeared at his bond hearing to show support, and after the hearing, the agents surrounded DeVecchio 'in a human blanket' so that he could not be questioned by reporters. One agent wrote, 'a few reporters received a few body checks out on the sidewalk' and that he 'was never prouder to be an FBI Agent.'" Grassley warns that "the public perception created by such aggressive and broad support" for DeVecchio, "could leave the impression that the FBI, as an institution, is circling the wagons to defend itself as well as DeVecchio against the charges."

May 30, 2006   The FBI admits that it has found no trace of missing Teamsters union president Jimmy Hoffa after dozens of FBI agents conducted a two-week search of a suburban Detroit horse farm. The Associated Press calls it "one of the most intensive searches in decades for the former Teamster boss who vanished in 1975."[63]

September 4, 2006   A study conducted by a private research group at Syracuse University finds that after surging in the months following 9/11, the number of terrorism cases brought by the Justice Department has dropped sharply since 2002 and federal prosecutors are reportedly turning down hundreds of cases due to weak evidence and other legal problems. For the first eight months of the current fiscal year, 91 percent of the referred cases were turned down.[64]

October 11, 2006   The *Washington Post* reports that five years after 9/11, the FBI has only thrity-three Arabic-speaking agents, and none of them work in Bureau sections that investigate international terrorism.[65]

What is the significance of all this when it comes to clearing the 9/11 "cold case?" The political and legal realities are that the men most responsible for the attacks of 9/11 now in U.S. custody may never get to trial. In the final chapter, we'll examine why.

42

THE 9/11
COLD CASE

In his series of speeches marking the fifth anniversary of 9/11, President Bush declared that "the families of those murdered that day have waited patiently for justice."[1] Announcing that he was transferring fourteen "high-value detainees," including Khalid Shaikh Mohammed and Ramzi bin al-Shibh, from secret CIA prisons to the U.S. Naval Base at Guantanamo Bay, Bush pledged that they would be "held in custody by the Department of Defense." As soon as Congress authorizes the military commissions he's proposed, said the president, "the men our intelligence officials believe orchestrated the deaths of nearly three thousand Americans on September the eleventh can face justice."

But the White House package sent to Congress to approve the tribunals retained several key provisions similar to those that had been struck down in June by the U.S. Supreme Court, including language that permits defendants to be excluded from their own trials. There was also a proposed modification of Common Article 3 of the Geneva Convention governing the treatment of POWs.[2]

The *New York Times* noted that the timing of the proposal before the elections put pressure on Democrats, who might risk being labeled as "weak on national security."[3] But the strongest reaction from Capitol Hill came from the president's own party. "I do not believe it is necessary to have a trial where the accused cannot see the evidence against them," said Sen. Lindsay Graham (R-SC), a former military prosecutor, who was joined by two other influential senators, John McCain (R-AZ) and John Warner (R-VA), chairman of the Senate Armed Services Committee.

Assertions in the president's September 6 speech that interrogation techniques of the fourteen "detainees" had led directly to the capture of a series of terrorists were also challenged. Bush had claimed that Abu Zubaydah, "a trusted associate of Osama bin Laden . . . disclosed [that] Khalid Sheikh Mohammed . . . used the alias 'Muktar'" after his capture, "a vital piece of the puzzle that helped our intelligence community pursue KSM."

But as Mark Mazzetti pointed out in the *New York Times* on September 8, even the 9/11 Commission noted that the CIA "knew of the moniker for Mr. Mohammed months before the capture of Mr. Zubaydah.

"Mr. Bush also said it was the interrogation of Mr. Zubaydah that identified [Ramzi] bin al-Shibh as an accomplice in the Sept. 11 attacks," wrote Marzetti, but "American officials had identified Mr. bin al-Shibh's role in the attacks months before Mr. Zubaydah's capture. A December 2001 federal grand jury indictment of Zacarias Moussaoui, the so-called 20th hijacker, said that Mr. Moussaoui had received money from Mr. bin al-Shibh and that Mr. bin al-Shibh had shared an apartment with Mohamed Atta, the ringleader of the plot."[4]

A week after the president's East Room address, McCain, Warner, and Graham made it clear that they would not go along with the White House proposals to redefine the Geneva Convention, which prohibits "outrages upon personal dignity, in particular, humiliating and degrading treatment" of war prisoners.[5] McCain, himself a former POW, insisted that a move like that might convey the wrong message about America's support for human rights. "Senator Warner and I and Senator Graham and others are not going to agree to changes in the definitions in Common Article 3, because that then sends the message to the world that we are not going to adhere fully to the Geneva Conventions. And we worry about, in the future, other nations maybe deciding to interpret Common Article 3 to their own purposes."

That conflict led Mr. Bush to accuse the three GOP senators of putting the nation at risk. In a Rose Garden speech on September 15, the president threatened to end the CIA interrogation program of high-value terror suspects if Congress passed the alternate rules package proposed by Graham, Warner, and McCain.[6]

"It's a debate that really is going to define how we protect ourselves," the president said.

But soon even Mr. Bush's former secretary of state, Colin L. Powell, the former chairman of the Joint Chiefs of Staff, sided with the opposition.

Now, in the weeks leading up to the midterm elections, in a debate Bush had hoped to be having with Democrats *alone,* he was effectively challenging the patriotism of Powell and three of the most senior Republicans charged with military oversight—suggesting that if they didn't accept his package, the nation's vulnerability to terrorism would increase. The dispute quickly developed into a thorny political problem for the White House.

Then, on September 21, the president blinked. The White House announced that it had reached a compromise agreement with the three senators, dropping its earlier demand for a watering-down of the Geneva Convention rules.[7] But in attempting a resolution on the due process issue, the GOP compromise may have created a legal problem that will prevent the fourteen Guantanamo suspects from ever reaching trial.

First, since *ex post facto* laws are prohibited by Article One of the U.S. Constitution, it is unlikely that the fourteen "high-value detainees," including KSM, will be tried under these new provisions, since they would go into effect years after their arrests.

Second, it's unlikely that the current Supreme Court, dominated by strict constructionists, will support any dilution of due process guarantees, even in the midst of a terror war.

Third, in announcing the settlement with the White House, Senator Graham noted that the GOP package contained new procedures in which certain classified or "sensitive" evidence could be withheld from terror suspects in order to prevent their use in future attacks.[8]

There are existing rules for the admission of classified evidence in U.S. legal proceedings under the Classified Information Procedures Act (CIPA).

But on the very same day that the White House reached its accord with the G.O.P. senators, a federal judge in another high-profile Washington case ruled that the use of classified evidence that might jeopardize national security could result in the dismissal of an indictment.

Ironically, the lead prosecutor in that case was none other than Patrick Fitzgerald.

Fitzgerald and the CIA Leak Scandal

On September 21, 2006, Judge Reggie Walton, presiding over the one public indictment in the CIA leak case—that of vice presidential counselor Lewis "Scooter" Libby, ruled that if Fitzgerald believes that admitting certain classified files in Libby's trial will threaten national security, he can move to dismiss the perjury charges.[9] If that happens, it will be just the latest stunning turn in the three-year investigation begun after Fitzgerald was appointed special prosecutor. Since the fall of 2003, he's been charged with determining whether Bush administration officials broke the law in leaking word to various reporters that Valerie Plame Wilson was a CIA employee. The motive for outing Mrs. Wilson—a potential crime—was thought to be a possible White House conspiracy to retaliate against her husband Joseph Wilson. A former ambassador under George Herbert Walker Bush, Wilson had openly criticized the second Bush administration in a July 6, 2003, op-ed piece for exaggerating the threat from Saddam Hussein in the months leading up to the invasion of Iraq.

After indicting Libby on the more limited charges of obstruction of justice and perjury, Fitzgerald had sought to narrow the definition of admissibility for classified evidence with a three-part test that Judge Walton rejected. It was a major victory for Libby's defense team, and that September 21 ruling gave Fitzgerald a legal out if he should decide to end the probe.[10]

Volumes have now been written about Fitzgerald's investigation as special prosecutor, and this book, which focuses largely on his involvement with Ali Mohamed, is not the place to tell that story in detail. But a brief review of the debate provoked by the $1.44 million investigation might shed some additional light on Fitzgerald's capabilities and motives, since he remains a senior Justice Department official in the Bush administration.

Perhaps the most astonishing revelation came as late as September 7, 2006, when Richard Armitage, the number two official at the State Department, admitted that he was the source of the leak that had triggered the probe after he disclosed Plame-Wilson's CIA identity to Bob Woodward of the *Washington Post* and syndicated columnist Robert Novak. It was Novak's July 14, 2003, column identifying Wilson's wife as an "agency operative on weapons of mass destruction," that initially touched off the grand jury investigation. Further, Armitage admitted that he had disclosed the leaks to the Justice Department as early as October 2003, months *before* Fitzgerald began submitting evidence to a grand jury on the third week in January 2004.

Throughout the investigation, Fitzgerald fired off subpoenas to a series of reporters, including Matt Cooper of *Time* and Judith Miller, a former *New York Times* reporter who spent almost three months behind bars for contempt after she refused to reveal her source on the leak, even though she'd never written a story about it.

"What did Patrick Fitzgerald know and when did he know it?" asked Reagan-era deputy assistant attorney general Victoria Toensing in a *Wall Street Journal* Op-Ed piece after the Armitage revelations.[11] "Put aside hundreds of thousands of dollars of taxpayer funds squandered on the investigation. . . . Judith Miller's 85 days in jail, the angst and legal fees of scores of witnesses, the White House held siege to a criminal investigation while fighting the war on terror, Karl Rove's reputation maligned, and 'Scooter' Libby's resignation and indictment. . . . What Mr. Fitzgerald knew, and chose to ignore, is troublesome. Despite what some CIA good ol' boys might have told Mr. Fitzgerald, he knew from the day he took office that the facts did not support a violation of the Intelligence Identities Protection Act; therefore, there was no crime to investigate. Although he claimed in Mr. Libby's indictment that Ms. Plame's employment status was 'classified,' Mr. Fitzgerald refuses to provide the basis for that fact and, even if true, can point to no law that would be violated by revealing a 'classified' (not covert) employment. It was this gap in the law that created the need to pass the act in the first place."[12]

Clearly Toensing falls on the "no crime was committed" side of the debate and she's protective of the White House. But accusing Patrick Fitzgerald—perhaps properly—of acting with negligence in the investigation, doesn't mean that laws weren't violated in Plame-Wilson's outing, or that there was no conspiracy to punish Plame or her husband at the White House level.

Toensing claimed in her piece that "The first journalist to reveal Ms. Plame was 'covert' was David Corn, on July 16, 2003, two days after Mr. Novak's column. [Novak] never wrote . . . that Ms. Plame was covert. However, Mr. Corn claimed Mr. Novak 'outed' her as an 'undercover CIA officer,' querying whether Bush officials blew 'the cover of a U.S. intelligence officer working covertly in . . . national security.'"

The same day Toensing's piece appeared in the *Journal*, Corn, the liberal Washington editor of the *Nation,* shot back in the *Huffington Post* that he was "disheartened to see [Toensig] embracing a rather idiotic conservative talking point and ignoring basic facts to tag me as the true culprit in the outing of Valerie Plame Wilson. . . . The fact that Novak did not state she was a 'covert' operative is utterly meaningless. (Does the CIA employ non-secret 'operatives'?)"[13]

The Chilling Effect

The determination of whether or not the Bush White House used its media influence to spank a critic who accused the administration of cooking the intelligence books in the lead-up to the war, and put a CIA employee (of any status) at risk, is a question worthy of investigation. If Patrick Fitzgerald botched it through negligence or intent, he ought to be held accountable. There seems to be bipartisan dissatisfaction about the way he's run the leak probe.

But until he issues other indictments, or backs out of the Libby case and shuts down the grand jury, he deserves the benefit of the doubt on whether his investigation will ever yield the full truth on the Plame-Wilson outing.

Having said that, one thing is very clear: Whether he's uncovered a convictable crime in the leak, Fitzgerald has chilled the press, and that may well be his most damaging legacy.

As recently as September 18, writing in the *New York Observer,* Michael Calderone noted that a number of *New York Times* reporters have had to adopt the techniques of drug dealers—literally resorting to disposable cell phones and erasable notes in their efforts to avoid subpoenas and "shake" the Feds.

In a 2006 memo, *Times* executive editor Bill Keller reportedly cited "the persistent legal perils that confront us."[14] On September 18, 2006, Keller found himself on the cover of *New York* magazine in a story head-lined "Times Under Siege." It detailed a December 2005 meeting at the White House in which Keller was confronted by the president, former counsel Harriet Miers, National Security Advisor Stephen Hadley, and former National Security Agency director (now CIA director) Michael Hayden. For a year, the *Times* had delayed publication of a story that the NSA had been monitoring the phone calls of U.S. citizens without court authorized warrants.

The December meeting in the Oval Office signaled a showdown over the possible publication of the piece. At one point in the meeting, accord-ing to reporter Joe Hagen, "Bush issued an emphatic warning: If [the *Times*] revealed the secret program to the public and there was another ter-rorist attack on American soil, the Paper of Record would be implicated. The basic message," recalls Keller, "was 'You'll have blood on your hands.'"[15]

Eleven days after that meeting on December 16, the *Times* ran a story at the top left of its front page headlined "Bush Lets U.S. Spy on Callers Without Courts."[16] It was written by reporters James Risen, who had done such seminal work on Ali Mohamed, and Eric Lichtblau, who was among the first reporters to reveal the failure of the Trilogy project at the FBI. That first piece, and their ongoing coverage of the NSA wiretap story, earned Risen and Lichtblau the 2006 Pulitzer Prize for National Report-ing. It also locked the "Grey Lady," as the *Times* is known, in a war with the White House that only escalated after the publication on June 23, 2006, of another piece by Lichtblau and Risen (with reporter Barclay

Walsh) revealing a secret Bush administration program to examine the bank records of thousands of Americans.[17]

The White House campaign against the *Times* has led to a grand jury probe of the NSA wiretap leak, and calls by conservative columnists to charge Keller and other *Times* editors under the Espionage Act.[18]

"The main worry these days is not libel, proving that you actually quoted something accurately," said Craig Witney, the standard's editor for the *Times*, "It's being subpoenaed."

Indeed, on August 12, 2006, in researching the Able Danger issue for this book, I placed a call to *New York Times* reporter Phil Shenon, who (with Douglas Jehl) was among the first to break the data-mining story a year earlier. There was a Fitzgerald-related angle that I wanted to pursue.

Shenon's response? "Peter, I'm sorry but I can't discuss anything that might even remotely involve [Patrick] Fitzgerald. He's subpoenaed my records."[19]

Also in August, in another case involving former *Times* reporter Judith Miller, a New York appeals court ruled that Fitzgerald could seize her phone records, as well as Shenon's, in connection with their reporting on Islamic charities.

As an author, I can only wonder whether hypersensitivity to Fitzgerald's tactics will cause the *New York Times* or other major media outlets to avoid coverage of the findings in this book. Time will tell, but I've already received a strong indication that they might.

Two months before publication, my findings on Fitzgerald were buried by a cable network in a two-hour documentary that was supposed to be based entirely on *Triple Cross*. The background on that scandal offers new insights into the power of the FBI and Justice Department to influence the media and rewrite the history on their al Qaeda related negligence.

Epilogue

THE FBI VERSION
OF *TRIPLE CROSS*

In the fall of 2005, I was approached by Jonathan Towers, producer of *Inside 9/11,* a four-hour documentary on September 11 for which I was one of sixty journalists and government officials interviewed. I told Towers that I was working on a new investigative book exposing FBI negligence in its nine-year failure to stop Ali Mohamed. Towers immediately optioned my research and flew me to Washington, where I presented my *Triple Cross* findings to John Ford, programming president of the National Geographic Channel (NGC), the cable network operated in conjunction with the National Geographic Society. Ford bought the project in the room, declaring, "I don't know how we can't do a documentary."

Over Christmas, I wrote a twelve-page, ten-act treatment outlining the two key parts of the Ali Mohamed story: first, his long run as al Qaeda's chief spy, and second, how the Feds, specifically Patrick Fitzgerald and the FBI's New York office, had allowed him to operate.[1]

Under a contract with Towers Productions, Inc., we went into production in the spring of 2006 on a documentary that I was supposed to narrate and co-executive produce. The two-hour program was to be based entirely on my research and writing. Towers hired a crew, and their line producer, Rachel Milton, flew to New York to meet me on March 30, 2006. We shot for an entire day, covering the hearing on the indictment of SSA Lin DeVecchio. Later, on the steps of Brooklyn federal court, I shot a series of on-camera "stand-ups," which were to provide bridging commentary for my narration of the documentary.

The final program was entitled *Triple Cross: Bin Laden's Spy in America*. But when it aired on August 28, 2006, not a word about the FBI-DOJ negligence could be found in the documentary. Except for a brief super at the top of the program, reading "Based in part on the book *Triple Cross* by Peter Lance," there wasn't a frame of my narration or on-camera presence—nor was the book even mentioned, even though the inclusion of the cover was specified in my contract with Towers Productions.

What ended up running on cable systems across the United States, and on television stations internationally, was a whitewash of my findings. Worse, the executives at NGC actually allowed Jack Cloonan to become the effective "voice" of the film.

As such, there wasn't a word about the DeVecchio scandal in the two-hour program. Nothing about the Able Danger cover-up or the burial by the Feds of that cache of al Qaeda related evidence from Yousef to Scarpa Jr. in 1996. Cloonan never mentioned the name of Ali's hapless West Coast control agent, John Zent, or that he'd been tied up for six years in that Ewell triple homicide case. Appearing on camera dozens of times in the two hours, Cloonan never once suggested that Patrick Fitzgerald was in any way at fault for failing to stop Mohamed prior to the African embassy bombings. In fact, when Cloonan recited Fitzgerald's statement about Ali following the October 1997 restaurant meeting in Sacramento, the producers of the Nat Geo documentary conveniently left out the most important part of his statement.

"Ali Mohamed is the most dangerous man I have ever met," Fitzgerald had said. "We cannot let this man out on the street."[2] But in the documentary as aired, the producers cut that second sentence—thus removing any hint of culpability from Fitzgerald, the Justice Department's bin

Laden "brain," in allowing Mohamed to remain free through the embassy bombings.

How did this happen? How could a cable network owned in part by a respected organization like the National Geographic Society get it so wrong? When the NGC greenlit the project in early 2006, approving a budget of more than $810,000, they knew I was going to tell both stories: how Ali did it, and how the FBI failed to stop him. But in June 2006, Towers Productions knuckled under to Cloonan and two other key Feds: former U.S. Attorney Mary Jo White and former NYO Joint Terrorism Task Force investigator Det. Tommy Corrigan.

My contract with Towers Productions stipulated that I was to get all interview transcripts immediately after on-camera shoots, in order to incorporate the details in the manuscript of this book. Yet these three ex-Feds demanded that Jonathan Towers keep the research from me—and the production executives at NGC simply *acquiesced.* I couldn't go on camera to narrate the documentary without these key interviews, so Towers Productions effectively cut me out of the production process. They even refused to send me a rough cut of the documentary for fact-checking unless I signed a nondisparagement agreement. All of this is documented in a series of letters between me and NGC executives, contained in an August 27, 2006, press release on my website.

In effect, NGC ended up replacing the principal author of the investigative report on Ali Mohamed with one of the very Feds that the author had concluded was negligent. Jack Cloonan had had two and a half years, from January 1996 to August 1998, to build a file on Mohamed and interdict the embassy plot; yet, despite evidence from Squad I-49's own files of Ali's direct links to senior embassy plotters, Cloonan, Fitzgerald, and other top Feds failed to detect the plot. In February 2001, Fitzgerald went on to prosecute three relatively peripheral players in the plot, and cemented his reputation by convicting them of an act of terror that his own "bin Laden squad" had failed to prevent.

The fourth operative, Wadih El-Hage, had been on the FBI's radar since 1991. Ali Mohamed had stayed in his Kenyan home in the mid-1990s as they plotted the bombings. Another agent in Fitzgerald's squad, Dan Coleman, had searched El-Hage's home a year before the bombings and found direct links to Ali Mohamed, and yet Fitzgerald failed to connect the dots. But the viewers of *Triple Cross*—the documentary—never saw any of my evidence that was critical of the Feds, because NGC allowed the story of FBI failures in the Ali Mohamed case to be told from the Bureau's point of view.

It's my belief that the casualty in all of this was the truth. Under the guise of a documentary that NGC claimed was "based in part" on my book, they had perpetrated a factual distortion virtually unprecedented in the recent history of broadcast journalism.

What's the significance of all this? Why is this more than a simple case of a disgruntled writer unhappy about a television adaptation of his work? Because from the start the Nat Geo Channel knew it was buying a documentary that would expose, once and for all, the negligence of the FBI and the Department of Justice on the road to 9/11. It matters because key Feds who covered up probative al Qaeda intelligence in 1996 remain in senior positions at Justice to this day. Most important, as I've discovered after five years of research, the FBI has failed to reform in the wake of 9/11. The Nat Geo documentary gave lip service to the tragic Ali Mohamed story, but failed to provide a single word of critical analysis to help viewers understand how Fitzgerald and Squad I-49 had failed to protect them against bin Laden's principal spy.

Now with this book, I've had a chance to connect the dots and set the record straight.

In my initial interview with Jack Cloonan on May 4, 2006, I was able to get a lot of the truth out of him, though he sugarcoated some of his criticism of the FBI later when he went before the cameras. In our interview, which lasted several hours and ran more than two hundred pages of transcript, Cloonan made one stunning admission to me that Towers Productions never got on tape.

"If you want to do something serious about counterterrorism," he said, "if you have any influence on Congress, tell them to take it away from the FBI. Bottom line."

I asked him why and he looked me straight in the eye.

"Because the culture is such that we just don't do it well. Yes, we've enjoyed some successes in the criminal process, but we were horrible at predictive analysis. The director, I suppose, and others are trying to recast the

Bureau as a domestic intelligence agency. [But] there is such a problem with leadership, and there has been for years."

With those few words, Jack Cloonan, the FBI's expert on Ali Mohamed and a veteran of I-49, the elite bin Laden squad, had summed it up: if Americans want to have an effective domestic counterterrorism system and thwart the al Qaeda threat, then *the FBI should be replaced.* Those aren't my words; they represent the sincere belief of a former agent who I believe may well be grappling with feelings of dismay over the FBI's inability to keep America safe while he was on the Bureau's terror watch.

Will We Ever Know the Full Truth?

We certainly know more of it now. The Ali Mohamed story offers a stunning illustration of how often the FBI and DOJ dropped the ball in underestimating the al Qaeda threat. The findings of the Able Danger team underscored the connections between al Qaeda's leadership and the Yousef/Rahman New York cell, and reinforced evidence disclosed by the Justice Department's own inspector general that the Feds should have had plenty of advance warning about the presence in the United States of key hijackers like al-Midhar and al-Hazmi in early 2000, more than a year and a half before the 9/11 attacks.

But on September 18, 2006, the inspector general for the Department of Defense told the Able Danger story another way. In a heavily redacted ninety-page report, the IG rejected claims by Lt. Col. Anthony Shaffer, Navy Capt. Scott Phillpott, and Congressman Curt Weldon that the Able Danger unit had tracked those two muscle hijackers, along with Marwan al-Shehhi and Mohammed Atta, prior to 9/11.

"We concluded that prior to Sept. 11, 2001, Able Danger team members did not identify Mohammed Atta or any other 9/11 hijackers," the report stated. "While we interviewed four witnesses who claimed to have seen a chart depicting . . . Atta and possibly other terrorists or 'cells' involved in 9/11, we determined that their recollections were not accurate."[3]

Further, the report concluded that "DIA officials did not reprise against LTC Shaffer, in either his civilian or military capacity, for making disclosures regarding Able Danger."

Reaction from Congressman Weldon was swift.

"The DOD IG cherry picked testimony from witnesses in an effort to minimize the historical importance of the Able Danger effort," said Weldon. "The IG narrowly focused their investigation on the witnesses' recollections of the 9/11 hijackers and a chart. The report trashes the reputations of military officers who had the courage to step forward and put their necks on the line to describe important work they were doing to track al-Qaeda prior to 9/11."[4]

Though the names of most witnesses were redacted, it's clear that the DOD IG's office conducted multiple interviews with Shaffer, Phillpott, and Dr. Eileen Preisser, who worked on the Able Danger team at LIWA and Garland, Texas. While each of them repeatedly insisted they had seen Atta's photo and/or name in the early Able Danger data harvest, the IG's investigators seemed bent on impeaching their accounts.

Potentially the most damaging allegation, singled out in the coverage of the IG's report in the *Washington Post,* had to do with Phillpott's allegedly varying accounts of Atta's picture.

"The report concludes that Philpott may have exaggerated knowing Atta's identity because he supported using Able Danger's techniques to fight terrorism. It shows that while Shaffer has consistently asserted that he believes he saw Atta's photograph, Philpott recanted his initial recollection."[5]

"If you read that *Post* story, it makes it seem like Scott lied," says Mike Kasper, a computer programmer who runs www.abledanger.com, a website dedicated to the scandal. "But when you study the report, you can see that Capt. Phillpott never denied seeing Atta's picture."

"In fact," says Congressman Weldon, "the IG's investigators came at Scott and Eileen Preisser more times than detectives would confront a suspect in an episode of *Law & Order.* They kept trying to get them caught up in inconsistent statements, but in the end, Capt. Phillpott said he saw Atta."

On page 18 of the report, there's a direct quote from Phillpott, who was to receive a new naval command at the time of the IG's investigation.

This is what he says after the IG's investigators have informed him that he's "changed his story":

> Well, I mean, obviously there's a compelling amount of evidence that would *make it appear* that I did not see Mohammed Atta. And I will absolutely grant you that based on what you're showing me, my recollection could have been wrong. But I still need to stress that *if I told you that I didn't think I saw Mohammed Atta's face, that in fact would be lying. . . . I honestly believe I saw Atta on the chart.* [emphasis added]

It's also clear that, in attempting to impeach Capt. Phillpott, the IG relied heavily on the word of Dietrich Snell, the 9/11 Commission senior counsel, who found Phillpott's account of the Able Danger findings "not sufficiently reliable to warrant revision of the [Commission] report or further investigation." That was Snell's conclusion following a July 12, 2004, meeting with Phillpott ten days before the Commission's "final report" was to go to press:

> We considered Mr. Snell's negative assessment of Capt. Phillpott's claims particularly persuasive given Mr. Snell's knowledge and background in antiterrorist efforts involving al Qaeda. Mr. Snell considered Capt. Phillpott's recollection with respect to Able Danger's identification of Mohammed Atta inaccurate because it was 'one hundred per cent inconsistent with everything we knew about Mohammed Atta and his colleagues at the time.' Mr. Snell went on to describe his knowledge of Mohammed Atta's overseas travel and associations before 9/11 noting the "utter absence of any information suggesting any kind of a tie between Atta and anyone located in this country during the first half of the year 2000," when Able Danger had allegedly identified him.

But in this book we've demonstrated that there was *massive* evidence on the high visibility of 9/11 hijackers al-Midhar and al-Hazmi, who were living openly in San Diego as early as January 2000. We showed how Atta himself entered the United States on June 3 and rented a room in Brooklyn near the Al Farooq Mosque, using his own name. Just how difficult would it have been for the Able Danger analysts to track his movements via airline reservations and immigration sources, since, according to the IG's report, the Able Danger data harvest was "collecting data from 10,000 websites each day"?

In an interview following release of the report, one operative close to the data-mining operation told me that "we also accessed INS databases in the data harvest, so picking up Atta who had to get airline tickets and a visa prior to his arrival in early June was no big deal."[6]

There's further evidence to assess the credibility of the IG's report.

It documents an expenditure of upwards of $1 million to fund the Able Danger operation when it moved from LIWA at Fort Belvoir, Virginia, to Garland, Texas, in the summer of 2000. The first appropriation signed off on by SOCOM was for $750,000; then, that fall, General Pete Schoomaker, the chief of SOCOM, was encouraged enough by the hits the team was getting that he approved another quarter million for an additional month. Yet the IG's report characterizes the data-mining operation as little more than "a proof of concept for data mining," lacking in any significant intelligence results.

Quoting an unnamed colonel, the report concludes that "in terms of . . . identifying al Qaeda and analyzing its vulnerabilities, the team was only '30 percent successful' and 'it was not validated.' " Another official is quoted as saying "We didn't get the mission accomplished."

"So what I want to know," says Weldon, "as a lawmaker with some oversight on Pentagon spending . . . if this program was so worthless, why did SOCOM spend a million dollars on it in a matter of a few months?"

Perhaps the most insidious aspect of the DOD report was its characterization of Lt. Col. Anthony Shaffer as "basically the delivery boy" for DIA on the Able Danger project. Shaffer was also described in the report as "minimally qualified" at HUMINT (human intelligence).

Yet a cursory examination of Shaffer's service record shows that he spent more than twenty-two years of his army career as a human intelligence officer. His decorations for HUMINT work include the Joint Commendation Medal, the Defense Meritorious Service Medal, and the Bronze Star. From 1993 to 1995, Shaffer was actually the chief of army-controlled HUMINT operations—in effect, the army's top human intelligence officer.* In his civilian capacity, Shaffer was selected as part of the Exceptional Intelligence Professional Program in 1998 for promotion to

---

*Controlled is a military term for "clandestine."

GS-14 by Lt. Gen. Patrick Hughes, director of the Defense Intelligence Agency. Only ten intelligence operatives out of a pool of ten thousand were selected for this highly competitive program.[7]

During the fall of 2003, Shaffer, then an army major, risked his life repeatedly after entering Afghanistan as part of Task Force 180, a clandestine operation to hunt down members of the Taliban. The commendation attached to his Bronze Star, which was awarded to him in secret, says:

> Major Shaffer had a major impact on Operation Mountain Viper, during which his actions contributed to TF-180 killing or capturing more than 100 Taliban fighters. He prepared, coordinated and successfully implemented a complex HUMINT collection plan in support of TF-180 decision operations. Maj. Shaffer participated in more than 20 SIGINT* reconnaissance missions in and around the Kabul area of operations, serving as the mission commander on the vast majority. His skill, leadership, tireless efforts and unfailing dedication were instrumental to the success of TF-180's mission and the continued strategic success of Operation Enduring Freedom. His performance reflects great credit upon him, TF-180, the U.S. Army and the Department of Defense.[8]

Another important measure of Shaffer's credibility is the fact that, in the midst of the Able Danger scandal, he was promoted from major to lieutenant colonel by the army and he remains on active duty today.

The report also denies that Shaffer ever worked to set up meetings between DIA brass and the FBI in the year 2000. But according to Weldon, "The FBI agent that was tasked with setting up meetings between Able Danger and FBI officials—was not interviewed in this Report."

The inspector general's report also denied that anyone in the Pentagon took retaliatory action against Shaffer, but Weldon says, "The I.G. never interviewed Wolf Blitzer [of CNN] or Brian Bennett [of *Time*] who both called my staff and said that DOD officials were spreading personal rumors about Shaffer to discredit him."[9] The report was supposed to include a full investigation of the three petty charges against Shaffer. But twenty-five pages on that issue, constituting more than one quarter of the report, have been entirely redacted or blacked out.

---

*According to the NSA's own website: "Signals Intelligence is technical and intelligence information derived from the exploitation of foreign electronic emissions which is comprised either individually or in combination of communications intelligence (COMINT), electronic intelligence (ELINT), and foreign instrumentation signals intelligence (FISINT)."

In support of Weldon's charge that the IG's investigators "cherry picked" evidence, the report seizes on a link chart entitled "The al Qaeda Network: Snapshots of Typical Operational Cells Associated with UBL," concluding that this was the chart that Shaffer and Phillpott had referred to as containing a picture of Mohammed Atta.

The chart on page eight of the DOD report appears to be identical in form to those created by Jacob L. Boesen, the contract employee from Orion Scientific who had worked with the FDNY's Ronnie Bucca at DIAC. As mentioned, Boesen sent me a number of charts, including the August 10, 1999, link chart reproduced as Appendix VIII, and the March 21, 2000, chart also reproduced as Appendix VIII.

"The I.G. set up this chart as the straw dog to knock down," says Weldon, "when in fact there were many, many Able Danger charts over the many months of its two incarnations. Just because this report says they couldn't find any evidence doesn't mean the evidence didn't exist. Remember, at the heart of this scandal was the destruction of massive amounts of data."[10]

On that issue, the report also claims that the destruction of the 2.5 terabytes of data "was carried out to comply with the ninety day limit imposed by DOD 5240.1-R [the Pentagon's embodiment of Executive Order 12333]. But the report doesn't contain a word about the two key 'U.S. person' exceptions to EO 12333 for open source and terrorism-related data."

"Just like the 9/11 Commission," says Mike Kasper, "the Inspector General knew the conclusions he wanted to reach and only looked for information that fit those conclusions.[11] Instead of investigating retaliation against members of the Able Danger team who have spoken out, the IG accuses Eileen Preisser, Scott Phillpott, and Tony Shaffer of inventing the story about Mohammed Atta in order to advance their personal agendas or their careers. That makes no sense. Each of them has been damaged because they had the guts to come forward about this."

Kasper has dug deeper into the details of the Able Danger scandal than most national security reporters, but the media coverage of the IG's report was universally pro-DOD. William A. Arkin, who writes a column on Homeland Security for the *Washington Post*, was typical:

The IG Report shows, however gingerly and circumspectly, that a principal public face of Able Danger, an Army reserve lieutenant colonel named Anthony Shaffer, who has worked in a variety of Defense Intelligence Agency "special" and secret projects as an officer on active duty and as a civilian, exaggerated, lied and possibly worse. Shaffer, who is shown in the IG's report to be peripheral to the Able Danger effort and less knowledgeable than he claims, also is shown to have a selective and inconsistent memory.[12]

"It's frankly outrageous," says Weldon, "that the IG's report would seek to attack the credibility of the Able Danger program by trashing the service record of an officer like Tony Shaffer. Even worse, that a columnist in a paper as widely read as the *Washington Post* would buy the IG's line hook, line and sinker."

It seems appropriate that Lt. Col. Shaffer, the man most maligned by the IG's report, should get the last word. This is what he told me in an interview on September 25:

> It is now clear that the DOD IG did not intend to conduct an investigation to seek the truth. Instead they acted to support the DOD bureaucracy's official party line that we did not ID Atta before the 9/11 attacks, and even if we had him in our database, it meant nothing.
>
> To support their findings they selectively interrogated witnesses. The DOD IG had obtained all the factual information they needed to prepare an accurate report by the spring of this year [2006]. But over the next six months, they spent time working to re-interview and intimidate witnesses to change their stories or to create information to undermine and discredit witnesses. It will be clear to any lay reader who looks at the report, that they excluded any information supporting our position while attempting to discredit those who came forward as "unreliable." The DOD IG ignored all classified information and testimony conducted in the closed hearings before the House Armed Services Committee in February. Not one bit of evidence from that hearing that supported our statements was referenced in the DOD's report.

Why This *Really* Matters

The Department of Defense controls some 80 percent of the U.S. intelligence budget.[13] The DOD asserted that level of dominance *beore* the 9/11 attacks and it has retained that same percentage in the five years *since,* despite the creation of a National Intelligence

Directorate in February 2005; one of the key recommendations of the 9/11 Commission.[14]

For years, as we've reported, the "war on terror" was fought as a series of criminal cases in the SDNY. But there's little doubt that today it's being defined almost exclusively in military terms.

In his prime time address on the fifth anniversary of 9/11, President Bush asserted that the United States was "engaged in a struggle for civilization," and he tied the security of this nation *directly* to the war in Iraq. "The safety of America depends," he asserted, "on the outcome of the battle in the streets of Baghdad."[15]

In these closing pages, we'll undertake a brief overview on the status of the military engagement in Iraq. But first, it's important to recall how we got there.

Beginning almost immediately after the 9/11 attacks, and in the eighteen months leading up to the invasion in March 2003, the Bush administration repeatedly cited two primary justifications for military intervention against Saddam Hussein: first, that there was a direct link tying the Iraqi dictator to the attacks of 9/11, and second, that he possessed weapons of mass destruction that would threaten not only America's allies in the region, but the U.S. homeland as well.

On the first issue, *Washington Post* managing editor Bob Woodward quoted former deputy defense secretary Paul D. Wolfowitz, chief advocate for the administration's get-tough policy on Iraq, as insisting that "There was a 10 percent to 50 percent chance Saddam was involved" in the 9/11 attacks.[16] A Fox News poll prior to the invasion found that 81 percent of those questioned "believe Saddam has ties to the al Qaeda terrorist group."[17]

On the issue of WMDs, President Bush alleged in an October 2002 speech that Saddam Hussein's government posed an immediate threat to the United States, and that Iraq had trained al Qaeda members "in bomb making and poisons and deadly gases."[18]

Declaring that "Iraq could decide on any given day to provide a biological or chemical weapon to a terrorist group," Bush insisted that "alliance with terrorists could allow the Iraqi regime to attack America without leaving any fingerprints."

In the weeks leading up to the invasion, as the administration sought consensus from the American people, both the White House and the Department of Homeland Security ratcheted up their public warnings about terrorism. In early February 2003, days after alleging links between Saddam and al Qaeda, U.S. intelligence officials began warning citizens that bin Laden's network might be in possession of "dirty bombs" encased in radioactive waste.[19] On February 7, former Homeland Security secretary Tom Ridge raised the terrorism Threat Advisory from yellow to orange, signaling a high risk of terrorist attacks.[20] Later, Ridge advised Americans to put together emergency supply kits that included a three-day supply of water, flashlights, and duct tape to seal doors and windows in the event of a radiological or biological attack.[21]

In a speech at FBI Headquarters, President Bush said, "We're trying to protect you. We're doing everything in our power to make sure the homeland is secure." Intelligence officials quoted at the time said they had identified six hundred to one thousand potential al Qaeda terrorists in cells around the United States.[22] Later, in answer to reporters' questions linking the al Qaeda threat to the impending Iraq invasion, Defense Secretary Donald Rumsfeld said, "Why now? The answer is that every week that goes by, [Saddam's] weapons of mass destruction programs become more mature [and] he has relationships with terrorist networks."[23]

A *Los Angeles Times* piece quoted supporters and critics of the potential Baghdad attack: "Of all the charges the United States has made, the most hotly debated are those linking Iraq and the al Qaeda network," the story said. "Without such a connection, the logic of invading Iraq as a response to September 11th seems weak to many Americans."[24]

Yet in his presentation to the UN Security Council on February 5, Secretary of State Colin Powell failed to produce any compelling proof that Baghdad was even remotely connected to the 9/11 attacks. Powell pointed to a suspected al Qaeda terror camp located near Kurdish-held northern Iraq.[25] Contending that the facility trained al Qaeda operatives to carry out attacks with explosives and poisons, Powell insisted that there was a "sinister nexus between Iraq and the al Qaeda terror network."[26]

That was the case for war. But in the previous five years, the State Department's own website had mentioned *nothing* about a threat to the U.S.

homeland from Iraq,[27] and according to the BBC, a classified British intelligence report showed no links between al Qaeda and the Iraqi regime.[28] By October 2004, the chief U.S. weapons inspector concluded that Iraq's nuclear capability had decayed, not grown, since the 1991 Gulf War that left Hussein in power.[29]

As to the alleged 9/11 link, as recently as August 21, 2006, Mr. Bush said that Saddam Hussein "had relations with [Abu Musab al-] Zarkawi," the late leader of al Qaeda in Iraq, killed on June 7.[30] But a CIA report completed in October 2005, and released by the Senate Intelligence Committee September 8, concluded that Hussein's government "did not have a relationship with, harbor or even turn a blind eye toward Zarkawi and his associates."[31]

Intelligence Committee ranking member Carl Levin, a Michigan Democrat, called the report "a devastating indictment of the Bush-Cheney administration's unrelenting, misleading and deceptive attempts to convince the American people that Saddam Hussein was linked with al Qaeda, the perpetrators of the 9/11 attacks."[32]

The Brink of Civil War

More than three and a half years after President Bush flew onto the deck of the U.S.S. *Abraham Lincoln* and stood under a banner that read "Mission Accomplished,"[33] Iraq teeters on the edge of civil war. The statistics are numbing:

- During the first six months of 2006, the civilian death toll from sectarian violence jumped more than 77 percent, from 1,778 in January to 3,149 in June. Some 14,338 civilians died violently in Iraq in the first half of this year according to UN statistics.[34]

- The violent death count in Bagdhad was particularly critical. While Iraqis across the country were being killed at the rate of 100 per day, an average of half had died in the capital, where the U.S. and coalition forces have the most troop strength.[35]

- In July 2006, the number of roadside bombs directed at U.S. forces in Iraq rose to the highest monthly total of the war, galvanizing evidence that the anti-American insurgency has only strengthened since the killing of Abu Musab al-Zarkawi. In July, 2,625 explosive devices were found, compared to 1,454 in January.[36]

- The death rate among U.S. troops has risen steadily, from 486 in 2003 to 559 by October 7, 2006, a total of 2,739. Casualties since the invasion have more than doubled.[37]

- On October 2, 2006, eight U.S. GI's were killed in Baghdad, the most in the capital in one day since July 2005.

- The death toll increase among coalition troops in Afghanistan is equally disheartening, up to 166 by early October 2006, compared to 12 in 2001, the year U.S. forces first landed in Kabul to root out the Taliban.[38]

- Meanwhile, the radical Islamic sect that had harbored Osama bin Laden for so many years in Afghanistan is enjoying a frightening resurgence, coupled with an explosion of drug cultivation. Across Afghanistan, roadside bomb attacks are up by 30 percent and suicide bombings have doubled.[39] The opium harvest this year reached the highest level ever recorded—an increase of 50 percent from last year, according to the UN's office on Drugs and Crime—signaling a potential worldwide heroin epidemic unseen since the Taliban were routed in the weeks following 9/11.[40]

- Multiple U.S. presidential administrations have failed to understand the Afghan Islamic terror threat. One of the prime examples is the re-emergence of Gulbuddin Hekmatyar, a Pashtun warlord with strong Pakistani connections. Having served twice as Afghan prime minister in the 1990s, Hekmatyar was the primary conduit for CIA covert aid during the war against the Soviets and a close associate of Sheikh Omar Abdel Rahman. In May 2005, a woman and her two daughters were beaten to death by his military faction, the Hezb al Islami. A letter found with their bodies said that the women had been murdered for their "whoredom."[41]

• Known as "Mr. Blowback" by some intelligence analysts,[42] Hekmatyar has joined forces with the Taliban leader Mullah Omar. Proving the old French saying *"Plus ça change, plus c'est la même chose."** Omar is believed to be holed up in Quetta, the Baluchistani capital that is Ramzi Yousef's hometown.[43] That the one-eyed Taliban leader is still on the loose is another example of the weakness of the intelligence communicated to Special Agent Jack Cloonan by Ali Mohamed—who gave details on Mullah Omar's whereabouts to the chief HUMINT officer from Delta Force in the weeks following the 9/11 attacks.[44]

• Meanwhile, a September 5 Pakistani cease-fire agreement signed with a series of pro-Taliban tribesman in semi-autonomous North Waziristan put pressure on the White House[45] as President Bush attempted to broker cooperation between Pakistani president General Pervez Musharraf and Hamid Karzai, the Afghan president. After a White House dinner in late September, Karzai openly attacked Musharaff, and charged that since his deal with the tribal chiefs, there has been a rise in attacks by Taliban sympathizers across the Pakistani border into Afghanistan of more than 300 percent.[46]

If President Bush is to be believed, and the safety of America is tied to the success of the U.S. military campaign in Iraq, the worst news yet came on September 24, from an unlikely quarter. The National Intelligence Estimate, representing the consensus of sixteen different U.S. spy services, concluded that the American invasion and occupation of Iraq since March 2003 has helped to spawn a new generation of Islamic radicals—effectively *increasing* the terror threat since the attacks of 9/11.[47]

Completed in April 2006, the NIE, as it's known, is the first formal assessment of global terrorism since the start of the Iraq war. Rather than being in *retreat*, as the White House has asserted, the NIE concludes that Islamic radicalism has metastasized and spread worldwide.

As Mark Mazzetti noted as he broke the story in the *New York Times,* "The Estimate's judgments confirm some predictions of a National Intelligence Council report completed in January 2003, two months before the

---

* "The more things change, the more they stay the same."

Iraq invasion," stating that "the approaching war had the potential to increase support for political Islam worldwide and could increase support for some terrorist objectives."[48]

The next day, the retired Maj. General John Batiste, who commanded the 1st Infantry Division in Iraq in 2004 and 2005 and served as an assistant to Paul Wolfowitz, placed the blame squarely on the shoulders of Defense Secretary Donald Rumsfeld.[49] Batiste, who'd called earlier in the year for Rumsfeld to step down, said that the SECDEF had refused to acknowledge the potential for insurgency after the invasion and had forbidden military planners from developing a blueprint for securing Iraq after the war.

"At one point, he threatened to fire the next person who talked about the need for a post-war plan," Batiste said.[50]

So where do we stand as we pass the fifth anniversary of the biggest unsolved mass murder in American history? If Iraq is the key to America's safety, how safe can this country be, given the state of the war? Administration spokesmen are quick to point out that there hasn't been an attack on the U.S. homeland since 9/11. But the assertion that al Qaeda has somehow deteriorated, or that a reform of U.S. intelligence agencies has kept us safer, recalls the short-sighted conclusion of FBI counterterrorism chief Dale Watson in 1998, three years before 9/11.

> I believe it is important to note that in the five years since the Trade Center bombing, no significant act of foreign directed terrorism has occurred on American soil.[51]

We know what the *costs* of the Iraqi invasion have been to U.S. forces and our treasury. What about the *benefits*? We have succeeded in creating a new, democratically elected government in Baghdad. But it is dominated by Shiites, who support our enemy, Iran. Saddam Hussein has been captured and put on trial, but his legal proceedings, now entering their second year, have given him a worldwide television platform to spout vitriolic condemnations of America, unlike any media access he commanded as an isolated despot. Meanwhile, anti-American resentment has grown to widespread hatred among many in the Iraqi civilian population, even as inflation in that country soars.

The cost of electricity in Iraq is up 270 percent from last year. The frail Iraqi national power grid produces electricity, at best, only six hours a day.[52] The very act of shopping for groceries, or sending one's children to school, can prove fatal as sectarian violence escalates against the common people. At the same time, unemployment is estimated at between 40 to 60 percent.[53] In the third richest oil nation on earth, the cost of a gallon of gasoline is up from $1.25 to $3.19—a price many Californians might envy, as America, too, grows weary of the way the Bush administration has conducted the terror war.

By late July 2006, 62 percent of those polled in the United States said that they disapproved of the way the president was handling the Iraqi situation.[54] In a poll of U.S. adults released September 25, 2006, 55 percent of respondents said that Iraq was not worth going to war over. Sixty-three percent of those questioned believed that neither side was winning.[55]

A Way Out

After five years of studying the intelligence failures on the road to 9/11 and beyond, I've come to believe that Americans have reached a state of numbness—a kind of cynical paralysis grounded in the belief that they will never know the real truth behind 9/11. After the whitewashes described in this book by the 9/11 Commission, the recent DOD IG's report—even the National Geographic Channel's documentary on my own work—it's easy to understand how the average citizen might feel hopeless about ever solving that cold case. But the first step toward a new examination of the crime is a push for accountability. The 9/11 Commission utterly failed on that point. In this investigation, by contrast, we have named names.

If the lawyers of the Brooklyn D.A.'s office persist in their prosecution of former Supervisory Special Agent Lin DeVecchio, and if that case is not removed to federal court—where it will very likely be buried—they will have the opportunity to shine a new light on the credibility of Greg Scarpa Jr. If the son of the "killing machine" can survive in the general population of the Supermax, and eventually get out to testify freely about what he learned from Ramzi Yousef in 1996, then a number of Justice Department and FBI officials will feel the pressure to come clean.

Will a legendary former FBI ADIC like James Kallstrom, now a vice president at MBNA in Delaware, fall on his sword if he's held accountable for burying that Scarpa Jr. intel? I don't think so. Nor will FBI general counsel Valerie Caproni or deputy New York attorney general Dietrich Snell. Will any of them go down without implicating a higher DOJ or FBI official?

And what of the man who became the second focus of this book, Patrick Fitzgerald? Will this son of Irish immigrants, who now holds the fate of Karl Rove in his hands, finally tell the truth about Ali Mohamed? Will a full vetting of the Mohamed story lead to a vindication of the Able Danger operatives?

And what of "Ali the American" himself? As he sits somewhere in custodial Witness Protection, will Mohamed ever see the light of day? He's a one-man 9/11 Commission, with more knowledge of how the FBI blew it on the road to September 11 than perhaps any senior operative of al Qaeda. Will he ever be persuaded to talk freely, or will he remain loyal to bin Laden, al-Zawahiri, and the jihad?

Back to Memorial Park

After five years, I decided to end this investigation where it began. In early 2002, Louis F. Garcia, the chief fire marshal of the FDNY, took me down to a kind of chilling graveyard tucked behind Bellevue Hospital, along the East River in Manhattan. In those days, months after the 9/11 attacks, there was still a series of makeshift morgue tables set up outside the office of New York's chief medical examiner across the street. I described that eerie place in the introduction to *1000 Years for Revenge:*

> It was a large, three-story-high white temporary structure tucked down behind Bellevue Hospital and the FDR drive. The structure was surrounded by a high fence topped with the flags of a dozen municipal and law enforcement agencies. There was a large garage door at one end of the structure. Inside, the floor was cov-

ered with green astro turf. An enormous American flag hung from a rafter over-head. Backed into the east and west sides of the structure were eight enormous white refrigerated trailers. Each had a small set of wooden stairs leading up to its back doors. The stairs were surrounded by dozens of funeral wreathes and standing bouquets of flowers. The trucks were covered with purple and black mourning crepe. Along the sides of the trailers, visitors had written their goodbyes: "Our hearts are crying," wrote one. "You're my heroes," wrote another. "No greater love than he who laid down his life, John 15:13" wrote a third. A detective named Moran had written, "God bless all my brothers." When I realized what this was, I stepped back. All I could say to Chief Garcia was, "My God . . ." We were standing inside an enormous makeshift mortuary. In each of those trucks were the 11,000 body parts of the World Trade Center 9/11 victims who had not yet been identi-fied. Each one had been assigned a DM (De Mort) number by the Medical Exam-iner's office in the hope that eventually through DNA comparison, the victims might be ID'd.

On the day I finished the principal reporting for this book I went back there. The flags around the perimeter of the fence are gone now. There are only three climate-controlled trucks left, but the number of unidentified body parts has actually grown to 13,790. A chapel has been created with an altar-like fountain and the big white temporary structure has turned grey on the outside from the city's soot. In perhaps the saddest statistic of all, only 1,598 of the 2,749 New York victims have been identified and laid to rest. The remainder—some 42 percent—stay here, locked in a state of perpetual anonymity. But that huge American flag still hangs from the rafters, a kind of sentinel guarding the dead. To me it symbolizes hope—that undying quality in the American spirit that demands justice, account-ability, and the truth.

For the sake of Ronnie Bucca, Louie Garcia's good friend, and for the sake of every man, woman, and child who died that day, the cold case of 9/11 needs to be reopened, and investigated with tenacity and courage. There has never been a crime in the history of this nation that deserves clearance more than the mass murders of September 11, 2001.

I sincerely hope this is my last 9/11 book. I don't want to have to write another one.

ACKNOWLEDGMENTS

Any investigative book on the subject of national security has the potential of being volatile; especially in a politically charged era like this. As the decision of the National Geographic Channel to bury my findings illustrates, it takes an executive with courage to publish a work that is critical of the Justice Department and the FBI. Fortunately, with this, my third book for her division at HarperCollins, I've got Judith Regan as a publisher. Not known for backing down in the face of controversy, she's the kind of publisher you want to have at your side if you're about to enter a war zone.

But without the two editors who sustain her company, Cal Morgan and Cassie Jones, this epic story of Ali Mohamed would never have seen print. This book, delayed due to the National Geographic controversy, was a bear to publish because I wanted to make sure that we could update the illustrated timeline that first appeared in *1000 Years for Revenge*. Allowing the reader a guide as they move through the story with so many twists, turns, and complicated names, the timeline was a mini-book in itself and Cal and Cassie, along with production editor Donna Lee Lurker and Cal's able assistant, Rachel Berk, produced it with the same level of professionalism they brought to the manuscript itself.

In a story that hinges on multiple legal issues, I have a number of attorneys to thank and for varied reasons. For the third time I've had the privilege of working with John Pelosi, who ensured that the narrative was factually bulletproof. Merril Sobie and John Moncrief assisted me with collateral issues that helped speed the writing.

Larry Stein and Bennett Bigman came in like white knights on another matter relating to an earlier work, and their tenacity yielded me the resources to see this book through to completion. I also want to single out Steve Kravit, the principal attorney at the Gersh Agency, and my longtime friend and agent Richard Arlook, whose assistant Eric Garfinkel did me a favor that literally helped to fund my research. And I want to extend a special thanks to Kevin Reilly at NBC, who has believed in my work for years.

John Berger and Paul Thompson, whom I've cited multiple times in the body of the book, brought a depth and breadth to my search for Ali Mohamed. Phyllis Reed did an early copy edit of the manuscript that was invaluable. She also provided a steady flow of open-source research over the past eighteen months.

Court reporters Sara Stanley and Joyce Fisher were the key to helping me assemble the Nosair trial transcript, along with Barbara Thompson of the Manhattan D.A.'s office.

Joe Murphy and Tim Gilman offered investigative help at key junctures in the process, as did A.J. Weberman, a natural-born detective who was key to unlocking many documents buried in the vaults in the Southern District of New York.

At one point my daughter Mallory spent hours with me in the clerk's office at 100 Centre Street feeding quarters into a primitive copy machine so that I could get the complete file on El Sayyid Nosair. She and her sister Ali helped me to organize the four-inch-thick binders of research that have now grown in number to forty-nine.

Jay Zeibarth, a brilliant animator and artist based in Toronto, deserves special thanks for maintaining my website over the past few years, and now that he's broken out and risen to new heights in the Great White North, Andrew Heuchert has redefined the site in a way that will allow me to make it more responsive to breaking news.

Eve Bucca and her children Jessica and Ronnie have remained a constant source of inspiration for me as they cope with the loss of "Big Ronnie" five years after 9/11. I kept a copy of his mass card on the wall next to my desk and did my best to channel his spirit each morning as I began to write.

Monica Gabrielle, whose husband Rich perished along with Ronnie in the South Tower that day and who worked with the Jersey Girls to push the 9/11 Commission into being, is another person who has helped to charge me as I sought to tell this story.

As I look back on the genesis of these three books, Maria Ressa, the former Manila bureau chief for CNN, deserves great thanks. She's the remarkable reporter who filed one of the first stories, September 18, 2001, on Col. Rodolfo Mendoza and how his interrogation of Abdul Hakim Murad might have led the U.S. Feds to the "planes-as-missiles" plot as early as 1995.

I'd like to acknowledge the great work on the Greg Scarpa Jr. story done by Angela Clemente and her late partner Dr. Stephen Dresch, who passed away far too early this past summer. Angela deserves credit for the opening of the Brooklyn D.A.'s investigation into Lin DeVecchio, more than any single citizen outside of government.

As I said in the preface, we stand on the shoulders of giants, and it was the great investigative work of reporters for the *New York Times, San Francisco Chronicle, Raleigh News & Observer, Wall Street Journal,* Associated Press, and *Chicago Tribune* who first began to draw the profile of the enigma named Ali Mohamed.

But in this book, the culmination of five years of investigative work, I'd like to reach back and acknowledge the great teachers, journalists, editors, and producers who helped to send me on my way as a reporter.

First, Gardner Dunton, the former bureau chief of the *Providence Journal-Bulletin* in my hometown of Newport, Rhode Island. As a paperboy, I would sit on the steps of my front porch folding copies of the paper each night for delivery, and Gardner would stop by on his way home to discuss the day's headlines with me. John Smith, my English teacher at Thompson Jr. High School in Newport, was the first to recognize that I could put words together.

In my first job as a cub reporter for the *Newport Daily News,* James G. Edwards taught me how to write a "five point lead." He also backed me when I had the audacity at the age of twenty to write my first investigative series—an exposé of slum housing called "Newport's Back Yard."

Later, while a student at Northeastern University, the adjunct professor who introduced me to broadcasting was Joseph R. Bailer, a man with the strongest work ethic of anyone I've encountered before or since. Professor Robert Cord, the poli-sci legend at Northeastern, gave me a deep respect for the U.S. Constitution and a healthy skepticism for officials who abuse their power. Dean Christopher Trump saw something in the pile of clippings that I would bring down to New York to show him each June, and he saw fit to allow me into the Journalism School at Columbia. There I had the amazing luck of drawing the great Fred W. Friendly as my adviser. He was a man of boundless enthusiasm and ethics of whom it was said, "He has five hundred ideas a day, and half of them are great ones."

The man who gave me my first real job in broadcasting was Jack Willis, then the program director at WNET, the PBS flagship in New York. He'd seen a couple of short films that I'd helped to "produce" for *The Great American Dream Machine* and took me on at $250.00 a week. The real auteur behind those 16-millimeter stories was Ron Finley, a writer, director, photographer, illustrator, and animator—truly a renaissance man. He and his wife Jean have been responsible for some of the most inspiring moments in my life, and although I had lost touch with them over the past few years, Ron was kind enough to take the photo for the jacket of this book.

At *ABC News* my two real mentors were Av Westin, who gave me my first on-camera job on *20/20*, and Bill Lord, who taught me what it took to be a correspondent when I worked for him on *Nightline*. But the great inspiration for me at 7 West 66th Street in those days was the late Roone Arledge, the broadcast icon who created much of live news and sports coverage as we know it. Few people realized it outside of the news division, but he was a real champion of investigative reporting, and even when the heat came down from the White House or some other federal agency, he always backed my play. An extraordinary new broadcast lab at Columbia University Graduate School of Journalism was recently opened in his name—so now other young journalists will be inspired.

Investigative reporting is nothing more than reporting when you have the time to do a thorough job. Daily deadline reporting simply doesn't allow a journalist the kind of perspective to connect the dots the way that

I've had the good fortune to do with this book and the two that came before it—all of which focused on the New York office of the FBI.

For most of the narrative I have been highly critical of the Bureau, particularly those officials known to street or brick agents as "management."

But there are a number of special agents for whom I have the highest regard and, as I close, I would like to single them out. The first is Nancy Floyd, who came as close as any FBI agent to derailing the first attack on the World Trade Center. Her mentor Len Predtechenskis, a Latvian émigré who was the first special agent with a "green card" ever to go through Quantico, became one of the top counterterrorism investigators in New York, keeping tabs on the Soviets at the height of the Cold War.

Jim Whalen, an eight-year veteran of the NYO, has helped to keep me up to date on a number of national security issues. Joseph F. O'Brien, a veteran organized crime investigator who tracked "Big Paul" Castellano, is another retired agent who watched my back at a critical time during my first investigation, and to him I'll always be grateful.

Finally, I owe everything that I've become as a reporter to my parents, Joseph and Albina Lance, both now departed. Every night at the dinner table when I was growing up, they would engage my sister Mary and me in a discussion of political issues. They never missed the television coverage of the political conventions or the space shots. My mother always worked at the polls. Election nights were an exciting time for us. Both of them imbued me with a sense of the importance of the political process and the role that a vigorous press should play in it. Mary went on to become a gifted and award-winning documentary film maker, and I've done my best to live up to the dictum of Finley Peter Dunne that it's the role of a newspaper—reporter in this case—"to comfort the afflicted and afflict the comfortable." To that I would add the admonition of Justice Benjamin Cardozo, that "sunlight is the best disinfectant."

I sincerely hope that Patrick Fitzgerald is listening.

NOTES

EPIGRAPH

1 Peter Waldman, Gerald F. Seib, Jerry Markon, and Christopher Cooper, "Sergeant Served U.S. Army and bin Laden, Showing Failings in FBI's Terror Policing," *Wall Street Journal,* November 26, 2001.

2 Steven Emerson, interview for *Triple Cross,* June 7, 2006.

3 Steven Emerson, testimony before Senate Judiciary Committee, December 4, 2001; "Abdullah Azzam: The Man Before Osama bin Laden," http://www.iacsp.com/itobli3.html.

4 Author's interview with Roger L. Stavis, March 17, 2006.

5 FBI special agent Jack Cloonan (ret.), interview for *Triple Cross,* June 1, 2006.

PREFACE

1 "Agent Who Arrested Moussaoui Blasts FBI," *Associated Press,* March 20, 2006.

2 Kate Zernike et al., "Rebuff for Bush on How to Treat Terror Suspects," *New York Times,* September 15, 2006.

3 Mark Mazetti, "C.I.A. Closes Unit Focused on Capture of bin Laden," *New York Times,* July 4, 2006.

4 Dan Eggen, "Bin Laden, Most Wanted for Embassy Bombings?" *Washington Post,* August 28, 2006.

5 In a *New York Times* interview in April 2004, 9/11 commissioner Jamie Gorelick admitted that "the vast preponderance of our work, including with regard to the Department of Justice, focuses on the period of 1998 forward." David E. Rosenbaum, "Threats and Responses: The Commissioners; For Members of Panel, Past Work Becomes an Issue in the Present Hearings," *New York Times,* April 14, 2004.

6 *9/11 Commission Report,* Footnote 116. On 9/11, NORAD was scheduled to conduct a military exercise, Vigilant Guardian, which postulated a bomber attack from the former Soviet Union. We investigated whether military preparations for the large-scale exercise compromised the military's response to the real-world terrorist attack on 9/11. According to General Eberhart, "it took about 30 seconds to make the adjustment to the real-world situation." Ralph Eberhart testimony, June 17, 2004. We found that the response was, if anything, expedited by the increased number of staff at the sectors and at NORAD because of the scheduled exercise. See Robert Marr interview (January 23, 2004). [Author's note: Vigiliant Guardian was one of at least three major war game exercises involving fighter aircraft on September 11.]

7   Mike Kelly, "Atlantic City F-16 Fighters Were Eight Minutes Away from 9/11 Hijacked Planes," *Bergen Record,* December 5, 2003.

8   Peter Lance, *First Degree Burn* (New York: Berkley, 1997).

9   Bob Drury, "Fireman Falls 5 Stories, Lives," *Newsday,* September 17, 1986; Cynthia Fagen, "Hero Fireman's Miracle Land," *New York Post,* September 17, 1986; Vincent Lee and Paul La Rosa, "As He Fell, Firefighter Heard Himself Screaming," New York *Daily News,* September 17, 1986; Vincent Lee and Tony Marcano, New York *Daily News,* September 17, 1986.

10 A *mufti* is an Islamic scholar with the authority to interpret Sharia or Islamic law, issuing *fatwas* (degrees or orders).

11 Peter Lance, *1000 Years for Revenge: International Terrorism and the FBI: The Untold Story* (New York: ReganBooks, 2003).

12 Letter from Gov. Tom Kean to the author, January 19, 2004.

13 9/11 Commission Staff Statement 15.

14 9/11 Commission Staff Statement 16.

15 Peter Lance, *Cover Up: What the Government Is Still Hiding About the War on Terror* (New York: ReganBooks, 2004).

16 *United States v. Ali Mohamed,* S(7) 98 Cr. 1023 (LBS) Sealed Complaint, September 1998. Affidavit of Daniel Coleman, FBI special agent; bin Laden unit, New York office.

17 Steven Emerson, *American Jihad: The Terrorists Living Among Us* (New York: Free Press, 2002).

18 Lance Williams and Erin McCormick, "Bin Laden's Man in Silicon Valley: 'Mohamed the American' Orchestrated Terrorist Acts While Living a Quiet Suburban Life in Santa Clara," *San Francisco Chronicle,* September 21, 2001; Lance Williams and Erin McCormick, "Al Qaeda Terrorist Worked with FBI," *San Francisco Chronicle,* November 11, 2001.

19 Joseph Neff and John Sullivan, "Al Qaeda Terrorist Duped FBI, Army," *Raleigh News and Observer,* October 24, 2001; Joseph Neff and John Sullivan, "An Al Qaeda Operative at Fort Bragg," *Raleigh News and Observer,* November 14, 2001.

20 Tom Hays and Sharen Theimer, "Egyptian Agent Worked with Green Berets, bin Laden," *Associated Press,* December 31, 2001.

21 Jerry Markon, "Zealous Prosecution Is Sure Bet in the Embassy-Bombing Trial," *Wall Street Journal,* January 3, 2001.

22 Andrew Martin and Michael J. Berens, "Terrorists Evolved in U.S. 2 Egyptians Set Stage for Attacks," *Chicago Tribune,* December 11, 2001.

23 Benjamin Weiser, "U.S. Sergeant Linked to bin Laden Conspiracy," *New York Times,* October 30, 1998; Benjamin Weiser, "Informer's Part in Terror Case Is Detailed," *New York Times,* December 22, 2000; Benjamin Weiser and James Risen, "The Masking of a Militant: A Special Report; A Soldier's Shadowy Trail in U.S. and the Mideast," *New York Times,* December 1, 1998; James Risen, "C.I.A. Said to Reject Bomb Suspect's Bid to Be a Spy," *New York Times,* October 31, 1998.

24 Name on Ali Mohamed's U.S. Army enlistment record as of August 15, 1986.

25 Identified by Khalid Ibrahim in testimony during *United States v. Osama bin Laden et al.,* S(7) 98 Cr. 1023 (LBS).

26 Ibid., *United States v. Osama bin Laden et al.,* testimony of L'Houssaine Kherchtou, February 23, 2001.

27 *United States v. Osama bin Laden et al.,* S(7) 98 Cr. 1023 (LBS). Docket.

28 Ibid., *United States v. Osama bin Laden et al.,* testimony of L'Houssaine Kherchtou, February 23, 2001.

29 Superior Court of California, County of Santa Clara, Petition for Name Change, May 14, 1993.

30 *United States v. Omar Abdel Rahman et al.,* S593CR.181 (MBM) testimony of Khalid Ibrahim, July 17, 1995.
31 Ibid., Kerchtou testimony.

PART I

1. THE DEEP BLACK HOLE

1 *United States v. Ali Mohamed,* S(7) 98 Cr. 1023 (LBS), transcript of plea session, U.S. District Court, Southern District of New York, October 20, 2000.
2 http://www.thesmokinggun.com/archive/jihadmanual.html.
3 A derivative of Ali Abul Saoud Mustafa, the name for Ali that surfaced during a 1999 Egyptian trial of 107 terrorists who were also affiliated with either al Qaeda or the Egyptian Islamic Jihad (EIJ), the group led by Dr. Ayman al-Zawahiri. Susan Sachs, "A Nation Challenged: Bin Laden's Allies; An Investigation in Egypt Illustrates Al Qaeda's Web," *New York Times,* November 21, 2001.
    Note: Of the 107 defendants, 43 were on trial and 64 were tried in absentia, including Dr. al-Zawahiri, 48 years old in 1999. It was the second biggest trial of fundamentalist organizations in Egypt since the Jihad Organization Trial of 1981 that followed the assassination of Anwar Sadat. The trial took place at the Higher Military Court at Haekstep base north of Cairo. See Khaild Sharaf-al-Din, "Surprises in the Trial of the Largest International Fundamentalist Organization in Egypt. Abu-al-Dahab: My Mission Was to Attack the Turah Prison After Dropping a Bomb from a Glider," *Al-Sharq al-Awsat,* March 6, 1999, FBIS translation from Arabic.
4 As we'll see, bin Laden achieved that goal after the invasion of Iraq in 2003 when the last remaining troops stationed in Saudi Arabia were withdrawn.
5 Author's interview with FBI special agent Jack Cloonan (ret.), May 4, 2006.
6 Steven Emerson, "Abdullah Assam: The Man Before Osama bin Laden," *Journal of Counterterrorism and Security International* vol. 5, no. 3, Fall 1998.
7 Lt. Col. Robert Anderson, U.S. Army (ret.), interview for *Triple Cross,* June 6, 2006.
8 Author's interview with confidential FBI source.
9 Steven Emerson, interview for *Triple Cross,* June 7, 2006.
10 Author's interview with Linda Sanchez, March 27, 2006.
11 Ibid., May 5, 2005.
12 Lance Williams and Erin McCormick, "Al Qaeda Terrorist Worked with FBI," *San Francisco Chronicle,* November 11, 2001.
13 Benjamin Weiser and James Risen, "The Masking of a Militant: A Special Report. A Soldier's Shadowy Trail in U.S. and the Mideast," *New York Times,* December 1, 1998.
14 Daniel Benjamin and Steven Simon, *The Age of Sacred Terror* (New York: Random House, 2002), pp. 82–83.
15 Yousef H. Aboul-Enein, "Islamic Militant Cells and Sadat's Assassination," *Military Review,* July–August 2004.
16 Ibid., Benjamin and Simon.
17 Michael Scheuer, *Through Our Enemies' Eyes* (Washington, D.C.: Brassey's, 2002), p. 270.
18 CNN.com, "Egyptian Doctor Emerges as Terror Mastermind," http://www.cnn.com/CNN/Programs/people/shows/zawahiri/profile.htm.
19 His aliases included: Abu Muhammad, Abu Fatima, Muhammad Ibrahim, Abu Abdallah, Abu al-Mu'iz, The Doctor, The Teacher, Nur, Ustaz, Abu Mohammed, Abu Mohammed Nur al-Deen, Abdel Muaz, http://www.fbi.gov/wanted/terrorists/teralzawahiri.htm.
20 Mary B. W. Tabor, "Slaying in Brooklyn Linked to Militants," *New York Times,* April 11, 1993.

21 Lance Williams, "Bin Laden's Bay Area Recruiter," *San Francisco Chronicle,* November 21, 2001.

22 Author's interview with FBI special agent Jack Cloonan (ret.), May 4, 2006.

23 Author's interview with confidential State Department source.

24 Joseph Neff and John Sullivan, "Al Qaeda Terrorist Duped FBI, Army," *Raleigh News and Observer,* October 24, 2001.

25 Ibid., Weiser.

26 Peter Waldman, Gerald F. Seib, and Jerry Markon, "Sergeant Served U.S. Army and bin Laden, Showing Failings in FBI's Terror Policing," *Wall Street Journal,* November 11, 2001.

27 Author's interview with Linda Sanchez, March 27, 2006.

28 Ibid., Neff and Sullivan.

29 Ibid.,Waldman et al.

30 Benjamin Weiser, "U.S. Sergeant Linked to bin Laden Conspiracy," *New York Times,* October 30, 1998.

31 Ibid., Cloonan, May 4, 2006.

32 Ibid., Cloonan.

2. A COMPANY JOB

1 "Remembering Bob Ames," *CBS News,* April 17, 2003.

2 CNN.com, "Iran Responsible for 1983 Marine Barracks Bombing, Judge Rules," 2003.

3 Author's interview with FBI special agent Jack Cloonan (ret.), May 4, 2006.

4 Sarah Baxter, "Iran's President Recruits Terror Master," *Sunday Times,* April 23, 2006.

5 Dana Priest and Douglas Farah, "Terror Alliance Has U.S. Worried: Hezbollah, Al Qaeda Seen Joining Forces," *Washington Post,* June 30, 2002.

6 Clifford Krauss, "2 Hostages, Slain in Beirut, Are Buried in U.S.," *New York Times,* December 31, 1991.

7 "A Nation Challenged: The Hunted; The 22 Most Wanted Suspects, in a Five-Act Drama of Global Terror," *New York Times,* October 14, 2001.

8 Benjamin Weiser and James Risen, "The Masking of a Militant: A Special Report; A Soldier's Shadowy Trail in U.S. and the Mideast," *New York Times,* December 1, 1998.

9 Ibid., Neff and Sullivan.

10 Paul Quinn-Judge and Charles M. Sennot, "Figure Cited in Terrorism Case Said to Enter U.S. with CIA Help Defense Says Defendants Trained by Him," *Boston Globe,* February 3, 1995.

11 The *Globe* piece did note that "There is thus far no indication that Mohamed's alleged activities after entering the United States were coordinated with—or even known to—the CIA," Ibid.

12 James Risen, "C.I.A. Said to Reject Bomb Suspect's Bid to be a Spy," *New York Times,* October 31, 1998.

   Note: In June 2006, I e-mailed *Boston Globe* reporter Charles M. Sennott, who cowrote the story. He was on a leave from the *Globe* but studying as a Neiman Fellow at Harvard University. I sent Sennott two queries asking if he stood by his story, but got no response.

13 Mary Ann Weaver, "Children of the Jihad," *New Yorker,* June 12, 1995.

14 Author's interview with confidential State Department source.

15 Robert Friedman, "The CIA's Jihad," *New Yorker,* March 17, 1995.

16 Weaver, "Children of the Jihad."

17 Charles M. Sennott, "Money, Loathing Fuel bin Laden's Network," *Boston Globe,* September 13, 2001.

18 Stephen Engelberg, "One Man and a Global Web of Violence," *New York Times,* January 14, 2001.

19 Author's interview with confidential Special Forces source.

20 Mary Anne Weaver, "Blowback," *Atlantic Monthly*, May 1996.

21 Steven Emerson, *American Jihad: The Terrorists Living Among Us* (New York: Free Press, 2002), pp. 128–130.

22 http://www.cooperativeresearch.org/searchResults.jsp?searchtext=al+Kifah&events=on &entities=on&articles=on&topics=on&timelines=on&projects=on&titles=on&descritions =on&dosearch=on&search=Go.

23 Roger Stavis, interview for *Triple Cross*, June 9, 2006.

24 Daniel Benjamin and Steven Simon, *The Age of Sacred Terror* (New York: Random House, 2002), p. 76.

25 Robert Friedman, "The CIA's Jihad," *New Yorker*, March 17, 1995.

26 Ibid.

27 The blind cleric's leadership of the IG was known to investigators in the NYPD-FBI Joint Terrorism Task Force (JTTF) as early as February 1992. Author's interview with JTTF Det. Lou Napoli, January 13, 2003.

28 Author's interview with confidential retired intelligence source.

29 Affidavit in Support of Criminal Complaint, *United States v. Benevolence International Foundation Inc. and Enaam M. Arnaout, aka Abu Mahmoud, aka Abdel Samia,* by FBI special agent Robert Walker, Northern District of Illinois, Eastern Division, April 29, 2002.

30 Bob Woodward, *Veil: The Secret Wars of the CIA* (New York: Pocket Books, 1989), p. 335.

31 http://en.wikipedia.org/wiki/List_of_Soviet_aircraft_crashes_in_Afghanistan.

3. "SO . . . CHARISMATIC"

1 Author's interview with Linda Sanchez, May 8, 2006; Ibid., Walden et al.

2 Author's interview with Linda Sanchez, March 27, 2006.

3 Steven Emerson, interview for *Triple Cross*, June 6, 2006.

4 Author's interview with Det. John P. Souza, Fresno Sheriff's Office (ret.), May 20, 2006.

5 Ibid.

6 Ibid., Neff and Sullivan.

7 Chapel of the Bells website: http://www.renochapel.com.

8 *United States v. Ali Mohamed,* S(7) 98 Cr. 1023 (LBS Sealed Complaint), September 1998; Affidavit of FBI special agent Daniel Coleman; bin Laden unit, New York office.

9 *Frontline*, "The Man Who Knew," PBS, http://www.pbs.org/wgbh/pages/frontline/shows/knew /etc/cron.html.

10 *United States v. Ali Mohamed,* S(7) 98 Cr. 1023 (LBS), transcript of plea session, U.S. District Court, Southern District of New York, October 20, 2000.

11 http://www.thesmokinggun.com/archive/jihadmanual.html.

12 Benjamin Weiser, "Informer's Part in Terror Case Is Detailed," *New York Times*, December 22, 2000.

13 Manual UK/BM-19; Victor Ostrovsky, *By Way of Deception* (Scottsdale, AZ: Wilshire Press, 2002).

14 Peter Waldman, Gerald F. Seib, and Jerry Markon, "Sergeant Served U.S. Army and bin Laden, Showing Failings in FBI's Terror Policing," *Wall Street Journal*, November 11, 2001.

15 Lt. Col. Robert Anderson, U.S. Army (ret.), interview for *Triple Cross*, June 6, 2006.

16 Author's interview with Linda Sanchez, May 8, 2006.

17 Alan Gathright, "Mosque Members Fear Backlash," *San Francisco Chronicle*, October 13, 2001.

18 Confession of Khalid Dahab, *Al-Sharq Al-Awsat*, October 10, 2001.

19   Lance Williams, "Bin Laden's Bay Area Recruiter," *San Francisco Chronicle,* November 21, 2001.

20   Dahab even calls himself "Khalid Mohamed." Calls he made to Ali using this name and the code name "Adam" to Wadih El-Hage in Kenya in November 1994, were referenced in *United States v. Osama bin Laden et al.,* S(7) 98 Cr. 1023, February 22, 2001, testimony of L'Houssaine Kherchtou. The other "Khalid Mohammed" was Ramzi Yousef's uncle Khalid Shaikh Mohammed, who spelled his last name with three m's vs. Ali Mohamed's spelling with two.

21   Jake Tapper, "Sleeper Cell or Foolish Pawns?" *Salon.com,* May 19, 2003.

22   Andrew Martin and Michael J. Berens, "Terrorists Evolved in U.S.: 2 Egyptians Set Stage for Attacks," *Chicago Tribune,* December 11, 2001.

23   Seth Hettena, "View of Neighbors Changes After Terror Attacks," *Associated Press,* December 29, 2001.

24   Ibid., Williams.

25   Steven Emerson, interview for *Triple Cross,* June 7, 2006.

4. PLACATING LINDA WITH GOLD

1   Lance Williams and Erin McCormick, "Bin Laden's Man in Silicon Valley 'Mohamed the American' Orchestrated Terrorist Acts While Living a Quiet Suburban Life in Santa Clara," *San Francisco Chronicle,* September 21, 2001.

2   Stephen A. Carnarota, "The Open Door: How Militant Islamic Terrorists Entered and Remained in the United States, 1993–2001," *Report of the Center for Immigration Studies,* May, 2002.

3   Ibid., Waldman et al.

4   Ibid., Williams and McCormick.

5   John J. Goldman, "Ex-Army Sergeant Admits Guilt in '98 Embassy Blasts: Egyptian Born Defendant Says He Conspired with Saudi Military Osama bin Laden to Bomb U.S. missions in Kenya and Tanzania," *Los Angeles Times,* October 21, 2000.

6   Service record of Ali Aboualacoud Mohamed.

7   Ibid., Sanchez, May 8, 2006.

8   Ibid., Cloonan, May 4, 2006.

9   B. Raman, "Taking Jihad to the U.S.," *Hindu Financial Daily,* November 8, 2000.

10   Ibid., Service record.

11   Lt. Col. Robert Anderson, interview for *Triple Cross,* June 6, 2006.

12   Steven Emerson, interview for *Triple Cross,* June 7, 2006.

13   Author's interview with confidential source, 5th Special Forces (ret.), March 12, 2005.

14   Ibid., Lt. Col. Robert Anderson interview.

15   Sean Webby and Rodney Foo, "Ali Mohamed, Who Lived in the South Bay During the Late 1980s and 1990s Has Long Played Vital Roles on Both Sides of the American Counterterrorism Campaign," *San Jose Mercury News,* November 12, 2001.

16   Ibid., Weiser.

17   Ibid., Neff and Sullivan.

18   Andrew Marshal, "Terror: 'Blowback' Burns CIA; America's Spies Paid and Trained Their Nation's Worst Enemies," *Independent,* November 1, 1999.

19   Interview with Norvell De Atkine for *Triple Cross,* April 21, 2006.

20   Benjamin Weiser and James Risen, "The Masking of a Militant: A Special Report; A Soldier's Shadowy Trail in U.S. and the Mideast," *New York Times,* December 1, 1998.

21   Author's interview with Linda Sanchez, May 8, 2006.

22   Interview with Norvell De Atkine for *Triple Cross,* April 21, 2006.

23   Ibid.

24 William K. Rashbaum, "City to Lose Man Who Led Terror Fight," *New York Times*, May 6, 2006.
25 Author's conversation with Michael Sheehan, Deputy Commission of Counterterrorism NYPD (ret.), January 3, 2006.
26 Joseph Neff and John Sullivan, "An Al Qaeda Operative at Fort Bragg," *Raleigh News & Observer*, November 14, 2001.
27 Ibid.
28 "Inside Story of the Hunt for Bin Laden," *Guardian*, August 23, 2003
29 Ibid., Neff and Sullivan.

5. LIT UP LIKE A CHRISTMAS TREE

1   Jim Garamone, "Bright Star Shines in Egypt," *American Forces Information Services*, October 22, 1999.
2   http://www.globalsecurity.org/military/ops/bright-star.htm.
3   Joseph Neff and John Sullivan, "Al Qaeda Terrorist Duped FBI, Army," *Raleigh News & Observer*, October 24, 2001.
4   Author's interview with FBI special agent Jack Cloonan (ret.), May 4, 2006.
5   Interview with FBI special agent Jack Cloonan (ret.) for *Triple Cross*, June 1, 2006.
6   Lt. Col. Robert Anderson, interview for *Triple Cross*, June 6, 2006.
7   Ibid., Weiser and Risen.
8   John Miller, Michael Stone, and Chris Mitchell, *The Cell: Inside the 9/11 Plot and Why the FBI and CIA Failed to Stop It* (New York: Hyperion, 2002), pp. 140–143.
9   Jailan Halawai, "Jihad Implicated in U.S. Embassy Bombings," *Al Ahram Weekly*, May 27–June 2, 1999.
10 Ibid., Williams and McCormick.
11 Ibid., Neff and Sullivan, October 24, 2001.
12 Stephen Engelberg, "One Man and a Global Web of Violence," *New York Times*, January 14, 2001.
13 Ibid., Engelberg.
14 Simon Reeve, *The New Jackals* (Boston: Northeastern University Press, 1999), p. 3.
15 Robert I. Friedman, "The CIA's Jihad," *New Yorker*, March 17, 1995.
16 The term first used to describe Gamal Abdel Nasser, Sadat's predecessor. Richard Bernstein, "On Trial: An Islamic Cleric Battles Secularism," *New York Times*, January 8, 1995.
17 Ibid., Emerson.
18 Robin Cook, "The Struggle against Terrorism Cannot Be Won by Military Means," *Guardian Unlimited*, July 8, 2005.
19 *United States v. Osama bin Laden et al.*, S(7) 98 Cr. 1023, February 21, 2001. Testimony of L'Houssaine Kherchtou.
20 *United States v. Omar Abdel Rahman et al.*, S(5) 93 Cr. 181 (MBM), January 30, 1995.
21 *The Cell*, pp. 140–143.
22 John Kinfer, "Police Say Kahane Suspect Took Anti-Depressant Drugs," *New York Times*, November 9, 1990.
23 Ibid., p. 66.
24 Ibid., *United States v. Omar Abdel Rahman et al.*, September 11, 1995.
25 Benjamin Weiser, "U.S. Sergeant Linked to bin Laden Conspiracy," *New York Times*, October 30, 1998.
26 *United States v. Omar Abdel Rahman et al.*, S(5) 93 Cr. 181 (MBM), February 7, 1995, pp. 14241–14242.
27 Ibid., July 13, 1995.

28 Author's interview with confidential FBI source.

29 *Two Seconds Under the World,* pp. 149–150; *The Cell,* pp. 50, 88.

30 John Rather, "Security Questions at Shooting Ranges," *New York Times,* October 5, 2003.

31 Ibid., *United States v. Omar Abdel Rahman et al.,* February 7, 1995.

32 Daniel Benjamin and Steven Simon, *The Age of Sacred Terror* (New York: Random House, 2002), p. 5.

33 *United States v. Omar Abdel Rahman et al.,* S(5) 93 Cr. 181 (MBM), February 7, 1995.

34 Roger Stavis, interview for *Triple Cross,* June 9, 2006.

35 M. A. Farber, "Kahane Trial Sets Off Squabbles by Lawyers," *New York Times,* December 9, 1991.

36 *United States v. Mohammed A. Salameh et al.,* S(5) 93 Cr. 180 (KTD).

37 *United States v. Omar Abdel Rahman et al.,* S(5) 93 Cr. 181 (MBM), February 7, 1995.

38 *United States v. Ali Mohamed,* S(7) 98 Cr. 1023 (LBS), transcript of plea session, U.S. District Court, Southern District of New York, October 20, 2000.

39 Richard Bernstein, "U.S. Has Kept 2 in Bomb Trial Under Surveillance Since 1989," *New York Times,* February 8, 1995.

40 Author's interview with Flora Edwards, April 27, 2004.

41 Interview with Tommy Corrigan, NYPD-JTTF (ret.) for *Triple Cross,* June 13, 2006.

42 *United States v. Omar Abdel Rahman et al.,* S(5) 93 Cr. 181 (MBM), February 7, 1995.

43 Author's interview with FBI special agent Jack Cloonan (ret.), May 4, 2006.

6. THE LONE GUNMAN

1 Neff and Sullivan, October 24, 2001.

2 Weiser and Risen, December 1, 1998.

3 Emerson, http://www.iacsp.com/itobli3.html.

4 Confession of Khalid Dahab, *Al-Sharq al-Awsat,* March 6, 1999, FBI's translation from Arabic.

5 *United States v. Ali Mohamed,* S(7) 98 Cr. 1023 (LBS Sealed Complaint), September 1998; Affidavit of FBI special agent Daniel Coleman, bin Laden unit, New York office.

6 Paul Thompson, *The Terror Timeline: Year by Year, Day by Day, Minute by Minute: A Comprehensive Chronicle of the Road to 9/11; And America's Response* (New York: ReganBooks, 2004).

7 Author's interview with Paul Thompson, May 28, 2006.

8 Questions about the Sheikh's U.S. entry surfaced publicly in early 1993 and continued throughout the year following the bombing of the World Trade Center on February 26, 1993, and the Sheikh's surrender to federal agents on July 3, 1993; Chris Hedges, "A Cry of Islamic Fury, Taped in Brooklyn for Cairo," *New York Times,* January 7, 1993; Timothy Carney and Mansoor Ijaz, "Intelligence Failure? Let's Go Back to Sudan," *Washington Post,* June 30, 2002; James C. McKinley Jr., "Islamic Leader on U.S. Terrorist List in Brooklyn," *New York Times,* December 16, 1990; James Risen, "Case of Spy in Anti-Terrorist Mission Points Up CIA's Perils," *Los Angeles Times,* February 11, 1996.

9 Alexander Yonah and Michael S. Swetnam, *Osama bin Laden's al Qaida: Profile of a Terrorist Network* (Ardsley, NY: Transnational Publishers, 2001), p. 38.

10 Interview with Tommy Corrigan, NYPD-JTTF (ret.) for *Triple Cross,* June 13, 2006.

11 The take was as much as $2 million a year by one account: Mary Ann Weaver, "Children of the Jihad," *New Yorker,* June 12, 1995.

12 Dwyer et al., *Two Seconds Under the World,* p. 151.

13 Notice of Federal Tax Lien, A. A. Mohamed, Form 668 (Y), October 25, 1990.

14 Base pay for an army E-5 with two years enlisted was only $1,814.00 a month or $21,769.00 in the year 2006. We don't know what kind of outside income Mohamed reported to the IRS but

it's clear that even with penalties, Mohamed never could have generated $10,458.55 based on his army salary alone.

15 FBI 302 memo re: the contents seized from Nosair's house on November 8 1998. The 302 was originally dated November 13, 1990.

16 Steven Emerson, interview for *Triple Cross,* June 6, 2006.

17 M. A. Farber, "Kahane Trial Sets Off Squabbles by Lawyers," *New York Times,* December 9, 1991.

18 Ibid., FBI 302 memo.

19 Joint Inquiry Statement, 10/8/02, p. 3.

20 Author's interview with William Greenbaum, October 11, 2005.

21 *The People of the State of New York v. El Sayyid Nosair,* bail hearing, December 10, 1991, p. 2356.

22 Ibid., p. 19.

23 FBI 302 memo re: the contents seized from Nosair's house on November 8 1998. The 302 was originally dated November 13, 1990.

24 FBI 302 interrogation of Ramzi Ahmed Yousef by Chuck Stern and Brian Parr, February 7 to 8, 1995. Transcribed February 28, 1995.

25 Ibid., p. 26.

26 "The Deadly Game of Cat and Mouse for al-Qaeda's No. 2," *London Sunday Times,* August 5, 2005.

27 *The People of the State of New York v. El Sayyid Nosair,* bail hearing, December 18, 1990, p. 43.

28 *Guardian,* March 31, 1998.

29 "Lawyer Confirms Omar Abdel Rahman's Deteriorating Health," *Arabic News.com,* October 11, 1997.

30 Rick Halperin, *Death Penalty News Worldwide,* November 18, 1997.

31 In the trial of Lynne Stewart, former attorney for the blind Sheikh, accused along with Ahmed Abdel Sattar of passing communiqués from the Sheikh to the violent IG, the government entered a Reuters article from June 18, 2000, that quoted the IG's head Rifa'I Taha. The article also mentioned a news conference attended by Abdullah Abdel Rahman, the blind Sheikh's son, who was accompanied by Abdel-Halim Mandour; *United States v. Ahmed Abdel Sattar,* Lynne Stewart and Mohammed Yousry, pp. 5576–5585, S(1) 01 Cr. 395 (JGK).

32 *The People of the State of New York v. El Sayyid Nosair,* bail hearing, December 18, 1990, pp. 4–8.

33 Ibid., Trial, November 27 1991, p. 1229.

34 Ibid., pp. 1231–1232.

35 Author's interview with William Greenbaum, October 11, 2005.

36 15 Diamond Street and 57 Prospect Park Southwest in Brooklyn; 11 Cater Avenue, and 288 Magnolia Street in Jersey City; in addition to 277 Olympia Avenue in Cliffside Park.

37 Ralph Blumenthal, "Clues Hinting at Terror Ring Were Ignored," *New York Times,* August 27, 1993.

38 Interview with Tommy Corrigan, NYPD-JTTF (ret.) for *Triple Cross,* June 13, 2006.

39 Miller, *The Cell,* pp. 55–56.

7. DEATH OF A "BAD MUSLIM"

1 Bill Turque, "The Trail to the Jihad Office," *Newsweek,* March 29, 1993.

2 Alison Mitchell, "After Blast, New Interest in Holy-War Recruits in Brooklyn," *New York Times,* April 11, 1993.

3 Dwyer, *Two Seconds Under the World,* p. 151.

4 Miller, *The Cell,* p. 66.

5   This fact alone defies the conclusion later reached by the 9/11 Commission that the original
    World Trade Center bombing cell was comprised of a "loosely based group of Sunni Islamists,"
    with little or no connection to al Qaeda. Evidence that al Qaeda controlled and financed the cell
    was laid out in the African Embassy bombing trial in the winter and spring of 2001. Still, days
    after 9/11, even the *New York Times* concluded that bin Laden's links to the Ali Mohamed-Shaikh
    Omar-Ramzi Yousef cell were "suggestive, but not conclusive." Stephen Engelberg, "One Man
    and a Global Web of Violence," *New York Times*, September 14, 2001.

6   Ibid., Engelberg.

7   Jailan Halawai, "Jihad Implicated in U.S. Embassy Bombings," *Al Ahram Weekly*, May 27–June 2,
    1999.

8   Dwyer, *Two Seconds Under the World*, p. 151.

9   Steven Emerson, interview for *Triple Cross*, June 7, 2006.

10 Interview with FBI special agent Jack Cloonan (ret.) for *Triple Cross*, June 1, 2006.

11 Ibid., Emerson.

12 Chris Hedges, "A Cry of Islamic Fury, Taped in Brooklyn for Cairo," *New York Times*, January 7,
    1993.

13 Interview with Tommy Corrigan, NYPD-JTTF (ret.) for *Triple Cross*, June 13, 2006.

14 Dwyer, *Two Seconds Under the World*, p. 151.

15 Mary B. W. Tabor, "Slaying in Brooklyn Linked to Militants," *New York Times*, April 11, 1993.

16 In 1993, post–World Trade Center bombing, when Abouhalima had been captured and tortured
    after fleeing to Egypt, he confessed that Sheikh Omar was behind the Shalabi hit.

17 Mary B. W. Tabor, "9th Held in Bomb Plot as Tie Is Made to 1991 Murder," *New York Times*,
    July 1, 1993.

18 Mary B. W. Tabor, "Inquiry into Slaying of Sheikh's Confident Appears Open," *New York Times*,
    November 23, 1993.

19 Orianna Zill, "Portrait of Wadih El-Hage," *Frontline*, http://www.pbs.org/wgbh/pages/frontline
    /shows/binladen/upclose/elhage.html.

20 Ibid., Corrigan.

21 *United States v. Ali Mohamed*, S(7) 98 Cr. 1023 (LBS), transcript of plea session, U.S. District
    Court, Southern District of New York, October 20, 2000.

22 Mimi Swartz, "The Terrorist Next Door," *Texas Monthly*, April 2002.

23 Ibid., Corrigan.

24 Testimony of then FBI director Louis Freeh before the Senate Judiciary Committee, September 3,
    1998.

25 Robert A. Martin, "Joint Terrorism Task Force: A Concept That Works–FBI–New York City Po-
    lice Department," *Law Enforcement Bulletin*, March, 1999.

26 Including U.S. Marshals Service; the U.S. Department of State's Diplomatic Security Service; the
    Bureau of Alcohol, Tobacco and Firearms; the Immigration and Naturalization Service; the New
    York State Police; the New York/New Jersey Port Authority Police Department; and the U.S. Se-
    cret Service; Ibid., Martin.

27 Testimony of FBI director Robert S. Mueller II before the Senate Judiciary Committee, March 4,
    2003.

28 Example: Within the FBI's Phoenix office in 1996, 60 of the 230 special agents were working
    drug cases at the same time that the Drug Enforcement Administration had jurisdiction.
    "Why is that," asked retired special agent James Hauswirth, a 27-year Bureau veteran, "If we have
    an agency called the DEA?" Author's interview with James. H. Hauswirth, November 1, 2002.

29 The rare military exception was when the Clinton administration fired a series of Tomahawk
    Cruise missiles into Sudan and Afghanistan on August 20, 1998, following the twin bombings of

the U.S. Embassies in Kenya and Ethiopia. "U.S.S. Missiles Pound Targets in Afghanistan, Sudan," *CNN.com,* August 20, 1988.

30 Statement of Patrick J. Fitzgerald, U.S. Attorney for the Northern District of Illinois, Senate Judiciary Committee, October 21, 2003.

31 Memo from Jamie S. Gorelick, Deputy Attorney General, to Mary Jo White, U.S. Attorney for the SDNY; Louis Freeh Director, FBI et al., March, 1995.

32 John Ashcroft, testimony before the 9/11 Commission, April 13, 2004.

33 James S. Gorelick, "The Truth About 'the Wall,'" *Washington Post,* April 18, 2004.

34 Author's interview with Det. Lou Napoli, NYPD (ret.), January 13, 2003.

35 Ibid.

36 Author's interview with confidential FBI source.

37 FBI 302 memo re: search of El Sayyid Nosair's home, November 8, 1990, p. 11.

38 The 302 memo actually misspells the name "Muterza" as "Murieza," substituting an "i" for a "t."

39 James C. McKinley, "Ex-Police Officer and Firearms Dealer Is Linked to Kahane Suspect,"*New York Times,* November 11, 1990.

40 Miller et al., *The Cell,* p. 65.

41 Dwyer, *Two Seconds Under the World,* pp. 151–152.

42 Ibid., pp. 143–146.

43 Ibid., p. 151.

8. FLIGHT TO KHARTOUM

1 Reeve, *The New Jackals,* p. 172.

2 Littlejohn, "Is Sudan Terrorism's New Mecca?" Marine Corps University Command and Staff College, 1997.

3 Steven Emerson, "Abdullah Assam: The Man Before Osama bin Laden," http://www.iacsp.com/itobli3.html.

4 Benjamin Weiser, "Informer's Part in Terror Case Is Detailed," *New York Times,* December 22, 2000.

5 Reeve, *The New Jackals,* p. 156.

6 Stephen Engelberg, "One Man and a Global Web of Violence," *New York Times,* January 14, 2001.

7 Jailan Halawai, "Jihad Implicated in U.S. Embassy Bombings," *Al Ahram Weekly,* May 27–June 2, 1999.

8 Indictment, *United States v. Wadih El-Hage et al.,* S(1) 98 Cr. 1023 (LBS), October 7, 1998.

9 Ibid., Engelberg.

10 http://www.metatempo.com/analysis-alqaida-tradecraft.html.

11 Author's interview with Special Agent Len Predtechenskis, FBI (ret.), August 27, 2002.

12 *United States v. Omar Abdel Rahman et al.,* March 7, 1995, p. 4589.

13 Author's interview with confidential FBI source.

14 Lance, *1000 Years for Revenge* (trade paperback edition), p. 56.

15 Author's interview with Det. Lou Napoli, January 10, 2003.

16 Ibid., Abdel Rahman.

17 Author's interview with FBI special agent Jack Cloonan (ret.), May 4, 2006.

18 Ibid., Abdel Rahman.

19 Author's interview with FBI ADIC Carson Dunbar (ret.), July 31, 2002.

20 *People v. El Sayyid Nosair,* trial transcript, December 10, 1991, p. 2421.

21 Robert D. McFadden, "For Jurors, Evidence in Kahane Case Was Riddled with Gaps," *New York Times,* December 23, 1991.

22   *The People of the State of New York v. El Sayyid Nosair,* bail hearing, December 18, 1990, p. 43.

23   Ibid.

24   Selwyn Raab, "Jury Acquits Defendant in Kahane Trial," *New York Times,* December 22, 1991.

25   Video, "Brooklyn Mosque Tape," *United States v. Omar Abdel Rahman et al.*

26   Anticev was reportedly out of work for many weeks during this period with a brain embolism. Author's interview with FBI confidential source.

27   Ibid., Predtechenskis.

28   Ibid., Napoli.

29   Ibid.

30   Author's interview with FBI source.

31   Ibid., Predtechenskis.

32   Author's interview with FBI source; *United States v. Omar Abdel Rahman et al.*

33   Ibid., Predtechenskis; Author's interview with FBI source.

34   Ibid., Napoli.

35   Interview with Tommy Corrigan, NYPD-JTTF (ret.), for *Triple Cross,* June 13, 2006.

9. IN COLD BLOOD

1   Pablo Lopez and Louis Galvan, "Three Members of Fresno Family Found Slain," *Fresno Bee,* April 22, 1992.

2   Tom Kertscher, "DA Says No on Ewell Sentence," *Fresno Bee,* June 20, 1998.

3   Author's interview with Det. John P. Souza, Fresno County Sheriff's Office (ret.), May 20, 2006.

4   Kraig Hanadel, *Catch Me If You Can* (New York: Avon, 2002).

5   Ibid., Souza, May 20, 2006.

6   Ibid., Hanadel, p. 85.

7   Ibid., Souza, May 20, 2006.

8   "Millions of Reasons to Kill," *American Justice,* Towers Productions Inc.

9   Steve Rosenlind, "The Mysterious Monica Zent," *Fresno Bee,* February 27, 1997. According to Rosenlind's report in the *Bee:*

> An investigation of 490 checks involving the Mitchell trust revealed that the money was used to pay Glee Mitchell's living expenses and to support the lifestyles of Dana Ewell, Monica Zent, and Joel Radovcich. Expenditures traced to the account include: $11,320 in flying lessons for Dana Ewell and Joel Radovcich paid for in advance with two checks dated June 25, 1992 and $234,000 to retain a lawyer for Dana Ewell. Money was transferred to the account of Fresno lawyer Richard Berman after Dana's arrest; $39,701 to Monica Zent. Includes checks on these dates: March 7, 1994—$5,000, Jan. 13, 1995—$9,950, [and] $17,014 to the University of San Diego, where Monica Zent was a law student. Detectives found more than 25 personal bank accounts used by Dana Ewell and Monica Zent at financial institutions in Fresno, Pasadena, Los Angeles, Woodland Hills, Beverly Hills, and Granada Hills. Many of the accounts contained money diverted from the Mitchell trust. (*Source:* Court documents, Doug Hansen, *Fresno Bee*)

10   Tom Kertscher, "Ewell Allegedly Misused $160,000," *Fresno Bee,* June 16 1995.

11   Ibid., Rosenlind.

12   Ibid.

13   Ibid., Souza.

14   Ibid., Hanadel, p. 229.

15   Ibid., p. 181.

16   Ibid., Souza.

17 Ibid., Hanadel, p. 251.

18 Ibid.

19 Royal Calkins and Steven Rosenlind, "Dana Ewell Held in Family's Slayings," *Fresno Bee,* March 12, 1995.

20 Author's interview with Det. Chris Curtice, Fresno County Sheriff's office, August 15, 2006.

10. INCIDENT IN ROME

1 Benjamin Weiser and James Risen, "The Masking of a Militant: A Special Report; A Soldier's Shadowy Trail in the U.S. and the Mideast," *New York Times,* December 1, 1998.

2 E-mail from Linda Sanchez to author, May 14, 2006.

3 Author's interview with FBI special agent Jack Cloonan (ret.), May 4, 2006.

4 Ibid., Sanchez e-mail.

5 Author's interview with Special Agent Joseph F. O'Brien (ret.), September 12, 2005.

6 E-mail from FBI special agent John Zent (ret.) to author, May 15, 2006.

7 Ibid., May 18, 2006, 12:41 P.M. PDT.

8 Ibid., 3:56 P.M. PDT.

9 Ibid., 5:21 P.M. PDT.

10 Author's interview with Det. John P. Souza (ret.), Fresno County Sheriff's Office, May 20, 2006.

11 Ibid.

12 Author's interview with Det. Souza, June 27, 2006.

13 Affidavit in Support of Criminal Complaint, *United States v. Benevolence International Foundation Inc. and Enaam M. Arnaout, aka Abu Mahmoud, aka Abdel Samia,* by Robert Walker, FBI special agent, Northern District of Illinois, Eastern Division, April 29, 2002.

14 *United States v. Mohammed A. Salameh et al.,* S(5) 93 Cr. 180 (KTD).

15 Benjamin and Simon, *The Age of Sacred Terror.*

11. THE GREAT ONE

1 His other aliases included: Azan Muhammed, Adam Ali Qasim, Naji Haddad, Dr. Paul Vijay, Dr. Adel Sabah, Amaldo Forlani, Muhammad Ali Baloch, Adam Baloch, Kamal Ibraham, Abraham Kamal, Rashed, Khurram Khan, Adam Ali, Dr. Alex Hume, and Dr. Richard Smith. *United States v. Ramzi Ahmed Yousef,* S(10) 93 (KTD) indictment and "wanted" poster, Dept. of Justice, U.S. State Dept. Office of Diplomatic Security.

2 Debriefing report, Philippines National Police Counter Intelligence Group, February 18 1995.

3 Simon Reeve, *The New Jackals: Ramzi Yousef, Osama bin Laden and the Future of Terrorism* (Boston: Northeastern University Press, 1999), p. 135.

4 FBI 302 interrogation of Ramzi Ahmed Yousef, February 7, 1995.

5 Christopher Dickey, "America's Most Wanted," *Newsweek,* July 4, 1994.

6 FBI Lab Report on Dona Josefa seizure, PNP documents on Room 603 search.

7 *United States v. Ramzi Ahmed Yousef et al.,* June 11, 1996 and July 17, 1996.

8 "Cold Blooded," PNP Superintendent Samuel Pagdilao; Simon Reeve, *The New Jackals,* "Diabolical," FBI asst. director Neal Herman; ibid., p. 249; "Evil Genius," Mary Ann Weaver; "Children of the Jihad," *New Yorker,* June 12, 1995.

9 Author's interview with U.S. Postal Inspector Frank Gonzalez (ret.), January 3, 2003.

10 Ibid., Weaver.

11 The World Trade Center urea-nitrate fuel oil bomb; *United States v. Ramzi Ahmed Yousef and Eyad Ismoil,* S(12) 93 Cr. 180 (KTD).

12 The Casio-nitroglycerine device Yousef planted aboard Philippine Airlines Flight #434 on December 11, 1994, in a test for the Bojinka plot; *United States v. Ramzi Ahmed Yousef et al.*, S(12) 93 Cr. 180 (KTD).

13 Samuel M. Katz, *Relentless Pursuit: The DSS and the Manhunt for the Al-Qaeda Terrorists* (New York: Forge, 2002).

14 Author's interview with Steve Legon, January 20, 2003.

15 Author's interview with U.S. Postal Inspector Frank Gonzalez (ret.), January 3, 2003.

16 *United States v. Mohammed A. Salameh et al.*, S(5) 93 Cr. 180 (KTD).

17 Lance, *1000 Years for Revenge* (trade paperback edition), pp. 98–100.

18 *United States v. Mohammed A. Salameh et al.*, S(5) 93 Cr. 180 (KTD), p. 2486.

19 Benjamin and Simon, *The Age of Sacred Terror*, p. 8.

20 *United States v. Omar Abdel Rahman et al.*, S(5) 93 Cr. 181 (MBM), July 17, 1995.

21 *United States v. Ali Mohamed*, S(7) 98 Cr. 1023 (LBS), Sealed Complaint, September 1998. Affidavit of Daniel Coleman, FBI special agent, bin Laden unit, New York office.

22 *United States v. Ali Mohamed*, S(7) 98 Cr. 1023 (LBS), transcript of plea session, U.S. District Court, Southern District of New York, October 20, 2000.

23 *9/11 Commission Final Report*, p. 73.

24 Ibid.

25 Ibid., Yonah and Swetnam, *Osama bin Laden's al-Qaida: Profile of a Terrorist Network*, p. 39.

26 *United States v. Omar Abdel Rahman et al.*, S(5) 93 Cr. 181 (MBM), testimony of Khalid Ibrihim.

27 *United States v. Osama bin Laden et al.*, S(7) 98 Cr. 1023, February 23, 2001.

28 "A Nation Challenged: The Hunted; The 22 Most Wanted Suspects, in a Five-Act Drama of Global Terror," *New York Times*, October 14, 2001.

29 Martin Bright, "MI-6 'Halted Bid to Arrest Bin Laden,'" *Observer*, November 10, 2002.

30 Alan Feuer and Benjamin Weiser, "Translation: 'The How-to Book of Terrorism,'" *New York Times*, April 5, 2001.

31 Interview with FBI special agent Jack Cloonan (ret.) for *Triple Cross*, June 1, 2006.

32 *United States v. Osama bin Laden et al.*, S(7) 98 Cr.1023 (LBS), February 23, 2001.

33 FBI 302 interview of Ramzi Yousef by FBI special agent Bradley Garrett, Islamabad, Pakistan, February 7, 1995.

34 *United States v. Ramzi Yousef et al.*, "The Bojinka Trial," S(12) 93 Cr. 180 (KTD), July 17, 1996.

35 *United States v. Mohammed Salameh et al.*

36 *United States v. Omar Abdel Rahman et al.*, March 13, 1995.

37 Alison Mitchell, "Before Bombing, Inquiry Sought Inroads into Enclave of Suspects," *New York Times*, April 1, 1993.

38 Author's interview with confidential FBI source.

12. GROUND ZERO PART ONE

1 Bill Gertz, *Breakdown: How America's Intelligence Failures Led to September 11* (Washington, D.C.: Regnery, 2002), pp. 27–28.

2 Alison Mitchell, "Before Bombing, Inquiry Sought Inroads into Enclave of Suspects," *New York Times*, April 1, 1993.

3 At one point, Yousef and Salameh tested the explosive at Liberty State Park in New Jersey, overlooking the Statue of Liberty. Yousef wasn't satisfied with the mixture's blasting radius so he decided to add aluminum power as an oxidizing agent; *United States v. Mohammed Salameh et al.*

4 Simon Reeve, *The New Jackals* (Boston: Northeastern University Press, 2000), p. 149.

5 *United States v. Ajaj*, 92-CR-993 EDNY, Addendum to the Pre-Sentence Report, December 8, 1992.

6 Ralph Blumenthal, "Tangled Ties and Tales of FBI Messenger," *New York Times,* January 9, 1994.

7 Reeve, *The New Jackals,* p. 143.

8 Richard Bernstein, "Testimony in Bomb Case Links Loose Ends," *New York Times,* January 19, 1994.

9 *United States v. Salameh,* U.S. Court of Appeals for the Second Circuit, August term.

10 *United States v. Ajaj,* 92-CR-993 EDNY, transcript of phone conversation with Ramzi Yousef aka Rashed.

11 U.S. Attorney for the EDNY, letter to Judge Reena Raggi, December 18, 1992.

12 Laurie Mylroie, *The War Against America* (New York: ReganBooks, 2002), p. 49.

13 FBI 302 interrogation of Ramzi Yousef, February 7, 1995, p. 21; "[Yousef] said his parents living in Iran part of Baluchistan were aware of his participation in WTC bombing. At one point post bombing, a female who claimed to rep a U.S. phone company telephoned his parents' residence and attempted to solicit information pertaining to whereabouts of RY claiming that Yousef owed the company a significant amount of money. The woman, rebuffed by Yousef's father, went on to inquire as to the whereabouts of numerous individuals which Yousef knew to be aliases he had used in past."

14 Interview with Tommy Corrigan, NYPD-JTTF (ret.) for *Triple Cross,* June 13, 2006.

15 Author's interview with Det. Lou Napoli, January 10, 2003.

16 Author's interview with confidential FBI source.

17 Author's interview with FBI agent Julian Stackhouse (ret.), June 3, 2003.

18 The FBI concluded that it was the "largest by weight and by damage of any improvised explosive device that we've seen since the inception of forensic explosion identification—and that's since 1925"; *The New Jackals,* p. 154.

19 Testimony of Dr. Jacqueline Lee at the second World Trade Center bombing trial, August 7, 1997.

20 Interview with Robert McLoughlin for *Triple Cross,* June 9, 2006.

21 Simon Reeve, *The New Jackals,* p. 40.

22 Miller, *The Cell,* p. 31.

23 FBI official bio John Miller "About Us: FBI Executives," http://www.fbi.gov/libref/executives/miller.htm.

24 Edward Wyatt, "More Questions of Accuracy Raised About ABC Mini-Series on 9/11 Prelude," *New York Times,* September 12, 2006.

25 FBI 302 interrogation of Ramzi Ahmed Yousef by Chuck Stern and Brian Parr, February 7 to 8, 1995, transcribed February 28, 1995.

26 FBI 302 interrogation of Ramzi Yousef a.k.a. Abdul Basit Mahmud Abdul Karim; in an interview on February 7, 1995, during an airborne rendition to the United States following his arrest in Pakistan, Yousef reportedly told FBI agent Bradley S. Garrett that he "operates independently." According to Garrett's FBI 302 memo summarizing the interrogation, "Muslim leaders/groups may be an inspiration for YOUSEF but YOUSEF stated that no particular individual or group controls or directs him." (FBI 302 memo, February 8, 1995, by Bradley S. Garrett.) In a subsequent and more lengthy interview during the same flight, Yousef reportedly told FBI agent Charles Stern and Secret Service agent Brian Parr that " 'The Liberation Army-Fifth Battalion' is a genuine organization, responsible for numerous bombings." (FBI 302 interrogation of Abdul Basit Mahmud Karim, February 7, 1995. Aircraft in Flight by special agent Charles Stern and Brian C. Parr; File #265A-NY-235983, p. 13.) But testimony in Yousef's two trials later suggested that "The Liberation Army" was Yousef's name for his own cell within al Qaeda. Early in the second airborne interview Yousef told the agents that he "became interested" in Sheikh Omar Abdel Rahman and had been introduced to him by Mohammed Salameh. He

said that he subsequently visited the Sheikh's Jersey City home and had dinner with him (Ibid. p. 8). In 1995, during the opening statement of the Sheikh's trial for a plot to bomb city landmarks, Asst. U.S. Attorney Robert Khuzami referred to Abdel Rahman as "the leader of the Jihad Army," operating in New York (*United States v. Omar Abdel Rahman et al.,* January 1, 1995). In 1996, during the summation for the first of Yousef's two federal trials, Asst. U.S. Attorney Lev Dassin told jurors that Yousef was part of a "self proclaimed army of terrorists" (*United States v. Ramzi Ahmed Yousef et al.,* August 5, 1996) and in the indictment of Osama bin Laden handed down secretly in June 1998 and unsealed that November, the U.S. Attorney for the SDNY declared that the alternate name for al Qaeda was the "Islamic Army." Indictment (*United States v. Osama bin Laden,* June, 1998). From testimony in the subsequent trial in February 2001, it became clear that bin Laden had directed an al Qaeda cell based at the Alkifah Center in Brooklyn from March 1991, when Mustafa Shalabi was killed. The blind Sheikh was spiritual adviser to the cell and Yousef was imported to build the WTC bomb. It's unknown where the bomb maker himself ranked in the al Qaeda power structure, but by 1994 he had become al Qaeda's chief operational point man. Not only did bin Laden finance Yousef's Manila-based Bojinka and Pope plots, he also underwrote Yousef's design of the 9/11 plot, which was executed by Yousef's uncle Khalid Shaikh Mohammed. Mohammed himself was described by intelligence officials as the "chief operating officer" of al Qaeda following his capture in March of 2003.

27 Author's interview with Eve Bucca, June 17, 2002. Bucca, who obtained Yousef's addendum, told dozens of people in the FDNY and New York law enforcement that Yousef was planning to return to the WTC. See also Peter Sleven and Walter Pincus, "Attackers Studied Mistakes in Previous Assaults," *Washington Post,* September 13, 2001.

28 9/11 Commission, Staff Statement 15.

29 Author's interview with Fire Marshal Robert McLoughlin (ret.), February 25, 2003.

30 Author's interview with Chief Fire Marshal Louis F. Garcia, April 9, 2002.

31 *United States v. Omar Abdel Rahman et al.,* January 30, 1995.

32 Ralph Blumenthal, "Tapes Depict Proposal to Thwart Bomb Used in Trade Center Blast," *New York Times,* October 29, 1993. The article discussed a conversation Salem taped with Anticev on his own equipment—one of many surreptitious recordings that would soon be known as Salem's "bootleg tapes."

33 *United States v. Omar Abdel Rahman et al.,* July 26, 1995.

34 Author's interview with NYPD Det. Lou Napoli (ret.), January 10, 2003.

35 *United States v. Omar Abdel Rahman et al.,* March 29, 1995.

13. BIN LADEN'S COPILOT

1 Author's interview with Col. Rodolfo B. Mendoza, Philippines National Police, March 19, 2002.

2 Transcript of interrogation of Abdul Hakim Murad, Philippines National Police, January 20, 1995.

3 FBI 302 on interrogation of Abdul Hakim Murad, April 12 to 13, 1995.

4 Ibid.

5 Ibid., Mendoza interview.

6 Steven Emerson, "Ihab Ali: Flight School," testimony before the Senate Judiciary committee, December 4, 2001.

7 Chuck Murphy, "Pilot Led a Quiet Life in Orlando," *St. Petersburg Times,* October 28, 2001.

8 Ibid.

9 State Department Cable. Document Number: 1994MANILA19999, p. 261. On March 20, 2002, U.S. Customs agents made a sweeping series of raids in 14, homes, charities, think tanks, and businesses in Herndon, Virginia, a town outside Washington, D.C., with a large Muslim population. According to http://www.cooperativeresearch.org, no arrests were made and no organizations shut down. But the 14 searches were related to an umbrella group of charities known as the Safa Group or SAAR network that included the MWL and IRRO as affiliated groups.

10 Steve Fairnaru, "Clues Pointed to Changing Terrorists Tactics," *Washington Post,* May 19, 2002.

11 Neil Mackay, "The Terror Trail," *Glasgow Sunday Herald,* September 16, 2001.

12 *United States v. Osama bin Laden et al.,* S(7) 98 Cr. 1023 (LBS), February 14, 2001.

13 Ibid., Fairnaru.

14 Ibid., Murphy.

15 http://www.cooperativeresearch.org/searchResults.jsp?searchtext=Nawawi&events =on&entities=on&articles=on&topics=on&timelines=on&projects=on&titles=on &descriptions=o&dosearch=on&search=Go.

16 Ibid., *United States v. Osama bin Laden et al.,* closing argument, May 1, 2001.

17 *United States v Ali Mohamed,* S(7) 98 Cr. 1023 (LBS), sealed complaint, September 1998. Affidavit of FBI special agent Daniel Coleman, bin Laden unit, New York office.

18 Estanislao Oziewicz and Tu Thanh, "Canada Freed Top Al Qaeda Operative," *Toronto Globe and Mail,* November 22, 2001.

19 Ibid.

20 Interview with FBI special agent Jack Cloonan (ret.) for *Triple Cross,* June 1, 2006.

21 "Ex-Sergeant's Ties to bin Laden Detailed," *Washington Post,* June 6, 1999.

22 Ibid., Oziewicz and Thanh.

23 Susan Sachs, "A Nation Challenged: Bin Laden's Allies; An Investigation In Egypt Illustrates Al Qaeda's Web," *New York Times,* November 21, 2001.

24 Ibid., Oziewicz and Thanh.

25 Ibid., Cloonan.

26 Ibid., Weiser and Risen, *New York Times,* December 1, 1998.

27 Williams and McCormick, *San Francisco Chronicle,* November 4, 2001.

28 Ralph Blumenthal, "Clues Hinting at Terror Ring Were Ignored, Officials Say: Sweeping Federal Indictment," *New York Times,* August 27, 1993; *United States v. Omar Abdel Rahman et al.,* January 30, 1995.

29 Dwyer et al., *Two Seconds Under the World,* pp. 154–156.

30 Robert McLoughlin, FDNY Fire Marshal (ret.), interview for *Triple Cross,* June 9, 2006.

31 Alison Mitchell, "U.S. Detains Cleric Linked to Militants: Sheikh to Be Held While Fighting Deportation," *New York Times,* July 3, 1993, p. 1.

32 Ibid.

33 Douglas Jehl, "U.S. Confirms FBI Alerted by Egyptians," *New York Times,* April 6, 1993.

34 Paul Quinn-Judge and Charles M. Sennot, "Figure Cited in Terrorism Case Said to Enter U.S. with CIA Help; Defense Says Defendants Trained by Him," *Boston Globe,* February 3, 1995.

35 FBI 302, detailing threat from Ramzi Yousef to FBI informant Greg Scarpa Jr., December 30, 1996; Presidential Daily Brief to President Clinton, 1998; Presidential Daily Brief to President Bush, August 6, 2001.

36 "Radical Muslim 'Demands' Have Foundation and History," *Agence France Press,* August 10, 1998.

37 *United States v. Ahmed Abdel Sattar et al.,* April 30, 2002.

38 Neil A. Lewis, "Moussaoui Tells Court He's Guilty of a Terror Plot," *New York Times,* April 23, 2005.

39 Steven Emerson, interview for *Triple Cross,* June 7, 2006.

40 Interview transcript, Patrick Fitzgerald videotaped for *Inside 9/11,* Towers Productions Inc., National Geographic Channel, 2005.

41 Author's interview with Paul Thompson, March 28, 2006.

42 The name was originally attached to Mahmud Abouhalima, "the Red," who for years eluded JTTF investigators Det. Lou Napoli and Special Agent John Anticev.

43 Interview with FBI special agent Jack Cloonan (ret.) for *Triple Cross,* June 1, 2006.

PART II

14. ANOTHER ALIAS

1 Santa Clara Court filing: In the Matter of the Application of Ali Abouelseoud Mohamed.

2 David Rose, "An Inconvenient Patriot," *Vanity Fair,* August 5, 2005.

3 Scott Shane, "Invoking Secrets Privilege Becomes a More Popular Legal Tactic by U.S.," *New York Times,* June 4, 2006.

4 Sibel Edmonds, interview for *Triple Cross,* June 6, 2006.

5 Steven Emerson, interview for *Triple Cross,* June 6, 2006.

6 Author's interview with confidential FBI source.

7 Interview with FBI special agent Jack Cloonan (ret.), May 4, 2006.

8 Peter Waldman, Gerald F. Seib, and Jerry Markon, "Sergeant Served U.S. Army and bin Laden, Showing Failings in FBI's Terror Policing," *Wall Street Journal,* November 11, 2001.

9 Affidavit in Support of Criminal Complaint, *United States v. Benevolence International Foundation Inc. and Enaam M. Arnaout, aka Abu Mahmoud, aka Abdel Samia,* by FBI special agent Robert Walker, Northern District of Illinois, Eastern Division, April 29, 2002.

10 *United States v. Ali Mohamed,* S(7) 98 Cr. 1023 (LBS), transcript of plea session, U.S. District Court, Southern District of New York, October 20, 2000.

11 Kathy Kiely, "Graham: Step Up Hunt for Terrorists, Scale Back on Iraq," *USA Today,* May 14, 2002.

12 "Khobar Towers Indictments Returned," *CNN.com,* June 22, 2001.

13 FBI 302 memo, July 2, 1996, account of intelligence received from Ramzi Yousef by Gregory Scarpa Jr., inmate 9, West Tier Metropolitan Correctional Center, New York.

14 *United States v. Ali Mohamed,* S(7) 98 Cr. 1023 (LBS), sealed complaint, September 1998. Affidavit of FBI special agent Daniel Coleman, bin Laden unit, New York office.

15 Author's interview with Congressman Curt Weldon (R-PA), June 6, 2006.

16 Steven Emerson, interview for *Triple Cross,* June 7, 2006.

17 Peter Baker, "15 Tied to Al Qaeda Turned Over to U.S. Arab Militants Caught in Georgian Gorge," *Washington Post,* October 22, 2002.

18 *United States v. Osama bin Laden et al.,* S(7) 98 Cr. 1023 (LBS).

19 Mark Bowden, *Black Hawk Down: A Story of Modern War* (Boston: Atlantic Monthly Press, 1999).

20 "Operation Restore Hope," http://www.wordiq.com/definition/Operation_Restore_Hope.

21 Mark Bowden was the author of a series of articles for the *Philadelphia Inquirer* that chronicled the Mogadishu incident. They were later assembled into the book *Blackhawk Down: A Story of Modern War* (Boston: Atlantic Monthly Press, 1999) http://inquirer.philly.com/packages /somalia/sitemap.asp.

22 Stephen Engelberg, "One Man and a Global Web of Violence," *New York Times,* January 14, 2001.

23 msnbc.com, "Hunt for Al-Qaida," *NBC News,* http://www.msnbc.msn.com/id/4677978.

24 Miller et al., *The Cell,* p. 196.

25 Yonah Alexander and Michael S. Swetnam, *Osama bin Laden's al-Qaida: Profile of a Terrorist Network* (Ardsley, NY: Transnational Publishers, 2001), p. 6.

26 Raghida Dirgham "Ramzi Yousef Discusses WTC Bombing, Other Activities," *Al Hayat,* translated in FBIS-NES-95-097, April 12, 1995; Author's interview with Raghida Dirgham, March 24, 2003.

27 Interview with FBI special agent Jack Cloonan (ret.) for *Triple Cross,* June 1, 2006.

28 *United States v. Ali Mohamed,* S(7) 98 Cr. 1023 (LBS), plea hearing, October 20, 2000; Colum Lynch and Vernon Loeb, "Bin Laden's Network: Terror Conspiracy or Loose Alliance," *Washington Post,* August 1, 1999; "The Man Who Knew," *Frontline,* PBS, http://www.pbs.org/wgbh/pages/frontline/shows/knew/etc/cron.html.

29 Ibid., *United States v. Ali Mohamed,* plea hearing; Lance Williams and Erin McCormick, "Bin Laden's Man in Silicon Valley 'Mohamed the American' Orchestrated Terrorist Acts While Living a Quiet Suburban Life in Santa Clara," *San Francisco Chronicle,* September 21, 2001.

30 *United States v. Ali Mohamed,* S(7) 98 Cr. 1023 (LBS), sealed complaint, September 1998. Affidavit of FBI special agent Daniel Coleman, bin Laden unit, New York office.

31 Ibid., *United States v. Ali Mohamed,* plea hearing.

32 *United States v. Osama bin Laden et al.,* S(7) 98 Cr. 1023, indictment, November 5, 1998, superseding indictment, S(10) 98 Cr. 1023 (LBS).

33 "The 22 Most Wanted Suspects in a Five-Act Drama of Global Terror," *New York Times,* October 14, 2001.

34 Statement of Patrick J. Fitzgerald, U.S. Attorney, Northern District Of Illinois, National Commission on Terrorist Attacks upon the United States, June 16, 2004.

35 *United States v. Osama bin Laden et al.,* S(7) 98 Cr. 1023 (LBS), testimony of L'Houssaine Kerchtou, February 21, 2001.

36 Ibid.

37 Ibid., Engelberg.

38 *United States v. Ali Mohamed,* plea hearing.

39 *United States v. Osama bin Laden et al.,* S(7) 98 Cr. 1023, indictment, November 5, 1998, superseding indictment, S(10) 98 Cr. 1023 (LBS).

15. THE SECOND FRONT

1 *United States v. Ali Mohamed,* S(7) 98 Cr. 1023 (LBS), transcript of plea session, U.S. District Court, Southern District of New York, October 20, 2000.

2 Author's interview with FBI special agent Jack Cloonan (ret.), May 4, 2006.

3 Susan Sachs, "A National Challenge: Bin Laden's Allies; An Investigation In Egypt Illustrates Al Qaeda's Web," *New York Times,* November 21, 2001.

4 Christopher Dickey, "America's Most Wanted," *Newsweek,* July 4, 1994.

5 Samuel M. Katz, *Relentless Pursuit the DSS and the Manhunt for the Al-Qaeda Terrorists* (New York: Forge, 2002).

6 Reeve, *The New Jackals,* p. 46.

7 David B. Ottoway and Steve Coll, "Retracing the Steps of a Terror Suspect: Accused Bomb Builder Tied to Many Plots," *Washington Post,* June 5, 1995.

8 Author's interview, confidential Pakistani source.

9 Associated Press, "Bhutto: New York Bombing Suspect Attempted to Assassinate Her," *Chicago Tribune,* March 19, 1995; "Bhutto Seeks U.S. Help," Associated Press Online, March 21, 1995; Simon Reeve, *The New Jackals,* p. 54.

10 Author's interview with Col. Rodolfo B. Mendoza, Philippines National Police, March 19, 2002.

11 In their summation for the Bojinka case, federal prosecutors described the C106D as Yousef's "signature" within the improvised explosive device, *United States v. Ramzi Ahmed Yousef et al.,* S(12) 93 Cr. 180 (KTD), August 26, 1996.

12 Terry McDermott, "The Plot: How Terrorists Hatched a Simple Plan to Use Planes as Bombs," *Los Angeles Times,* September 1, 2003; Mitch Frank, "Four Dots American Intelligence Failed to Connect," *Time,* April 26, 2004 (Bojinka = "explosion"); Steve Fairnaru, "Clues Pointed to Changing Terrorist Tactics," *Washington Post,* May 18, 2002 (Bojinka = "loud bang"); David Horowitz, "Why Bush Is Innocent and the Democrats Are Guilty," *Frontpagemagazine.com* May 20, 2002 (Bojinka = "big bang"); http://en.wikipedia.org/wiki/Talk:Oplan_Bojinka.

13 http://www.eudict.com/?lang=croeng&word=boānica.

14 Ibid., Yousef et al., July 30, 1996.

15 Ibid., June 11, 1996.

16 Ibid., May 29, 1996.

17 Ibid.

18 Although federal prosecutors argued to a jury in the Southern District of New York that it was Yousef's intent for all 12 planes to blow up over the Pacific during a two-day period, it's now clear from evidence seized by the FBI that the plot envisioned a series of jumbo jet explosions that would play out for months. Further, the April 2002 BIF affidavit describes the plot as one in which the planes would blow up over U.S. "cities." See: Affidavit in Support of Criminal Complaint, *United States v. Benevolence International Foundation Inc. and Enaam M. Arnaout, aka Abu Mahmoud, aka Abdel Samia,* by FBI special agent Robert Walker, Northern District of Illinois, Eastern Division, April 29, 2002.

19 Author's interview with U.S. postal inspector Frank Gonzalez (ret.), January 3, 2003.

20 Scott Shane, "Scale and Detail of Plane Scheme Recall Al Qaeda," *New York Times,* August 11, 2006; Raymond Bonner and Benjamin Weiser, "Echoes of Early Design to Use Chemicals to Blow Up Airliners," *New York Times,* August 11, 2006.

21 Wali Kahn was also linked by the FBI to BIF, the Benevolence International Foundation, another bin Laden NGO; Ibid., Arnaout affidavit, April 29, 2002.

22 Maria Ressa, "Investigators Think Sept. 11, 1995 Plot Related," *CNN.com,* February 25, 2002; Mark Fineman and Richard C. Paddock, "Indonesia Cleric Tied to '95 Anti-U.S. Plot," *Los Angeles Times,* February 7, 2002; Raymond Bonner, "How Qaeda Linked Up with Malaysian Groups," *New York Times,* February 7, 2002.

23 Ibid., Yousef et al., May 29, 1996.

24 Ibid., August 15, 1996.

25 Log book, Dona Josefa Apartments, December 1994 to January 9, 1995; obtained by author.

26 *United States v. Ramzi Ahmed Yousef et al.,* June 3, 1996.

27 Ibid.

28 The evidence proving the origin of the plot in 1994 is contained in *1000 Years for Revenge* and it's based on dozens of interviews with sources inside the Justice Department and the U.S. intelligence community as well as once-classified documents obtained from the Philippines National Police. As we'll see later in this book, the direct al Qaeda ties to the Yousef-Shaikh Omar Abdel-Rahman 1993 World Trade Center bombing cell and the Yousef-KSM, Murad-Wali Khan Manila cell (which hatched the 9/11 plot) were confirmed in the year 2000 by the Defense In-

telligence Agency (DIA) and the U.S. Army's Special Operations Command in an al Qaeda targeted operation called Able Danger. See declassified March 21, 2000 link chart pp. 570–571.

16. LOSING THE AL QAEDA KEY

1 Eric Brazil, "Terror Suspect OKs Deportation," *San Francisco Examiner,* April 27, 1995.

2 Philippines National Police (PNP) Person Report on Mohammed Jamal Khalifa, August 25, 1996.

3 Col. Rodolfo B. Mendoza, senior superintendent, provincial director, Philippines National Police, Pampanga PPO, Philippine Jihad Inc., September 11, 2002, p. 50.

4 *United States v. Soliman S. Biheiri,* 03-365A, Declaration in Support of Pre-Trial Detention, August 14, 2003.

5 PNP: Initial results re: Investigation on Suspected Islamic Extremists. January 6, 1995; PNP Network Diagram of the International Terrorists' ("Liberation Army") Connections.

6 Ibid., PNP Person Report, August 25, 1996.

7 Affidavit in support of criminal complaint, *United States v. Benevolence International Foundation Inc. and Enaam M. Arnaout, aka Abu Mahmoud, aka Abdel Samia,* by FBI special agent Robert Walker, Northern District of Illinois, Eastern Division, April 29, 2002; *The 9/11 Commission Report,* p. 106.

8 FBI property receipt pursuant to search warrant, December 20, 1994.

9 Ibid., Arnaout affidavit, April 29, 2002.

10 State Department Cable, Document Number: 1994MANILA19999, p. 261. American Embassy in Manila to Sec, State "A Saudi Arabian-based relief agency operating in Manila had been coordinating with and helping Muslim Secessionist factions in Mindanao and the ASG [Abu Sayyaf Group]. The head of the Agency (Islamic Relief Organization [IIRO]) is identified as a Saudi named Muhamad Jammal (Khalifah)." Cited by Steven Emerson in testimony before the House Committee on Financial Services; Subcommittee on Oversight and Investigations, February 12, 2002; Miller et al., *The Cell,* pp. 138–139.

11 Wali Khan escaped from the custody of the Philippines National Police at Camp Crame on January 11, 1995, and wasn't apprehended until the following December in Malaysia. Simon Reeve, *The New Jackals,* p. 94; Nancy Reckler, "Man Arrested in Malaysia Charged in N.Y. with Plot to Bomb U.S. Airliners," *Washington Post,* December 14, 1995; Ibid., Arnaout affidavit.

12 State Department Cable; Document Number: 1994STATE335575.

13 Certificate of Revocation, U.S. Department of State, signed by Diane Dillard, December 16, 1994.

14 Philip C. Wilcox, Jr. Coordinator for Counterterrorism, U.S. State Department, December 23, 1994 to "Executive Office for Immigration Review," Immigration and Naturalization Service, San Francisco, CA.

15 "Saudi Convict Surrenders to Jordanian Authorities," *Associated Press,* May 5, 1995.

16 Letter from Secretary of State Warren Christopher to Attorney General Janet Reno, January 6, 1995.

17 Rick DelVecchio, "Saudi Businessman Denies Link to Terrorism," *San Francisco Chronicle,* April 18, 1995.

18 Letter from Jamie S. Gorelick, Deputy Attorney General, to Office of Immigration Judge, re: Mohammed Jamal Khalifa, January 6, 1995.

19 Author's interview with Jacob L. Boesen, February 16, 2003.

20 Eric Brazil, "Saudi Faces Extradition to Jordan," *San Francisco Examiner,* April 26, 1995.

21 "Suspect in Terror Gang Being Held in Dublin," *San Francisco Chronicle,* April 17, 1995.

22 "Jailed Saudi Denies Terrorism, Fights Deportation to Jordan," *San Francisco Examiner,* April 18, 1995.

23 Joe Thomas, "Sightings of John Doe No. 2 in Blast Case, Mystery No. 1," *New York Times,* December 3, 1995; John Kifner, "FBI Seeking 2 in Blast. Search for Bodies Is Slow," *New York Times,* April 21, 1995; Interpol Report "Regarding: Update of Oklahoma Bombing to Include New Composite Sketch For 'John Doe' Suspect #2." Marked: Critical Urgent. From: Interpol Washington. To: Secretary General, Interpol. Attention: Anti-Terrorism. Date: May 6, 1995.

24 Peter Lance, *1000 Years for Revenge,* Chapter 30, "John Doe No. 2," pp. 308–318.

25 Author's interview with Stephen Jones, May 15, 2003.

26 In his own handwriting fixed with his thumbprint, Angeles wrote: "I certify that Terry Nichols was known to me personally during our meeting w/Abdul Hakim Murad, Wali-Khan + Ahmed Yousef in . . . Davao City in 1991. *Note:* Terry Nichols introduced himself to me as a farmer," Affidavit of Edwin Angeles, Philippines National Police Station, Basilan, the Philippines, November 3, 1996.

27 *United States v. Timothy McVeigh,* May 12, 1997.

28 *United States v. Ramzi Ahmed Yousef et al.,* August 9, 1996, pp. 3953–3989.

29 Passport of Terry Lynn Nichols, visa granted November 4, 1994.

30 Summary of telephone activity on Daryl Bridges' account spotlight prepaid card, December 7, 1993 through April 17, 1995. (Prepared August 16, 1996.)

31 FBI 302, Philip Rojas re: conversation with Abdul Hakim Murad, April 19, 1995, by FBI agent Frank Pellegrino and secret service agent Brian Parr. (Transcribed April 20, 1995.)

32 Stephen Jones and Peter Israel, *Others Unknown: The Oklahoma City Bombing Case* (New York: Public Affairs, 1998).

33 Author's interview with Congressman Dana Rohrabacher (R-CA), June 9, 2006.

34 Richard Clark, *Against All Enemies: Inside America's War on Terror* (New York: Free Press, 2004), p. 127.

35 Bureau of Prisons Public Information Inmate Data for Mohammed Jamal Khalifa, July 23, 2004.

36 Eric Brazil "Saudi Faces Extradition to Jordan," *San Francisco Examiner,* April 26, 1995.

37 Eric Brazil "Terror Suspect OKs Deportation," *San Francisco Examiner,* April 27, 1994.

38 Ibid.

39 Ibid.

40 Ibid., April 26, 1995.

41 "Alleged Terrorist Deported to Jordan," *UPI,* May 5, 1995.

42 "Saudi Convict Surrenders to Jordanian Authorities," *Associated Press,* May 5, 1995.

43 Memo to author from John Berger, March 20, 2006.

44 Ibid., Bureau of Prisons Public Information Inmate Data for Mohammed Jamal Khalifa, July 23, 2004.

45 Author's interview with Mike Scheuer, July 17, 2005.

46 "U.S. Advising Philippines on Terrorism War: Abu Sayyaf Rebels Linked to Bin Laden," *San Francisco Chronicle,* November 24, 2001.

47 Declaration of Mohammed Jamal Khalifa, re: Terrorist Attacks of September 11, 2001, *Thomas E. Burnett Sr. et al. v. Al Baraka Investment and Development Corporation et al.,* Case No. CV9849 RCC, April 8, 2004.

48 Author's interview with Terry McDermott, July 16, 2005; Terry McDermott, *Perfect Soldiers, Who They Were, Why They Did It* (New York: HarperCollins, 2005).

49 Steven Emerson, interview for *Triple Cross,* June 6, 2006.

50 Ibid.

51 Jamie S. Gorelick, Memorandum to Mary Jo White, Louis Freeh, et al., March 1995. Declassified, April 2004. http://www.globalsecurity.org/security/library/report/2004/1995_gorelick_memo.pdf.

52 See list of 172 unindicted coconspirators in *United States v. Omar Abdel Rahman et al.*, S(5) 93 Cr. 181 (MBM), Appendix X, p. 574.

53 Dan Eggen and Walter Pincus, "House Member Seeks Gorelick's Resignation," *Washington Post*, April 15, 2004.

54 Ibid., Eggen and Pincus.

55 David E. Rosenbaum, "Threats and Responses: The Commissioners—For Members of Panel, Past Work Becomes an Issue in the Present Hearings," *New York Times*, April 14, 2004.

56 *The 9/11 Commission Report* (New York: W.W. Norton, 2004).

17. HIDING BEHIND THE WALL

1 Andrew C. McCarthy, "The Wall Truth," *National Review Online*, April 19, 2004.

2 *United States v. Omar Abdel Rahman et al.*, S(5) 93 Cr. 181 (MBM), January 30, 1995.

3 Author's interview with Roger L. Stavis, March 17, 2006.

4 *United States v. Ali Mohamed*, S(7) 98 Cr. 1023 (LBS), sealed complaint, September 1998. Affidavit of FBI special agent Daniel Coleman, bin Laden Unit, New York office.

5 Author's interview with FBI special agent Jack Cloonan (ret.), May 4, 2006.

6 *United States v. Ali Mohamed*, S(7) 98 Cr. 1023 (LBS), transcript of plea session, U.S. District Court, Southern District of New York, October 20, 2000.

7 *United States v. Osama bin Laden et al.*, S(7) 98 Cr. 1023 (LBS), testimony of L'Houssaine Kerchtou, February 22, 2001.

8 Ibid., plea session transcript.

9 *United States v. Osama bin Laden et al.*, S(7) 98 Cr. 1023, March 26, 2001, February 22, 2001.

10 Ibid.

11 Ibid., Coleman affidavit.

12 U.S. military enlistment oath, http://usmilitary.about.com/od/joiningthemilitary/l/blenlistoath.htm.

13 *United States v. Omar Abdel Rahman et al.*, S(5) 93 Cr. 181 (MBM), January 30, 1995.

14 Ibid., plea session transcript.

15 Handwritten note of Ibrahim El-Gabrowny attached as exhibit to the appeal of his conviction in *United States v. Omar Abdel Rahman et al.*, S(5) 93 Cr. 181 (MBM).

16 Laural L. Hooper, Jennifer E. Marsh, and Brian Yeh, Treatment of *Brady v. Maryland*, Material in U.S. District and State Courts' Rules, Orders, and Policies Report to the Advisory Committee on Criminal Rules of the Judicial Conference of the United States, October 2004.

17 *United States v. Omar Abdel Rahman et al.*, S(5) 93 Cr. 181 (MBM), transcript p. 14165, July 13, 1995.

18 Ibid., Stavis.

19 Ibid., plea session transcript.

20 *United States v. Osama bin Laden et al.*, S(7) 98 Cr. 1023 (LBS), May 1, 2001.

21 Ibid., March 26, 2001, pp. 3337–3338.

22 Ibid.

23 Ibid., plea session transcript.

24 Letter to Judge Leonard B. Sand from Mary Jo White, U.S. Attorney for the SDNY, and Alan R. Kaufman, Chief of the Criminal Division, requesting that Ali Mohamed's letter and attachments remain under seal, August 27, 1999.

25 *United States v. Ramzi Ahmed Yousef et al.,* S(12) 93 Cr. 180 (KTD), June 24, 1996.

26 PNP Memorandum: Initial Results re: Investigation on Suspected Islamic Extremists, January 6, 1995.

27 FBI 302 interrogation of Ramzi Yousef, February 7 to 8, 1995, p. 17.

28 Ibid., *United States v. Yousef et al.*

29 Author's interview with Col. Aida Fariscal, PNP (ret.), April 18, 2002.

30 1995 President Lingkod Bayan Awardee, Aida Fariscal; autobiography and character.

31 Ibid., Fariscal.

32 Ibid.

18. THE THIRD PLOT

1 *United States v. Ramzi Ahmed Yousef et al.,* S(12) 93 Cr. 180 (KTD), July 18, 1996.

2 Author's interview with PNP Col. Rodolfo B. Mendoza, April 19, 2002.

3 Memo from Capt. Aida Fariscal, PNP National Capitol Regional Command, to President Fidel Ramos.

4 Ibid., Mendoza, April 19, 2002.

5 Ibid.

6 Maria Ressa, "U.S. Warned in 1995 of Plot to Hijack Planes, Attack Buildings," *CNN.com,* September 18, 2001; transcript of interview with Secretary Rigoberto Bobby Tiglao, by *CNN,* September 18, 2001.

7 Jim Gomez and John Solomon, "Authorities Warned of Hijack Risks," *Associated Press,* March 3, 2002.

8 *United States v. Ramzi Yousef et al.,* July 17, 1996, p. 2387.

9 Ibid., July 22, 1996. p. 2552.

10 Ibid., July 23, 1996. p. 2612.

11 Ed Offley, "First Questions for the Inquests into 9–11," *Defense Watch,* January 9, 2002.

12 Luis H. Francia, "Local Is Global," *Village Voice,* September 26, 2001.

13 Rafael Garcia III, "Decoding Bojinka," *Newsbreak,* November 15, 2001.

14 Author's interview with Rafael Garcia III, March 27, 2005.

15 Author's interview with Rafael Garcia III, May 19, 2005.

16 At the time of the Dona Josefa fire, Col. Avelino "Sonny" Razon was deputy commander of the Presidential Security Group. He was promoted to general after running the Bojinka investigation and in 2005 was serving as police chief of Manila.

17 Author's interview with Rafael Garcia III, March 27, 2005.

18 Alexander Cockburn, "Ex-State Department Security Officer Charges Pre-9/11 Cover-Up," *Counterpunch,* March 9, 2006.

19 Ibid.

20 Thomas Sancton, "Anatomy of a Hijack," *Time,* January 9, 1995.

21 Specialoperations.com, GIGN at Marseilles Airport, December, 1994.

22 In CNN.com's *9/11 Timeline,* the reported Marseilles hijacking incident with the Eiffel Tower as a possible target is considered the first early warning sign, http://www.CNNcom/interactive/us/0205/intelligence.timeline/content..1..html.

23 FBI SECRET/NOFORN memo: Ramzi Ahmed Yousef: A New Generation of Sunni Islamic Terrorists. NOFORN is a designation indicating "no distribution to foreigners." Bob Woodward, *Veil: The Secret Wars of the CIA* (New York: Simon & Schuster, 2005), p. 418.

24 9/11 Commission, Staff Statement #15.

25 *The 9/11 Commission Report, Authorized Edition.* Endnote 1 to Chapter 5, p. 488.

26 Thomas Jocelyn, "The Moussaoui Dossier," *Weekly Standard,* May 30, 2006. Yahoo News.
27 White House press briefing, May 17, 2002, CNN.com.
28 9/11 Commission, testimony of Condoleezza Rice, April 8, 2004.
29 Final Declassified Report of the Joint Inquiry, July 24, 2003, pp. 209–215.
30 Lance Williams, "Bin Laden's Bay Area recruiter," *San Francisco Chronicle,* November 21, 2001.

19. RED CRESCENT TOUR

1   Author's interview with FBI special agent Jack Cloonan (ret.), May 4, 2006.
2   Lawrence Wright, "How an Egyptian Doctor Became a Master of Terror," *New Yorker,* September 9, 2002.
3   "A Nation Challenged: The Hunted; The 22 Most Wanted Suspects, in a Five-Act Drama of Global Terror," *New York Times,* October 14, 2001.
4   "The World's Most Wanted," *CNN Presents,* June 11, 2006.
5   Ibid.
6   Patrick E. Tyler, "Feeling Secure, U.S. Failed to Grasp bin Laden Threat," *New York Times,* September 8, 2002.
7   Susan Sachs, "A Nation Challenged: Bin Laden's Allies; An Investigation in Egypt Illustrates Al Qaeda's Web," *New York Times,* November 21, 2001.
8   Lance Williams and Erin McCormick, "Top bin Laden Aide Toured State, Special Report: Al-Zawahiri Solicited Funds Under the Guise of Refugee Relief," *San Francisco Chronicle,* October 11, 2001.
9   Author's interview with Linda Sanchez, March 27, 2006.
10 http://www.kasralainy.edu.eg/english.
11 Website of Dr. Ali Zaki, http://dralizaki.com/about.aspx.
12 HealthGrades.com Report on Dr. Ali Zaki, MD, June 11, 2006, http://www.healthgrades.com /consumer/index.cfm?fuseaction=frame&modtype=PRC&modact=PRC_profile_report&hgi =HGPY9623386A875647053&requesttimeout=300&Iid=1055997.
13 Ibid., Williams and McCormack.
14 Ibid.
15 Peter Waldman, Gerald F. Seib, Jerry Markon, and Christopher Cooper, *Wall Street Journal,* November 26, 2001.
16 Ibid.
17 It was the FBI office in Charlotte, North Carolina, where Ali Mohamed said he'd applied for a job as a translator. There is no evidence that he got the job.
18 Lance Williams and Erin McCormick, "Bin Laden's Bay Area Recruiter Khalid Abu-al-Dahab Signed Up American Muslims to Be Terrorists," *San Francisco Chronicle,* November 21, 2001.
19 Author's interview with Linda Sanchez, May 8, 2006.
20 "Anti-Terror War's Missteps Detailed Ex-NSC Staffers," *Washington Post,* October 2, 2002.
21 Ibid., Cloonan interview.
22 Ibid.
23 Interview with Steven Emerson for *Triple Cross,* June 7, 2006.
24 Reeve, *The New Jackals,* pp. 104–106.
25 According to a database of open-source and declassified CIA files compiled by Boston-based researchers Ed and Donna Basset, Yousef later added the name "Baluch," a reference to the Baluchistan province where his family is based. Also at the Su Casa, Yousef showed a Pakistani identity card issued in Pasni. His fake Pakistani passport reportedly gave his address as the Usmania Mosque in Islamabad, frequented by Baluchis.

26 Bill Keller, "Self-Portrait of an Informer: An Innocent," *New York Times,* February 21, 1995.

27 Ibid., *The New Jackals,* p. 65.

28 Author's interview with Jeanne Smith, July 10, 1999; Author's interview with DSS agent Rob Born (ret.), May 5, 2002.

29 Affidavit of Bradley Smith, EEOC complaint, August, 31, 1998.

30 Bill Keller, "Terror Case Informer Is No Hero in His Homeland; Man's Actions in Capturing Accused Trade Center Bomber Draw Scorn in South Africa," *New York Times,* February 15, 1995.

31 Samuel M. Katz, *Relentless Pursuit: The DSS and the Manhunt for the Al-Qaeda Terrorists* (New York: Forge, 2002).

32 *United States v. Ramzi Ahmed Yousef et al.,* S(12) 93 Cr. 180 (KTD), August 9, 1996.

33 "How the FBI Gets Its Man," *60 Minutes II,* October 10, 2001.

34 The account was first revealed in a story by Christopher John Farley, "The Man Who Wasn't There," *Time,* May 20, 1995, and later published in a piece by Terry McDermott and other reporters for the *Los Angeles Times* on December 21, 2002. Terry McDermott, Josh Meyer, and Patrick J. McDonnell, "The Plots and Designs of Al Qaeda's Engineer: Khalid Shaikh Mohammed, the Man Believed to Be behind 9/11, Hides in Plain Sight; And Narrowly Escapes Capture in Pakistan," *Los Angeles Times,* December 22, 2002.

35 "The Mastermind," *CBS News,* March 5, 2003.

36 FBI 302 interrogation of Ramzi Ahmed Yousef by Bradley J. Garrett, February 7, 1995, transcribed February 10, 1995.

37 Jane Mayer, "Outsourcing Torture: The Secret History of America's 'Extraordinary Rendition' Program," *New Yorker,* February 14, 2005.

38 Author's interview with confidential DSS source, February 18, 2000.

39 FBI 302 interrogation of Ramzi Ahmed Yousef by Chuck Stern and Brian Parr, February 7 to 8, 1995. Transcribed February 28, 1995.

40 Lou Michel and Dan Herbeck, *American Terrorist: Timothy McVeigh and the Tragedy at Oklahoma City* (New York: ReganBooks, 2001), uses the wording attributed to William A. Gavin, the ADIC of the FBI's New York office, who was quoted by Simon Reeve in *The New Jackals,* pp. 108–109. In my interview with the retired ADIC on June 15, 2003, he said that he lifted Yousef's blindfold and gestured to the Towers with the line, "They're still standing." Yousef reportedly said, "They wouldn't be, if I had had enough money and enough explosives." But in *The Cell,* by Miller, Stone, and Mitchell, FBI agent Chuck Stern is cited as the agent who lifted the blindfold and reminded Yousef that the Trade Center was "still standing." In that version, Yousef replied, "They wouldn't be, if I'd gotten a little more money."

41 Peg Tyre, "An Icon Destroyed," *Newsweek,* September 11, 2001.

20. THE COVER-UP BEGINS

1 *United States v. Omar Abdel Rahman et al.,* S(5) 93 Cr. 181 (MBM), February 7, 1995, p. 2311.

2 Paul Quinn-Judge and Charles M. Sennot, "Figure Cited in Terrorism Case Said to Enter U.S. with CIA Help," *Boston Globe,* February 3, 1995.

3 *United States v. Ali Mohamed,* S(7) 98 Cr. 1023 (LBS), sealed complaint, September 1998. Affidavit of FBI special agent Daniel Coleman, bin Laden unit, New York office.

4 Ibid.

5 Ibid.

6 Steven Emerson, interview for *Triple Cross,* June 7, 2006.

7 Ibid., Coleman Affidavit.

8 Ibid.

9 Declaration of Mohammed Jamal Khalifa, In re: Terrorist Attacks of September 11, 2001, *Thomas E. Burnett Sr. et al. v. Al Baraka Investment and Development Corporation et al.*, Case No. CV9849 RCC, April 8, 2004.

10 See http://www.pinkertons.com. Burns International and American Protective Services are all under the umbrella of Securitas Security Services, USA, Inc. It includes Pinkerton, Wells Fargo Burns, America Protective Services, First Security, and other companies.

11 Author's interview with Linda Sanchez, May 8, 2006.

12 Author's interview with FBI special agent Jack Cloonan (ret.), May 4, 2006.

13 Author's interview with Lt. Col. Anthony Shaffer, June 29, 2006.

14 Ibid., September 11, 2006.

15 *United States v. Omar Abdel Rahman et al.*, S(5) 93 Cr. 181 (MBM), September 1, 1995, pp. 18, 418.

16 As a general matter, a trial judge has discretion to give a missing witness instruction "if a party has it peculiarly within his power to produce witnesses whose testimony would elucidate the transaction." *Pennewell v. United States*, 353 F.2d 870, 871 (D.C. Cir. 1965) (quoting *Graves v. United States*, 150 U.S. 118, 121 (1893)). "If such a person does not appear and one of the parties had some special ability to produce him, the law permits the jury to draw an inference—namely, that the missing witness would have given testimony damaging to that party," *United States v. Pitts*, 918 F.2d 197, 199 (D.C. Cir. 1990). The *Pitts* and *Pennewell* decisions also make clear, however, that "no inference can fairly be drawn against defendant from his failure to call [a witness] to the stand to incriminate himself," *Pennewell*, 353 F.2d at 871. Cited in *United States v. Eric Glenn*, 93CR00250.

17 Sean Webby and Rodney Foo, "Ali Mohamed, Who Lived in the South Bay During the Late 1980's and 1990's, Has Long Played Vital Roles on Both Sides of the American Counterterrorism Campaign," *San Jose Mercury News*, November 12, 2001.

18 Joseph P. Fried, "Sheik and 9 Followers Guilty of a Conspiracy of Terrorism," *New York Times*, October 2, 1995.

19 Steven Emerson, interview for *Triple Cross*, June 7, 2006.

20 *United States v. Omar Abdel Rahman et al.*, S(5) 93 Cr. 181 (MBM), July 26, 1995, p. 15252; Richard Bernstein and Ralph Blumenthal, "Bomb Informer's Tapes Give Rare Glimpse of FBI Dealings."

21 Colin Miner, "Temptress and the Spy," *New York Post*, March 12, 1994.

22 Author's interview with Diane Bodner-Duhig, December 19, 2002; Author's interview with Richard Swick, December 17, 2002.

23 *United States v. Cecil Ray Price et al.*, Criminal Action Number 5291, U.S. Court for the Southern District of Mississippi, October 7, 1968.

24 FBI AIRTEL re: Top Echelon Informant, June, 6, 1962. Payment authorization from Asst. Director Evens to Director J. Edgar Hoover.

25 Author's interview with Judge W. O. "Chet" Dillard, June 11, 2004.

26 Testimony of Marty Light, Gregory Scarpa Sr.'s former attorney, at hearings before the President's Commission on Organized Crime, Washington, D.C., January 29, 1986.

27 Fredric Dannen, "The G-Man and the Hit Man," *New Yorker*, December 16, 1996.

28 Author's interview with Alan Futerfas, May 24, 2004.

29 Author's interview with Det. Joseph Simone, April 30, 2004.

30 Affirmation of Flora Edwards; author's interview with Flora Edwards, April 26, 2004; author's interview with Det. Joseph Simone, NYPD (ret.), April 30, 2004.

31 Affidavit of Gregory Scarpa Jr., April 29, 1999; affidavit of Gregory Scarpa Jr., 2002.

32 FBI 302 reports re: interview of Christopher M. Favo, November 16, 1995; December 8, 1995; Alan J. Futerfas, pros. memo, *United States v. Anthony Russo et al.;* FBI 302 interrogation of Larry Mazza, April 28, 1994.

33 In a later trial, Victor M. Orena Jr., son of the Colombo boss, and six codefendants were acquitted based on the defense that they were merely defending themselves against Scarpa Sr.'s murderous attacks.

34 Author's interview with Flora Edwards, June 3, 2006.

35 Author's interview with Ellen Resnick, May 24, 2004.

36 *United States v. Michael Sessa,* CR-92-351, September 24, 2001, pp. 19–20.

37 FBI 302 memo re: contents retrieved in search of Nosair's residence. By FBI special agent Leonard P. Mleczkowski, dictated November 9, 1990, dated November 13, 1990.

21. THE BIN LADEN SQUAD

1 President Bill Clinton, PDD-39. Unclassified. Signed June 21, 1995.

2 James Bamford, *A Pretext for War: 9/11, Iraq, and the Abuse of America's Intelligence Agencies* (New York: Anchor Books, 2005).

3 Steve Coll, *Ghost Wars: The Secret History of the CIA, Afghanistan, and Bin Laden from the Soviet Invasion to September 10, 2001* (New York: Penguin, 2004).

4 Henry Schuster, "The Al Qaeda Hunter," *CNN.com,* March 2, 2005.

5 Author's interview with FBI special agent Jack Cloonan (ret.), May 4, 2006.

6 David Margolick, "Mr. Fitz Goes to Washington," *Vanity Fair,* February 2006.

7 Official biography, Office of the U.S. Attorney for the Northern District of Illinois.

8 Ibid.

9 Patrick J. Fitzgerald, U.S. Attorney, Northern District Of Illinois, U.S. Senate Committee on the Judiciary, Hearing: "Protecting Our National Security from Terrorist Attacks: A Review of Criminal Terrorism Investigations and Prosecutions," October 21, 2003.

10 *United States v. Ali Mohamed,* S(7) 98 Cr. 1023 (LBS), sealed complaint, September 1998. Affidavit of FBI special agent Daniel Coleman, bin Laden unit, New York office.

11 Author's interview with FBI Special Agent Jack Cloonan (ret.), May 4, 2006.

12 Timothy Carney, Mansoor Ijaz, "Intelligence Failure? Let's Go Back to Sudan," *Washington Post,* June 30, 2002.

13 Chris Floyd, "Kean Insight: Bush, bin Laden, BCCI and the 9/11 Commission," *Counterpunch,* January 31, 2003.

14 But in 1999 the Egyptian government brought 107 al Qaeda and Islamic Jihad terrorists to trial, including Ali Mohamed and Dr. Ayman al-Zawahiri (*in absentia*). Seventy-eight of the defendants were given prison sentences. Eleven were sentenced to death, including Mohamed and the Egyptian surgeon who was bin Laden's number two. Jailan Halawai, "Jihad Émigrés Sentenced to Death," *Al-Ahram Weekly,* April 22, 1999.

15 Miller et al., *The Cell,* pp. 151–152.

16 Susan Page, "Why Clinton Failed to Stop bin Laden," *USA Today,* November 12, 2001.

17 Ibid., *The Cell,* p. 66.

18 Mary Ann Weaver, "Blowback: The CIA Poured Billions into a Jihad Against Soviet-Occupied Afghanistan, Creating a Militant Islamist Abraham Lincoln Brigade Believed to Have Been Involved in Bombings from Islamabad to New York; Is Bosnia Next?" *Atlantic Monthly,* May 1996.

19 Steven Emerson, testimony before Senate Judiciary Committee, December 4, 2001.

20 Susan Sachs, "An Investigation in Egypt Illustrates al Qaeda's Web," *New York Times,* November 21, 2001.

21 *United States v. Osama bin Laden et al.*, S(7) 98 Cr. 1023 (LBS), February 21, 2001.

22 Ibid., January 8, 2001.

23 Brian Ross, "Al Qaeda Ally? Member of Qatari Royal Family Helped Senior Al Qaeda Official Get Away," *ABC News*, February 7, 2003.

24 Steve Coll, *Ghost Wars: The Secret History of the CIA, Afghanistan, and Bin Laden from the Soviet Invasion to September 10, 2001* (New York: Penguin, 2004), p. 325.

25 Pepe Escobar, "Kabul Diary, Part 3: Air Osama," *Asia Times*, November 30, 2001.

26 Ibid., February 22, 2001.

27 Chapter 7 bankruptcy filing by Khaled E. Mohamed and Karie A. Mohamed, U.S. Bankruptcy Court, Case # 96-53312, Judge James R. Grube.

28 Author's interview with Paul Thompson, June 14, 2006.

29 http://cooperativeresearch.org/timeline.jsp?timeline=complete_911_timeline&other_al-qaeda _operatives=aliMohamed.

30 *United States v. Ramzi Ahmed Yousef et al.*, S(12) 93 Cr. 180 (KTD), May 29, 1996.

31 Indictment, *United States v. Ramzi Ahmed Yousef et al.*, S(12) 93 Cr. 180 (KTD).

32 PNP transcript of interrogation of Abdul Hakim Murad, January 7, 1995. Government's Exhibit 760-T, *United States v. Ramzi Ahmed Yousef et al.*

33 Larry Silverman, interview for *Triple Cross*, June 12, 2006.

34 FBI 302, Gregory Scarpa Jr. re: Ramzi Yousef intelligence, March 5, 1996, p. 3.

35 Fredric Dannen, "The G-Man and the Hit Man," *New Yorker*, December 16, 1996.

36 Letter from Scarpa Jr.'s attorney, Jeremy Orden, to Judge Reena Raggi, April 29, 1999, *United States v. Gregory Scarpa Jr.*, 94 Cr. 1119 (S-5).

37 FBI 302 memo, March 5, 1996.

38 Author's interview with Larry Silverman, April 13, 2004.

39 Author's interview with Det. Joseph Simone, April 30, 2004.

40 Author's interview with Flora Edwards, April 27, 2004.

41 Interview with James Kallstrom for documentary *Conspiracy?* The History Channel, 2005.

22. "HOW TO BLOW UP AIRPLANES"

1 David Stout and Mark Mazzetti, "Dry Run Was Planned in Bomb Plot, Officials Say," *New York Times*, August 10, 2006. Quoting from the *New York Times* story: "The FBI and homeland security memo said the plotters expected to use peroxide-based explosives that are 'sensitive to heat, shock and friction and can be initiated simply with fire or an electrical charge and can also be used to produce improvised detonators.' Other officials in London said the plotters planned to smuggle the liquids in drink bottles."

2 Kim Murphy, "Bomb Plot Evidence 'Immense,' British Say," *Los Angeles Times*, August 22, 2006.

3 FBI 302 interview with Greg Scarpa Jr. re: Ramzi Yousef intelligence, May 5, 1996.

4 The conventional wisdom, which was ratified by then-National Security Advisor Condoleezza Rice in her April 8, 2004, testimony before the 9/11 Commission, was that until the attacks of September 11, any warnings of a threat to the United States, specifically New York City, were "historic" and devoid of "actionable intelligence." See Rice testimony at: http://www.cnn.com /2004/ALLPOLITICS/04/08/rice.transcript.

5 John Kifner, "Kahane Suspect Is a Muslim with a Series of Addresses," *New York Times*, November 7, 1990.

6 See list of 172 unindicted coconspirators in *United States v. Omar Abdel Rahman et al.*, S(5) 93 Cr. 181 (MBM) at Appendix X, p. 574.

7　Yousef's handwritten notes March 27–28, 1996, FBI 302 memo, September 7, 1996, re: Angela Clemente and Associates, "The Scarpa Intelligence on the Terrorist Threat: An Evaluative Report," February 20, 2005.

8　FBI 302, March 5, 1996, p. 4.

9　Roma Corp. "kite," May 9, 1996. See *Cover Up*, Appendix II, p. 301.

10　Author's interview with confidential FBI source.

11　Final Declassified Report of the Joint Inquiry, July 24, 2003.

12　Terry McDermott, "The Plot: How Terrorist Hatched a Simple Plan to Use Planes as Bombs," *Los Angeles Times*, September 1, 2002.

13　Ibid., Coll, *Ghost Wars*, p. 326.

14　Bill Gertz, *Breakdown: How America's Intelligence Failures Led to September 11* (Washington, D.C.: Regnery, 2002).

15　Seymour Hersh, "Missed Messages," *New Yorker*, June 3, 2002.

16　Ibid., Ross.

17　Ibid., McDermott.

18　"Qatar Interior Minister Asks U.S. Judge to Scrap 9/11 Case Against Him," *Associated Press*, June 8, 2006.

19　http://www.qatarembassy.net/emir.asp.

20　Hugh Miles, "Al-Jazeera: The inside Story of the Arab News Channel that Is Challenging the West," *Denver Post*, May 26, 2005.

21　Author's interview with Bathiya Coomasaru, February 6, 2005.

22　U.S. Department of State, *Background Note: Qatar*, November, 2005.

23　Josh Meyer and John Goetz, "War with Iraq: Qatar's Security Chief Suspected of Having Ties to Al Qaeda; Interior Minister Reportedly Sheltered Terrorists, Including 9/11 Plotter; U.S. Military Campaign's Headquarters Are in the Gulf Nation's Capital," *Los Angeles Times*, March 28, 2003.

24　Author's interview with Lt. Col. Anthony Shaffer, June 15, 2006.

25　FBI 302 interview with Greg Scarpa Jr. re: Ramzi Yousef intelligence, July 2, 1996.

26　Dan Eggen, "9/11 Panel Links Al Qaeda, Iran," *Washington Post*, June 26, 2004.

27　Ibid., Shaffer, June 15, 2006.

28　Greg Smith, "Terrorist Called Pals on Feds' Line," New York *Daily News*, September 24, 2000; Greg Smith, "FBI's Chilling Terror Leads on '96 Tapes," New York *Daily News*, January 21, 2002.

29　Pat Milton, *In the Blink of an Eye: The FBI Investigation of TWA Flight 800* (New York: Random House, 1999), p. 51.

30　Matthew L. Wald. "The Fate of TWA 800: The Overview: Flight 800 Flew for 24 Seconds After the Initial Catastrophe," *New York Times*, July 27, 1996.

31　Ibid., Milton, p. 21.

32　Author's interview with James K. Kallstrom, FBI ADIC, NYO (ret.), July 12–13 2004.

33　FBI 302, March 5, 1996.

34　Christopher S. Wren, "Judge to Ask Bomb Trial Jury About Prejudice from Crash," *New York Times*, July 23, 1996; *United States v. Ramzi Ahmed Yousef et al.*, S(12) 93 Cr. 180 (KTD), July 18, 1996.

23. BOJINKA FULFILLED

1　Ibid., Kallstrom interview.

2　Author's interview with Larry Silverman, April 13, 2004.

3　Author's interview with Larry Silverman for *Triple Cross*, June 12, 2006.

4　Louis M. Freeh, "Report to the American People on the Work of the FBI 1993–1998."

5 Ibid., Kallstrom interview.

6 Milton, *In the Blink of an Eye*, pp. 182–183.

7 Author's interview with Kenneth Maxwell, March 29, 2003.

8 Sylvia Adcock and Al Baker, "Probe Turns to Athens for Answers," *Newsday*, September 16, 1996.

9 Author's interview with William Tobin, July 14, 2004.

10 Matthew L. Wald, "Fate of Flight 800: The Overview: Jet's Landing Gear Is Said to Provide Evidence of Bomb," *New York Times*, July 31, 1996; Don Van Natta Jr., "More Traces of Explosive in Flight 800," *New York Times*, August 31, 1996; Silvia Adcock and Knut Royce, "Two Traces Found," *Newsday*, August 31, 1996.

11 *United States v. Ramzi Yousef et al.*, testimony of Steven Burmeister, August 15, 1996, court transcript, p. 4502.

12 Don Van Natta Jr., "Prime Evidence Found That Device Exploded in Cabin of Flight 800," *New York Times*, August 23, 1996.

13 Ibid.

14 Michael Arena and Silvia Adcock, "Probers Kept in the Dark," *Newsday*, August 24, 1996.

15 Milton, *In the Blink of an Eye*, pp. 227–228.

16 Ibid., Kallstrom.

17 Dan Barry, "FBI Says 2 Labs Found Traces of Explosive on TWA Jetliner," *New York Times*, August 24, 1996.

18 Author's interview with confidential FBI source.

19 "Ill-Fated TWA Plane Used for Troop Transport in the Gulf War," *CNN.com*, August 26, 1996.

20 Milton, *In the Blink of an Eye*, p. 230.

21 Matthew Purdy, "Bob Security Test on Jet May Explain Trace of Explosives," *New York Times*, September 21, 1996.

22 Testimony of James Kallstrom before the House Subcommittee on Aviation, July 10, 1997.

23 On September 20, 1996, a patrolman for the St. Louis Airport Police Department (SLAPD), who was assigned to the canine unit, was interviewed by FBI agents in St. Louis. The patrolman advised that his responsibilities included maintaining the training for his explosives sniffing dog on a daily basis so that he could meet FAA requirements for training and certification. According to the patrolman, it is normal procedure to conduct training for the dogs on virtually a daily basis on available aircraft.

On the morning of June 10, 1996, while working the day shift at the St. Louis International Airport, the patrolman placed a call to the manager on duty at TWA Line Service to determine if they had an aircraft available on which the patrolman could conduct some training for his bomb-sniffing dog. The manager on duty, whose name the patrolman could not recall, told him that a "wide body" was available at gate 50 at the St. Louis Airport, and that the patrolman could use this aircraft to conduct his training. The patrolman recalled that he was particularly enthused because it is rare that "wide-body" aircraft become available for such training at St. Louis.

The patrolman retrieved four types of explosives from the SLAPD explosives bunker for use in the training. The explosives retrieved were water gel, C-4, det cord, and ammonia dynamite. He also used smokeless powder, which was stored in the trunk of his patrol car, in the training. The officer noted that the explosives bunker contains a variety of military and commercial type explosives for use in training, and opined that the bunker would very likely contain residue of these explosives. After retrieving the explosives, the patrolman proceeded in his patrol car to Gate 50 where he found a 747 parked.

The patrolman parked his vehicle at the base of the stairway at the outside of the jetway and entered the aircraft. The patrolman determined that the electric power was on and that no one else was present on the plane. He returned to his patrol car to bring the explosives on board the aircraft, which he believes he accomplished in two trips. The explosives were initially placed on the counter in the galley just inside the main entry door to the aircraft. The patrolman then proceeded to place the explosives around the aircraft interior for the training/certification exercise as follows:

1. The smokeless powder was on its side with the cap unscrewed inside the center armrest of row 2, seat 2 of the first class section.

2. The water gel was placed on the floor inside a tall, narrow closet/storage bin at the rear of the upper level first class section.

3. A 1.4 pound block of C-4, covered with a thin covering of clear cellophane type material, which the patrolman described as being in poor condition and allowing some of the explosive to be exposed, was placed in the pouch on the back of the backrest of row 10, seat 9.

4. The det cord, which was described by the patrolman as a thirty foot piece in extremely poor condition with cracks every few inches, was brought in its container to row 20 of the main cabin. The patrolman said that he believes he went to the side of the cabin opposite from the side where he placed the C-4, since it was his practice to place the explosives in a zig-zag pattern within the aircraft. The patrolman placed the container in which the cord was stored on the floor in the aisle, removed the cord and placed it in an overhead compartment in row 20. The patrolman noted that the can containing the det cord contained quite a bit of powder from the det cord and said if one were to wave it in the air it would create a visible cloud of powder.

5. One stick of ammonia dynamite was partially concealed in a groove in the flooring near an emergency door labeled "PRE" on the same side of the aircraft as he placed the C-4. The patrolman believes the door was located over the wing. The patrolman advised that he began the placement of the explosives at 10:45 A.M. and is required by FAA regulation to wait 30 minutes from the first placement before commencing the training exercise with the dog.

At 11:45 A.M., the patrolman began the exercise by bringing the dog into the aircraft and working him through the three areas of the aircraft where the explosives were placed. The exercise lasted fifteen minutes and the dog located all the explosives. After returning the dog to his patrol car, the patrolman proceeded to remove the explosives from the aircraft in the same order in which he placed them, using the galley as the center of his movements. The patrolman stated that he did not enter any areas of the aircraft other than those described and specifically stated that he did not enter any cargo areas. He also stated that he was the only person involved in the exercise. The patrolman provided the FBI with the can of smokeless powder used in the exercise and advised that all the other explosives had been replaced by either the FAA or exchanged locally for fresh material since the time the exercise was conducted.

The FAA in St. Louis provided the FBI with a copy of a TWA document listing gate assignments for June 10, 1996. This document shows that a 747 bearing tail number 17119 (which is the tail number for the 747 that was Flight 800) was parked at gate 50 from shortly before 700 hours (7 A.M.) until approximately 1230 hours (12:30 P.M.) on that date.

24 Richard Clarke, *Against All Enemies: Inside America's War on Terror* (New York: Free Press, 2004).

25 Bill Clinton, *My Life* (New York: Knopf, 2004), p. 718.

26 Miller et al., *The Cell,* p. 170.

27 David Rohde, "November 9–15; FBI Ends Flight 800 Inquiry," *New York Times,* November 16, 1997.

28 Appendix VII, p. 567.

29 Ibid.

30 Both planes were built at Boeing's plant in Everett, Washington, and commissioned in October 1971 (Milton, p. 48).

31 Author's phone interview and correspondence with Herman Burnett, May 5, 2004.

32 Author's interview with Flora Edwards, April 27, 2004.

33 Interview with James Kallstrom for documentary *Conspiracy?* The History Channel, 2005.

34 Author's interview with Noel Downey, Assistant District Attorney and First Deputy of the Rackets Bureau, Kings County District Attorney's Office, March 30, 2006.

35 *The People of the State of New York against Roy Lindley DeVecchio, John Sinagra,* indictment no. 6825/2005, March 23, 2005.

36 Interview with Tommy Corrigan, NYPD-JTTF (ret.) for *Triple Cross,* June 13, 2006.

37 David Johnston, "The Crash of Flight 800: The Possibilities; Tips, Leads and Theories Are Flooding In," *New York Times,* July 21, 1996.

38 Ibid.

39 Patricia Hurtado, "Bomb Suspect's Letter Revealed," *Newsday,* July 10, 1998.

40 Joseph Fried, "Conflict Portraits of Bomb Suspects," *New York Times,* July 5, 1998.

41 Author's interview with confidential retired NSA source, July 27, 2006.

24. CROSSING THE LINE

1 Simon Reeve, *The New Jackals,* p. 237.

2 *United States v. Ramzi Ahmed Yousef et al.,* S(12) 93 Cr. 180 (KTD), May 29, 1996.

3 *United States v. Ramzi Ahmed Yousef et al.,* S(12) 93 Cr. 180 (KTD), July 17, 1996.

4 Author's interview with PNP Col. Rodolfo Mendoza, April 19, 2002.

5 Letter from Jamie S. Gorelick, deputy attorney general, to Office of Immigration Judge, re: Mohammed Jamal Khalifa, January 6, 1995.

6 *United States v. Ramzi Ahmed Yousef et al.,* S(12) 93 Cr. 180 (KTD), August 26, 1996.

7 Ibid, August 26, 1996.

8 Author's interview with confidential DSS source.

9 Christopher John Farley, "The Man Who Wasn't There," *Time,* May 20, 1995.

10 Benjamin Weiser, "U.S. to Offer Detailed Trail of bin Laden in Bomb Trial," *New York Times,* January 13, 2001.

11 Letter from Patrick Fitzgerald to Michael Young, November 13, 1999, on Wadih El-Hage.

12 Author's interview with FBI special agent Jack Cloonan (ret.), May 4, 2006.

13 CNN.com, Khobar indictments returned, June 22, 2001.

14 FBI 302, December 30, 1996, p. 2.

15 Angela Clemente and Association, "The Scarpa Intelligence on the Terrorist Threat: An Evaluative Report," February 20, 2005.

16 FBI 302, March 7, 1996.

17 David Margolick, "Mr. Fitz Goes to Washington," *Vanity Fair,* February 2006.

18 Author's interview with FBI special agent Jack Cloonan (ret.), May 4, 2006.

19 Author's interview with confidential source in FBI's NYO, May 5, 2006.

20 Patrick J. Fitzgerald, U.S. Attorney, Northern District of Illinois, U.S. Senate Committee on the Judiciary, Hearing: "Protecting Our National Security from Terrorist Attacks: A Review of Criminal Terrorism Investigations and Prosecutions," October 21, 2003.

21 Author's interview with Richard Swick, December 17, 2002; author's interview with Diane Bodner-Duhig, December 19, 2002.

22 Author's interview with FBI Special Agent Len Predtechenskis (ret.), August 27, 2002.

25. VICTORY DECLARED

1 *United States v. Ramzi Ahmed Yousef et al.,* September 5, 1996.

2 Christopher S. Wren, "Jury Convicts 3 in a Conspiracy to Bomb Airliners," *New York Times,* September 6, 1996.

3 *United States v. Osama bin Laden et al.*, S(7) 98 Cr. 1023 (LBS), February 6, 2001.

4 Reference to the title character in the film written and directed by Woody Allen in 1983. Zelig, like Forrest Gump after him, was a fictional character who was a witness to many of the great events in twentieth-century history.

5 Ibid., *United States v. Osama bin Laden et al.,* February 6, 2001.

6 Author's interview with FBI special agent Jack Cloonan (ret.), May 4, 2006.

7 Patrick Fitzgerald, interview for *Inside 9/11,* Towers Productions, Inc., for the National Geographic Channel.

8 In Staff Statement 15, the 9/11 Commission concludes: "Ramzi Yousef, who was a lead operative in both plots, trained in camps in Afghanistan that were funded by bin Ladin and used to train many al Qaeda operatives. Whether he was then or later became a member of al Qaeda remains a matter of debate, but he was at a minimum part of a loose network of extremist Sunni Islamists who, like bin Ladin, began to focus their rage on the United States. Khalid Shaikh Mohammed, who provided some funding for Yousef in the 1993 WTC attack and was his operational partner in the Manila plot, later did join al Qaeda and masterminded the al Qaeda 9/11 attack. He was not, however, an al Qaeda member at the time of the Manila plot. A number of other individuals connected to the 1993 and 1995 plots or to some of the plotters either were or later became associates of bin Ladin. We have no conclusive evidence, however, that at the time of the plots any of them was operating under bin Ladin's direction."

9 Press Release, U.S. Attorney for the Northern District of Illinois, "Benevolence Director Indicted For Racketeering Conspiracy; Providing Material Support to Al Qaeda and Other Violent Groups," October 9, 2002.

10 Robert Walker, affidavit in support of criminal complaint, *United States v. Benevolence International Foundation Inc and Enaam M. Arnaout,* April 29, 2002.

26. TAPPING THE CELL

1 *United States v. Ali Mohamed,* S(7) 98 Cr. 1023 (LBS), transcript of plea session, U.S. District Court, Southern District of New York, October 20, 2000.

2 FBI executive summary of findings, international bulletin, November 18, 1998.

3 Ibid., plea session, October 20, 2000.

4 Author's interview with FBI special agent Jack Cloonan (ret.), May 4, 2006.

5 *United States v. Ali Mohamed,* S(7) 98 Cr. 1023 (LBS), Sealed Complaint, September 1998. Affidavit of FBI special agent Daniel Coleman, bin Laden unit, New York office.

6 *United States v. Osama bin Laden et al.,* S(7) 98 Cr. 1023 (LBS), February 21, 2001.

7 Ibid., plea session, October 20, 2000.

8 Ibid., Coleman affidavit.

9 *United States v. Osama bin Laden et al.,* S(7) 98 Cr. 1023, indictment, November 5, 1998, superseding indictment, S(10) 98 Cr. 1023 (LBS).

10 Benjamin Weiser, "U.S. to Offer Detailed Trail of bin Laden in Bomb Trial," *New York Times,* January 13, 2001.

11 *United States v. Wadih El-Hage et al.,* S(1) 98 Cr. 1023, Indictment (LBS).

12 *United States v. Osama bin Laden et al.,* S(7) 98 Cr. 1023 (LBS).

13 Ibid., Cloonan.

14 Ibid.

15 Title IX U.S. Code Sections 9-110.00 to 9-1110.900.

16 Christopher Wren, "Case Accusing 3 of Plotting to Bomb Jets Shows a Flaw," *New York Times,* August 8, 1996.

17 Author's interview with FBI special agent Jack Cloonan (ret.), May 4, 2006.

18 *United States v. Osama bin Laden et al.*, S(7) 98 Cr. 1023, May 1, 2001; government's closing remarks by Kenneth Karas.

19 Ibid.

20 *United States v. Osama bin Laden et al.*, S(7) 98 Cr. 1023, February 22, 2001, testimony of L'Houssaine Kherchtou, examination by Patrick Fitzgerald.

21 Author's interviews with Harry Ellen, February 25, 2003, and April 18, 2004.

22 James Risen, "Before Bombings, Omens and Fears," *New York Times,* January 9, 1999.

23 U.S. State Department Press Release, "U.S., Saudi Arabia Freeze Assets of Saudi Charity Branch Offices," January 23, 2004.

24 Interview with FBI special agent Jack Cloonan (ret.) for *Triple Cross,* June 1, 2006.

25 Ibid.

26 Peter Arnett, interview with Osama bin Laden, *CNN,* March 20, 1997.

27 Ibid.

28 In Staff Statement 16, authored principally by Snell as Senior Counsel to the 9/11 Commission, Yousef's uncle KSM was described as a "veteran jihadist." Although the statement admits that KSM "provided a small amount of funding" for the World Trade Center bombing in 1993, it alleges that it wasn't until 1996 that KSM sought to "renew" his acquaintance with bin Laden, whom he first met "in the 1980's" and first "pitched" the idea of the "planes operation" to bin Laden, which wasn't approved until 1999, after the previous year's East African embassy bombings. Staff Statement 15 maintains that whether Ramzi Yousef "became a member of al Qaeda remains a matter of debate." It claims further that "Khalid Shaikh Mohammed, who provided some funding for Yousef in the 1993 WTC attack and was his operational partner in the Manila plot, later did join al Qaeda and masterminded the al Qaeda 9/11 attack. He was not, however, an al Qaeda member at the time of the Manila plot."

29 Ibid., Cloonan, June 1, 2006.

27. THIRD AND FINAL WARNING

1 James Risen, "Before Bombings, Omens, and Fears," *New York Times,* January 9, 1999.

2 Raymond Bonner and James Risen, "Nairobi Embassy Received Warning of Coming Attack," *New York Times,* October 23, 1998.

3 Ibid., Risen, January 9, 1999.

4 Ibid.

5 *United States v. Osama bin Laden et al.*, S(7) 98 Cr. 1023, indictment, November 5, 1998, superseding indictment, S(10) 98 Cr. 1023 (LBS).

6 *United States v. Osama bin Laden et al.*, S(7) 98 Cr. 1023, May 3, 2001.

7 *United States v. Ramzi Ahmed Yousef and Eyad Ismoil,* S(12) 93 Cr. 180 (KTD), January 8, 1998.

8 Ibid.

9 Sharon Walsh, " 'Proud' Terrorist Gets 240 Years in N.Y. Bombing," *Washington Post,* January 9, 1998; Larry Neumeister, " 'Apostle of Evil' Terrorist Sentenced to Life in Prison," *Associated Press,* January 9, 1998.

10 Ibid.

11 Benjamin Weiser, "Mastermind Gets Life for Bombing of Trade Center," *New York Times,* January 9, 1998, p. 1.

12 The Egypt-based Brotherhood, whose leading theoretician, Sayyid Qutb, had also influenced Osama bin Laden, espoused a militant return to the strict principles of Islam. See Paul Berman, "Al Qaeda's Philosopher," *New York Times Magazine,* March 23, 2003.

13 PNP Debriefing report, Counter Intelligence Group, February 18, 1995.

14 PNP SECRET briefing entitled "Chronological Activities of Rose Mosquera."

15 Jim Gomez, "Police: Suspected Sept. 11 Mastermind Was Uncle to 1993 World Trade Center Plotter," *Associated Press,* June 25, 2002.

16 Matthew Brezinski, "Bust and Boom," *Washington Post,* December 30, 2001.

17 Joint Inquiry Statement of Staff Director Eleanor Hill, October 8, 2002, p. 16.

18 Louis Freeh, *My FBI: Bringing Down the Mafia, Investigating Bill Clinton, and Fighting the War on Terror* (New York: St. Martin's Press, 2005).

19 Author's interview with FBI special agent Len Predtechenskis (ret.), August 27, 2002.

20 Testimony of J. T. Caruso, acting assistant director, Counter Terrorism Division, FBI, before the Subcommittee on International Operations and Terrorism, Committee on Foreign Relations, U.S. Senate, "Al-Qaeda International," December 18, 2001.

21 Timothy Carney and Mansoor Ijaz, "Intelligence Failure? Let's Go Back to Sudan," *Washington Post,* June 30, 2002.

22 *United States v. Osama bin Laden et al.,* S(7) 98 Cr. 1023, May 1, 2001; government's closing remarks by Kenneth Karas.

23 Paul Thompson, "December 1997–Spring 1998: Urgent Requests for Embassy Security Go Unheeded," Cooperativeresearch.org.

24 Kraig Hanadel, *Catch Me If You Can* (New York: Avon, 2002).

25 Pablo Lopez, "Ewell Family Rift Continues over Grandmother's Estate," *Fresno Bee,* April 7, 1996.

26 Steve Elliott, "Ewell 'Burglary' Staged, Zent Says," *Fresno Bee,* April 9, 1998.

27 Ibid.

28 Steve Elliott, "Rebuttal Focuses on Agent's Credibility," *Fresno Bee,* April 15, 1998.

29 Ibid., Hanadel, pp. 386–387.

30 Ibid., p. 396.

31 John Miller, interview with Osama bin Laden, *ABC News,* May 28, 1998 (air date).

32 Mike Davis, "Car Bombs with Wings," *Asia Times Online,* April 18, 2006.

33 FBI 302 interrogation of Abdul Hakim Murad by SA Frank Pellegrino and SA Thomas Donlon, April 12–13, 1995, transcribed May 11, 1995.

34 "Report of the Joint Inquiry into the Terrorist Attacks of September 11, 2001, by the House Permanent Select Committee on Intelligence and the Senate Select Committee on Intelligence (The Joint Inquiry)," *CNN Intelligence Timeline,* http://www.cnn.com/interactive/us/0205/intelligence.timeline/content.1.html.

35 Tim Weiner, "U.S. Fury on 2 Continents: The Protagonist; Man with Mission Takes on the U.S. at Far Flung Sites," *New York Times,* August 21, 1998; "World's Most Wanted," *CNN Presents,* June 11, 2006; Interview with David Ruhnke, attorney for Kalfan Khanis Mohammed in *United States v. Osama bin Laden et al.,* June 13, 2006.

36 *United States v. Osama bin Laden et al.,* S(7) 98 Cr. 1023 (LBS).

37 Author's interview with confidential FBI source.

38 Benjamin Weiser, "U.S. to Offer Detailed Trail of bin Laden in Bomb Trial," *New York Times,* January 13, 2001.

39 Steven Emerson, testimony before Senate Judiciary Committee, December 4, 2001; "Abdullah Azzam: The Man Before Osama bin Laden," http://www.iacsp.com/itobli3.html.

28. THE SPY WHO WASN'T THERE

1 *United States v. Ali Mohamed,* S(7) 98 Cr. 1023 (LBS) Sealed Complaint, September 1998. Affidavit of FBI special agent Daniel Coleman, bin Laden unit, New York office.

2   *United States v. Osama bin Laden et al.,* S(7) 98 Cr. 1023, indictment, November 5, 1998, superseding indictment, S(10) 98 Cr. 1023 (LBS).

3   *United States v. Ali Mohamed,* Defense affidavit, p. 15.

4   *United States v. Osama bin Laden et al.,* S(7) 98 Cr. 1023 (LBS), March 20, 2001.

5   *United States v. Ali Mohamed,* S(7) 98 Cr. 1023 (LBS), transcript of plea session, U.S. District Court, Southern District of New York, October 20, 2000.

6   Author's interview with FBI special agent Jack Cloonan (ret.), May 4, 2006.

7   Statement of Patrick J. Fitzgerald, U.S. Attorney, Northern District of Illinois, before the Senate Judiciary Committee, October 21, 2003.

8   Interview with FBI special agent Jack Cloonan (ret.) for *Triple Cross,* June 1, 2006.

9   Benjamin Weiser, "Terror Suspect's Indictment to Be Sought as Talks Fail," *New York Times,* May 18, 1999.

10 Jerry Capeci, "My Father Did It," "Gang Land," New York *Daily News,* September 28, 1998.

11 *United States v. Mohammed Ajaj,* 92-CR-993 EDNY, addendum to the pre-sentence report, December 8, 1992.

12 *United States v. Mohammed Ajaj,* transcript of motion hearing before Judge Reena Raggi, December 22, 1995.

13 U.S. Attorney for the EDNY, letter to Judge Reena Raggi, December 18, 1992.

14 *United States v. Gregory Scarpa Jr.,* trial transcript, p. 3037.

15 Larry Silverman, interview for *Triple Cross,* June 12, 2006.

16 *United States v. Ramzi Ahmed Yousef et al.,* S(12) 93 Cr. 180 (KTD), August 26, 1996.

17 Pete Yost, "FBI Unit Probes Intercepted Package Case," *Washington Post,* April 23, 2003.

18 "A.P. Protests Government Seizure of Package Sent from One Reporter to Another," *Associated Press,* May 13, 2003.

29. THE "HOAX" AND THE "SCAM"

1   *United States v. Ramzi Ahmed Yousef et al.,* decision, U.S. Second Circuit Court of Appeals, August Term 2001, Decided April 4, 2003, p. 171.

2   Jerry Capeci, "Mobster Gets 40-Year Term," New York *Daily News,* May 9, 1999.

3   Ibid.

4   Greg B. Smith, "Terrorist Called Pals on Feds' Line," New York *Daily News,* September 24, 2000.

5   Patrick Fitzgerald, sealed affidavit, June 25, 1999.

6   According to a related court decision, "Napoli ultimately contacted the Government himself [and] admitted that Scarpa had attempted to enlist him in a scheme where: (1) Napoli would provide information to the Government about Yousef, which Napoli understood to be false (2) Scarpa would tell Napoli what Napoli would tell the Government. (3) Napoli might thereby earn a reduction of his sentence under USSG Sec 5K1.1. and (4) Napoli, in turn would be required to testify falsely on Scarp's behalf at an upcoming trial." The court's conclusion about the "false" information, however, related only to Scarpa Jr.'s organized crime charges, and in no way invalidated the 11-month intelligence initiative between Scarpa Jr. and Ramzi Yousef. The June 25, 1999, affirmation by Patrick Fitzgerald (Appendix VI, p. 559) underscores that point.

7   Denial of Recusal Motion. Judge Kevin Duffy, *United States v. Ramzi Ahmed Yousef and Eyad Ismoil,* S(12) 93 Cr. 180 (KTD).

8   *John Napoli v. United States,* "Petitioner's Supplement and Reply to Government's Memorandum in Opposition to Section 2255 Petition and Request for Evidentiary Hearing," Neil M. Shuster, August 2003, citing *United States v. Ramzi Ahmed Yousef,* 327 F. 3rd, 166–170 (C.A.2; N.Y. 2003), Gov. App. pp. 581–82, Napoli Ex F.

9   Author's interview with Larry Silverman, April 14, 2004.

10 Ann Imse, "Supermax 'Security Risk,'" *Rocky Mountain News,* July 1, 2006.

PART III

30. THE TEN-MONTH DANCE

1   "U.S. Charges bin Laden, Aide with Murder in Africa Bombings," *CNN,* November 4, 1998.

2   Author's interview with confidential FBI source.

3   CNN, "Ex-Green Beret Linked to Terror Attacks," October 30, 1998, from Associated Press and Reuters.

4   Steven Emerson, interview for *Triple Cross,* June 6, 2006.

5   CNN, November 4, 1998.

6   Benjamin Weiser, "Informer's Part in Terror Case Is Detailed," *New York Times,* December 22, 2000.

7   Benjamin Weiser, "Terror Suspect's Indictment to Be Sought as Talks Fail," *New York Times,* May 18, 1999.

8   Interview with FBI special agent Jack Cloonan (ret.) for *Triple Cross,* June 1, 2006.

9   Ibid.

10 Ibid., Weiser.

11 Ibid.

12 Lance Williams, "Bin Laden's Bay Area Recruiter," *San Francisco Chronicle,* November 21, 2001.

13 Lance Williams and Erin McCormick, "Top bin Laden Aide Toured State," *San Francisco Chronicle,* October 11, 2001.

14 Jailan Halawai "Jihad Emigrés Sentenced to Death," *Al-Ahram Weekly,* April 22–28, 1999.

15 Ibid., Al-Ahram.

16 Ibid.

17 Author's interview with confidential source.

18 Ibid.

19 Interview with David Ruhnke, attorney for Kalfan Khanis Mohammed in *United States v. bin Laden,* June 13, 2006.

20 Ibid., Cloonan interview June 1, 2006.

21 Ibid., Weiser, December 22, 2000.

22 *United States v. Ahmed Abdel Sattar et al.,* April 9, 2002.

23 Michael Powell and Michelle Garcia, "Sheikh's U.S. Lawyers Convicted of Aiding Terrorist's Activity," *Washington Post,* February 11, 2005; "N.Y. Attorney Lynne Stewart Convicted of Aiding Terrorist Group," *Bloomberg,* February 10, 2005.

24 Peter Lance, *1000 Years for Revenge* (New York: ReganBooks, 2003), Chapters, 2, 11, 13, 18, 24, 37.

25 Bureau of Fire Investigation "face sheet" reports on Ahmed Amin Refai, August 26 to September 1, 1999.

26 Author's interview with FDNY Deputy Commissioner Kay Ellis, July 30, 2002. An FDNY Bureau of Fire Investigation report describing the incident put the date at 1991, based on Woods's earlier recollection, but after checking her records in 2003 she told the author that she believed that Refai obtained the blueprints between July and August 1992. Author's interview with Kay Ellis, June 15, 2003.

27 Author's interviews with Fire Marshal Mel Hazel FDNY (ret.), July 18 and September 20, 2002; Fire Marshal Bobby Greene, July 16 and 30, 2002.

28   Jim Hickey, report on arrest of Mohammed Salameh, *ABC News*, March 4, 1993. See still frame from the video in the Timeline on page 10.

29   Author's interview with Joseph F. O'Brien, FBI (ret.), July 8, 2003.

30   Author's interview with Det. Lou Napoli, January 10, 2003.

31   Author's interview with Lt. Col. Anthony Shaffer, November 28, 2005.

32   Author's interview with Congressman Curt Weldon (R-PA), November 28, 2005.

33   Author's interview with Jacob L. Boesen, February 16, 2003.

34   Steven Emerson, interview for *Triple Cross*, June 10, 2006.

35   Testimony of Lt. Col. Anthony Shaffer, House Armed Services Committee hearing, February 15, 2006.

31. OPERATION ABLE DANGER

1   Ibid., Lt. Col Shaffer interview.

2   Ibid.

3   William M. Arkin, *Code Names: Deciphering U.S. Military Plans, Programs, and Operations in the 9/11 World* (Hanover, NH: Steerforth Press, 2005).

4   Shane Harris, "Intelligence Designs," *National Journal*, December 3, 2005.

5   Ibid., Curt Weldon interview.

6   Testimony of Eric Kleinsmith, U.S. Army (ret.), at Senate Judiciary Committee hearing, September 21, 2005.

7   Author's interview with confidential IDC source.

8   Shane Harris, "Intelligence Designs," *National Journal*, December 3, 2005.

9   Author's interview with Lt. Col. Anthony Shaffer, July 5, 2006.

10   Keith Phucas, "Testimony Barred by Pentagon," *Times Herald*, September 22, 2005.

11   Paul Thompson, "Khalid al-Midhar and Nawaf al-Hazmi," 9/11 Complete Timeline, www .cooperativeresearch.org.

12   Lawrence Wright, *The Looming Tower: Al Qaeda and the Road to 9/11* (New York: Knopf, 2006).

13   Lawrence Wright, "The Agent," *New Yorker*, July 10 and 17, 2006.

14   Author's interview with FBI special agent Jack Cloonan (ret.), May 4, 2006.

15   David Kaplan, "Pieces of the 9/11 Puzzle," *U.S. News and World Report*, March 15, 2004.

16   Michael Isikoff and Daniel Klaidman, "The Hijackers We Let Escape," *Newsweek*, June 2, 2002.

17   Author's interview with FBI special agent Jack Cloonan (ret.), May 4, 2006.

18   Nick Fielding and Gadhery Dipesh, "Al-Qaeda's Satellite Phone Records Revealed," *Sunday Times*, March 24, 2002; Terry McDermott, "The Plot: How Terrorists Hatched a Simple Plan to Use Planes as Bombs," *Los Angeles Times*, September 1, 2002.

19   Barry Wigmore, "9/11: The 7 Missed Clues," *Mirror*, June 9, 2002.

20   9/11 Commission public hearing; Ibid., www.cooperativeresearch.org.

21   Oliver Laabs, "The Deadly Mistakes of the U.S. Intelligence Agency (Part 1)," *Stern*, August 13, 2003.

22   Ibid., Cloonan interview; James Bamford, *A Pretext for War: 9/11, Iraq, and the Abuse of America's Intelligence Agencies* (New York: Anchor Books, 2005), p. 224.

23   *The 9/11 Commission Report*, p. 502.

24   "Report of the Joint Inquiry into the Terrorist Attacks of September 11," 108th Congress, First Session, July 24, 2003.

25   Phil Shenon and David Johnston, "Malaysian Acknowledges Al Qaeda Ties," *New York Times*, January 31, 2002.

26 Mark Fineman and Bob Drogin, "Indonesian Cleric Had Roles in Skyjackings," *Los Angeles Times*, February 2, 2002; Maria Ressa, "The Quest for SE Asia's Islamic 'Super' State," *CNN*, August 30, 2002; Maria Ressa, "Uncovering Southeast Asia's Jihad Network," November 7, 2002.

27 Brian Blomquist, "Meeting That Spawned 9/11," *New York Post*, July 10, 2003.

28 Dr. Zachary Abuza, *Militant Islam in Southeast Asia: Crucible of Terror* (Boulder, CO: Lynne Rienner, 2003).

29 Dr. Zachary Abuza, e-mail to author, July 7, 2006.

30 Michael Isikoff and Mark Hosenball, "Terror Tort Reform," *Newsweek*, July 9, 2003.

31 "Yemeni Pair Charged in USS *Cole* Bombing," *CNN.com*, May 15, 2003.

32 James Bamford, *A Pretext for War: 9/11, Iraq, and the Abuse of America's Intelligence Agencies* (New York: Anchor Books, 2005).

33 Ibid., Bamford.

34 *United States v. Zacarias Moussaoui*, 1:01CR445, March 7, 2006, p. 171.

35 David Kaplan and Kevin Whitelaw, "Pieces of the 9/11 Puzzle," *U.S. News and World Report*, March 15, 2004.

36 Lawrence Wright, *The Looming Tower: Al Qaeda and the Road to 9/11* (New York: Knopf, 2006).

37 *The 9/11 Commission Report*, pp. 160–168.

38 "A Decade of Warnings: Did Rabbi's Assassination Mark Birth of Islamic Terror in America?" *ABC News*, August 16, 2002.

39 Maria Ressa, *Seeds of Terror: An Eyewitness Account of al Qaeda's Newest Center of Operations in Southeast Asia* (New York: Free Press, 2003).

32. OBLITERATING THE DOTS

1 Author's interview with Congressman Curt Weldon (R-PA), November 28, 2005.

2 Testimony of Maj. Eric Kleinsmith, U.S. Army (ret.), before the Senate Judiciary Committee, September 21, 2005.

3 The Pentagon's order implementing the Order is DOD 5240.1-R, entitled "Procedures Governing the Activities of DOD Intelligence Components That Affect United States Persons."

4 Testimony of William Dugan, acting assistant to the secretary of defense for intelligence oversight, before the Senate Judiciary Committee, September 21, 2005.

5 Ibid., Kleinsmith.

6 Author's interview with Congressman Curt Weldon (R-PA), May 15, 2006.

7 Executive Order 12333 provides that U.S. intelligence agencies may retain U.S. person data from:

(a) Information that is publicly available or collected with the consent of the person concerned;

(b) Information constituting foreign intelligence or counterintelligence, including such information concerning corporations or other commercial organizations. Collection within the United States of foreign intelligence not otherwise obtainable shall be undertaken by the FBI or, when significant foreign intelligence is sought, by other authorized agencies of the Intelligence Community, provided that no foreign intelligence collection by such agencies may be undertaken for the purpose of acquiring information concerning the domestic activities of United States persons;

(c) Information obtained in the course of a lawful foreign intelligence, counterintelligence, international narcotics or international terrorism investigation;

(d) Information needed to protect the safety of any persons or organizations, including those who are targets, victims or hostages of international terrorist organizations;

(e) Information needed to protect foreign intelligence or counterintelligence sources or methods from unauthorized disclosure. Collection within the United States shall be undertaken by the FBI except that other agencies of the Intelligence Community may also collect such information concerning present or former employees, present or former intelligence agency contractors or their present or former employees, or applicants for any such employment or contracting;

(f) Information concerning persons who are reasonably believed to be potential sources or contacts for the purpose of determining their suitability or credibility;

(g) Information arising out of a lawful personnel, physical or communications security investigation;

(h) Information acquired by overhead reconnaissance not directed at specific United States persons;

(i) Incidentally obtained information that may indicate involvement in activities that may violate federal, state, local or foreign laws; and

(j) Information necessary for administrative purposes.

8   9/11 Commission public hearing; Ibid., www.cooperativeresearch.org.

9   Amy Goldstein, "Hijackers Led Core Group," *Washington Post,* September 30, 2001.

10 Rohan Sullivan, "Officials Watched 9–11 Plotters," *Associated Press,* September 20, 2002; testimony before Congressional Joint Inquiry, July 24, 2003.

11 Congressional Joint Inquiry, September 20, 2002.

12 Congressional Joint Inquiry Report; Michael Isikoff and Daniel Klaidman, "Failure to Communicate," *Newsweek,* July 28, 2003.

13 *United States v. Zacarias Moussaoui,* 1:01CR445, March 7, 2006, p. 250.

14 Bassey Amardeep, "Students Links to Pentagon Hijackers: Arrested Man Rented Rooms to Terrorists," *Sunday Mercury,* Birmingham, U.K., October 21, 2002; http://cooperativeresearch.org /searchResults.jsp?searchtext=Bayoumi&events=on&entities=on&articles=on&topics=on &timelines=on&projects=on&titles=on&descriptions=on&dosearch=on&search=Go; Jerry Seper, "Princess's Cash Went to Al Qaeda Advance Man," *Washington Times,* November 26, 2002; Michael Isikoff, "9/11 Hijackers: A Saudi Money Trail?" *Newsweek,* November 22, 2002; Julian Borger, "Mystery Men Link Saudi Intelligence to Sept. 11 Hijackers," *Guardian Unlimited,* November 25, 2002.

15 www.cooperativeresearch.com.

16 Amy Goldstein and William Booth. "Hijackers Found Welcome Mat on West Coast," *Washington Post,* December 29, 2001.

17 Kelly Thornton, "Ex-San Diegan Suspected as 'Terrorist's Advance Man," *San Diego Union Telegram,* October 25, 2001.

18 Kelly Thornton, "Local Probes Active, Quiet," *San Diego Union Telegram,* September 14, 2002.

19 Ibid., Thornton, September 14; Joint Inquiry Report.

20 Frank J. Murray, "Killers in the Cockpit: Who and Why?" *Washington Times,* September 10, 2002.

21 Mitch Lipka, "Multiple Identities of Hijack Suspects Confound FBI," *South Florida Sun-Sentinel,* September 28, 2001.

22 Edward Helmore and Ed Vulliamy, "Saudi Hijacker 'Was Key Link to bin Laden,'" *Guardian Unlimited,* October 7, 2001.

23 Congressional Joint Inquiry, July 24, 2003.

24 Oliver Schrom, "Deadly Mistakes," *Die Zeit,* October 2, 2002.

25 Kelly Thornton, "FBI Following of SD Hijackers Financial Trail," *San Diego Times Union,* September 21, 2001.

26 Author's interview with Congressman Curt Weldon (R-PA), May 15, 2006.

27 Michael Isikoff, "The Informant Who Lived with the Hijackers," *Newsweek,* September 9, 2002.

28 Ibid., Isikoff, September 9, 2002; Seth Hettena, "San Diego Represented Best Chance to Foil September 11 Plot," *Associated Press,* July 25, 2002; Congressional Joint Inquiry, July 24, 2003.

29 Ibid., Isikoff.

30 Ibid., Congressional Joint Inquiry.

31 H.G. Reza, Rich Connell, and Robert J. Lopez, "Hijackers in San Diego Weren't Hiding," *Los Angeles Times,* July 25, 2003; Ibid., Congressional Joint Inquiry.

32 Ibid., Congressional Joint Inquiry.

33 James Risen, "Congress Seeks FBI Data on Informer: FBI Resists," *New York Times,* October 6, 2002.

34 Jose Meyer, "Graham Alleges a 9/11 'Cover-up,'" *Los Angeles Times,* May 12, 2003.

33. ABLE DANGER PART TWO

1 Author's interview with Congressman Curt Weldon (D-PA) and Lt. Col. Anthony Shaffer, November 28, 2005.

2 Author's interview with Lt. Col. Anthony Shaffer, July 5, 2006.

3 Testimony of Lt. Col. Anthony Shaffer before the House Armed Services Committee, February 15, 2006.

4 Author's interview with Congressman Curt Weldon (D-PA), May 15, 2006.

5 Ibid.

6 Lawrence Wright, "The Counter-Terrorist," *New Yorker,* January 14, 2002.

7 Mary Jo White, "Prosecuting Terrorism in New York," *Middle East Quarterly,* March 1, 2001.

8 Larry Neumeister "Anti-Terror Squad Produced Patrick Fitzgerald and a Blueprint for Prosecutions," *Associated Press,* December 20, 2005.

9 World Islamic Front statement "Jihad Against Jews and Crusaders," *Washington Post,* February 23, 1988.

10 *United States v. Ahmed Abdel Sattar et al.,* April 30, 2002.

11 Woolsey wrote the Foreword to *The War Against America* (New York: ReganBooks, 2001), a book by Laurie Mylroie, a scholar with the conservative American Enterprise Institute. Mylroie espouses the theory that Ramzi Yousef was an Iraqi agent who actually stole the persona Abdul Basit from a Kuwait. The theory first appeared in an article entitled "The World Trade Center Bomb: Who Is Ramzi Yousef? Why It Matters," published in the Winter 1995–1996 edition of *The National Interest.* An expanded version of that piece became a book entitled *A Study of Revenge,* published in 2000 by AEI Press, an imprint of the American Enterprise Institute. *The War Against America* was a retitled 2001 trade paperback edition of *A Study in Revenge.* In the acknowledgments, Mylroie wrote that Clare Wolfowitz "fundamentally shaped this book." Wolfowitz, who taught at the Johns Hopkins School of Advanced International Studies, was the wife of Paul Wolfowitz, the deputy secretary of defense, largely considered the architect of the Bush administration policies that led to the March 2003 invasion of Iraq. In the same acknowledgments Mylroie thanked Mr. Wolfowitz for reading the manuscript prior to publication.

12 Executive Summary, "U.S.S. *Cole* Commission Report," Department of Defense, January 9, 2001.

13 Speech by Congressman Curt Weldon, February 23–26, 2006.

14 Josh Meyer, "Officials Say Bush's Illegal Wiretap Program Unnecessary: Court OK Is Easy to Get," *Los Angeles Times,* December 21, 2005.

15 Interview with FBI special agent Jack Cloonan (ret.) for *Triple Cross*, June 1, 2006.

16 *United States v. Ali Mohamed*, S(7) 98 Cr. 1023 (LBS), transcript of plea session, U.S. District Court, Southern District of New York, October 20, 2000.

17 David Ruhnke, interview for *Triple Cross*, June 10, 2006.

18 Benjamin Weiser, "Informer's Part in Terror Case Is Detailed," *New York Times*, December 22, 2000.

19 Confession of Khalid Dahab, *Al-Sharq al-Awsat*, March 6, 1999, FBIS, translation from Arabic.

20 Author's interview with confidential FBI source, June 12, 2006.

21 Author's interview with confidential defense source, May 28, 2006.

34. THE SECRET WITNESS

1 Larry Neumeister, "4 Convicted in Bombings of Embassies," *Associated Press*, May 30, 2001.

2 Jerry Markon, "Zealous Prosecution Is Sure Bet in the Embassy-Bombing Trial," *Wall Street Journal*, January 3, 2001.

3 Ibid., Weiser.

4 Ibid., Markon

5 *United States v. Osama bin Laden et al.*, S(7) 98 Cr. 1023 (LBS).

6 Author's interview with FBI agent Joseph F. O'Brien (ret.), January 4, 2006.

7 Mary Jo White, interview for *Triple Cross*, June 8, 2006.

8 Benjamin Weiser, "U.S. to Offer Detailed Trail of bin Laden in Bomb Trial," *New York Times*, January 13, 2001.

9 Author's interview with FBI special agent Jack Cloonan (ret.), May 4, 2006.

10 *The 9/11 Commission Report*, pp. 8–9.

11 Ibid., p. 158.

12 Toni Locy, Kevin Johnson, and Richard Willing, "Al-Qaeda Records Solve Many 9/11 Puzzles, but Others Linger," *USA Today*, August 29, 2002.

13 Ibid., Neumeister.

14 Ibid.

15 Robert Windrem, "U.S. Knew of bin Laden Kenya Cell," *NBC News*, October 24, 2003.

16 *The 9/11 Commission Report*, Chapter 8.

17 Rice made this admission at a White House press briefing eight months after 9/11 on May 16, 2002.

18 Barton Gellman, "Before Sept. 11, Unshared Clues and Unshaped Policy," *Washington Post*, May 17, 2002.

19 Steve Fainaru and James V. Grimaldi, "FBI New Terrorists Were Using Flight Schools," *Washington Post*, September 23, 2001.

20 Letters of endorsement for Harry Ellen (Abu Yusef) from Shoeil Juma al-Gool, September 21, 1999, and Major General Mahmoud Abu Marzoug, Director General of Civil Defense, Palestinian National Authority, October 20, 1999.

21 Author's interview with Harry Ellen, April 18, 2004.

22 Author's interview with Harry Ellen, February 25, 2003.

23 Mark Flatten, "A World of Intrigue: Valley Couple Take on FBI in Tale of Espionage, Betrayal, Romance"; "Documents, Letters Back Fantastic Story of Intrigue," *East Valley Tribune*, July 29, 2001; Mark Flatten, "FBI Entanglement Blocks Charity's Efforts in Gaza," *East Valley Tribune*, July 30, 2001.

24 Mark Flatten, "Could We Have Stopped Attacks? Hindsight Reveals McVeigh, Hanjour Left Clues in Arizona," *East Valley Tribune*, October 14, 2001.

25   "A Terrifying Plot Years in the Making," *U.S. News and World Report,* June 20, 2004.

26   A.P. "Report Says FAA Got 52 Warnings Before 9/11," *Washington Post,* February 11, 2005.

35. SECOND TO LAST CHANCE

1   Testimony of Detective Fred Ernest, Patterson, New Jersey Sheriff's Department, *State of New Jersey v. El-Atriss,* transcript, November 19, 2002.

2   Robert Hanley and Jonathan Miller, "4 Transcripts Are Released in Case Tied to 9/11 Hijackers," *New York Times,* June 25, 2003.

3   Ibid., Ernst.

4   Author's interview with confidential FBI source.

5   Robert Schwaneberg, "Six Months in Jail on a False Assumption," *Newark Star-Ledger,* October 20, 2003.

6   Ibid., Hanley and Miller.

7   http://www.gwu.edu/~nsarchiv/NSAEBB/NSAEBB116/pdb8-6-2001.pdf.

8   "Omar Abdel-Rahman Taliban's Likely Choice," *Frontier Post,* September 10, 2001; Kate Clark, "Revealed: The Taliban Minister, the U.S. Envoy, and the Warning of September 11 That Was Ignored," *The Independent,* September 7, 2002.

9   "Agent Who Arrested Moussaoui Blasts FBI," *Associated Press,* March 20, 2006.

10   *United States v. Zacarias Moussaoui,* 1:01CR455, penalty phase, March 9, 2006.

11   Neil A. Lewis, "Agent Says He Thought Moussaoui Knew About Plot," *New York Times,* March 10, 2006.

12   Joint Inquiry Staff Statement, October 17, 2002, p. 17.

13   Title 50 U.S. Code Chapter 36, Subchapter I, Section 1801.

14   Neil A. Lewis, "Superior Says He Didn't See Agent's Report on Moussaoui," *New York Times,* March 22, 2006.

15   Neil A. Lewis, "FBI Agent Testifies Superiors Didn't Pursue Moussaoui Case," *New York Times,* March 21, 2006.

16   Joint Inquiry Staff Statement, September 24, 2002, p. 20.

17   Neil A. Lewis, "Moussaoui Tells Court He's Guilty of a Terror Plot," *New York Times,* April 23, 2005.

18   Author's interview with FDNY fire marshal Andy DiFusco, June 23, 2002.

19   Author's interview with FDNY fire marshal Jimmy Devery (ret), June 21, 2002.

20   David Margolick, "Mr. Fitz Goes to Washington," *Vanity Fair,* February, 2006.

36. FINALLY, MOHAMED SPEAKS

1   Interview with FBI special agent Jack Cloonan (ret.) for *Triple Cross,* June 1, 2006.

2   Press conference of Condoleezza Rice, *CNN.com,* May 17, 2002.

3   http://www.pbs.org/wgbh/pages/frontline/shows/terrorism/interviews/sheehan.html.

4   Ibid.

5   Larry C. Johnson, e-mail to Peter Lance, May 24, 2002. In the e-mail, Johnson writes: "With respect to the 9/11 warning. Just before I left [Manila] I received the complete debriefing reports of Murad by the Philippine police. Murad said two things of relevance on this point. First, he said they had a plan (but not further specified) to fly a plane into CIA headquarters. He provided no more details about that. This info in and of itself would not have prevented 9/11 nor does it provide a heads up."

6   Benjamin Weiser, "The Terror Verdict: The Organization; Trial Poked Holes in Image of bin Laden's Terror Group," *New York Times,* May 31, 2001.

7   Larry C. Johnson, "The Declining Terrorist Threat," *New York Times,* Op-ed, July 10, 2001.
8   Transcript of interrogation of Abdul Hakim Murad by the Philippines National Police, January 20, 1995.
9   Joint Inquiry Statement, September 18, 2002.
10 9/11 Commission Staff Statement 9, April 13, 2004.
11 Matthew Brezinski, "Bust and Boom," *Washington Post,* December 30, 2001. The article reported that the CIA official "dismissed the connection to Bojinka as a 'hindsight is cheap' theory."
12 Press Release on Kallstrom appointment, October 10, 2001.
13 Author's interview with confidential FBI source.
14 Jake Tapper, "Senate Report: FBI Still Unprepared," *Salon.com,* March 3, 2003.
15 Remarks prepared for delivery by Robert S. Mueller at the Commonwealth Club, April 19, 2002.
16 John Solomon, "Rumsfeld, Others Swiped 9/11 Evidence as Souvenirs," *Associated Press,* March 12, 2004.
17 http://www.giulianipartners.com/press.aspx.
18 Romesh Ratnesar and Timothy Burger, "The FBI: Does It Want to Be Fixed?" *Time,* December 30, 2002.
19 http://www.pbs.org/newshour/bb/middle_east/july-dec03/saudi_07-29.html.
20 Michael Isikoff, "The 9–11 Report. Slamming the FBI," *Newsweek,* July 21, 2003.
21 Greg Miller, "Page After Page, the Mysteries of Sept. 11 Grow," *Los Angeles Times,* July 27, 2003.
22 Sheryl Gay Stolberg, "9/11 Widow Skillfully Applies the Power of a Question: Why?" *New York Times,* April 1, 2004.
23 Author's interview with Sally Regenhard, November 19, 2003.
24 Philip Shenon, "9/11 Commission Says U.S. Agencies Slow Its Inquiry," *New York Times,* July 9, 2003.
25 Scott J. Paltrow, "White House Hurdles Delay 9/11 Commission Investigation," *Wall Street Journal,* July 8, 2003.
26 Peter Lance, *Cover Up: What the Government Is Still Hiding About the War on Terror* (New York: ReganBooks, 2004), p. 208.
27 Author's interview with Congressman Curt Weldon (R-PA), May 15, 2006.
28 Letter from Gov. Tom Kean to Peter Lance, January 19, 2004, reproduced in *Cover Up,* p. 296.
29 Author's interview with confidential 9/11 Commission staff source, November 8, 2003.
30 Author's interview with Lt. Col. Anthony Shaffer, November 28, 2005.

37. THE BRIEFING IN BAGRAM

1   Journal of Lt. Col. Anthony Shaffer.
2   Author's interview with Lt. Col. Anthony Shaffer, November 28, 2005.
3   "Inside Able Danger: The Secret Birth, Extraordinary Life and Untimely Death of a U.S. Military Intelligence Program," *Government Security News,* August 23, 2005.
4   Philip Shenon, "Office Says Pentagon Barred Sharing Pre-9/11 Qaeda Data With FBI," *New York Times,* August 16, 2005.
5   Ibid., Shaffer interview.
6   Author's interview with Congressman Curt Weldon, November 28, 2005.
7   Author's interview with Congressman Curt Weldon, May 15, 2006.
8   Douglas Jehl, "Four in 9/11 Plot Are Called Tied to Qaeda in '00," *New York Times,* August 9, 2005.
9   Ibid., Shaffer interview.

10 Ibid.

11 Pat Milton, "Investigator: Atta Visited New York," *Associated Press,* December 8, 2001.

12 Ibid., Jehl.

13 Keith Phucas, "Missed Change on Way to 9/11," *Norristown Herald,* September 22, 2005.

14 The testimony is published as Appendix I to *Cover Up,* pp. 273–293.

15 *The 9/11 Commission Report,* Chapter 4, Footnote 33.

16 Philip Shenon and Douglas Jehl, "9/11 Panel Seeks Inquiry on New Atta Report," *New York Times,* August 10, 2005.

17 Niles Lathem, Fredrick U. Dicker, "Eliot KO'd Fed Grilling of Aide," *New York Post,* February 15, 2006.

18 John Schiffman, Mitch Lipka, and Patrick Kerkstra, "FBI Raids Four Homes, Two Offices in Weldon Probe," *Philadelphia Inquirer,* October 16, 2006.

19 Ken Silverstein, Chuck Neubauer, and Richard T. Cooper, "Kric's Lobbyist Karen Weldon," *Los Angeles Times,* February 21, 2004.

20 Author's interview with Congressman Curt Weldon (R-PA), October 16, 2006.

38. THE PUBLIC WHITEWASH

1 Testimony of Special Agent Mary Debbie Doran before the 9/11 Commission, June 16, 2004, http://www.washingtonpost.com/wp-dyn/articles/A46525-2004Jun16.html.

2 Testimony of Patrick Fitzgerald before the 9/11 Commission, June 16, 2004, http://www.washingtonpost.com/wp-dyn/articles/A46525-2004Jun16.html.

3 Author's interview with confidential FBI source.

4 Peter Dale Scott, "9/11 Commission Misses FBI's Embarrassing Al Qaeda Dealings," *Pacific News Service,* June 27, 2004.

5 "He comes to the United States and applies for jobs as an FBI translator and as a defense contractor," Roemer said. Hearing transcript, National Commission on Terrorist Attacks upon the United States, June 16, 2004.

6 Testimony of Dietrich Snell before the 9/11 Commission, June 16, 2004, http://www.washingtonpost.com/wp-dyn/articles/A46525-2004Jun16.html.

7 9/11 Commission, Staff Statement 15.

8 John Crewdson, "Waterboarding Use on 9/11 Mastermind, Who Eventually Talked," *Chicago Tribune,* December 28, 2005.

9 Douglas Jehl and David Johnston, "CIA Expands Its Inquiry into Interrogation Tactics," *New York Times,* August 29, 2004.

10 Douglas Jehl, "The Reach of War: Intelligence; Al Qaeda-Iraq Link U.S. Cited Is Tied to Coercion Claim," *New York Times,* December 9, 2005.

11 Churchill is remembered for stating that "In wartime, truth is so precious that she should always be attended by a bodyguard of lies." That same metaphor became the title of the April 2003 CIA report that was referenced in the following footnote regarding Khalid Shaikh Mohammed in *The 9/11 Commission Report:*

> Chapter Six, Note 513: "In an assessment of KSM's reporting, the CIA concluded that protecting operatives in the United States appeared to be a 'major part' of KSM's resistance efforts. For example, in response to questions about U.S. zip codes found in his notebooks, KSM provided the less than satisfactory explanation that he was planning to use the zip codes to open new e-mail accounts; CIA report, Intelligence Community Terrorist Threat Assessment, 'Khalid Shaikh Mohammed's Threat Reporting: Precious Truths, Surrounded by a Bodyguard of Lies,'" April 3, 2003, pp. 4–5.

12 http://www.rcfp.org/moussaoui.

13 "Defense Wants Bush to Testify at German 9/11 Trial," *Reuters,* March 8, 2005.

14 CNN interview with Henry Kissinger, September 11, 2001.

15 William B. Scott, "Exercise Jump-Starts Response to Attacks," *Aviation Week and Space Technology,* June 3, 2002; Mike Kelly, "Atlantic City F-16 Fighters Were Eight Minutes Away from 9/11 Hijacked Planes," *Bergen Record,* December 5, 2003.

16 John J. Lumpkin, "Agency Was to Crash Plane on 9/11," *Associated Press,* August 22, 2002; Pamela Hess, "U.S. Agencies: Strange 9/11 Coincidence," *United Press International,* August 22, 2002.

17 "9/11: Interviews by Peter Jennings," *ABC News,* September 11, 2002.

18 "Officials: Government Failed to React to FAA Warning," *CNN,* September 17, 2001; 8:53; "Timeline in Terrorist Attacks of Sept. 11, 2001," *Washington Post,* September 12, 2001; Bradley Graham, "Military Alerted Before Attacks; Jets Didn't Have Time to Intercept Hijackers Officers Say," *Washington Post,* September 15, 2001; 8:52; "9/11: Interviews by Peter Jennings," *ABC News,* September 11, 2002.

19 Tech. Sgt. Rick DelaHaya, "F-15 Eagle Celebrates Silver Anniversary," *Air Force News,* July 30, 1997.

20 "9/11: Interviews by Peter Jennings," *ABC News,* September 11, 2002.

21 Kevin Dennehy, "I Thought It Was the Start of World War III," *Cape Cod Times,* August 21, 2002.

22 CNN reported in 1999, "Only the president has the authority to order a civilian aircraft shot down." Judy Woodruff, Charles Zewe, and Jaime McIntyre, "Investigation into Mysterious Crash of the Famous Payne Stewart Learjet Begins: Unusual Circumstances of Crash Raises Disturbing Question," *World View,* CNN, October 26, 1999.

23 Mike Kelly, "Atlantic City F-16 Fighters Were Eight Minutes Away From 9/11 Hijacked Planes," *Bergen Record,* December 5, 2003.

24 Philip Shenon, "9/11 Panel Choose Publisher for Report," *New York Times,* May 25, 2004; Philip D. Zelikow, Timothy Naftali, and Ernest May, *The Presidential Recordings: John F. Kennedy: Volumes 1–3, The Great Crises* (New York: W.W. Norton, 2001).

25 http://www.nationalbook.org/nba2004_911.htm.

26 FBI 302, March 7, 1996, Appendix VI, p. 554.

39. EXPLOSIVES THE FBI MISSED

1 Edna Fernandes, "Supermax Prison: The Alcatraz of the Rockies," *Sunday Times,* May 4, 2006.

2 Jim Hughes, "The Feds Plan to Make the Supermax the Nation's Premier Prison for Terrorists: 'Alcatraz of the Rockies,'" *Denver Post,* August 3, 2003.

3 Stephen P. Dresch, "Report of Explosive Cache Secreted by Terry Lynn Nichols," March 23, 2005; author's interview with Angela Clemente, April 8, 2005.

4 Ibid., Clemente.

5 Ibid.

6 Ibid.

7 Jones and Israel, *Others Unknown,* pp. 79, 272, 304.

8 Mark Sherman, "FBI Waited to Check Out Tip on Nichols," *Associated Press,* April 14, 2005.

9 Ibid., Clemente.

10 John Solomon, "Explosives Found in Former Home of Terry Nichols," *Associated Press,* April 2, 2005.

11 Ibid., Sherman.

12 Robert Vosper, "The Chosen One," *Corporate Legal Times,* October 4, 2004.

13 Author's interview with Larry Silverman, April 13, 2004.

14 FBI 302 interview with Special Agent Christopher Favo, November 16, 1995.

15 Ibid.

16 Ibid.

17 Affirmation of Valerie Caproni, May 28, 1996; *United States v. Anthony Russo et al.*, 92 CR351 (S9) (CPS).

18 FBI 302 on phone call between Valerie Caproni, Chief of Criminal Division EDNY, by S. A. Thomas Fuentes, January 21, 1994.

19 Ibid.

20 Frederic Dannen, "The G-Man and the Hit Man," *New Yorker,* December 16, 1996.

21 Greg B. Smith, "7 Cleared in Brooklyn Mob Case," New York *Daily News,* July 1, 1995.

22 J. R. de Szigethy, "Partners in Crime: The Mafia Cops," AmericanMafia.com, April 2006. http://www.americanmafia.com/Feature_Articles_346.html.

23 Ibid., de Szigethy.

24 Ed Bradley, "Mafia Cops," *60 Minutes,* April 10, 2005; Jerry Capeci, "Cousin Got the Mafia Cop Started," Gangland, *New York Sun,* March 17, 2005.

25 Kati Cornell Smith, "No Retrial for Wiseguy Killer," *New York Post,* January 16, 2004.

26 Alan Feuer, "Statute of Limitations Still an Issue for Ex-Detectives," *New York Times,* September 21, 2005.

27 Jose Martinez and William Sherman, "Hit Man Is Singing FBI Song," New York *Daily News,* January 6, 2006.

28 Author's interview with Flora Edwards, April 27, 2004.

29 Author's interview with Det. Joseph Simone, April 30, 2004.

30 *United States v. Gregory Scarpa Sr.,* CR 93 124, May 6, 1993.

31 FBI 302 memo re: testimony of Christopher Favo, June 1 to 2, 1994.

32 Jeff Harrell, "Fired Cop with Mob Rap Could Have Been Set Up by FBI," *Staten Island Advance,* January 6, 2006.

33 *United States v. Joseph Simone,* transcript of cross examination of Special Agent Lynn Smith, pp. 665–669.

40. FOUR COUNTS OF HOMICIDE

1 Indictment No. 6825/2005, *People of the State of New York v. Roy Lindley DeVecchio and John Sinagra,* March 23, 2006.

2 Frederic Dannen, "The G-Man and the Hit Man," *New Yorker,* December 16, 1996.

3 Ibid.

4 Charles J. Hynes, "Former Agent DeVecchio Charged with Aiding Mafia Hits," press release from D.A.'s office, March 20, 2006.

5 William K. Rashbaum and Janon Fisher, "FBI Colleagues Help Ex-Agent Post Bail," *New York Times,* March 21, 2006; "The Bail Hearing," The Friends of Lin DeVecchio Trust, http://www.lindevecchio.com/bailhearing_report.htm.

6 Tom Hays, "Suit Alleges FBI Agent Assisted Mob Hit," *Associated Press,* January 7, 2006.

7 Jerry Capeci, "From 'Drop Dead Gorgeous' to DOA," *New York Sun,* February 16, 2006.

8 Alan Feuer, "Inquiry in 1992 Mob Killing Focuses on Ex-FBI Agent," *New York Times,* January 5, 2006.

9 Alan Feuer, "A Tale of Cops and Mobsters Who Failed to Overlap," *New York Times,* January 6, 2006.

10 Ibid., Rashbaum and Fisher.

11 E-mail from Chris Mattiace to various agents, January 7, 2006, obtained by author from confidential FBI source.

12 Alan Feuer, "For Ex FBI Agent Accused in Murders: A Case of What Might Have Been," *New York Times,* April 15, 2006.

13 *Pasquale Amato and Victor Orena v. CV-96-1461;* CV-96-1474, affirmation of Flora Edwards, Habeas Petition. Exhibit M, p. 9, January 7, 2004.

14 Ibid., Feuer, April 15, 2006.

15 Michael Brick, "Agent Accused in Mob Murders Seeks Immunity," *New York Times,* April 11, 2006.

16 Anthony DeStefano, "Ex-Agent Seeks to Switch Courts," *Newsday,* April 11, 2006.

17 Author's interview with Andrew Orena, July 2, 2006.

18 Alan Feuer, Colin Moynihan, and Andy Newman, "2 Ex-Detectives Guilty in Killings," *New York Times,* April 7, 2006.

19 *United States v. Michael Sessa,* CR-92-351, September 24, 2001, pp. 19–20.

20 John Marzulli, "Judge Rubs Out Mob Cob Verdict," *New York Daily News,* July 1, 2006.

21 Ibid., Feuer, July 1, 2006.

22 Ibid., Feuer, September 21, 2005.

23 http://www.lindevecchio.com/motives.htm.

24 Andy Kurins, e-mail to the author, June 14, 2006.

25 Murray Weiss, Alex Ginsberg, and Marsha Kranes, " 'Tipster' Slay Try on G-Mom, 'Mob Fed' Buster Choked, Left for Dead," *New York Post,* June 17, 2006.

26 Author's interview with Angela Clemente, July 15, 2006.

27 Kerry Burke, Alison Gendar, Nancie L. Katz, and William Sherman, "FBI Prober Attacked," New York *Daily News,* June 17, 2006.

28 Jerry Capeci, "Cops Probing Sleuth's Beating Story," *New York Sun,* June 29, 2006.

29 Jerry Capeci, "Bloody War Still Plays Out in Court," *New York Sun,* July 20, 2006.

30 Author's interview with Angela Clemente, July 21, 2006.

31 Brad Hamilton and Alex Ginsburg, "Choked G-Mom: I'm Set to Quit." *New York Post,* June 18, 2006.

41. WHY ANY OF THIS MATTERS

1 Don Van Natta Jr., Elaine Sciolino, and Stephen Grey, "In Tapes, Receipts, and a Diary, Details of the British Terror Case," *New York Times,* August 28, 2006.

2 Ibid.

3 Brian Bennett and Douglas Waller, "Thwarting the Airline Plot: Inside the Investigation," *Time,* August 10, 2006.

4 Karen Kaplan and Denise Gellene, "Humble Ingredients for a Deadly Purpose," *Los Angeles Times,* August 11, 2006; http://www.globalsecurity.org/military/systems/munitions/tatp.htm.

5 Alan Cowell and Dexter Filkins, "Terror Plot Foiled, Airports Quickly Clamp Down. Plan Was to Sneak Liquid Explosives on Planes," *New York Times,* August 11, 2006.

6 Alan Cowell, Dexter Filkins, and Mark Mazzetti, "Figure Is Described as Liason in Plot to Bomb Planes," *New York Times,* August 12, 2006.

7 Ibid.

8 Ibid, Van Natta Jr., Sciolino, and Grey.

9 Maria Ressa, "Sources: Reid Is Al Qaeda Operative," *CNN,* December 6, 2003.

10 Brian Bennett and Douglas Waller, "Thwarting the Airline Plot: Inside the Investigation," *Time,* August 10, 2006.

11 Kirk Johnson, "Crackdown Costs Travelers Time, Lipstick, Hair Gel . . ." *New York Times,* August 11, 2006.

12 Author's interview with Dick Doubrava, Delta Airlines, March 13, 2000.

13 Author's interview with Glen Winn, United Airlines, March 14, 2000.

14 Author's interview with Paul Thompson, August 15, 2006.

15 Terry McDermott, "Echoes of '95 Manila Plot," *Los Angeles Times,* August 11, 2006; Raymond Bonner and Benjamin Weiser, "Echoes of Early Design to Use Chemicals to Blow Airliners," *New York Times,* August 11, 2006.

16 Josh Meyer, "Al Qaeda Imprint Debated," *Los Angeles Times,* August 11, 2006.

17 Author's interview with Angela Clemente, September 15, 2006.

18 Ibid.

19 Author's interview with Bernard V. Kleinman, August 15, 2006.

20 Craig Gordon, Earl Lane, and Knut Royce, "PETN: What It Might Mean," *Newsday,* August 24, 1996; Silvia Adcock and Knut Royce, "Two Traces Found," *Newsday,* August 31, 1996; Liam Pleven and Al Baker, "Probe Follows Chemical Trail," *Newsday,* August 27, 1996.

21 Bill Bleyer, "TWA Flight 800 10 Years Later: Conspiracy Theorists Still See It Differently," *Newsday,* July 17, 2006.

22 Nelson DeMille, *Night Fall* (New York: Warner Vision, 2005).

23 David Evans, "Federal Agencies Disagree over Need to Eliminate Vapors from All Airliner Fuel Tanks," *Newsday,* August 1, 2006.

24 Jack Cashill and James Sanders, *First Strike* (Nashville: WNB Books, 2003).

25 Author's interview with Jack Cashill, September 20, 2006.

26 Ibid., Clemente.

27 Sheryl Gay Stolberg, "Bush Assures That the Nation Is Safer as Memories Turn to a Day of Destruction," *New York Times,* September 8, 2006.

28 Robert S. Mueller III, "FBI Reorganization," testimony of Robert S. Mueller III, Director, FBI, before the Senate Committee on the Judiciary May 8, 2002.

29 Eric Lichtblau and Charles Piller, "War on Terrorism Highlights FBI's Computer Woes," *Los Angeles Times,* July 28, 2002.

30 Richard B. Schmitt, "FBI's Computer Upgrade Develops Its Own Glitches," *Los Angeles Times,* January 28, 2003.

31 "Keystone Komputers," *New York Times,* March 27, 2006.

32 9/11 Commission, Staff Statement 9, April 13, 2004.

33 "Washington in Brief," *Washington Post,* December 11, 2003.

34 "A Review of the FBI's Trilogy Information Technology Modernization Program," *National Research Council,* May 10, 2004.

35 Ibid., *New York Times,* March 27, 2006.

36 Eric Lichtblau, "At FBI Translation Lags, as Does the System Upgrade," *New York Times,* July 28, 2005.

37 Eric Lichtblau, "Cost Concerns for FBI Computer Overhaul," *New York Times,* March 14, 2006.

38 "Some New York FBI Agents Lack E-Mail," *Associated Press,* March 21, 2006.

39 Author's interview with FBI special agent James Whalen (ret.), September 21, 2006.

40 "9/11 Panel Peport: 'We Must Act.'" *CNN,* July 23, 2004.

41 "Alleged FBI Negligence in investigation of Hamas and al Qaeda Before 9/11," *Federal News Service,* May 30, 2002.

42 Eric Lichtblau, "Another FBI Employee Blows Whistle on Agency," *New York Times,* August 2, 2004.

43 Eric Lichtblau, "Report Finds Cover-Up in an FBI Terror Case," *New York Times,* December 3, 2005.

44 Eric Lichtblau, "Inspector General Rebukes FBI over Espionage Case and Firing of Whistle-Blower," *New York Times,* January 15, 2005.

45 Chitra Ragavan, "Fixing the FBI," *U.S. News and World Report,* March 28, 2005.
46 Chris Strohm, "Report: FBI Falls Short in Hiring, Retaining Intelligence Analysts," *Government Exec.com,* May 5, 2005.
47 Dan Eggen, "FBI Fails to Transform Itself, Panel Says," *Washington Post,* June 7, 2005.
48 Eric Lichtblau, "Report Details FBI's Failures on 2 Hijackers," *New York Times,* June 11, 2005.
49 Jerry Markon, "Post 9/11 Probe Revived Stolen-Cereal Incident," *Washington Post,* June 12, 2005.
50 David Johnston, "FBI Counterterror Officials Lack Experience, Lawyer Says," *New York Times,* June 20, 2005.
51 John Solomon, "FBI Says Counterterror Experts Not Crucial," *Associated Press,* June 20, 2006.
52 William Odom, "Why The FBI Can't Be Reformed," *Washington Post,* June 29, 2005.
53 Eric Lichtblau, "At FBI Translation Lags, as Does the System Upgrade," *New York Times,* July 28, 2005.
54 Ibid.
55 Eric Lichtblau, "FBI Found to Violate Its Informant Rules," *New York Times,* September 13, 2005.
56 Linda Greenhouse, "Justices Reject FBI Translator's Appeal on Termination," *New York Times,* November 29, 2005.
57 Eric Lichtblau, "FBI Watched Activist Groups, New Files Show," *New York Times,* December 20, 2005.
58 David Stout, "Inquiry Says FBI Erred in Implicating Man in Attack," *New York Times,* January 7, 2006; Jerry Seper, "FBI Error Cited in Lawyer's Arrest," *Washington Times,* January 7, 2006.
59 Richard A. Serrano, "Al Qaeda Expert Offers Few Details at Moussaoui Trial," *Los Angeles Times,* March 8, 2006.
60 Scott Shane, "FBI Is Seeking to Search Papers of Dead Reporter," *New York Times,* April 19, 2006.
61 John O'Neill, "FBI Director Is Bombarded by Stinging Questions at Senate Hearing," *New York Times,* May 3, 2006.
62 Sen. Chuck Grassley, Statement, FBI Oversight, U.S. Senate Committee on the Judiciary, May 2, 2006.
63 "FBI Comes Up Empty-Handed in Hoffa Search," *Associated Press,* May 30, 2006.
64 Eric Lichtblau, "Study Finds Sharp Drop in the Number of Terrorism Cases Prosecuted," *New York Times,* September 4, 2006.
65 Dan Eggen, "FBI Agents Still Lacking Arabic Skills," *Washington Post,* October 11, 2006.

42. THE 9/11 COLD CASE

1 George W. Bush. "Creation of Military Commissions to Try Suspected Detainees," East Room speech, September 6, 2006.
2 Sheryl Gay Stolberg, "President Moves 14 Held in Secret to Guantanamo," *New York Times,* September 7, 2006.
3 Ibid.
4 Mark Mazzetti, "Questions Raised About Bush's Primary Claims in Defense of Secret Detention System," *New York Times,* September 8, 2006.
5 Kate Zernike, "Deal Reported Near on Rights of Suspects in Terror Cases," *New York Times,* September 13, 2006.
6 Jim Rutenberg and Sheryl Gay Stolberg, "Bush Says GOP Rebels Are Putting Nation at Risk," *New York Times,* September 16, 2006.
7 Kate Zernike, "Top Republicans Reach an Accord on Detainee Bill," *New York Times,* September 22, 2006.
8 Ibid.

9   Joel Siedman, "Fitzgerald Given Way out of Libby CIA Leak Case," *NBC News,* September 21, 2006.

10 Ibid.

11 Victoria Toensing, "What a Load of Armitage!" *Wall Street Journal,* September 15, 2006.

12 Ibid.

13 David Corn, "WSJ and Toensing: I Outed Plame (Here We Go Again)," *Huffington Post,* September 15, 2006.

14 Michael Calderone, "Times Studies How to Shake Feds: Disposable Phones, Erasable Notes: Act Like a Drug Dealer," *New York Observer,* September 18, 2006.

15 Joe Hagen, "Times Under Seige," *New York,* September 18, 2006.

16 James Risen and Eric Lichtblau, "Bush Lets U.S. Spy on Callers Without Courts," *New York Times,* December 16, 2005.

17 Eric Lichtblau and James Risen (with Barclay Walsh), "Bank Data Sifted in Secret by U.S. to Block Terror," *New York Times,* June 23, 2006.

18 Gabriel Schoenfeld, "Has the New York Times Violated the Espionage Act?" *Commentary,* March 2006; Cliff Kincaid, "Prosecute the New York Times, Part One," *Accuracy in Media,* June 19, 2006.

19 Author's phone conversation with Phil Shenon, August 12, 2006.

EPILOGUE

1   Peter Lance, "Triple Cross: A National Geographic Channel Special About Al Qaeda's Master Spy and the Untold Story Behind the 9/11 Attacks," treatment. Included with press release dated August 27, 2006, at www.peterlance.com.

2   FBI special agent Jack Cloonan (ret.), interview for *Triple Cross,* June 1, 2006.

3   Department of Defense, Report of Investigation, Case Number: H05L97905217, September 18, 2006. Accessible at www.peterlance.com.

4   Curt Weldon, "Weldon Rejects DOD Report on Able Danger and Harassment of Military Officer," press release, September 21, 2006.

5   Josh White, "Hijackers Were Not Identified Before 9/11, Investigation Says," *Washington Post,* September 22, 2006.

6   Author's interview with confidential Able Danger source, September 25, 2006.

7   Service record and commendations of Lt. Col. Anthony Shaffer.

8   Col. Jose R. Olivero, "Narrative for Bronze Star Medal Awarded to Maj. Anthony Shaffer, U.S. Army Reserve."

9   Author's interview with Congressman Curt Weldon, September 24, 2006.

10 Ibid.

11 Author's interview with Mike Kasper, September 23, 2006.

12 William A. Arkin, "The Final Verdict on Able Danger," *Washington Post,* September 25, 2006.

13 Seymour M. Hersh, "The Coming Wars," *New Yorker,* January 24, 2005.

14 Douglas Jehl, "Early Clues to a New Spy Chief's Muscle," *New York Times,* February 20, 2005.

15 Jim Rutenberg and Sheryl Gay Stolberg, "In Prime-Time Address, Bush Says Safety of U.S. Hinges on Iraq," *New York Times,* September 12, 2006.

16 Bob Woodward, *Bush at War* (New York: Simon & Schuster, 2002), p. 83.

17 "Study Finds Widespread Misperceptions on Iraq Highly Related to Support for War," http://groups.google.com/group/uk.currentevents.terrorism/browse_thread/thread/4b3ac67199 d9e12d/3e9af38aa361dd23%233e9af38aa361dd23.

18 Walter Pincus, "Report Casts Doubt on Iraq-Al Qaeda Connection," *Washington Post*, June 22, 2003.

19 Josh Meyer, "Al Qaeda Feared to Have 'Dirty Bombs,'" *Los Angeles Times*, February 8, 2003.

20 Press Release, "Agency Actions in Response to the National Elevated Alert Level," U.S. Department of Homeland Security, February 7, 2003.

21 John J. Lumpkin, "No Need to Panic over Alerts," *Associated Press*, February 14, 2003.

22 Richard Simon "Bush Urges Americans to Be Alert, Stay Calm," *Los Angeles Times*, February 16, 2003.

23 Doyle McManus and Robin Wright, "Is War Necessary? Why Now? Who Agrees?" *Los Angeles Times*, February 16, 2003.

24 Ibid.

25 Remarks of Secretary of State Colin Powell before the UN Security Council, February 5, 2003.

26 Brian Ross, "Weak Link? Radical Islamic Leader Denies Powell's Link Between Al Qaeda and Iraq," *ABCNEWS.com*, February 5, 2003.

27 "Patterns of Global Terrorism," www.fas.org/irp/threat/terror.

28 "Leaked Report Rejects Iraqi Al-Qaeda Link," *BBC.com*, February 5, 2003.

29 "Report Concludes No WMD in Iraq," *BBC News*, October 7, 2004.

30 Mark Mazzetti, "CIA Said to Find No Hussein Link to Terror Chief," *New York Times*, September 9, 2006.

31 Carl Levin (D-MI), "Senate Floor Statement on the Senate Intelligence Committee's Phase II Report," September 8, 2006.

32 Ibid.

33 "Mission Accomplished Whodunit," *CBS News*, October 29, 2003.

34 Kirk Semple, "Iraqi Death Toll Rises Above 100 per Day, U.N. Says," *New York Times*, July 19, 2006.

35 Richard A. Oppel Jr., "On Another Grim Day, Bodies Lie Everywhere in Baghdad," *New York Times*, September 14, 2006.

36 Michael R. Gordon, Mark Mazzetti, and Thom Shanker, "Insurgent bombs directed at G.I.'s Increase in Iraq," *New York Times*, August 17, 2006.

37 Source: http://www.icasualties.org/oif.

38 Source: http://www.icasualties.org/oif.

39 David Rohde, "An Afghan Symbol for Change, Then Failure," *New York Times*, September 5, 2006.

40 Carlotta Gall, "Opium Harvest at Record Level in Afghanistan," *New York Times*, September 3, 2006.

41 "Killing Highlights Vulnerability of Afghan Women," Agence France Press, *Middle East Times*, September 26, 2006.

42 Gary Leupp, "Meet Mr. Blowback," *Counterpunch*, February 14, 2003.

43 Peter Bergen, "Source Mullah Omar in Pakistan," *CNN*, September 9, 2006.

44 Author's phone interview with FBI special agent Jack Cloonan (ret.), May 2, 2006.

45 David Sanger, "Musharraf Defends Deal with Tribal Leaders," *New York Times*, September 23, 2006.

46 "Hamid Karzai Slams Musharraf," *The Hindu*, September 28, 2006.

47 Mark Mazzetti, "Spy Agenices Say Iraq War Worsens Terrorism Threat," *New York Times*, September 24, 2006.

48 Ibid.

49 William Branigan, "Three Retired Officers Demand Rumsfeld Resignation," *Washington Post*, September 25, 2006.

50 "Iraq War Fueled Islamic Radicals: Retired U.S. General," *Reuters*, September 25, 2006.

51 Matthew Brezinski, "Bust and Boom," *Washington Post*, December 30, 2001.

52 Kirk Semple, "As Iraqi Lights Flicker, 'Generator Man' Feels Heat," *New York Times*, September 25, 2006.

53 Damien Cave, "Weary Iraqis Finds New Foe: Rising Prices," *New York Times*, August 26, 2006.

54 *New York Times*/CBS News poll, "Poll Shows Growing Skepticism in U.S. Over Peace in The Middle East," *New York Times*, July 27, 2006.

55 "Americans Remain Upset with Iraq War," *Angus Reid Global Monitor*, September 25, 2006.

Appendix I:
El Sayyid Nosair Documents

Documents found in El Sayyid Nosair's house after the murder of Rabbi Meier Kahane.

CHAPTER 2

LOCATION OF SELECTED UNITS ON 05 DEC 1988

قواعد جوية

Section I.

Special Operations Forces (SOF)

1. SOCCENT   MACDILL AFB, FL

2. ARSOF الاركان   المخطط المصري   الحربة
   وحدات متقدمة

Unit Forward	Location	Lat/Long	Mission
B-120, B-1-21 A-122, B-1-21 A-216, A-2-21	Muscat, Oman عمان	Vic 23N/58E	DFT MAROPS
A-125, B-1-21	Al Kharj, Saudi Arabia سعودية	Vic 24N/48E	MTT HALO
A-126, B-1-21	Al Hufuf, Saudi Arabia	Vic 25N/50E	MTT REDEYE
A-235, C-2-21	Iscia Baidoa, Somalia صومال	Vic 03N/48E	DFT MEDCAP
A-236, C-2-21	Rocca Litterio, Somalia صومال	Vic 07N/47E	DFT MEDCAP
B-230, C-2-21	Al Mukhha, North Yemen اليمن الشمالي	Vic 13N/43E	DFT LT INF TACTICS
A-231, C-2-21			
A-232, C-2-21	Sanaa, صنعاء North Yemen	Vic 15N/44E	
A-313, A-3-21	Dongola, Sudan سودان	Vic 19N/30E	MTT NCO LDRS
B-210, A-1-21 A-211, A-1-21 A-212, A-1-21	Cairo West		JTX/Isol.

قوّ.ا.

توو.ا.

تو.ب.

(نار عنب فقمرة)

3. NAVSOF

   CDR, NAVSPECOPSCOM   Coronado, CA   توين

   NSWG-4   Little Creek NAB, VA   كريم

   SEAL-7, SEAL-9, SPEC BOAT
   SDN 5, SBU 31, SBU 33   Little Creek NAB, VA   2-L

FOR TRAINING PURPOSES ONLY

١ تتعارض الاسباب / لكنهم الاقتناع حول لديه السبب بأنه عليا الاتجاه عليا لازمهم فعال

A. Location of Selected Special Forces units on December 5, 1988, from Fort Bragg, with Ali Mohamed's Arabic notations.

APPENDIX III

JCS WARNING ORDER

002725

أ مراانذارريم ميادة لقوات المشتركة

مرسم قيادة لقوات المشتركة العملية

نجلت من قبل ا هتحدث العملية

والعواصم العربية التابل:

بنية وتتم البلاغ الغارات

نزلح مصر - السودان

مان - السعودية - لبن البنان

FROM JCS WASHINGTON DC//CJCS//
TO   USCINCCENT MACDILL AFB FL
     USCINCSOC MACDILL AFB FL
     USCINCTRANS SCOTT AFB IL
     CINCSAC OFFUTT AFB NE
     USCINCLANT NORFOLK VA
     USCINCEUR VAIHAGEN GE
     USCINCPAC HONOLULU HI
     USCINCSO QUARRY HEIGHTS PN
     WHITE HOUSE SITROOM WASH DC
     SECSTATE WASHINGTON DC
     NSA/CSS FT GEORGE G MEADE MD
     DIA WASHINGTON DC
DISTR: CJCS/DJS/SJCS/J1/J3/J4/J5/C3S/SOD/DIA/SECDEF/USDP/
       ASD:PA/ASD:SOLIC/J3:NMCC/NIDS/JDA:LO/DOCDIV
WRITER: LT COL W.M.SHRIVER,USAF
        J-3, EXT 53406
INFO: CSA WASHINGTON DC
       CNO WASHINGTON DC
       CSAF WASHINGTON DC
       CMC WASHINGTON DC
       DMA WASHINGTON DC
       DNA WASHINGTON DC
       COMUSARCENT FT MCPHERSON GA
       COMUSNAVCENT PEARL HARBOR HI
       COMUSCENTAF SHAW AFB SC
       CG IMEF CAMP PENDLETON CA
       CG FMFLANT
       CINCPACFLT PEARL HARBOR HI
       CINCPACAF HICKAM AFB HI
       CG FMFPAC
       CINCUSNAVEUR LONDON UK
       JCSE MACDILL AFB FL
الغارة: AMEMBASSY CAIRO
       AMEMBASSY KHARTOUM
       AMEMBASSY MOGADISHO
       AMEMBASSY MUSCAT

B. JSC Warning order from Joint Chiefs of Staff to all key U.S. commands, from Fort Bragg, with AM's Arabic notations.

Appendix II:
FBI 302 Document

FBI 302 from JTTF Det. Lou Napoli, November 13, 1990, on surveillance of the High Rock shooting range and ex-cop Raymond Murteza.

FD-302 (Rev. 3-10-82)

FEDERAL BUREAU OF INVESTIGATION

- 1 -

Date of transcription   Nov 13, 1990

On Nov 13, 1990, Det. Louis Napoli conducted the following interview of JOE NORTON, of telephone

Norton advised that he was the Range Officer at the HIGH ROCK STATE PARK, located at Hunter's Mountain Road, Naugatuch, Conn. from April 1987 to Dec.1989.

Norton advised that a Raymond Murtzea who was also a Range Officer at the HIGH ROCK RANGE, started to train a group of Mid-Easterners in the in the art of shooting and the handling of firearms on every Saturday and Sunday from 1988 to 1990. The group would average about 15 persons at any one time. These Mid-Easterners would come to the range and use RAYMOND MURTZEA permit in order to shoot. Norton also advised that MURTZEA would personnally train these Mid-Easterners on an individual bases.

NORTON advised that when these Mid-Easterners came up on the weekends, that MURTZEA would supply them with shotguns and hand-guns (9mm,357cal and 45cal) which he would bring to the range in a dufflebag. NORTON advised that he saw some of the Mid-Easterners bring up AK47 which they would remove from the trunks of their vehicles. NORTON could not remember any plate numbers but he did remember that they were New York State Licence Plates.

NORTON advised that MURTZEA and the Mid-Easterners would shoot over one thousand (1000) rounds per day, and that they shot at silhouette targets instead of bulleye targets. Norton stated that MURTZEA would train them to shoot for the head and hearth areas.

Norton, after viewing photos of several Mid-Easterns, identify EL-SAYYID A. NOSAIR as one of the Mid-Easterners who came to the HIGH ROCK RANGE to shoot with MURTZEA.

Investigation on   Nov 13, 1990   at   New York N.Y.   File #   265A-(NY195576)

by   Det. Louis Napoli   Date dictated

Appendix III:
Khalifa Letter

Letter from Philip C. Wilcox Jr., the State Dept.'s senior adviser, regarding terrorism, to an unnamed immigration judge, declaring that Mohammed Jamal Khalifa has "engaged in serious terrorist offenses" and that his release "would endanger U.S. national security."

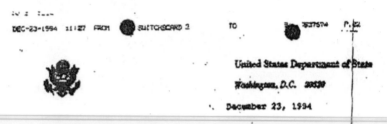

DEC-23-1994 11:27 FROM SWITCHBOARD 2 TO 5337574 P.02

United States Department of State

Washington, D.C. 20520

December 23, 1994

Dear Immigration Judge:

The Department of State is the Administration's "lead agency" regarding international terrorism. I serve as the Secretary of State's senior adviser regarding terrorism as well as U.S. foreign policy practices and initiatives intended to counter this threat to American interests and citizens. I will hold the personal rank of Ambassador, upon Senate confirmation. Prior to this current assignment, I served as the senior career official in the Bureau of Intelligence and Research. The bureau is responsible for analysis, on behalf of the Secretary, of intelligence products collected by the U.S. Government. In preparation for this letter, moreover, I have been in close contact with the Department of State's Bureau of Near Eastern Affairs, which coordinates U.S. foreign policy in the Middle East, including with the Hashemite Kingdom of Jordan.

In my letters to you of December 16 and 20, I provided you substantial information regarding the terrorist connections of Mohammad Jamal Khalifa. In the last two days there has been a significant additional development in this matter. On December 21 the State Security Court in Jordan found Mohammad Jamal Khalifa guilty of the charges for which he was indicted and imposed a capital sentence.

Based on my experience as a specialist in Middle Eastern affairs and service as U.S. Consul General in Jerusalem and Deputy Assistant Secretary of State in the Bureau of Near Eastern and South Asian Affairs, it is my view that a conviction by the competent Jordanian authorities provides strong evidence that Mohammad Jamal Khalifah has, in fact, engaged in serious terrorist offenses. I further believe that Mr. Khalifah's release in the United States under these circumstances would endanger U.S. national security, and would significantly damage U.S. foreign policy interests, particularly with respect to the Hashemite Kingdom of Jordan.

Sincerely,

Philip C. Wilcox, Jr.
Coordinator for Counterterrorism

Executive Office for Immigration Review
Immigration and Naturalization Service,
Federal Building,
San Francisco, CA.

Appendix IV:
The Infamous Wall Memo

Deputy Attorney General Jamie Gorelick's memo regarding "Separation of Certain Foreign Counterintelligence and Criminal Investigations." Though ignored by units like the FBI's Squad I-49, after 9/11 the memo gave FBI and DOJ officials an excuse for their failures to stop al Qaeda.

~~SECRET~~

Office of the Deputy Attorney General

Washington, D.C. 20530

MEMORANDUM

TO: Mary Jo White
United States Attorney
Southern District of New York

Louis Freeh
Director
Federal Bureau of Investigation

Richard Scruggs
Counsel of Intelligence Policy and Review
Office of Intelligence Policy and Review

Jo Ann Harris
Assistant Attorney General
Criminal Division

FROM: Jamie S. Gorelick
Deputy Attorney General

RE: Instructions on Separation of Certain Foreign
Counterintelligence and Criminal Investigations

      The United States Attorney's Office for the Southern District of New York and the FBI have been conducting criminal investigations of certain terrorist acts, including the bombing of the World Trade Center, and potential obstruction of the indicted case of United States v. Rahman, et al. During the course of those investigations significant counterintelligence information has been developed related to the activities and plans of agents of foreign powers operating in this country and overseas, including previously unknown connections between separate terrorist groups. Although information and evidence relevant to possible future criminal prosecutions is still being

SECRET

Classified by: Deputy Counsel for Intelligence Operations,
Office of Intelligence Policy and Review, Department of
Justice
Declassify on: OADR

Declassified by James A. Baker
Counsel for Intelligence Policy
OIPR/USDOJ
Date: April 10, 2004

SECRET

- 2 -

sought, it has become overwhelmingly apparent that there is a compelling need to further develop and expand that foreign counterintelligence information. Consequently, the FBI has initiated a separate full field counterintelligence investigation.

Although the counterintelligence investigation may result in the incidental collection of information relevant to possible future criminal prosecutions, the primary purpose of the counter-intelligence investigation will be to collect foreign counterintelligence information. Because the counterintelligence investigation will involve the use of surveillance techniques authorized under the Foreign Intelligence Surveillance Act (FISA) against targets that, in some instances, had been subject to surveillance under Title III, and because it will involve some of the same sources and targets as the criminal investigation, we believe that it is prudent to establish a set of instructions that will clearly separate the counterintelligence investigation from the more limited, but continued, criminal investigations. These procedures, which go beyond what is legally required, will prevent any risk of creating an unwarranted appearance that FISA is being used to avoid procedural safeguards which would apply in a criminal investigation.

(1) The focus of the Foreign Counterintelligence (FCI) investigation will be on preventing future terrorist acts and obtaining foreign counterintelligence information about the individuals and groups engaging in, or preparing to engage in, terrorist activities in the United States and abroad.

(2) The criminal investigations will focus on the indicted cases of United States v. Yousef, et al. and United States v. Rahman, et al., and the potential obstruction of the Rahman case. The criminal investigations will also focus on the conspiracy to bomb United States airlines recently uncovered in the Philippines and the bombing of a Philippine airliner.

(3) No "pro-active" investigative efforts or technical coverages are presently contemplated in any of the ongoing criminal investigations, which primarily focus on past criminal conduct, with the exception of the obstruction investigation. If in the future, the criminal investigations develop information requiring "pro-active" efforts or technical coverages, the United States Attorneys Office (USAO) and the criminal agents will consult with the Office of Intelligence Policy and Review (OIPR), and the FCI agents before undertaking such efforts, absent exigent circumstances, in order to determine the impact, if any, on the FCI investigation.

SECRET

Appendix V:
DeVecchio Documents

Documents regarding the case against SSA R. Lindley DeVecchio.

U.S Department of Justice

United States Attorney
Eastern District of New York

VC:GAS:EMC
F.#9305994
Devecchi.lt

United States Attorney's Office
225 Cadman Plaza East
Brooklyn, New York 11201

May 8, 1995

BY ~~TELEFAX ONLY~~ HAND

Gerald L. Shargel, Esq.
1585 Broadway, 19th Floor
New York, New York 10036

James M. LaRossa, Esq.
LaRossa, Mitchell & Ross
41 Madison Avenue, 34th Floor
New York, New York 10010

Alan S. Futerfas, Esq.
260 Madison Avenue, 22nd Floor
New York, New York 10016

Steve Zissou, Esq.
42-40 Bell Boulevard
Suite 302
Bayside, New York 11361

James Neville, Esq.
8 West 40th Street,
9th Floor
New York, New York 10018

Emanuel A. Moore, Esq.
89-17 190th Street
Hollis, New York 11423

Bettina Schein, Esq.
41 Madison Avenue,
34th Floor
New York, New York 10010

     Re: United States v. Victor M. Orena, et al.
           Criminal Docket No. 93-1366 (ERK)

Dear Ms. Schein and Messrs. Shargel, LaRossa, Futerfas, Zissou,
Neville and Moore:

        In accordance with the ruling of Judge Korman, in lieu
of disclosing an affidavit that had been presented to Judge
Korman _ex parte_, please be advised that the following constitutes
our knowledge of the items that Special Agent R. Lindley
DeVecchio may have disclosed to Gregory Scarpa, Sr. and the
approximate time of the disclosure:

        a. the planned 1987 arrest by DEA of Gregory
Scarpa, Jr., and his crew, and that law enforcement
believed that Cosmo Catanzano was a "weak link," who
might cooperate with authorities if arrested;

A. Letter from EDNY ASUA Ellen Corcella to defense attorneys on May 8, 1995, listing
eight possible disclosures by SSA Lin DeVecchio to Gregory Scarpa Sr. The information,
including details on mob associates who may have been cooperating with law enforcement officers, was potentially fatal to Scarpa's enemies.

2

    b.   on or about February 27, 1992, that Carmine Imbriale was cooperating with law enforcement;

    c.   during the Colombo Family war, information on at least one member of the Orena faction who had a hit team that was looking for members of the Persico faction;

    d.   following the arrest of Joseph Ambrosino, that there were arrest warrants outstanding for Lawrence Mazza and James DelMasto (two of Scarpa's closest associates), but that if they stayed away from their normal "hangouts" they could avoid being arrested;

    e.   in or around January 1992, that it was believed that Orena was staying at his girlfriend's house, the location of which (as then known by some in law enforcement)[1] was also conveyed;

    f.   in or around January 1992, the address of the house in which Salvatore Miciotta was residing; and

    g.   in early 1992, subscriber information for telephone numbers of two of Scarpa's loanshark customers;

    h.   in the mid to late 1980s, that Scarpa's social club was subject to court-ordered electronic surveillance and that he would soon be arrested on charges involving dealing with fraudulent credit cards.

Very truly yours,

ZACHARY W. CARTER
UNITED STATES ATTORNEY

By: *Ellen M. Corcella*
Ellen M. Corcella
Assistant U.S. Attorney

cc: Clerk of Court (ERK)

---

[1]   In January 1992, certain FBI agents had incorrect information on the location of the house of Orena's girlfriend.

(3 31/31)

FEDERAL BUREAU OF INVESTIGATION

Precedence: IMMEDIATE   Date: 04/10/1996

To: DIRECTOR, FBI   Attn: ASSISTANT DIRECTOR, INSPECTION
                                   DIVISION

From: ADIC, NEW YORK
           Contact: JAMES J. ROTH

Approved By: ROTH JAMES J

Drafted By: ROTH JAMES J:jjr

File Number(s): 263- (Pending)

Title: SUPERVISORY SPECIAL AGENT R. LINDLEY DEL VECCHIO
        OPR MATTER

          NY requests that whatever investigation is to be
conducted as a result of this letter be conducted expeditiously,
with the results provided to DOJ, and that DOJ be strenuously
pressed to provide a prosecutive opinion regarding this matter so
that it may be resolved. NY believes, based on the investigative
results to date and assuming this latest information does not
change the result, that there is insufficient evidence to take
prosecutive action against SSA DelVecchio. The failure of the DOJ
to provide a prosecutive opinion or for the FBI to
administratively resolve this matter continues to have a serious
negative impact on the government's prosecutions of various LCN
figures in the EDNY and casts a cloud over the NYO.

B. Memo from FBI NYO ADIC James Kallstrom (per his top lawyer, James J. Roth) to FBI director Louis Freeh on April 10, 1996, urging that the Feds "resolve" the DeVecchio OPR. Coming eleven months after Corcella's letter specifying leaks believed to have come from DeVecchio to Scarpa Sr., Kallstrom's conclusion that "there is insufficient evidence to take prosecutive action against SSA DelVecchio" (sic) suggests that he wants to end the OPR in order to remove the "cloud over the NYO" caused by the DeVecchio scandal.

Appendix VI:
Yousef-Scarpa Intelligence

The Ramzi Yousef-Gregory Scarpa Jr. intelligence.

- 1 -

FEDERAL BUREAU OF INVESTIGATION

Date of transcription ___3/7/96___

            At the request of GREGORY SCARPA, JR., Date of Birth:
August 3, 1951, he was interviewed at the Office of the United
States Attorney, Eastern District of New York, Brooklyn, New
York. Present at this interview was SCARPA's Attorney, Lawrence
Silverman, Assistant United States Attorneys (AUSA) DEITRICH
SNELL and PATRICK FITZGERALD, Southern District of New York and
EVELYN CORCELLA, and VALERIE CAPRONI, Chief of the Criminal
Division, Eastern District of New York, and Special Agents PAMELA
M. McDAID and HOWARD LEADBETTER II (FBI); and RICHARD CORAGGIO
(INS).

A. FBI 302 from March 7, 1996, recording a session between Scarpa Jr. and his lawyer, Larry Silverman, with a host of key Feds. Present at this meeting was Patrick Fitzgerald, head of Organized Crime and Terrorism in the SDNY along with Valerie Caproni, head of the Criminal Division in the EDNY; Dietrich Snell, the AUSA who was about to co-prosecute Yousef in the Bojinka case; Ellen Corcella, the AUSA running many of the Colombo war prosecutions in the EDNY; and Howard Leadbetter II, one of the original three FBI agents whose allegations about DeVecchio and Greg Scarpa Sr. led to the opening of the FBI OPR. Both Fitzgerald and Caproni had multiple meetings with Scarpa Jr.

How To Smuggle Explosives Into an Airplane   Sun. 5/19

1. When Talking about Smuggling Explosives into an Airplane, it is meant By That, Explosive Substances which are going To Be placed into an airplane Later, To Be used For Blowing up The airplanes. Therefore The quantity of Explosive Substances Which We'll Be Talking about, is The quantity needed To Blow-up an airplane, Which is equivelant To 300 gm of TNT. For 747-400 airplanes, at 30,000 Feet altitude. For Substances Which are more powerful Than TNT, The quantity needed Would Be Less Than 300 gm. depending on it's power compared To TNT.

2. All metalic Substances, or Substances which contains metals, cannot Be used or smuggled into The airplane Because They are easily detected By X-Ray machines and Metal Detectors, Therefore, all Azides and mercury Compounds Explosive Substances should Not Be used.

3. All Explosive Substances of A Density higher Than 2 Kg/L should Not Be used due To The possibility of Detecting Them by X-Ray Machines.
   The Following Explosive Substances Have a Density Less Than 2 gm can Easily Be Smuggled. 1. Tetrazene (Guanyl Nitrosaminoguanylтетrazene)
   2. Acetone Peroxide
   3. R.D.X.
   4. H.M.T.D. (Hexamethylenetriperox-idediamine)
   5. DDN.P (Diazodinitrophenol)
   6. HMX (Cyclotetramethylenetetra-anitramine)

All Liquid Explosives Can Be used
1. When an Explosive Substance is smuggled into an Airplane, Then it Can Be assembled easily inside The airplane.
2. A Detonator can Be hid in a Heel of a Shoe.
3. The Wiring and 9V Battery Can Be Hidden inside a Shaving machine or a Toy.
        The above Explosive Substances which are in powder Form can also Be Smuggled in an Airplane easily By Hiding Them in The Holes in The Heal of a Shoe, or By putting Them in Medicine Capsules.

B. May 19, 1996, "kite" from Ramzi Yousef to Greg Scarpa Jr. entitled "How to Smuggle Explosives Into An Airplane." The note suggests several alternatives to nitroglycerine as a high explosive, including RDX and "acetone peroxide," later suspected by British authorities of being one of the key ingredients in the August 2006 transatlantic airliner bombing plot.

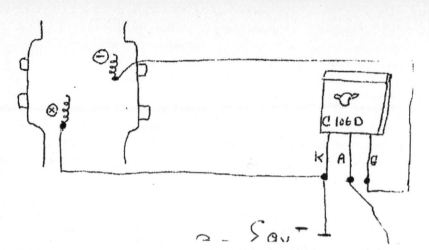

C. Schematic of Yousef's Casio-nitro bomb trigger, passed to Scarpa Jr. in a kite, May 1996. No high school-educated wiseguy could ever have fabricated such evidence; nor did Yousef have any motive for revealing this design to the Feds, since it would have ensured a guilty verdict at his trial.

At the trial, months after Scarpa Jr. retrieved this schematic, with its specific mention of a C106D semi-conductor, AUSAs Dietrich Snell and Mike Garcia referred to the use of that device, soldered inside a Casio DBC-61 watch, as Yousef's unique "signature"—a position that clearly undercut the Feds (including Patrick Fitzgerald) who later tried to dismiss the Yousef-Scarpa Jr. intelligence as a "hoax" and a "scam."

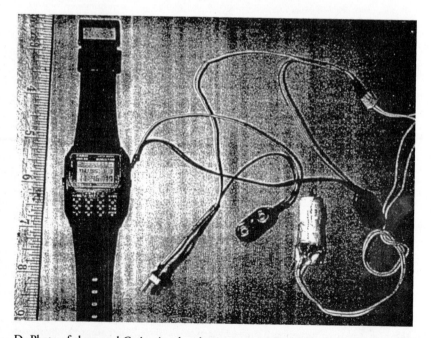

D. Photo of the actual Casio-nitro bomb trigger seized from Yousef's "bomb factory," Room 603 at the Dona Josefa apartments in Manila. Its design was a precursor to the schematic in Yousef's kite.

265A-NY-252802

Continuation of FD-302 of __GREGORY SCARPA, JR._____ .On __3/5/96____ . Page __

SCARPA advised that YOUSEF began slipping papers to him, 1/2 sheet of paper rolled up with writing on them. According to SCARPA, YOUSEF writes in sentences. SCARPA advised that when YOUSEF slips him these papers he writes on the paper that he wants them back. SCARPA advised he has only kept the notes for a matter of minutes, approximately 10 minutes, just long enough to write some things down. SCARPA advised he may get one note a day or one every couple of days. According to SCARPA, the number of notes varies according to the circumstances at the mcc. SCARPA advised YOUSEF does not give his notes back to him, but expects SCARPA to return YOUSEF's notes quickly. SCARPA believes YOUSEF throws the notes in the toilet.

SCARPA advised these notes, referred to as "kites" are passed from inmate to inmate, in newspapers, or through holes in the walls of the cells.

SCARPA advised that there is a guard permanently assigned to both ISMAIL and YOUSEF and sometimes they check the newspaper before its given to ISMAIL or YOUSEF and sometimes they do not.

According to SCARPA, YOUSEF told him, "if you're interested, I'll teach you things nobody knows."

YOUSEF told SCARPA I'll teach you how to blow up airplanes, and how to make bombs and then you can get the information to your people (meaning SCARPA's people on the outside). YOUSEF told SCARPA I can show you how to get a bomb on an airplane through a metal detector. YOUSEF told SCARPA he would teach him how to make timing devices.

According to SCARPA, YOUSEF wants to hurt the United States Government and wants to teach SCARPA how. SCARPA advised YOUSEF has not asked for any specific help. SCARPA advised that YOUSEF wants to blow things up, but he does not say why.

YOUSEF told SCARPA that during the trial they had a plan to blow up a plane to show that they are serious and then make their demands, or kidnap and hurt a judge or an attorney so a mistrial will be declared. SCARPA advised that blowing up an airplane during the trial seems easy to YOUSEF. YOUSEF never mentioned a specific airline as a target.

According to SCARPA, YOUSEF believes that SCARPA is in touch with people on the outside. YOUSEF told SCARPA if things get going we may be able to hook up, if you're serious my people and your people can meet. SCARPA believes YOUSEF needs help

E. FBI 302 of March 5, 1996, recording the threat communicated by Ramzi Yousef to Greg Scarpa Jr. The 302, which notes how Yousef "began slipping papers" to Scarpa Jr., is the first of many recording Yousef's "plan to blow up a plane . . . so that a mistrial will be declared" in the Bojinka case. TWA 800 blew up on the night before Murad's confession to Col. Mendoza—among the most damning evidence against Yousef—was to be entered at trial. The morning after the crash, July 18, 1996, Yousef moved for a mistrial.

May 9

How are you Buddy?
I Hope your CASE Went Well For you ToDay.
Listen Bo as I ToLD you My Lawyer is pretty GooD,
as Soon as He Received The INFO From my people, He
Brought it right up

Phone- AS I alReaDy gave you
FAX
You're To Say; Bonnie CALLing - I'De Like To make a phone
Call:
You SenD your FAX To;
George Smith
C/o RoMa CoRP
Suite 2252
N.Y. N.Y. 10010

F. The kite from Scarpa Jr. to Yousef on May 9, 1996, announcing the creation of "Roma Corp.," the front company devised by the FBI for intercepting Yousef's outside calls to his "people" in New York and aboard. This intelligence initiative, which continued throughout the summer of 1996—well past the crash of TWA 800—further proves that the FBI believed in the legitimacy of Greg Jr.'s intelligence from Yousef.

UNITED STATES DISTRICT COURT
SOUTHERN DISTRICT OF NEW YORK
- - - - - - - - - - - - - - - - x
UNITED STATES OF AMERICA   :   **AFFIRMATION**

. -v.-   :

RAMZI AHMED YOUSEF,   93 Cr. 180 (KTD)
EYAD ISMOIL,   :

           Defendants.   :
- - - - - - - - - - - - - - - - x

STATE OF NEW YORK   )
COUNTY OF NEW YORK   )   ss:
SOUTHERN DISTRICT OF NEW YORK)

       PATRICK J. FITZGERALD, pursuant to Title 28, United States Code, Section 1746, hereby affirms under penalty of perjury:

       1.   I am an Assistant United States Attorney ("AUSA") in the office of Mary Jo White, United States Attorney for the Southern District of New York ("SDNY"). I have personal knowledge of the information set forth below, and I submit this affirmation in opposition to: (i) the motion by the defendants Ramzi Yousef and Eyad Ismoil to compel the Government to disclose materials arising from the purported cooperation of Gregory Scarpa, Jr. (the "Scarpa material"); and (ii) recuse the Court from consideration of the motion to compel and any subsequent motion for a new trial based on the Scarpa material. As is set forth more fully below, it is respectfully submitted that the motion be denied for, among other reasons, there is no legal requirement providing for discovery of the Scarpa material, and, under the circumstances, it would be entirely inappropriate to

G. June 25, 1999, sealed affirmation of Patrick Fitzgerald. After admitting that an investigation of the Yousef-Scarpa Jr. intel "appeared to corroborate Scarpa's information," Fitzgerald cites reputed mob wiseguy John Napoli for his assertion that the treasure trove of intel gathered by Scarpa Jr. over eleven months was a "scam in collusion with Yousef and others." Yet Napoli maintains that he never told the Feds the Yousef-Scarpa Jr. intel was fraudulent, and that "at no point did [Greg Scarpa Jr.] have a deal with Yousef to give false information." Napoli insists that the Yousef-Scarpa Jr. intel "wasn't a hoax" and that Scarpa Jr. was "legitimately trying to help" the Feds.

disclose it.

Background

2.   I became familiar with Scarpa in or about March
1996. I understood Scarpa to be a member of the Colombo Organized
Crime Family who was detained in the MCC while awaiting trial on
racketeering charges, including murder conspiracy, in the Eastern
District of New York. Scarpa's father had also been a member of
the Colombo Family and had died of natural causes. I met with
Scarpa on a number of occasions during 1996 and also spoke
regularly with Special Agents of the FBI who debriefed Scarpa on
other occasions during 1996. In addition, I received some
additional information concerning Scarpa from periodic
conversations with his counsel, Larry Silverman, Esq.

3.   During the debriefings of Scarpa, Scarpa alleged
that Ramzi Yousef and others were planning terrorist activity
from within the Metropolitan Correctional Center - New York
("MCC"). Scarpa alleged, among other things, that: (a) Yousef was
planning to assassinate an Assistant United States Attorney in
the Southern District of New York ("SDNY") as well as certain
witnesses, including an FBI supervisor; (b) Yousef's associates
were planning to conduct a terrorist attack at the 1996 summer
Olympics in Atlanta; and (c) Yousef was planning to blow up
airplanes and/or kidnap ambassadors or other high officials of
the United States Government to disrupt his imminent trials. In
addition, Scarpa claimed in mid-1996 that Ismoil and Yousef had
discussed the advisability of kidnaping and possibly hurting a

2

federal judge in an effort to obtain a mistrial. Scarpa also claimed, however, that this notion was rejected by the defendants because of a perception that security for judges was too tight. While Scarpa's apparent criminal history made the Government skeptical of his information at first, the Government could not fail to follow up on the information provided, given the past criminal behavior of the incarcerated terrorists and the grave consequences if any of the allegedly contemplated conduct was carried out. The follow-up investigation appeared to corroborate Scarpa's information. In particular, Scarpa provided "kites" (notes exchanged between inmates in the MCC) which bore Yousef's handwriting and whose contents were consistent with Scarpa's account of terrorist machinations. By way of example, one such note bore the name of an Assistant United States Attorney; another note sought access to a friend of Scarpa on the outside who could connect Yousef by telephone from the MCC to outside contacts -- a method Yousef had earlier used to contact an incarcerated associate while Yousef was plotting the bombing of the World Trade Center. Moreover, some details provided by Scarpa of Yousef's impending plans were consistent with information we had earlier received from a confidential source whose information was not in the public domain.

The Agreement with Scarpa

    4. Because the United States Attorney's Office for the Eastern District of New York ("EDNY") had a pending prosecution against Scarpa on very serious charges, it was explicitly agreed

3

between and among the SDNY, the EDNY, and Scarpa (through his attorney Silverman) that, as a result of the first meeting, a firewall would be established whereby Scarpa would be debriefed by prosecutors from the SDNY (who were not participants in the impending trials of either Scarpa or Yousef), who would maintain contact with Valerie Caproni, then Chief of the Criminal Division of the EDNY.

The Purported Cooperation

5. As a result of the information provided by Scarpa, the Government spent considerable resources to attempt to investigate the allegations and to take measures to thwart any potential terrorist attacks. Those efforts, which included, but were not limited to, providing an undercover telephone for Yousef to "patch through" calls to his associates, are described in additional detail in an accompanying *ex parte* affidavit.

6. In addition to the information provided about terrorist plots, Scarpa also provided information concerning the fact that Yousef tampered with some trial exhibits by, among other things, causing himself to bleed and then placing his blood on certain exhibits seized at or about the time of his arrest overseas in order to create the impression that he had been tortured during post-arrest questioning in Pakistan. While this information appeared to be accurate, the SDNY did not call Scarpa as a witness at Yousef's trial or otherwise put such evidence before the jury.

7. The Government passed along the threat information

4

to appropriate security officials. The resulting precautions diverted resources that would otherwise have been directed elsewhere and caused great expense to the Government and private industry. By late summer 1996, the Government made an investigative decision that it no longer wished to pursue the investigation of Yousef using the "patch through" telephone, for reasons briefly explained in the _ex parte_ affidavit. In fact, during the course of the investigation no terrorist attacks were prevented and no one was arrested. Since then, special restrictions have been placed on the defendants and some of their associates, pursuant to 28 C.F.R. § 501.3, to ensure as much as possible that they do not plot any violence from within Bureau of Prisons facilities.

Subsequent Revelations

8. I have since learned information which convinced me that Scarpa's effort at "cooperation" was a scam in collusion with Yousef and others. The Government learned of the fraudulent nature of Scarpa's purported cooperation from two different sources. First, in the latter part of 1996, Scarpa had told the Government that an inmate, John Napoli, had even better access to Yousef and his colleagues than Scarpa himself. Indeed, Scarpa urged the Government to contact John Napoli. Meanwhile, John Napoli also sought to make contact with the Government. I was advised by the EDNY that Napoli had a very checkered history of cooperating with law enforcement and that the EDNY did not wish

to enter into a cooperation agreement with Napoli. After some delay, Napoli was finally debriefed and admitted the following: (i) that Scarpa had approached him with the idea that if Napoli provided information to the Government about Yousef -- which Napoli understood to be false -- then Napoli might earn a Section 5K1.1 letter; (ii) Scarpa would tell Napoli what to tell the Government; and (iii) in turn, Scarpa wanted Napoli to testify falsely at Scarpa's upcoming trial to indicate that Scarpa's father, as opposed to Scarpa, had carried out the murders Scarpa was charged with. Napoli understood that Yousef was witting of the scam being perpetrated by Scarpa on the Government. Napoli initially intended to go along with the scam by Yousef and Scarpa but then decided not to pursue the idea and advised the Government of the scam.

9. Thereafter, the Government learned additional information from a confidential source further indicating that Scarpa's purported cooperation was a scam. To protect the confidentiality of the source, the additional information is set forth in the accompanying ex parte affidavit.

10. The Government would respectfully request that if the instant affidavit is to be filed publicly, that it be filed in slightly redacted form. In particular, to avoid public confirmation of the fact that the Government has used an

---

¹ I understand generally that the EDNY was concerned that Napoli had a history of cooperating with the Government to reduce his sentencing exposure -- and a history of committing further crimes while cooperating.

6

undercover "patch through" telephone as an investigative technique, it is respectfully requested that the second sentence in paragraph 5, the third sentence in paragraph 7, as well as this sentence, be redacted.

I affirm under penalty of perjury that the foregoing is true and correct.

Dated: New York, New York
           June 25, 1999

                              PATRICK J. FITZGERALD
                              Assistant United States Attorney
                              United States Attorney's Office
                              Southern District of New York

07/07/2004 09:34   7197845298   ADX WARDEN   PAGE 02/02

U.S. Department of Justice

Federal Bureau of Prisons

United States Penitentiary
Administrative Maximum

Office of the Warden   *P.O. Box 8500*
                                          Florence, CO 81226-8500

July 6, 2004

Peter Anthony Lance
c/o Regan Books
Harper Collins
18th Floor
10 East 53rd St.
New York, NY 10022

Dear Mr. Lance:

This is in response to your correspondence dated July 1, 2004, received by fax on July 2, 2004, in which you request permission to conduct an interview with inmate Gregory Scarpa.

The Bureau of Prisons makes every effort to accommodate media personnel as long as the request does not negatively affect the security and operation of our institutions. It is my determination, based on my sound correctional judgement, that to grant your request at this time could pose a risk to the internal security of this institution and to the safety of staff, inmates and members of the public. Therefore, your request has been denied and you will not be permitted to conduct an interview with inmate Scarpa at this time.

Please feel free to contact my Executive Assistant and Public Information Officer, Wendy Montgomery, at 719/784-9464, if you have any further questions regarding this letter.

Sincerely,

Robert A. Hood
Warden

by fax (212)734-0056

H. Response from the warden of the ADX Florence (Supermax) to the author's July 2004 request for an interview with Greg Scarpa Jr. Prison officials failed to respond to a second interview request from the author submitted as late as September 20, 2006.

Appendix VII:
Flight 800 Documents

Documents regarding the 747 that became TWA 800.

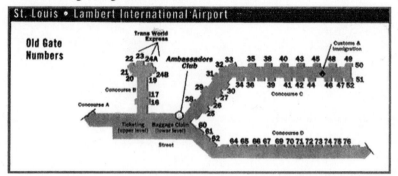

A. Illustration of the C concourse at St. Louis Lambert International Airport as it was in June 1996. The 747 that became TWA Flight 800 (N-93 17119) was parked at Gate 50, while an almost identical 747 (N-93 17116) was parked at Gate 52 around the corner.

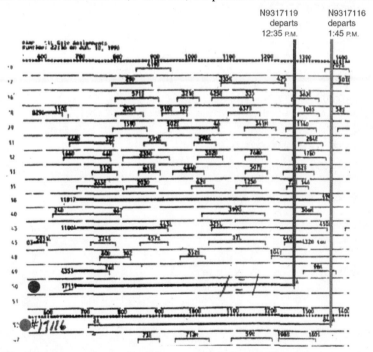

B. The TWA gate assignment from June 10, 1996, showing that N-93 17119, the aircraft that exploded as TWA 800 on July 17, 1996, left Gate 50 at 12:35 P.M. on June 10, and took off fully catered and crewed bound for Honolulu only 35 minutes after K-9 Officer Herman Burnett finished his test. Yet the 747 around the corner at Gate 52 (N-93-17116) didn't leave until 1:45 P.M. more than 90 minutes later. Officer Burnett later recalled that his "notes and memory at the time . . . told [him] that it had to be the other plane" [93-17116] on which he'd performed the K-9 test.

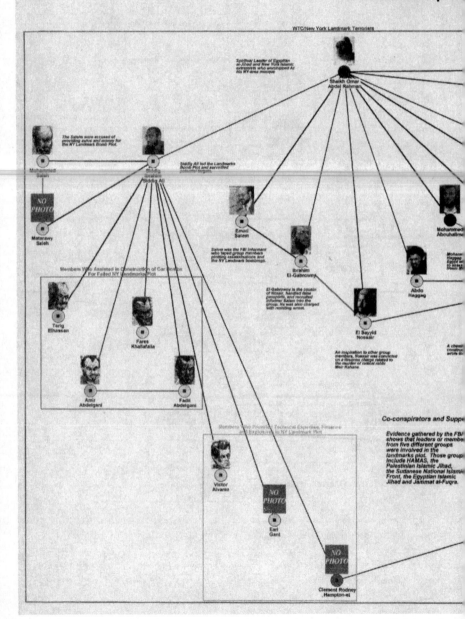

A. The DIAC link chart of August 10, 1999, showing connections between Ali Mohamed in Africa (center right) and the Rahman/Yousef New York cell.

nera̶d by the DIAC.

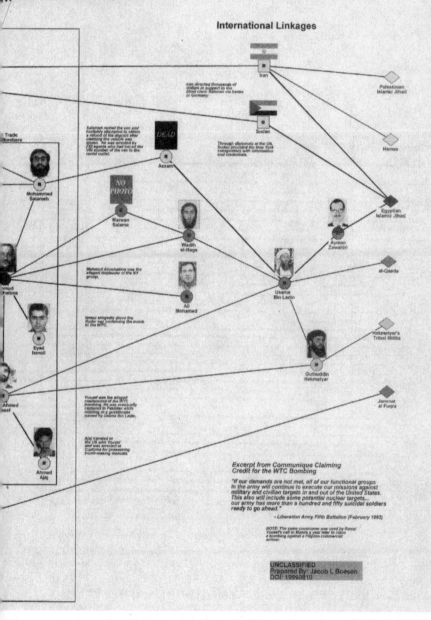

New York Landmarks Bomb Plot:
International Linkages

International Linkages

Iran

Iran directed thousands of
dollars in support to the
blind cleric Rahman via banks
in Germany

Palestinian
Islamic Jihad

Sudan

Through diplomats at the UN,
Sudan provided the New York
conspirators with information
and credentials.

Hamas

World Trade
Center Bombers

Salameh rented the van and
foolishly attempted to obtain
a refund of his deposit after
claiming the vehicle was
stolen. He was arrested by
FBI agents who had traced the
VIN number of the van to the
rental outlet.

DEAD

Azzam

Mohammed
Salameh

NO
PHOTO

Marwan
Salama

Wadih
el-Hage

Egyptian
Islamic Jihad

Ayman
Zawahiri

Mahmud Abouhalima was the
alleged ringleader of the NY
groups.

al-Qaeda

Mahmud
Abouhalima

Ali
Mohamed

Usama
Bin Ladin

Ismoil allegedly drove the
Ryder van containing the bomb
to the WTC.

Eyad
Ismoil

Hekmatyar's
Tribal Militia

Yousef was the alleged
mastermind of the WTC
bombing. He was eventually
captured in Pakistan while
residing in a guesthouse
owned by Usama Bin Laden.

Gulbuddin
Hekmatyar

Ahmed
Yousef

Jammat
al Fuqra

Ajaj traveled to
the US with Yousef
and was arrested at
Customs for possessing
bomb-making manuals.

Ahmed
Ajaj

Excerpt from Communique Claiming
Credit for the WTC Bombing

"If our demands are not met, all of our functional groups
in the army will continue to execute our missions against
military and civilian targets in and out of the United States.
This also will include some potential nuclear targets...
our army has more than a hundred and fifty suicidal soldiers
ready to go ahead."

- Liberation Army Fifth Battalion (February 1993)

NOTE: The same codename was used by Ramzi
Yousef's call in Manila a year later to claim
a bombing against a Filipino commercial
airliner.

WORLD TRADE CENTER BOM

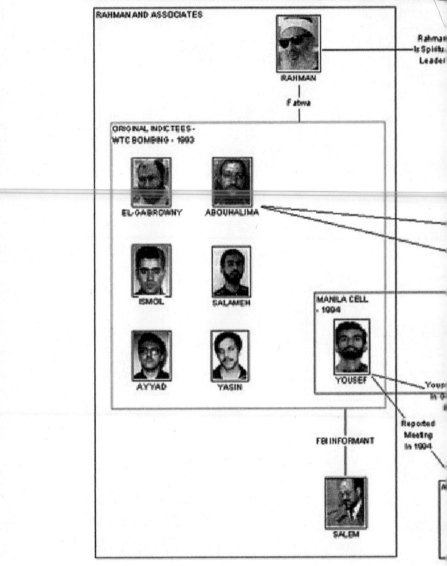

B. Published here for the first time, a second link chart, this one declassified by Jacob L. Boesen on March 21, 2000, just weeks before the Able Danger intel on al Qaeda was ordered destroyed by the Pentagon. The chart, which shows Ali Mohamed, a former U.S.

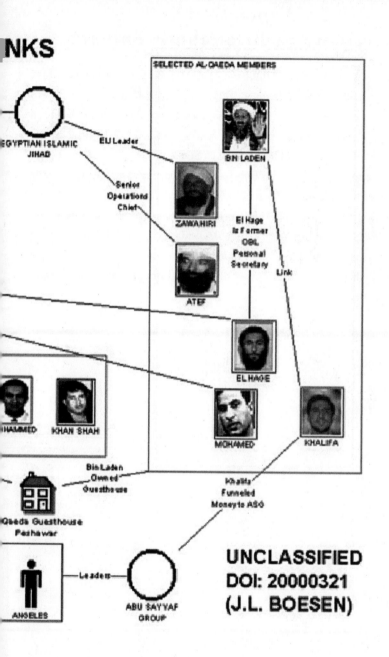

NKS

SELECTED AL-QAEDA MEMBERS

EGYPTIAN ISLAMIC JIHAD

EU Leader

BIN LADEN

Senior Operational Chief

ZAWAHIRI

El Hage Is Former OBL Personal Secretary

Link

ATEF

EL HAGE

HAMMED   KHAN SHAH

MOHAMED

KHALIFA

Bin Laden Owned Guesthouse

Khalifa Funneled Money to ASG

Qaeda Guesthouse Peshawar

ANGELES

Leaders

ABU SAYYAF GROUP

UNCLASSIFIED
DOI: 20000321
(J.L. BOESEN)

Army Sergeant who penetrated the JFK SWC at Fort Bragg, as a member of al Qaeda's inner circle, would have proven enormously embarrassing to the U.S. Army Special Operations Command (SOCOM) that commenced the Able Danger operation.

Appendix IX:
Presidential Brief about Rahman

The infamous Presidential Daily Brief of August 6, 2001, which the Bush White House tried to keep from the 9/11 Commission, discussed a plot to hijack a plane to free the blind Sheikh and a "senior EIJ member" living in California. Given to the president just weeks before the 9/11 attacks, the PDB, entitled "Bin Laden Determined to Strike in U.S.," underscores not only the importance of Sheikh Rahman to al Qaeda; vindicating the Able Danger intelligence, but it references Ali Mohamed as both a senior Egyptian Islamic Jihad member and one of the al Qaeda members found guilty in the embassy bombing, noting that al Qaeda members have maintained a support structure in the United States. The memo also vindicates Greg Scarpa Jr., who learned from Yousef of at least four al Qaeda operatives in NYC in 1996.

Bin Ladin Determined To Strike in US

Clandestine, foreign government, and media reports indicate Bin Ladin since 1997 has wanted to conduct terrorist attacks in the US. Bin Ladin implied in US television interviews in 1997 and 1998 that his followers would follow the example of World Trade Center bomber Ramzi Yousef and "bring the fighting to America."

> After US missile strikes on his base in Afghanistan in 1998, Bin Ladin told followers he wanted to retaliate in Washington, according to a ▓▓▓▓▓▓▓▓▓▓ service.

> An Egyptian Islamic Jihad (EIJ) operative told an ▓▓▓▓▓ service at the same time that Bin Ladin was planning to exploit the operative's access to the US to mount a terrorist strike.

The millennium plotting in Canada in 1999 may have been part of Bin Ladin's first serious attempt to implement a terrorist strike in the US. Convicted plotter Ahmed Ressam has told the FBI that he conceived the idea to attack Los Angeles International Airport himself, but that Bin Ladin lieutenant Abu Zubaydah encouraged him and helped facilitate the operation. Ressam also said that in 1998 Abu Zubaydah was planning his own US attack.

> Ressam says Bin Ladin was aware of the Los Angeles operation.

Although Bin Ladin has not succeeded, his attacks against the US Embassies in Kenya and Tanzania in 1998 demonstrate that he prepares operations years in advance and is not deterred by setbacks. Bin Ladin associates surveilled our Embassies in Nairobi and Dar es Salaam as early as 1993, and some members of the Nairobi cell planning the bombings were arrested and deported in 1997.

Al-Qa'ida members—including some who are US citizens—have resided in or traveled to the US for years, and the group apparently maintains a support structure that could aid attacks. Two al-Qa'ida members found guilty in the conspiracy to bomb our Embassies in East Africa were US citizens, and a senior EIJ member lived in California in the mid-1990s.

> A clandestine source said in 1998 that a Bin Ladin cell in New York was recruiting Muslim-American youth for attacks.

We have not been able to corroborate some of the more sensational threat reporting, such as that from a ▓▓▓▓▓▓▓▓▓▓ service in 1998 saying that Bin Ladin wanted to hijack a US aircraft to gain the release of "Blind Shaykh" 'Umar 'Abd al-Rahman and other US-held extremists.

Appendix X:
Unindicted Coconspirators in the
Day of Terror Trial

A 1994 List of 172 Unindicted Coconspirators in the Day of Terror Trial, including Osama bin Laden, Mohammed Jamal Khalifa, Ali Mohamed, the Murteza Brothers, Waleed al-Noor, co-owner of Sphinx Trading and the long-deceased Abdullah Azzam and Mustafa Shalabi.

1 Ahmed Muhammad Aasran	35 Mohammed Azzam	68 Fathy M. Hassan
2 Mohammed Yousef Abbas	36 Ahab Ashraf Abdul Azziz	69 Sabri Hassan (John Kinard)
3 Jamal Abdelgani	37 Hasab el Rasoul	70 Ibrahim Higazi
4 Mohammed Hassan Abdou	Mohamed Babiker	71 Nasser Homosany
5 Emad Abdou	38 Abdul Basir (Tito)	72 Khalid LNU
6 Amad Elden Abdou	39 Ahmed Bilal	73 Alaa Ibrahim
7 Abdalhele A. Abwalannen	40 Adnan Constantine	74 Khalid Ibrahim
8 Dawud Adib	41 Fawaz Damra	75 Mamdouh Ibrahim
9 Hosni Ahmed	42 Ahmed Al Dalta Daota	**76 Muhammad Shawqi**
10 Mohssen Ahmed	43 Halim Abul Efni	**Islambouli**
11 Nasser Al Din Alamani	44 Moustafa Elaebrak	77 Abdel Rahman Ja'afar
12 Majdi Alghamrawi	45 Mahmud Elder	78 Al Sayyid Sami Jamal
13 Hekmat Alhadashek	46 Nimmer Elder	79 Mahir Al Jamal
14 Abd Al Hafez Mustafa Ali	47 Ahmed Mansour El-Eslah	80 Kamal Al Jayh
15 Atif Ahmed Ali	48 Ali El-Gabrowny	81 Ali Abdul Kareem
16 Hamdi Ali	49 Mohammed El-Gabrowny	82 Ahmed Kazalek
17 Samy Ali	50 Ahmed Elganainy	83 Abdel Khalek
18 Sharif Ali	52 Ali Al Faqueer	84 Walid Khalid
19 Mike Alkam	53 Shawki Abd Al Fariz	85 Yah Yah Ibn Khalid
21 Hassan Karim Allah	54 Umar Faruqq	**86 Mohammed Khalifa**
22 Abu Abdullah	55 Abu Al Walid Gizeh	87 Ashraq Kahlil
23 Othman Abdullah	56 Abdel Hafez	88 Samir Khalil
24 Abu Abdulla Alnagar	57 Sahied Hahmad	89 Abd Al Khaliq
25 Raef Alwishe	58 Mohamed Ahmed Al Haj	90 Atif Mahmood Khan
26 Saleem Amin	59 Isam Abdul Hakim	91 Ahmed Khatteria
27 Hiam Arazy	60 Saad Hanafi	92 Tareq Khatteria
28 Mustafa Assad (Boriqua)	61 Esteshamel Haque	93 Lawrence L. Khidr
29 Moneeb Ashraf	62 Quazi Haque	94 Y'aqub Kursam
30 Mohammed Atiyah	63 Hameed LNU	**95 Osama bin Ladin**
31 Sami Atiya	64 Hesham El Hamamey	96 Khalil Lahoud
32 Amin Awad	65 Hammid Hammid	97 Yousef Maani
33 Mona Awad	66 Jack Hamrick	98 Mokhtar Mahmoud
34 Abdullah Azzam	67 Mohammed Al Hanooti	99 Adel Mahroud

100 Hamam Sayeed Mahseen
101 Ahmed Abd Al Majeed
102 Abd Al Manaâm
103 Abd Al Halimi Mansour
104 Said Mansour
105 Hassan El Mansouri
106 Safullah McNeil
107 Ahmed Megali
108 Mohamed Mehdi
109 Ali A. Mohamed
110 Arioua Mostafa
111 Adel Said Mohammed
112 Ashraf Mohammed
113 Mouaki Benani Mohammed
114 Mohmoud Mohmoud
115 Hassan Mousa
116 Mohammed Mousa
117 Sami Mousa
118 Ahmed H. Moustafa
119 Assan Muhammad
120 Hanif Muhammad
    (Abu Hanif)
121 Moustafa Muhammad
122 Ahmed Muneer

123 Daniel Murteza
124 Raymond Murteza
125 Hamdi Musa
126 Omar Mohammed Musa
127 Majed Mustafa
128 Adel El Nasser
129 Mustafa Dauod Mustafa
    Nassar
130 Waleed A. Noor
131 Kamal Muhamad Omar
132 Bilal Phillips
133 Fatahi Qoura
134 Nabig Ragab
135 Mikial Abdur Rahim
    (Richard Smith)
136 Nabir Abu Abd Al Rakhi
137 Frank Ramos
138 Abu Obaida Rouas
139 Yehyeh Sabor
140 Hussein Saffan
141 Mustafa Saif
142 Saifuldin
143 Tharwat Saleh
144 Tariq Mustafa Salem

145 Muhammad Samir
146 Ahmed Samy
    (Samy Mohammed Ali)
147 Ahmed Abdel Sattar
148 Sabir Shakir
149 Mustafa Shalabi
150 Mustafa Al Shareef
158 Sirraj Wahhaj
159 Sudanese Mission to the
    United Nations
160 Abdul Wali
161 Madha Warda
162 Seraj LNU
163 Shawkat M. Wehidy
164 Khalid Younis
165 Nasser Younis
166 Ahmed Yousef
167 Mahmud Yousef
168 Yousef Bin Yousef
169 Zakariah
170 Badre Zhony
171 Ahmed Zidan
172 Ibrahim Foxmanef
    (Abe Foxman)

Appendix XI:
FBI NO/FORN Memo 1995

This once-secret 1995 FBI memo proves that the Bureau had received intelligence from the PNP that Ramzi Yousef intended to fly planes into buildings in the U.S. Beyond the early notion of flying a small plane into CIA headquarters, the memo acknowledges the Yousef-Murad plot to attack a U.S. nuclear facility uncovered by Col. Rodolfo B. Mendoza. It also notes that Murad, a pilot trained in four U.S. flight schools, had chosen the WTC as a target.

SECRET/NOFORN REL TO THE PHILIPPINES

RAMZI AHMED YOUSEF: A NEW GENERATION OF SUNNI ISLAMIC
                    TERRORISTS

INTRODUCTION:

        RAMZI AHMED YOUSEF FIRST CAME TO OUR ATTENTION WITH THE
BOMBING OF THE WORLD TRADE CENTER (WTC) BUILDING ON 26 FEBRUARY
1993. AFTER THE ATTACK, HE DISAPPEARED FROM OUR SCREENS. YOUSEF
REAPPEARED IN THE PHILIPPINES IN JANUARY 1995 WHEN YOU
SUCCESSFULLY UNCOVERED HIS PLOT TO ATTACK U.S. AIRLINES AND THE
POPE. THE 7 FEBRUARY ARREST OF YOUSEF IN PAKISTAN, AND YOUR
JANUARY ARREST OF ABDUL HAKIM MURAD, ARE MAJOR COUNTERTERRORISM
VICTORIES. WE BELIEVE THE INFORMATION WE HAVE LEARNED TO DATE
ABOUT YOUSEF AND HIS PLANS TO LAUNCH ATTACKS, HOWEVER,
UNDERSCORES A LARGER THREAT FROM ISLAMIC TERRORISTS. WE CONTINUE
TO TRACK DOWN LEADS FROM THE INVESTIGATION AND ARE STILL
ATTEMPTING TO IDENTIFY AND LOCATE OTHER ASSOCIATES OF YOUSEF.

    A. NORTH AMERICA

        1) THE WTC BOMBING IN 1993 CLEARLY DEMONSTRATES
YOUSEF'S ABILITY TO ENTER THE UNITED STATES, ESTABLISH A SUPPORT
STRUCTURE, RECRUIT A TERRORIST TEAM, AND SUCCESSFULLY CARRY OUT
AN ATTACK.

        2) YOUSEF IS ABLE TO USE HIS FRIENDS AND ASSOCIATES IN
FOREIGN COUNTRIES TO IDENTIFY POSSIBLE TARGETS. AN EXAMPLE OF
THIS IS YOUSEF'S REQUEST TO MURAD, WHILE HE (MURAD) WAS IN THE
U.S. FOR PILOT TRAINING, TO CHOOSE AN APPROPRIATE SITE FOR AN
ATTACK. MURAD CHOSE THE WTC BUILDING.

        3) YOUSEF AND MURAD ALSO DISCUSSED FUTURE ATTACKS IN
THE U.S. INCLUDING POSSIBLY FLYING A PLANE FILLED WITH EXPLOSIVES
INTO THE CIA BUILDING. MURAD ALSO MENTIONED THAT IN JUNE OF THIS
YEAR HE WAS TO TRAVEL TO THE U.S. AND POSSIBLY ATTACK A U.S.
NUCLEAR FACILITY.

        --THOSE INVOLVED IN THE WTC BOMBING AND A SECOND GROUP OF
EXTREMISTS WHO PLOTTED TO BOMB OTHER LANDMARKS IN NEW YORK CITY,
INCLUDING THE UNITED NATIONS BUILDING, DID NOT BELONG TO A
SINGLE, COHESIVE ORGANIZATION, BUT RATHER WERE PART OF A LOOSE
GROUP OF POLITICALLY COMMITTED MUSLIMS LIVING IN THE AREA. THEY
WERE OF VARYING NATIONALITIES INCLUDING EGYPTIAN, SUDANESE,
PAKISTANI, PALESTINIAN, AND IRAQI.

INDEX